THE ILLUSTRATED VETERINARY GUIDE

Chris C. Pinney, DVM

New York   San Francisco   Washington, D.C.   Auckland   Bogotá
Caracas   Lisbon   London   Madrid   Mexico City   Milan
Montreal   New Delhi   San Juan   Singapore
Sydney   Tokyo   Toronto

To Tracy and the kids

Library of Congress Cataloging-in-Publication Data

Pinney, Chris C.
    The illustrated veterinary guide / Chris C. Pinney.
        p.   cm.
        ISBN 0-07-135186-8
    1. Pets—Diseases. 2. Pets—Health. 3. Veterinary medicine. I. Title.
SF981 .P55 2000

636.089—dc21   99-058867
                                                                CIP

McGraw-Hill

A Division of The **McGraw·Hill** *Companies*

    2 3 4 5 6 7 8 9 0   AGM/AGM   9 0 9 8 7 6 5 4 3 2 1

ISBN 0-07-135186-8

The sponsoring editor for this book was Zoe G. Foundotos, the editing supervisor was Caroline Levine, and the production supervisor was Pamela Pelton. It was set in Melior per the Mod. CMS design by Joanne Morbit and Michele Pridmore of McGraw-Hill's Professional Book Group composition unit, Hightstown, N.J.

Printed and bound by Quebecor/Martinsburg.

This book is printed on recycled, acid-free paper containing a minimum of 50% recycled, de-inked fiber.

CONTENTS

Part 3   Birds   537

ACKNOWLEDGMENTS

The author would like to thank the following contributors for their part in the development of this book:

Bob Rogers, DVM, for providing a multitude of reference resources as well as his valuable insights into practical care of pets.

Elizabeth M. Hodgkins, DVM, of Hill's Pet Products for her contributions on canine and feline nutrition.

Claudia L. Barton, DVM, for her contributions on cancer in companion animals.

Larry P Tilley, DVM Diplomate, ACVIM for his contributions on cardiology and heart disease in dogs.

James R. Smith, DVM for his contributions on dermatology and skin diseases.

Lon D. Lewis, DVM, Mark L. Morris Jr., DVM, and Michael S. Hand, DVM of Mark Morris Associates for their input regarding canine and feline nutrition.

Michael O. Woolley, DVM, for his contributions on geriatric care and behavioral problems in pets.

INTRODUCTION

It's a proven fact: People love pets! And regardless of whether they're furred, feathered, or finned, companion animals serve vital roles, both physical and psychological, in our society. Certainly the popularity of dogs and cats as pets is ever on the rise. In fact, in American households, cats have surpassed dogs in popularity! But don't get the idea that dogs and cats monopolize the hearts of all pet owners. The appeal of birds and less conventional pets such as small rodents, rabbits, ferrets, fish, and pigs—that's right, pigs!—is growing. Furthermore, the households that harbor these birds and exotic pets are often inhabited by dogs and/or cats as well. Because of the multipet fancies exhibited by numerous pet owners, a need was seen for a resource that contained information on all types of pets, all condensed into one layperson volume. It was for this reason that *The Complete Home Veterinary Guide,* a comprehensive, up-to-date guide to companion house pets, was written.

The Complete Home Veterinary Guide is loaded with illustrations and covers important topics concerning husbandry and health care for all popular species of pets. Written from a veterinary perspective, this book provides an objective "nuts and bolts" look at pet care. It doesn't matter if you own one pet or multiple species of pets, *The Complete Home Veterinary Guide* covers them all.

Just look at some of the subjects presented and questions answered:

Ten strategies for reducing pet care costs that you can implement today

How to treat annoying behavioral problems in pets

Are we vaccinating our pets too much?

New steroid-free treatments that can be used for canine skin allergies

Serious breakthroughs in the treatment of arthritis in pets

Recognizing the signs of illness in pet birds

Vital first aid procedures, all of which could save your pet's life some day

Seven ways to help our pets live longer and healthier lives

Protecting your family and yourself from zoonotic (petborne) diseases

Do holistic approaches to pet care work?

Care and husbandry of exotic pets, from rabbits to tarantulas

How to maintain high water quality in aquariums

And much more

Part I of the book deals with our best friend, the dog. Information ranging from selecting a dog to preventing disease are covered in this section. Fighting fleas, managing allergies, and coping with arthritis are just a few of the topics that will prove valuable to everyone who owns one or more of these "classic" pets.

Part II is dedicated to—you guessed it—the cat. For centuries, this creature has been a faithful companion to humans and has sparked the fancy of millions of pet owners throughout the world. In this section, you'll learn how to properly care for your own cat, with subjects again ranging from the selection process to coping with a diabetic feline. There are even tips on training these often independent creatures!

The popularity of pet birds is quickly closing the gap on that of dogs and cats. Part III covers important information regarding the selection, housing, feeding, breeding, and preventive

health care of pet birds, as well as select diseases and disorders. There are even sections on hand-raising baby birds and on emergency and first aid procedures for our feathered friends.

For those pet fanciers who prefer less conventional choices for companionship, Part IV is where it's at! This section deals with "exotic" or "alternative" pets, including rabbits, guinea pigs, small rodents, chinchillas, prairie dogs, hedgehogs, ferrets, miniature pot-bellied pigs, reptiles, amphibians, and invertebrates. For tropical fish lovers, there is also a chapter (Chap. 55) on aquarium maintenance and disease prevention in fish.

Part V presents a variety of topics of interest to pet owners. With the growth and popularity of holistic approaches to health care among people, it is no wonder that many satisfied followers are seeking such approaches for their pets. As a result, therapies such as acupuncture, herbal medicine, homeopathy, chiropractic, and nutritional medicine are presented as they relate to the health and well-being of our pets. What you read may surprise you!

Saving money seems to be first and foremost on everyone's mind these days. And by following the 10 super strategies suggested in Chapter 57 for reducing the cost of pet ownership, you'll quickly realize that this book was one of the best investments you ever made! Chapter 58, on increasing your pet's longevity, summarizes key points presented in the book that have direct bearing on the health and longevity of our companions.

Take them to heart, and you'll enjoy a long, fruitful relationship with your companion. Chapter 59, on zoonotic diseases, or diseases that can be transmitted from pets to people, is sure to open some eyes! Although the chances of transmission can be minimized through good preventive health-care, many pet owners fail to realize the importance of such care. As a result, they can be inadvertently placing their health and indeed, that of their families, in jeopardy! Finally, a comprehensive look at cancer in dogs and cats (see Chap. 60) will increase owner awareness and understanding of this universal disease challenge.

You may have wondered how to administer cardiopulmonary resuscitation (C.P.R.) to a dog or a cat, or what to do if your pet swallows a poison. The appendix covers those and other important topics regarding emergencies and first aid for dogs and cats. In fact, this could very well be the most important section of the book, since in emergency situations, timing is of the essence. As a result, foreknowledge of the material presented in the appendix could very well save your pet's life one day.

The Complete Home Veterinary Guide contains two additional valuable features that make it a must for all pet owners. The first is the multitude of illustrations that accompany the text of the book. Someone once said, "A picture is worth a thousand words," and this advice was kept in mind when preparing this book. The second special feature is the complete and comprehensive index.

Of course, despite all the features mentioned above, this book is not designed to replace quality veterinary care for pets, but rather to supplement it. If your pet is exhibiting signs of injury or illness, always consult your veterinarian. Remember: The sooner a correct diagnosis can be made by a qualified veterinarian, the greater the chances are for a successful treatment.

Now get set for an informative voyage into the world of pets with the *The Complete Home Veterinary Guide* as your guide. Regardless of your pet fancy, this book is sure to enrich the relationship you have with your loving companion!

DOGS

The Dog: What can be said about this magnificent creature? For 10,000 years, it has been an integral part of human social and cultural development. Its blood and toil has helped humans discover new lands and build civilizations; its effectiveness in war has helped topple the same. It has hunted alongside humans for centuries and has been hunted by them for food. As eyes for the blind and ears for the deaf, the dog has become an indispensable member of our modern society. But what really sets the dog apart from all the rest? Millions of dog lovers will agree that it's the special loyalty and devotion the dog exhibits toward members of our own species—*homo sapiens*—a characteristic that has justly earned it the proper title of "[hu]man's best friend."

All dogs are thought to originate from a common ancestor called *Miacis,* a carnivorous creature that lived over 40 million years ago.

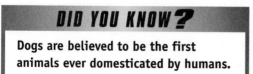

DID YOU KNOW?

Dogs are believed to be the first animals ever domesticated by humans.

There are many theories regarding the evolutionary process that concluded with the domestic dog as we know it. One popular theory is that the modern-day dog descended from the wolf, which, over time, gave rise to four separate groups of dogs.

The first group, the *dingo group,* is descended from the wolves of Asia. Its members were dispersed throughout the Asian, African, and Australian continents. Modern-day descendants of this group include Rhodesian ridgebacks, basenjis, and the dingoes of Australia. One distinguishing characteristic of this group is that they don't like to bark too much.

A second group of dogs, the *greyhound group,* is believed to have evolved from wolves inhabiting the open plains of Asia, Africa, and the Middle East. The oldest member of this group, the saluki, is thought to have originated prior to 1400 B.C.! Distinguishing features of the greyhound group include a keen eyesight and incredible speed, two characteristics the Egyptians found especially useful for hunting purposes. Besides the saluki, other modern representatives include the Afghan hound, the borzoi, and, of course, the greyhound.

The *Northern dog group* is believed to have evolved from the large gray wolf of northern Europe. Generally regarded as one-master dogs, descendants of this group have been used by humans for a variety of functions, including pulling sleds (Alaskan malamutes, Siberian huskies), hunting game (Norwegian elk hound), and guarding flocks (collies).

A final group, the *mastiff group,* arose from wolves occupying the mountainous regions of Eurasia. Gifted with a keen sense of smell, members of this group were commonly used as war dogs and as hunting dogs. We still utilize the hunting skills of retrievers, setters, and pointers today. The mastiff, the St. Bernard, and the Great Pyrenees are a few of the more sizable members of this group.

Choosing the Right Dog for You

Because the ancestry of the dog is so diverse, all shapes, sizes, colors, coat lengths, and personalities abound (Fig. 1.1). With such a multitude of groups and types from which to select your pet, how do you know which dog is going to be just right for you and for your particular situation? Questions you should ask yourself include the following :

FIGURE 1.1   Dogs are believed to be descended from wolves.

- Why do I want a dog in the first place?

- What type of dog do I want?

- Do I want an indoor or outdoor dog?

- How will my new dog affect my existing pets?

- Am I willing to devote the time and money needed to be a responsible pet owner?

Your answers to these questions will have great bearing on the type of dog you will ultimately choose.

Why Do You Want a Dog?

Regardless of breed, whether they are genetically pure or genetic blends, dogs make great companions and can fulfill a variety of roles (Fig. 1.2). After all, they weren't coined "[hu]man's best friend" for nothing! Obviously, when making your selection, keep your particular wants and needs in mind. Although you may want your dog to fulfill several roles, know what the primary one will be, and base your selection on that.

For instance, do you want an exercise companion? If so, you will want a larger dog with a stride length and aerobic capacity that won't slow you down. On the other hand, you might want a cute lap warmer just to keep you company. If so, toy breeds weighing less than 10 pounds were bred specifically for this purpose. By going into the selection process knowing why you want a dog in the first place, chances are you won't be disappointed with your results.

FIGURE 1.2 Companionship is the number one reason for dog ownership.

Dogs as Protectors

Many persons want a dog for protection purposes. If you envision your new acquisition roaming your backyard, lunging and snarling at anyone or anything that approaches your gate, then forget it. Obtaining a dog under such pretenses is only asking for trouble (and a lawsuit), and is heartily discouraged. If, on the other hand, you plan to treat your dog as a true companion and household member, as well as protector, then your qualifications for ownership are acceptable.

It stands to reason that an 85-pound rottweiler with glistening white teeth would certainly be more imposing to an intruder than would an 11-pound Lhasa apso (not that the latter wouldn't tear into him—Lhasa apsos were originally bred for this purpose)! However, it is instinctive that all dogs, regardless of breed or size, will actively defend pack members (and, like it or not, you are a pack member) or territory if threatened. If you want your dog to protect you, it is important that it recognize what does and does not constitute a threat. And this is where professional protection training will come in handy.

All dogs to be used for protection purposes must be properly socialized to people. Military and police dogs are perfect examples. These dogs are trained to attack on command only. Off duty, most are gentle as lambs. This is how your dog should be. Not only will it ensure your safety and that of your family and friends, but it also might prevent a lawsuit! Remember: A socialized dog can be a great protector; an unsocialized dog is downright dangerous!

Dogs as Child Companions

Dogs are an excellent means for educating children about responsibility and about unconditional love! As a result, many parents opt to purchase a new dog for their children (Fig. 1.3). If this is your reason for wanting a dog, keep these guidelines in mind.

First, for maximum benefit and enjoyment, wait until your children are at least 5 years old before acquiring a new pet. Younger children, some of whom might just be starting to crawl or walk, stand a greater chance of being accidentally hurt by a playful pooch than do older children. On the contrary, older children are better equipped to learn about and/or undertake responsibilities associated with pet ownership, and can become active participants in the care of your new dog. And that is why you wanted the dog in the first place, right?

FIGURE 1.3   Dogs are an excellent way to teach children about responsibility and unconditional love!

Choose a pup with an outgoing personality, one that can stand up to the rigors of ownership by a child. Shy, introverted pups rarely satisfy the energy requirements of children. Such dogs might be difficult to socialize and could turn aggressive if mentally traumatized by an overzealous child.

As far as size is concerned, medium to medium-large breeds are preferred for children. Small dogs and toy breeds, because of their small stature, are more susceptible to accidental injury at the hands and feet of young ones. They are also more likely to become aggressive if mishandled. On the other hand, while one of the giant breeds can be gentle as a lamb, such a pet could still pose a significant health threat to your child due to sheer mass.

Personality features to look for include low aggressiveness, high tolerance, and low excitability. Golden retrievers are a favorite among parents, owing to their reputation for gentleness with children. Basset hounds, Labrador retrievers, and collies are also popular picks for children.

If purchasing a puppy, limit your selection to one that is between 8 and 12 weeks old. Because socialization naturally occurs during this time, a greater bond will form between it and your child. Along the same lines, a dog older than 12 weeks of age should not be placed with children unless it is correctly socialized to children. One word of caution: Be certain that your child is not allowed to abuse or hurt the new pet during this sensitive socialization period. Such adverse interaction could ruin their relationship for years to come, as the puppy will have learned to associate your child with pain and abuse. It is every parent's responsibility to teach their children that their cuddly new friend is not a toy, and that it needs to be handled with loving kindness and gentleness.

FIGURE 1.4   As hunting partners, dogs have no equals!

Dogs as Hunters or Exercise Partners

If you are in the market for a hunting dog, there are many from which to choose. Setters, pointers, retrievers, hounds, and spaniels are available in a wide variety of types, shapes, sizes, and abilities. For upland game hunting, setters, pointers, and spaniels fit the bill. For waterfowl, retrievers won't hesitate to plunge into the water to retrieve a fallen bird. For tracking larger game, one of the keen-scented hound breeds might be what you require. Some hunting dogs will do it all!

Keeping your particular needs in mind, research your options thoroughly, and talk with local gun club, hunting club, and/or breed club members to assist you in the decision-making process (Fig. 1.4).

DID YOU KNOW?

The excellent tracking skills of hunting dogs arise in part from their ability to detect distinct volatile fatty acids located on the surface of game or left over on the ground, brush, and/or trees.

As mentioned earlier, if you are interested in an exercise or jogging companion, stick to those dogs that have the size and aerobic capacity to keep up with your exercise pace! Recognize that for your safety, proper command training and equipment is essential before taking your partner on a fitness excursion.

Dogs as Income Sources

Unless you are planning to become (or are already) a professional dog breeder, don't purchase a dog with visions of large profits from the sale of future litters. Most novices find out real fast that breeding operations, if done correctly and humanely (and they should always be), represent a considerable investment in time and money. Be sure to find out what these investments are prior to plunging into the dog-breeding business.

If you are a novice, confine your efforts to one of the medium to large top ten AKC breeds rather than some exotic, delicate breed. As a rule, you'll be rewarded with larger litters and fewer problems with dystocia (difficult or complicated birthing). In addition, the more popular the breed, the greater the demand will be for your puppies, resulting in greater financial rewards.

But beware: When selecting your initial breeding stock, closely scrutinize the pedigree of the dog's parents. All that it takes is one genetic defect to appear in one or more of your dog's offspring, and your reputation as a breeder could be ruined!

Dogs as Competitors

For many, the pleasure of dog ownership is compounded by the thrill of competition in the field or show ring (Fig. 1.5). Thousands of events are sanctioned each year by the American Kennel Club (AKC), an organization dedicated to the advancement of purebred dogs in the United States. Breeders are motivated by these events as well, for earning the reputation of producing champion-quality dogs is rewarding not only to the ego, but to the pocketbook as well.

If you are interested in entering your dog into a competitive event, contact your local kennel club or the American Kennel Club. Check out their Websites on the Internet. These can be valuable sources of information regarding types of competitive events, rules and qualifications, and event schedules.

FIGURE 1.5   The thrill of competition.

Dogs as Gifts

Although your intentions might be pure and from the heart, never surprise someone with a new dog or puppy unless you are positively,
absolutely sure that they actually want one. Think about it; your gift to
them includes not only that furry bundle of energy but also a hearty commitment to training, time, and money. Unfortunately, too many people
do fail to think about it that way, and as a result, our nation's pounds and
shelters are overflowing with unwanted pets turned in by disgruntled or
disinterested gift recipients. As a result, it is always best to allow other
people to come to a decision about pet ownership by themselves, and not
to force it on them by your good intentions. Believe me, everyone will be
happier in the long run!

What Type of Dog Do You Want?

Once you have figured out why you want a dog, you must further narrow your choices as to the type of dog you want. For starters, both purebreds and "mutts" can make great pets, and the decision concerning genetic purity pedigree is entirely up to you. If you choose to go the purebred route, expect to pay more up front for your purchase. In addition, you run greater risk of facing genetic disorders inherent to that particular breed. Being very cautious and prudent in your selection process can minimize this risk. If you don't have your heart set on any breed in particular, publications by the American Kennel Club and other books or Internet sites that discuss the individual breeds and their special characteristics can help you narrow the field.

If you are like many dog fanciers, you might be less finicky about a lengthy pedigree and instead prefer a dog with a more mysterious gene pool. In fact, there are several advantages to owning mixed-breed dogs. First, because of their diluted, colorful ancestries, they exhibit a unique genetic phenomenon known as *hybrid vigor.* Because of hybrid vigor, mixed-breed dogs as a group tend to be healthier and live longer than their purebred cousins.

Another obvious advantage of choosing a hybrid is that they cost less to purchase than do their papered peers. Ask yourself, "What type of purebred breed(s) do I like best?" Then start looking in newspapers, pet stores, and pounds for crosses that contain the genes of your favored breed. In many instances, the genetic makeup of the parents is not known, yet you can usually guess the genetic background of the candidate by its anatomic features or by its behavior.

For instance, let's say you notice that its ears stand erect, yet are folded halfway. There is a good chance that this mystery breed is part terrier. Does it enjoy lounging around in its water dish? It could contain some retriever blood. Chances are, your particu-

FACT OR FICTION

A dog with AKC "papers" is of higher quality than one without papers.
FICTION. . Because the AKC has no real regulatory enforcement of quality standards outside its sanctioned events, purchasing a pet with "papers" is not a guarantee of quality.

lar mixed-breed will be a cross between one or more of the top 10 most popular AKC breeds. Contact the AKC for the most current standings.

Of course, space limitations will play an important role in the type of dog you'll ultimately choose. Obviously, apartment dwellers will probably want to select a smaller dog than do those living in homes. However, there are exceptions to every rule!

Do You Want an Indoor or Outdoor Dog?

When choosing a dog, consider carefully where it will live. All dogs, even if you plan on housing yours outside, should be first trained as indoor dogs. That way, if the need ever arises, it is easier (and certainly more sanitary) to later convert a dog accustomed to the rules of the house into an outdoor one rather than vice versa. Moreover, dogs raised as indoor dogs will respond more favorably to training and generally have less behavioral problems than do those who are perpetually banished to the backyard from day 1. The reason: Dogs crave the attention and company of people, and, in most instances, a backyard existence does not fulfill this need. Problem behaviors and disobedience frequently result from such discontent.

Excitability, size, and coat length are certainly three important considerations when deciding where to house your dog. As a rule, the more excitable the dog, the more attention that dog will crave. Isolate an excitable dog in a backyard away from human contact, and you are just begging for behavioral problems. At the same time, selecting a large dog for a house pet and failing to housetrain or command-train it properly could lead to some very disturbing and destructive confrontations. If you are not willing to devote the time to properly train an indoor dog, you should stick to one of the smaller breeds in order to limit the damage that is bound to happen to your carpet and furniture!

Depending on the type of climate in which you live, haircoat length becomes an important factor to consider when deciding on an indoor versus outdoor pet. In colder climates, dogs with long coats and dense undercoats can withstand the outdoor chill much better than can their shorthaired counterparts. Conversely, dogs such as the Siberian husky and the chow chow may have a difficult time coping with Southern (U.S.) heat without the benefits of air conditioning (Fig. 1.6).

FIGURE 1.6 Dogs with long coats and/or thick undercoats should not be housed outdoors in hot climates.

Outdoor dogs with long haircoats will also require more grooming time and effort to keep their coats healthy than if they were housed indoors (Fig. 1.7). Are you willing to devote this time each day? If not, either select a dog with a shorter coat, or plan on bringing your dog inside.

How Will Your New Dog Affect Existing Pets?

Are there other pets in your household already? Jealousies or incompatibilities could arise that need to be anticipated before a new dog is brought home. Household cats and small pocket pets can harbor a particular aversion to such new additions to the family!

Another important question to ask yourself if you already own a dog is whether it has ever been socialized to other dogs. If your existing dog is the type that attacks anything that barks or moves on four legs, it might do the same to your new arrival. Unsocialized dogs (and even some that are properly socialized) might refuse to accept another dog into its territory without a fight.

FIGURE 1.7   Plan on brushing your dog every day!

All newcomers should be gradually introduced to existing pets one day at a time. Keep your new dog in a separate room or enclosure, allowing initial interactions to take place only under your direct supervision. These gradual encounters should eventually help break the ice between the two and help establish a social pecking order within your furry family.

Are You Willing to Be a Responsible Pet Owner?

By nature, dogs are pack animals (Fig. 1.8), and they crave attention from their human pack members. Certainly one of the easiest ways to upset a dog is to habitually ignore it. In fact, this lack of owner attention underlies many of the problem behaviors seen in dogs. Regardless of whether you keep your dog indoors or outdoors, consider how much quality time you will be able to spend with it each day. If your projections are low because of your job or other commitments, oftentimes two dogs are better than one. The company that one provides

DID YOU KNOW?

A dog and cat that are correctly socialized to one another can become best of buddies, whereas the same two animals, if socialization does not occur, often become bitter enemies!

FIGURE 1.8   Dogs are pack animals, and they crave attention.

the other while you are away can be an effective substitute for your affections.

Another factor to consider is how much time you will have to devote to training. It cannot be stressed enough how important this is to your future relationship with your dog. One of the major causes of owner dissatisfaction is an unruly pet. As a result, training is definitely one aspect of pet ownership that should never be neglected.

The financial aspect of pet ownership is a major consideration if you are in the market for a dog. The actual cost of owning a dog, including food, supplies, training, and veterinary care, can cost hundreds of dollars each year, assuming it stays healthy. Are you willing to accept financial responsibility for your pet's preventive health care or for treatment in an event of an injury or illness? If not, you are not ready to own a dog.

Finding the Right Dog

Once you have decided on a particular type or breed of dog, it is time to start your search. Newspapers, reputable pet stores, veterinary hospitals, the Internet, and word of mouth are fruitful avenues for information. If you're not interested in a registered dog, check with the local humane society or animal shelter in your area. These are excellent places to start and are often jam-packed with mixed-breed and purebred dogs alike, all eager to be adopted into happy homes. Usually, one can be yours to love for only a nominal adoption fee. As an added benefit, you will feel good knowing that you've saved an unwanted pet from an uncertain future.

If a registered purebred fits your fancy, check pet stores or contact dog breeders within your area. Local veterinarians and groomers can often provide specific recommendations. Magazines catering to dog owners or outdoorsmen can also be excellent reference sources for purebred dogs and professional breeders. Finally, dog shows and other competitive events provide a means of giving you a first-hand glimpse of the cream of the crop and can give you the opportunity to meet prominent dog breeders and handlers in person.

Before you go shopping, do your homework. Find out what the going rate is for the particular breed you want. Beware of the small-time operator who advertises or offers you a great deal on a "registered" pup. These "great deals" can end up costing you more in the long run in medical bills and emotional drain. Where quality counts, stick with reputable breeders who can provide you with the complete pedigrees of both parents and references of satisfied clients. This rule holds true for pet store purchases as well. Before buying from a pet store, ask where the pup came from and who the breeder was. Ask to see the pedigrees of both parents. Reputable pet stores will have all this information readily available for your inspection.

And don't hesitate to ask for references from satisfied customers. If the store is unwilling or unable to divulge such information, look elsewhere.

Whatever you do, don't rush your decision. Remember: You are making a long-term commitment. Take your time, and pick out that special puppy or dog just right for you!

The Prepurchase Exam

Once you think you've finally found the perfect companion, now what? For starters, you want to be sure you are getting a healthy specimen. Be sure to inquire as to the dog's vaccination and deworming history. You might be told that all of the "shots" and dewormings have been given. This might be true, but don't hesitate to ask for, in writing, dates and names of products used. Your veterinarian can then review this list for completeness during the professional prepurchase exam.

Even before your veterinarian gets involved, you should perform your own prepurchase exam on the prospect. It is easy to do on site and will help clarify many problems that might otherwise elude the untrained eye.

1. *Environment.* For starters, take note of the surrounding environment in which the puppy or dog is being kept. Does it look and smell clean, or is it filthy, with urine and feces lying all around? If the latter is true, you should question the integrity of the seller. Observe all the pups and dogs in the litter or group. Do any appear sickly, depressed, or otherwise unhealthy? An infectious disease can run rampant through such a congregation of canines, and it could be just beginning to rear its ugly head within the group.

2. *Attitude.* Now focus your attention on the actual candidate. Start with overall attitude. Does it appear active and healthy, or is it lethargic and depressed? Are breathing problems evident? Does it seem friendly and outgoing to people and to the other dogs in the group, or does it seem shy and introverted? Dogs destined to be good pets should take an instant fancy to people, and should outwardly display this affection. At the same time, avoid those individuals with overbearing and domineering personalities. Observe how your favorite

Table 1.1 Congenital/Inherited Disorders in Dogs*

Eyes	Microphthalmia (small eyes)
	Juvenile cataracts
	Entropion/ectropion
	Glaucoma
	Prolapsed third eyelid
	Tear duct deformity
Ears	Congenital deafness
Nervous system	Epilepsy
	Brain underdevelopment
	Hydrocephalus
	Invertebral disk disease
Integument	Umbilical hernia
	Inguinal hernia
	Demodectic mange
Digestive system	Cleft palate
	Abnormal dentition
	Overbite/underbite
Musculoskeletal system	Dwarfism
	Joint dislocations
	Patellar luxation
Cardiovascular system	Blood clotting disorders
	Heart murmurs
	Anemia
Respiratory system	Collapsed trachea
Reproductive system	Retained testicles (cryptorchidism)

*For ethical purposes, all pets with congenital or inherited disorders should be neutered.

treats other members of its group. Domineering personalities are usually quite evident. As a general rule, choose one that is "middle of the road," that is, not too domineering, yet not too shy.

3. *Skin and coat.* Once attitude and personality have been evaluated, check out the skin and coat. Any fleas or ticks present? How about any hair loss, scabs, or signs of infection? These could be indicators of diseases such as mange or ringworm, both of which can be zoonotic.

4. *Lumps, bumps, or swellings.* Run your hands over the umbilical area and, on both sides, over the points where the inner thighs connect with the abdominal wall. Notice any soft, fluctuant masses? These could be herniations, especially in young pups. Run your hands over the entire body surface, feeling for other types of lumps and bumps. Note the location of any you find. Does the belly seem distended? If so, it could be full of food, or it could be full of worms? Check beneath the tail, looking for tapeworm segments and for evidence of diarrhea. Soiling on and around the hair in this area should tip you off to a potential intestinal disorder.

5. *Other anatomical considerations.* Observe leg conformation and the way the puppy or dog walks and runs. Any obvious deformity and/or lameness should be noted. In male dogs, check for descent of the testicles. Both testicles should be present at birth. If they aren't, be prepared to neuter at a later date, not only for health reasons, but also to prevent the passage of this inheritable trait to future generations.

6. *Head region.* Now focus in on the head region. Using your eyes and your nose, check the ears for discharges or strong odors (usually a sign of infection). Both eyes should be free of matter, with no cloudiness or redness. Compare both eyes, making sure that they are of the same size, and that the pupils are of the same diameter. Glance at the nose, noting any discharges or crusts. Finally, look into the mouth. The gums should be pink. If they are white, the dog could be anemic. Look for any severe underbites or overbites, or any missing teeth. Also glance at the roof of the mouth. In young puppies, a cleft palate is a serious birth defect, and unless it is surgically corrected, it will lead to secondary aspiration pneumonia and ultimately death.

Consulting Your Veterinarian

Let's say you've completed the exam described above and have found some potential problem areas. What do you do next? First, don't be discouraged. Many of these conditions have quick, inexpensive solutions. This is where your veterinarian comes in handy.

Don't feel awkward asking the seller to pick up the tab for a professional prepurchase exam by a veterinarian of your choice. Those sellers confidant in the quality of their dogs should have no qualms about this. If they balk, a warning light should flash in your head. And don't get suckered into a "money back" or "lifetime" guarantee on a pet as an alternative to a professional prepurchase screen. Such a guarantee doesn't protect you against the emotional distress caused by having to return a pet to which you've already grown attached.

Follow your veterinarian's recommendations as to the purchase quality of the dog in question. If the one you have your heart set on does have medical problems that can be easily corrected, negotiate with the seller to deduct these costs from the purchase price. The seller isn't legally (only morally, perhaps) obligated to do so; as a result, you must decide on your next move if the seller refuses or fails to compromise. The extra expense out of your own pocketbook might be worth it if you think you have truly found the dog of your dreams! You be the judge.

Dogproofing Your Home

If you choose to allow your new pet to have the run of the house, be sure to take proper steps to petproof your home. For instance, be sure to place all plants out of reach. Dogs have an instinctive craving for vegetation, and puppies are no exception. As a result, they could harm themselves if they ingest one of the many poisonous ornamental varieties.

Keep all electrical cords well out of reach. This might mean banishing your playful pet from certain areas of the house, but it is a minor inconvenience compared to a potentially fatal accident. Again, puppies love to chew, and electrical cords can be mighty appetizing.

Puppies explore with their mouths, and will pick up anything. Keep everything that's not a toy out of reach, including spare change.

Also, be careful when putting out roach or rat poisons, as these can attract curious mouths.

You will probably want to confine unsupervised puppies to non-carpeted floors until proper housetraining has been accomplished. Even so-called stain-resistant carpets can buckle under the strain of repeated bombardments.

Your Dog's Outdoor Home

No doubt there will undoubtedly be special situations which prohibit the indoor dwelling of a grown dog. In these instances, outdoor accommodations provided for your dog must take into account its comfort and well-being. Remember that dogs get hot and cold just as we do, and when housed outdoors, need to be provided a means of protection against extremes in the weather. Your friend is entitled to a sturdy, well-insulated shelter. It should be positioned in a relatively shady area of the yard, and should also be elevated a few inches off of the ground using bricks or wood to prevent flooding in the event of a rain storm. Ideally, the shelter should have a short, enclosed porch which leads into the main house. This will help keep wind drafts from penetrating into the main living area. The main living quarters should be large enough to allow your dog to turn around comfortably within, yet confined enough to provide it a sense of security and to concentrate heat during cold winter days. Finally, a ramp should be included to allow your dog easy access into its elevated home.

If you build the house yourself, select sturdy building materials, remembering that they must be able to withstand constant punishment from teeth and claws. If fiberglass insulation is to be used, make certain it remains well contained and sealed within the walls and roof, since such material can cause severe gastrointestinal upset if swallowed.

If you plan to further confine your dog to a pen or run, use a smooth concrete or quarry tile as flooring on which to place the doghouse. Although such surfaces may not be the most comfortable for your pet, they are the most sanitary and easy to clean. Floors consisting of grass, sand, pebbles, and/or just plain dirt only serve to trap and accumulate filth and disease, and should be avoided.

The fence surrounding the enclosure should be made of wire chain link and be tall enough to prevent escape. Exposed metal points from the chain links at the top of the fencing material should not extend above the metal support bar in order to prevent injuries if your dog does try to jump. The same rule applies for the bottom perimeter of the fence as well, just in case your dog tries to squeeze its way out.

Naming Your Dog

Naming your new pet should be fun and involve the entire family. You can even find entire books dedicated to choosing the right name for your dog at your favorite bookstore. When deciding on a name, stick to one that has two syllables. This will enable your dog to tell the difference between its name and those one-syllable commands it must learn. You can make the name sound even more unique by adding a vowel sound to the end of it.

Always be consistent when calling your dog by name. If you name your dog "Beverly," don't shorten it to "Bev." You'll only confuse your pet as to its true identity!

Introducing Your Dog to Its New Home

You will want to do everything in your power to make your new dog feel comfortable and secure in its new home (see Table 1.2). Establish an area in the house that your dog can call its own and completely dog-proof it. When you first get your dog home, introduce it to its special room immediately. Allow it some time to scope out the new surroundings, including the sleeping accommodations you have provided.

Your new dog's first encounters with the rest of your family are important. Be sure initial introductions, be they with children or other adults in the family, turn out to be positive ones. Carefully supervise child-pet interactions, and stress to your children the importance of gentle play and handling. Instruct your children and other adults on the proper way to pick up and hold a new puppy. Dogs should not be picked up solely by the front legs or by the neck. Instead, the entire body should be picked up as one unit, with the hind end supported, not left dangling in midair.

Table 1.2 Supply Checklist for Your New Dog

Food and water bowls	Brush
Dog (puppy) food	Comb
Collar	Bed or dog house
Leash	Travel kennel
Training lead and rope	Nail trimmers
Identification tag	Ear cleanser
City license (if required)	Toothbrush/paste
Proof of rabies vaccination	Toys
Heartworm preventative	Flea control products

If they had it their way, most children, and some adults, for that matter, would choose to play with a new puppy 24 hours a day. However, you need to stress the importance of a rest time for the new puppy after periods of play, and lay down strict ground rules against disturbing it during this downtime (Fig. 1.9).

Rules of Play

Puppies love to play. In fact, it's part of their normal behavioral development. However, realize that there is a right way to go about it and a wrong way. Follow these "rules of play" to be sure your approach is the correct approach (Fig. 1.10).

To begin, toys that you purchase for your dog to play with should be made of nylon, rawhide, or hard rubber. Of the three, hard nylon is most desirable because it is most easily digested if swallowed. Rawhides are fine if the dog takes its time and chews slowly. For those dogs that don't take the time to chew, avoid giving them rawhides because they can cause serious stomach upset and even intestinal blockages if swallowed whole. Also, some dogs have difficulty differentiating rawhide from refined leather, which could put your new pair of shoes in serious jeopardy! Rubber chew toys should be solid and sturdy so that they cannot be easily

FIGURE 1.9 Puppies need their rest, too!

ripped apart by sharp puppy teeth. Avoid chew toys with plastic "squeaks" in them. Most dogs can extract these too easily, only to swallow or aspirate them into their airways. Regardless of the type of chew toy you pick, choose it as you would a child's toy. If its design is such that it could cause suffocation or serious problems if swallowed, put it back and choose a safer one.

Avoid using old socks, shoes, or sweatshirts as substitute toys for your dog because it won't be able to tell the difference between old and new. Allow a puppy to chew on an old shoe or sweatshirt while still an

FIGURE 1.10   Make sure your puppy learns the rules of play early!

adolescent, and you might find it fancying your expensive leather shoes or tennis warmups when it grows up.

It is okay to play hard with your puppy, but overt rough-housing should be avoided. If a play session progresses from a friendly romp to an all-out frontal assault, end it immediately. Your puppy needs to learn how to keep its activity level to a socially acceptable intensity. Also, be sure that your puppy gets plenty of time to rest after an especially active play period.

The same rules of moderation apply to chewing. It is perfectly natural for a puppy to want to explore its environment with its mouth. During play, there will be times when the pup will bite and nip too much or too hard. When this occurs, shout "No," pull your arm or leg away, and provide a chew toy as a substitute. In essence, what you want to tell your pup is that it is fine to use its mouth to explore, just as long as it knows its limits. You'll be surprised how quickly it will learn!

Traveling with Your Dog

When transporting a dog by car, the comfort and safety of both driver and passenger must always be considered. Whether you are bringing your dog home for the first time, or simply taking it on a Sunday afternoon drive, keep these principles in mind to make the trip pleasant and safe for the both of you.

To begin, it is always recommended that, when transporting a pet by automobile, a travel carrier or kennel be used. Not only will your pet feel more secure in a carrier, helping to reduce stress associated with the ride, but it will help minimize jostling and jolting movements that could injure your dog. This carrier should be just large enough for your dog to stand up and turn around in (Fig. 1.11). If your dog is too large to fit comfortably into one of these carriers, or if the carrier is too big for your car, then the back seat is the place to be, not the front seat! An excited or stressed-out, unrestrained pet in the passenger seat of an automobile creates a very dangerous driving condition. In addition, dogs allowed to ride in front seats can suffer serious or even fatal injuries should airbags deploy in an accident. Special canine restraint harnesses or seat belts are available commercially and should be used to secure your dog to its assigned seat.

Even though dogs love to stick their heads out of car windows while cars are in motion (it reminds them of the wind in their faces while they are chasing prey), don't let yours do it. Dogs with long, floppy ears can suffer trauma to their earflaps. Also, both ear and eye injuries from insects and flying road debris can easily occur in dogs allowed such freedoms.

For truck owners, never allow any dog to ride in the bed of a pickup truck unless it is confined to a carrier. Many of the dogs you see lying dead along the highway met their fate as a result of owners failing to heed such commonsense advice!

You shouldn't have to be told to keep the interior of your car well ventilated and cool. Excited or stressed dogs forced to travel in hot, stuffy cars, or ones filled with cigarette or cigar smoke, are likely to suffer ill effects. Cigarette smoke in itself can be quite irritating to the eyes, nose, and mucous membranes of your dog. As a result, as a courtesy to your canine friend, refrain from smoking until you have reached your final destination. Car exhaust fumes can have the same effect as cigarette smoke. As a result, if stopped in traffic for any appreciable amount of time, crack the car windows and keep the air within the car circulating.

Never leave your dog in a parked car unattended for more than 5 minutes on days when environmental temperatures exceed 72 degrees or drop below 55

FIGURE 1.11 When traveling by car, always confine your pet to a travel carrier.

degrees Fahrenheit, as heat stroke or hypothermia (respectively) could result (Fig. 1.12). If you do have to leave your pet for a few minutes, be sure to leave two or more windows partially opened to allow for air

FIGURE 1.12 Leaving your dog in a parked car even with the windows cracked can be hazardous to its health.

Dr. P's Vet Tip

When transporting your pet by air, book nonstop flights to reduce the chances of your pet becoming lost luggage. In addition, during the summer, book flights early in the mornings or late in the evenings to avoid exposing your pet to midday heat.

circulation. In addition, the use of window shields and sun visors is strongly recommended to help temporarily keep temperatures within the car at acceptable levels.

For trips over two hours, be sure to take plenty of breaks to give your dog water and to relieve itself. Ice can also be offered along the way to keep your dog's thirst at bay. If your dog gets carsick, try feeding a small amount of food about 30 minutes prior to your trip. Often, an empty stomach coupled with stress can predispose a pet to motion sickness. If this fails to work, an antihistamine may be administered prior to travel. Contact your veterinarian concerning the various over-the-counter medications you can use and their dosages.

For those dogs absolutely terrified of the car, a stronger tranquilizer prescribed by your veterinarian may be needed. Although this should be used only as a last resort, it can be an effective tool for taking the edge off your phobic pooch and thereby make the ride much less stressful for everyone concerned.

When transporting your dog by airplane, special precautions should be taken. Always consult your veterinarian beforehand to determine whether any medical conditions your pet may have could be exacerbated by such a trip. For example, high-altitude flying and potential temperature and pressure fluctuations could prove to be harmful to a dog that may be suffering from an underlying heart disorder. Speak with your airline representatives concerning their accommodations and restrictions for traveling pets. Most will require a current health certificate prior to transport and will restrict travel if environmental temperatures are too extreme.

CHAPTER 2

Training Your Dog

Proper training is definitely the key to a happy owner-pet relationship. It establishes your dominance in the relationship between you and your pet right from the start, and it can help prevent many behavioral challenges from rearing their ugly heads later on. Not only that, solid training can also keep your pet out of troublesome situations that could threaten both its health and yours (Fig. 2.1)!

There is one characteristic exhibited by every good trainer: patience. Without this virtue, you're going to have a tough time teaching your dog anything. You need to set aside time each day for training and resolve to stick to it. Keep in mind that it will only be a temporary dip into your time budget. After all, the more time you devote from the start, the quicker and more satisfying the results will be.

What about training school? Is it worth the time and the money? The answer is "Yes" if it will motivate you to devote the time for the task at hand. You still have to be physically present during the training (you can't have someone else train your dog, then expect your star pupil to respond likewise to your commands). If you choose this route, enroll in an active-participation class in which an instructor directs you and your dog through the training session. However, keep in mind that such a class doesn't relieve you of your homework duties. You still need to practice with your dog daily on your home turf.

FIGURE 2.1 Proper training will enhance the relationship that you have with your dog.

DID YOU KNOW?

Dogs learn in primarily two ways. The most basic type of learning, called *habituation,* is characterized by a diminishing response to a repeated stimulus over time. In the second type of learning, called *associative learning,* a dog creates a "link" between two or more different types of actions, results, and/or stimuli (e.g., food rewards for desired behavior). Socialization is regarded as a form of this associative learning.

Main Principles of Training

To be effective, any training method needs to follow some basic principles to ensure its success. These principles include the following:

Consistency and Repetition

The magic success formula for all training endeavors is derived from two key concepts: consistency and repetition. Consistency provides the building blocks; repetition is the mortar that holds the program together. Without the two, you might as well try to teach a rock how to fetch. The results will be the same!

Consistency means more than just using the same commands over and over again. It also means using the same praises and corrections each time and keeping your voice tones consistently unique for each. Even your body language and postures used during training should remain uniform between sessions. As trivial as it might seem, dogs pick up on stuff like that. Dogs like routine, so stick to it. Train at the same hour each day and for the same length of time for each daily session.

DR. P's VET TIP

When training, always end your session on a positive note. This will greatly accelerate your results.

Just as important as consistency to a dog's learning process is repetition. Repeating an action or training drill over and over will help reinforce the positive response you are looking for. Furthermore, the more repetition you implement in training, the leaner and more refined your dog's learned skills become.

Verbal Praise

Use verbal praise instead of physical pain in your training sessions. Dogs, especially puppies, should always be rewarded for a job well done with lots of praise and attention. Food treats are fine as a reward supplement, but they should never replace verbal compliments. Punishment might be warranted if your puppy or dog purposely disobeys a command or commits an undesirable act, but this should never take the form of physical punishment. There are alternative means, each of which is just as effective as—if not more effective than—physical violence.

Punishment

Dogs can be reprimanded effectively with a sharp verbal "No." Water sprayers, air horns, a can full of coins, handheld vacuums, and so on can all be used to gain your dog's attention quickly without inflicting any pain.

If you decide to use punishment, be sure to institute it quickly, preferably within 5 seconds of the act. If you don't apply it before this time expires, any punishment thereafter might satisfy your anger, but it will serve no useful training purpose.

FACT OR **FICTION**

Sticking a dog's nose in its stool or urine is an effective form of punishment. **FICTION**. C'mon, who thought of this one? For some reason, this type of punishment is still quite popular among pet owners, even though it serves no useful purpose. Dogs are attracted to the smell of this stuff, anyway!

Don't extend your punishment past a few seconds. Prolonged exhortations will only confuse your pet (and cause you to lose your voice).

Never use your pet's name during the negative reinforcement. If you do, your dog might begin to associate its name with the bad act and eventually become a basket case whenever the name is called. Reserve this name calling for positive, happy experiences only.

If you do punish, always follow it up shortly thereafter with a command or drill that will lead to a praise situation. Remember: The most effective training programs rely on praise more than they do on punishment. For some dogs, simply withholding praise from them is punishment enough to modify their behavior! By rewarding your dog for doing good rather than punishing it for doing bad, you'll get the positive results you are looking for much faster.

Get the Whole Family Involved

In any training situation, always try to involve all members of the family. An all-too-common scenario is one in which a dog virtually ignores the commands of anyone except the one person who trained it. To avoid this, get the whole family involved. Just be sure to remain consistent within the family with regard to the training methods and commands used.

Use Short Commands

All verbal commands you employ need to be kept short and sweet. Using slightly different voice tones for each command will help prevent confusion. If verbal punishment is to be used, make certain that it is totally different in tone and in presentation than the other commands.

Start Young

Always start your dog's training at an early age. While it is true that certain advanced training techniques can be best taught at around 6 months of age, basic training, including house training, should be started as early as 8 weeks of age. If basic command training is not taught this early in life, poor habits arise later on, some of which can put a damper on future training efforts.

Keep Training Sessions Short

Try to keep the training sessions short and to the point. For puppies 8 to 12 weeks of age, devoting 10 minutes two to three times daily will yield excellent results. As your dog matures, the length of each of these sessions can increase. Let your dog's attitude be your judge. If it seems bored, indifferent, or has become totally unruly, you have probably exceeded its attention span.

End on a Good Note

Always end your training session on a good note. Doing so is very constructive in terms of your pet's mental development, and effectively sets the tone for the next session.

Asserting Your Dominance

One of the purposes of training a dog is to establish your dominance in the relationship right from the start. Your dog needs to realize who is boss and who is the head of the pack. There are five effective ways to assert this dominance during your training sessions.

   1. *Control your dog's neck region.* It is especially important in the early stages of training to maintain control of your dog's head region. The collar and leash were originally developed with this principle in mind. Dogs are naturally very protective of their neck regions because in a fight, this is often the first area that the opponent will attack. You've probably noticed that most dogs will lower their heads in a menacing gesture if they feel threatened. Puppies grasped by the scruff of the neck by their mother become limp in willful submission. Along these same lines, when your dog allows you to put a collar on and maneuver it with leash pressure applied to the neck region, it is in essence submitting itself to your dominant position. Your dog's new collar should be fitted in such a way that you can easily slip your fingers between the buckled collar and the neck. If you've got a puppy, make certain to check the collar's tightness on a weekly basis. As the puppy grows, the collar must be loosened periodically to accommodate for an increasing neck diameter.

2. *Apply pressure along the back region.* As you will see, this concept comes in handy when teaching your dog to sit or lie down. In nature, a dog will assert its dominance over another by mounting its back with his forelegs. By applying direct pressure on the back (e.g., teaching it to sit) or by simply petting your dog along the neck and back region, you are essentially doing the same.

3. *Stay calm and relaxed during training.* Dogs can sense nervousness or distress on your part. Overbearing and stubborn dogs might try to take advantage of such a situation and refuse to submit to authority. Exhibit an air of confidence and control around your dog, and it will catch on quickly that you mean business.

4. *Avoid physical or painful punishments.* As mentioned before, physical punishment really serves no purpose and could trigger retaliatory attacks, which will completely ruin your training sessions, not to mention the relationship you have with your dog. In addition, such behavior on your part could turn your pet into a sniveling, cowering mass of extreme submissiveness, which also will hinder your training efforts. Your dog will be more worried about when the next punishment is coming rather than about learning the training material.

5. *Establish direct eye contact.* Always establish and maintain direct eye contact with your dog when giving a command. Don't be the first to look away, for the one who wins the stare-down wins the dominance play. Use caution: An overly aggressive dog might refuse to submit, and may interpret your eye contact as a direct challenge. For these dogs, it's best to avoid the confrontation and seek professional training assistance.

Basic Commands

Some tools of the trade you'll want to acquire to assist you in your training efforts include a leash, a 20- to 25-foot rope with an end clasp attached, and a sturdy collar. You can substitute a harness if you desire.

If you decide to use a slip or choke chain collar, read the package directions and make certain you know how to use it properly; otherwise, serious damage to your pet's neck and trachea could result. Because this device can be easily misused, many veterinarians recommend not using them unless you are a seasoned trainer. If your new puppy or dog is not used to wearing a collar or leash, you must get it accustomed to these two devices prior to any training efforts (Fig. 2.2). Start by placing a collar on your dog and allowing it to wear it for a few days. Once you think your dog feels fairly comfortable with it on, attach a leash to the clasp and allow your dog to walk around with the leash dragging behind. To protect your dog from snagging furniture or other objects with the leash and hurting itself, be sure you supervise these sessions. After about six to eight sessions over the course of 2 days, your dog should feel more comfortable with its leash being attached to its collar, and should be ready for further instruction.

Heel

The first command you will teach your four-legged student is to heel, or walk at your side (Fig. 2.3). To begin, position yourself on your dog's right side facing forward, with its shoulders even with your left knee. Take up the slack on the leash to prevent your dog from becoming entangled in the excess. Now, in simultaneous fashion, give a quick forward tug on the lead, say "heel," and start forward with your left foot leading. As your dog follows, keep its head level and in control using the leash. Start out by going five yards at a time, then stopping to praise for a job well done.

If your dog refuses to move on your initial command, go back to the starting

FIGURE 2.2 All dogs should be taught to walk on a leash.

FIGURE 2.3 Teaching your dog to "heel."

line and set up again. This time, if needed, follow the quick tug with an encouraging pull on the lead to initiate movement. Start and stop frequently, praising your dog as you go. As your dog starts to catch on, increase the distance you go each time. The ultimate goal is to have your dog walk briskly by your side until a command is given to do otherwise.

If your dog gets too far out in front of you, a quick, backward tug on the lead should be used to correct the discrepancy. For those trainees more interested in playing rather than learning, stop the training session temporarily until your dog settles down. Don't scold or show any other acknowledgment of its antics. It will soon learn that you mean business!

Once your dog has become comfortable walking in straight lines by your side, take it through some turns both to the right and to the left. During the turns, your dog's shoulder should remain aligned with your knee.

Stop

Once your dog responds favorably to the heel command, it is time to teach it the command "stop." With your dog heeling at your side, give a sharp backward tug on the leash as you say "stop," and halt your forward motion. (The verbal exclamation differentiates this from the backward tug used to slow an overenergized heeler.) Hold the stop for

3 seconds, then praise heavily for compliance. Afterward, have your dog heel again, and repeat the process over and over again, gradually increasing the amount of time you require your pet to remain still.

Sit and Stay

From the stop position, pull upwards on your dog's lead while at the same time saying "sit," and pushing down on its rear end to achieve the sitting position (Fig. 2.4). Have your dog maintain this posture for a good 5 seconds, then break into a heel. Gradually increase the sitting interval as your training progresses.

FIGURE 2.4   The "sit" command.

When your dog has learned what "sit" and "stop" mean, it's time to teach the "stay" command (Fig. 2.5). This is where your 20-foot rope lead comes in handy. Attach this to the collar and walk your dog again through the heel-stop-sit routine. Once your dog is in the sitting position, place your left

FIGURE 2.5   The "stay" command.

hand in front of its face and say "stay." Now slowly walk about 3 yards away, keeping your back to your dog. If it breaks its "stay" when you move, reel your dog in with the lead, and make it immediately return to the sitting position. Then try again.

If the student stays in place even for three seconds after you walk away, heap on bundles of praise. If your dog still disobeys, walk it through your heel-stop-sit routine a few more times before returning to the "stay" command. As your pet starts to catch on, you can begin increasing the distances you go and time intervals for it to stay put.

Other Commands

Heel, stop, sit, and stay are the basic obedience commands that you should start teaching your dog as early as 8 weeks of age. Two other commands that are optional, yet could come in handy in certain instances, are "down" and "come."

"Down" should be included as an adjunct to the "sit" command. After your dog is in the sitting position, say the command while applying downward pressure with your free hand to its shoulder region. Note the difference from the "sit" command, in which downward pressure is applied to the hind end. Now, from this down position, you can proceed into the "stay" drill.

"Come" can be taught as a continuation of the "stay" command. With your dog sitting or lying at rope's length, give a quick forward tug while uttering the command "come." Again, use the lead to reel it in if it decides to wander off track. Praise your dog only if it comes directly to you from its original starting position.

When, and only when, your dog has mastered these commands and responds to them consistently can you discard the leash or lead. For off-leash training, repeat each command sequence as before. Don't hesitate to put the lead back on if your dog fails to cooperate. At first, it is especially important to hold all off-leash training sessions in enclosed areas or fenced-in yards to prevent your star pupil from dashing off into the sunset!

Housebreaking Your Puppy

Puppies should be housebroken at an early age, preferably as close to 8 weeks old as possible because this is when the period of stable learning begins in adolescent dogs. Their minds are wide open to suggestions, and they learn quite quickly at this early stage of life.

If you expect to yield successful results, you must be willing to devote some quality time to the task. Recognize that puppies have four fairly predictable elimination times:

1. After waking

2. After eating

3. After exercising

4. Just before retiring for the night

Make a concerted effort to take your puppy outside at these times, and every 3 to 4 hours in between. When you suspect that it has to go (excrete), take your pup outside and set it down in the grass. If elimination takes place, praise your puppy, and then take it immediately back inside the house. By doing so, you will help it associate the act with the location (Fig. 2.6).

If a minute passes and your puppy hasn't gone (excreted), take it back inside. Don't leave it outside to play or roam. Puppies trained in this manner soon realize that their primary business for being outside is to eliminate, not to play. What happens if you catch your puppy in midact? If this is the case, go ahead and rush it outside. The puppy might finish what it started before you make it out, but don't get upset. Again, praise it immensely for going outside, and then bring it immediately back inside.

If you happen to miss an accident altogether, don't fret. If you saw it happen, a verbal punishment is warranted. On the other hand, if you didn't see it happen, do nothing. Simply try to be more attentive next time.

Other housetraining tips to remember are

1. Be sure your puppy is current on its vaccines (since it will be

FIGURE 2.6 When housebreaking a puppy, use lots of praise and avoid punishment.

going outside) and is free of intestinal parasites. The latter is very important because the presence of worms in the intestinal tract will cause unpredictable urges to eliminate.

2. Always use lots of praise; never physically punish. Again, remember that puppies crave praise, and if they don't get it, they feel punished. Give plenty of praise when they deserve it; hold it back when they don't.

3. When verbal punishment is indicated, avoid associating your puppy's name with the reprimand. For instance, simply say "bad," instead of "bad dog, Sugar." By leaving names out of it, the puppy won't associate its name with the bad behavior.

4. Establish a regular feeding schedule for your new puppy. Feed no more than twice daily, and take your puppy outside after it finishes each meal. It is preferable to feed the evening portion before 6:00 P.M. in order to help reduce the number of overnight accidents that can occur otherwise.

5. To help prevent accidents, keep your puppy in a confined area at night. It should be puppyproofed and have a floor that won't be damaged if a slipup occurs. Utility rooms and half-bathrooms work well for this purpose, as do kitchens if they can be cornered off. If accidents occurs during the night or while you are away, don't get upset. As your training sessions progress, you'll find that this will become less and less of a problem. A natural instinct of any canine is to keep its "den" clean. These inherent instincts, combined with correct house-training efforts on your part, will help fuel the success of your training efforts.

6. When cleaning up an accident, always use an odor neutralizer rather than a deodorizer on the area in question. These are available at most pet stores, and will usually eliminate any lingering scents that can lure your pet back to the same spot. Avoid using ammonia-based cleaners, since ammonia is a normal component of canine urine. Such cleaners might serve to attract, rather than to repel, repeat offenders.

Socializing Your Dog

There is no doubt that the most important time in a new puppy's life is between the ages of three and 12 weeks. During this short time span, a puppy will learn who it is, who you are, and who and what all of those other living, moving beings surrounding it are as well. This stage of life in which such vital learning takes place is called the *socialization period* (Fig. 2.7).

If for some reason a puppy fails to be properly introduced to members of its own species or to other

FIGURE 2.7 All dogs must be properly socialized to children.

species (including children) during this time, then there is a good chance that it will not recognize these individuals for what or who they are, and it might even show aggressiveness toward them (Fig. 2.8). For example, dogs intended for breeding purposes must be properly socialized to members of their own species if they are to be

FIGURE 2.8 Dogs and cats can become best of friends if socialized at an early age.

expected to breed with one of these members. Good examples of dogs not properly socialized include those that show extreme aggressiveness to men only, or those aggressive to children. Dogs see people as two species: big people and little people. As a result, while a dog might recognize an adult person as the one who feeds and commands it, it might not recognize a small toddler as one who commands the same respect if the pet is never properly socialized to small children. Some dogs aren't fit for any type of human interaction at all. These have absolutely no socialization whatsoever and could pose a threat to humans.

Improper or negative socialization is even worse than no socialization at all. Any traumatic experience or physical punishment that occurs between 8 and 12 weeks of age could permanently scar a dog's personality relative to a specific group or species for life. For instance, many dogs that fear certain humans were actually abused by a member of this group during the socialization period. This is one reason why all physical punishment should be avoided during this time in your puppy's life. Such activity could damage the pup's relationship with the person doing the punishing for life!

The existence of this socialization period is one reason you should select puppies less than 12 weeks of age when choosing a new companion. If you don't, you have no way of knowing whether proper socialization has taken place, and you might be faced with behavioral problems in the future. Socializing a puppy is not difficult if you remember to keep all interactions positive and to guard against any physically and emotionally traumatic situations.

Before introducing a new puppy to other dogs, it should have had at least two of its series of puppy shots and be current on its vaccination schedule. In addition, always be sure that the animals you are planning to introduce it to are socialized themselves, or else you could have a battle on your hands.

Weekend excursions to a park and/or neighborhood strolls with your puppy are some of the more opportune ways of introducing it to other animals and to other adults and children. Allow children to freely interact with your pup, but again, be sure none gets too rough. For best results, you should repeat such encounters throughout your pup's socialization period. And by all means praise your puppy for good behavior during these interactions. It will leave a lasting impression on its personality!

One word of caution: Socialization, like any personality skill, can eventually be lost if it is not reinforced periodically. As a result, even as your dog matures, don't just discard those trips to the park or strolls through the neighborhood. Remember: You have to use it or lose it!

Solving Challenging Behaviors

When searching for the leading cause of dissatisfaction among dog owners, problem behaviors top the list. Each year, a multitude of dogs are abandoned, evicted from their homes, or even put to sleep because of annoying behavioral activity. However, by understanding and employing special training techniques and/or therapy to correct such vices, and by allowing veterinarians to play active roles in the treatment process, dog owners can often avoid such drastic actions.

Separation Anxiety

It has happened to many of us—we leave the house, sometimes for only a few minutes, and our "best friend" proceeds to chew up the furniture, bark or howl, and/or eliminate in the house. If your dog behaves this way when you leave your home, it is probably suffering from the behavioral problem known as separation anxiety. [*Note:* Medical problems can be the cause of such aberrant behavior; these must be ruled out before you can safely assume that you are dealing with a case of separation anxiety.] Before you can successfully treat a problem like separation anxiety, it is helpful to know what causes it (Fig. 2.9).

Dogs are considered pack animals; that is, they

FIGURE 2.9   **Dogs enjoy spending time with other members of their "pack."**

DR. P's VET TIP

For cases of separation anxiety that are refractory to conventional management, veterinarians can prescribe specific antianxiety medications to help effect a cure.

prefer to associate in groups rather than act as loners. Because you are its owner, a dog will consider you part of its "pack" and will constantly want to associate with you. When you leave, you separate the dog from its pack, and this creates separation anxiety. This behavior will be magnified if you tend to make a big fuss over the dog when leaving or returning to the house. Furthermore, certain other behavioral patterns on your part, such as rattling the car keys or turning off the television, can be associated to your departure by the dog.

When treating separation anxiety, you must remember that it is an instinctive behavior; it is not due to disobedience and/or lack of training. As a result, overt punishment for the act tends to be unrewarding. In fact, most of these dogs would rather be punished than left alone! The key to treating this problem lies in planning short-term departures, then gradually lengthening them until your dog gets used to your absence.

Begin by stepping out of the house for 10 seconds at a time for the first few days or so. Hopefully this will allow your dog to get used to you leaving the house, since it will learn that you will return soon. Vary your training session times throughout the day. The idea is to gradually lengthen your leaves of absences (30 seconds at first, then 1 minute, then 2 minutes, etc.) so that your departures soon become second nature to the dog.

Points to keep in mind when attempting to break your dog of this annoying behavior are as follows:

1. Don't make a fuss over your dog within 5 to 10 minutes of your arrival to or departure from home. This will help keep the excitement and anxiety levels in your dog to a minimum. During your training sessions, try not to reenter the house while the dog is performing the undesirable act. Doing so will only serve to positively reinforce the dog to repeat the act.

2. Eliminate any behavior that might key the dog off to your departure, such as rattling your car keys, saying "goodbye" to your dog, and so on.

3. For the dog that likes to chew a lot, provide plenty of nylon chew bones to occupy its time.

4. Leaving the television or radio on while you're gone seems to help in some cases.

Excessive (Nuisance) Barking

Let's face it: Some dogs just love to hear their own voices! Unfortunately, most owners and their neighbors hardly share the same adoration. There is no doubt that dogs that bark excessively are a nuisance and can cause many a sleepless night. For this reason, correction of the problem is essential to your sanity, and that of those who live around you.

A dog might bark excessively for a number of reasons. The first is boredom. Dogs that have nothing else to do might simply "sing" to themselves to whittle time away.

Another potential cause is territoriality. Outsiders, whether human or animal, will almost always elicit a bark out of a dog if threatening to encroach on its territory. Dogs can also use the bark indiscriminately as a communiqué to other outsiders to stay away. In such instances, the far-off bay of a neighborhood dog or the slamming of a car door down the street can trigger a barking episode.

Separation anxiety is another common source of nuisance barking. Some dogs have it so bad that they bark continuously when their owner leaves them, even for a short period of time. Often, owners return home to find their dogs hoarse from so much barking.

When attempting to break your dog of this annoying habit, always remember this one principle: If you respond to your dog's barking fit by yelling at it or physically punishing it, you are going to make the problem worse. Dogs that are isolated from their owners for most of the day do not care what kind of attention they receive (positive or negative), as long as they get some. Dogs that are barking out of boredom or from separation anxiety will soon learn that their actions will eventually get them attention, and they'll keep doing it. Even dogs that are barking for other reasons can catch on quickly that such vocalization will bring them a bonus of attention from their beloved owners. As a result, no matter how angry you become, or how sleepy you are, avoid the urge to punish your dog for its barking.

The first thing you need to determine is whether separation anxiety has anything to do with the problem. If you think it does, treat it as you would any other case of separation anxiety. In many cases, dogs that bark for this reason alone can be broken of their habit.

Keep in mind, though, that the source of the barking might involve a combination of the factors, not just one. Dogs that bark for reasons other than separation anxiety need to be given more attention throughout the day. A dog that tends to bark through the night should be given plenty of exercise in the evening to encourage a good night's sleep. A nylon or rawhide chew bone can be helpful at diverting its attention. Feeding its daily ration later in the evening can also promote contentment for the night.

For those times of the day or night that the barking seems the worst, consider bringing the dog inside the house or at least inside the garage. This, of course, will not be possible if you failed to instruct your dog as to the ways of household living when it was a puppy. Nevertheless, removing your dog from its primary territory and/or increasing the amount of contact with members of its pack can help curb the urge to bark. Also, if possible, encourage your neighbors to keep their pets indoors at night, since nighttime roaming of neighborhood dogs and cats are major causes of nuisance barking.

House Soiling

It has happened to many of us: the early morning encounter in the family room or the unexpected (or sometimes expected) surprise awaiting our arrival home from work—house soiling. It is a dirty habit, yet one that millions of pet owners have to put up with each day. In many of these cases, the problem had an origin traceable to puppyhood; for others, it results from developmental behavioral and/or health problems. Regardless of the cause, pet owners can take an active role in most cases to minimize or completely stop this annoying habit.

Don't think you will break your dog of this nasty habit by sticking its face and nose in the excrement after the fact. Not only is this action illogical and inappropriate for the particular situation; some dogs might even enjoy it! Instead, pet owners need to take a more rational approach to identifying the cause and solving the problem. To do that, you must first determine what is causing it (Fig. 2.10).

Lack of or Improper Housetraining

The most common case of house soiling is undoubtedly the failure of an owner

FIGURE 2.10 The cause of housesoiling must be determined before effective treatment can be instituted.

to housetrain the dog properly during its puppyhood. Many pet owners can't understand why their puppies have no problems going on newspapers, but just can't get the knack of going outside. They seem to forget that, to a puppy, newspaper and grass are two different surfaces with different smells. To paper-train a puppy and then expect it to switch easily to another type of surface is asking a lot, and this often presents a confusing dilemma to the poor creature.

Puppies need to be taught right from the start to go outside to use the bathroom instead of encouraging them to go within the confines of the home. At the same time, dogs that will spend a great deal of time outside need to be housetrained as puppies, just in case the need arises later in life to bring them indoors for whatever reason. If you miss this chance when it is a puppy, you could be in for trouble later on.

Contrary to popular opinion, you *can* teach an old dog new tricks, it just takes longer! With older canines that weren't properly potty-trained, proceed with training or retraining as you would with a puppy. Along with lots of praise, a favorite treat or snack can also be used to reinforce desired behavior. For those times you can't be at home to monitor indoor activity, confine your dog to a travel kennel or small bathroom, since dogs are less likely to have premeditated accidents in such confined spaces. Just be reasonable as to the amount of time you make it wait between eliminations.

Separation Anxiety

Inappropriate elimination activity can, as do many other behavioral problems, result from separation anxiety. Dogs left alone may become frustrated and soil one or more parts of the house. Some dogs can even become downright spiteful, targeting favorite furniture, bedding, and, if kept in the garage, even the roofs of automobiles. If your dog is truly suffering from separation anxiety, most of its adverse behavior will occur within 15 to 20 minutes of your departure. This predictability can assist in efforts to correct the problem. Treat this as you would any other case of separation anxiety.

Desire to Delineate Territory

The desire to delineate territory is another reason why a dog may choose to urinate (or sometimes defecate) indiscriminately. Certainly, intact (nonneutered) male dogs are more prone to this instinctive activity. Dogs have such a keen sense of smell that the mere presence of a canine trespasser around the perimeter of the home can set off a urine-marking binge. Owners who move into preowned homes often find out the hard way that the previous owners had a poorly trained or highly territorial pet housed within.

Neutering your pet may or may not help solve this problem, depending on its age. In many older males, house soiling has become more habitual than hormonal, and neutering does little to prevent it.

Use of a pet odor neutralizer on the carpet and baseboards is warranted if you suspect that a previous occupant is to blame. Use of fencing or dog repellent (not poison!) around the perimeter of the house may also help keep persistent urine-markers away from your house.

Extremely Submissive Behavior

Extremely submissive behavior often results in a cowering dog that urinates whenever anyone approaches. This type of adverse elimination is common in dogs that have been abused as puppies or have spent most of their growing years in a kennel or pound facility.

Management of such behavior depends on your actions and body language when approaching or greeting such a dog. Try to avoid direct eye contact and sudden physical contact with such dogs, for by doing so, you can send them into immediate submissiveness. If you've been gone from the house for a while, avoid sudden and exuberant greetings when you get home. By ignoring your dog initially, you'll lower its excitement level, reduce the immediate threat, and give it no reason to urinate.

One trick you can try is to immediately and casually walk over to your dog's food bowl and place some food or treats in it. The idea is to distract your dog's attention away from the excitement of your arrival and create a more comfortable, pleasing situation for it. Once you've been home a while, then you can (and should) offer more of your attention.

Illness or Disease

Finally, don't forget that some diseases or illnesses can cause a pet to urinate or defecate indiscriminately. For instance, dogs that tend to defecate inside the house should be checked for internal parasites. Diets with increased fiber content can also increase the number of trips your pet will need to take outdoors.

Certainly if the stools are semi-formed or seem to differ from normal appearance or consistency, an underlying medical reason should be suspected. In addition, some of the conditions that can increase the frequency and/or urge to urinate include urinary tract infections, kidney disease, and diabetes mellitus. Urinary incontinence, characterized by the inability of the bladder to retain urine as a result of poor sphincter function, is common in older dogs. For these reasons, don't assume that your dog's soiling problem is purely mental. Have the potential medical causes ruled out first, and then you can concentrate on behavioral modification.

Just a word about cleaning up an accident in the house: When using cleaners to tackle the initial mess, be sure that they don't contain ammonia. Dog urine contains a form of ammonia, and such products might actually attract your dog back to the same spot later on. Along this same line, after the initial manual cleaning, your next job is to ensure that residual smell doesn't attract your pet back to the same spot. To accomplish this, you need to employ a product containing odor neutralizers specifically targeted for dogs. These products are available at grocery stores or pet shops. Deodorizers should not be

FIGURE 2.11 Digging behavior is often caused by instinct or by sheer boredom.

used, for it is virtually impossible to completely mask or hide a scent from the keen canine nose.

Digging

Although separation anxiety can cause digging episodes, its influence on this behavior is much less than with other problem behaviors. Instead, sheer boredom and/or instinctive behavior are the two common states of mind that compel a dog to dig (Fig. 2.11).

Dogs with nothing else to do might opt for yard excavation simply to help pass the time or to use up extra energy. The urge to break out of confinement and roam the neighborhood can also compel a dog to start digging. Finally, as you might have already experienced, many dogs like to bury personal items such as bones or toys for exhumation at a later date. Such instinctive behavior, although aggravating, can hardly be considered abnormal, and is difficult to totally eliminate.

Increasing your dog's daily dose of exercise may help resolve its boredom and release any pent-up energy. Diverting the attention of a chronic digger is another plausible treatment approach. For instance, some troublesome cases have responded very well to the addition of another canine playmate. Rawhide bones and other chewing devices can also be used as attention-grabbers, but only if they don't end up underground themselves. If most of the digging occurs at night, overnight confinement to the garage might be the answer to spare your yard from the ravages of claws. Finally, if you haven't already done it, neutering can sometimes help snuff out the strong urge to dig in those dogs wanting to escape the yard and roam the neighborhood.

Destructive Chewing

Many canines are literally "in the doghouse" with their owners because of their destructive chewing. No one wants a pet that seeks and destroys any inanimate object into which it can sink its teeth. However, the urgency for dealing with such behavior is not governed merely by personal property damage. Many of these chewers also end up in veterinary hospitals suffering from gastroenteritis or intestinal obstructions. Hence, such adverse activity can cost more than the replacement value of furniture or fixtures. It can even sometimes cost the life of a pet!

In puppies, destructive chewing can easily arise from lack of training and from inappropriate selection of toys. Although puppies will naturally explore their environment with their mouths, they need to learn at an early age what is and isn't acceptable to chew on. Solid command training is a must in these little guys.

Avoid providing normal household items such as old shoes, T-shirts, or sweatshirts as toys to play with. Puppies can't tell the difference between an old shoe and a new shoe, and they might decide to try out your new pair for a snack one afternoon!

Objects that repeatedly bear the brunt of your dog's teeth should be placed as far out of reach as possible. For furniture or immovable objects, special pet repellents should be sprayed around their perimeters to make a mischievous puppy think twice before sinking its teeth into the item.

In young to middle-aged adults, separation anxiety is probably the number one cause of destructive chewing. As with all cases of separation anxiety and the behavior it provokes, correction of the problem should focus on correction of the anxiety attack. Finally, as with problem barking, boredom plays a leading role in destructive chewing in some adult dogs (Fig. 2.12). If you think this might be the case, increase your dog's daily activity, and provide it with plenty of alternative targets, such as rawhides or nylon bones, on which to chew. Divert its attention, and most likely it will divert its chewing.

Jumping

Talk about annoying behavior! Jumping is right up there with house soiling and incessant barking. Jumpers are usually right there at the door when visitors call and have this innate tendency to spoil a perfectly cordial greeting. After all, nobody wants a dog with dirty paws to jump on their nice, clean clothes, especially if the dog weighs 50 pounds or more!

FIGURE 2.12 Destructive chewing is an annoying behavior that can lead to serious health challenges.

This is one challenging behavior that should never be allowed to gain a firm root in a puppy. Probably the best way to assure this is through strict command training, starting at an early age. Until it learns its commands, be sure to discourage your dog from jumping on you or family members when the occasion arises. When it does jump at or on you, quickly push it off with your hands and shout "No." Or, as an alternative, flex your knee and make sudden contact with its chest, making it fall backward. Just don't overdo it and injure your pet!

For adult dogs that never learned their manners, a refresher course in command training is the most effective method of curing the chronic jumper (Fig. 2.13). Sometimes dogs that jump are simply trying to tell their owners that they want more attention. In such cases, a few more moments of your time devoted to your furry friend each day is an important adjunct to therapy.

Fear of Loud Noises

Fear induced by loud noises such as thunder or gunshots can be a common cause of aberrant behavior in canines. Many people argue that because of the ultrasensitive hearing of dogs, pain induced by the noise or a pressure change might play a bigger role than fear itself. Regardless of the reason, when confronted with the disturbing sound, these dogs often become hysterical and quite destructive in their attempts to escape. Many might even injure themselves or their owners in the process.

In the case of the hunting dog that shies away when a gun is fired, training sessions involving repeated, gradual increases in exposure to the sound of gunfire is an effective method of ridding the dog of its fear. For dogs that fear the sound of thunder, fireworks, and other explosive noise, owners must avoid direct attempts at comforting the pet, since by doing so would be indirectly rewarding the undesirable behavior. If your dog is the

FIGURE 2.13 Proper obedience training is the key to curing the "jumper."

type that comes unglued in these situations, consider letting it "ride out the storm" in a travel kennel. In addition, playing a radio or television loudly in the room where your pet is being kept might help muffle some of the fearful sounds, as well as make your dog feel more at ease.

Your veterinarian can prescribe antianxiety medications for your dog if it has an exceptional fear of loud noises. In any event, these should be used sparingly and only as needed.

Aggressiveness

Of all the undesirable behaviors a dog can exhibit, this one is certainly the most disturbing and the most unacceptable. Aggressiveness can be directed toward other dogs or toward other species, including humans. Certainly dogs harboring an uncontrollable inherent aggressiveness toward the latter pose special problems to their owners in terms of liability as well.

DOMINANCE

This certainly plays an important role in canine aggressiveness. Some dogs refuse to submit to authority and will lash out at anyone or anything that attempts to exert such. In many instances, these dogs were not properly socialized and/or trained when they were young. In others, sex hormones, namely, testosterone, can exert a strong influence as well.

Treatment for such aggressiveness consists of a return to basic command and obedience training. In addition, exercises designed to reestablish dominance should be performed as well. If the aggression is directed toward a particular person in general, he/she too should be included in these exercises. Remember: Extreme caution and a good, strong muzzle are both advised before any attempts at such dominance assertion are made! For domineering male dogs, neutering is recommended prior to any attempts at retraining.

FEAR AND PAIN

Fear and pain are the two other common causes of aggressive showings in canines. If a dog feels threatened or overwhelmingly fearful, it naturally experiences a "fight or flight" syndrome, and might choose the former option over the latter, depending on how it perceives its situation. In addition, dogs have been known to naturally lash out in fear at humans or other animals on being startled, or more frequently, when they are experiencing pain. For this reason, sudden aggressive changes in personality with or without other signs of illness warrant a complete checkup by your veterinarian.

Treating fear-induced aggression is aimed at reducing the threat you or others pose to your pet. If fear aggression is induced by some outside stimulus, such as thunder, then proper restraint and isolation is recommended while the stimulus lasts. If a dog suffers from a vision or hearing deficit, attempts should be made to capture the dog's attention prior to approach. Also, remember that not only is physical punishment a useless tool for training, it can in itself lead to natural, aggressive backlashes due to pain (and fear). This is just one more reason why such punishment should be avoided. Finally, for those dogs suffering from injuries or illnesses, owners should remember to always approach and handle them with caution, for although they might not mean to, they could exhibit aggressive tendencies due to the pain associated with the disease.

Territorial Defense

Dogs, male or female, will certainly defend that property they deem theirs, and they might not hesitate to fight for it. Territorial aggressiveness toward unwelcome animals or people is not uncommon, as many utility-meter readers or mail carriers would attest to! Such aggressive behavior can be just as easily sparked by a perceived encroachment while the dog is eating, or while it is playing with its favorite toy. Many bite wounds to humans have been inflicted because of such actions.

Again, a return to the basics of command training should help curb some of the territorial aggressiveness that might be exhibited by some canines. Certainly, showing some respect for a dog's "private property" (toys, bowls, etc.) and its eating privacy is a commonsense way to avoid this type of aggressive behavior. It is important to impress this concept on children, too, because they are often the most frequent violators of this rule. If a dog seems particularly possessive over toys, bones, and so on, then the number of these objects should be reduced to only one or two items. Also, consider feeding the dog in an isolated area of the house, free from interruptions.

"Mean Streaks"

Finally, certain breeds and canine family lines can have inherent "mean streaks" in them. For instance, chow chows are notorious among veterinary circles for their aggressiveness toward strangers. In addition, pit-bull terriers, because of selective breeding, pose a real threat to any other dog that might cross their paths.

In many instances, this inherent aggressiveness can be harnessed by way of proper socialization and by strict command training. Neutering can be of assistance as well in select instances.

Treatment

The best treatment for most types of aggression is prevention. By adhering to the principles of proper socialization and by proper command training, most behavioral problems related to aggressiveness can be controlled or avoided altogether.

However, for any dog exhibiting aggressiveness, a thorough physical examination and consultation with a veterinarian is warranted. Ruling out underlying medical causes is certainly one reason for this; the other is that your veterinarian might choose to prescribe medications to assist in retraining efforts or as a direct attempt to curb the psychological aspects of your dog's aggressiveness. Antianxiety medications and behavior modification drugs are now commonly used in veterinary medicine to help assist in the correction of many behavioral problems, including aggressiveness. Don't hesitate to ask your veterinarian for more details.

CHAPTER 3

Preventive Health Care

When it comes to health, dogs are similar to people. Some will go through their entire lives without any health problems along the way; others just seem to be prone to every illness that comes along. A number of factors play a role in the susceptibility of dogs to illness, including genetics, environment, nutrition, immune system competence, and, very importantly, the extent of preventive health care provided to them by their owners. In fact, for a dog that is genetically prone to illness, this latter factor can do wonders to help counteract some of these inherent effects. Unfortunately, many pet owners fail to realize the importance of preventive health care; as a result, their pet can ultimately pay the price later in life.

At-Home Physical Exam

Do you worry about your dog's health even when it appears healthy? Your veterinarian can ensure that your dog is thriving by performing a thorough checkup, but what can you do between visits? Dogs cannot verbalize their discomforts, and people often worry that they'll miss the early signs of illness. If you learn to examine your dog at home, you can have that all-important peace of mind between visits to the vet (Fig. 3.1).

FIGURE 3.1 Periodic physical exams performed at home are a vital part of your pet's preventive health care program.

During your next visit to the pet clinic, the veterinarian will probably begin with an examination of your dog. Watch how your veterinarian performs the exam and ask to participate in the process. Discuss your desire to supplement the vet's exams with at-home checks that you will make. Your veterinarian should be pleased with your desire to provide such attention to your dog's health and should be happy to help develop your skills. Your teamwork will provide the consistent attention to details that could prevent a tragedy.

At-home examinations are no substitute for a veterinary checkup, but doing them might one day give you a jump on treating a minor or serious condition. For convenience, these exams can be combined with regular grooming sessions (Table 3.1).

1. *Observe your dog.* Begin the exam by looking at your pet from a distance. Observe its general appearance. Watch it move back and forth. An abnormal gait with or without limping or lameness could indicate such things as nervous system problems or musculoskeletal disorders. Does your dog stand erect and relaxed? Abnormal postures such as a wide stance with the neck extended could indicate breathing difficulties. An arching of the back could indicate abdominal pain. Note the position of your dog's head. A tilted head is often characteristic of a dog with an irritated or infected ear canal. A droopy head can signify depression and overall malaise. What is your pet's attitude? Is it alert, active, and friendly, or is it lethargic, depressed, or aggressive?

Table 3.1 Physical Exam Checklist for Dogs

Date_____	Temperature_____	Weight_____

General evaluation

__Alert	__Disinterested
__Active	__Lethargic
__Healthy appetite	__Poor appetite
__Playful	__Weight loss/gain
__Lameness	__Abnormal posture
__Abnormal aggressiveness	

Skin and haircoat

__Appears normal	__Shedding
__Hair loss	__Mats
__Dull; unkempt	__Tumors or warts
__Scaly	__Parasites
__Dry	__Abnormal lumps under the skin
__Oily	__Pustules
__Itching	

Eyes

__Appear normal	__Haziness/cloudiness
__Clear discharge	__Unequal pupil size
__Mucus discharge	__Discoloration
__Redness	__Squinting
__Eyelid abnormalities	__Protruding third eyelids

Ears

__Appear normal	__Hair loss on pinnae
__Red; swollen	__Bad odor

Table 3.1 Physical Exam Checklist for Dogs (*Continued*)

__Itchy	__Masses
__Creamy, yellow discharge	__Excessive hair
__Brown to black discharge	__Tender
__Head shaking	__Head tilt
Nose and throat	
__Appear normal	__Ulceration on nose
__Nasal discharge	__Crusty nose
__Enlarged lymph nodes (Feel on either side of the neck just under the jaw)	
Mouth, teeth, and gums	
__Appear normal	__Tooth loss
__Broken, discolored, or loose teeth	__Inflamed gums
__Retained deciduous teeth	__Excess salivation
__Tartar accumulation	__Pale gums
__Growths or masses	__Ulcers
__Foul odor	
Miscellaneous	
__Abdominal tenderness	__Increased water consumption
__Coughing	__Decreased water consumption
__Breathing difficulties	__Genital discharge
__Abnormal stools	__Mammary lumps
__Abnormal urination	__Scooting

Sick or injured animals, especially those in pain, often show aggressive behaviors; therefore, handle them with caution. Keep in mind that normal behavior will vary among individuals and in different situations.

2. *Look for warning signs.* Dog owners should be aware of certain clinical signs that could signify serious problems in their pets. Weakness, shortness of breath, coughing, labored breathing, and, as mentioned before, a wide-based stance could be the first signs of heart or lung problems. A pale blue or purple tongue (except in chow chows and shar-peis) can signify poor tissue oxygenation, often the result of circulation problems. If your dog shows any of these signs, obtain a pulse by gently pressing your fingers against the upper, inner portion of a back leg, or on either side of the neck next to the trachea. Normal resting pulse for a dog ranges from 60 to 120 beats per minute. An abnormal pulse or any other signs of heart or lung problems should be reported to your veterinarian immediately. A dog's normal temperature ranges from 99.5 to 102.5 degrees Fahrenheit. Excited or nervous animals might have elevated temperatures, but a temperature due to excitement should rarely exceed 103.5 degrees Fahrenheit (Table 3.2). To take your dog's temperature, lubricate the tip of a plastic electronic thermometer with a water-soluble lubricant. Insert the thermometer into the dog's rectum and hold it in place for at least 2 minutes (Fig. 3.2). If the reading is higher than 103.5 degrees Fahrenheit, you should call your veterinarian for advice. Get into the habit of weighing your dog every 3 months and record your readings. Unexplained weight loss or weight gain that is greater than 5 pounds (2 pounds for small dogs) or a pattern of continual loss or gain should prompt you to contact your veterinarian. Such fluctuations or patterns could signify some underlying medical disorder. Dogs 8 years old or older should be weighed monthly, and unexplained changes in weight should be reported to the veterinarian. Additionally, keep in mind that obesity poses the same health hazards in animals that it does in humans. An overweight dog should be put on a diet and an exercise program formulated and prescribed by its veterinarian.

Table 3.2 Potential Causes of Elevated Body Temperature in Dogs

Fear or excitement
High environmental temperature
Exercise
Infection
Tissue inflammation or trauma
Autoimmune disease
Cancer
Drug reactions
Endocrine disorders

FIGURE 3.2   Use a digital thermometer to obtain your pet's temperature.

3. *Inspect the head region.* Using a systematic approach when performing the examination, start at the head and working toward the rear. As you go, check each body part for abnormalities. A check sheet might be helpful to remind you of each stop along the way, and it will be an excellent record for future reference.

Eyes. Any abnormalities you detect involving the eyes should be brought to the attention of your veterinarian. Redness, cloudiness, discharge (or drainage), squinting, or unequal pupil sizes could signify trouble. The white of the eye, called the *sclera,* should be just that—white. If inflammation is present, the scleras are usually reddened. Yellow-tinged or jaundiced scleras indicate the presence of a serious condition, such as liver failure. A thorough exam by a veterinarian is the only way to determine the cause of the jaundice. Check the dog's eyelids. Be sure that no foreign objects are irritating the surfaces of the eyes. Constant, untreated irritation can lead to corneal injuries, which are extremely painful. Eyelid abnormalities require immediate veterinary attention to prevent significant eye damage.

Ears. Inspect the ears and note any foul smell or discharge. A black or brown discharge could signify an ear mite infestation or a yeast infection. A yellowish, creamy discharge means a bacterial infection is present. Other signs of ear disease include constant scratching at the ears, head shaking, and head tilting. Ear problems are very common in dogs; therefore, every dog owner should implement a program of ear cleaning to prevent problems from arising. Never insert anything directly into the ear canal. This would only push debris further into the canal and increase the chance of injury to the eardrum.

Excessive hair growth in or around the ear canal traps moisture and can lead to the development of infections. Breeds such as poodles, cocker spaniels, Maltese, bearded collies, and other longhairs should receive special attention. Hair should be plucked, not cut, from the ear canal. Cut hair can lodge in the ear and is very difficult to remove. A veterinarian or a qualified groomer can remove the accumulated hair, or he/she can instruct you in how to keep the area clean.

Nostrils. Discharges from the nostrils should alert you to a potential disease condition. Clear discharges usually indicate either allergies or viral infections. A green, mucus discharge usually indicates bacterial infection, which can be caused by a variety of diseases or a lodged foreign object. Bleeding from the nose could result from trauma, tumors, foreign bodies, or a blood-clotting disorder. Look for tumors and ulcerations affecting the mucous membranes of the nose.

Mouth. Gently open your dog's mouth by grasping the head and upper jaw with one hand, tilting the head back, and using your other hand to separate the jaws. The gums and mucous membranes should be moist and pink (except in animals with very dark pigmentation). Pale, dry mucous membranes might indicate anemia, dehydration, or shock. If you suspect a problem, obtain a capillary refill time by pressing on the upper gum with your index finger. The gum region under your finger should turn white. Release the pressure and the gum should return to a pink color within two seconds. If it takes longer, consult your veterinarian. Check the mouth for swollen gums, foreign objects, tumors, ulcerations, and sores. A foul odor can be caused by excessive dental tartar or by tumors or infections in the mouth.

4. *Inspect the body.* Run your hands over your pet's entire body and feel for lumps or bumps. If you have any doubt that what you feel is normal, you should consult your veterinarian. Lumps can indicate abscesses, enlarged lymph nodes, cysts, foreign bodies, soft tissue swellings (such as hernias and bruises), or cancer. The earlier you detect and treat cancer, the better the chances are for complete recovery. Be sure to check for lumps in the mammary region of female dogs (especially if they have not been spayed). The testicles of intact male dogs should be examined for abnormal swellings and masses. Intact males and females run higher risks of developing certain types of cancer than do neutered animals. Note any discharges from the reproductive tract. Not all discharges are abnormal, but some discharges indicate the presence of infections. For example, female dogs coming into heat can have a normal bloody discharge lasting up to 2 weeks. Also, an intact male dog may have a slight green discharge around the opening of its prepuce, yet this rarely denotes a problem. Often an odor is the first noticeable sign of infection of the reproductive tract. If you have any doubt as to whether a discharge is normal, consult your veterinarian. The stomach, intestines, liver, pancreas, spleen, and kidneys are all located in the abdomen. Gently press both sides of the abdomen just behind the ribcage. (*Note:* Some dogs immediately become tense when you do this.) Slowly work your way to the hip region, gently pressing as you go. Unless you have training in palpation (the act of feeling with the hand to determine physical diagnosis), don't expect to know what you are feeling. The purpose of doing this is to detect any swelling, tenderness, pain, or obvious masses involving the abdomen. If you feel anything strange, seek the opinion of your veterinarian.

5. *Inspect the skin and coat.* Evaluate your dog's skin and coat carefully. Signs of skin problems include hair loss, itchiness, redness, oiliness, scaliness, crustiness, and infection. Look closely for parasites, such as fleas and ticks, which can cause a number of skin problems. Poor nutrition or metabolic disorder (abnormal thyroid function, for example) can cause a dog's hair to become dull and lifeless. The potential causes of skin and coat disorders are so numerous that a veterinarian should diagnose all such disorders. Your early-warning system will enable you to treat the problems before they become serious.

6. *Other observations.* If your dog scoots its rear across the floor, continually bites at its rear end, or has difficulty defecating, it could have impacted anal sacs. These sacs are located at the four and eight o'clock positions beneath the dog's anus. Normally, the dog will empty the sacs when it defecates. Occasionally, fluid can accumulate in the sacs, and they will need to be manually expressed by you, your vet, or your dog's groomer. If left untreated, the sacs could become infected, and could eventually rupture.

If your dog struggles against your attempts to examine it, you might consider reevaluating your obedience training. If you dislike struggling with your pet, so will your veterinarian. A dog that will not cooperate during the examination is difficult to diagnose and treat. This regular examination should teach your dog to cooperate with handling, which in itself is a very valuable lesson.

Remember: Your veterinarian wants to keep your dog in top condition but cannot do it alone. With a little practice, you should be able to complete your physical examination in a matter of minutes. This is time well spent when your dog's health is at stake.

The ABCs of Immunity

The theory behind vaccinating any pet is to provide artificial exposure to certain disease-causing organisms, thereby priming the body's immune system before actual exposure occurs. Doing so will allow for a rapid, effective immune response if this exposure does happen, without the lag time associated with a first exposure.

If their mother has been properly vaccinated prior to pregnancy, most puppies receive protective antibodies from their mother through nursing, primarily during the first 24 hours of life. These "passive" antibodies are important, since the immune system of a neonate less than 6 weeks of age is incapable of mounting an effective response to any antigen (foreign organism or substance). Around 8 weeks of age, levels of these antibodies begin to taper off, leaving the puppy to fend for itself.

If a puppy that still has adequate levels of passive antibodies present in its system is immunized, the vaccination will be rendered ineffective. For this reason, initial vaccinations for such puppies are

Vaccines given to puppies 8 weeks of age or younger are generally ineffective. **F**ACT. Vaccines administered before a puppy is 8 weeks old are rendered useless by antibodies that the puppy received from its mother while nursing. In addition, even if the puppy did not receive such antibodies, its immune system is often too immature at 6 weeks of age to respond effectively to antigenic stimulation.

usually given around 8 weeks of age, when levels of passive antibodies begin to decrease. Vaccination as early as 6 weeks of age is indicated in those instances where the mother was not current on her vaccinations, or if lack of passive antibody absorption is a possibility (i.e., inadequate nursing during the first hours of life).

Those diseases that can be vaccinated against in dogs include

Distemper

Parvovirus

Infectious canine hepatitis

Parainfluenza

Rabies

Canine contagious respiratory disease (kennel cough; *Bordetella*)

Leptospirosis

Coronavirus

Lyme disease

Giardia

The first five vaccinations are considered core vaccines, and should be administered to all dogs. The remaining vaccines are optional, and can be given at your veterinarian's discretion. Depending on the type of vaccination that is being given, booster immunizations of the core vaccines are normally given every 3 to 4 weeks until a puppy reaches 16 weeks of age. The purpose of this schedule is to successively prime the immune response to a higher level with each booster given to ensure that, if the puppy eventually meets up with one of the diseases in question, a maximized immune response will be achieved.

Dogs may receive boosters on these vaccines; the frequency depends on a variety of factors. Many veterinary practitioners and specialists are opting to use extended vaccination schedules for dogs in lieu of the traditional "yearly booster" approach. These changes in traditional protocol are based on research indicating that

■ Certain vaccines may provide extended immunity, and in some cases, lifelong immunity after an initial series of immunizations.

■ Vaccines administered after this immunity has been established may be neutralized and rendered ineffective by the dog's immune system.

■ Repeated immunizations using certain vaccine agents have been linked to an isolated number of cases of autoimmune hemolytic anemia, arthritis, kidney disease, and other autoimmune disorders.

One example of an extended vaccination schedule used for dogs is as follows. Core vaccines, including distemper, parvovirus, and canine infectious hepatitis, are administered to puppies at 8 weeks of age, and then repeated at 12 and 16 weeks of age, for a total of three puppy immunizations. A fourth core vaccine, rabies, is administered between 12 and 16 weeks of age.

All core vaccines are boostered at 1 and 2 years of age. After 2 years of age, boosters are administered every 3 years for the remainder of the dog's life. The exception to this would be the rabies vaccine, which may need to be administered each year, depending on the laws of the state in which the owner lives.

As an alternate approach, some practitioners opt to rotate the vaccinations every 3 years. For instance, a distemper booster may be given at 3 years of age, a parvo booster at 6 years of age, an infectious canine hepatitis booster at 9 years of age, and so on.

As for the optional (noncore) vaccines, they are used at the discretion of each individual veterinarian. For instance, the intranasal vaccine for canine contagious respiratory disease (kennel cough) need only be administered in those dogs that are going to be boarded or grouped with other dogs. If this is the case, and a dog has not received the vaccine within the past 6 months, it should receive a vaccination at least one week prior to the scheduled event.

On a final note, research is also suggesting that individual vaccines that provide protection against a single type of disease ("univalent" vaccines) should be administered in lieu of those containing multiple agents that stimulate immunity against more than one type of disease ("multivalent" vaccines). The traditional "five-way" and "seven-way" vaccines used in dogs for years are examples of multivalent vaccines. Even though it may mean more needles for your pet, the protection conferred by univalent vaccines is deemed superior to that of the multivalent varieties.

As you can see, much is changing regarding the principles behind immunizations in dogs. Continuing research is being performed to determine the best vaccine protocol for this species. Regardless of types of vaccines used and frequency of immunizations, such a protocol must be one that provides maximum protection with minimum risk to the pet. Be sure to ask your veterinarian about the latest research findings regarding canine immunology, and about the best vaccination protocol for your particular pet.

Staying Ahead of Internal Parasites

Left undetected and untreated, intestinal parasites can rob your dog of much-needed nutrients, can cause severe gastrointestinal upset, and can predispose it to secondary disease, such as parvovirus. Internal parasites are widespread throughout the canine population. To make matters worse, many internal parasites of dogs are also classified as zoonotic diseases; that is, they can be directly communicable to humans, especially children. As a result, controlling canine intestinal parasites is a vital part of any preventive health care program.

Management of canine intestinal worms should begin when a puppy is as young as 3 weeks of age. At this age, these puppies can harbor immature hookworms and roundworms without any evidence of eggs shed in the stool. Puppies should receive medications for these parasites at 3, 6, and 9 weeks of age, regardless of whether eggs are detected in the pup's stool.

Stool Examinations

More treatments might be necessary for those puppies found to be actually harboring worms. Stool examinations on such a pup should be performed by a veterinarian at 6, 9, and 12 weeks of age to ensure that your pet is indeed free of these parasites and is not shedding eggs into the environment.

Frequent stool checks such as these will also assist in the detection of two other common intestinal parasites: tapeworms and coccidia. The latter parasite can especially cause severe gastroenteritis and sometimes even neurological problems in puppies if left undetected and untreated.

Most heartworm preventives available also contain medication to protect against common intestinal parasites in dogs. As a result, if your dog is taking such medication (and it should be!), it does not need to be routinely dewormed. However, your pet's stools should still be examined for parasite eggs at least once a year, just to be safe. Stool exams should also be conducted on any ill animal, regardless of clinical signs. Even when the worms do not directly cause the illness, their mere presence and effect on the host's immune system can exacerbate any disease, regardless of cause.

Sanitary Environment

Aside from routine stool checks, good environmental sanitation is another way to lessen the impact of canine intestinal parasites. Many parasite eggs that are shed into the environment via feces take days of sitting in the sunlight or in other favorable environmental conditions before becoming infective to other dogs. As a result, keeping all fecal matter (whether your dog's or that of an unwelcome visitor) cleaned up out of your dog's environment on a daily basis is a very effective way of protecting your pet (and yourself) from these worms.

Staying Ahead of Fleas and Ticks

Much confusion exists in the proper approaches to external parasite control and prevention in dogs. Many different products are now available for external parasite control. The key to successful control is choosing and properly using the products that provide the best possible results for the specific external parasite and environment involved.

Flea Control

Fleas are by far the most common external parasites with which your dog will have to contend. Effective flea control entails not only treatment for fleas on the pet, but environmental control as well (Fig. 3.3). Consult with your veterinarian concerning the best approach to take to relieve your dog of these pesky parasites.

Insecticide Sprays, Powders, Collars, and Dips

Once comprising the vanguard in the war against fleas and ticks, these products are being replaced by newer, more effective agents. However, some can still be helpful in certain situations, and warrant mention here.

Flea and tick sprays, available in both liquid and aerosol forms, are useful for spot treatments. Sprays containing natural chemicals called *pyrethrins,* derived from chrysanthemums, are the preferred products over others for flea control due to their safety and efficacy if used properly. The big advantage of natural pyrethrins is that they are relatively safe for use on pets of all ages. The disadvantage is that they have poor residual flea-fighting activity, lasting only a day or so. Newer, synthetic pyrethrin products available on the market today have improved this residual activity while still maintaining a good safety margin. If pyrethrin products are used, frequent spray application on both the dog and in its environment (bedding, carpet, etc.) is imperative for effective flea control. In some instances, this means on a daily basis. Just be sure before doing so to check the label on the particular product you are using to confirm the safety of this practice. If you are in doubt, always follow label directions!

FIGURE 3.3   With the advent of sophisticated methods and products, flea control has never been easier!

As with the sprays, pyrethrin-containing powders are preferred over others because of their low-toxicity potentials. Powders do not evaporate as do liquid products; therefore, under dry conditions, powders stay active on the hair and skin somewhat longer than sprays. Again, frequent application is required for best results. Exposure to water inactivates most insecticide powders.

Insecticide shampoos and collars are common items in retail stores and in most veterinary clinics. However, since frequent shampoo can lead to excessively dry skin, and collars are of little use to begin with, these products are not recommended for flea control. Dips, which consist only of highly concentrated preparations of insecticides, are also no longer recommended for flea and tick control, because of their highly toxic nature and with the advent of newer, safer products.

Second-Generation (Once-a-Month) Products

When treating for parasites on your dog, a number of products designed to be administered only once per month are now available. For instance, fipronil (marketed under the trade name Frontline, etc.) kills adult fleas on dogs and helps to break the flea life cycle by killing immature fleas before they can lay eggs. This product is also effective against ticks that your dog may encounter in the woods or field. Applied as a spray or topical drops, fipronil collects within the hair follicles and sebaceous glands of the skin, providing good residual action after initial application. Imidacloprid is yet another addition to the flea control arsenal that can be incorporated into a comprehensive flea control program. Imidacloprid (e.g., Advantage) works by killing adult fleas on contact, before they can lay eggs. Applied as topical drops on the back, the manufacturer of this product claims that it retains its effectiveness even after shampooing or repeated swimming. Lufenuron (e.g., Program) is a product designed to be taken internally by your dog. Available in tablet form, lufenuron exerts its flea control action by sterilizing the fleas that bite the dog. Since they cannot reproduce, fleas are eventually eliminated (in a contained environment) via attrition. It is important to remember that lufenuron does not actually kill fleas. As a result, products that kill adult fleas must be used in conjunction with this treatment in order to achieve effective flea control. As one might expect, many veterinarians recommend this product for those dogs kept in an indoor (contained) environment.

Natural Remedies

Throughout the years, countless natural remedies for parasite control have been touted as effective alternatives to insecticides. Some of these substances or devices are worn or applied externally; some are designed to be taken internally.

Products such as brewer's yeast, garlic, and B vitamins have all been implicated at one time or another as flea-control remedies. Unfortunately, controlled scientific studies indicate little to no benefit in flea control with these products.

Certain products containing abrasive-type ingredients (e.g., silica gel and diatomaceous earth) are available for external flea control. These noninsecticidal products act by damaging the chitin exoskeleton of the flea, leading to desiccation (drying up) and death of the flea.

Moderate success has been reported with these abrasive-type products. Drying and/or mild irritation of the pet's skin may occur with these products. Frequent application (four to seven times weekly) is required if these are to be used.

Electronic flea collars have limited popularity, as well as limited benefits. Although manufacturers may stand by their efficacy, scientific studies have shown that their worth in controlling external parasites is minimal. The idea behind them is that the device emits a high-frequency sound that can't be heard by humans or dogs, yet it drives fleas away. Unfortunately, aside from their relative ineffectiveness, some models might indeed deliver an audible pitch that can be heard by—and might be quite discomforting to—the dog wearing the collar.

Environmental Control

Environmental control of fleas begins in the home (Fig. 3.4). You can use insecticidal foggers to get the job done, or you can employ a professional exterminator. For excellent results, you can also use polymerized borate compounds, available under various brand names from your veterinarian or favorite pet supply store. Sprinkled on the carpets, baseboards, and/or furniture, these compounds will kill all fleas that come in contact with them. Noticeable results are usually obtained within a week after application. Best of all, these powders are odorless, easy to use, and safe for pets and children. Under normal conditions, application of this product must be performed every 6 to 12 months. Carpets must remain dry for continued efficacy; if the carpet becomes damp or is shampooed, reapplication will be necessary.

Your yard should be treated with insecticidal granules every 6 to 8 weeks during the warm months of the year. Alternating the types of insecticidal granules used with each treatment (several different types are available commercially) can improve effectiveness of your overall control program.

Tick Control

Besides fleas, the next most prevalent external parasite that your dog will likely encounter is the tick. Controlling ticks on your dog and in your environment is important not only for your pet's health, but for yours as well. These unsightly parasites, which attach themselves to their host via sucking mouthparts, can transmit serious diseases such as Rocky Mountain Spotted Fever and Lyme disease to pets and to people. As far as their canine hosts are concerned, untreated infestations can also lead to skin irritation and in severe cases, blood-loss anemia.

Female ticks lay their eggs in and under sheltered areas in the environment, such as wood stumps, rocks, and wall crevices. Once hatched, the larvae, called "seed ticks," will crawl up onto grass stems or bushes and attach themselves to a host that may happen to pass by. Depending on their life cycle, immature ticks may seek out one to three different host animals to complete the maturation process into an adult.

Since ticks are sensitive to the same type of chemicals as are fleas, treatment and control is basically the same. Certain topical once-a-month treatments for fleas in dogs can be effective in controlling ticks as well.

FIGURE 3.4 Environmental treatment is required for effective flea control.

Ask your veterinarian for details. Flea and tick collars are sometimes effective at keeping ticks out of the ears. A pyrethrin spray can also be applied to your dog's haircoat prior to a trip to the field to discourage ticks from attaching.

Certainly a thorough and consistent treatment of the yard (and sometimes the house) with an approved insecticide is the cornerstone of an effective control program. Since ticks can live for months in their surrounding habitat without a blood meal, treatment should be performed every 2 to 4 weeks during the peak tick seasons in your area.

If a tick happens to attach itself to your dog, use a pyrethrin spray to kill it. Never attempt to remove ticks from your dog by applying manual pressure alone, or by applying a hot match or needle to the tick's body. Most ticks first killed by the application of a pyrethrin spray will eventually fall off after they die. In some cases, you may need to manually remove the dead tick after spraying. When picking them off your dog, never use your bare hands in order to prevent accidental exposure to disease. Instead, use a pair of gloves and tweezers to grasp the dead tick as close to its attachment site as possible, then pull straight up using constant tension. Once the tick is freed, wash the bite wound with soap and water and then apply a first aid cream or ointment to prevent infection. Again, be sure the tick is completely dead before removal; this will insure that the tick's mouthparts come out attached to the rest of the body. If left behind, the mouthparts can cause an irritating localized skin reaction.

Preventing Canine Heartworm Disease

Heartworm disease is a devastating disease of dogs, responsible for tens of thousands of deaths each year. Most of these occur due to the destruction that these worms do not just to the heart, but the lungs, liver, and kidneys as well. In some cases, the worm burden within the heart and blood vessels can become so great that circulation of blood is actually compromised, resulting in sudden death. Other infected dogs can go years without showing any signs of heartworm disease, seemingly forming a symbiotic relationship with the parasites. Regardless of its presentation, the presence of heartworm disease puts a tremendous burden on the body's organs and immune system. (For more information regarding canine heartworm disease, see Chap. 7.)

The good news is that this destructive disease is completely and easily preventable! The most popular heartworm preventive medications come in tablet form, and are designed to be given only once a month. If your dog is not currently on a heartworm prevention program, call right now and schedule an appointment with your veterinarian to start one. As a responsible pet owner, you owe it to your companion (Fig. 3.5)! In warmer climates where mosquitoes are present nearly year-round, a heartworm preventive needs to be given 12 months out of the year. In contrast, in those regions that experience seasonal changes and cooler temperatures, the preventive need not be

FIGURE 3.5 All dogs should be taking heartworm preventive medicine.

given the entire year but only during the warmer mosquito season. Be sure to consult your veterinarian as to the proper preventive schedule to follow in your particular area.

Before starting a dog on heartworm preventive medication, a simple blood test needs to be performed to determine whether exposure to heartworms has already occurred (Fig. 3.6). If the test results are negative, then

DR. P'S VET TIP

Even if heartworm preventive medication is not required year-round in your area, you should still give it to your pet all throughout the year. The reason: Most preventatives sold on the market today also prevent infestations with intestinal parasites (some of which can be zoonotic, including roundworms), providing an important source of continual protection for not only your dog but for you and your family as well.

FIGURE 3.6   Drawing blood for a heartworm test.

your dog may be started on a preventative. However, if the test returns positive for heartworms, then treatment options must be discussed. Furthermore, if you are currently giving your pet preventive medication and you miss a scheduled administration, consult your veterinarian prior to resuming the treatments. Depending on how late you are on the treatment, retesting may be recommended. For those dogs on a seasonal prevention program, blood retesting should be performed before the first preventive of the season is given.

Dental Care

Periodontal disease, or tooth and gum disease, is one of the most common diseases affecting dogs today. In fact, most canines show some signs of this disease after they reach 3 years of age. Signs can include tender, swollen gums, excessive drooling, loss of appetite, and bad breath (Fig. 3.7).

FIGURE 3.7   Calculus buildup starts at the gumline.

A complete dental exam should be performed on all dogs at least once a year. For smaller breeds more prone to periodontal disease, these exams should be done every 6 months. If dental calculus is present at the gumline, your veterinarian should professionally clean the teeth. Because this cleaning can be a painful procedure, especially if periodontal disease already exists, a short-acting sedative or anesthetic is essential for your dog's comfort and safety. An ultrasonic dental scaler, combined with manual scaling instruments, is used to break apart and remove the hard calculus and deposits from the tooth surfaces (Fig. 3.8). Afterward, the teeth are polished with a special paste to restore their natural smooth surfaces.

FIGURE 3.8   Professional cleaning will be needed to effectively remove dental calculus from your pet's teeth.

Your pet's dental care doesn't stop there, though! At-home aftercare is a vital part of your dog's dental health. Toothpaste, gels, and rinses formulated for use in canines are readily available from pet stores or from veterinary offices. Choose one that contains chlorhexidine, as this antibacterial compound can remain effective for up to 12 hours after application. Human toothpaste should not be used, as it can cause stomach upset if swallowed by your pet. Also, the much-advocated home formula mixing baking soda and salt in water can be effective as a toothpaste alternative, yet because of the high sodium content of this mixture, it should not be used in older dogs or in those dogs suffering from heart ailments. A regular, soft-bristled, human toothbrush can be used to apply the dental product. For smaller dogs, a child's toothbrush can be substituted. However, for best results, purchase a special "finger" brush that fits on the end of your finger. These can be purchased at any pet supply. Apply the paste, gel, or solution to the brush, and proceed to brush as you would your own teeth, concentrating on the gumline as well as the outsides of the large premolars and canine teeth. No rinsing is necessary.

What about flossing? Yes, you can floss your dog's teeth, but not in the conventional way. Flossing devices in the form of chew toys have been developed to assist in dental hygiene (Fig. 3.9). Don't laugh; such devices can have a significant impact on dental health, assuming, of course, that your pet will play with them.

Rawhides, nylon chew bones, and urethane chewing devices can also prove helpful in mechanically removing plaque from dental sur-

FIGURE 3.9   Dental floss for dogs.

faces. Contrary to popular belief, feeding hard chew biscuits does little by itself to prevent periodontal disease; in fact, the starchy nature of such food items can promote plaque formation. The same holds true for most hard dog foods, although most contain substantially less plaque-promoting sugar than do their moist counterparts. Special diets do exist that contain ingredients to help control tartar buildup in dogs. Ask your veterinarian if such a diet would be right for your pet.

Remember: Good dental hygiene is important to the health of your pet. In fact, it can help it live a longer, happier life. If you have any questions concerning your pet's dental health, don't hesitate to confer with your veterinarian.

Feeding Your Dog

There can be little doubt that proper nutrition is the cornerstone of a long, healthy life for all pets. As our understanding of the link between diet and health increases each day, so does the quality of foods that are available to feed your pet. Not long ago, the diet of most dogs consisted primarily of table scraps, supplemented by whatever other foods they could find while roaming freely. Today, most pets live indoors with their owner, and it is much more practical to feed them commercially prepared food that is complete and balanced for the particular stage of life of each pet.

While the quality of nutrition for dogs has improved considerably with the increasing use of prepared pet foods, there remains a great deal you should know about choosing the proper diet for your pet from among the many thousands of brands available in this country alone. Because dogs move through several "life stages" as they age, it is easiest to discuss the nutritional needs of these different life stages separately and in the order in which the dog experiences them.

Nutrition for Puppies

For most dogs, puppyhood lasts for about the first year of life, although very large breed dogs (Great Danes, Newfoundlands, St. Bernards, etc.) may continue to grow rapidly until they are 18 to 24 months of age. During this time, the puppy requires higher levels of minerals such as calcium and phosphorus, protein, vitamins, and energy (calories) than it will as an adult. Therefore, foods fed to young, growing dogs should contain these higher levels in balance with each other and with all other dietary nutrients. Such a pet food will carry a designation such as "canine growth" or "puppy food," to distinguish it from diets that contain levels of nutrients that are right for some other life stage, such as adult maintenance.

Please note that the commonly held belief that "if a little is good, more must be better" is not true when it comes to feeding pets. Diets that contain very high levels of minerals, protein, and certain vitamins are not superior to those that contain only the amounts required for growth. Excesses can actually be harmful to the growing pup, as can the practice of supplementing a good growth diet with various human foods or vitamin-mineral preparations. Scientific studies have shown that high calcium and phosphorus intakes by young dogs can lead to a variety of bone problems, especially in large, rapidly growing dogs. In addition, research has also shown that allowing your puppy to overeat even a high-quality, well-balanced growth diet can lead to some of these same problems because the pup grows too rapidly as a result of the increased food intake.

To be sure your puppy gets all the good nutrition it needs for good growth and development, but never too much, follow these simple guidelines:

1. Feed a high-quality, balanced commercial dog food that specifically states on the label that it is intended for growth in dogs. Your veterinarian, who should examine, vaccinate, and deworm your pup, can recommend an appropriate brand. Remember that your puppy's nutrition will influence its lifelong health and happiness. It is very important that you invest in good nutrition at this crucial life stage.

2. If you own a large breed puppy that will have an adult weight exceeding 55 pounds, consider feeding it a diet specially designed for its growth needs. These diets contain controlled levels of fat, calories, and minerals when compared to conventional puppy foods in order to promote a proper growth rate, thereby guarding against bone and skeletal disorders that can be caused by extrafast growth in large-breed puppies. Ask your veterinarian to recommend such a diet for your dog.

3. Do not feed your puppy free-choice. Most pups are very eager eaters and will tend to eat too much of a high quality, highly palatable (good-tasting) diet. It is much better to put down half of the recommended daily ration amount (as stated on the bag or can) for a limited time period, say, 30 minutes. Allow your pup to eat all that it wishes

FIGURE 3.10   For better health, consider offering your dog filtered water instead of plain tap water.

to eat in that time, and then pick up any uneaten food and save it until the next feeding. Later on in the day, feed the second-half of the daily ration, along with the food not eaten at the first sitting. As always, keep fresh, clean water (preferably filtered) available at all times (Fig. 3.10).

4. Do not supplement a quality, balanced food; you will almost certainly create an imbalance in your pet's diet if you do. Avoid giving table food, table scraps, or treats and snacks to your puppy for the same reason (Fig. 3.11).

Nutrition for Adult Dogs

At about 12 months of age, switch your pet to a maintenance diet for adults. Once your puppy is grown, its nutritional needs are reduced considerably from those during the rapid development of that first year. Continuing to feed your adult dog high levels of minerals (particularly calcium and phosphorus), protein, and energy (calories) could lead to problems later in life. Just as we are finding that excess intake of certain dietary nutrients (e.g., phosphorus, sodium, fat) are harmful for humans over long periods, certain excesses might also contribute to diseases such as kidney failure, heart failure, obesity, and diabetes in adult and older dogs. Also, we know that reducing the level of key nutrients in the adult's diet to meet but not greatly exceed its needs is never harmful. Good-quality, scientifically designed, adult-maintenance diets always contain these reduced and balanced nutrient levels.

S. Pinson

FIGURE 3.11 **Feeding table scraps will promote an annoying begging habit.**

Guidelines for feeding adult dogs include

1. Feed a high-quality, complete, and balanced diet specifically designed for adult dog maintenance. Be aware that foods that say they are "complete and balanced for all life stages" are actually puppy foods, since they have been formulated to meet the needs of the most demanding life stage: growth. They contain excesses of most nutrients for the adult or older dog.

2. It is best not to give supplements or treats to your adult dog. If you must give an occasional food snack, either use a small amount of the regular food, or fresh, unsalted vegetables cut up in bite size pieces. Most dogs like vegetables, and eating them often satisfies the craving for snacks.

3. Most dogs can be fed their allotted daily ration at one sitting. Use the manufacturer's recommended feeding amounts as a starting point only. If your pet gains weight, reduce the portion offered. If your pet starts to lose weight, increase the amount you feed. Your veterinarian can help you decide what your pet's optimum weight should be. Once you know this, weigh your pet periodically to prevent weight loss or gain from becoming a problem.

4. Some dogs show a pronounced tendency to gain weight as they grow older, despite eating only moderate amounts of an adult

maintenance diet. For these, follow the instructions for over-weight dogs in this chapter.

5. Dogs that are very active, work regularly, have nervous disposi-tions, or are simply not eager eaters should be fed a ration that contains extra calories. In addition, pregnant females will need extra nutrition during the last few weeks of pregnancy and throughout lactation (Fig. 3.12). Puppy growth diets fulfill this role well. Feed such a food starting in the last trimester of preg-nancy and continue it until all puppies are weaned. Also, feed her free-choice, and do not add vitamin or mineral supplements unless your veterinarian recommends it.

6. Keep fresh, clean water (preferably filtered) available at all times.

Now a word about bones is in order. To get to the point, natural bones should not be fed to dogs. Now some might scoff at this, saying that dogs have been surviving on bones for centuries. While this is true, we still don't know how many of those dogs succumbed to impactions and to intestinal perforations. Why take a chance?

Bones, regardless of type, can splinter, causing penetrating wounds within the gastrointestinal tract. They can also add unwanted amounts of minerals to the diet. Nylon and/or rawhide substitutes more than adequately satisfy that bone-chewing urge and are much safer (Fig. 3.13).

Nutrition for the Older Dog

Once your pet is 7 years old (5 years old for larger-breed dogs), another dietary change becomes necessary. As people and animals age, many organ systems begin to show the effects of wear and tear. The kidneys especially begin to lose the ability to handle waste materials that must be removed from the bloodstream and excreted in the urine. Even older dogs that appear to be in perfect health could have kidneys that function much less effectively than they used to.

Guidelines for feeding the older dog include

1. Feed a high-quality pet food specifically designed for the older dog. Your veterinarian can advise you of any special health prob-lems that your pet already has and any other dietary changes that

FIGURE 3.12   Pregnant and lactating females should be fed a "growth" formula to provide added nutritional support.

might be necessary. In many cases of "old age" diseases, special foods can be prescribed along with medication to help manage these conditions.

2. If you notice your older dog gaining or losing weight, consult with your veterinarian about any changes in diet that can correct the problem. At the same time, your vet will check for any medical problem that might be contributing to the change in weight.

3. Do not supplement your older dog's diet with anything unless your veterinarian specifically recommends it. The older dog is even more sensitive than the young dog to the unbalancing effects of frequent snacks, treats, and table food added to the diet.

FIGURE 3.13 Rawhide bones are relatively safe alternatives to real bones.

4. Take your "senior" for regular (at least once a year) medical checkups to catch problems early or prevent them altogether. The right diet throughout life is an important part of a sound preventive medicine program to safeguard the health and long life of your treasured pet.

5. Keep fresh, clean, filtered water available at all times.

Dietary Management of Disease

For years, medical research has been telling us about the benefits of a well-balanced diet for good health. In addition, we also know that special modification of the dietary intake in the presence of a disease state can be helpful in the treatment and/or long-term management of the condition. This same nutritional health concept can be applied to dogs as well.

Many disease conditions in dogs, such as obesity (yes, obesity is a disease!), heart disease, kidney disease, and gastrointestinal disease, can be effectively controlled, and sometimes even cured, through diet modulation alone.

For example, obesity, constipation, certain types of colitis, and diabetes mellitus all warrant an increase in the amount of fiber present in the ration. Dogs suffering from diarrhea, excessive gas production, and/or pancreatic problems can benefit from diets that are more easily digestible than standard maintenance rations. Finally, recommended management of dogs suffering from kidney disease includes diets low in phosphorus.

These special diets or rations aimed at fighting or counteracting canine diseases can be purchased through your veterinarian, or can be prepared at home via veterinary-supplied recipes. In general, the commercially prepared products are preferred over the homemade rations. The cost of these diets is negligible when compared to continuing veterinary bills and the poor quality of life that would result by not providing them. Just remember to follow your veterinarian's directions closely as to amounts and frequency of feeding of these diets if they are indeed used.

Battling Obesity in Dogs

Obesity is certainly one of the most prevalent diseases affecting the dog population today. For years, the frequency of this health disorder was skyrocketing at an alarming pace, owing primarily to improper feeding practices and inadequate time spent exercising due to owners' perceived lack of time. Sounds a lot like the cause of most obesity in humans, doesn't it? In fact, dogs are not much different than us in this respect. The problem, however, is that most overweight dogs were made that way not by themselves, but by their owners! Unfortunately, few owners realize that by encouraging their pet to get fat, they are at the same time endangering its health and unfairly reducing its quality of life.

The health-related ramifications in dogs are the same as they are in people. Although dogs don't suffer from atherosclerosis and "heart attacks" as humans do, obesity does place a great strain on their cardiovascular systems. Other internal organs suffer the consequences as well. For instance, obesity promotes pancreatitis in dogs, among other gastrointestinal disturbances. Obese canines seem to suffer from more skin ailments and coat disorders than do their slim-and-trim counterparts. Musculoskeletal disorders, including intervertebral disk disease, occur with greater frequency in dogs carrying around excessive weight. In summary, it is safe to say that the overall quality of and length of life for these dogs is reduced, owing to these side effects of obesity.

Visually, dogs that are overweight will sport a waist that is barely discernable. In addition, their ribs can barely be felt when their chest is touched, and their abdomens may be noticeably distended. Finally, fat dogs will carry prominent fat deposits along the hips and at the base of their tails.

Causes of Obesity

The causes of obesity in dogs are numerous, but the first and foremost of them is plain, old dietary indiscretion (also known as too many table scraps)! Realize that when you feed 10-pound Ginger that tiny piece of hot dog, that is equivalent to you eating two to three! In other words, it won't take many of these tiny pieces to make Ginger fat. Feeding one innocent cheese curl to a dog might be the same as eating half a bag ourselves, depending on the dog's size! Table scraps do nothing but promote obesity and create an annoying beggar out of your dog.

Feeding dogs table scraps is no doubt the biggest culprit causing obesity in pets, but simply feeding the wrong type of dog food can do the same. Most dog food manufacturers produce products geared for different stages of a dog's life. For instance, on the market today you have growth formulas, high-protein rations, "light" formulas, adult-maintenance formulas, geriatric formulas, and so on. The choices are so numerous that pet owners often become confused as to which type their particular pooch should be on, and this could lead to improper feeding practices and obesity.

The only dogs that need to be on a growth formula of dog food are puppies under one year of age, pregnant and lactating dogs, and, in certain instances, dogs that are recovering from or fighting off illness. Because energy requirements drop considerably as a dog matures, feeding high-energy, high-calorie growth formulas to an otherwise healthy adult dog can inadvertently cause obesity. The same holds true for geriatric pets over 8 years of age. These dogs should be on "less active" or senior-type diets containing higher fiber and fewer calories instead of the regular adult-maintenance rations.

Failure to adjust dietary requirements to specific individual needs is another predisposing cause of obesity. As far as how much you should be feeding your pet, the first place to start is to consult a breed-specific book or your veterinarian and find out what the ideal weight should be for your dog. Then look at the recommendations printed on the label of the dog food you are using. Even these printed guidelines should be considered averages, since the needs of each individual will vary, depending on individual metabolic rates, exercise levels, and eating habits (Fig. 3.14).

For adult and senior dogs, the best approach is to feed the recommended amount of food over a 3-week period, monitoring your dog's weight each week. If weight gain is noted, cut back on the rations fed. If the opposite is true, then increase the rations slightly.

For puppies, follow the manufacturer's recommendations as to how much to feed. When your dog is still a pup, instilling solid feeding habits is more important than worrying about how much to feed.

FIGURE 3.14 While automatic feeders may be convenient, they can predispose dogs to obesity.

Weight Reduction

If your dog is overweight, simply cutting back on the amount you feed will not do the trick. In fact, doing so could conceivably lead to a mild state of malnutrition and cause your dog to be constantly hungry (and begging!). Many dogs that are not receiving adequate nutrition will try to eat anything, which in itself can lead to a serious case of gastroenteritis.

PROPER DIET

Instead of cutting back on its ration, switch your dog's feed to one that is specially formulated for weight loss. These diets are readily available from your veterinarian. They might cost a bit more than what you are accustomed to paying for dog food, but the switch is only temporary and the benefits to your pet are immense. These special foods have a high fiber content, which allows for calorie reduction while still giving your dog that feeling of fullness after eating.

Your veterinarian can assist you as far as how much to feed and how often to feed. Spreading out the total daily food amount over two to three feedings during the day might help satisfy your pet even more. Be patient with the results. You might not realize it, but even one pound of weight loss is significant in a dog.

It is vital that during the weight reduction period that you remain consistent with the feedings and avoid giving any snacks (a few kibbles of the special diet now and then can provide an excellent snack substitute). Rawhide bones are okay to give your dog to chew on during this time, but keep in mind that dogs that gulp down rawhides in a ravenous fashion can be susceptible to gastritis and intestinal blockages.

EXERCISE

As with people, lack of exercise does its part to promote obesity. House dogs kept indoors most of the time are the ones at greatest risk. Many are lucky if they just get acknowledged when their owner steps in the door from a hard day's work. When they do get to go outside, it is often just to go to the bathroom, then back inside.

Regardless of whether your dog is kept indoors or out, make it a habit to devote a specific amount of time each day to social activity and exercise with your dog. This is not only important for its peace of mind, but it will keep its body fit and will keep the fat away.

A brisk, 15-minute aerobic walk or jog twice a day is all that should be needed. When exercising your dog, be sure not to overdo it. Stride for stride, most dogs need to work twice as hard to keep up with the pace you set. Avoid exercising during those times of the day when the heat and humidity are highest. And remember to keep plenty of water available for your dog. Drinking water prevents these dogs from becoming dehydrated, and provides a cooling mechanism for their bodies.

RULING OUT MEDICAL REASONS FOR OBESITY

Finally, just to be fair, pet owners can't be saddled with the blame for their dogs' obesity in all cases. There can be medical reasons behind a dog's weight problem. Hypothyroidism is a common condition in dogs, and it can lead to weight gain and lethargy by lowering the body's metabolic rate. One

DID YOU KNOW?

Dogs can't sweat like people do; thus they pant to dissipate heat via the mouth and tongue.

unique finding in hypothyroid dogs is that these dogs will gain weight despite a poor appetite.

The signs associated with this condition can be quite subtle and might lead you to believe that improper diet is the cause of your dog's weight problem. Because of this, all dogs that have a problem with their weight should have their thyroid function tested. Most veterinarians now offer a simple, inexpensive in-house thyroid screen that can detect problems if they exist. In these cases, supplementing thyroid hormone by mouth not only makes the pet feel better, but also helps conquer the weight disorder at the same time.

In summary, follow these guidelines to protect your dog from the health risks caused by obesity:

1. Be strict when it comes to your dog's diet. Keep it regular and feed a formulation suited for its stage of life and physical activity. Avoid feeding table scraps! If your dog needs to lose weight, don't just cut back on its ration. Switching to a specially formulated high-fiber diet is a must. Eliminate all treats and special snacks during the weight reduction period, and never feed free-choice.

2. If you haven't already done so, implement an exercise program for your dog. You will not only help control your dog's weight but also prevent potential behavioral problems. Don't overdo the exercise, and always keep plenty of water available at all times.

3. Always have a medical checkup performed on your pet before embarking on any weight-loss program. Your veterinarian can tell you if your dog is actually overweight, and can give you specific guidelines for weight reduction in your pet if needed.

Caring for the Canine Ear

Because of the unique anatomy of the canine ear, routine preventive ear care, involving cleaning, drying, and, when applicable, plucking, is recommended.

Cleaning

Many different types of ear cleansers and drying agents are available from pet stores, pet supply houses, and veterinary offices. Liquid cleansers are preferred over powders; powders can become quickly saturated with moisture, trapping it within the ear canal. Most liquid ear cleansers contain wax solvents as well as built-in astringents (drying agents) that help promote a healthy environment within the ear.

Cotton balls, cotton-tip applicators, and tissues are also helpful accessories to have available. These are used to clean around the outer portions of the ear canal and surrounding structures. In no instances should a cotton-tipped applicator be placed down into an ear canal; you'll only serve to pack wax and debris down deep next to the eardrum or actually rupture the eardrum itself.

Be sure to consult your veterinarian before putting any medications or solutions into your pet's ears. This is especially important if those ears are inflamed or infected, since many solutions designed for use in healthy ears can cause serious problems if used in ears with unhealthy or ruptured eardrums.

Restraint during Cleaning or Treatment

The most important part of any preventive or treatment program for the ears is proper restraint of the patient. This is essential for effective application of medications, as well for the safety of both owner and dog. If necessary, don't hesitate to use a muzzle. Unfortunately, many dogs object to having their ears medicated, especially if the ears are already sore from inflammation.

If at all possible, obtain assistance from a friend or family member for that extra set of hands. Smaller dogs can be placed atop tables or washing machines for a better working angle. This unfamiliar ground usually serves to pacify a fidgety protester.

Use good judgment; if all-out war appears to be imminent, abandon your efforts and seek the assistance of your veterinarian. Having to make repeated weekly trips back and forth from the veterinary office might be inconvenient, but try to keep the benefits afforded to your pooch's ears in mind. If

Dr. P's Vet Tip

A 50:50 mixture of isopropyl alcohol and white vinegar can be used as a routine ear cleanser for healthy ears or those with mild yeast infections. (*Caution:* Alcohol will sting an inflamed ear.)

your dog is suffering from an ear infection, consider leaving it at the hospital or clinic for a few days to make sure those ears are treated properly.

Proper Procedure

The procedure for cleaning and/or applying medication to the ears is easy. To begin, the pinna (ear flap) should be pulled gently toward the handler in an outward, not upward, direction. By extending it in this fashion, the external-ear canal will be straightened, allowing easy access of the cleanser to the deep portions of the canal. On the other hand, if the pinna is pulled upward, the ear canal will become flattened against the skull, rendering cleansing efforts ineffective (Fig. 3.15).

Now carefully place the cleanser or medication into the external ear opening and squeeze a liberal amount of solution into the ear. The next step is to feel for the cartilage supporting the ear canal and, keeping the pinna extended outwards, gently massage the ear canal for a good 15 to 20 seconds. Once this time is up, the dog should be allowed to shake its head before proceeding to the next ear.

After both ears have been treated, cotton balls, cotton applicators, or tissue can be used to wipe up excess cleanser, medication, or waxy debris stuck to the inside folds of the pinnae and the very outer portions of the ear canals. Again, never stick anything down into the ear canal itself. Serious injury could result! Most commercial ear cleaners contain or come with drying agents, which makes manual drying of the ear canals unnecessary.

Hair in the Ear Canal

In some breeds, hair can occlude the ear canal, predisposing to inflammation and infection. Poodles, terriers, and schnauzers are notorious for this. In cases where excessive hair is visualized in the ear canal, your veterinarian should perform an ear pluck (Fig. 3.16).

FIGURE 3.15 When cleaning your dog's ear, pull the pinna straight out (not up) to allow the medication to get down deep into the ear canal.

Why not do it yourself? Well, there are three good reasons not to. First, ear plucking is a painful procedure, especially if inflammation is already a factor. As such, it requires effective restraint. In some instances, sedation might even be required to do the job.

Also, if done properly, an ear pluck should be focused not just on the hair visibly occluding the outside of the ear canal, but on the hair down deep within the canal as well. Special instruments are needed for this; the kind used by your veterinarian. Finally, if done improperly, ear plucking can lead to

FIGURE 3.16   Excess hair occluding the external ear canal should be plucked.

infection within an ear canal. Since the act of forcibly removing hair from their follicles causes inflammation, the entire length of the plucked canal needs to be medicated afterward to reduce this inflammation and prevent a secondary infection from occurring. The bottom line is that ear plucks done improperly and without proper medicating afterward can actually do more harm than good!

Routine weekly application of an ear solution can help keep ear canals healthy. In addition, using a drying agent in the ears after a pet goes swimming or receives a bath is also a good idea. Daily or alternate-day preventive treatment is not needed unless prescribed by a veterinarian; in fact, such frequent application could conceivably alter the normal flora and environment within the ear enough to allow disease-causing bacteria to proliferate. Routine ear plucks should be performed on an as-needed basis. In most cases, this means every 4 to 6 weeks.

If the ears are being treated for an infection, follow the dosage and frequency guidelines prescribed by your veterinarian for the particular medications you are using. See Chap. 15 for more information regarding diseases and disorders that can affect the canine ear.

Maintaining a Healthy Skin and Coat

Routine grooming is essential for maintaining healthy hair and skin in dogs. Be sure to allot some time each day for this task.

Brushing

Whether your dog has short hair or long hair, brushing the coat thoroughly on a daily basis will aid in its appearance as well as promote healthy skin. It does this by

- Removing telogen (dead) hairs from the coat, making way for new ones to grow in.

- Preventing tangles and mats.

- Stimulating sebaceous gland activity, which keeps the skin moisturized and the haircoat shiny. Brushing also helps to spread these oils across the entire skin and coat.

- Removing scale (excess keratin), which could lead to itching.

- Increasing owner awareness of the presence of external parasites or other skin-related problems.

Long-haired and/or thick-coated breeds require more diligent brushing than do shorter-coated dogs. Minor shedding is normal year-round in all breeds. However, because the shedding cycle in dogs is stimulated by changes in day length, most will occur during the spring and fall months, when the days become longer and shorter, respectively.

Be sure to choose the right type of brush for your pet. In general, the wider

FACT OR FICTION

Dogs should be bathed at least once a week. **FICTION**. Dogs with healthy skin and haircoats rarely require routine bathing. Daily brushing and application of a coat conditioner will accomplish the same results! In fact, indiscriminate bathing can dry out the skin and predispose an otherwise healthy skin to disease.

the bristles or pins are placed on the brush, the longer the coat it is designed to be used on. Brush your medium- and long-haired dogs, as well as those breeds with thick coats, using a wire-pin brush. For dogs with short haircoats, brushing with a bristle-type brush will work best (Fig. 3.17).

In addition to the wire-pin brush, the slicker brush is another very popular type of device. Most of these con-

FIGURE 3.17   Be sure to use the right type of brush for your pet's particular haircoat.

sist of a square head containing lots of tiny wire projections, and they can be used on almost any type of haircoat for removing shed hair and tangles.

Purchase of a comb is optional, unless you own one of the silky-coated breeds with a coat might be too delicate for many standard brushes. Combs can also come in quite handy for removing tangles and mats when used in conjunction with scissors. Like brushes, the teeth of combs are set at different widths apart for different types of coats; widely-spaced for thicker coats and closely spaced for longer, silkier hair. Just keep in mind that using the wrong type of brush or comb can be painful to your pet and actually damage the haircoat. For this reason, choose grooming tools with care.

Always use firm, short strokes when brushing, never forcing the brush through the coat. For dogs with short- to medium-length hair, brush with the grain of the hair. To help in the removal of shed hair, use towels or disposable gloves to buff the coat after brushing. For those canines with thick undercoats, the initial direction of brushing should be against the grain of the hair. Once the undercoat has been groomed, then you can brush the outer coat with the grain.

If you encounter a mat, don't try to forcefully remove it with the brush. Instead, try to work it free with your fingers, using one hand to

...nd the other to stabilize the tuft of hair to keep it from ... . If the mat or tangle still can't be freed, insert a comb ...at and the skin surface, then take a pair of blunt-nosed ...ip as much of the mat off as you can between the comb and u... ...nd of the hair. Don't worry about cosmetic appearances. It will grow back! Mats that are left in place can promote infection involving the skin beneath. And always remember that if you brush your dog as often as you should, you won't have a problem with matting!

Bathing

Dogs should be bathed when one or more of the following situations develop:

- Accumulation of excessive dirt, grease, or other foreign substances (e.g., skunk odor) on the skin and coat
- Buildup of waxy sebum (seborrhea), which often leads to body odor
- Accumulation of skin scale (dandruff)
- Skin infections

Hypoallergenic or other mild dog shampoos are ideal for bathing dogs with otherwise healthy skin and coats. For medical conditions involving skin infections and seborrhea, use only those shampoos prescribed by your veterinarian. Using the wrong type of shampoo on such skin disorders will yield poor results and might even exacerbate them. Even if your dog appears to have perfectly healthy skin, it is still prudent to consult your veterinarian in choosing a specific shampoo for it. The vet will be able to recommend products and give you valuable tips on how to continue to keep your dog's integument (skin) in the top shape (Fig. 3.18).

Before you put your pooch into the tub, brush it out thoroughly and remove

Dr. P's Vet Tip

To remove skunk odor, mix one quart of 3% hydrogen peroxide with 1/4 cup of baking soda and one teaspoon of mild liquid dish soap. Apply liberally to the coat, then rinse thoroughly.

any mats and tangles. In addition, always apply some type of protection to both eyes to prevent accidental soap burns. Mineral oil has been used for this purpose; however, a sterile ophthalmic ointment is preferred. Such ointment is readily available from your veterinarian or favorite pet store, and provides greater eye protection than does plain mineral oil.

FIGURE 3.18 Contrary to popular belief, dogs do not need to be bathed on a regular basis.

After you've treated the eyes, stick some cotton balls into the outer portion of each ear canal to keep bath water out. If the nails need trimming or the anal sacs need emptying, do this before the bath as well. Once these preparatory measures have been taken, you can now proceed with the shampoo and rinse.

If you are using a medicated shampoo, allow it to remain in contact with the skin for at least 10 minutes prior to rinsing. After rinsing, a towel, chamois cloth, or brush and blow dryer (on the low-heat setting only) can be used for drying.

Nail Trimming

As part of a routine grooming program, you should perform a nail trim on your dog every 4 to 6 weeks. The procedure itself is easy, assuming that you have the right equipment and your dog agrees to cooperate. If your pooch refuses to stand still for its manicure, let your veterinarian perform the deed. It will be less stressful on both you and your dog.

There are many types and style of nail trimmers on the market today. The preferred choice is the guillotine-type nail trimmers with replaceable blades. These are available at pet stores everywhere.

The procedure itself is simple on clear nails. Observe the nail to be clipped and identify the endpoint of the blood supply, or the quick. Then, staying just in front of the quick, snip off the end portion of the nail.

FIGURE 3.19 When trimming nails, trim back just far enough so that when your dog's paw is flat against a surface, the nails are just off the surface.

On dark nails that don't have readily identifiable quicks, start snipping back the end of the nail in small portions at a time. Stop just when the nail is too short to contact the ground when weight is placed on the paw (Fig. 3.19).

Invariably, the time might come when you accidentally "quick" your pet's nail, causing it to bleed. If this occurs, there is no cause for panic. Using a clean cloth or gauze pad, apply direct pressure to the bleeding nail for 5 minutes to stop the bleeding. Alternatively, you can apply clotting powder or clotting sticks, both of which can be purchased at pet stores, to the end of the affected nail to quickly stop the bleeding. If none of these are handy, ordinary flour can be used as an effective substitute.

Occasionally, a dog's nails might have grown so long that the quick has extended far down the nail, making it virtually impossible to clip without making it bleed. In these instances, you might wish to employ the help of your veterinarian, who can sedate your pet and perform a short nail trim.

FACT OR FICTION

A dog that scoots its rear end on the floor has worms. **FICTION.** A dog that scoots its rear end on your floor has distended anal sacs and is trying to empty them on your floor or carpet!

Expressing Anal Sacs

The anal sacs are structures located on either side of the anal opening in dogs. Filled with a foul-smelling fluid that dogs use for intraspecies identification, these sacs normally empty with each bowel movement. Contrary to popular belief, these do not have to be manually emptied on a routine basis whenever a dog is bathed. In fact, by manually expressing healthy anal sacs, you could inadvertently cause inflammation and predispose to secondary impaction. Anal sacs require attention only if

FIGURE 3.20   Anal sacs should be expressed only if they are impacted.

a dog is showing signs of impaction or anal sac irritation (Fig. 3.20). These signs usually appear in the form of scooting the rear end across the floor or excessive licking of that region.

Mildly impacted anal sacs can be expressed by applying gentle, inward and upward pressure at the four and eight o'clock positions surrounding the anal opening, using your thumb and forefinger, respectively. If this fails to empty the sacs, or if the sacs are especially tender, stop what you are doing and call the pet clinic. In these instances the procedure is better performed at the veterinarian's office.

(*Note:* If you happen to get anal sac secretion on your skin or clothes, you might lose your friends quickly unless you take appropriate action to neutralize the odor. Isopropyl alcohol can be used to get rid of the smell. Better yet, many commercial odor neutralizers that are available at pet stores can do the job even more effectively.)

Geriatrics: Caring for Your Older Dog

It is estimated that in the United States alone, over 35 percent of all pets owned are geriatric. Depending on which veterinarian you talk to, dogs are considered geriatric when they reach 7 to 9 years of age (5 to 7 years for larger breeds). Understand, though, that breed, genetics, nutrition, and environmental influences will all ultimately affect the aging process in a particular dog (Table 3.3).

body of waste products. As a result, care taken early to help ease the burden placed on the aging kidneys using special diets and medications will greatly enhance the longevity of a dog.

5. *Urinary incontinence.* Older dogs, especially spayed females, may begin to lose control of their bladders as they enter their teens. This is usually the result of weakened sphincters that normally prevent the involuntary outflow of urine from the bladder. Medications are available that can increase sphincter tone and help curb this problem.

6. *Reproductive challenges.* Female dogs that were not spayed at an early age are more prone to uterine diseases and mammary cancer as they enter into their geriatric years. At the same time, most older male dogs are afflicted with some degree of prostate enlargement. Furthermore, as one might expect, fertility and reproductive performance tend to decrease with advancing age.

7. *Intestinal challenges.* The aging gastrointestinal tract might begin to show signs of reduced efficiency and intolerance to excesses. For this reason, flare-ups of gastritis, colitis, and constipation can become more prevalent as a pet enters into its golden years. At the same time, liver function can decrease, making it more difficult to metabolize nutrients and detoxify wastes within the body.

8. *Weakened immune systems.* It is well documented that the efficiency and activity of the immune system is compromised with age. As a result, geriatric pets are more susceptible to disease, especially viruses and cancer. For this reason, preventive health care takes on an even more important meaning in these pets.

9. *Endocrine challenges.* As dogs mature, the activity of the glands within the body may start to decrease, leaving the pet with hormone-related challenges. For example, hypothyroidism is a common condition seen in maturing dogs. Diabetes mellitus can occur secondarily to aging of the insulin-producing cells within the pancreas, or to repeated bouts of pancreatitis over the years. In contrast, age-related tumors affecting glands within the body can lead to oversecretion of hormones, resulting in illness. Canine Cushing's disease is a prime example of this type of illness.

10. *Vision challenges.* Most older dogs will likely develop a slight grayish white or bluish haze to the lenses of both eyes. This change, termed *nuclear sclerosis,* is brought on by a complex deposition of body metabolites into the eye lenses. It is a normal change and should not be confused with a cataract. Unlike cataracts, nuclear sclerosis affects vision only mildly. Dogs with decreased visual acuity might not be able to focus on an object rapidly, so they might react suddenly if approached. Don't confuse this with crankiness or irritability. A slow approach with a gentle hand accompanied by a calm voice will allow a dog with failing vision to hear and smell the familiar person approaching.

11. *Hearing loss.* Partial or total hearing loss is common in geriatric dogs. It is often related to long-term, irreversible nervous changes in the inner ear. Further hearing loss occurs with senile changes or damage to the eardrum or ossicles (the bones of vibration conduction) housed within the middle ear. Wax accumulation within the ears can play a role in deafness as well.

12. *Dependence on sense of smell.* The sense of smell is usually the last sense to fail in a dog. For this reason, the geriatric dog depends more and more on its sense of smell to identify people, objects, and food. Also, the senses of taste and smell are highly dependent on one another. As a result, the appetite of an older dog will taper off as the sense of smell becomes compromised.

13. *Cognitive dysfunction syndrome (senility).* Signs of senility in older dogs can include changes in sleep patterns, changes in the levels and types of social interaction desired, increased housesoiling, and disorientation. Your veterinarian can prescribe medications to help ease these symptoms and improve your pet's quality of life.

The changes that occur with aging warrant special adjustments in husbandry practices and preventive health care for geriatric pets. The following are five steps you can take to be sure your pet's geriatric years are filled with health and happiness:

1. Adjust your dog's diet to match its health needs. Your veterinarian can assist you with this switch. If your pet suffers from a specific ailment, such as heart disease, special diets can be prescribed to reduce the wear and tear on the affected organ systems. For the otherwise healthy dog, provide a diet that is higher in fiber and reduced in calories. Don't forget to weigh your dog on a regular basis. Obesity is an enemy, and can significantly shorten your dog's life.

2. Maintain a moderate exercise program to keep your dog's bones, joints, heart, and lungs conditioned. Always consult your veterinarian first as to the type and amount of exercise appropriate for your particular pet.

3. Be sure to brush your pet daily. Skin and coat changes secondary to metabolic slowdown or adjustments within the body can often be managed with a stepped-up home-grooming program. In addition, keep those toenails trimmed short. Older dogs suffering from arthritis don't need the added challenge and pain of having to ambulate on nails that have grown to the floor.

4. Along with grooming and brushing, be sure to give your geriatric pet plenty of attention each day. As the senses start to fail, pets can become frightened by the gradual loss of sensory contact with their owners. As a result, you need to reinforce the care and companionship you are offering.

5. Semiannual veterinary checkups and periodic at-home physical examinations for aging pets are a must. Remember that early detection of a disease condition is the key to curing or managing the disorder. Also, because of the effects aging has on the immune system, be sure to keep your pet current on its vaccinations.

Breeding Your Dog

Since the early days of domestication, humans have sought to understand and assist in the propagation of their canine companions. From acquired knowledge gathered throughout the ages, new breeds and favorable characteristics were created, designed to meet the needs of each civilization. As creatures of status and show, dogs became the compatriots of kings and queens, who appointed royal breeders to oversee the task of maintaining the form and functional purity of their favored breeds (Fig. 4.1).

Today, a sound knowledge of canine reproductive principles constitutes the livelihood of the professional dog breeder. But professional breeders are not the only ones who need to know about these matters. All dog owners desiring to breed their pet should do their homework first prior to proceeding with such plans. For this purpose, this chapter will come in quite handy. For an overview of canine reproductive anatomy, see Chap. 13.

Puberty and the Reproductive Cycle

Puberty is defined as the age at which female dogs first come into heat, and when the male testicles first begin to produce spermatozoa. The time at which this event occurs is not sex-dependent, but is governed

FIGURE 4.1   Breeding your dog can have its rewards!

by other factors, including age, size, and breed. In general, the smaller the breed, the earlier puberty is reached. For toy breeds, this can mean at 6 to 7 months of age; for giant breeds, it can take up to 2 years! On the average, though, most dogs reach puberty around 8 to 10 months of age. However, just because puberty is reached does not mean that they have reached breeding age.

As a general rule, owners should wait until a male dog (sire) reaches 12 to 14 months before using it for breeding purposes. For females, breeding attempts should not be made until the second or third heat cycle. Even these guidelines can vary, depending on the dog's level of maturity, both mentally and physically.

The optimum breeding age for female dogs is between 3 to 6 years of age. Puppies born to females in these age groups tend to be healthier at birth, grow faster, and wean much easier when compared to others. After 6 years, reproductive performance in the female begins a steady decline.

Male dogs, on the other hand, have greater sexual longevity than do females, yet this, too, begins to decline as the dog advances in years.

The Female Estrous Cycle

The term *estrous cycle* is used to describe a series of events that occurs within the female reproductive tract between actual heat periods. On the average, this cycle lasts from 6 to 8 months in the female dog (bitch). Contrary to popular belief, smaller breeds do not have shorter, more frequent estrous cycles than do larger ones. The basenji, which averages only one heat period per year, is a prime example. As with breed size, seasonal changes also have no significant effect on the length of the estrous cycle.

There are four phases to the canine estrous cycle: anestrus, proestrus, estrus, and metestrus.

1. *Anestrus.* This is the period of time in which there is no reproductive activity going on in the ovaries. The duration of anestrus is typically 4 to 5 months in the average dog.

2. *Proestrus.* From anestrus, the reproductive cycle enters the period of proestrus. Signs seen during proestrus are related to the ovaries' increased production of the hormone estrogen, and they include vaginal bleeding and a gradual swelling of the vulva. Proestrus can last anywhere from 7 to 14 days. Normally, females will not stand to be mated until the waning days of this phase.

3. *Estrus.* As vaginal bleeding subsides and proestrus ends, estrus, or true heat, begins. (The term *estrus* should not be confused with *estrous cycle.*) As with proestrus, this heat period can last 1 to 2 weeks

FACT OR *FICTION*

Once a female dog starts bleeding from her vagina, she is "in heat." **FICTION.** In reality, such females are beginning their proestrual period and won't enter into true heat until the bleeding stops. Unfortunately, many pet owners trying to guard against accidental pregnancies learn this fact 2 months later when an unexpected litter arrives!

and is characterized by sexual receptivity of the bitch to the sire and by ovulation of unfertilized eggs from the ovaries. Some breeds of dogs, particularly husky-type breeds and basenjis, can undergo a phenomenon known as "wolf heat." Thought to be a carryover from their wild ancestors, dogs exhibiting such a pattern might not enter directly into heat after the proestrual period. Instead, the estrous cycle actually comes to a halt for 2 to 3 weeks before starting up again in estrus. Another interesting fact about the heat period in the dog is that eggs that are ovulated from the ovaries can mature and be fertilized at different times. As a result, it is possible for mixed litters to occur if the female dog happens to be bred by more than one male.

4. *Metestrus.* The last stage in the estrous cycle is metestrus, which can last from 2 to 3 months. This stage begins when the female refuses to accept the sire for further breeding. It is the period of uterine repair or, if fertilization is achieved, the period of pregnancy. False pregnancies appear during this phase as well.

When to Breed

The following can identify females entering into heat:

- The vaginal discharge changes from a red color to a brown or tan color as estrus arrives.

- The vulva will turn flaccid in appearance.

- A female entering estrus will often flag her tail; that is, she will move her tail to the side of her body when touched around her posterior.

Another parameter used by some breeders is to start counting the days from when the first signs of proestrual bleeding appeared. Usually by the tenth day after this bleeding starts, the female becomes willing to accept a male dog, and attempts should be made to breed. If the female refuses to mate at this time, wait 2 days and try again. After the first mating occurs, a second mating should be performed 3 to 4 days later.

Your veterinarian can help you decide the best time to breed your female about to enter into heat. By microscopically examining slides containing smears of vaginal cells (vaginal cytology), your vet can pin-point the exact dates when proestrus and estrus begin. This informa-tion is especially helpful for those female dogs that tend to exhibit subtle proestrual and estrual signs.

Where and How to Breed

When deciding where exactly the breeding should take place, it is wise to take the female dog to the male's own environment, rather than vice versa. Males tend to feel more comfortable in their own territory, and will perform their duties with fewer problems and distractions.

The male and female should be first introduced restrained by leashes and with owners present. That way, if personality conflicts arise, they can be quelled quickly, before a fight breaks out (such con-flicts may arise if the female is not yet ready to accept a male).

If the two seem compatible, then breeding can be allowed to take place. Some experts recommend muzzling both dogs prior to breeding to prevent accidental injuries or personality surges. Whether you actu-ally stick around for the mating is up to you; some of the more inexpe-rienced dogs might need assistance. Most dogs don't mind the presence of a third party, but some might become uncomfortable.

A key point to remember is that once mounting takes place, it's best to leave the two alone from then on. After mounting, the two will "lock" together, forming a "tie." While intercourse is maintained via the tie, the male might manipulate himself around so that both dogs' posteriors are facing each other, with their heads pointed in opposite directions. This is a normal mating position, and dogs so locked together should not be disturbed until the mating process has been voluntarily completed.

Normal ties will last from 10 seconds to 3 minutes, although longer ones are not uncommon. After the male releases the tie, the two will separate, and breeding is complete.

Breeding Challenges

Occasionally, you will find that some dogs cannot breed properly due to personality problems or physical defects. In these cases, artificial insemination offers a viable way to obtain a litter from the impotent pooch.

Gestation

The gestation period for dogs ranges from 59 to 65 days; the average is 63 days. Unfortunately, there are few accurate blood tests that can confirm whether a dog is pregnant, and this problem is certainly compounded by the fact that dogs can experience false pregnancies that can mimic the real thing. As a result, alternate means of pregnancy diagnosis must often be utilized.

Ultrasonography provides a reliable way to confirm pregnancy status as early as 28 days. If an ultrasound is not available, abdominal palpation by trained hands can often achieve similar results. However, there is much room for error with this method, especially if the female dog is tense during the examination. Abdominal enlargement and mammary development usually become noticeable after the first month of pregnancy. If an uncertainty still exists, radiographic X rays can be used to confirm pregnancies as early as 42 days.

Care of the Pregnant Dog

Care of the pregnant dog consists of nothing more than maintaining a good plane of nutrition and reducing stress as much as possible. Pregnant bitches should be placed on a growth-type ration, similar to those used for puppies, during the gestation and lactation periods. Vitamin and mineral supplements are seldom required; however, if your dog is at risk of developing eclampsia, your veterinarian might elect to start her on a calcium supplement a few weeks before parturition and continuing as such through the lactation period.

Stressful situations should be avoided if at all possible. Moderate exercise (two 15-minute walks daily) is certainly acceptable and encouraged during your dog's pregnancy. However, intense exercise and/or play sessions should be avoided.

While your dog is pregnant, administer all medications only with your veterinarian's direct consent or direct supervision. Many drugs can harm both mother and unborn pups if given during pregnancy.

Always check the labels on insecticide products used for flea and tick control before applying these products to pregnant pets. The label should state whether that product is safe to use on pregnant pets. If it doesn't say anything about it at all, play it safe: Don't use it.

Most heartworm prevention medications on the market are safe for use during pregnancy and can be used without interruption. Again, check the label.

The Birthing Process

One of the most fascinating and rewarding experiences associated with pet ownership occurs when a female pet undergoes parturition, the birthing process. In most instances, you need only to sit back and let nature take her course. While dystocia, or difficult parturition, is not especially common in dogs, it is important to be able to recognize problem situations that might arise in order to protect the health of both mother and offspring.

Dystocia can occur in any type of dog, yet smaller breeds and those that become pregnant during their first heat cycle might be more prone to these birthing difficulties.

It is important to record the actual breeding date of your dog to accurately predict when parturition will occur. If your dog is not already acquainted with the surroundings, be sure to allow her 3 weeks prior to the due date to become familiar and comfortable with her new environment. In addition, in order to satisfy her "nesting" instinct, provide her with plenty of clean towels and some sort of enclosure (a covered box or travel kennel) into which she can retire if she so desires.

Interestingly, the season of the year can affect what time during the day that your dog will whelp. For instance, during the spring and summer months, whelping tends to occur during the early-morning hours. Whelping during the fall and winter months commonly occurs in the late afternoon or evening hours.

A yellow, gelatinous vaginal discharge might appear up to 2 days prior to whelping. In addition, 12 to 24 hours prior to parturition, the rectal temperature of your dog will drop to as low as 97 degrees Fahrenheit. This sign alone should alert you of impending parturition.

Stages of Parturition

Stage 1: prelabor. This stage might last anywhere from 2 to 36 hours. Signs associated with this stage include pacing, anxiety, nest building, loss of appetite, vomiting, and/or shivering.

Stage 2: true labor. Signs seen when a dog enters into true labor include straining, abdominal contractions, the appearance of the placental sac, and the actual birth of the puppy. Be aware that up to 40 percent of pups might be delivered "feet first."

Stage 3: expulsion. The placenta might be passed with the puppy or soon after its birth. A greenish fluid should accompany a normal delivery.

The following guidelines are written in a quick reference, logarithmic format to help you through your dog's special time. If you ever have any questions or doubts concerning the health of your dog or one of its pups, don't hesitate to contact your veterinarian for advice.

FIGURE 4.2 To stimulate a newborn pup to breathe, hold it upside down in your hands and supporting its head, swing your arms up and down several times to help clear fluid from its lungs and airways.

Care of Neonatal Puppies

This section is included to alert you to proper handling of (e.g., see Fig. 4.2) and potential health problems that might arise in neonatal puppies. If you suspect that something is wrong, consult your veterinarian immediately. Normally, healthy newborn puppies should be doing one of two things: eating or sleeping. Crying usually indicates hunger, and should cease when the puppy is allowed to nurse (Fig. 4.3). If it doesn't, something might be wrong.

Flowchart for parturition in dogs

Has your dog started to show signs of stage 1 labor? ——▶ No. ——▶ Review this section and watch for signs of stage 1 labor. Contact your veterinarian if pregnancy lasts more than 63 days.

Yes.

Is there any evidence of a green, black, or red foul-smelling discharge from the vulva? ——▶ Yes. ——▶ Contact your veterianarian.

No.

Don't intervene prematurely. Leave your dog alone in a quiet environment with minimal interruptions. Many dogs have the ability to delay parturition if interrupted by the unnecessary presence of an owner.

Has your dog started to show signs of stage 2 labor? ——▶ No. ——▶ Contact your veterinarian if stage 1 lasts more than 36 hours.

Yes.

Has a puppy been born within 2 hours after the onset of stage 2 labor? ——▶ No. ——▶ Contact your veterinarian.

Yes.

Immediately after giving birth, has the bitch removed the placental membranes surrounding the newborn? ——▶ No. ——▶ Put on disposable gloves and manually remove the membranes.

Yes.

Flowchart for parturition in dogs (*Cont.*)

Has the puppy started breathing within one minute after birth? ⟶ No. ⟶ Hold the puppy upside-down to allow the fluid to drain from the lungs and vigorously massage the skin. A bulb syringe can be used to suction excess fluid out of the mouth and nose. If this approach is not working within 2 to 3 minutes, institute artificial respiration (see CPR, Appendix), and gently expand the lungs, taking care not to blow too hard into the nostril. Avoid overinflating the lungs. Continue artificial respiration and massage until the puppy is breathing on its own.

Yes.

Has the bitch severed the umbilical cord? ⟶ No. ⟶ Tie off the cord with thin gauze or thread by making a knot about ½ inch from the body wall of the newborn, then sever the cord between the knot and the membranes. Discard the membranes. Treat the end of the umbilical stump with tamed iodine.

Has greater than 2 hours elapsed between births? ⟶ Yes. ⟶ Contact your veterinarian.

No.

Following delivery and cleanup by the mother, newborn puppies will usually find their way to their mother's milk supply. You should, however, keep an eye out for puppies that might be rejected and ignored by the mother for one reason or another. For instance, this rejection might occur if the newborn's body temperature is lower than normal, if it is the runt of the litter, or if it has any physical abnormalities.

Do you suspect a rejection ———→ Yes. ———→ Try warming the puppy
of a newborn?   with a blanket or well-
                                               insulated heating pad (use
                                               the low setting!), then place
                                               it back with the mother and
                                               the rest of the litter. If this
                                               does not work, you might
                                               need to hand-feed the pup
                                               yourself. Contact your
                                               veterinarian.

No.

It is wise to have your dog examined by your veterinarian once you think that
parturition is complete. A dark, red discharge might be seen from the vulva
following the last birth. On the average, an entire litter is usually born within 12
hours after the onset of parturition.

Hypoglycemia

Hypoglycemia, or low blood
sugar, can result from lack
of adequate intake of the
mother's milk. It is often
seen in orphaned puppies
too weak to nurse. This condition requires immediate
attention, for it can lead to
profound weakness, convulsions, and death.

Commercial formulas
available at your veterinarian or pet store are ideal milk
substitutes. The amounts
needed by the puppy are
printed on the label. However, in emergency situa-
tions, you can prepare a
homemade formula from
one large egg yolk and
enough homogenized milk

FIGURE 4.3   A newborn puppy that continues
to cry even after it has eaten could be ill.

FIGURE 5.2   If desired, tails should be docked and dewclaws removed prior to one week of age.

snagged and torn on carpet, furniture, and underbrush. Secondary infections can develop if this trauma is repeated. For this reason, removal of dewclaws is a good idea if this is the case.

Tail docking and dewclaw removal are best performed within the first week of life (Fig. 5.2). The operations simply involve snipping off the dewclaws and the desired length of tail (per breed standards) with surgical scissors. One to two sutures are usually placed in the tail; the site of the dewclaw removal is often cauterized and left open.

If tail docking or dewclaw removal is not performed within 7 days after birth, anesthesia will be required for the surgery. As a result, the procedures must be postponed until the pet is 5 to 6 months of age.

Cosmetic Ear Trimming

Cosmetic ear trimming, or ear cropping, is the surgical alteration of the normal anatomy of the ear pinnae in dogs to conform to accepted breed standards (Fig. 5.3). Many people feel that ear trimming puts a dog through needless pain and suffering. Veterinarians and veterinary organizations are even joining the bandwagon and are advising against cosmetic ear trims, since they serve no useful purpose. In certain countries, cropped ears are no longer considered an acceptable breed standard, and cosmetic ear trimming has been officially banned.

The choice of whether to have it done is strictly up to you. If your pet's breed standard calls for it and you plan on competing on the show circuit, then you'll need to have your dog's ears cropped. In these cases, the surgery is best performed between 12 and 14 weeks of age. If, on the other hand, your dog is strictly for companionship, then such a procedure is not necessary.

Postsurgical Care for Dogs

Following any type of surgery, you should receive specific instructions from your veterinarian as to the type of postsurgical care your pet requires. It is important to follow these instructions closely to ensure an uneventful recovery. Postsurgical instructions include the following:

FIGURE 5.3 Cosmetic ear trimming has sparked much controversy among the dog-owning population.

■ Do not give your dog food or water for 30 minutes after arriving at home. To do so can cause nausea and vomiting.

■ Restrict your pet's activity for 8 to 10 days or until the sutures are removed. Protect your pet from stress, such as extreme exertion, excitement, temperature fluctuations, and drafts. Traveling should be kept to a minimum.

■ Check incision sites twice daily for any swelling and/or discharge. Keep them clean and dry at all times. Avoid bathing your pet until all sutures have been removed.

■ Unless otherwise instructed, return to your veterinarian in 8 to 10 days for suture removal.

■ If medications are dispensed, follow all label directions closely.

■ Don't hesitate to call your veterinarian if any problems arise or if you have any questions regarding your pet's recovery.

Infectious Diseases

nfectious diseases are those diseases directly communicable between pets. They are certainly among the most common canine illnesses seen by veterinarians. Infectious organisms responsible for diseases in dogs include a multitude of viruses, bacteria and bacteria-like organisms, and fungi. Multiple organ systems can be affected when an infectious disease is involved, resulting in a potpourri of clinical signs (Fig. 6.1).

Viral Diseases

Viruses account for the majority of infectious disease seen in the canine population. Treatment for these agents is usually supportive in nature, owing to a lack of specific antiviral medications. Fortunately, most can be prevented through proper vaccination.

Distemper

This infamous viral disease of dogs used to be one of the leading causes of death in unvaccinated puppies throughout the world. Although the incidence of this disease has decreased dramatically over the years as a result of vaccination programs, the distemper virus is still out there and can strike without warning.

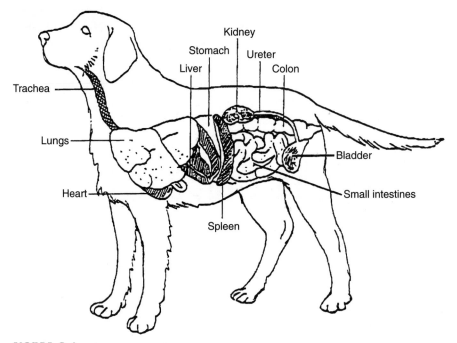

FIGURE 6.1   The internal organs of the dog.

The virus itself is related to the human measles virus and can produce a number of different disease patterns in canines. Infected dogs shed the disease in all body excretions, and transmission usually occurs via airborne means. As a result, like canine cough, it is highly contagious and can travel some distance on an air current.

Distemper is considered a multifaceted disease; that is, it can affect a number of different body systems, including the respiratory, gastrointestinal, and nervous systems.

Early signs of the disease include fever, loss of appetite, and a mild conjunctivitis (eye inflammation). These signs can come and go, lasting only a few days. As a result, pet owners often miss or ignore this early phase of the disease.

As the disease progresses, signs become more serious and extensive. They can include coughing, breathing difficulties, eye and nose discharges, vomiting and diarrhea, blindness, paralysis, and seizures. The seizures associated with this disease often have their own unique presentation, called "chewing gum fits." As the name implies, pets stricken as such will look as if they are chewing gum during the attack. In fact, many owners, when they see this, immediately think of rabies.

The final outcome of an infection with the canine distemper depends on the extent of exposure, the strain of the virus involved, and the ability of the dog's immune system to mount a defense against the virus (with the help of supportive treatment). Depending on these factors, the outcome of such an infection can present itself in one of four ways:

1. Death

2. Recovery with no lasting side effects

3. Recovery, with non-life-threatening side effects

4. Recovery, with life-threatening sequela

The first and second outcomes are fairly self-explanatory. Non-life-threatening side effects that can result from distemper can include such conditions as hard pad and enamel hypoplasia. The former is characterized by a prominent thickening and proliferation of the pads of the feet, hence the name.

Enamel hypoplasia is a term used to describe the lack of normal enamel covering the tooth surfaces. This occurs in puppies stricken with distemper at an early age, before their permanent teeth have erupted. What happens is the virus attacks and kills off those cells responsible for manufacturing the tooth enamel, hence the new teeth grow in lacking this vital component. Needless to say, teeth lacking enamel are not very strong and tend to erode quickly, becoming brownish in color.

These innocuous side effects might be all that linger, or they might be coupled with more serious sequela. One such side effect that could become life-threatening to some recovered cases is a degeneration of the nervous system, which can occur slowly or very rapidly. Dogs so affected sometimes show a progressive deterioration of both their motor skills and their mental abilities. Rhythmic muscle twitching can become so severe that it totally disables the unfortunate pet. Seizures, paralysis, and incoordination can also become factors as deterioration proceeds.

A diagnosis of canine distemper is based on a history of exposure, the absence of proper vaccination, and classic clinical signs associated with the disease (eye and nasal discharges, chewing gum fits, enamel hypoplasia, hard pad, etc.). In addition, direct microscopic evidence of the virus within blood cells, or within scrapings of the conjunctiva of the eye or tonsils, can help out the veterinarian in his/her diagnosis.

There is no specific treatment for the canine distemper virus; as a result, supportive care with antibiotics, fluids, and anticonvulsants is indicated. Unfortunately, the overall prognosis is poor, with over 50 percent of dogs that exhibit severe signs dying in spite of good supportive care. Of those dogs that do recover, about 50 percent can be expected to develop some form of nervous system complication down the line.

With recent advancements in veterinary dentistry, enamel restoration with artificial compounds has become available for those cases involving hypoplasia, and it is a viable way to prevent further tooth deterioration.

Immunization at an early age with a canine distemper vaccine is the cornerstone for preventing this disease. Any puppy or dog suspected of having the disease should be immediately isolated from its pack members. Disinfection of the contaminated premises with bleach (1 part bleach to 30 parts water) will also help reduce spread.

Parvovirus

First identified in 1977, this virus, which is related to the feline panleukopenia virus, usually strikes young, unvaccinated puppies under the age of 6 weeks, although all ages can be susceptible to infection. It is highly contagious, spreading from host to host via oral contamination with infected feces. Parvovirus affects the intestines, the immune system, and/or the heart of infected canines and can quickly be fatal if neglected.

The parvovirus is attracted to those areas of the body wherein normal cells are actively dividing and multiplying. In dogs, the lining of the intestines, lymph nodes, and bone marrow are targeted areas. In addition, in puppies under 6 weeks of age, the virus can infect heart cells, causing irreparable damage to this organ.

The intestinal form of the disease is by far the most common. Signs seen include loss of appetite, persistent vomiting, and profuse, odiferous diarrhea, often streaked with blood (Fig. 6.2). In severe cases, the actual lining of the intestines may be shed in the stool. As these signs develop, dehydration and secondary bacterial infection can rapidly occur, especially in the young pup. If not treated immediately, both conditions can lead to organ failure and death.

FIGURE 6.2 **Bloody diarrhea accompanies acute parvovirus infections.**

The cardiac, or heart, form of the disease is usually characterized by sudden death for no apparent reason, and often with no outward signs to indicate the virus's involvement. In a few cases, severe breathing problems may arise as the heart is attacked, which may then be followed up by vomiting and diarrhea as the disease progresses into its intestinal stage.

Diagnosis of parvovirus infection is based on clinical signs, vaccination history, and laboratory tests. A declining white blood cell count, which reflects the virus's invasion into the bone marrow, is one of the most consistent signs seen with parvovirus. In fact, this parameter is used as a prognostic indicator by veterinary clinicians for determining the severity of a particular infection. In general, if this white cell count continues to fall even after 3 days from the onset of clinical signs, the prognosis for recovery is poor. On the other hand, if the count rebounds, and starts its way back up by day 3, recovery can usually be expected, provided, of course, that supportive treatment is continued.

Because there are no specific antiviral agents available for this disease, treatment for parvovirus infection involves supportive care and the prevention of secondary complications. Success of treatment depends on many factors, including how quickly it is instituted after the onset of signs, how aggressively treatment is applied, and which strain of the virus is involved.

Intravenous fluids are a must to treat existing dehydration and to prevent further dehydration from occurring. Supplementation with potassium, a substance vital to the normal motility of the intestinal tract, is also used to replace the amount that was lost due to vomiting and diarrhea.

Since an infected puppy or dog cannot keep any food down, a dextrose or sugar supplement and vitamins may be given intravenously as well. Antibiotics and drugs designed to control vomiting are also part of the support plan. Good nursing care to maintain an adequate body temperature and reduce stress is also a must. Finally, injections with special preparations of antibodies (immunoglobulin injections) are showing great promise in the active treatment of parvovirus infections.

Starting immunizations at a young age is the most effective way to prevent serious complications associated with parvovirus exposure and infection. To help reduce the chances of puppies contracting the heart form of this disease, bitches should be current on vaccinations prior to breeding to ensure that optimum amounts of protective maternal antibodies will be passed on to the offspring.

Minimizing exposure is also an important control measure for parvovirus. This virus survives relatively well in the environment outside its host, so its contagiousness can last for days. All puppies and dogs, even those vaccinated, should be kept well away from dogs infected with the virus. Owners should also realize that some of these infected dogs can even shed the virus in their stools for weeks after clinical recovery. Puppies should be restricted in their contact with other dogs and with stressful situations until their vaccination program is complete. Contaminated environments can be cleaned with a 1:3 dilution of bleach to help inactivate the virus.

Coronavirus

Coronavirus infection is a highly contagious disease of puppies that can cause minor gastrointestinal illness. The virus is transmitted via contact with shed fecal material containing the virus. This can present a problem when large groups of puppies are housed together, since viral shedding from one infected animal can continue for several weeks even after clinical signs have abated.

Coronavirus cause mild, self-limiting diarrhea and occasional vomiting in affected puppies. However, if a puppy contracts parvovirus, the resulting immune suppression can allow the coronavirus to replicate unchecked and exacerbate the clinical signs seen due to the parvovirus.

Diagnosis is afforded by a good history, clinical signs seen, and laboratory tests. There is no specific treatment for coronavirus itself. If the coronavirus is coupled with parvovirus, then treatment approaches will be the same as those for the latter disease.

The need for vaccination against coronavirus is questionable. As a rule, puppies that are properly vaccinated against parvovirus rarely suffer from coronavirus enteritis.

Infectious Canine Hepatitis (ICH)

This disease is caused by the canine adenovirus 1, an organism found worldwide and known for its stability outside its host environment. (It can survive up to 2 weeks!) The virus is shed in all body excretions, and can be found in the urine of a recovered dog for up to 6 months. Direct contact with such secretions by an unsuspecting dog, usually under one year of age and unvaccinated, is the method of disease transmission.

As the name implies, once the organism enters the body, it can set up a severe inflammation of the liver, or hepatitis. ICH does not, however, stop there. Other organ systems, including the eyes and kidneys, can be affected as well.

Loss of appetite, depression, and fever, sometimes reaching 106 degrees Fahrenheit, are initial symptoms seen. Enlargement of the tonsils and other lymph nodes occurs as the virus multiplies in these regions. As the liver is attacked, abdominal pain and jaundice become evident. In addition, inflammation of the blood vessels within the body can lead to clotting problems and internal bleeding.

One characteristic lesion of infectious canine hepatitis that can develop later as the disease progresses is called blue eye. In this condition, one or both eyes can take on a blue appearance due to fluid buildup and inflammation within the eye(s).

Diagnosis of infectious canine hepatitis is based on the age of the animal involved, vaccination history, and laboratory data. Such data will reveal elevated liver enzyme levels, a lowered white blood cell count, and increased clotting time. Biopsy samples might reveal the actual presence of the virus within the tissue itself.

Treatment aims are preventing secondary complications, such as bacterial infections, and giving intravenous fluids to combat dehydration. In severe cases, blood transfusions could be required. Even when vigorous therapy is instituted, prognosis for recovery remains very guarded in the majority of cases.

Vaccination is the best way to prevent this disease.

Canine Contagious Respiratory Disease

Canine contagious respiratory disease (CCRD; also known as "canine cough" or "kennel cough") is a highly contagious disease transmitted by air and wind currents contaminated with cough and sneeze droplets from infected canines. It occurs with high frequency in boarding kennels, dog shows, and other areas where dogs may be congregated. There is no one organism on which to solely place the blame for this disease. In fact, over six different causative agents have been isolated, including several types of adenoviruses and reoviruses, the canine herpesvirus, the parainfluenza virus, and a bacterium called *Bordetella bronchiseptica.* All these agents can cause disease by themselves or in combination with the others. The *Bordetella* organism is related to the bacterium that causes whooping cough in humans, and can cause permanent damage to the airways of affected dogs if not detected and treated soon enough.

The classic clinical sign associated with an uncomplicated case of CCRD includes a relentless dry, hacking cough, usually nonproductive (Fig. 6.3). Occasionally, a clear discharge from the nose might appear. Gagging or retching might be noted at the end of a coughing spell and is often mistaken for vomiting. Affected dogs usually don't run a fever or seem to "feel bad," nor is it common for them to lose their appetite—that is, if the case doesn't become complicated with secondary infections.

Complicated cases of CCRD are characterized by a greenish eye and nasal discharge, and by obvious breathing difficulties as pneumonia rears its ugly head. In these instances, affected animals do run fevers, do lose their appetites, and do appear sick.

Diagnosis of CCRD is based on the presence of the classic clinical signs, plus a recent history of exposure to other dogs. Radiographs might be required to evaluate the extent of the lung and airway involvement in complicated cases. Bacterial cultures are also indicated in these latter instances.

Treatment of the disease consists of antibiotic therapy, and, in the case of nonproductive coughs, cough suppressants. Owners need to realize that coughing can persist for up to 3 weeks, even after treatment.

If complications exist, more specific therapy will be needed to battle the pneumonia and fever and to prevent dehydration. Vaporizers are often used to liquefy secretions in the airway, allowing for greater

FIGURE 6.3   A dry, hacking cough is characteristic of "kennel cough."

ease of passage. A similar effect can be obtained by placing the affected pet in a steam-filled bathroom for 10 to 15 minutes. Just be sure the temperature within the room doesn't get too hot; drinking water should be provided to the dog to help prevent overheating.

An intranasal vaccine can be administered to provide some protection against CCRD. If a dog has not been vaccinated within the past 6 months, it should be administered no later than 1 week prior to a scheduled boarding or event.

Herpes Virus

This virus poses no real threat to adult dogs. In fact, it is thought to be a natural inhabitant of the respiratory tract and sometimes the reproductive tracts of these adults. Its main importance rests in the disease it causes in puppies under 2 weeks of age.

As it turns out, this herpes virus does not multiply well in the higher body temperatures normally found in adult dogs. However, neonatal puppies, whose ability to maintain this body temperature is poor, are prime targets for the virus. They can become infected with it directly inside the mother's uterus, or they can become exposed after birth. Unfortunately, once clinical signs appear in these young puppies, there is not much that can be done to save them.

The time from exposure to the appearance of clinical signs is about 7 to 10 days. Afflicted puppies will cry constantly, become depressed, and stop nursing, Death usually occurs within 24 hours after the signs begin.

Because of its age specificity, herpes virus infection should be suspected anytime puppies under 2 weeks of age become ill and cry constantly. Further diagnostics performed on tissue samples after death can help confirm the diagnosis and shift focus on saving the remaining members of the litter.

As mentioned before, once signs appear in an individual, death is inevitable. However, there are steps owners can take to try to spare the other puppies in the litter from the same fate. Be sure to provide a source of heat (*remember—never* allow a heating pad to come in direct contact with the body surface, and always keep heating pads on their low setting) to the puppies to maintain their body temperatures above 100 degrees Fahrenheit. This will help slow the multiplication of the virus. If indicated, supportive fluids and force-fed nutrition can also be helpful as well.

There is no vaccine available to help combat this disease.

Rabies

If there was ever a disease to strike fear into the hearts and minds of pet owners everywhere, this is it! Rabies is a deadly viral disease that can infect any warm-blooded mammal, including domesticated animals such as dogs, cats, horses, and cattle. As a disease to be avoided, rabies is one of the earliest ever recorded, dating back to almost 2000 B.C. It is found worldwide, except in a few countries, such as Great Britain and Japan, which have strict laws designed to keep their countries rabies-free.

The incidence of rabies within the United States varies with each state, depending on the normal fauna found in that state and on existing vaccination laws. It is estimated that over 86 percent of all rabies cases occur in wildlife species of animals, with about 14 percent spilling over into the domestic pet and livestock population. It is certainly these latter groups that pose the greatest threat to public health. Species that are commonly culprits of spreading wildlife rabies include skunks, raccoons, coyotes, foxes, and bats. Opossums are noted for their resistance to this virus, and they rarely become infected. Rodents, such as rats and mice, are not significant carriers of the disease, either, since most don't survive encounters with rabid animals in the first place.

Skunk rabies is most prevalent in the midwestern and southwestern states and California; raccoon rabies, in the mid-Atlantic and southeastern United States; fox rabies in the eastern states; and bat rabies—well, it's found in all states. Most cases seem to occur during the spring and fall months of the year.

The rabies virus is usually transmitted via the infected saliva of affected animals through a bite wound or contamination therewith of an open wound or mucous membranes. The disease is uniformly fatal once contracted.

Dogs are a leading host for this killer, and are a major vector for transmission of the disease to humans. Studies have shown that rabies occurs in higher incidence in younger dogs, with a median age of about one year. In addition, as a result of hormonally related roaming and territorial instincts, male dogs are at greater risk of exposure than are females.

Traditionally, when speaking of rabies, most people visualize a snarling, frothing dog snapping at anything in sight. While this is true in some instances, pet owners should understand that this represents only one of three stages that are part of the overall disease process. Depending on each individual case, viciousness might take on a prominent role, or might not occur at all. These three stages of rabies include the prodromal stage, the furious stage, and the "dumb" or paralytic stage.

The first stage, which might last from 1 to 3 days, is characterized by a change in the overall behavior of the animal. Normally friendly dogs might suddenly exhibit aggressive tendencies toward their owners or toward other pets in the household. Affected individuals might also hide a lot, preferring to be left alone, and becoming upset when disturbed. Loss of appetite might become apparent, and owners might notice an increased sexual arousal and/or frequency of urination.

Once the prodromal stage is complete, the victim then enters into the furious stage. This is the stage most persons equate with a traditional rabies presentation. Dogs in this

DID YOU KNOW ❓

Contrary to popular belief, a bite wound or direct contamination of an open wound isn't the only way a person can be exposed to the rabies virus. Aerosol transmission has been known to occur as well (e.g., breathing air in caves heavily populated by bats).

stage often become quite restless, excitatory, and aggressive, losing fear of natural enemies. They might wander about aimlessly, snapping and biting at anything that moves. The character of the animal's vocalizations might noticeably change. In dogs especially, *pica,* or an abnormal desire to eat anything within reach (rocks, wire, dirt, feces, etc.), might become apparent. As the disease enters the third stage, the swallowing reflex becomes paralyzed, making it impossible to eat, drink, or swallow saliva. This is what accounts for the excessive drooling seen in rabid animals.

The furious stage might last for up to a week before progressing into stage 3, the paralytic stage. Pet owners should be aware of the fact that some animals, especially dogs, might skip the furious stage entirely, going directly from the prodromal stage into the paralytic stage. When this happens, the disease can be easily mistaken for other nervous system disorders if the diagnostician is not careful. Because this quick transition can occur, the risk of human exposure is greatly increased. The paralytic stage presents itself as a general loss of coordination and paralysis. A droopy lower jaw with the mouth hanging open is often characteristic. A general paralysis and death usually overtakes the unfortunate animal in a matter of hours.

Rabies should be suspected anytime a dog exhibits behavioral changes with unexplained, abnormal nervous system signs. Unfortunately, the only way to definitively diagnose a case of rabies is to have a laboratory analysis performed on the animal's brain tissue, which means, of course, euthanasia of the animal in question.

There is no known treatment for this fatal disease; as a result, stringent control and vaccination measures are a must. All puppies should receive a rabies immunization between 3 and 4 months of age. In most states, a licensed veterinarian must administer this vaccine. Depending on the vaccine used and on the state in which you live, a booster immunization is required every 1 to 3 years. Owing to the public health implications of this disease, dog owners who fail to keep their pets current on this immunization are putting their own health at risk!

Other preventive control measures that can be taken include discouraging night roaming and keeping all pets restrained on a leash when walking outside. Repairing or constructing fences and enclosures to help keep wild animals out of a pet's play area or living area will also help reduce chances of exposure.

If a stray or wild animal bites a dog, the wound needs to be seen immediately by a veterinarian, and, depending on when the last one was given, a booster rabies immunization should be administered. The animal should also be placed in quarantine for a minimum of 90 days, unless the particular animal that did the biting can be found and its rabies status confirmed as negative.

If the dog that was bitten by a known rabies carrier has never been vaccinated before, immediate euthanasia is warranted. If an owner of such a pet refuses to do so, then, for safety reasons, the pet should be quarantined for at least 6 months before it is declared uninfected.

Laws in most states spell out regulations concerning vaccinations, bites involving humans, and the ownership of wildlife in order to curb the impact of this disease. Any vaccinated dog that bites a human being needs to be placed in quarantine for a minimum of 10 days to observe for signs of rabies. If suspicious signs appear, the animal is then euthanized, and samples are sent to the laboratory. If there is no history of the dog ever having a rabies vaccine in the past, or if a wild animal is involved, euthanasia and prompt laboratory examination of the brain tissue is warranted to expedite the diagnostic process.

Euthanasia should be carried out only by veterinarians or other public health and/or wildlife officials to ensure that the sample that reaches the lab has been properly handled and stored. Certainly any person bitten by an animal should contact a physician immediately. If the situation warrants it, prophylactic rabies treatment will be started on the bitten individual until the quarantine period is over or until the specific laboratory test results are in.

It is interesting to note that because the concentration of the rabies virus in the infected dog's saliva might be low or even absent in some cases, less than 50 percent of all bites from rabies-positive animals will result in the transmission of the disease. Yet because there is no way of knowing which fall into this category, prophylactic treatment is a must, just to be on the safe side!

Finally, ownership of wild animals, especially skunks (descented or not) and raccoons, should be avoided for a number of reasons. First, there are no licensed vaccines available for these wild pets. Second, because the incubation period of rabies can last for months, owners might be exposing themselves to rabies right from the start without knowing it. Finally, in many states, it is in fact illegal to own such pets without a permit.

Parents should always discourage children from interacting with stray animals or wildlife. Their natural curiosity could lead to a serious bite wound and much anxiety, especially if the offender is not found.

Bacterial Diseases

Primary infections caused by bacterial organisms are uncommon in dogs. In most instances, bacterial infections occur secondarily to other disease conditions, such as stress, viral infections, and parasites. As a result, whenever a bacterial disease is present, treatments should be directed against any underlying problems as well.

Bacterial Skin Disease

Bacteria can play an important role in diseases and disorders of the skin in dogs. For more information on bacterial skin diseases and their treatment, see Chapter 14.

Leptospirosis

Canine leptospirosis is a bacterial disease of dogs characterized by jaundice, vomiting, and kidney failure. At least four different groups of leptospirosis organisms, all belonging to the genus and species *Leptospira interrogans,* have been implicated in this disease in dogs. Remarkably, most infections are subclinical; that is, few show clinical signs of disease. When clinical signs do arise, however, the results can be serious, even life-threatening. Leptospirosis becomes more of a problem in kennels where animals are kept together under poor sanitary conditions. Animals become infected with the organisms through contact with infected urine.

Leptospirosis is found primarily in young animals between the ages of 1 to 4 years. In addition, males seem to be more commonly affected than females. Signs associated with the disease reflect the damage done by the organisms to the body's blood, liver, and kidneys.

Fever, depression, vomiting, and diarrhea might be early signs that become noticeable. Anemia might set in as red blood cells are destroyed by the invading organisms, and distinct bruising on the skin surface becomes evident as the body's blood clotting mechanisms are impaired. In severe cases, liver failure and/or kidney failure appear, leading to rapid dehydration and to a urine with an orange-brown color, a feature characteristic of this disease. Left untreated, death will often result.

To diagnose this disease, veterinarians rely on a thorough history (including potential exposure to livestock), clinical signs, and special laboratory tests. The white blood cell count is usually elevated, in contrast to those seen with viral diseases. Blood and urine cultures might be used to confirm a diagnosis. Antibody levels measured at 2-week intervals have been used as well for this purpose.

Treatment of leptospirosis consists of high levels of specific antibiotics, combined with fluid therapy to combat dehydration and medications to stimulate kidney function. Unfortunately, unless treated early enough, the kidneys could suffer irreparable damage, leading to unavoidable failure.

Because of the serious nature of this disease, dog owners need to focus their attention on prevention. Since cross-protection against this disease is not afforded by most leptospirosis vaccines, preventing is aimed at limiting access to potentially infected livestock and water sources they may frequent.

Higher Bacteria

A special group of bacteria, called "higher bacteria," which share characteristics of both standard bacteria and fungi, can cause significant disease in exposed dogs.

Two of the more prevalent organisms in this class include *Nocardia* and *Actinomyces*. These agents, found in soil, are transmitted primarily via traumatic wounds. Draining, painful skin lesions, and severe pneumonia are consequences of higher bacterial infections in dogs. Diagnosis and treatment for these diseases are similar to that of standard bacterial infections; however, surgical removal of infected tissue is often required to afford a complete cure.

FIGURE 6.4   Microscopic appearance of ringworm spores.

Fungi and Yeast

Along with viruses and bacteria, fungal organisms can produce infectious disease (mycoses) in dogs. Probably the most common one pet owners are familiar with and have heard about is dermatophytosis, or ringworm. In addition, yeast infections can be a common problem in the ears of dogs. These types of yeast and fungi that affect mainly the outer skin surfaces are termed *superficial mycoses.*

Ringworm

The most prevalent fungal disease that afflicts dogs is ringworm. Three different organisms—*Microsporum canis, Trichophyton mentagrophytes,* and *Microsporum gypseum*—can actually cause ringworm (Fig. 6.4). The first two are contracted from infected animals, the third from contaminated soil.

In dogs, ringworm causes patchy hair logs with or without an accompanying lesion on the skin beneath. Since humans can be susceptible to the same type of ringworm, reddened, circular lesions occurring on the owner as well might support a diagnosis.

Diagnosis of ringworm is confirmed by a fungal culture. Treatment can consist of iodine or chlorhexidine shampoos and topical and/or oral antifungal medications.

Subcutaneous and Deep Mycoses

In contrast to ringworm, fungal and yeast infections involving the deeper tissues of the body are termed subcutaneous or deep mycoses, depending on the depth of tissue involvement. These diseases, including sporotrichosis, aspergillosis, blastomycosis, histoplasmosis, coccidioidomycosis, and cryptococcosis, can be quite severe, and even life-threatening at times.

Inhalation of fungal spores from infected soil through the respiratory tract is the primary mode of transmission for the majority of these deeper fungi and yeast (with the exception of sporotrichosis). As a result, the first clinical signs usually seen relate to some type of respiratory problem. Many of these dogs just seem to do poorly, and often suffer from chronic weight loss. Others are presented to the veterinarian for a skin disorder or abscess, when in fact the skin problem is actually being caused by underlying drainage from the deeper fungal involvement.

Sporotrichosis

The fungus that causes sporotrichosis in dogs, *Sporothrix schenckii,* can gain entrance into the body via a direct injury to the skin or by inhalation, and then spread throughout the body by way of the lymphatic system.

Dogs afflicted with this soilborne organism can exhibit numerous and tender lumps, nodules, and/or ulcerations anywhere on the body surface, but particularly on the extremities. Some of these lumps might actually resemble warts. In severe instances, liver, lungs, and other body organs can become involved as well. Inorganic iodide compounds, such as sodium or potassium iodide, are the treatments of choice for sporotrichosis.

Blastomycosis

Blastomyces dermatitidis is the organism responsible for this disease in dogs. Of all dogs affected, 80 percent will show some type of respiratory signs, such as a nonproductive cough. Skin involvement can occur with numerous draining lesions and abscesses, along with lymph node enlargement. Other organ systems can be affected as well. Blindness can result if the organisms spread to the eyes, and lameness, especially in the hind legs, occurs secondary to bone involvement.

Histoplasmosis

Histoplasmosis is caused by the organism *Histoplasma capsulatum.* Soil contaminated with the droppings of starlings and other birds appear to be an important source of this disease in dogs. Like blasto-mycosis, histoplasmosis can strike the respiratory system of affected dogs, leading to coughing and breathing difficulties. The gastrointesti-nal tract is often involved as well, resulting in chronic diarrhea. Bone, eye, and skin lesions call also result from a histoplasmosis infection.

Coccidioidomycosis

Infections with the fungus *Coccidioides immitis* are associated more with the dry, desert regions of North America. Hunting dogs and other canines allowed access to rodent burrows are most susceptible to exposure, since the soil in these areas might have a high concentration of fungal spores. As with other deep fungi, these spores are inhaled into the lungs, where the organisms set up housekeeping.

If the disease remains localized in the lungs, the clinical signs usu-ally reflect this respiratory involvement. Coughing and breathing diffi-culties result from invasion of the lung tissue and from enlargement of lymph nodes within the chest cavity. If the coccidioidomycosis dis-seminates throughout the body via the blood and lymphatics, bone infection is common. Lameness, pain, and joint swelling usually occur as a result. Often, draining tracts originating from the bone infection break through the skin and create unsightly lesions.

Cryptococcosis

Unlike the three conditions just mentioned, this disease is caused by a yeast organism, *Cryptococcus neoformans,* rather than a fungus. Soil contaminated with pigeon and bat feces is a main source of these yeast organisms.

Cryptococcosis in dogs is mainly an upper respiratory and nasal problem. A thick, copious, continuous nasal discharge usually results, and sneezing can be a clinical sign. From the nasal passages, crypto-coccosis can spread throughout the body and cause lameness, enlarged lymph nodes, nervous system impairment, blindness, and skin infections.

Diagnosis and Treatment for Fungal Infections

History, physical exam findings, and laboratory tests, including radi-ographic X rays, and biopsies of affected regions, can lead the veterinary practitioner to a tentative diagnosis of a fungal infection within the body. Microscopic examination of body fluids or drainages for fungal spores or yeast can also be helpful. In most cases, a definitive diagnosis is made by testing a blood serum sample for antibodies against the fungal organisms in question, or, less commonly, by culturing for growth.

A number of antifungal medications are available and can be used to treat such infections in dogs. Depending on which agents are used (many are used in combination with one another), duration of treatment required is often 1 to 3 months to effect a complete cure.

Radiographs and special immunologic tests can be used to monitor the response to treatment. In many cases, surgical excision of those regions infected with the fungus can result in faster recovery. The prognosis for dogs is good when fungal infections are detected and treated in their early stages; guarded to poor, if dissemination throughout the body has occurred.

Parasitic Diseases

A long with infectious diseases, internal and external parasites are responsible for the vast majority of illnesses and disorders seen in dogs. As a result, timely diagnosis and treatment for these pests is vital to the health of the dog.

Fleas

Ctenocephalides canis (common dog flea) is by far the most common external parasite seen on dogs (Fig. 7.1). As every pet owner will attest to, these pests are the number-1 health problem facing these pets. However, aside from causing relentless chewing and scratching, fleas are also disease carriers, and can threaten the dog owner's health as well. For these reasons, the development of a good control program to combat these irritating pests is a must.

It is important to understand that fleas spend the vast majority of their time off of the pet, reproducing and maturing in the pet's environment. As a result, environmental control measures are essential for successful flea control.

The flea life cycle includes four major stages: egg, larva, pupa, and adult stages. Both the egg and pupa stages are very resistant to insecticides, which can make complete flea control difficult. During summer

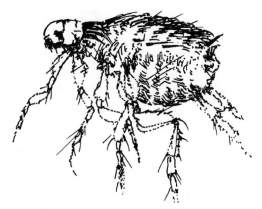

FIGURE 7.1 The flea is the most common parasite of dogs.

DID YOU KNOW?

For every one flea seen on your dog, there are nine more in your house or yard!

months, the entire flea cycle (egg to adult) might be completed in 16–21 days. Heat and humidity tend to shorten this cycle period. In addition, fleas are most prolific during hot, humid weather.

A complete approach to flea control should always involve three steps:

1. Treating the home
2. Treating the yard
3. Treating the pet

Because fleas, on the average, will only spend about ten percent of their time on dogs, treating the surrounding environment is probably more important than treating the actual pet. For more information regarding flea control, see Chapter 3.

Ticks

Ticks, unlike fleas, attach themselves to the pet's skin via their mouthparts. Ticks generally remain attached in one spot for long periods. The head, neck, and interdigital (between the toes) areas of the pet are the most common sites of severe infestation. Ticks produce local irritation and even anemia in heavy infestations (Fig. 7.2). Ticks might serve as intermediate hosts for disease-producing microorganisms and might transmit these "germs" (such as Lyme disease) to the infested pet. For more information on tick control, see Chapter 3.

Mites

Mite infestation is commonly known as mange and requires the diagnostic and treatment expertise of a veterinarian. The common mites infecting dogs are microscopic requiring skin scrapes and subsequent microscopic examination by the veterinarian for diagnosis. The three most common forms of mange and pertinent facts concerning each are listed below.

Sarcoptic Mange (Scabies)

Caused by the organism *Sarcoptes scabiei var. canis,* sarcoptic mange is characterized by a sudden onset of severe itching. Direct exposure to an infected animal is required for transmission (Fig. 7.3).

The mite burrows into the host's epidermis and tunnels. Severe itching results, particularly on the abdomen, chest, legs, and ears. Thickening and scaling of elbows, hocks, and ear tips might be noted. Hair loss and skin irritation often results from the almost constant scratching and biting (Fig. 7.4).

Scabies is highly contagious to other dogs. In addition, it might temporarily produce chiggerlike bites and itching on exposed human family members.

Pet treatment consists of proper diagnosis, miticidal dipping, and/or systemic miticides. All dogs in the household should be

FIGURE 7.2　Female ticks engorged on blood can reach relatively enormous sizes!

FIGURE 7.3　The sarcoptic mange mite.

FIGURE 7.4 Facial crusting caused by sarcoptic mange.

treated because of the highly contagious nature of the scabies mite. If pet-to-human transmission occurs, contact your physician.

Cheyletiella Mange

The mange mite *Cheyletiella* can cause skin scaling, intense itching, and hair loss in affected dogs. The common name for this parasitism is "walking dandruff," since the flakes and scales produced by the disease, when observed closely, appear to be in motion. Like sarcoptic mange, this mite can temporarily infest people who become exposed. Diagnosis and treatment of *Cheyletiella* is the same as that for sarcoptic mange.

Demodectic Mange

Demodectic mange is also called *follicular* or "red mange." The demodectic mange mite, *Demodex canis,* might be found in the hair follicles of normal dogs in low numbers (Fig. 7.5). However, in cases where demodectic mange develops, normal immunity to the mite either fails to develop or is suppressed, resulting in pathogenic proliferation of the mite within the hair follicles.

The majority of demodectic mange cases occur in dogs less than 2 years of age with immune systems that are immature or temporarily suppressed. The first symptom observable is usually small areas of hair

FACT *OR* **FICTION**

Mange is always contagious from dog to dog. **FICTION.** Although many types of mange mites are indeed contagious, one of the most infamous, *Demodex,* is not. This type of mange causes problems only in dogs with compromised immune systems.

loss (alopecia). The lesions might occur anywhere on the body but often begin in the head area. Diagnosis requires a skin scraping and microscopic exam by a veterinarian.

The lesions (areas of hair loss) might be localized to one area or generalized over the body. Secondary bacterial hair follicle infections (folliculitis) are common sequela to some localized and most generalized cases. The inflammatory skin reaction that ensues might result in the reddened skin referred to by the term "red mange."

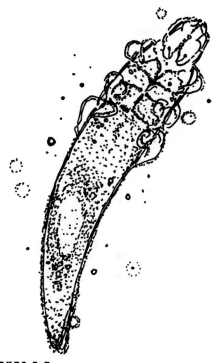

FIGURE 7.5   The demodectic mange mite.

With correct diagnosis and appropriate treatment, 80 to 90 percent of young dogs with demodicosis will recover. Maturation of the immune response plays a vital role in cases of complete recovery. Relapse might occur but is infrequent. However, unlike sarcoptic mange (caused by *Sarcoptes scabiei* infestation), demodicosis often requires long-term therapy

Demodectic mange in older dogs might reflect immunologic suppression elicited by an underlying disease. Liver disorders, viral infections, malnutrition, heat-cycle changes, neoplasia, hypothyroidism, diabetes, and other problems might lead to impaired immune responses and demodicosis. A thorough physical examination is important in such cases. The success of the treatment varies being dependent on the cause of immunodeficiency.

Special insecticidal medications, both topical and systemic, are available for demodectic mange through a veterinarian.

Factors concerning a dog's immunologic ability to protect it from developing demodectic mange are considered hereditary. However, since most cases of demodicosis resolve on patient maturity, the significance of its inheritable nature is questionable.

Lice

Lice infection, or pediculosis, in dogs is usually seen in young animals kept in unclean breeding or kennel environments (Fig. 7.6).

Signs of such an infestation can include itching and reddened skin, with or without secondary bacterial infection. As with mites, lice can be identified by performing a skin scraping on an affected area and looking for the organisms under the microscope. In addition, the eggs of lice can often be visualized attached to hair shafts near their attachments to the hair follicles.

Lice are treated effectively with insecticidal dipping. These dippings should be performed on a weekly basis for three or four treatments. In addition, the pet's environment should be treated as well to prevent reinfestation.

Esophageal Worms

The esophageal worm of dogs, *Spirocerca lupi,* is found primarily in the southeastern and southwestern portions of the United States. These worms, which are red and coiled in appearance, burrow into and inhabit the wall of the esophagus, and sometimes the stomach, of their host.

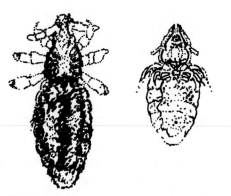

FIGURE 7.6 Left: sucking louse; Right: biting louse

Direct transmission from dog to dog does not occur; rather, beetles, chickens, amphibians, and rodents all can act as intermediary hosts for this worm. When dogs come in oral contact with one of these hosts, infection can result. Once ingested, the worms migrate through blood vessels within the body, eventually ending up in the esophageal wall. From here, they produce more eggs, which are coughed up and swallowed, and then passed out in the feces.

Because the nodules formed by the worms interfere with swallowing, vomiting after meals is the most prevalent clinical sign seen with *Spirocerca* infections. To make matters worse, these nodules can have a propensity for becoming cancerous in a small percentage of cases. In addition, bony lesions along the vertebral column and in the bones of the arms and legs can result from the migratory habits of these parasites.

Diagnosis of esophageal worms involves a fecal exam, radiographs, and direct examination of the esophagus and stomach using an endoscope. Unfortunately, once the owner notices clinical signs, the majority of the damage has already been done, and treatment attempts are futile. Surgery can sometimes be used to actually remove the nodules and provide relief, yet it rarely affords a total cure. And considering the number of possible transport hosts for this parasite, environmental control is difficult at best.

Tapeworms

Tapeworms are considered segmented flatworms, belonging to a class of organisms called *Cestoda*. One important characteristic of this class is that all utilize intermediate hosts in their transmission cycle. Intermediate hosts can include rodents, fleas and other insects, rabbits, sheep, swine, cattle, and in some instances, even humans!

Tapeworm segments containing eggs are shed in fecal material. When these eggs are accidentally or voluntarily consumed by an intermediate host, they hatch and the resulting larvae migrate into the body tissues and begin their development. Yet they won't reach their adult stage inside the tissues of this intermediate host. Instead, the life cycle is completed when this host or portions thereof is (are) consumed by another, called the *definitive host.* Inside this new host environment, the larvae then proceed to develop into adult tapeworms, which attach to the intestinal wall, eat, and repeat the life cycle all over again.

The extent of disease caused by tapeworms depends on the type of worm involved, and whether the affected individual is an intermediate or final host. As a rule, adult tapeworms living within the intestines of a definitive host are rarely life-threatening, causing varying degrees of gastroenteritis and malnutrition. Larval forms, on the other hand, tend to do more damage, simply because they migrate through the body tissues. Furthermore, if these larvae gain entrance into the tissues of an animal (or human) that is not a normal intermediate host for that tapeworm, the results can sometimes be deadly.

By far the most prevalent species of tapeworm seen in dogs is called *Dipylidium caninum,* the double-pored tapeworm. It is so common because it uses the flea as an intermediate host (the dog louse can also be a carrier).

Segments from the tapeworm are passed in the feces or actually "crawl" out onto the haircoat of an infested animal. Once outside, the segments dry out and release egg baskets into the environment. Flea larvae looking for food then ingest these eggs, and a new tapeworm begins its development. If the flea happens to be ingested by a dog during chewing or self-grooming episodes, the tapeworm larvae will continue their development into adult worms within the pet's small intestine.

Although less frequent, dogs can become infected with other types of tapeworms besides *Dipylidium,* depending on potential exposure to intermediate hosts. For instance, dogs fed raw meat or garbage are at risk. *Echinococcus granulosus,* the tapeworm responsible for hydatid cyst disease, is often transmitted to dogs in this way.

Dogs infested with adult tapeworms may or may not exhibit the typical signs associated with gastroenteritis, such as vomiting and diarrhea. Weight loss certainly can occur as the worms absorb nutrients from within the gut. Often, scooting and other signs related to anal sac discomfort might also alert an owner as to the presence of these pesky parasites.

Diagnosis of a tapeworm infestation can be confirmed by actually seeing the white, moving, wormlike segments in fresh fecal material or on the haircoat around the hind region. Segments might also be seen on anal sac expression. If dried, the segments will take on a brownish, "ricelike" appearance.

Microscopic examination of the stool might be helpful as well; however, because the shedding of the segments is sporadic, a negative finding cannot totally rule out an infestation.

Tapeworms can be difficult pests to treat and totally eliminate. Praziquantel and epsiprantel are two effective medications used by veterinarians to eliminate tapeworms from the intestines. Other drugs are available as well. Repeating the treatment in 2 to 3 weeks helps ensure thorough elimination.

Flea control is the best way to prevent *D. caninum.* Other tapeworms, including *Echinococcus,* can be prevented by denying access to garbage and/or raw meat.

Roundworms

Roundworms, known as *ascarids* or "spool worms," are thick-bodied, whitish-to-cream-colored worms that can inhabit the small intestine of dogs. This is one of the most common intestinal parasites affecting dogs and young puppies. In fact, research has demonstrated that over 95 percent of all puppies are born with roundworms.

Adult worms exist unattached within the intestinal lumen and can grow up to 8 inches in length. If present in large enough numbers, adult roundworms can cause prominent malnutrition and gastroenteritis. In some severe instances, rupture of an intestine jam-packed with roundworms has been known to happen. Immature roundworms can cause problems too, since they might migrate throughout the lungs, liver, and other tissues of the body before settling down as adults within the intestines.

Unlike the tapeworm, roundworms do not require an intermediate host for their transmission. Each female worm sheds thousands of eggs into the environment by the way of feces. These eggs, which are covered by a thick shell, are very resistant and might remain viable in an environment for years prior to being consumed by an unsuspecting dog.

> ## Dr. P's Vet Tip
>
> Even if heartworm preventive medication is not required year-round in your area, you should still give it to your pet all throughout the year. The reason: Most preventatives sold on the market today also prevent infestations with intestinal parasites (some of which can be zoonotic, including roundworms), providing an important source of continual protection for not only your dog, but for you and your family as well.

After consumption of a roundworm egg, it is possible for the hatched larvae to develop into adults without ever leaving the intestine. However, this is the exception rather than the rule. What usually happens is the larvae penetrate the bowel wall and migrate to the liver and the lungs, maturing and growing along the way. Once inside the lungs, they can enter the airways, be coughed up and swallowed again, allowing them to finish their development into adults within the intestines.

Alternatively, from the lungs, these larvae can enter the bloodstream and circulate throughout the body. In female dogs, these larvae might settle down and become dormant within the mammary tissue until such time as lactation begins. In this way, newborn pups can ingest roundworm larvae through their mother's milk. But this isn't the only reason for the high incidence of roundworms in neonatal puppies. They can also be exposed to the circulating roundworm larvae via the umbilical cord while they are still in the womb, and actually be born with active infestations!

The clinical signs seen with a roundworm infestation depend on the age of the dog affected, the stage of maturity that the worms are in, and their location within the body. As a general rule, the younger the dog, the more severe the signs tend to be. In fact, some older dogs can actually develop a resistance to these parasites. If adult worms are within the intestines, signs often include stomach pain with a prominent "bloated" appearance to the abdomen, vomiting, and diarrhea. In many instances, actual adult worms might be revealed within the vomitus or stool. Ruptured bowels and intestinal obstructions can result if not treated promptly.

Because of the migration through the lungs, coughing, breathing difficulties, and other signs of pneumonia might be present. In severe cases, seizures and other nervous system problems can occur.

Veterinarians can diagnose roundworms by using a microscope to look for eggs in a sample of stool. Clinical signs and the dog's history are helpful in those cases where eggs might be absent from such a sample.

There are many commercially available deworming drugs effective at removing roundworms from the intestines. You can buy relatively inexpensive dewormers at grocery stores and pet supply stores. Be sure, however, to consult a veterinarian before using one of these to be certain that it contains the correct ingredients for your pet's particular problem. Repeat deworming should be performed 3 weeks later to ensure that any migrating larvae that reached the intestines since the first deworming are killed.

Young puppies suffering from roundworm-induced pneumonia require intensive veterinary supportive care to prevent life-threatening complications from arising. Most will recover with such care.

All puppies should be dewormed for these parasites, even if parasite eggs are not seen on an initial stool exam. These dewormings should commence at 3 weeks of age, and should be repeated at 6 and 9 weeks of age. Periodic stool exams are warranted to confirm a puppy's negative status.

Good sanitation procedures will help prevent reinfections and spread to other dogs. Realize, however, that once roundworms enter an environment, they are almost impossible to totally eliminate because of the hardy nature of the eggs. As a result, annual stool checks by a veterinarian are indicated to ensure pets remain parasite-free.

Visceral larval migrans, a human disease syndrome caused by migrating roundworm larvae, does pose a serious public health threat. As a result, good personal hygiene after handling pets, plus routine stool exams and treatments are a must to minimize the threat from this disease.

Most heartworm preventive medications on the market today also help prevent roundworm infestations if given on a regular basis. In those instances where environmental contamination is difficult to control, administering such a preventive agent year-round is one way to keep a dog free of these parasites.

Hookworms

The hookworm (*Ancylostoma, Uncinaria*) is another type of parasite that inhabits the small intestine of dogs. Unlike the roundworm that floats unattached within the intestinal lumen, absorbing nutrients through its skin, the hookworm actually uses teeth to attach itself to the wall of the intestine. Once attached, it begins to suck blood from vessels within the wall. In fact, it can become so severe that anemia and eventual death of the host animal could result if the hookworms are left untreated.

Compared to roundworms, hookworms are fairly small and thread-like, measuring up to 1 inch in length. Their life cycle begins with adult worms within the gut laying eggs, which are then passed out in the stool. If environmental conditions are sufficiently warm and humid, the eggs hatch and give rise to larvae, which then search for a host canine.

Once a host comes along, the larvae can gain entrance into the body in a number of ways. They can be picked up by way of mouth, or they can actually penetrate the skin (usually the footpads) and migrate through tissue before reaching the small intestine. Like roundworms, some of these migrating larvae might decide to stop and settle for a while within the tissues, making it possible for puppies of such females to become infected while still in the womb, or through nursing infected milk. As a result, puppies can be born with these blood-sucking parasites.

The severity of clinical signs depends largely on the amount of worms present in the gut and the age of the dog infected. Generally speaking, young puppies suffer from more severe disease than do adults.

Lethargy, loss of appetite, and pale mucous membranes due to loss of blood are not uncommon in canines harboring a large worm burden. A dark, tarry diarrhea may be present. If skin penetration has taken place, the footpads or other areas might be reddened, bleeding, and/or infected because of the larvae. Intense itching can also be noted as a result of this penetration.

Diagnosis of a hookworm infestation is based upon an examination of a stool sample for the presence of hookworm eggs.

There are a number of safe dewormers available from veterinarians that can help eliminate a hookworm infection. After the initial dose is given, a follow-up deworming should be administered 2 to 3 weeks later to kill any migrating larvae that have since reached the intestines.

In dogs suffering from anemia, supportive veterinary care is needed. This might include blood transfusions if blood loss is severe enough. Intravenous fluids and antibiotics might also be used to combat dehydration and secondary infections. Vitamin and iron supplements, combined with a high-quality diet, are fed to anemic dogs to provide building blocks within the body for new blood to be produced.

It is known that some dogs can actually develop an immunity to hookworms after an initial infection has taken place. However, this does not preclude routine periodic stool checks by a veterinarian, since those individuals that actually develop immunity can be difficult to identify. Hookworm eggs are not as hardy as their roundworm counterparts; hence, environmental control can be an effective way to prevent reinfection or spread to other dogs. Since the eggs require optimum environmental conditions before hatching will occur, keeping fecal material picked up daily in and around the premises will reduce chances of exposure. Studies have also shown that outdoor dogs kept on concrete stand less chance of infection than do dogs housed in kennels with dirt or grassy floors. Again, this is assuming that daily removal of contaminated fecal material is performed.

Deworming female dogs prior to pregnancy will help reduce the chances of puppies being born with hookworm infections. However, because deworming will not eliminate larvae within the mother's tissues and mammary glands, all neonatal pups should be routinely dewormed for these parasites starting at 3 weeks of age.

Most heartworm preventive medications on the market today also help prevent hookworm infestations if given on a regular basis. In those instances where environmental contamination is difficult to control, administering such a preventive year-round is one way to keep a dog hookworm-free.

Some hookworm larvae have the ability to penetrate the skin of humans, causing severe itching and dermatitis. In humans this condition is known as *cutaneous larval migrans,* or "creeping eruption." It is seen most often in tropical climates and in the southeastern portions of the United States. Since hookworm larvae thrive in warm sandy soils, this disease is one major reason why in most areas, pets are denied access to public beaches.

Whipworms

Trichuris vulpis, the dog whipworm, is a slender parasite that can reach 4 inches in length. Unlike tapeworms, hookworms, and roundworms, which inhabit the small intestine, whipworms colonize the large intestine, particularly the cecum (this structure corresponds to the human appendix).

The life cycle of this parasite is fairly simple. Eggs are passed in fresh feces into the environment. These eggs are then swallowed by an unsuspecting dog, and hatch within the dog's gut. From there, they set up housekeeping within the large intestine and grow to maturity, sometimes taking up to 3 months to do so. Adult females then produce more eggs, and the cycle is repeated. Note that unlike hookworms and roundworms, whipworms are not known to undergo tissue migration.

Light to moderate infections with whipworms might not give any outward hints of their presence. Sometimes dogs so affected might develop rough, unkempt haircoats and lose weight. Diarrhea might be a clinical sign. When it does occur, the stools are often blood-tinged.

Like other intestinal parasites, definitive diagnosis of a whipworm infestation is made by identifying whipworm eggs in stool under a microscope. Whipworms don't seem to be as prolific as other gut parasites; as a result, multiple samples might need to be examined before any eggs are seen.

Since whipworms are a common cause of chronic colitis in dogs, many practitioners opt to deworm for these parasites in such cases, even if eggs are not seen on a fecal exam. In those instances where whipworms are indeed to blame, the condition responds quite favorably to this empirical therapy.

Several different types of dewormers are effective at expelling whipworms. Some require only a single treatment; others need to be repeated months later. As seen with hookworm infections, many heartworm preventive medications on the market today also help prevent whipworm infestations if given on a regular basis. In those instances where environmental contamination is difficult to control, administering such a preventive agent year-round might be useful.

Threadworms

Threadworm infestations usually limit themselves to tropical climates. These worms live within the small intestines as adults, and, like canine lungworms, produce eggs that hatch before being passed out in the stool. These active larvae that are passed can then enter a new host through oral ingestion, or, like hookworms, can penetrate the skin or be acquired through the milk of infected females.

Parasitism is most common in puppies under 4 months of age. Profuse diarrhea often results from such an infestation. In addition, if skin penetration occurred, intense itching at the sites of entry is seen. Following skin invasion, coughing might become a problem as the larvae migrate through the lungs on their way to the intestines. In severe cases, pneumonia can result.

Diagnosis is made by direct microscopic examination of the live larvae in the feces. Treatment of threadworms can be difficult, requiring more potent compounds than those used to treat roundworms and hookworms. If diarrhea and/or coughing are severe, supportive veterinary care is also indicated.

Because threadworms thrive in warm, humid, unsanitary conditions, sound environmental management can help curb the spread of these parasites. This is especially important for public health reasons, since cross-infection between humans and dogs has been known to occur.

Lungworms

Lungworm infections in dogs are uncommon, yet worth mentioning. These delicate, transparent worms live within the respiratory tract of affected canines, burrowed within the wall of the trachea. Eggs are coughed up and swallowed. Hatching then takes place within the gut, and live larvae are passed out in the feces. As a result, contact with the latter is the mode of transmission from dog to dog.

Relentless coughing is the number one sign caused by this parasite. In severe infestations, actual suffocation resulting in death has been known to occur, especially in young pups. Because eggs are passed in the stool, veterinarians can use fecal examinations to diagnose an infestation. Direct endoscopic examination of the airway nodules caused by the worms also provides definitive answers.

Levamisole is one of several dewormers commonly used to tackle lungworm infestations in dogs.

Heartworms

When we hear of parasites or worms, our natural inclination is to think of those that inhabit the gastrointestinal tract. However, there is one parasite that, instead of residing within the gut, prefers the heart instead. That parasite is *Dirofilaria immitis,* the canine heartworm.

Heartworm disease is a devastating disease of dogs, responsible for tens of thousands of deaths each year. Most of these deaths occur as a result of the destruction that these worms cause not only to the heart but the lungs, liver, and kidneys as well. In some cases, the worm burden within the heart and blood vessels might become so great that circulation of blood is actually compromised, resulting in sudden death. Other infected dogs might go for years without showing any signs of heartworm disease, seemingly forming a symbiotic relationship with the parasites.

Regardless of its presentation, heartworm disease puts a tremendous burden on the body's organs and immune system. The good news is that this destructive disease is completely preventable!

Heartworm disease is transmitted through the use of a vector, the mosquito. When a mosquito feeds on a dog infected with heartworms, it picks up heartworm larvae (microfilariae) through its blood meal. Inside the insect, the microfilariae begin to undergo primary development. Now when the mosquito gets hungry again, the larvae exit the feeding mouthpart of the mosquito and are deposited on the skin of the new host canine. From here, they gain access into the dog's tissue through the feeding port created by the mosquito, and begin a 6-month migration to the heart, growing and developing along the way.

Once they reach the heart, the worms set up housekeeping and mature into adults. Some of these can reach up to 14 inches in length! Once mature, they start reproducing and the new larvae produced are deposited into the bloodstream (Fig. 7.7), just waiting to be picked up by a hungry mosquito.

Heartworm disease is found worldwide, anywhere mosquitoes are found. In North America, the southeastern and Gulf Coast regions of the United States have a greater prevalence of the disease than other areas. However, infections have been documented as far north as Canada. The incidence of this disease seems to be higher in dogs between the ages of 4 and 7 years. Males are more likely to contract the disease than are females. Larger breeds that, as a general rule, spend more time outdoors are also more susceptible to heartworms. Of

FIGURE 7.7 Larval forms of the heartworm, not adults, are found circulating in the bloodstream.

course, this does not mean that small, indoor lap dogs are safe from exposure, since they can't be totally shielded from the wayward mosquito that happens to find its way indoors. Interestingly, the length of a dog's haircoat does not figure in when determining a dog's risk of contracting heartworm disease.

Canines are the primary host of *Dirofilaria immitis*; however, other mammals can become infected, including cats and foxes. Humans have even been known to become accidental hosts for this parasite. In these instances, the larvae will migrate into the lungs, where they are sealed off by the body and subsequently cause no clinical problems. The lung lesions created, however, might be easily confused with tuberculosis or cancer, causing some consternation in physicians and in the patients so affected.

Clinical signs of heartworm disease can include exercise intolerance, coughing and breathing difficulties, or sudden death. The worms primarily reside in the right portion of the heart and in the lungs. Heartworms cause thickening of the lung's blood vessels, causing an increase in blood pressure and the workload on the heart (Fig. 7.8). Congestive heart failure is not an uncommon sequela in these individuals as the heart eventually becomes unable to compensate for such an increased workload. This in itself has a "snowball" effect, causing fluid buildup

FIGURE 7.8 As one might imagine, heartworms can drastically reduce the heart's ability to pump blood effectively.

FIGURE 7.9 Dogs with advanced heartworm disease often appear emaciated.

within the lungs and a disruption of blood circulation to the vital organs. Damage to the liver and kidneys is an ultimate consequence (Fig. 7.9).

Occasionally, the number of heartworms becomes so great that they can actually block the return flow of blood from other parts of the body to the heart. This condition and the resulting clinical signs are termed caval syndrome. Whereas the onset of clinical signs with a typical heartworm infection might be slow and gradual, the signs seen with caval syndrome occur abruptly and with fury. Dogs so affected might suddenly collapse, unable to breath, and in advanced organ failure. Actual surgical removal of the offending heartworms can be used to save the life of some of these dogs; in most, how-

ever, the disease is too far advanced to even attempt treatment.

Diagnosis of an active heartworm infestation can be made utilizing blood tests, radiographs, and/or ultrasound results. The blood tests are designed not only to detect microfilariae that may be in the blood but also to detect occult infections (infections characterized by the absence of circulating microfilariae, even though adults are present within the heart) (Fig. 7.7). These types of infections can occur in 15 to 30 percent of all heartworm-infected dogs. They can result from a number of factors, including the presence of immature adult worms in the heart that are not yet reproducing, infections involving worms of all the same sex, the destruction of those microfilariae that are produced by the dog's immune system, and/or the elimination of larvae as a result of giving heartworm preventive medication to an infected dog.

Safe and successful treatment of a heartworm infection depends on prompt diagnosis in the early stages of the disease, before secondary organ damage has occurred. A special drug can be administered to a dog to kill the adult worms within the heart and lungs.

Prior to treating a dog for heartworms, a complete laboratory workup, including radiographic X rays and/or ultrasound, should be performed to determine the status of the internal organs, especially the heart, lungs, liver, and kidneys. If potential problems do exist, a "priming" dose of medication might be administered to allow the body to adjust to the drug. Then in a month or so, if all looks well, a standard treatment is attempted.

Because of the high potency of the drug used to treat heartworm disease, complications from the drug therapy can arise, prompting immediate cessation of the treatment series. These can include loss of appetite, vomiting, and/or the development of icterus, indicating liver inflammation. As the adult worms die, pieces of their bodies might lodge within the blood vessels of the lungs, and if penetration is extensive, protracted coughing and lung hemorrhaging can result.

If all goes well with the treatment series, patients are usually discharged from the hospital 2 to 3 days after the treatments are started to begin convalescence at home for the next 4 to 6 weeks. During this time, supportive treatments consisting of antibiotics, aspirin, and/or special diets might be prescribed.

It is of the utmost importance that a strict limitation of exercise and stress be employed during this convalescent period. In addition, preventive heartworm medication is not to be administered during this time.

Depression, loss of appetite, bleeding, and/or protracted coughing during this time should alert dog owners to potential posttreatment complications and warrant prompt veterinary attention.

Four to six weeks after treating the adult heartworms, special medication is administered to eliminate any circulating microfilariae that are present in nonoccult cases. Once this is performed, preventive medication can then be given on a routine basis. At 12 weeks post-treatment, another heartworm test should be done to be certain that the infection was completely eliminated by the treatment. If not, the treatment series might need to be repeated, generally 6 to 8 months after the first.

For information on preventing heartworm disease, see Chapter 3.

Flukes

Flukes are small, flat, tongue- or leaf-shaped parasites that inhabit the liver and/or lungs of parasitized dogs. Snails and fish can act as intermediate hosts for flukes, and dogs often become exposed by eating raw fish that is infected with the parasite. One such fluke, *Nanophyetus salmincola,* is also responsible for transmitting the organism that causes "salmon poisoning" in dogs. Seen primarily in canines living in or visiting California and other portions of the Pacific Northwest, the disease is contracted when these dogs consume raw or cold-smoked salmon or trout containing flukes. The disease syndrome seen somewhat resembles distemper and can cause a profuse, bloody diarrhea in affected individuals. Most dogs so affected will die unless treated promptly by a veterinarian.

Kidney Worms

As with flukes, dogs can become infected with the canine kidney worm, *Dioctophyma renale,* by eating raw fish. These worms are exceptionally large (some can grow up to 3 feet in length!) and cause damage to the tissues of the kidneys simply by their size. Bloody urine is a common clinical sign seen, and eggs from the kidney worms can be visualized in the urine under a microscope. If parasites are found, surgical removal is warranted. Untreated dogs will eventually succumb to kidney failure.

Coccidia

Coccidia belong to a group of microscopic parasites called *proto-zoans.* These organisms primarily inhabit the small intestine of affected dogs. The disease caused by coccidia (coccidiosis) is rarely severe, yet the resulting diarrhea it causes can rapidly dehydrate a young puppy. Overcrowding and poor sanitation greatly contribute to the spread of these organisms within a group of canines. Eggs passed in fecal material can be directly ingested by another dog, leading to the development and maturation of the organisms within the gut of their new hosts.

If coccidia are ingested by animals other than their normal host (e.g., if the feline *Toxoplasma* coccidia is ingested by a dog), tissue migration might occur, similar to that seen with roundworms. In most cases, this migration causes no problems, and the infection is quickly eliminated by the animal's immune system. However, if a young puppy is involved, or an animal with a compromised immune system, severe disease might result.

In younger dogs, diarrhea, abdominal pain, and weight loss are the most consistent clinical signs seen in an overwhelming case of coccidiosis. Older dogs might not show any signs at all. If tissue migration has occurred (toxoplasmosis), other signs might be seen, including fever, muscle soreness, and convulsions.

A microscopic examination of a stool specimen will detect coccidia eggs if present. Treatment consists of administering an anticoccidia drug in proper dosages. If dehydration is present, intravenous fluids are indicated to correct the disorder.

Good sanitation practices are the best ways to prevent exposure to coccidiosis. Routine stool checks performed by a veterinarian should also be utilized to ensure dogs remain parasite-free.

Ehrlichiosis

Ehrlichiosis, also known as canine typhus, is caused by the bacterial organism *Ehrlichia canis.* One of many tickborne diseases, Ehrlichia is spread from dog to dog by the bite of the brown dog tick, *Rhipicephalus sanguineus.* First reported in the United States in 1963, this disease is most prevalent in the midwestern and southern states. Left undetected, ehrlichiosis can be quite devastating and ultimately fatal to its host.

Once they gain entrance into the body, these parasitic bacteria set up housekeeping in various organ systems throughout the body within a week or two. As a result, clinical signs can be quite variable once they start to appear.

Acute signs of infection include general depression, weakness, fever, weight loss, eye and nose discharges, and swollen lymph nodes. As the disease progresses over time and the organisms colonize the bone marrow, dogs will often become anemic and immunosuppressed. As a result, secondary pneumonia is a frequent finding in infected canines. Nosebleeds and bruising of the skin might also become apparent as the body's blood clotting mechanisms are interfered with. Finally, in severe instances, the kidneys and brain might become affected, leading to kidney failure and nervous system disorders.

A noticeable drop in the total number of white blood cells, red blood cells, and platelets (structures that play a vital role in the body's blood clotting mechanism) within an obtained blood sample are usually the first parameters that alert veterinarians to a possible infection with *Ehrlichia*. In fact, in many cases, the *Ehrlichia* organisms can be seen microscopically within the actual white blood cells themselves. Clinical signs related to a bleeding disorder or involving a high fever also provide clues leading to such a diagnosis. Specific *Ehrlichia* antibody detection tests are also available through veterinarians, and can help confirm what is already suspected.

Current treatment of ehrlichiosis in dogs employs high doses of special antibiotics until clinical signs go into remission. Owing to the organism's ability to hide within blood cells and bone marrow, ehrlichiosis is difficult to treat. The sooner treatment is instituted after the appearance of clinical signs, the better the chances are for a complete recovery.

Chronic long-term infections, however, might never clear up totally with antibiotic therapy. Experimental drugs such as imidocarb diproprionate have shown some promise in many of these cases. Continuous low-dose administration of antibiotics, combined with supportive therapy, including occasional blood transfusions, might be needed to keep these long-term infections under control.

To date, there is no vaccine available to protect against ehrlichiosis. As a result, a good tick-control program is still the best way to prevent this disease.

Rocky Mountain Spotted Fever

Rocky Mountain Spotted Fever is another tickborne illness that can be transmitted to dogs. Many different tick species, including the brown dog tick, can be carriers of the bacteria that can cause this illness. The incidence of this disease in the United States peaks during the late summer, and then drops off as fall and winter arrive. As far as breed susceptibility to this disease is concerned, it is seen mostly in sporting breeds of dogs, simply because of their increased risk of tick exposure.

The clinical signs seen with Rocky Mountain Spotted Fever are very similar to those seen with ehrlichiosis. Bleeding, high fever, swollen lymph nodes, pneumonia, and seizures can all be seen with this disease. Yet unlike with ehrlichiosis, these clinical signs relate to an intense inflammation involving the blood vessels throughout the body. This can also result in marked abdominal pain, complete with vomiting and diarrhea.

Rocky Mountain Spotted Fever should be suspected whenever there is high fever, swollen lymph nodes, abdominal pain, and bruising of the skin and mucous membranes together with a history of tick infestation. Unlike ehrlichiosis, this disease is characterized in its later stages by an increase in the number of circulating white blood cells in the body, a clue that can help a veterinarian differentiate between the two diseases. Specific antibody tests can also be employed to obtain a definitive diagnosis.

Treatment of this disease involves the use of high levels of special antibiotics for a minimum of 14 days. In many instances, response to treatment is slow, and favorable results might not be seen for some time. As with ehrlichiosis, there is no vaccine available for this disease. As a result, tick control is essential.

Lyme Disease

In recent years, Lyme disease has come to the forefront in public awareness because of its ability to cause human illness. The disease, caused by the bacteria *Borrelia burgdorferi,* is spread to dogs and humans primarily through the bite of an infected tick. Many different species of ticks can be involved, including the deer tick, the black-legged tick, and the Western black-legged tick.

Ticks, however, are not the only way the disease can be spread; fleas and other biting insects are capable of its spread as well. In addition, Lyme disease has also occasionally been transmitted via direct contact with infected body fluids. Because of this ease of transmission, Lyme disease is one of the most commonly reported tickborne diseases, and it has been diagnosed in many states across the country.

Clinical signs of Lyme disease in dogs include loss of appetite, lethargy, high fever, swollen lymph nodes and joints, and/or a sudden onset of lameness. This lameness often resolves on its own accord, only to recur weeks to months later. In untreated dogs, kidney disease and heart disease can be unfortunate sequela.

Diagnosis of Lyme disease is based on a history of exposure to ticks and of recurring lameness. Veterinarians now have the ability to test for this disease in house.

Rapid treatment of a diagnosed case of Lyme disease is essential to prevent permanent damage to the joints or internal organs from resulting. Many different types of antibiotics can be used to treat this disease, and acute signs will usually disappear within 36 hours of instituting such therapy. Long-standing infections might not respond as well and require a more vigorous treatment approach.

A vaccine against Lyme disease is available for use in dogs living in endemic areas. Tick control is another important control measure to prevent Lyme disease. Since a tick must feed for about 24 hours before spread of the disease will take place, prompt removal of ticks will help break the transmission cycle.

The signs of this disease in humans are similar to those found in dogs. Vaccination of the family dog should help prevent it from becoming a source of human infection. In addition, prompt removal of ticks from the skin will help ensure the same protection in people as it does in dogs.

CHAPTER 8

The Immune System

Without a functioning immune system, our pets would easily fall prey to every hostile organism that came around. Immunity is designed to protect against such infectious invaders and eliminate any foreign matter or cells that somehow gain entrance into the body. Preventing the growth of cancer cells and tumors is also in the immune system's job description.

Although the immune system serves a rough and rugged function, a delicate balance does exist as far as its activity is concerned. Stress, poor nutrition, and hormone fluctuations are only some of the many factors which can deleteriously alter this activity, leading to a weakened defense system. As if this weren't enough, certain viruses, such as the canine parvovirus, have the ability to suppress the immune system. Such an overwhelming impact on the body's natural defense mechanisms can only lead to one outcome, and it isn't good.

This balance can be thrown the other way as well. Certain disease conditions can be caused by an overactive, overworking immune system. Allergies are a good example of this. Allergic reactions can even turn deadly if the response is exaggerated enough.

At other times, the immune system, in carrying out its duties, will destroy or damage normal healthy tissue in the process. These autoimmune diseases usually result from the body's inability to turn off the immune response, with disastrous consequences.

Anatomy and Physiology

The immune system itself is a complex network of cells, organs, and special chemicals. No one division overshadows another; each team member relies on the others for support. In this way, they all work in unison toward a common goal.

Cells of the Immune System

Special cells, called *stem cells,* located within the bone marrow give rise to all the cells of the immune system. The cells that are produced by these stem cells are referred to as *white blood cells.* Within this general category there are numerous types, each serving distinct functions.

The neutrophil functions to gobble up bacteria that gain entrance into the body. Also assisting in this function are white blood cells called *macrophages.* These cells usually come after the neutrophils are already engaged. In addition to bacteria, macrophages also have the capability to eat viruses, fungal organisms, and foreign matter.

When a dog is vaccinated, special immune cells called *lymphocytes* are stimulated. B lymphocytes are responsible for producing actual antibodies in response to the vaccine or foreign organism; T lymphocytes don't produce antibodies per se, yet they assist the B lymphocytes in doing so, and help modulate the immune response. They also have the ability to attack and kill cells within the body that are cancerous or infected with viruses.

Both B and T lymphocytes are said to possess "memory"—that is, they remember the various organisms and invaders that they're fighting against. That way, if they reappear again at a later date, they will be attacked without hesitation. Yet even with memory, this response can become slower and weaker over time if the immune system remains idle. This is why certain vaccination boosters are needed periodically.

Another important lymphocyte of the immune system is called the *natural-killer cell.* These cells search out and destroy tumor cells and cells infected with viruses. Unlike their T-cell counterparts, natural-killer cells do not possess memory, yet at the same time, most do not require a previous exposure to a foreign agent to respond effectively.

Organs of the Immune System

The organs of the immune system include the bone marrow, the thymus, the spleen, and the various lymph nodes and aggregates of lymph tissue spread throughout the body.

BONE MARROW

As mentioned before, all cells of the immune system originate within the bone marrow. Many stay put and undergo maturity right where they are; other cells are shuttled off to the thymus.

THYMUS

The thymus is an organ located in the neck region of young animals. As that individual grows older and the immune system undergoes a mature development, the thymus gland gradually disappears. It is in this organ that most of the T cells undergo their maturation.

LYMPH NODES AND TISSUE

From the thymus and the bone marrow, the cells of the immune system are then shipped to the front-line defenses, including the lymph nodes, tonsils, and other lymph tissue lining the gastrointestinal and respiratory tracts. This latter tissue, owing to its strategic location, comprises a first line of defense against organisms that try to gain entrance into the body. B lymphocytes in this tissue produce special antibodies that coat the surface of the tract, and block such access.

Lymph nodes and tissue are responsible for filtering the body's blood and lymph for foreign agents and cells. Lymph is a special type of fluid that circulates throughout the body within its own separate channels or vessels, called *lymphatic vessels.* Fats that are absorbed via the intestinal tract enter into this lymphatic system, as do lymphocytes on their way to and from the front-line defenses.

THE SPLEEN

The spleen is an organ most have heard about; its various functions include filtering blood and providing a storehouse for blood cells.

Chemicals of the Immune System

Special chemicals produced by the cells of the immune system serve to assist them in their protective function. Among those chemicals generated are interferon, interleukins, and complement.

Interferon is a protein that is produced and released by cells that have been invaded by or come in contact with a virus. Released within 2 hours after the cell is invaded, it acts as a messenger to surrounding healthy cells and stimulates the immune system to respond. It even has antitumor effects, preventing tumor cell replication in some instances.

Interleukins are chemicals produced by macrophages that help control and modulate the activity of the T cells during an immune response. Interference with the release of interleukins, which can occur with many viral diseases, can lead to immunosuppression.

Complement is a special protein produced by the body that attaches itself to the surface of antibodies. When these antibodies bind to a bacterium or infected cell, the complement serves to "burn" a hole in the cell membrane, leading to the cell's destruction. In some instances, complement doesn't need the help of antibodies to fulfill this function.

Antigens

An *antigen* is defined as any substance capable of eliciting an immune response. Infectious organisms—such as bacteria, foreign matter, and even tumor cells—have antigens within their makeup and lining their outer surfaces. Since the body does not recognize such an antigen as one of its own, it mounts an immune response against it to try to eliminate it.

On initial exposure to an antigen, B lymphocytes start to divide and differentiate into their antibody-producing form. It might take up to 7 days before antibody production can be achieved. Even then, production is only moderate, and adequate levels generally last only about 3 weeks. In the meantime, however, other immune components, such as neutrophils, macrophages, and killer cells, are called in to fight off the invader.

If the invader is a tumor cell, foreign body, or an organism that lives and multiplies within body cells (such as viruses do), then the T lymphocytes start to multiply and prepare themselves for battle as well. As with the B lymphocytes, they are specific for each antigen; that is, such a lymphocyte that responds to one type of antigen will not respond to any others. As a result, each different antigen that enters the body will stimulate its own group of antagonistic B and T lymphocytes.

Following this first exposure, the lymphocytes that have been primed to the antigen retain "memory" of the experience. Sent to the front-line defenses, they simply wait for the antigen to show up again. Now if it ever does, the lymphocytes are ready for it, without the 7-day lag time. Antibodies are produced in high levels almost immediately, and the T cells are primed and sent into action with minimal delay.

Immunosuppression

As pointed out previously, the immune system is a complicated and delicately balanced system that performs a vital function within the body. If this balance is disrupted, serious trouble can develop.

A suppressed immune system leaves the body wide open to invasion by foreign organisms and cancer cells. This immunosuppression can occur secondarily to viral infections (such as parvovirus or canine distemper), drug therapy (including steroid treatments), severe stress, and disorders of the bone marrow. In addition, dogs can actually inherit poorly functioning immune systems. For instance, the incidence of an underactive immune system seems to be higher in Doberman pinschers and rottweilers than in other breeds.

Allergies and Autoimmune Disease

Both allergies and autoimmune diseases are characterized by an overactive immune system that can irritate or damage its host's own tissues in response to an antigen invasion within the body. For example, atopic (allergic) dermatitis in dogs results from an overactive immune response to inhaled pollens. Lupus erythmatosis and pemphigus are two autoimmune disorders in dogs that, aside from causing significant skin lesions, can damage other organs of the body as well.

In autoimmune hemolytic anemia, the immune system actually destroys the body's own red blood cells, leading to anemia. Myasthenia gravis, a disease characterized by profound muscle weakness after only minimal exertion, is also classified as an autoimmune disease. Immune mediated kidney disease and arthritis can also afflict dogs stricken with a genetic predisposition for these disorders. Finally, many cases of hypothyroidism are caused by an overactive immune system attacking and inactivating the thyroid hormone produced within the body.

Allergies and autoimmune reactions can be controlled with corticosteroid medication, which, at sufficiently high dosages, has a suppressive effect on the immune system. However, because these steroids can have significant side effects, such treatments should be performed only under the close, continual supervision of a veterinarian.

The Cardiovascular and Hemolymphatic Systems

The systems responsible for the effective transmission of oxygen and/or nutrition to all organs and tissues of the body are the cardiovascular and hemolymphatic systems. These systems comprise the heart and vessels, located within the chest or thoracic cavity, and the vessels that carry blood and lymph throughout the body.

Anatomy and Physiology

The *heart* is a hollow organ that serves as a double pump and is located approximately in the center of the thoracic cavity. Its walls consist of muscular tissue called myocardium. The pumping action of the heart causes blood to flow through the circulatory system, supplying oxygen and nutrients to the body tissue. Inside the heart a wall of tissue separates the heart into two sections of pumps: the "right heart" and the "left heart."

Each side of the heart is made up of two hollow chambers. The upper chamber is the *atrium*, which receives blood; the lower chamber is the *ventricle*, which pumps blood from the heart. The cavities of the atrium and ventricle on each side of the heart communicate with each other, but the right chambers do not communicate directly with those on the left. Thus, right and left atria and right and left ventricles are distinct.

Blood flow is directed by a series of valves that have nothing to do with the initiation of flow. The driving force for blood comes from the active contraction of cardiac muscles. The valves only prevent the blood from flowing in the opposite direction. Heart murmurs are caused by the backflow of blood through defective or diseased heart valves.

A drop of blood that is in the right atrium is first pumped through a valve into the right ventricle. The ventricle then pumps the droplet to the pulmonary arteries and lungs. In the lungs, the blood takes on oxygen and releases the waste product carbon dioxide. The oxygen-rich droplet is now ready to nourish cells of the body, but first it must return to the heart. This time the droplet enters the pulmonary veins and goes into the left atrium. The atrium pumps it through a valve into the left ventricle. The left ventricle then pumps it out to the cells, tissue, and organs of the body.

Arteries are blood vessels that carry oxygen-rich blood from the heart to the tissues. As these vessels approach their targets, they progressively branch out, creating smaller arterioles. Actual exchange of oxygen, nutrients, and waste products between the blood and the tissues occurs through microscopic, thin-walled vessels that originate from the arterioles called *capillaries.* Once this exchange has taken place, the capillary beds coalesce to form venules, which eventually empty into even larger veins. Blood is carried back to the heart via these veins.

The walls of arteries are much thicker and elastic than those of veins primarily to accommodate for the increased blood pressure within the arterial system caused by the pumping heart. Pets can suffer the same ill effects from high blood pressure as do humans. Although stress can cause the blood pressure to rise, some type of impedance to normal blood flow—such as heart failure, liver disease, and/or kidney disease—is the most common cause of its occurrence in animals.

Blood consists of a variety of cellular elements, including *erythrocytes* (red blood cells), which transport oxygen with the help of hemoglobin molecules contained within; *leukocytes* (white blood cells), which fight infections and foreign invaders; and tiny cell fragments called *platelets,* which initiate the blood clotting cascade.

Plasma is the noncellular portion of the blood. It consists of water, nutrients, waste products, and a wide variety of hormones, enzymes, and electrolytes. Plasma also contains three special plasma proteins: albumin, globulin, and fibrinogen.

Albumin is a transport protein that escorts large molecules, including some hormones, through the bloodstream. *Globulins* include antibodies formed by the immune system and certain proteins needed for normal blood clotting. *Fibrinogen* is a plasma protein also involved in the body's blood clotting scheme. Serum is the term given to plasma that has had this clotting component removed.

The lymphatic system is an entirely different type of circulatory system found within the body. Lymphatic vessels that course throughout the body carry not blood, but a special substance called *lymph,* a plasmalike substance derived from fluid and protein that normally leaves the bloodstream at the capillary level to enter into tissues. Lymph components that are not used by the tissues enter into special lymphatic vessels, which carry them back into circulation. Lymph also contains fats absorbed from the small intestine.

Lymph nodes are special structures found all along the lymphatic chain that serve to filter bacteria and contaminants out of the lymph, while at the same time adding special immune cells called *lymphocytes* to the fluid for transport to the blood circulatory system. In dogs, edema—fluid retention within the tissues—can be caused by parasites or tumors obstructing normal lymph flow through the lymphatic vessels.

Heart Disease and Heart Failure

Heart disease, with subsequent heart failure, is one of the most frequent problems in small-animal medicine. Because the heart functions to supply oxygen and nutrients to the rest of the body via the blood, serious ramifications result if this function is interfered with by disease. In addition, the decreased movement of blood through the circulatory system caused by a faulty heart leads to high blood pressure, and fluid buildup within the abdomen and/or the lungs (congestive heart failure), depending on which side of the heart is involved. If the latter structures do become waterlogged, oxygen exchange is reduced even further.

Mitral Insufficiency

Different diseases involving the heart valves or heart muscle can lead to heart failure. By far the most common type of heart disease seen in dogs, aside from that caused by heartworms, is called *mitral insufficiency,* which involves the heart valve separating the left atrium from the left ventricle. If this valve becomes diseased and fails to close properly when it is supposed to, blood is allowed to flow back into the left atrium when the left ventricle contracts.

This has two effects: (1) the amount of blood pushed forward into circulation by each heart contraction is greatly reduced, which means that the heart (which, remember, is diseased) must work harder than it did when it was healthy to keep up with the body's demand for blood; and (2) the backup of blood that occurs as a result of the inefficient heart contraction leads to fluid buildup within the lungs, interfering with oxygen exchange between the blood and the lungs. As a result, a vicious cycle develops.

Mitral insufficiency can result from normal wear and tear associated with age, or—more importantly—it can appear secondary to other diseases, including periodontal disease. Bacteria from the diseased teeth and gums can enter the bloodstream and attach to the heart valve, setting up infection and inflammation. Over time, the heart valve becomes damaged and scarred, making it unable to function properly. The end result is often heart failure.

Other Valve-Related Diseases

Although their frequency is much less, diseases involving the other valves in the heart can nevertheless occur. Disease of the tricuspid valve, which separates the right chambers of the heart, can occur secondary to age or infection and can interfere with the normal return of blood to the heart from the body. Defects in the pulmonic or aortic valves, which separate the ventricles from the pulmonary vessels and aorta, respectively, are usually congenital (present at birth) and might not be detectable when the dog is young. However, as the dog matures and the requirements placed on the heart increase, signs of heart disease or failure could become apparent.

Cardiomyopathies

Diseases involving the actual heart muscle itself can also lead to heart failure. First, cardiomyopathies are diseases of the heart muscle that lead to enlargement of the heart. *Dilatative cardiomyopathy* is characterized by a thinning of the wall of the heart; *hypertrophic cardiomyopathy* refers to an abnormal enlargement and thickening of the heart muscle.

In either case, normal contractility of the heart is disrupted, with end results similar to those caused by valvular diseases. Next, although dogs rarely suffer from overt heart attacks, microinfarctions (tiny regions of injury to heart muscle) resulting from diminished blood and oxygen flow to the heart muscle can be featured in any of the various forms of heart disease and can further interfere with heart's ability to contract. Infectious diseases such as parvovirus and Lyme disease can also have a predilection for heart muscle and seriously damage cardiac function.

Birth Defects

Birth defects involving the heart wall (septal defects), the heart valves (valvular stenosis), or the vessels leaving the heart (patent ductus arteriosus) can increase the workload placed on the heart and can lead to heart failure as the affected animal gets older. If detected early enough, many of these defects can be surgically corrected at a young age, before associated signs become severe. In those that cannot be repaired, treatment is similar to that of other forms of heart disease.

Symptoms of a Failing Heart

Regardless of the inciting cause, the clinical signs associated with a failing heart include coughing, especially at night and after exercise; breathing difficulties, distended abdomen; weight loss; and exercise intolerance. Suffering dogs might stand with their front legs spread wide apart and necks lowered and extended to afford the passage of more air into the lungs. Affected dogs might collapse even after the slightest exertion or excitement.

If the right side of the heart is involved, owners might notice a bulging abdomen. This occurs secondarily to a backup of blood within the abdominal vessels, leading to a fluid buildup within the abdominal cavity.

All of these signs might start off subtly, yet they usually become increasingly severe as the disease progresses and failure begins.

Detection of Heart Disease

Diagnosis of heart disease or heart failure is made using clinical signs, radiographs, ultrasound, and/or electrocardiogram findings. In addition

FIGURE 9.1 Heart murmurs can be detected by your veterinarian using a stethoscope.

to the classic clinical signs listed above, many forms of heart disease are accompanied by heart murmurs, which can be detected by a veterinarian on listening to the chest using a stethoscope (Fig. 9.1)

A *heart murmur* is simply an irregular sound caused by the disruption of normal blood flow within the heart. By far the majority of heart murmurs heard are caused by diseases of the heart valves and the abnormal blood flow through these valves that results. Still other murmurs can originate from the defects in the heart muscle or vessels that alter normal blood flow. Unusually forceful and rapid heart contractions, such as those seen within overly excited animals or in dogs suffering from anemia, can even lead to an irregular heart sound. Interestingly, murmurs are not commonly detected in dogs suffering from heartworm disease, even when their hearts are full of the parasites.

Heart murmurs are usually classified according to their intensity as heard through a stethoscope. A trained veterinarian can identify which portion of the heart is affected and arrive at a diagnosis just by pinpointing the area on the chest where the murmur is the loudest, and by determining when the murmur occurs, whether it is during the heart's contraction phase, relaxation phase, or both.

Other Diagnostic Tests

One parameter that cannot be determined from the intensity of a heart murmur is the stage of heart disease or failure the animal is in. For instance, severe mitral insufficiency might not be associated with any murmur whatsoever, whereas a loud one might accompany an early case. This is because in the later stages, the valve might become so

DID YOU KNOW?

Atherosclerosis, characterized by a buildup of fat, calcium, and cellular debris within the vessels, is not a significant problem in pets as it is in people.

diseased and worn that it could offer such little resistance to blood flow back through it that a murmur-causing disruption of blood flow might not arise.

Radiographs and/or ultrasonography of the chest are essential for establishing a diagnosis of heart disease. Animals with primary lung disease, including pneumonia, can exhibit clinical signs very similar to those seen in patients with heart failure, and these tests are needed to differentiate the two. Diseased hearts will appear abnormally enlarged on both tests. This enlargement can occur in response to the increased workload on the heart to pump blood, or it could be due to a thinning and bulging of the heart wall resulting from constant bombardment with high-pressure streams of blood escaping through faulty heart valves. Regardless of the cause, an enlarged heart, combined with clinical signs or murmurs, signifies heart disease. If such a combination exists, the next test most practitioners will perform is an electrocardiogram.

The *electrocardiogram* (ECG) is a test used widely to assess the condition of the heart (Fig. 9.2). Remember that a heartbeat is produced when a wave of electrical energy moves through the tissues of the chambers, starting in the atria and moving down to the ventricles. This electrical wave then causes the muscle wall of these chambers to contract, pumping out the blood contained within. The ECG helps evaluate the status of this electrical conduction system, and at the same time, can give the veterinarian useful information regarding the size of the heart itself, and indirectly, the

FIGURE 9.2   An electrocardiogram (ECG) measures electrical conduction within the heart.

condition of the heart as a pump. In addition, with the information gained from an ECG, proper drug treatment dosages can be more easily established.

Treatment for Heart Disease

Because most cases of heart disease or failure are nonreversible, the treatment goal for any dog suffering from such is to create an environment that relieves some of the workload on the heart and slows the progression of the disease.

Canines with heart conditions need to be fed special diets that are low in sodium to help reduce blood pressure and discourage the accumulation of fluid within the lungs and/or the abdomen. Diets formulated especially for this purpose are available from veterinarians.

Diuretic drugs are also used in heart failure patients to help mobilize and get rid of excessive fluid that might be accumulating within the body. In many instances, this diuretic therapy, combined with a low-sodium diet, might be all that it takes to relieve the coughing and discomfort seen in affected dogs. Be sure to remember that a dog on diuretic medication will drink lots of water and urinate with greater frequency, so be sure to provide it with plenty of water to drink at all times, and be prepared to walk it outside more often.

Medications designed to dilate the blood vessels, making it easier for the diseased heart to pump blood through them, are usually the next in line if the special diet and diuretics don't seem to be enough to correct the problem.

If none of these treatment regimens prove effective, the final medicating step often taken to manage the heart failure is to give a drug designed to help slow and strengthen the heart's contraction. Such medications can have many undesirable and serious side effects if a veterinarian does not carefully monitor therapy but, on the average, they will prolong the life of a dog in heart failure for an average of 4 to 6 months.

Anemia

Anemia is defined as an overall reduction in the number of red blood cells within the bloodstream relative to normal levels within that pet. This reduction can occur from a number of processes, including an increased destruction or decreased production of red blood cells within the body. The overall consequence of anemia is the inability of the blood to supply desired levels of oxygen to the tissues.

Signs seen in an anemic dog include intense lethargy, weakness, increased respiratory and heart rates, and a pallor of the mucous membranes. Depending on the cause of the anemia, signs related to a blood clotting disorder might be seen as well. Finally, if red blood cells are being destroyed within the body, the skin and mucous membranes might become jaundiced.

A simple blood test performed by your veterinarian can tell you if your dog is anemic. Treatment of anemia depends on the underlying cause. In severe cases, blood transfusions and oxygen therapy might be required to save the pet's life until the cause can be identified and treated. Therapy utilizing special compounds called *colloids* and oxygen-carrying solutions can be lifesaving as well.

Bleeding Disorders

Whenever an injury or illness compromises a blood vessel and leads to bleeding from that vessel, a remarkable mechanism or chain reaction begins within the body in an effort to stop the leakage of blood from the damaged vessel and prevent the individual from bleeding to death. This mechanism is known as *hemostasis*.

When a blood vessel is compromised, the first reaction that occurs is constriction of the vessel to help slow blood loss. Following this, special blood cells called *platelets* begin to adhere to the injured vessel wall, forming a temporary plug. At the same time, a coagulation (clotting) pathway is activated within the body, involving a complex interaction of blood and tissue components, as well as calcium and vitamin K. The end result of this pathway is the formation of a more permanent clot at the site of injury.

Bleeding disorders can occur whenever any part of the clotting mechanism is interfered with. Diseases or substances such as toxins, drugs, cancers, autoimmune hemolytic anemia, and infectious agent such as *Ehrlichia canis* can interfere with platelet numbers or function. In addition, kidney disease and certain inherited defects can also lead to poor platelet function and secondary bleeding.

FIGURE 10.2 The lungs sound harsh in dogs suffering from pneumonia.

mucus within the respiratory tree might be performed as well. Blood work will usually show an elevated white blood cell count.

With infectious pneumonia, high doses of appropriate antibiotics and/or antifungal medications will be required to bring it under control. Drugs designed to expand the airways are helpful in improving airflow into and out of the lungs. Intravenous fluids are also useful to replace important body fluids lost in the increased respiratory secretions and to prevent existing secretions from becoming thickened as a result of dehydration. (*Note:* In dogs, medication designed to suppress coughing should not be used, in most cases, since this only serves to prevent the removal of mucus and other respiratory secretions from the lungs.)

Cases of aspiration or inhalation pneumonia are treated in a similar fashion, yet these carry a much poorer prognosis. Attempts can be made to suction the foreign material out of the lungs through the trachea are often unsuccessful. Dogs that survive are often afflicted with a residual cough for the rest of their lives.

Chronic Obstructive Pulmonary Disease

Chronic obstructive pulmonary disease (COPD) is a disorder of the lungs and respiratory tree often linked to aging in dogs. COPD is actually a catchall phrase for all those conditions that affect and restrict normal air movement into and within the lungs. Chronic bronchitis, as well as age-related scarring of the actual lung tissue, are the two most common causes of COPD in canines.

COPD is characterized by persistent coughing, mucus buildup within the airways, and breathing difficulties. Definitive diagnosis of chronic obstructive pulmonary disease can be made by ruling out other potential causes of the clinical signs (pneumonia, canine cough, etc.), evaluating the duration of the clinical signs, and by obtaining biopsy samples of lung tissue to determine whether scar tissue is indeed present. Unfortunately, if diagnosed, there is no treatment that can reverse the effects of COPD. However, medications designed to dilate the airway passages can provide some degree of respiratory relief to the affected pet. In addition, antiinflammatory medications can also be utilized to reduce inflammation and slow scar tissue formation that may be contributing to the COPD.

Metastatic Lung Disease

One characteristic of most highly malignant tumors, regardless of their point of origin, is that they invariably spread to and end up in the lungs if not detected and treated soon enough. Some cancers spread, or metastasize, more readily to the lungs than others. For instance, malignant melanoma of the skin might be present in the lungs even before the actual skin tumor becomes noticeable.

The clinical signs exhibited by dogs afflicted with metastatic lung disease can be similar to those seen with pneumonia. Unfortunately, the prognosis for dogs harboring such tumors in their lungs is grave, even with specific cancer treatment.

The Digestive System

The digestive system of the dog is made up of a collective network of organs designed to supply the body with the nutrition it needs for growth, maintenance, and repair. It also functions to rid the body of waste. Because of this, diseases involving the digestive system can have a profound effect not only on the region so afflicted but on the entire body as well.

Anatomy and Physiology

Those organs or regions of the body categorized under the digestive system include the oral cavity (teeth, tongue, salivary glands, etc.), esophagus, stomach, small intestine, large intestine, rectum, anus, pancreas, liver, and gall bladder. In order to understand diseases and their adverse effects, a brief overview of the digestive process is warranted. Keep in mind, however, that the following description is an oversimplification; the actual digestive process is so complex and involved that it warrants the devotion of an entire book in itself!

Once food enters the oral cavity, the process of digestion begins. The teeth mechanically rip, crush, and grind down the food, while the saliva secreted by the salivary glands into the mouth moistens and partially digests carbohydrate portions of the food before it is swallowed.

As digested nutrients are absorbed, they enter into either the circulatory system or the lymphatic system. End products of protein and carbohydrate digestion travel by way of the blood to the liver, where any toxic by-products are promptly eliminated. Other functions of the liver include the production of serum proteins, the storage of vitamins and other nutrients, the destruction and removal of old red blood cells from the bloodstream, and the secretion and excretion of bile into the small intestine to aid in the digestive process.

Fatty acids, resulting from fat digestion, travel initially via the lymphatic vessels and later enter the bloodstream, where they are broken down and absorbed into the body tissues. The lymphatic system also plays an important role in immunity.

Digesta and waste that are not absorbed from within the small intestine then pass into the large intestine, which is responsible for removing water and electrolytes from the material and lubricating it for passage out of the body through the rectum and anus.

One special portion of the canine large intestine is called the *cecum,* which corresponds to the human appendix. In dogs, whipworms inhabit this portion of the large intestine and exert their deleterious effects from within.

Gastrointestinal Response to Disease

Considering what they have to go through each day, the stomach and intestines represent a remarkable organ system. In the performance of their daily nutritional functions, they must be on constant guard to protect themselves from autodigestion by digestive acids and enzymes produced and must constantly battle foreign organisms and agents that are inadvertently taken in by mouth.

When the stomach and/or intestines become acutely diseased, three major factors come into play that can quickly turn a sometimes seemingly harmless situation into a life-threatening predicament; these include pain, secondary bacterial invasion, and dehydration (Fig. 11.2).

Pain

Any inflammation and/or excessive smooth-muscle contractions occurring within the gastrointestinal system can be quite discomforting and painful. In fact, in severe cases of viral enteritis, intestinal obstructions, and intussusceptions, this pain can be so great as to send the patient into life-threatening shock. As a result, the sooner therapeutic measures are undertaken to correct the problem and stifle the pain associated with it, the less are the chances of complications.

Secondary Bacterial Invasion

FIGURE 11.2 Dogs with gastrointestinal disturbances invariably lose their appetites.

The second factor to contend with is secondary bacterial invasion. Normally, the intestines are inhabited by billions of bacteria that peacefully reside within without causing any problems whatsoever. In fact, the very presence of these non-disease-causing bacteria actually helps prevent the growth of pathogenic, or disease-causing, bacteria within the intestinal setting. However, if disease strikes the small or large intestines, these "friendly" bacteria can be wiped out, allowing pathogenic ones to proliferate and cause disease themselves. If the inflammation persists, or if an intestinal perforation occurs, these and any other bacteria within the intestines can leak out of the gut and even gain entrance into the bloodstream, causing a life-threatening systemic infection and shock.

For these reasons, it is obvious that antibiotics become very important in the treatment of moderate to severe cases of gastroenteritis, even if the original cause is nonbacterial in origin.

Dehydration

The final threatening factor that arises when acute gastroenteritis strikes a pet is dehydration. Pets suffering from vomiting and/or diarrhea can quickly become dehydrated because of water loss through the bowels. Since inflamed bowels cannot regulate water absorption as

DID YOU KNOW?

If bright red blood appears in the stool, it has originated from somewhere along the large intestine. On the contrary, when bleeding originates within the small intestine, the blood that is passed in the stool is often partially digested, giving the latter a black, tarry appearance.

they do when they are healthy, any fluid intake that indeed occurs will usually pass out of the body via vomiting and/or diarrhea without being absorbed.

In fact, the disruption of normal motility and distension occurring within the affected bowel can actually attract and draw water out of the body and directly into the intestinal lumen. As a result, dogs that have become dehydrated or are on the verge of dehydration due to gastroenteritis require intravenous fluids to correct the dehydration occurring within their body cells, at least until the gut has healed sufficiently to resume these functions once again.

Treatment

Once the gastrointestinal system is on the mend, and all vomiting has been brought under control, a good plane of nutrition is required to counteract any malnutrition induced by the disease. Bland diets that are easily digested are prescribed until complete healing of the stomach and/or intestinal linings have taken place. Offering a convalescent dog some type of electrolyte replacement drinks during these first few days can also promote rapid recovery. Feeding plain yogurt is also helpful toward repopulating the gastrointestinal tract with nonpathogenic bacteria.

Disorders of the Teeth and Oral Cavity

Diseases and disorders affecting the teeth or oral cavity interfere with a pet's ability to prehense and process food for digestion. In addition, other general signs associated with conditions involving these areas usually include increased salivation, swallowing difficulties, bad breath, gagging, and decreased appetite.

Malocclusion

Malocclusion occurs when the teeth lining the upper jaw fail to line up and fit properly with the teeth of the lower arcade. In the normal canine bite, the upper canine teeth should rest immediately behind the lower canines. Disruption of the normal bite pattern can be caused by trauma, by improper tooth eruption, and by genetics.

> ## FACT OR FICTION
>
> **Force-feeding water can help correct dehydration in a sick pet. FICTION. Whenever a pet reaches a state of true clinical dehydration, intravenous fluids are required to correct the problem. This is especially true for dehydration caused by vomiting or diarrhea. Most fluids given orally to such animals will pass right through their diseased digestive systems without being absorbed and could actually make the dehydration worse.**

Brachygnathism refers to a condition in which an overbite, or overshot upper jaw, exists. Conversely, *prognathism* refers to a condition involving an undershot jaw (underbite). Both conditions are inheritable traits, passed from one generation to another. In fact, malocclusions are considered normal for certain breeds, such as pugs, boxers, and bulldogs. Although not life-threatening, these anatomic maladies can interfere with normal biting action and eating, and can predispose to dental and jaw problems in affected dogs. As a result, dogs suffering from distinct overbites or underbites (unless normal for the breed) should be surgically neutered to prevent the propagation of these undesirable traits.

Malocclusion can also result from improperly positioned deciduous teeth creating abnormal eruption pathways for the permanent ones. Dental examination of the deciduous teeth performed on puppies as early as 8 weeks of age can help identify potential problems. In many instances, simply removing the offending deciduous tooth clears the path for the proper eruption of its permanent successor.

Surgical repair or reconstruction of the jaw can be used to repair trauma-induced malocclusions. Orthodontic correction of brachygnathism and prognathism have been utilized in select cases, yet for ethical reasons, such procedures should be performed only for medical purposes, not for cosmetic gains.

Supernumerary Teeth

Supernumerary teeth are extra teeth within the mouth. These can be retained deciduous teeth, or can actually be permanent ones.

Retained deciduous teeth are not uncommon in smaller breeds, including miniature poodles and Yorkshire terriers. In these dogs, the deciduous canine teeth have the greatest propensity for remaining behind (Fig. 11.3). Such retained teeth can crowd the permanent ones, creating abnormal eruption pathways. In addition, because of their close proximity with their permanent counterparts, these extra teeth can serve as niduses for dental calculus buildup and infection. As long as the eruption pattern for the corresponding permanent tooth is not being interfered with, most veterinarians will postpone removal of the retained tooth (teeth) until another elective procedure, such as neutering or teeth cleaning, is performed. However, if the permanent tooth is being interfered with in any way, immediate removal is recommended.

In rare instances, duplicated permanent teeth, consisting of one or two isolated ones, or an entire arcade, can erupt. Removal of these

FIGURE 11.3   A retained deciduous upper canine tooth.

permanent supernumerary teeth is usually not necessary unless they interfere with the normal biting action of the dog. Because of the genetic predisposition of this condition, affected dogs should not be bred.

Enamel Hypoplasia

This unfortunate condition involves the incomplete development of the hard, protective layer of enamel that normally surrounds the crown of the tooth. Enamel hypoplasia results when the enamel-producing cells within the dental arcade, called *ameloblasts,* are injured or destroyed prior to eruption of either the deciduous or permanent teeth. The canine distemper virus is the most notable culprit, causing enamel hypoplasia to occur; other causes can include severe malnutrition and fluorine toxicity.

Teeth lacking in enamel have coarse textures (due to exposed dentin) and tend to stain brown. The absence of the protective enamel coating renders these teeth especially susceptible to decay and to traumatic fractures.

For puppies suffering from enamel hypoplasia on their permanent teeth, enamel restoration procedures (such as crowning) performed by a veterinary dental specialist can add a protective layer to exposed surfaces. Ask a veterinarian for more details regarding these dentistry procedures now available for dogs.

Broken Teeth

Occasionally, teeth will break or fracture as a result of trauma or disease (such as in enamel hypoplasia). If the pulp cavity of the tooth is not exposed by the break, treatment measures, aside from filing down any sharp edges, are seldom required. However, if the damage does extend down into the pulp cavity, inflammation, infection, and pain could result.

Endodontic therapy, or root canals, can be performed to salvage teeth with exposed or infected pulp cavities and dentin. The procedure involves the removal of the pulp tissue and infected dentin, thereby alleviating pain and the further progression of disease within the tooth. Cracks and fractures in the tooth can then be filled, completing the restoration procedure.

Discolored Teeth

The administration of certain antibiotics to a pregnant dog can result in yellow-stained dentin within the teeth of her offspring. The same holds true for adolescent puppies administered these drugs prior to eruption of their permanent teeth. Although this staining has no effect on the health of the teeth, it can be unsightly, and detrimental in the show ring.

Calculus buildup can certainly discolor teeth so affected. If allowed to persist on a long-term basis, the tooth surface can often take on a yellow hue, even after the calculus has been removed. In these instances, the complete removal of the calculus is far more important than any discoloration left behind.

As mentioned previously, a brownish discoloration to the teeth could be the result of enamel hypoplasia. Enamel restoration procedures can be employed to deal with this problem.

Finally, a bluish-gray discoloration to a tooth is indicative of inflammation within the pulp cavity, warranting endodontic management if the tooth is to be saved.

Dental Caries (Cavities)

Because of a uniquely high pH of the saliva, cavities rarely form in the teeth of dogs. When they do, they are often secondary to some trauma that has disrupted the continuity of the dental enamel. Cavities in dogs are managed the same way as they are in people, with dental fillings.

Periodontal Disease

Periodontal disease, or tooth and gum disease, is one of the most prevalent health disorders in dogs. Studies have shown that most canines show some signs of this disease by 3 years of age. Early signs can include tender, swollen gums, and, most commonly, bad breath. More importantly, though, left untreated, periodontal disease can lead to secondary disease conditions that can seriously threaten the health of affected pets (Fig. 11.4).

It all begins with the formation of plaque on tooth surfaces. This plaque is nothing more than a thin film of food particles and bacteria. Over time, however, plaque mineralizes and hardens to form calculus.

An owner who lifts up the dog's lip and glances at its teeth, especially near the gum line, might notice brownish to yellowish buildup of calculus on the outer surface of the teeth.

Calculus tends to accumulate worse on the outer surface of the large fourth upper premolars and on the inner surfaces of the lower incisors and premolars. This is because canine saliva is conducive to calculus formation, and the

FIGURE 11.4 Receding gums caused by periodontal disease.

ducts from the salivary glands empty into the mouth at these particular sites. Buildup of this substance tends to be worse in smaller breeds of dogs, such as miniature poodles, Yorkshire terriers, Maltese, and schnauzers. In fact, it is not at all unusual for some of these dogs to start losing teeth by 4 to 5 years of age without at-home preventive dental care!

Along with these breed predispositions, diet can play an important role in the development of periodontal disease. For instance, moist foods high in sugar content promote plaque formation much more readily than do the dry varieties. In addition, diets containing too much phosphorus (such as all-meat rations) have been linked to periodontal disease.

Certain underlying disease conditions might also promote periodontal disease as a side effect. For example, hypothyroidism can lead to gingivitis and dental complications associated with it. Periodontal disease can also occur incidentally with tumors involving the gum tissue and/or teeth.

Dogs suffering from periodontal disease can exhibit a diverse selection of clinical signs. Early periodontal disease might be marked only by a decreased appetite due to swollen, painful gums. Dog owners often complain of bad breath in their pets, and might notice signs of gagging or retching as secondary tonsillitis sets in.

As the disease progresses, these signs might worsen, and other symptoms, such as gum recession, gum bleeding, and tooth loss, might arise. Infected teeth that do not fall out can form abscesses, marked by sinus infections, nasal discharges, and/or draining tracts appearing on the face.

Unfortunately, the damage caused by periodontal disease doesn't stop there. Bacteria can gain entrance into the bloodstream by way of the teeth and gums, seeding the body with infectious organisms. In advanced cases, these bacteria can overwhelm the host's immune system and set up housekeeping on the valves of the heart. The resulting valvular endocarditis can, in turn, lead to heart murmurs and eventual heart failure.

Besides the heart, the bacteria that gain access to the body because of periodontal disease can lodge in the kidney, causing infection, inflammation, and acute damage. Over time, signs related to kidney failure might develop in affected dogs.

Early cases of periodontal disease can be treated by a thorough scaling and polishing of the teeth to remove the offending calculus. This scaling needs to be performed professionally under sedation or anesthesia to ensure complete removal of the calculus under the gumline.

Using special instruments to hand-scale a pet's teeth at home without anesthesia is not only dangerous but also highly ineffective at cleaning the teeth where it counts the most, up under the gumline. Furthermore, such scaling, if not followed by polishing, will leave etches in the enamel covering of the teeth that can serve as foci for future plaque and calculus buildup.

Antibiotics will also be prescribed for dogs suffering from moderate to advanced periodontal disease to combat the associated bacterial infection. Teeth that are excessively loose within their sockets serve only to propagate infection, and should be extracted. For infected teeth that are still deemed viable, a root canal can be performed as a salvage procedure. See Chap. 3 for prevention tips to help protect pets against the adverse effects of periodontal disease.

Tonsillitis

The tonsils are lymphoid tissues located in the back of the oral cavity near the esophagus. Since they are lymphatic tissues, tonsils have an immune function. Tonsillitis refers to the inflammation and/or swelling of these lymphoid structures in response to infections, foreign bodies, and sometimes even noninfectious diseases. For instance, long-term coughing, such as that seen in cases of canine cough, can result in a secondary tonsillar inflammation. Periodontal disease is another common cause of tonsillar swelling. Finally, certain tumors, such as lymphosarcoma and squamous cell carcinoma, can cause the tonsils to swell and should always be kept in mind anytime a dog develops tonsillitis.

Signs of tonsillitis in dogs include gagging, retching, and difficulty swallowing. Affected animals might also go off feed and have a tendency to salivate excessively. Because tonsillitis is usually secondary in nature, other signs of illness related to the primary disease might be present as well.

Diagnosis of tonsillitis is easy based on clinical signs and actually visualizing the swollen tonsils within the oral cavity. Treatment depends upon the underlying cause. For example, if the disease is infectious, appropriate antimicrobial therapy will clear up the tonsillitis. If a tumor is suspected, or if a seemingly simple case of tonsillitis is refractory to standard treatment, then the tonsils should be removed and biopsied.

Cleft Palate

The palate is a fleshy structure located at the roof of the mouth that separates the oral cavity from the nasal passages. The firm portion located forward-most in the mouth is termed the *hard palate,* whereas the softer, flexible portion towards the back of the mouth is called the soft palate. *Cleft palate* is a disease condition in which the palate fails to fully develop, leaving a communication gap between the mouth and the nasal passages. This condition is inheritable in breeds such as English bulldogs, Boston terriers, and cocker spaniels. It can also be acquired secondary to foreign bodies puncturing the palate, or by burns caused by puppies chewing on electrical cords.

Neonatal puppies born with cleft palates often die because they are unable to suckle properly. Pups that do survive initially can develop nasal infections and aspiration pneumonia if the problem is not surgically corrected in time. The recommended time of surgery for these puppies is around six weeks of age. Until then, daily feedings using a tube passed directly into the esophagus is indicated to prevent these secondary complications.

Oral Tumors and Gingival Hyperplasia

Like other regions of the body, the oral cavity is not immune to its share of tumors and growths. A wide variety of tumors, including melanomas, sarcomas, papillomas, and carcinomas, can arise within the oral cavity of dogs. In contrast, *epulis,* or gingival hyperplasia, is a type of benign proliferation of the gum tissue within the mouth.

Signs associated with oral tumors and gingival hyperplasia in dogs can include bad breath, oral bleeding, excessive salivation, and/or swallowing difficulties. In severe cases involving malignant tumors, actual facial deformities could occur secondary to the tumor growth.

Rapid recognition of the presence of an oral tumor and concurrent treatment are essential, since malignant oral tumors in dogs will spread very rapidly to other areas of the body, including the lungs.

Gingival hyperplasia, on the other hand, requires no specific treatment unless the proliferation is so great as to interfere with normal function. In these instances, surgical removal of the overgrown gum tissue is indicated.

Esophageal Disorders

Disorders involving the esophagus will manifest themselves as difficulty in swallowing. Effortless regurgitation of solid food, which must be differentiated from vomiting and its associated abdominal spasms, often alerts the pet owner and veterinary practitioner to an existing problem with the esophagus. Because they are unable to properly swallow food, dogs afflicted with esophageal disease are at high risk of accidentally aspirating food into their lungs, causing serious, life-threatening pneumonia.

Megaesophagus

In *megaesophagus* the esophagus becomes generally enlarged and distended and is unable to push food into the stomach. This condition might be inherited, or seen secondary to esophageal obstructions or neuromuscular diseases such as myasthenia gravis.

Diagnosis of megaesophagus is made by taking radiographs of the esophagus or actually visualizing the enlargement with an endoscope inserted into the esophagus through the mouth. Those dogs diagnosed with this disorder must be fed with their front ends elevated on a chair or table to encourage gravity flow of food and water into the stomach. Feeding liquid or semisolid food will also help facilitate this passage into the stomach. Depending on the cause, some individuals do improve with time. In select cases, surgery might be performed to help improve esophageal function.

Esophagitis

Inflammation occurring anywhere along the esophagus is termed *esophagitis.* Esophagitis can be instituted by foreign bodies that injure the organ's lining, ingestion of caustic substances, and reflux of stomach contents and acids up into the esophagus. In keeping with the latter cause, chronic, long-term vomiting can also lead to esophagitis.

Regurgitation, loss of appetite, and weight loss are the most frequent signs seen. If left untreated, damage to the lining of the esophagus could occur, causing strictures and secondary megaesophagus.

As with megaesophagus, diagnosis is made using clinical signs, physical exam findings, and endoscopic exam or radiographic X rays of the esophagus using a barium isotope as a contrast medium. Treatment of esophagitis consists of treating any primary problems that might be present, and, if stomach acid reflux is to blame, reducing the amount of stomach acid secretions and increasing the rate of stomach emptying.

Esophageal Obstructions

Obstructions can occur secondary to tumors, infections, strictures, and the ingestion of foreign objects (especially bones). As with megaesophagus, obstructions can be diagnosed using radiographs and/or endoscopy (Fig. 11.5). Treatment is aimed at the surgical removal of the offending agent.

Gastric Dilatation–Volvulus Complex

Gastric dilatation–volvulus complex (GDV), or "bloat," is a serious, life-threatening disorder that can strike the gastrointestinal system of dogs, particularly that of large, deep-chested breeds. Great Danes, St.

FIGURE 11.5 **An endoscope is useful for retrieving foreign objects in the upper airways, esophagus, and stomach.**

Bernards, Irish setters, standard poodles, boxers, and English sheepdogs are only a few of the many breeds that can be suddenly afflicted with GDV. Although they don't fit the anatomical mold of these other breeds, dachshunds and Pekinese also have a higher incidence of GDV than do other similar-sized breeds. Regardless of the size and age, death can quickly ensue in these dogs if the condition is not recognized and treated with speed.

Rapid ingestion of a large amount of food and water, followed by exercise, is an important predisposing cause for this disorder. As the stomach dilates to accommodate the large food and water content within, and with the gas formed within the stomach secondary to vigorous exercise, the stomach can rotate or twist in such a way as to block off its entry and exit outlets. The condition snowballs as the food, water, and gas within the stomach are not allowed to escape, and more and more gas and fluid are produced by the churning action and secretions of the distressed stomach. In addition, as the stomach dilates and/or rotates, it can effectively put pressure on the large blood vessels located within the abdomen and seriously reduce blood flow through these vessels. This in turn places almost every major organ within the abdomen in serious jeopardy.

Dogs suffering from an acute case of GDV will exhibit signs such as a distended or bloated abdomen, vomiting, excessive salivation, and rapid breathing. In the early stages, the dog will be quite restless because of the pain; as the disease progresses, weakness, recumbency, and shock set in.

A diagnosis of GDV is based on history and clinical signs seen. As mentioned before, treatment must be instituted in earnest to save the life of the pet. The attending veterinarian will try to pass a tube into the stomach to relieve the stomach distension; however, if the stomach is twisted, this passage might be impossible. In these cases, immediate surgical intervention is required. Intravenous fluids, antibiotics, and steroids to combat shock are among the medications used in these patients. The prognosis is guarded with any dog presented with GDV, and recurrence is not uncommon.

If a dog likes to gulp down its food as soon as it is set down, protect it from the dangers of GDV by feeding smaller portions at more frequent intervals throughout the day. In addition, discourage exercise for at least one hour after mealtime. For dogs that have recurring bouts with GDV, surgery can be performed as a preventive measure to "tack" the stomach down to the inner abdominal wall, thereby preventing it from twisting if bloating occurs.

Gastrointestinal Ulcers

An ulceration within the stomach or intestines occurs when the protective barrier of mucus covering the inner surfaces of the gastrointestinal tract is lost or destroyed, allowing stomach acids and bile acids to erode the gastrointestinal lining. The same type of heartburn humans can sometimes experience with this problem can affect dogs as well, leading to inappetence, vomiting, and lethargy.

Ulcers actually are indicators of disease rather than distinct disease syndromes in themselves. Sharp foreign bodies or harsh chemicals that are swallowed can scrape, injure, and—in the case of the latter—burn the gastrointestinal lining and cause a primary ulceration.

Ulcers occur secondary to stress, infectious diseases, intestinal parasites, bacteria (including *Helicobacter*), and metabolic diseases such as Cushing's disease and kidney disease. Certain drugs, such as aspirin, can also have a deleterious effect upon the stomach lining when given orally.

Diagnosis of an ulcer relies heavily on clinical signs seen and the history or evidence of an underlying disorder. Radiographs taken after the oral administration of barium can be used to pinpoint the exact location of an ulcer. In addition, direct visualization of the actual stomach or intestinal lining using an endoscope is another means of diagnosing ulcers in a pet.

Obviously, when formulating any treatment regimen for ulcers, any underlying source for the ulceration must be identified and treated. Specific ulcer treatment is aimed at reducing the amount of stomach acid secretion and providing a protective coating over the existing ulcer until it has time to heal. Medications used to treat ulcers in humans are very effective at treating the same in dogs.

Hemorrhagic Gastroenteritis

Hemorrhagic gastroenteritis is a life-threatening condition that can be rapidly fatal if not treated promptly. Characterized by an explosive onset of bloody diarrhea, hemorrhagic gastroenteritis can quickly cause dehydration, depression, shock, and toxemia in affected dogs. It is most often seen with dietary indiscretions and/or bouts of pancreatitis. Toxins produced by bacteria within an irritated gut cause such extensive inflammation that overt bleeding within the digestive system results. Toxins and bacteria may then permeate these blood vessels and gain entrance into the body, with serious consequences.

Diagnosis of hemorrhagic gastroenteritis is based on history and clinical signs observed, as well as ruling out other causes of digestive system disturbances. Treatment consists of intravenous fluids to control dehydration, high levels of antibiotics to combat infection, high dosages of steroid anti-inflammatory agents, and other medications to control shock and counteract the effects of toxemia.

Intussusception

As with GDV, intussusception is a life-threatening condition involving the gastrointestinal tract of dogs. An *intussusception* is abnormal invagination of a portion of small or large intestine into a dilated portion of bowel situated just ahead of it, causing obstruction to normal flow within the intestine (Fig. 11.6). Peristalsis involving the affected gut segments further aggravates the intussusception, causing it to worsen with time. In especially severe instances, the blood supply to the portion of the intestine involved will be cut off, resulting in the death of that tissue (necrosis) and serious health consequences. The site at which an intussusception is most likely to occur in dogs is where the small intestine links up with the large intestine.

The causes of an intussusception can include any type of inflammation within the gut, viral infections, parasites, tumors, and swallowed foreign objects. Signs seen in dogs affected include lethargy, abdominal pain, fever, and vomiting.

Radiographs are the most useful tools in the diagnosis of an intussusception, since this disorder has its own characteristic appearance on a radiograph. If intussusception is suspected or diagnosed, immediate surgery is necessary to correct the invagination and to remove any dead portions of bowel that might be present. Obviously, the underlying problem that initially caused the intussusception must be corrected as well.

FIGURE 11.6 An intussusception occurs when a portion of the bowel folds over and invaginates on itself.

FIGURE 11.7 Characteristic "hunched up" appearance of a dog with an intestinal obstruction.

Intestinal Obstructions

In addition to intussusception, other items can obstruct normal flow through the gut and result in clinical signs, such as lethargy, vomiting, and black, tarry stools (Fig. 11.7). Swallowed foreign bodies (such as bones, rubber balls, and stones), tumors, fungal infections, and herniations are all capable of causing either partial or complete obstructions if sufficiently large or extensive. Unless the obstruction is relieved in a timely fashion, usually through surgical means, loss of blood supply to the affected portion can occur, resulting in the death of that portion of bowel, systemic infection, and shock.

Inflammatory Bowel Disease

A special type of enteritis, termed *inflammatory bowel disease* (IBD), is a poorly understood disease that evokes much controversy among researchers. The hallmark characteristic of IBD is an infiltration of the gut wall with large numbers of lymphocytes, which suggests that this disease might have an immune component. An overactive immune response to certain dietary ingredients, parasites, and/or bacteria within the intestines is believed to be the underlying cause for this source of chronic diarrhea in dogs.

Clinical signs related to IBD are similar to those seen with other cases of colitis. Interestingly, IBD can strike dogs as young as 8 months of age!

A diagnosis of PLC can only be made after obtaining a biopsy of the affected portion of the gut. Before attempting this, however, other laboratory work, including stool exams and blood profiles, should be performed to rule out the other multitude of causes of bowel inflammation.

Dogs that are diagnosed with IBD should be placed on hypoallergenic diets to rule out food allergies as a potential cause. If they respond favorably, then dietary management might be all that is needed to control the disease. Fiber supplementation has also been used with some effectiveness in the management of IBD, with the added fiber helping normalize the motility within the intestines. However, if needed, drugs are available to help treat cases of IBD nonresponsive to dietary manipulation.

Unfortunately, because of the apparent immune system component to this disease, a complete cure for IBD is usually unobtainable. However, with appropriate treatment, most cases can be managed enough as to allow the affected pet to live a relatively normal life otherwise.

Colitis

Problems involving the large intestine of dogs are common in veterinary medicine. *Colitis* refers to the inflammation of the lining of the large intestine, resulting in diarrhea, with the feces often containing an abundance of red blood and mucus. *Tenesmus,* or straining to defecate, is another prevalent sign that is often mistaken for constipation.

Acute colitis refers to a sudden onset of signs that usually lasts only a short period of time with proper treatment. *Chronic colitis* is a long-term, recurring condition that might last the entire lifetime of the pet.

Parasites such as whipworms and coccidia are common causes of acute colitis in dogs. Dietary indiscretions and stress-induced situations are two other prevalent sources. Less commonly, fungal infections, foreign bodies, intussusceptions, polyps, food allergies, immune system disorders, and tumors can all result in signs related to a chronic colitis.

Because of the variety of potential causes, colitis can strike a dog of any age. As far as breed dispositions to chronic colitis are concerned, boxers seem to be highly susceptible.

Diagnosis of colitis is made from a predisposing history (such as dietary indiscretion), existing clinical signs, and physical examination. Stool examinations and other laboratory tests should be performed in an attempt to identify the underlying cause of the colitis. Radiographs, including barium contrast studies, are indicated in nonresponsive, recurring cases. Biopsies obtained using an endoscope or through exploratory surgery can also prove to be helpful for establishing a definitive diagnosis. In some cases, an exact cause of the inflammation can never be discerned, even with extensive laboratory tests.

Treatment of acute colitis is aimed at eliminating the inciting cause. Parasites should be treated using proper dewormers and antiparasitic medications. Antibiotics can be used to help remove any disease-causing bacteria within the colon, and steroid anti-inflammatory agents might prove to be helpful in diminishing clinical signs. If polyps or tumors are presented, surgical removal might be necessary to effect a cure.

However, understand that in many cases of chronic colitis, especially those caused by stress or by immune system disorders, a complete cure cannot be achieved. In these pets, treatment goals are aimed at managing flare-ups as they occur and maintaining a good quality of life for the dog. Anti-inflammatory agents, antibiotics, and local protectants such as kaolin and pectin can help provide relief from these intermittent episodes.

Dietary management is an important component of colitis treatment. Acute cases of colitis caused by dietary indiscretion or some infectious process respond well to feeding a bland, easily digestible diet available from your veterinarian.

Chronic, recurring bouts with colitis might be managed by increasing the fiber content in the diet to normalize the gut motility. Finally, for those cases in which food allergy origins are suspected, a hypoallergenic diet can help eliminate the effects of the allergy.

Anal Sac Disease

The anal sacs are special structures located at the eight and four o'clock positions below the anus. These sacs are lined with special cells that secrete an odiferous liquid into the lumen of each sac, where it is stored. As feces pass out of the anus, these sacs are emptied of their stored material via small ducts located immediately below the anal opening. Some dogs even have the skunklike ability to express these sacs on their own free will! No one knows quite for sure what the purpose of the anal sacs and their secretions are in dogs, but many suspect that they serve as a means of communication and identification between dogs.

Anal sac infections and irritation can occur if the material within the sacs isn't emptied on a regular basis. Secretions that are allowed to remain within the sacs for long periods of time often become thick and gritty, making future emptying that much harder. Any inflammation of the skin caused by allergies, fleas, and other sources can lead to this problem. Changes in frequency or consistency of bowel movements caused by diarrhea, constipation, or dietary changes, can also result in improper emptying of the sacs and secondary anal sac disease. Tapeworm segments are notorious for finding their way into the sacs and causing marked irritation. Small breeds of dogs under 15 pounds seem to have more problems with their anal sacs than do larger breeds because the sacs' emptying ducts are also smaller.

Dogs suffering from anal sac irritation often show obvious signs of discomfort, including constant licking in that region, and "scooting" their hind end along the floor in an attempt to empty the sacs (Fig. 11.8). In these instances, manual emptying of the sacs often leads to dramatic improvement in the pet's overall disposition.

FIGURE 11.8   A dog with impacted anal sacs will "scoot" along the ground in an attempt to empty them.

If one or more anal sacs become infected, actual pus or draining tracts might be observed around the affected region. These dogs are in a great deal of pain and will resist attempts at inspection. The amount of licking activity will also increase.

Infected anal sacs need to be treated with topical antibiotics instilled directly into the affected sac(s) on a daily basis. In extensive cases, oral antibiotics might also be used to hasten the cure.

Anal sac problems can be prevented in a number of ways. Increasing the fiber and bulk content in the diet, and hence in the fecal material, will promote a thorough emptying of the sacs with each bowel movement. If a dog is showing early signs of anal sac problems, such as scooting, prompt evacuation of the sacs by a veterinarian can help prevent further progression of the disorder.

Routine expression of healthy anal sacs is not advised, since, if done improperly, it could actually inflame these sacs and lead to impaction. Surgical removal of the anal sacs is certainly an option for those dogs that suffer miserably from this affliction. If infection is present, it must be cleared up before this type of surgery is performed.

Pancreatitis

Inflammation of the pancreas, or *pancreatitis,* is a painful condition characterized by an overproduction of digestive enzymes by the pancreas, which actually begin to damage the pancreatic tissue itself. This disorder tends to strike middle-aged, overweight dogs. In addition, female dogs seem to have a greater propensity for pancreatitis than do males. Dogs that are fed poor quality, high-calorie diets with or without table scraps are also at high risk of developing pancreatitis. Finally, heredity can come into play with certain breeds, such as schnauzers, which are at greater risk than are some of their counterparts.

Signs of a pancreatitis attack include loss of appetite, excessive salivation, vomiting, diarrhea, depression, and marked pain in the abdominal region on the right side immediately behind the rib cage (Fig. 11.9). Animals so afflicted will sometimes assume a "praying" posture, with the front legs bent and the hind end stuck up in the air, in an attempt to alleviate some of the pain.

With severe involvement, shock and death can result if the pain and inflammation are not relieved promptly. Diabetes mellitus can also be an unfortunate consequence with repeated bouts of pancreatitis as digestive enzymes destroy the insulin-producing cells within the pancreas. Because of the similarity of the clinical signs, acute bouts of

FIGURE 11.9   Pancreatitis causes severe vomiting in dogs so affected.

pancreatitis must be differentiated from GDV, intestinal obstructions, and intussusceptions.

Dogs suffering from mild flare-ups of pancreatitis will often recover spontaneously when food and water is withheld. In fact, this is one method of diagnosing this condition. Measuring the blood levels of the pancreatic enzymes amylase and lipase can also be a helpful diagnostic tool, since both tend to be elevated during an acute attack. Radiographs are useful for ruling out other potential causes of the clinical signs, such as intestinal obstructions.

When treating pancreatitis, it is imperative that all food, water, and even oral medication be discontinued for a period of 48 to 72 hours. This will help lower the amounts of digestive enzymes being produced by the pancreas. Intravenous fluids are required to prevent dehydration during this time of fasting.

Pain relievers and medications designed to reduce pancreatic secretions are very important to prevent secondary complications from arising. Since the gastrointestinal tract is involved, antibiotics are indicated as well to prevent secondary bacterial infections.

Pancreatitis is usually a recurring problem that can never be eliminated completely. However, owners can institute certain measures at home to protect pets from acute flare-ups and the health problems associated with them.

Canines with a history of this disorder should be fed low-calorie, easily digestible diets that don't require much pancreatic effort for their breakdown within the intestines. Such a diet, or a recipe for its formulation, is available from veterinarians. All table scraps should cease; even sneaking a small treat from the table could result in a life-threatening pancreatitis attack.

Increasing exercise levels and promoting weight loss will also serve protective functions against recurrence of this disorder.

Hepatitis and Liver Disease

While *pancreatitis* means inflammation involving the pancreas, *hepatitis* involves inflammation of the liver. Contrary to popular belief, not all cases of hepatitis are infectious and contagious in nature (e.g., infectious canine hepatitis, roundworms). There can be numerous noninfectious causes of liver inflammation as well. Some of these include diabetes mellitus, heart disease, accidental poisonings, starvation, and cancer.

As an organ responsible for metabolism of the multitude of nutrients absorbed from the intestines, and detoxification of poisons and drugs circulating in the blood, it is remarkable that the liver is normally very resistant to injury or breakdown resulting from its normal day-to-day functions. Unfortunately, because of this heartiness, clinical signs of liver inflammation usually won't appear until serious damage to liver function has already taken place.

Like so many other diseases affecting the gastrointestinal tract, acute flare-ups of hepatitis can cause loss of appetite, vomiting, diarrhea, and fever in affected dogs. One unique sign often seen with hepatitis, both acute and chronic, is jaundice, or *icterus. Jaundice,* caused by elevated levels of bile pigments in the bloodstream, is characterized by a yellow discoloration of the skin, mucous membranes, and the liquid portion of the blood.

Other clinical signs that can result from chronic, long-term hepatitis and liver disease include a fluid buildup within the abdominal cavity (ascites) due to increased resistance to blood flow through the liver, bleeding tendencies, and anemia. Seizures and other neurologic disorders can also appear with advanced cases as blood levels of ammonia are allowed to build up.

Diagnosis of hepatitis is made on the basis of clinical signs, elevated serum levels of liver enzymes, and/or the demonstration of an enlarged liver on radiographs. For those more subtle cases, special liver function tests and even biopsies might be required to confirm a diagnosis of hepatitis or discover its cause.

Treatment objectives for hepatitis and liver disease are aimed at eliminating the injurious agent and its harmful effect on the liver tissue and at promoting the healing of the affected tissue. The liver is one of the few organs within the body that can actually regenerate itself after injury, provided, of course, that the source of the injury is dealt with properly (Fig. 11.10).

If vomiting is a problem, intravenous fluids might be needed until the stomach settles down enough for oral food and water. An easily digestible diet with high biological value (available through veterinar-

FIGURE 11.10   Acute liver disease requires intense veterinary support.

ians) is ideal for patients suffering from a liver disorder. Oral antibiotics designed to eliminate ammonia-forming organisms are useful for those cases exhibiting neurological signs. Ascites can be treated with diuretic drugs and by reducing the amount of sodium in the dog's diet.

Finally, in chronic cases of hepatitis, steroids might be warranted to increase appetite and counteract the loss of protein that can occur with liver disease. In addition, certain drugs for liver disease designed for use in humans are being used in dogs with variable success.

The Urinary System

In the normal, day-to-day functioning of the body, lots of waste material is formed as a result of metabolic activity. It is the function of the urinary system to handle and to rid the body of these waste products. In addition, through its ability to dilute or concentrate the urine, it serves to regulate fluid levels within the body.

Anatomy and Physiology

The urinary system of dogs is composed of two kidneys, the ureters, a bladder, and a urethra. The kidneys are composed of cells called *nephrons,* which are responsible for filtering the waste material out of the blood and returning vital fluids and nutrients back into the bloodstream that would otherwise be lost in the urine (Fig. 12.1). Those solids and fluids not put back into the blood by the nephrons will eventually make up the urine. All the nephrons empty urine into a specific portion of the kidney, which then empties into the ureter for transport to and storage in the bladder.

The bladder wall is composed of smooth muscle and is capable of expanding to enormous sizes. Special muscular sphincters prevent the urine from passing out of the bladder prematurely. Urinary incontinence, characterized by an inability to voluntarily hold urine within

FIGURE 12.1 **The kidneys function to filter waste material out of the bloodstream.**

the bladder, can result from malfunction of these sphincters. Once the bladder is ready to release its contents, the urine passes out of the body by way of the urethra.

Because of its vital function, any interference or alteration of urinary system function can quickly lead to serious health consequences. For this reason, prompt and proper diagnosis of urinary tract disorders in dogs is essential. Periodic checkups by a veterinarian can help detect potential problems before they reach such a magnitude as to threaten the health of the pet.

Kidney Disease

The kidneys are responsible for eliminating waste products produced by the body's normal metabolism. If they fail to perform this function adequately, the body will literally poison itself. For this reason, special attention must be directed at keeping these organs healthy, or—if a disease state already exists—at treating to prevent further functional deterioration.

In dogs, kidney (renal) disease is the most common disorder associated with old age. In essence, through normal wear and tear, the kidneys become unable to perform their functions in the same way that they did when they were young. Worn-out kidney cells die and are replaced by scar tissue, which can't filter out toxins from the blood. When enough of these nephrons die and the buildup of toxins in the blood increases to a certain degree, the pet begins to exhibit signs of kidney failure.

But don't get the idea that older dogs are the only ones that can suffer from kidney impairment. Young dogs might be born with inadequate kidney function, or they might suffer from other diseases or toxic agents that kill nephrons and impair renal performance.

For example, systemic infections, heat stroke, heart disease, and autoimmune diseases are only some of the acquired conditions that can lead to kidney disease and kidney failure. Many therapeutic drugs, such as aspirin and certain antibiotics, can be damaging to the kidneys if used indiscriminately. Antifreeze, or ethylene glycol, is deadly to dogs when ingested because of the profound damage it causes to the kidneys. Finally, periodontal disease, with its associated complications, can predispose dogs, both young and old, to kidney problems in the future.

The clinical signs associated with kidney disease can be quite variable depending on the extent of damage to the kidneys. Interestingly, dogs rarely show outward signs of kidney disease until at least 75 percent of the function in both kidneys is lost! As a result, when signs do finally become apparent, it is vital that therapeutic measures be taken quickly to prevent the loss of the remaining 25 percent.

Sudden, acute kidney failure—the type that can result from the ingestion of a poison such as antifreeze—can lead directly into intense dehydration, shock, unconsciousness, and death without manifestation of any other signs.

Chronic, longer-term kidney disease and kidney failure rarely have such a dramatic presentation, yet such conditions can eventually turn into acute kidney failure if measures aren't instituted to prevent this progression. Dogs with chronic renal failure will exhibit an increased thirst and an increased desire to urinate. Depression and loss of appetite might also set in. In addition, since renal disease can cause stomach ulcers, vomiting might occur.

Veterinarians can diagnose kidney disease through a series of laboratory tests performed on the blood and the urine. Two blood parameters, blood urea nitrogen (BUN) and serum creatinine, will be elevated if the kidneys are failing.

The urine specific gravity is also an important parameter that helps the veterinary practitioner determine the extent of damage to the kidneys. Under normal circumstances, the specific gravity of the urine, which measures how concentrated the urine is, should fluctuate depending on the body's own needs for water. Diseased kidneys, however, are unable to conserve water for the body; hence, the specific gravity of the urine in a dog with advanced kidney disease will be diluted, even if the pet is clinically dehydrated.

Dogs suffering from acute renal failure must be hospitalized and placed on intravenous fluids to correct dehydration. Other medications designed to stimulate kidney function will be given as well. If the dog survives this acute attack, support measures for chronic kidney failure must then be implemented.

Stress reduction is vital in dogs with chronic renal disease and/or failure. Unlimited access to clean, fresh water should be provided at all times, since water deprivation could lead into an acute kidney failure crisis. Special diets that are low in phosphorus and protein should be fed to help reduce toxin buildup within the bloodstream. These are available from veterinarians. Vitamin supplementation should also be considered to replace those lost in the increased urine flow.

Since renal disease can alter, among other things, the blood levels of calcium and phosphorus, medications designed to keep levels of these electrolytes constant are used as well. If a pet is having trouble with vomiting, human antiulcer medications can be employed to help settle the stomach.

Finally, since kidney disease places an incredible burden on the affected pet's immune system, all underlying disease processes and disorders (such as periodontal disease) need to be addressed.

Urinary Incontinence

Dogs that are unable to willfully control their urination habits are said to be suffering from incontinence. Pets with urinary incontinence might simply urinate spontaneously without warning, or might drip urine continuously throughout the day. Inappropriate urination while sleeping is another common complaint. Dermatitis in the genital and hind leg regions can also be seen as a result of incontinence and urine scalding in these areas.

The potential causes of urinary incontinence are numerous; as a result, a proper veterinary workup is essential to obtain a correct diagnosis. Spinal trauma; anatomical changes or irritation caused by inherited defects, infections, tumors, or urinary calculi; and metabolic diseases such as diabetes mellitus or diabetes insipidus can all be underlying causes of incontinence. In these instances, treatment is geared toward correcting the underlying cause if possible.

It has been noted that a small number of female dogs that are spayed at an early age can suffer from incontinence when they enter their geriatric years. Although the exact cause of this incontinence is unknown, it can usually be controlled with medications designed to increase sphincter tone within the lower urinary tract.

Puppies and even some adult dogs might urinate spontaneously when they become excited or frightened. Most puppies will "grow out" of this problem as they mature. For these and others, treatment for behavioral incontinence is directed toward minimizing the stimuli that cause the incontinence in the first place. For instance, when dealing with dogs that urinate when excited, avoiding eye contact or exaggerated greetings when approaching the pet often help to curb excitement and prevent urination. For those dogs that urinate when frightened, easing their fear through behavioral modification is the key to a cure.

Urolithiasis (Urinary Stones)

Urinary tract infections that go unnoticed for a period of time can predispose a dog to urolithiasis. A *urolith* or "stone" results from the coalescing of crystals that form within the bladder environment. In dogs, these stones form more readily within the bladder than they do in other portions of the urinary system. Urolithiasis presents itself in dogs in two forms: cystic (bladder) calculi and urethral calculi.

The first of these, *cystic calculi,* are found mainly in females and appear when infectious bacteria within the bladder cause an increase in the urine pH, which in turn causes the crystals to form. The most common types of crystals generated are termed struvite crystals. Stones formed by these crystals are often discoid in shape.

Urethral calculi occur in male dogs and are typically composed of cystine or urate crystals instead of struvite. This type of urolithiasis is seldom caused by infections; rather, an inherent metabolic disorder is responsible for their formation. If these stones lodge in the male urethra, they can prevent normal urination, and can seriously threaten the life of the pet.

Straining to urinate, bloody urine, constant licking at the urethral opening, and/or frequent unsuccessful attempts to urinate are all signs of a urinary problem. Stones might or might not be present in a dog first line of defense. Sphincter systems, controlled by contracting smooth muscle, help seal off the different portions of the tract from one another. An acidic pH to the urine is another safeguard against the multiplication of undesirable organisms. Finally, normal, frequent urination is also very effective at eliminating undesirable bacteria from the bladder and other parts of the system. For this reason, any disruption in the normal urination routine (not taking a dog outside enough, dehydration, etc.) can predispose an individual to a bacterial infection.

Clinical signs of urinary tract infection will vary, depending on the region(s) involved. Signs associated with infections of the bladder and urethra include straining when trying to urinate (often mistaken for constipation), passage of only small amounts of urine at a time, and/or bloody urine. In the latter case, blood noted at the beginning of urination often signifies a urethral infection, whereas blood noticed near the end of elimination might mean that the bladder is involved. In many cases, dogs won't show any other signs of illness or fever.

If the kidneys or ureters are involved, similar clinical signs might be noticed, along with other obvious signs of illness, such as fever, depression, vomiting, abdominal pain, and/or back pain. In cases of upper urinary tract infections, it is vital that treatment be instituted at once to prevent permanent damage to the kidneys.

A urinary tract infection can be associated with other disease processes as well, so its presence can sometimes be overshadowed by clinical signs associated with another primary disease. For instance, diabetes mellitus can predispose to urinary tract infections because of the high sugar content in the urine caused by the disease (sugar can provide an ideal growth medium for bacteria). Disorders of the nervous system can even lead to urinary infections if the nerve supply to the muscles and sphincters of the tract are disrupted, thereby eliminating some of the body's natural means of defense.

One unfortunate sequela that can result from any type of urinary tract infection that is not treated promptly is *urolithiasis,* or urinary stones. Stones have a propensity to form when an increase in urine pH occurs, often as a result of bacteria acting within the urinary tract to break down urine. When this breakdown occurs, ammonia is released, increasing the pH of the bladder environment.

Diagnosis of a urinary tract infection is based on clinical signs, urinalysis, and urine cultures designed to identify the actual bacteria involved. In addition, a veterinarian might choose to order a blood workup done on a pet to rule out any disorders, such as diabetes mellitus, that might be underlying the infection. Furthermore, if crystals are noted on microscopic examination of the urine, radiographs will be needed to rule out the presence of any bladder or kidney stones.

Treatment for a urinary tract infection involves the use of an appropriate antibiotic for a minimum of 10 days. Since bacteria can become resistant to certain antibiotics over time, urine cultures to determine antibiotic sensitivity should be performed if a response to treatment with a particular antibiotic is poor.

Large urinary stones might need to be removed surgically. Smaller stones and crystals can often be dissolved by providing a special type of diet designed to accomplish this task.

For those dogs that suffer from chronic, recurring flare-ups of urinary tract infections, long-term, low-dose antibiotic therapy might be prescribed by a veterinarian. This involves the administration of a single dosage of antibiotic just before the pet's bedtime. Because of the overnight buildup of urine within the bladder, the antibiotic is allowed to reach high concentrations within the urine, effectively combating any bacteria that might be present. It is important to take a dog outside to eliminate just before bedtime, to assure that the new urine that is formed will contain high levels of the medication.

Owners can help prevent the occurrence of a urinary tract infection in their dogs by providing plenty of fresh water to drink at all times, and by encouraging frequent urination. Special diets that promote a healthy environment within the urinary tract and help discourage infections are available from veterinarians.

For dogs with long hair, especially females, keep the hair trimmed up around the external urinary structures to reduce the chances of bacteria gaining entrance to the urinary system via contamination by this hair.

Finally, because uncomplicated urinary tract infections might not show any outward signs, a routine urinalysis on a pet is encouraged on an annual basis along with its regular checkup.

The Reproductive System

Diseases and conditions involving the reproductive tract are not uncommon in dogs that have not been neutered. Most of the problems that arise tend to be either infectious or anatomical in nature. Prompt medical attention is warranted in any disorder involving the reproductive tract.

Anatomy and Physiology

The Male Reproductive System

Starting with the male, or sire, the major parts of the reproductive system include the testicles (with associated epididymis and ductus deferens), the scrotum (containing the testicles), the penis (containing the urethra), and the prostate gland.

The testes are the organs responsible for the production of spermatozoa. This production is directly influenced by the hormone testosterone, also produced by the testicles. Aside from regulating sperm production, testosterone is also responsible for normal male sexual behavior, as well as the aggressive, territorial behavior exhibited by some male dogs.

Normally, the testicles should descend into the scrotum shortly after birth, usually no later than 8 weeks of age. If this event fails to occur, the dog is said to be *cryptorchid,* and surgical removal of the testicles is required to prevent medical problems in the future and the passage of that undesirable trait to offspring.

From the testicle, sperm is shunted into the *epididymis,* a structure closely attached to each testicle, where it finishes its maturation process. On copulation, the mature sperm is transported from the epididymis through the ductus deferens and to the tubelike urethra coursing within the penis.

The canine penis, contained within a sheath of skin known as the *prepuce,* has the uncommon ability to swell near its origin during erection, effecting the unique interlocking "tie" with the female during reproduction. In addition, the dog's penis contains a bony structure called the *os penis,* which is grooved underneath to allow for the passage of the urethra. If its support function seems somewhat sedentary, its medical significance is not. Because the penis and urethra are parts of both the urinary and the reproductive systems, this os penis can exacerbate complications associated with certain urinary disorders, including urethral calculi.

The prostate gland, considered an accessory sex gland, is located surrounding the urethra near the neck of the bladder. It functions to produce prostatic fluid, which mixes with sperm to form semen, and helps increase the survivability of the sperm within the female reproductive tract. Enlargement or inflammation of this gland can occur as intact male dogs mature. Constipation, discharges from the penis, and painful urinations can be clinical signs of a prostatic disorder.

The Female Reproductive System

The major reproductive organs of the female dog, or bitch, include the ovaries, the oviducts, the uterus, the vagina, the vulva and the mammary glands. The ovaries are responsible for the production and release of eggs destined to be fertilized by the male sperm. In addition, several important reproductive hormones are produced by these structures.

Unfertilized eggs are released, or *ovulated,* by the ovaries, and pass into the small oviducts. It is within these oviducts that fertilization takes place. The fertilized egg, or *embryo,* continues its passage down the oviducts on its way to the uterus.

When an embryo reaches the uterus, it attaches itself to the uterine wall and begins to develop. If fertilization has not taken place, this attachment won't occur and the body will eventually resorb the egg.

The uterus is separated from the vagina by a ring of muscle known as the *cervix.* Most of the time, this cervix remains open. During pregnancy, however, the cervix will close, preventing outside access to the uterine environment. At time of parturition, the cervix relaxes, allowing the birth to take place.

The external opening of the vagina is termed the *vulva.* As a female dog enters into her heat cycle, the vulva will begin to swell, tipping off owners to the impending heat.

Dogs typically have a total of 8 to 10 mammary glands (4 to 5 on each side), designed to supply newborn offspring with life-sustaining milk. The size of these glands will fluctuate, depending on the stage of the estrous cycle and the pregnancy status of the bitch.

Accidental Mating (Mismating)

The issue regarding what to do with the female dog that is accidentally bred is not an easy one to resolve (Fig. 13.1). Many years ago, dog owners needed only to take her in to the veterinarian for a "mismating" shot or pill. These treatments consisted simply of formulations of the female hormone estrogen, which, if given within the first 36 hours after mating occurred, would effectively terminate a pregnancy.

However, it is now known that significant side effects can occur if such drugs are used. For starters, external sources of estro-

FIGURE 13.1   Be on guard: Male dogs will go to great lengths to be with a female in heat.

gens have been demonstrated to actually cause infertility in some female dogs, rendering them unable to conceive at later dates. On a more serious note, estrogens can also cause a life-threatening anemia in sensitive cases. And if that weren't enough, they can also predispose a dog to pyometra after administration.

To be safe, use of such estrogen-containing drugs is not an acceptable method for dealing with mismatings in dogs. So what are the options open to pet owners? To begin, valuable breeding females should be allowed to just go ahead and have the litter of puppies instead of chancing it with mismating medications. If this is not acceptable, then either surgical removal of the puppies from the uterus at a later stage of development or an actual ovariohysterectomy is warranted.

Remember: All of this is assuming, of course, that a viable mating did indeed take place and that a pregnancy resulted from it! Many mismatings do not result in pregnancy, and cause needless grief among their owners.

False Pregnancy (Pseudopregnancy)

When the ovaries of a female dog release eggs to be fertilized, they then start to produce a hormone called *progesterone.* The function of this progesterone is to maintain pregnancy if egg fertilization occurs. However, a unique feature about dogs is that even if fertilization does not occur, progesterone levels will remain high for up to 10 weeks after heat is over. It is precisely this behavior that is responsible for the condition dog owners know as *pseudopregnancy,* or "false" pregnancy.

All female dogs exhibit some form of pseudopregnancy after they come out of heat. In most, signs associated with it go unnoticed by the owner. However, some dogs do exhibit marked changes as a result of these high progesterone levels, including mammary gland enlargement with or without the production of milk, and behavioral changes that include restlessness, nesting, mothering of inanimate objects, and loss of appetite. In short, they might actually appear to be expectant mothers! Often, there is no way to be sure that they are not, without the use of ultrasound or radiographic X rays. Dogs that undergo marked false pregnancies are also prime candidates for mastitis, a common sequela.

Therapy to control signs associated with pseudopregnancy is rarely needed, unless mastitis becomes a recurring problem, or if marked behavioral changes occur. Hormones prescribed by your veterinarian can provide relief in many cases, yet prolonged use of these can have undesirable side effects, especially in females used for breeding. Because of this, unless you have a valuable breeder on your hands, ovariohysterectomy is the safest and most effective way to deal with pseudopregnancy.

Eclampsia

Eclampsia is a serious, sometimes life-threatening disease that can occur in the bitch either just prior to giving birth or within 3 weeks after parturition has taken place. More common in the smaller, toy breeds, it is characterized by abnormally low levels of blood calcium in their systems.

Early signs seen with eclampsia include nervousness, whining, pacing, and trembling. This might progress into incoordination, muscle spasms, and seizurelike activity. Left untreated, death can result from respiratory difficulties and high fevers (Fig. 13.2).

FIGURE 13.2   Eclampsia causes rigid (spastic) convulsions in affected female dogs.

Diagnosis of eclampsia is based on history, clinical signs, and blood calcium levels. Luckily, treatment consisting of intravenous injections of calcium is highly effective and provides instant relief from the life-threatening signs seen.

After treatment is performed, and clinical signs have abated, owners need to take special precautions to ensure that a relapse does not occur, For starters, puppies should not be allowed to nurse for 24 hours after such an episode. Instead, a commercial milk replacement formula should be fed to them. In fact, periodic supplementation should continue even after the puppies are placed back on their mother's milk to reduce the load on her. In some cases, putting the puppies back on their mother's milk will cause another episode of eclampsia, in which case they should be permanently placed on supplements.

Bitches that are prone to eclampsia should be placed on oral calcium supplements throughout the nursing period. In fact, if there is a past history of such a problem, calcium supplementation started during the last 2 weeks of pregnancy and continued throughout lactation can be quite helpful in preventing a recurrence.

Placental Subinvolution

Normally, after a bitch gives birth to a litter of pups, she might experience a thin blood-tinged discharge from the vulva for up to 6 weeks after whelping. If the discharge persists for longer than this, however, your dog could be suffering from a condition called *subinvolution of placental sites.* In lay terms, this means that the uterus fails to repair itself properly after the birthing process, resulting in a low-grade blood loss. Over time, this blood loss could conceivably cause anemia if left unchecked. In addition, such a condition predisposes the female to uterine infections.

Most cases of placental subinvolution will resolve automatically within a few months, yet oral iron supplements should be given to the bitch to help prevent anemia. Antibiotics are required as well if infection is present. Finally, in recurring cases, or situations where the bleeding is severe, an ovariohysterectomy is recommended.

Vaginitis and Metritis

Inflammation involving the uterus is termed *metritis*; those involving the vagina are properly termed *vaginitis.* Both vaginitis and metritis can occur either independently of each other or together. Causes of vaginitis and metritis can include venereally transmitted organisms, metabolic diseases such as diabetes mellitus, retained fetuses or placentas, and, as mentioned earlier, treatment with estrogen-type drugs.

Female puppies under one year of age can suffer from a condition termed *juvenile vaginitis,* characterized by a thick, greenish vaginal discharge. Aside from the discharge, affected puppies generally show no other ill effects, and the condition will, in most instances, spontaneously resolve on its own when the puppy enters into her first heat cycle.

Classic signs of vaginitis and metritis include a thick, yellow-to-green discharge from the vagina. Owners might notice their pets licking excessively around this area. In especially dour metritis cases, loss of appetite with an increased water intake, fever, and abdominal pain might become apparent. The discharge might also become discernibly blood-tinged. Because of the intimacy of the urinary tract with the reproductive tract in females, bladder infections that occur secondary to vaginitis and metritis are also common.

The type of treatment used for reproductive tract infections depends on which portions are involved. For instance, in mild cases of vaginitis, including juvenile vaginitis, direct infusion of the vagina with antibiotics or povidone-iodine douches provides effective results. If the vaginitis is severe or if the uterus is involved, high doses of antibiotics given orally or by injection are required. To determine which antibiotics will work best, a bacterial culture is indicated. Certainly, if there are any puppies nursing on the affected bitch, they should be removed and placed on formula.

In critical metritis cases, intravenous fluids might even be required for support. Unless the bitch is a valuable breeding animal, an ovariohysterectomy should be performed on these dogs to directly eliminate the source of the problem, and to prevent metritis from recurring at a later date. For those dogs that are considered too valuable to be spayed, special medications called *prostaglandins* can be utilized to help the uterus contract and empty. These, however, must be used with extreme care under the direct supervision of a veterinarian, and even then, only as a last resort.

Cystic Endometrial Hyperplasia (Pyometra)

In older dogs that have experienced numerous heat cycles, *cystic endometrial hyperplasia complex* (CEHC), or pyometra, can develop.

Because of repeated hormonal stimulation of the uterus year after year, glands lining the inside wall of the uterus become larger and more active with each heat cycle. Large amounts of fluid are secreted into the uterus by these glands, which can then accumulate, causing uterine swelling. Obvious problems can arise if this fluid is not allowed to drain out of the uterus. Unfortunately, this is precisely what happens in many instances. Because of high progesterone levels associated with metestrus, the cervix remains closed, prohibiting drainage from the uterus. At the same time, the trapped fluid provides an ideal medium for bacteria to grow in, leading to bacterial infections and pus formation. As a result, the uterus literally becomes a bag full of pus. And because of the continued buildup of fluid and pus, an infected uterus can reach an enormous size within the dog's abdomen. In advanced cases, actual rupture of the uterine wall might result, often with fatal consequences for the unfortunate dog.

Bitches afflicted with pyometra usually exhibit the classic signs of metritis, including depression, loss of appetite with a markedly increased thirst, and abdominal pain. As mentioned earlier, a discharge might or might not be associated with pyometra, and the lack thereof might be associated with the more serious form of the disease.

Abdominal enlargement due to uterine filling might also become apparent, with radiographs revealing a huge uterine outline. Blood work performed on these patients will reveal an enormously elevated white blood cell count and mild anemia (due to the long-term nature of the disease). Pyometra has also been shown to induce kidney disease in affected dogs; as a result, increased urinations, vomiting, and dehydration might also be present.

Complete ovariohysterectomy is the treatment of choice for pyometra. Those cases involving a grossly enlarged uterus filled with pus and fluid should be regarded as emergencies, and the surgery should be performed as soon as possible.

Spaying nonbreeding females at an early age can prevent pyometra and its associated complications. For those bitches used for breeding purposes, spaying is recommended after their useful breeding life is finished (usually around 8 years of age).

Phimosis and Paraphimosis

Phimosis and paraphimosis are two conditions that occur in male dogs resulting from a preputial opening that is too small.

The first, *phimosis,* refers to the inability to extrude the penis through the opening, effectively interfering with reproductive activity. The second, *paraphimosis,* is exactly the opposite: The inability to retract the penis back into the prepuce once extruded. The exposed organ is very susceptible to trauma and lacerations, which can exacerbate the problem even more.

Phimosis can be treated by having the prepucial opening surgically enlarged. In cases of paraphimosis, reducing the penile swelling by soaking it in Epsom salts will usually allow the replacement of the penis back into the prepuce. Antibiotic ointment can then be instilled into the prepuce to speed healing.

Prostate Disorders

The prostate gland in male dogs lies at the base of the bladder at the origin of the urethra. Its normal function is to produce secretions that make up a portion of the semen. Disorders that can affect the prostate include bacterial infections, benign prostatic enlargement, cysts, and tumors. Signs of prostate disease include straining to urinate, painful urinations, blood in the urine, abdominal pain, and/or hind-limb lameness.

Prostate pain or enlargement can be detected on a physical exam using rectal palpation and/or radiographs. If an infection is present, treatment consists of antibiotic therapy. If a tumor or cyst is suspected, surgical treatment is necessary. Neutering should be performed on all dogs that suffer from prostate problems to help prevent recurrences in the future.

The Skin and Haircoat

The skin, or *integument,* functions to protect the body from outside foreign invaders and from water loss. It provides a focus for the sense of touch and assists in the regulation of the temperature within the body. In addition, special modifications of the skin, such as claws and pads, provide a means of traction and defense, as well as shock absorbency.

Anatomy and Physiology

The skin of the dog is composed of three layers: the epidermis, the dermis, and the hypodermis. The epidermis is the outermost layer of the skin. Beneath the epidermis lies the dermis and hypodermis, which are composed of, among other things, an array of connective and fatty tissue. Sebaceous glands, embedded within these layers, secrete natural oils out onto the skin surface that lubricate and moisturize the skin.

The hair of canines consists of guard hairs, which make up the rougher outer coat, and the wool hairs, which constitute the fine dense undercoat of most breeds. In addition, special hairs called *tactile hairs* (more commonly known as "whiskers") can be found on the head region. These fulfill a sensory function.

A hair cycle exists in dogs that is responsible for the seasonal shedding of old hair and replacement by new hair. This cycle is dependent on light, not on temperature, and increasing or decreasing amounts of daylight trigger it. As a result, peak shedding periods for the dog occur in the springtime, when the days begin to lengthen, and in the fall when the days shorten. Of course, as more dogs spend more time indoors with artificial lighting, the hair cycle can be altered, with shedding occurring year-round.

Hair color is dependent on the amount of pigment present within the hair shaft. Large amounts of pigment result in black hair; hairs that lack pigment are white. Different levels of pigmentation that fall between these two result in all other coat colors. Changes in the natural color of the hair can occur with inflammation, trauma, or constant licking of a particular region or regions of the coat. Of course, as a dog enters its senior years, the appearance of gray hairs is not an uncommon sight as well.

The Itchy Dog

Many disease conditions can produce itching in the dog. However, only a few disorders result in severe and/or prolonged itching. The primary symptoms of the "itchy dog" are scratching and biting of the skin. Early signs that might be noticed include wet hairs, reddened skin, and hair loss in the areas of biting and scratching. Prolonged itching results in further hair loss, excessive scaling and thickening, and discoloration of the involved skin. Secondary skin infections are common.

Severe and/or prolonged itching is almost always a symptom of an underlying skin disorder. As a result, correction of the underlying problem is imperative if the symptom of itching is to be successfully controlled.

External Parasites

Refer to specific discussions of external parasites found in this book (Chap. 10).

Inhalant Allergic Dermatitis (Canine Atopic Dermatitis; Atopy)

Inhalant allergic dermatitis represents one of the most common causes of itching in dogs across the United States. Atopy often produces severe itching and is frequently accompanied by skin infection (folliculitis), scaling, hair loss, and discoloration. Atopy parallels human hay fever with the exception of itching being the primary symptom in the dog rather than the respiratory symptoms exhibited by people. Licking and chewing of the feet and legs are common symptoms reported by owners, along with generalized scratching.

Atopy is inherited and usually develops between the ages of 6 months to 4 years, following exposure to immune-system-stimulating substances called *allergens.* Because it is seasonal, sporadic, and relatively mild in its early stages, atopy often becomes perennial, and worsens in severity with time. Unfortunately, dogs do not outgrow these allergies. Dust (and dust mites), fungal spores, and pollens from trees, shrubs, and grasses can all initiate an allergy in dogs (Table 14.1). Since these substances are present in the air and can be carried hundreds of miles by wind, trying to avoid them by restricting a dog's environment is not possible.

Diagnosis of atopy in dogs is based on clinical signs seen, seasonality of such signs, and allergy testing. There are currently two methods of allergy testing available: intradermal skin testing and serum testing.

Intradermal skin testing involves injecting a number of different allergens into the skin of the patient and observing the injection sites for a corresponding allergic reaction. This type of testing has been used effectively for allergy diagnosis for years and provides the most definitive way to find out what a pet is actually allergic to.

Serum testing is also used to diagnose allergies. These tests involve the evaluation of a serum sample from the allergic dog for antibodies to substances to which it might be allergic. The advantage such testing affords over skin testing is that it is much easier to perform and causes little discomfort to the patient. However, since the accuracy of such tests is still being debated within the veterinary community, intradermal skin testing is still considered by some experts to be the most definitive way to diagnose atopy in dogs.

There are four ways to approach treatment for atopy in dogs, described in the following paragraphs.

STEROID ANTI-INFLAMMATORY AGENTS

These cortisone-type drugs temporarily suppress the itching sensations produced by the allergy. Steroid anti-inflammatory drugs are never curative, yet they can offer effective relief from itching for days

Table 14.1 Wind-Pollinated Plants and Trees that Can Lead to Atopy in Dogs

Red-root pigweed	Common sagebrush
Meadow fescue	Wild oat
Bermuda grass	Short ragweed
Johnson grass	Kentucky bluegrass
Sweet vernal grass	Redtop
Quackgrass	Smooth brome
Velvetgrass	Broncho grass
Ryegrass	Prairie ragweed
Russian thistle	Cocklebur
Lamb's quarter	Sheep sorrel
Western waterhemp	Annual June grass
Box elder	Oak
Silver maple	White elm

to weeks. Increases in water consumption, urination frequency, and appetite are sometimes seen in dogs placed on steroid therapy. Unfortunately, prolonged steroid usage over months might produce side effects much more unpleasant than these, including bloating (water retention), muscle atrophy, skin thinning, hair loss, and decreased resistance to infection. In addition, while these steroids are being administered to a dog, its body's ability to produce its own cortisone is suppressed, and might not return even when the steroid therapy is discontinued. If this happens, the dog could go into shock and die. As a result, long-term usage of these drugs for allergic dermatitis should be done only under the close scrutiny of a veterinarian.

ANTIHISTAMINE AND FATTY ACID THERAPY

Scientific studies have shown that antihistamine medications alone do little to suppress itching caused by atopic dermatitis. Because antihistamine drugs can cause drowsiness, they can be useful for helping calm down a frustrated dog that can't stop itching and chewing on itself.

Omega-3 fatty acids can be quite beneficial to atopic dogs. It seems that these fatty acids, which are derived from cold-water fish such as salmon, do have the ability in some cases to reduce inflammatory responses and stop itching. Some allergic dogs do fantastically well on these agents alone. Others require additional medications, such as antihistamines, in order to achieve an acceptable comfort level for the pet. Although the effectiveness of this therapy can vary between cases, it does provide a unique alternative to steroid therapy.

FACT OR **FICTION**

The type of steroid used to treat allergies in dogs is different from those commonly used by people to build muscle and strength. **FACT**. The steroids used to treat allergies in dogs (glucocorticosteroids) are actually *catabolic* in nature, meaning that they tend to diminish muscle size and strength with prolonged use. Steroids used to increase muscle size and strength are called *anabolic steroids*, which, by the way, are sometimes used in veterinary medicine to counteract the effects of aging in older pets.

TOPICAL THERAPY

Topical treatments by themselves do little to provide lasting relief to the atopic dog. However, when used in combination with other forms of therapy, they can potentiate the effects of these other treatments. One such topical product, a colloidal oatmeal conditioner, can provide effective topical relief for atopic dogs. Along with applying it after bathing, it can also be used as a daily spray (mixed 50:50 with filtered water and placed in a spray bottle) as well. The advantage of using oatmeal conditioners versus shampooing is twofold: (1) a conditioner will help moisturize and soothe the skin with repeated use, whereas shampoos can dry out the skin; and (2) colloidal oatmeal is known to be an effective anti-itch agent and can be applied as many times during the day as necessary to provide relief. Just be sure to brush your pet thoroughly after each application to work the conditioner down to the skin.

ALLERGY SHOTS AND HYPOSENSITIZATION

An alternative approach to treating allergies aside from the ones just mentioned is to hyposensitize the pet using allergen injections. This approach requires allergy testing to be performed, followed by a series of injections of the exact allergens or agents causing the reaction. Although not effective in all instances, some veterinary dermatology specialists do report at least an 85 to 90 percent success rate—this rate is based on greater than 50 percent overall improvement in the allergic pet's condition. However, since inhalant allergens are poor stimulators of immunity, this improvement takes some time. Owners should allow anywhere from 1 to 6 months before making a final judgment as to the effectiveness of the treatment. In most cases, maintenance injections given monthly will be required for the lifetime of the pet.

Fleabite Hypersensitivity

Aside from the discomfort caused by the actual bite of a flea, dogs might develop an allergic response to the flea's saliva deposited in the skin during feeding. Moderate to severe itching and hair loss can result, especially along the back near the tail, hips, and rear leg areas (Fig. 14.1).

Some allergic dogs can harbor staphylococcal bacteria not found on the skin of nonallergic dogs. Irritation resulting from fleabites can produce a skin infection (folliculitis) on the damaged skin surface and the hair follicles. Toxins released from these bacteria might further intensify the itch-scratch cycle. As one might

FIGURE 14.1 A flea allergy causes characteristic hair loss from the hips, tail base, and lower portion of the back.

guess, successful treatment of a flea allergy is heavily dependent on the ability to control fleas on the pet and in the environment.

DID YOU KNOW?

Of all the different types of allergies that can affect pets, food allergies are among the rarest!

Food Hypersensitivity (Food Allergies)

Food allergies are a potential cause of nonseasonal itching in dogs. Other dermatological symptoms might include hives, facial swelling, and chronic ear infections as well. And besides these skin-related problems, food-related allergies have also been implicated in gastrointestinal disorders, such as diarrhea, vomiting, and/or excess gas.

Diagnosis of food hypersensitivity requires an 8-week regimen of an exclusively hypoallergenic diet containing a protein source that is not commonly used in commercial pet foods. Such diets are available through veterinarians.

If a positive diagnosis is made, the dog will need to remain on the hypoallergenic diet indefinitely. Simply changing food brands or types seldom benefits food allergy cases since most commercial foods contain similar ingredients. Food items such as milk, animal proteins, and vegetable proteins are the most common culprits, causing food-induced allergies in dogs.

Contact Hypersensitivity (Contact Allergy)

The haircoat of dogs offers an efficient protective barrier to many substances and agents that could produce an allergic reaction simply by coming in contact with the skin. Therefore, those areas relatively devoid of hair such as the chest, abdomen, and feet are more susceptible to contact allergies.

The most common contact-allergy-producing agents are detergents, shampoos, pet sprays, insecticides, and other agents, which, in liquid form, can penetrate the normally protective haircoat. In addition, bedding that is moldy or has been chemically treated can cause contact hypersensitivity.

Symptoms of such exposure include redness and swelling of the skin and intense itching. These signs will generally develop 24 to 72 hours after exposure.

Chemicals that can normally irritate the skin might produce similar symptoms immediately after contact. Such reactions are not to be confused with slower developing hypersensitivity. Treatment of contact allergies requires the removal of the offending agent and administration of topical and/or systemic anti-inflammatory drugs. A thorough history of the pet's exposure to chemicals and exposure to any environment vegetation is imperative in the veterinarian's effort to identify the allergy-producing agent.

Bacterial Infections

Bacterial infections involving the skin are itchy in themselves. As a result, when they occur secondarily to an allergy or parasitic infestation, it can mean sheer misery for a dog. It is for this reason that many treatments for other skin ailments are combined with antibiotic therapy.

Hair Loss (Alopecia)

Loss of hair either locally or generalized over the coat of a dog is another type of skin problem owners may face. As with itching, the causes of hair loss can be quite numerous, and sometimes very complex. A proper diagnosis is essential for restoring a full-bodied haircoat.

Shedding

Though the normal shedding cycles for dogs tend to occur in the spring and fall, some pets, especially those kept indoors, might actually shed year-round. In fact, some of these dogs can fill a brush with hair every day! If the dog is otherwise healthy and is on a good nutritional program, this seemingly excessive shedding is of no real consequence. If normal shedding is truly the cause of the hair loss, rarely do raw spots or patches of exposed skin appear. If they do, another cause of the hair loss should be suspected. If the dog is of the type that sheds excessively, be sure to brush it daily to remove the dead hairs and make way for the new ones. Failure to do so can predispose the pet to skin infections.

Any event that is associated with abnormally high amounts of stress can cause increases in shedding activity and, in some cases, overt alopecia. A good example of this is a female dog undergoing pregnancy or lactation. The physiological stress and demands placed on her body might lead to an accelerated hair-loss situation. Fortunately, in most instances, the hair will return once the stress abates.

Malnutrition

The hair cycle in dogs is dynamic and active, with new hairs constantly growing in to replace old, dead hairs that are naturally shed. These new hairs require a bounty of protein and other nutrients for their proper formation and development. If these are not supplied, the replacement hairs might not grow in at all, or they might be weak, brittle, and easily broken. As a result, dogs suffering from poor nutrition often have scanty, lackluster haircoats, not to mention unhealthy skin. Since the source of the problem is internal in nature, the distribution of this hair loss tends to be symmetrical over the entire body.

Feeding the wrong type of diet is not the only way to cause nutritionally related hair loss. Failure to have a pet checked routinely for internal parasites can also lead to malnutrition secondary to parasitism. Because intestinal parasites can steal vital nutrients, the haircoat can become deprived of essential nutrients and bear the brunt of the consequences.

Obviously, providing a good plane of nutrition and correcting any internal parasite problems that might exist are the two key means of restoring normal hair growth in these cases.

Itching

Virtually all the disorders that cause itching can cause loss of hair as well. This hair loss might be due to self-trauma from licking, chewing, and/or scratching, or it might be secondary to inflammation affecting the hair follicle (e.g., demodectic mange, folliculitis). The distribution of the hair loss can be localized or diffuse, symmetrical or asymmetrical, depending on the extent of the causative disorder. For instance, if allergies are to blame, the resulting hair loss is often symmetrical, affecting both sides equally. On the other hand, hair loss caused by mange or bacterial folliculitis usually appears localized to certain portions of the body at first, although this hair loss can spread to other parts if the disease is left unchecked.

Identifying and correcting the underlying problem is the most important step to take for restoring the scanty coat (Fig. 14.2). Realize that in many conditions involving inflammation of the hair follicle, the coat might look worse with treatment before it improves, because of treatment-induced shedding of dead or damaged hair. A good plane of nutrition, one that is adequate in protein and fatty acids, will also speed replacement of the lost hair in recovered pets.

Hormonal Imbalances

Symmetrical, nonitchy hair loss in middle-aged to older dogs might be the result of hormonal disturbances within the body. Abnormally low amounts of thyroid hormone, deficiencies in insulin, and/or unusually high amounts of steroid hormones in circulation can all cause this type of alopecia.

Although one would expect to see other signs associated with such disorders, this is not always the case. Imbalances in circulating amounts of sex hormones (estrogen and testosterone) have also been implicated in some cases of alopecia. Regardless of which hormone(s) are involved, stabilization and normalization of their circulating levels within the body are needed to correct the existing alopecia.

FIGURE 14.2 A special test called a "skin scraping" is needed to definitively diagnose mange in a dog.

Ringworm

Fungal infections involving the skin and hair can cause hair loss without associated itching. Certainly the most prevalent fungal infection affecting the integument of dogs is ringworm. For more information on ringworm, see Chap. 6.

Treatment of Hair Loss

As illustrated, canine itching and hair loss can be a complex challenge to diagnose and treat. Owners should no longer ignore or simply blame external parasites in all cases of itchy or balding pets. A complete and thorough history provided to a veterinarian, combined with the vet's dermatological examination, are important first steps in all cases of problem itching and/or alopecia.

Seborrhea

The term *seborrhea* refers to an abnormality in the normal turnover of skin cells, which can lead to excessive secretion of sebum by the sebaceous glands in the skin. Dogs afflicted with seborrhea might have dry, flaky skin (*seborrhea sicca*), or, if the sebaceous glands are active, greasy skin with a rancid odor to it (*seborrhea oleosa*). Itching and infections can also be unpleasant components of both types.

Seborrhea can be caused by a number of diseases, including allergies, fleas, and poor thyroid function. It can also be a primary disease entity, with no apparent underlying cause. Cocker spaniels and Doberman pinschers are two examples of breeds that can suffer from primary seborrhea.

Diagnosis of a seborrheic condition is not difficult; what can be challenging is determining the underlying problems if they exist. Laboratory tests, including skin biopsies, might be needed to determine whether the seborrhea is primary or secondary; this knowledge would increase the chances for a successful treatment.

Successful treatment of seborrhea depends on correcting any underlying sources (secondary seborrhea), and then focusing attention on normalizing the abnormal cell turnover occurring in the skin. Special medicated shampoos containing chlorhexidine, tar and sulfur, and/or selenium disulfide have all been used to clear up infections and remove dead epithelial cells and excessive oils associated with seborrhea.

In cases of dry seborrhea, moisturizing skin rinses and fatty acid supplements (available from veterinarians) can be helpful. In especially tough cases, prednisolone can be used to lessen the severity of signs and help stop the itching.

Because of its inherent nature, a complete cure will rarely be possible in those cases of primary seborrhea. However, veterinary researchers are looking with interest at a new treatment for primary seborrhea utilizing vitamin A derivatives called *retinoids.* Although research is still ongoing, the results so far at least look promising.

Acanthosis Nigricans

Acanthosis nigricans is a hormonal condition seen primarily in dachshunds and cocker spaniels, and characterized by hair loss, increased pigmentation, and thickening of the skin. This increased pigmentation usually begins in the armpit region and spreads to the chest and other regions of the body As the skin thickens, it becomes itchy and inflamed. Seborrhea and secondary bacterial skin infection could also result.

The exact cause of this disease is unknown, but a hormonal imbalance resulting in increases in the melanin pigment is suspect. Hyperthyroidism, although rare in dogs, must be ruled out as the cause of the increased pigmentation; so must allergic skin disorders. Skin biopsies can be used to help confirm or rule out cases of acanthosis nigricans.

Treatment of acanthosis nigricans is nonspecific, using corticosteroids to reduce pain and inflammation, and antibiotics to combat skin infection. Aloe vera gels applied topically can also be used to soothe and comfort irritated regions. Finally, if seborrhea is present, antiseborrheic shampoos should be used on a weekly or twice-weekly basis.

Bacterial Skin Disease

Bacterial skin disease in dogs seldom occurs unless there is some underlying disorder promoting it. Trauma, malnutrition, parasitism, hormonal abnormalities, and immune system malfunctions can all predispose to the proliferation of bacteria on the skin.

Healthy skin has several mechanisms by which it resists infectious organisms. A dry, outer layer of keratin, combined with periodic shedding of dead skin cells, helps discourage population of the skin surface with harmful bacteria. Even sebum, produced by the sebaceous glands of the skin, is antibacterial at normal concentrations. Finally, a normal population of bacteria that resides on the skin surface and in the hair follicles competitively inhibits the growth of disease-causing bacteria.

Problems can start to occur when the integument becomes traumatized, or underlying disease alters the normal integrity of the skin. If the skin's defenses are penetrated in such a way, disease-causing bacteria found naturally in the environment can set up housekeeping.

Superficial bacterial skin disease can take on a number of appearances. These infections are limited to the outermost layers of the skin, although, if left untreated, they can spread to the inner layers, making treatment difficult and lengthy.

Acute Moist Dermatitis

Acute moist dermatitis (hot spots) is characterized by moist, weeping lesions with hair loss and noticeable redness and swelling of the skin. These lesions are quite itchy and painful to the touch, and can spread rapidly over the dog's body if not treated soon enough. Although any breed can be affected, thick-coated breeds such as golden retrievers and chow chows seem to suffer from these the most.

Impetigo

Impetigo, also known as "milk rash," is a bacterial skin disease affecting puppies 6 weeks to 6 months of age. Characterized by small pustule formations, especially in the abdominal region, impetigo is usually an aftereffect of some debilitating disease that stresses the immune system, such as intestinal parasites or viruses. Few puppies seem irritated by their presence, and with proper treatment, cases of impetigo clear up very rapidly.

Skin-Fold Pyodermas

Skin-fold pyodermas can strike those breeds with lots of extra skin. This type of infection occurs secondary to moisture, warmth, and friction occurring within prominent folds of skin. Many breeds and breed crosses can be affected by skin-fold pyoderma. For instance, cocker spaniels can have this problem in their lip region, Pekinese and similar flat-nosed breeds in their facial region, pugs in their tail region, and bulldogs and shar-peis just about anywhere on their bodies! Keeping these areas clean and dry can help discourage this problem. In some cases, plastic surgery to remove the skin fold in question is truly the only way to effect a cure.

Folliculitis

Folliculitis is a bacterial infection that affects the hair follicles. Because the hair within the follicle suffers from the infection, the coats of dogs with folliculitis often develop a moth-eaten appearance as the damaged hair falls out. In addition, as the inflammation progresses, pustules and small crusty lesions often form over the hair follicles. The amount of itching seen with folliculitis can range from mild to severe. One special type of folliculitis, called *bacterial hypersensitivity,* is a type of allergic reaction to the bacteria residing on the skin. Dogs affected with bacterial hypersensitivity exhibit severe itching and hair loss. In fact, because the hair loss is usually in a circular pattern, bacterial hypersensitivity is often mistaken for a case of ringworm.

Canine acne is another form of folliculitis that can affect the chin and lips of dogs. Seen primarily in young dogs, this condition will usually clear up once puberty is reached.

Deep Pyodermas

Deep pyodermas extending into the depths of the skin layers warrant prompt attention. Unless hit hard with treatment, these infections can spread throughout the body. As mentioned above, superficial pyodermas can easily become deep if neglected.

Juvenile pyoderma is a form of deep pyoderma that can strike young dogs less than 6 months of age. Affected dogs have marked swelling, inflammation, and pain in the facial and ear regions. Lymph nodes in the neck

DID YOU KNOW?

Most bacterial skin infections in dogs occur secondary to other underlying disorders.

region might be noticeably swollen as a result of such infections, and these dogs are noticeably depressed, sometimes running fevers of up to 104 degrees Fahrenheit. Unless juvenile pyoderma is treated promptly and aggressively, permanent scarring and hair loss around the face and head can be an unfortunate side effect.

Cellulitis and abscesses are types of deep pyodermas that appear secondary to tissue injury. *Cellulitis* involves a poorly defined region of inflammation involving the deeper layers of the skin with no apparent rim or border, whereas *abscesses* do have a well-demarcated line of surrounding inflammatory cells that make them stand out. Both can be characterized by a painful buildup of pus, and usually cause fever and depression. Both can also lead to blood poisoning if not treated. Because of their isolated nature, veterinarians often lance and flush out abscesses to help speed the healing process.

Other types of deep pyoderma are named for the region of the body affected. These include, among others, nasal pyoderma, interdigital or foot pyoderma, and elbow callus pyoderma. *Generalized pyoderma* refers to a deep bacterial infection involving all areas of the body.

Treatment of Bacterial Skin Disease

Prompt treatment of bacterial skin disease is a smart idea to prevent unnecessary complications. For all types, both superficial and deep, there are certain principles that should be followed when treating such diseases.

If there is an underlying cause for the infection, it *must* be identified and corrected first. For instance, if fleas seem to be the source, insecticidal treatment is warranted. If this problem is not controlled, the infection will recur after other treatments are stopped.

Skin lesions should be kept clean and dry at all times. This is especially true for cases of acute moist dermatitis. Astringents (drying agents) should be applied daily to assist in healing and prevent further spread. Many of the car cleansers available have excellent drying properties and can be used topically for such a purpose. Creams and ointments should not be used on moist skin lesions, since such vehicles are counterproductive to drying efforts. Ideally, bacterial skin lesions should be allowed direct access to surrounding air, which means that the hair in the affected region(s) should be shaved and bandages avoided.

High doses of antibiotics used for extended durations are the mainstay of treatment for bacterial skin infections. Mild, superficial infections might require only 10 to 14 days of medication to afford a cure; severe, deep infections might require antibiotic therapy that can last as long as 8 weeks!

In recent years, bacterial resistance to the effects of certain antibiotics has become an unfortunate reality. As a result, do not be surprised if a veterinarian elects to perform a bacterial culture/sensitivity to determine the exact antibiotics that are effective against that particular infection. If a dog is placed on oral antibiotic therapy for a skin infection, it is imperative that owners complete the entire prescription as directed, even if the skin clears up after only a few days of medication.

Topical therapy for bacterial skin infections is an important adjunct to any treatment regimen. Many medicated shampoos are available that can be used to help speed healing. Those shampoos containing chlorhexidine are preferred, since this substance has excellent antibacterial properties. In some cases, these medicated shampoos should be used daily until the infection is brought under control. For best results, medicated shampoos should be allowed to remain in contact with skin in the affected area(s) for at least 15 minutes before rinsing. Remember to follow all veterinary recommendations concerning the frequency and duration of this type of topical therapy.

Pets should be shampooed and rinsed thoroughly, then dried off completely. This last step is vital because moisture will only serve to promote the infection. If needed, a handheld blow dryer set on low can assist in this task.

Medicated creams and ointments are also popular therapeutic additions for dogs with skin infections. Triple antibiotic formulations available over the counter or by prescription are preferred, and should be applied three to four times a day to the lesions. As mentioned before, use these products only on lesions that have been properly dried; do not use on moist lesions.

When using a medicated cream or ointment, avoid those preparations containing hydrocortisone or other steroid anti-inflammatory drugs unless specifically prescribed or recommended by veterinarians. Indiscriminate use of such products could actually delay healing and allow the infection to worsen.

Skin Lumps and Masses

Whenever a lump or mass appears on/or beneath the skin of a dog, five possibilities exist as to its source:

1. An abscess
2. A hematoma or seroma
3. A cyst
4. A granuloma
5. A tumor

Obviously, because the cause can vary, owners will need to employ the help of a veterinarian for identification of the mass. A fine-needle aspirate of the mass, or an actual biopsy sample will assist in a diagnosis (Fig. 14.3).

Abscesses

Abscesses are usually painful to the touch and are often associated with other signs, such as fever, depression, and loss of appetite. They also tend to be fluctuant when direct pressure is applied to them.

Hematomas and Seromas

Hematomas and seromas result from leakage of blood or serum, respectively, from damaged blood vessels. Traumatic blows to the skin can result in hematoma or seroma formation beneath the affected area of skin. The swellings caused by these are also fluctuant, and because of the traumatic nature of their occurrence, they can be painful as well.

FIGURE 14.3 Cell and fluid samples taken from an unidentified lump can be used to assist in a definitive diagnosis.

In most cases, the swellings caused by hematomas and seromas will resolve on their own with time, assuming that infection does not occur in the meantime.

Cysts

A cyst is nothing more than a well-defined pocket filled with fluid, secretion, or inflammatory debris. Unlike abscesses, cysts are usually not painful to the touch.

Sebaceous cysts or epidermoid cysts develop within the skin of dogs when the sebum normally formed within sebaceous glands is not allowed to escape. There does seem to be a breed predisposition for this problem, with cocker spaniels, springer spaniels, terriers, and shepherds most commonly affected.

Sebaceous cysts can arise in multiple locations over the body of these dogs, and can recur constantly throughout the life of the pet. Although they pose no specific danger to the health of a dog, extra-large cysts should be surgically excised.

Granulomas

Granulomas are firm, raised masses consisting chiefly of inflammatory cells sent to the particular area by the body in response to skin penetration by a foreign substance or infectious agent. In essence, the body attempts to quickly surround and wall off the foreign invader before it can spread to other parts of the body. Thorns, insect stingers, vaccines, fungal organisms, and certain bacteria are only a few of the things that can trigger granuloma formation.

If a pet develops one of these growths, an attempt should be made to determine the cause of its appearance. If an infectious agent is suspected, appropriate antimicrobial therapy is warranted to prevent further development of the granuloma.

Granulomas might recede with time, depending on the cause. In some cases, surgical removal of the mass gets rid of the unsightly lump and its cause all at the same time.

Tumors

Skin tumors or cancers can appear in a variety of types, sizes, and shapes. Common tumors that might appear as a lump or mass on or beneath the skin of a dog include sebaceous adenomas, lipomas, carcinomas, sarcomas, and most cell tumors. It is imperative that a biopsy be performed in all instances to determine whether the tumor is malignant.

Sebaceous gland tumors are among the most prevalent of all skin tumors. These wartlike growths are especially common in cocker spaniels and poodles. They can appear anywhere on the body, including the eyelids. The vast majority of these growths are benign and cause no problems whatsoever, unless they become traumatized because of their sheer size. Excision of these tumors is curative locally, but others often appear elsewhere with time.

Lipomas are benign, soft, fatty tumors that often form beneath the skin of dogs and cause noticeable lumps. They occur with greater frequency in older dogs that have weight problems. Although a diagnosis of lipoma might seem obvious, a fine-needle aspirate should always be performed to rule out the presence of its less common malignant counterpart, liposarcoma. Lipomas can be surgically removed, yet because they can infiltrate into the muscle bundles and surrounding tissue, this removal might be unknowingly incomplete, with the recurrence of the tumor. As a result, many practitioners will choose to remove only those lipomas that are extra large or those diagnosed as malignant.

Histiocytomas are classified as skin tumors, yet many researchers believe they represent instead inflammatory reactions by the body to some foreign invader or substance. Although they can develop at any age, most histiocytomas occur in dogs less than 2 years of age. These tumors are disk-shaped and often reddened and ulcerated. The head, ears, and/or extremities are the prevalent sites of appearance. For more information on tumors, refer to Chap. 60.

The Eyes and Ears

THE EYES

The visual acuity of the average dog has been compared to that of a human at sunset. Most see only generalized forms rather than distinct images or features. Exceptions to this rule include the sight hounds (greyhounds, afghans), which indeed have keen eyesight.

Contrary to popular belief, dogs might not be as colorblind as people think. In fact, the canine eye possesses all of those structures necessary to perceive their world in color. Now, whether they take full advantage of this is still a matter of speculation. It seems, however, that since the sense of sight is not as vital to most dogs than, let's say, the sense of smell, there might be no real need for color perception.

Anatomy and Physiology

Each eye (Fig. 15.1) is housed within a bony socket of the skull, and is surrounded by an upper eyelid and a lower eyelid. In addition, a nictitating membrane, or third eyelid, is located on the inside corner of each eye. Serving a protective function similar to the conventional lids, this third eyelid will passively extrude over the eye in the event of injury or illness. Special glands lining the inside portion of this lid also bear significance in the disease condition known as "cherry eye."

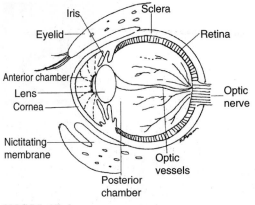

FIGURE 15.1   **The canine eye.**

The *conjunctiva* is the delicate membrane seen lining the pink inner portion of the eyelid and a substantial portion of the eyeball itself. *Conjunctivitis* is the term applied to inflammation involving this membrane. It often results in red, weeping eyes.

The white portion of the eyeball is properly termed the *sclera*. Changes in the color of the sclera can be indicative of underlying disease. For instance, a sclera that is yellow-tinged could be reflecting a serious underlying liver or bleeding disorder.

The *cornea* is the clear, transparent structure at the front of the eye through which the colored iris and black pupil can be seen. When light passes through the cornea, it enters into the fluid-filled anterior chamber of the eye, which is located between the cornea and the iris.

Monitoring the pressure maintained within the eyes by this fluid is a valuable diagnostic tool for the veterinarian trying to diagnose eye disorders in pets. For instance, glaucoma, or increased pressure within the eye, is a serious disease that can lead to blindness if not treated promptly. It can originate as a result of increased amounts of this anterior chamber fluid. On the contrary, a decreased pressure reading signifies active inflammation within the eye itself (uveitis), prompting appropriate treatment measures.

The *iris* is the structure that contains the pigment that gives the eye its characteristic color. In dogs, brown is by far the dominant eye color seen, with a few blue eyes interspersed here and there.

The *pupil* is a hole formed by the iris. The size of the pupil is determined by the contraction and expansion of the iris in response to varying degrees of light. Thus, the iris serves to regulate the amount of light that is actually allowed into the eye.

Injury or illness can affect pupil size. For example, poisonings caused by organophosphate insecticides can cause the pupils to be pinpoint in size. Furthermore, pupils that are unequal in size can be indicators of a primary neurological disease, including disorders of the middle ear.

Once through the pupil, light enters into the posterior chamber of the eye, containing the lens and the retina. The lens serves to gather incoming light and then focus it in on the retina, which lines the back surface of the eye. Special fibers attaching to the lens allow it to change sizes to accommodate for distances.

The *retina* contains a multitude of nerve endings that, when stimulated by light, send nervous impulses that feed into the optic disk and then into the brain. The end result is a visualized, perceived image. The appearance of the retina can be altered by a variety of disease states, offering valuable diagnostic insight to the veterinarian attempting to pinpoint the source of a canine illness.

The *tapetum* is a specially pigmented structure that lines the back surface of the eye along with the retina. The tapetum serves as a light-gathering, reflective device that improves night (nocturnal) vision in the dog. It is responsible for the characteristic green color seen when light from approaching automobile headlights or other sources reflect off of it.

Corneal Ulcers

The transparent cornea enclosing the front portion of the eye is a remarkable organ in itself. Responsible for gathering light and directing it into the eye, healthy corneas are essential for proper vision. It stands to reason, then, that ulcerations (loss of surface epithelium) or scratches involving one or more corneal surfaces can seriously threaten eyesight if not managed promptly.

Corneal ulcerations in dogs can occur secondary to poor tear production, entropion or ectropion, dust and foreign debris in the eye(s), nail scratches and other direct trauma, and infections.

One of the most common sources of corneal ulceration seen by veterinarians is the soap or shampoo burn caused by inadequate eye protection when bathing. Dog owners should always apply a sterile ophthalmic ointment to their pet's eyes prior to any procedure that involves potentially caustic substances around the eyes. Since canine corneas are so sensitive that even shampoos with touted "no tears" formulations should never be used without applying this protection first.

Clinical signs of a corneal ulcer include squinting and aversion to light, ocular discharge, and obvious discomfort, often signified by pawing at or rubbing the affected eye. A change in the normal color or transparency of the corneal surface is also an indicator that something is wrong.

Definitive diagnosis of a corneal ulcer is made by veterinarians using special fluorescein dyes to stain the corneal surfaces. Dead, diseased corneal tissue will readily take up such stain whereas healthy tissue will not.

Luckily, the cornea is one organ that will heal quite rapidly if treatment is administered quickly and vigorously (Fig. 15.2). For ulcers involving only the superficial layers of the cornea, topical antibiotic ointments or solutions designed for use in the eyes and applied three to six times daily will help speed healing.

Of course, if an underlying cause, such as foreign debris, still exists in the eye, it must be removed before proper healing can take place. Superficial ulcers can heal in 36 to 48 hours with proper treatment applied.

Deep Corneal Ulcerations

Deep corneal ulcerations are treated the same way that superficial ulcerations are, yet these require close observation for progression or worsening of the ulcer. Bacterial cultures of such ulcers are necessary to be certain that the antibiotics being used are effective against any organisms involved.

For deep ulcers that worsen or fail to respond to conventional treatment, additional procedures might be necessary to speed healing or to prevent the cornea from actually rupturing. A favorite procedure among

FIGURE 15.2   All corneal ulcers must be treated aggressively.

veterinarians consists of surgically freeing and extending a portion of the thin conjunctiva over the ulcer and actually tacking it down against the ulcer using suture material (conjunctival flap). The flap of conjunctiva provides nutrition and speeds healing to the ulcer, and also allows any medications applied directly to the eye(s) to reach the ulcer without hindrance. Once healing has been accomplished, the flap is released, and excess conjunctival tissue is trimmed away from the healed surface.

Special contact lenses and/or corneal tissue adhesives can also be applied over the damaged surface of the cornea. These serve to protect it from further degradation and help promote rapid healing. For difficult ulcers, actual grafts using fresh or frozen corneal tissue may be required.

Conjunctivitis

Inflammation of the thin, transparent mucous membrane lining the inner portion of the eyelids and front part of the sclera is termed *conjunctivitis.* Conjunctivitis is the most common cause of "red eyes" in dogs. Other signs seen with conjunctivitis include discharge, swelling, and pain.

The type of discharge present can sometimes give a clue as to the underlying cause of the conjunctivitis. For instance, a watery discharge can indicate irritation from an allergy, virus (canine distemper), or contact with dirt or dust; a mucuslike discharge often links the problem to abnormal tear formation ("dry eye") or to a bacterial infection, either primary or secondary to any of the causes previously mentioned.

Because conjunctivitis can be secondary to other problems, diagnostic tests performed by veterinarians should be directed at identifying any underlying causes. Corneal staining using a fluorescent stain is usually performed to determine whether the cornea is affected. If a mucuslike discharge is present, a tear flow test should be performed to rule out dry eye as the cause of the conjunctivitis.

In cases of conjunctivitis that don't respond to conventional therapy, a bacterial culture or sensitivity assay should be performed to ensure that the treatment measures being used are correct.

Treatment of conjunctivitis is aimed at treating or eliminating any inciting causes, and at controlling the localized inflammation. If dust or pollen are the source of the conjunctivitis, daily flushing of the eyes with a sterile saline solution designed for use in the eyes or daily

FIGURE 15.3 Antibiotic drops can be used to combat conjunctivitis.

application of a sterile ophthalmic lubricant can help reduce the irritation caused by these offenders.

Ophthalmic drops or ointments containing antibiotics are necessary if a bacterial infection is present (Fig. 15.3). In addition, ophthalmic preparations containing steroids can be used to reduce the inflammation present, provided the surface of the cornea is intact. A number of preparations containing both antibiotics and steroid compounds for use in the eyes are readily available for pets through a prescription from a veterinarian.

Glaucoma

Glaucoma is a condition characterized by an increase in fluid pressure from the aqueous humor within the eye(s). In the normal eye, pressure and aqueous levels are maintained at a constant level by the continual drainage of excess aqueous humor out of the eye through tiny ports (drainage angles) located where the edge of the iris meets the cornea. If this drainage is obstructed or altered in any way, a rise in pressure within the eye can result. Unfortunately, even short-term rises in this pressure can lead to irreversible damage if not detected and treated in a timely fashion.

Conditions such as a buildup of inflammatory material within the eye, luxation of the lens due to trauma or cataracts, and synechia, where the iris "sticks" to the lens or cornea, can all effectively prevent the normal drainage of the aqueous humor from the eye.

Heredity is also thought to play a role in some cases of glaucoma, with basset hounds, beagles, and cocker spaniels having a higher incidence of the disease because of improper development of the drainage angles. In addition, a predisposition for lens luxation has been identified along family lines for many of the terrier breeds, predisposing them to glaucoma.

Finally, allergies and overactive immune system responses are also thought to be important precursors to glaucoma in dogs.

Clinical signs of a glaucomatous eye include a marked redness affecting both the conjunctival tissue and the sclera; a blue, hazy cornea; a dilated, unresponsive pupil; and apparent blindness due to the pressure the fluid is placing on the optic nerve. In instances where the glaucoma has been present for quite some time, enlargement of the affected eyeball might become noticeable, and actual rupture of the cornea could occur.

Diagnosis of glaucoma can be easily confirmed by a veterinarian through the use of an instrument called a *tonometer*. This instrument, when placed directly on the cornea surface, measures the exact pressure within the eye. If the pressure reading is indeed elevated, then treatment should be instituted immediately to prevent lasting damage to the eye.

Treatment for glaucoma is aimed at decreasing the pressure within the eye to an acceptable level as quickly as possible, and then stabilizing this pressure to prevent future increases.

Drugs designed to quickly draw fluid out of the eye and into the bloodstream will initially be used to reduce the pressure within a pet's eye(s). Other drugs that act by decreasing the production of aqueous humor and by increasing the size of the drainage angles are then prescribed for the long-term management and prevention of recurrence. At the same time, anti-inflammatory medications can be used topically on the eye to clear up any primary or secondary inflammation that might be aggravating the glaucoma.

In instances where a luxated lens is causing the increase in pressure, surgical removal of the offending lens should always be performed. Cryotherapy (freezing) can be used as well. This involves surgically inserting a special needle within the eye and freezing the cells within the eye responsible for the production of aqueous humor. With this technique, aqueous production can be reduced by up to 30 percent in some patients.

Cataracts

An opacity involving the lens of the eye that prevents light from reaching the retina is termed a *cataract.* Cataracts can be inherited (juvenile cataracts) or might develop secondary to eye trauma, infections, or metabolic disease, such as diabetes mellitus. As lens opacity increases, the amount of light allowed to reach the retina is diminished, and partial blindness ensues.

Cataracts can also predispose to rotation or luxation of the lens. Such lens movement can disrupt normal fluid flow within the eye and lead to secondary glaucoma.

True cataracts must be differentiated from lenticular sclerosis seen in older dogs. Lenticular sclerosis is a lens opacity caused by a normal hardening of the lens material due to age. It is a normal aging change seen in some dogs, and rarely leads to loss of sight as can occur with cataracts. As a result, no specific treatment is required for most cases of lenticular sclerosis. Lenticular sclerosis and cataracts can be differentiated with an ophthalmologic examination performed by a veterinarian.

Treatment for cataracts usually involves surgical removal of the offending lens or lenses. A less invasive surgical technique for cataract removal is called *phacofragmentation.* This procedure employs the use of ultrasound to break up the lens material into small pieces, which can then be drawn or sucked out of the eye using special instrumentation. Once cataracts are removed, vision is effectively restored in the affected pet.

Keratoconjunctivitis Sicca (Dry Eye)

Keratoconjunctivitis sicca (KCS), or "dry eye," is a condition affecting the cornea and conjunctiva of the eye resulting from inadequate tear production. In actuality, only the water portion of the tear film is deficient; the mucus portion is still produced in adequate quantities. This leads to the characteristic green, mucoid buildup in and around eyes affected with KCS. The lack of adequate tear moisture also predisposes the cornea to damage and ulcers. Long-term sequelas include pigmentation of the corneal surface and blindness.

KCS can have a number of underlying causes. In many breeds—such as Yorkshire terriers, schnauzers, cocker spaniels, bulldogs, and beagles—KCS can be an inherited trait. Other potential causes include canine distemper, certain medications (such as sulfa drugs), hypothyroidism, diabetes mellitus, and autoimmune disease.

Diagnosis of KCS is made using tear flow tests to determine the amount of tear production (Fig. 15.4). Treatment of KCS involves the use of tear replacement drops, followed by an application of a tear replacement ointment to seal in the drops. These replacements must be applied every 3 to 4 hours to be truly effective. If infection or inflammation is present, antibiotics and anti-inflammatory medications should be instilled into the eyes as well.

FIGURE 15.4 Special test strips can be used to check for tear production in suspected cases of "dry eye."

Medications designed to stimulate more tear production have been used for treatment in the past with varying success. Also, the drug cyclosporine can be quite effective at stimulating renewed tear production in some dogs with KCS. For more information on cyclosporine, owners should contact their veterinarians.

In especially advanced cases of KCS, surgical intervention might become necessary. The standard surgical treatment used, called *parotid duct transposition,* involves repositioning a duct from a salivary gland to the corner of the affected eye(s), thereby providing a constant source of moisture (saliva) to the eye.

Retinal Degeneration and Disease

Retinal degeneration and disease can be a cause of blindness in dogs. For instance, *progressive retinal atrophy* (PRA) is a hereditary condition that can strike middle-aged to older dogs and produce blindness over a period of several months to years. Breeds that are predisposed to this condition include Gordon setters, Irish setters, poodles, Norwegian elkhounds, Labrador retrievers, collies, cocker spaniels, and malamutes. Characterized by a slow degeneration of the receptor cells making up the retina, PRA in its early stages often leads to nightblindness in affected dogs. These dogs tend to fear or shy away from poorly lighted areas. As PRA progresses, it eventually causes the pupils to remain dilated and fail to respond to light, creating complete blindness.

Retinal function may also be partially or completely lost due to underlying disease or injury. For example, glaucoma affecting an eye can place so much pressure on the blood vessels supplying the retina of that eye that secondary retinal degeneration results. *Sudden acquired retinal degeneration* (SARD) is another nonhereditary condition that can cause blindness in dogs, yet its exact cause remains a mystery. Interestingly, this disease is often accompanied by an increase in thirst and appetite in those dogs so affected. Infectious diseases such as ehrlichiosis, Rocky Mountain Spotted Fever, and fungi can also adversely affect the region of the retina where the optic nerve exits, leading to inflammation and subsequent loss of vision. In addition, neoplasms such as lymphosarcoma can infiltrate the retinas of dogs and inhibit retinal function. Finally, trauma, immune-mediated diseases, and certain toxins can cause retinal injury and lead to blindness.

Diagnosis of retinal disease and degeneration is made using history, physical exam findings, and information obtained from an ophthalmic examination of the retinas themselves. In addition, an *electroretinogram,* which measures the electrical activity taking place within the retinas, will provide a definitive diagnosis of retinal degeneration and retinal blindness. If a disease condition such as glaucoma, infection, neoplasia, or toxicity is suspected, other diagnostic testing procedures specific to these conditions may be required as well to confirm a diagnosis.

Unfortunately, there are presently no known treatments for PRA and SAR, and the prognosis remains grave for the restoration of sight in affected dogs. Other diseases involving the retina may respond favorably to treatments specific for the particular disorder; however, it must be remembered that the longer such treatments are delayed or neglected, the greater the chances are of permanent loss of vision.

Prolapse of Third Eyelid Gland (Cherry Eye)

The third eyelid of dogs contains a gland that might occasionally become inflamed and protrude over the edge of the third eyelid, producing a classic "cherry eye" appearance. Certain breeds—such as the cocker spaniel, Lhasa apso, Pekinese, and beagle—seem to be more predisposed to this condition than others.

In the past, treatment for a prolapsed gland of the third eyelid involved complete surgical removal of the gland. However, researchers agree that the gland might play an important role in tear production; hence, complete removal of the gland might predispose a pet to keratoconjunctivitis sicca. As a result, favored surgical procedures involve removal of only a portion of the gland, or actually tacking down the prolapsed portion of the gland to the inner surface of the third eyelid.

Entropion

Entropion is an ophthalmic condition in which the eyelids roll inward, allowing lashes and hair to irritate the surface of the eyes. The condition is inheritable, or it can occur secondary to other types of eye irritation (spastic entropion) or eyelid injury. Congenital entropion has a high incidence in chow chows, shar-peis, English bulldogs, poodles, and rottweilers.

Signs of entropion include excessive tearing, squinting, constant rubbing of the affected eye(s), excessive redness to the eye(s), and a noticeable inward roll to the eyelid, especially the lower lid.

If a pet is suffering from entropion, surgical treatment might be essential to prevent lasting damage to the surface of the eye(s). Some puppies afflicted with this disorder might grow out of it as they mature; hence, surgery is usually delayed in these young animals until they are at least 6 months old, unless the damage to the eye is severe.

In the meantime, topical lubricants designed to protect the corneas can be used on a daily basis in these patients. In some pups, especially shar-peis, temporary eversion of the offending lids with sutures implanted in the skin of the lids can also help prevent complications until they grow out of the entropion or until they are old enough for the surgery.

Entropion surgery involves the removal of a flap of skin just beneath (lower lid) or above (upper lid) the inverted lid. Suturing close the resulting gap of skin will then provide enough tension to roll the lid back out. In many instances, more than one surgery is necessary to achieve just the right amount of eversion.

After surgery is performed, care must be taken to prevent the dog from irritating the incision line and causing swelling. Hospitalization for a few days after the procedure is performed will help reduce this occurrence.

Because of the inheritable nature of this disorder, all dogs affected with entropion should be neutered to prevent its passing to future generations. When selecting a new pet, especially one that falls into the high-risk category, owners should examine the pup's parents closely for any signs of entropion or for evidence that surgical correction has been previously performed.

Ectropion

Ectropion is the exact opposite of entropion; it is the outward rolling of the eyelid(s), which exposes the pink conjunctival lining within. As with entropion, this condition is inheritable, with cocker spaniels, St. Bernards, and bloodhounds having a high incidence. Facial nerve paralysis, such as that seen secondary to otitis media can also result in ectropic lids.

Mild cases of ectropion usually cause no problems whatsoever in affected individuals. Moderate to severe cases are often accompanied by conjunctivitis, excessive lacrimation, and eye discharges.

Keeping the eye(s) clean and free of discharge on a daily basis using saline solution or medicated drops or ointments will help keep minor cases of ectropion under control. For more extensive involvement, surgical correction designed to release the tension placed upon the skin of the eyelid, allowing it to roll back to its correct position, might be required.

Masses Involving the Eyelids

The integrity of the eyelids is vital to protect the eyes from environmental hazards. Any disruption or alteration in the normal lid anatomy can place vision in jeopardy. And certain masses involving the lids can do just that if they become large enough.

Chalazion are masses involving the eyelid that originate from the small meibomian glands that line the edge of the lid. They result from a buildup of secretion within the glands due to blockage of the ducts leading from the gland. Chalazion appear as yellow-to-white swellings beneath the conjunctiva on the inner lid margin. Puncturing or incising these to remove the trapped contents will afford a cure.

Hordeolums are pus-filled masses caused by infections within the meibomian glands or hair follicles lining the lid margin. As with chalazion, these can be punctured and expressed to help speed healing. Topical or systemic antibiotics are also used to eliminate infection.

Tumors that affect the eyelid can be very serious because of the inability to remove them surgically without disrupting the integrity of the lid. Sebaceous gland adenomas are common lid tumors, especially in older dogs. Others include adenocarcinomas, papillomas, and melanomas. As an alternative or adjunct to surgical removal, radiation therapy, chemotherapy, or cryotherapy (freezing) can be used as well, depending on which type of tumor is involved.

THE EARS

The sense of hearing in the average dog is much more fine-tuned than that of a human, allowing it to detect much higher sound pitches. The upper range of canine hearing is thought to be around 50,000 kHz, almost 30,000 kHz higher than that of people.

Silent dog whistles were invented on the basis of this principle; the pitch emitted is just above the human hearing range but well within that of the dog being summoned. Unfortunately, the high pitch emitted by many of the new electronic flea collars available on the market often falls within the dog's hearing range, raising serious questions as to their safe use.

Anatomy and Physiology

The canine hearing apparatus can be divided into three portions: the inner ear, the middle ear, and the external ear canal and associated structures.

The *inner ear* is that portion containing the nerve endings responsible for the sensation of hearing. It also plays a leading role in maintaining balance and equilibrium in your pet (dogs can get carsick, too!). The inner ear apparatus lies protected within the bony confines of the skull. The nerves and associated structures within the inner ear are very sensitive and can be damaged through continued exposure to loud, high-pitched noises, infections, and/or toxic medications.

The *middle ear* communicates directly with the inner ear and is contained within a pear-shaped bony cavity called the *tympanic bulla* originating from the skull. This middle-ear cavity is normally filled with air and contains blood vessels and nerves that supply the head and face. Inflammation involving the middle ear can adversely affect these nerves, leading to paralysis of the muscles of the face.

The *eardrum,* or *tympanic membrane,* separates the middle ear from the external ear canal. This external canal directly communicates to the outside world, but not without first going through some significant anatomical changes along the way. A horizontal portion of the canal courses a short distance directly away from the eardrum before angling sharply upward to form a long vertical portion. This distinct bend has medical significance in that it can lead to the entrapment of wax, hair, and debris deep within the ear, predisposing to inflammation and infection.

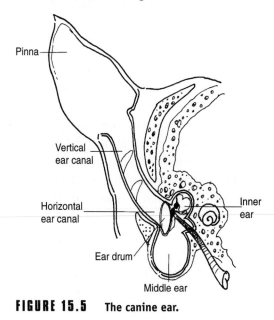

The vertical external ear canal—and to a lesser extent, the horizontal ear canal—are lined with special glands that produce ear wax, or cerumen. In the past, cerumen was thought to exert some beneficial antibacterial effects in the ear. Yet research has disproved this theory and has shown that too much of a waxy buildup can actually

Pinna

Vertical ear canal

Horizontal ear canal

Ear drum

Middle ear

Inner ear

FIGURE 15.5 The canine ear.

promote bacterial growth and infections. In the healthy ear with normal amounts of cerumen produced, this doesn't present much of a problem. Yet when an ear becomes inflamed, wax production increases, and can predispose to infectious complications.

Surrounding the opening of the external ear canals is the ear flap, or pinna, which come in all sorts of sizes and shapes, both natural and synthetic. Each pinna is supported by a sturdy band of cartilage that courses from the vertical ear canal to the tip of each flap (Fig. 15.5). Long

FIGURE 15.6   Dogs with erect ears are less prone to ear problems than are dogs with droopy ears.

droopy car flaps that hang down over the ear openings can effectively cut off proper air circulation within the ear canal (Figs. 15.6 and 15.7). This can potentially lead to ear problems in these dogs unless preventive measures are instituted on a routine basis.

Otitis Externa

Inflammation involving the external-ear canal is called *otitis externa*. It is estimated that up to 20 percent of the dog population in the United States alone suffers from some form of otitis externa. Anatomical features that predispose certain breeds to ear disorders include long, pendulous ears (cocker spaniels), long, narrow ear canals (poodles), and excessive hair within the ear canal that entraps wax and restricts air circulation (poodles). Dogs that spend a lot of time in the water, such as hunting retrievers and spaniels, are also prone to otitis externa.

FIGURE 15.7 Long, floppy pinnae can reduce air circulation within the ear canal and predispose the dog to infections.

Since the external canals are merely inward extensions of the skin, conceivably anything that can cause skin to become inflamed can cause otitis externa. This can include allergies, metabolic diseases (hypothyroidism, seborrhea), trauma, foreign bodies such as grass awns and twigs, and parasites such as ticks and mites. Anal sac disease has even been implicated in cases of otitis externa, even though the exact mechanism of involvement is not completely understood.

Signs of otitis externa involving one or both ears include head shaking, itching, painful ears, personality changes, and/or odiferous discharges coming from the ear canal(s). Hair loss might be noticed around the pinnae as a result of scratching. Aural hematomas might also develop in the wake of such self-trauma.

Diagnosis of otitis externa is based on clinical signs, physical exam, and selected laboratory tests if needed to determine the underlying cause of the inflammation. An otoscopic (ear) exam performed by a veterinarian will help rule out foreign bodies and parasites. This exam is also needed to assess the health of the eardrums. Since many medications cannot be used if the eardrum is torn or ruptured, never attempt to treat otitis externa at home without first having a veterinarian perform this otoscopic exam.

The type of medications prescribed by a veterinarian for the treatment of otitis externa will vary, depending on the nature and extent of the causative agent or condition. See Chap. 3 for proper techniques for instilling medications into the ears.

Yeast Infections

Malassezia pachydermatis is a yeast organism most commonly involved in otitis externa. This is not sur-

prising, since *Malassezia* is normally found within the ear canals of healthy dogs, causing no problems whatsoever. However, if inflammation strikes for whatever reason, the yeast takes advantage of a good situation and begins to proliferate. When this growth reaches a certain level, it, too, can promote inflammation. A characteristic brownish discharge is seen with a buildup of yeast within the ears.

Ear ointments or solutions containing miconazole, thiabendazole, or nystatin can be used to effectively treat yeast infections in the ear. Treating the ears twice daily for 10 to 14 days will clear up most infections.

Because *Malassezia* is considered an opportunist, it is important that the underlying source of the inflammation that led to the yeast infection be identified and treated concurrently.

Bacterial Infections

Failure to detect and treat inflammation within the external ear canal early enough can lead to the establishment of a bacterial infection within the ear. Often, these infections result when the harmless bacteria that normally inhabit the ear become overwhelmed by the inflammation, allowing their not-so-peaceful counterparts to proliferate and take over.

A creamy brown-to-yellow discharge carrying a foul odor is characteristic of a bacterial disorder within the ear. Bacterial infections can even be found together with yeast infections within the same ear(s), leading to a discharge having characteristics of both types.

If not treated promptly and vigorously, bacterial infections can become firmly entrenched within the ear canal, making a complete cure difficult. For this reason, veterinary practitioners rely heavily on bacterial cultures and sensitivity tests to tell them which bacteria are involved and which antibiotics will be most effective.

Otic preparations containing appropriate antibiotics, often combined with anti-inflammatory medications, are used to combat cases of bacterial otitis externa; 5% vinegar (acetic acid) solutions have also been used with effectiveness against bacteria within the ear.

If a ruptured eardrum is suspected, selection of treatment agents must be made carefully. For example, antibiotics belonging to the class known as *aminoglycosides* (examples include gentamycin and neomycin) should not be used in the ear directly, since they can cause nerve deafness if exposed to the inner ear. The same holds true for astringent preparations and acetic acid solutions. In addition, if a ruptured eardrum is suspected, only water-soluble treatment solutions should be used. Ointments should be avoided, as they can become entrapped within the middle ear.

In especially severe cases of bacterial otitis, oral antibiotics might be given concurrently with topical ear medications to expedite results. In chronic long-standing infections that can't be cleared up with antibiotics, a surgical procedure known as a *lateral ear resection* might be necessary to increase the treatment effectiveness. This involves the surgical reconstruction of the external-ear canal to eliminate the vertical portion, allowing easy, direct access to the horizontal portion and the eardrum. Although the results might not be the most cosmetic, a lateral ear resection can mean the difference between a life of misery or comfort for a dog afflicted with chronic otitis externa.

Ear Mites

Otodectes cynotis is the name of the most common mite that inhabits the canine ear canal. These tiny parasites, which are transmitted by close contact with other infected animals, live on the skin surface within the ear and feed on body fluids. Their presence irritates the glands lining the ear canal, leading to an increased cerumen production. Secondary infections with the *Malassezia* yeast are not uncommon, leading to the brown, crusty discharge so often seen with ear mite infestations. In isolated cases, intense allergic reactions to ear mites can occur, causing severe inflammation and secondary infection.

Diagnosis of an ear mite infestation is confirmed by identification of the mites directly on otoscopic exam or through a microscopic examination of an ear swab. Treatment involves the use of medications containing antiparasitic compounds, such as pyrethrins, rotenone, and/or thiabendazole. Mineral oil has also been employed as a home remedy for killing mites by suffocation. Since secondary yeast infections are commonly found with ear mite infestations, an antiyeast medication should be used concurrently with antimite preparations.

Ear mites can be difficult pests to eliminate. Daily treatment for 3 to 4 weeks might be needed to ensure a complete kill. All animals in the household, regardless of whether they are exhibiting signs of infestation, should be treated at the same time. In addition, to prevent reinfestation from the haircoat, an insecticidal spray or shampoo should be used at least twice during the treatment period.

Otitis Media and Interna

Otitis media, infection involving the middle ear, usually results from a chronic, untreated or recurring otitis externa. In such cases, the eardrum might become so diseased as to tear or rupture completely, allowing direct access of infectious organisms into the middle-ear chamber.

The clinical signs of otitis media are essentially the same as those for otitis externa, with a few notable additions. Dogs so afflicted will usually exhibit a head tilt toward the side of the affected ear.

In severe cases, paralysis of the facial muscles on the side of the lesion might be seen as the nerves passing through the middle ear become involved. This can result in a characteristic drooping of the eyelids, cheeks, and lips. In addition, a decreased tear production, pinpoint pupil, and protrusion of the third eyelid might be noted in the eye on the affected side.

If the infection extends from the middle ear into the inner-ear apparatus, the signs become even more pronounced. Since the inner ear functions in maintaining balance and equilibrium as well as hearing, dogs suffering from otitis interna tend to become very uncoordinated and might fall down frequently or move in circles to the affected side. A characteristic twitching of the eyeball, called *nystagmus,* also becomes more noticeable.

Although the clinical signs seen are often diagnostic, radiographs of the skull are quite helpful at confirming a diagnosis of otitis media or interna and determining the extent of the disorder.

Therapy for otitis media or interna must be instituted promptly to prevent permanent damage to the hearing apparatus. Oral antibiotics should be started immediately. In cases of otitis interna, continued treatment with antibiotics might be required for up to 30 days for a complete cure. In select cases, anti-inflammatory medications have been used to reduce signs associated with inflammation. If not already ruptured, the eardrum on the affected side is usually punctured to allow for thorough drainage of the middle ear cavity and direct infusion of medications. Of course, such treatment steps must be carried out in a veterinary hospital under heavy sedation or anesthesia. In tough, refractory cases, surgical placement of a drain in the bony tympanic bulla affords excellent exposure to the middle and inner ear spaces.

Ruptured Eardrums

Eardrums can tear or rupture as the result of direct trauma from a foreign body (such as a twig, cotton-tip applicator, etc.), sudden pressure changes, or, most commonly, as a secondary complication due to otitis externa. Although it is a serious and painful condition, a torn eardrum will heal quite quickly provided the underlying cause of the perforation is eliminated.

Medications designed for use in the ears must be used with caution if a dog suffers from a ruptured eardrum. Not only can their application be painful, but also, as mentioned previously, certain antibiotics and solutions, if allowed direct access into the middle- and inner-ear chambers, can cause damage to the auditory nerve endings, resulting in deafness. As a result, be certain to follow a veterinarian's recommendations closely.

Deafness

Veterinarians are often confronted by frustrated owners claiming that their dog is going deaf! Now, whether this is a valid claim or rather an actual ploy conceived by a defiant Fido will not be known until a thorough ear examination is performed. A dog's apparent inability to perceive sounds can result for a number of reasons.

First, there might be impedance to the sound waves traveling through the ear. An external ear canal clogged with wax and debris can certainly be the culprit, as can constrictive swelling of the ear canal caused by otitis externa. Torn or ruptured eardrums can also diminish the effective transmission of sound waves to the middle and inner ears.

Interestingly, some researchers feel that a dog's eardrums are not altogether necessary for efficient conduction of sound waves; rather, sound waves permeating the bony, air-filled tympanic bullae directly fulfill a major portion of this conductive function. Nevertheless, researchers do know that sound waves must pass through the middle ear cavity before reaching the inner ear, and that fluid or inflammation secondary to otitis media can lead to diminished hearing.

Besides interference with the transmission of sound waves, deafness in dogs can also be caused by developmental defects or damage involving the actual nerve endings within the inner ear.

Congenital nerve deafness has been reported in some breeds, including dalmatians, collies, and rottweilers. Certain drugs, such as the aminoglycoside antibiotics, are well known for their adverse effects upon the hearing function in dogs. Chronic, untreated bacterial and fungal infections within the middle and inner ears can undoubtedly lead to nerve deafness, as can certain viral organisms, including canine distemper.

Diagnosis of nerve deafness is based on history and special hearing tests. One such test, the brain stem auditory evoked response test (BAER), measures the brain's response to auditory stimuli and is quite helpful in the detection of hearing defects, determining the extent of any defect, and pinpointing its location.

Unfortunately, no known treatment exists for true nerve deafness. Hearing aids designed especially for dogs are now commercially available, and may help improve hearing in select instances.

Aural Hematomas

Fractures or trauma to the cartilage supporting the pinna of the ear can lead to the accumulation of blood and serum within the affected flap. These aural hematomas cause the pinna to swell, sometimes to enormous sizes. In the majority of cases, the fluid accumulation occurs on the inside portion of the earflap.

Researchers don't know what precipitates many cases of aural hematomas, but they do have a few suspicions. Since these hematomas are often accompanied by otitis externa, many feel that the trauma induced by scratching and shaking the head predisposes to aural hematomas, especially in those dogs with pendulous ears. Still others suspect that an overactive host immune system is the culprit behind this disorder. Regardless of the cause, aural hematomas are painful and irritating, and need to be drained as soon as possible after initial appearance.

Surgical drainage of the hematoma has been the standard treatment for years. This involves making an elliptical incision in the skin on the inner portion of the pinna, then tacking down the remaining skin tightly to the underlying cartilage. The procedure results in a portion of the cartilage remaining exposed to the outside, allowing for continued drainage to occur. In time, the wound heals over, hopefully with enough scarring to keep the skin and cartilage bound together.

Another form of management involves draining the hematoma with a needle and syringe, then injecting anti-inflammatory medications directly into the affected part of the pinna. This noninvasive procedure has shown promise in the treatment of aural hematomas, prompting support for the "overactive immune system" theory.

The Musculoskeletal System

The musculoskeletal system in mammals is responsible for locomotion, plus support and protection of vital internal organs. The components of this system include muscles, bones, and a variety of supportive structures, including ligaments, tendons, and cartilage. Disorders of the musculoskeletal system can be quite debilitating to a dog and be accompanied by a lot of pain.

Anatomy and Physiology

The type of muscle involved in skeletal locomotion is termed *striated muscle.* This type of muscle is in contrast to the cardiac muscle found in the heart and the smooth muscle found in many of the internal organs, both of which are under involuntary control by the nervous system. Striated muscle consists of interlocking bands of cells capable of contracting with great force, thereby achieving movement. Tendons are those tough, fibrous bands that anchor the striated muscle to bone and allow this movement to occur. A strain is said to have occurred on injury to a muscle or a tendon.

The axial skeleton of the dog consists of the skull, the vertebrae, and the ribcage. The appendicular skeleton consists of the bones making up the front and hind limbs, as well as the pelvis.

Each type is made up of a hard mineralized matrix with bone cells interspersed within. The centers of most bones are hollow and filled with soft bone marrow. This substance is an important component of the host immune system as the location for white blood cell production. Red blood cells and platelets, those structures involved in the blood-clotting scheme, are also produced exclusively within the bone marrow.

Bone is a dynamic tissue, constantly being reabsorbed and regenerated throughout the life of the individual. Long bones grow in length by means of a special structure called an epiphyseal plate, located at the ends of the bones. It is interesting to note that overall health and growth patterns of bony tissue are very dependent on proper nutrition; malnutrition and vitamin and mineral deficiencies can wreak havoc on the development and/or integrity of the skeletal system.

A ligament is different from a tendon in that it connects bone to bone, not muscle to bone. Injuries involving ligaments are properly termed *sprains.*

A *joint* is simply a site at which two bones meet. Not all joints are movable, such as those making up the skull. However, for purposes of discussion, the types of joints referred to most are called *synovial joints.* These joints, found throughout the body, allow for free movement between bones and also serve a shock-absorbing capacity. Each synovial joint consists of ligaments, cartilage on which the ends of the bones move or articulate, joint fluid designed to lubricate the joint and provide nutrition to the articular cartilage, and a tough, fibrous capsule surrounding it all. In addition, some synovial joints contain special pads of cartilage, called *menisci,* which act as super shock absorbers. The knee joint, or stifle, is a good example of such a joint.

Arthritis and Degenerative Joint Disease

Arthritis is the term used in both human and veterinary medicine to describe any type of joint inflammation. *Polyarthritis* describes inflammation involving multiple joints throughout the body. This inflammation might be accompanied by loss of cartilage or bony changes within the joint(s) in question. Causes of arthritis in dogs include infections, autoimmune diseases, and trauma. Even certain drugs, such as sulfa antibiotics, can promote joint inflammation if used indiscriminately.

Osteoarthrosis, or degenerative joint disease, describes the condition in which a cartilage defect or cartilage erosion occurs within a given joint. Though not considered a true inflammatory condition, many people use the term interchangeably with *arthritis.* Osteoarthrosis often occurs as a result of a hereditary defect that may show up at any age. For instance, hip dysplasia is one of the more infamous forms of inheritable degenerative joint disease, and it's one most dog owners have heard of.

But osteoarthrosis doesn't always have to be inherited; it can also occur secondary to joint injury, or it can even be a part of the normal aging process in older dogs.

Regardless of the cause, the clinical signs associated with joint disease are basically the same. Stiffness or lameness involving one or more limbs is often the most obvious sign of a joint problem. In many instances, cold weather and/or exercise aggravate this lameness.

Affected pets might be reluctant to play or jump, and they might become more irritable because of pain. If the hips are involved, inability to rise after lying down is a common clinical complaint. Joints can be swollen and painful to the touch, especially with infectious or autoimmune etiologies. Depression, fever, and loss of appetite could become apparent with the latter as well.

Diagnosis of a joint disorder is based on physical palpation of the joint(s) in question, observing the abnormal gait or movement associated with the disorder, and by obtaining radiographs.

Treatment approaches for arthritis and osteoarthrosis depend on the cause and severity of the condition. In recent years, new medications and innovative surgical techniques have been introduced which show promise in the treatment of canine joint disease and alleviation of the pain associated with it.

Infectious Arthritis

As mentioned above, joint inflammation can be secondary to an infectious process. Bacteria that gain

DID YOU KNOW?

The onset of hip lameness in an older dog may not necessarily be due to arthritis. Vertebral spondylosis also causes similar signs. Radiographs should be used to differentiate the two conditions since treatment modalities are different for each.

entrance into the body's bloodstream can circulate to one or more joints of the body, setting up housekeeping within the joint fluid. Bacterial endocarditis caused by periodontal disease can be an important source of these organisms.

Arthritis can also be a prominent sign in ehrlichiosis, Rocky Mountain Spotted Fever, and Lyme disease. Left untreated, permanent damage to the cartilage and other joint structures can result.

Fever, depression, and painful, swollen joints are prominent clinical signs seen in most cases of infectious arthritis. Laboratory testing, including cultures of the fluid within the joint, may be needed to positively identify the offender. Once this identification is accomplished, specific treatment, usually involving high doses of antibiotics, can be instituted.

Arthritis Due to Autoimmune Disease

Sometimes, an overactive immune system can lead to an arthritic condition. In these instances, immune complexes consisting of antibodies coalesce within the joints of the body, causing inflammation. The resultant polyarthritis can be very painful and debilitating. Fever and a generalized depression are also features of these diseases.

Dogs can get rheumatoid arthritis just as people can. In dogs, this autoimmune-related disease is seen more frequently in the toy breeds than in any others. Another autoimmune disease in dogs that can cause arthritis is called *systemic lupus.* In contrast to rheumatoid arthritis, systemic lupus usually favors the larger breeds of dog, such as German shepherds and St. Bernards.

Special blood tests and/or tests on joint fluid are used to diagnose autoimmune disorders in canines. Treatment usually consists of high dosages of steroid anti-inflammatory medications designed to curb the body's overactive immune response.

Hip Dysplasia

Hip dysplasia refers to an inherited arthritic condition involving one or both hip joints of affected dogs. It presents itself as a partial dislocation, or in severe cases, a complete dislocation of the hip joints. With time, the cartilage lining the joint surfaces wear down because of the abnormal stress and strain placed on the joint, and arthritis results (Fig. 16.1).

FIGURE 16.1 Hip dysplasia is a crippling and painful genetic disease.

Although hip dysplasia can be a problem in any breed, it is seen most often in larger purebred dogs, such as German shepherds, golden retrievers, Labrador retrievers, and St. Bernards. In German shepherds alone, the incidence is thought to be as high as 80 percent!

Because of its inherited nature, signs associated with hip dysplasia may appear as early as 4 weeks of age, although as a rule, most cases show up around 8 to 12 months of age. These clinical signs consist of posterior pain, unsteadiness on the hind limbs, difficulty in rising from a prone position, and a reluctance to move or exercise. Manipulation of the hip joints will reveal obvious pain. In less severe cases, signs might appear only after intense activity and exercise.

Diagnosis of hip dysplasia is achieved by radiographing (X-raying) suspected joints and from a history of this disorder in the dog's genetic bloodline. Several registries aimed at controlling genetic diseases in dogs have developed guidelines and testing procedures for veterinarians in an effort to detect this disease in puppies and young dogs before clinical signs even appear.

In otherwise healthy dogs exhibiting marked lameness due to dysplasia, a number of different surgical techniques can be employed to help relieve pain and lameness caused by the disease, and/or to actually do not have to carry as much weight around on their knee joints as do larger dogs have the most satisfactory postsurgical results.

Following surgical repair, disease-modifying osteoarthritis drugs (DMOADs) can be used to accelerate the healing of any cartilage damaged as a result of the injury.

Hip Luxation

One common sequela to car accidents and other types of trauma involving dogs is dislocation, or *luxation,* of one or both hip joints. These dogs usually have a non-weight-bearing lameness on the affected leg, and it is quite painful. Diagnosis can be made with a physical examination and radiographic X rays of the hips and pelvis.

Treatment involves realigning the hip joints under sedation and strict cage confinement for a period of 3 to 4 weeks as healing takes place. If indicated, special slings designed to prevent reluxation can be applied as well. In severe cases, orthopedic surgery is often needed to stabilize the joint.

Fractures

Most bone fractures in dogs are trauma-related. In isolated instances, metabolic diseases, such as nutritional osteodystrophy and bone cancers, can also be underlying causes as well. A fracture will present itself as a non-weight-bearing lameness, with noticeable swelling and pain in the region of the affected bone. *Crepitus,* or the grinding feel made by broken ends of bone rubbing together, and an anatomical distortion of the site, such as a shortening of an affected limb, might be seen as well.

Diagnosis of a fracture is based on physical exam findings and radiographic X rays. Treatment depends on the type of fracture and the region involved, and it consists of any combination of cage rest, bandaging and splinting, and surgery to reduce and stabilize the fracture.

Minor fractures involving the pelvis will often heal up nicely with cage rest alone, whereas displaced fractures of one or more limbs might require surgical fixation using orthopedic pins, screws, and/or bone plates. In general, uncomplicated fractures usually heal quite readily in dogs.

Osteomyelitis

Infections involving bony tissue within the body are termed *osteomyelitis.* Bacterial osteomyelitis in dogs can occur secondary to a deep bite wound or some other type of penetrating trauma. Open fractures can also predispose to bone infections. Furthermore, fungal organisms, such as histoplasmosis and blastomycosis, can also spread from other areas of the body via the blood and infect bony tissue in dogs.

Dogs with osteomyelitis are lame and feverish, and the affected site is usually quite painful. These signs, combined with the localized swelling that often occurs, can easily be mistaken for a fracture and must be differentiated from such. To do this, radiographic X rays should be taken of the suspected skeletal region. In addition, bone biopsies might be necessary to differentiate some cases of osteomyelitis from bone tumors, and to collect samples for bacterial or fungal cultures.

Because infections that become embedded in bone can be difficult to clear up with antibiotics alone, surgery is usually needed to actually remove those portions of bone severely affected. Drain tubes are placed as well to allow for postsurgical drainage and flushing of the site with medicated solutions. Following surgery, antibiotic therapy might be required for 1 to 2 months. If a fungal organism is involved, medications might need to be given for 4 to 6 months.

Spondylosis Deformans

Spondylosis deformans is a degenerative bone condition that seems to be related to the aging process in some dogs, especially the larger breeds. It is characterized by the development of bony spurs that originate from intervertebral disks and grow to bridge the gap between adjacent vertebrae (Fig. 16.5). These spurs are evident on radiographic X rays. Most dogs afflicted with this disorder show no clinical signs whatsoever. However, in some dogs, pressure and pain originating from these bony growths can cause prominent hind-end weakness and reluctance to move.

Unfortunately, there is no cure for spondylosis deformans. Discomfort associated with the condition can be temporarily relieved with aspirin or other anti-inflammatory medication.

FIGURE 16.5 Bony spurs bridge the gap between vertebrae in dogs with spondylosis deformans.

Metabolic Bone Disease

Metabolic bone diseases are characterized by a thinning and loss of bony mass, predisposing the bone to fractures and to growth deformities. The most common metabolic bone disease seen in dogs is hyperparathyroidism. This condition is characterized by a calcium deficiency within the body that leads to abnormal bone growth and bone resorption as the body tries to correct the low calcium levels in the bloodstream. Hyperparathyroidism can result from feeding dogs all-meat diets (which are naturally low in calcium), or it can result secondary to kidney disease.

Puppies and dogs, who are afflicted with metabolic bone diseases, exhibit lameness, weakness, bone and joint deformities, and spontaneous fractures. Diagnosis is based on radiographic X-ray findings and on blood calcium measurements. Treatment for nutritionally related bone disease obviously involves changes in the diet and calcium supplementation. There is no effective treatment for kidney-related hyperparathyroidism.

Myositis and Myopathies

Myositis is inflammation of muscle tissue that results in pain, weakness, and muscle atrophy (shrinking). Dogs suffering from severe bouts of myositis are reluctant to move and can actually appear as if they are paralyzed by the inflammatory effects on the muscles.

Myositis in dogs can be caused by a number of different disease entities, including toxoplasmosis, leptospirosis, bacterial infections (abscesses), and autoimmune disease. One special type of myositis, called *masticatory myositis,* affects the facial muscles of the affected dogs, causing atrophy and the inability to chew normally. This autoimmune disease is seen most frequently in German shepherds.

Myositis is diagnosed using clinical signs and blood tests designed to detect increased levels in muscle enzymes within the blood. In especially elusive cases, biopsy samples taken from suspected muscle tissue can help veterinarians obtain a definitive diagnosis.

Treatment for myositis is aimed at the underlying cause. If infections are to blame, appropriate antimicrobial or antiparasitic therapy will help relieve the myositis. Anti-inflammatory medications can also be used to relieve the pain and discomfort associated with the inflammation until the underlying cause is treated.

Autoimmune myositis, such as masticatory myositis, is treated with high levels of glucocorticosteroids (such as prednisolone) in an effort to suppress the immune response originally causing the inflammation. The prognosis for complete recovery in dogs with autoimmune myositis is poor, yet with medications, the signs associated with the disorder can be kept under control.

The term *myopathy* refers to abnormal anatomy and/or function of skeletal muscle tissue within the body. Most myopathies in dogs are inherited. Chow chows, golden retrievers, and Irish terriers are examples of breeds that can suffer from inherited myopathies. Dogs suffering from myopathies exhibit abnormal postures, stiff gaits, and generalized shrinking or atrophy of the muscles. Because of the inherited nature of these diseases, the onset of clinical signs usually occurs within a year of age. Unfortunately, there is no effective treatment to stop the progression of these myopathies.

Hernias

A hernia results from a tear or defect in a muscular wall, allowing the contents contained behind the wall to protrude through the opening in the muscle. In dogs, the four most common types of hernias include umbilical hernias, inguinal hernias, perineal hernias, and diaphragmatic hernias.

Umbilical hernias occur on the midline of the dog's stomach at the location of the umbilicus, or the belly button. These usually result from trauma to the muscle wall in this area that occurs as when the bitch severs the umbilical cord after birth. Umbilical hernias pose no real health problems, since fatty tissue is usually the only item to protrude through the opening. These hernias can be sutured and repaired at the time of other elective surgeries.

Inguinal hernias occur in the inguinal region of the abdomen, or that region where the abdominal musculature meets that of the hind legs. They are seen as birth defects or secondary to trauma. These hernias are more serious than umbilical hernias, since the herniated material often includes intestines. As a result, normal digestive processes can be disrupted. Treatment involves surgical replacement of the herniated material back inside the abdomen and suturing the defective muscle.

Perineal hernias result from a weakening of the musculature in the region located beneath the tail on either side of the anus. Seen primarily in older male dogs that have not been neutered, perineal hernias can involve portions of the colon and cause impactions and elimination problems if not surgically corrected. Because the hormone testosterone seems to play a role in the development of these hernias, neutering these dogs is also recommended to prevent a recurrence.

By far the most serious type of hernia is the diaphragmatic hernia. The diaphragm is the thick wall of muscle that separates the thorax or chest cavity from the abdominal contents. Tears or ruptures occurring in this band of muscle, resulting from either inherited defects or traumatic incidents, can allow liver, intestines, and/or other abdominal contents to herniate through into the chest cavity. When this happens, the pressure applied to the crowded lungs and heart results in, among other things, breathing difficulties, weakness, and/or gastrointestinal disturbances.

Definitive diagnosis of a diaphragmatic hernia can be made by coupling history, clinical signs, and a physical examination with radiographic X-ray findings. Surgical repair of the torn diaphragm will alleviate the signs and usually result in a complete recovery.

The Nervous System

The nervous system involves a complex interaction between special elements designed to originate or to carry unique electrochemical charges to and from the various organs within the body. Like its endocrine counterpart, the nervous system initiates and regulates bodily functions and ensures its owner of an awareness to the surrounding environment.

Anatomy and Physiology

The smallest component of the nervous system is the *neuron.* There are over 10 billion of these dynamic cells in the body, and they have the ability to originate and propagate nerve impulses. These result from changes in electrolyte ratios, namely, those of sodium and potassium, occurring across the cell membrane of the neuron. For this reason, abnormalities in the amounts of sodium and potassium within the body can have devastating effects on nervous system function.

Generated impulses are transmitted to their respective targets along special cellular projections, originating from the cell body, called *nerve fibers.* Speeds of transmission along these nerve fibers can reach over 110 meters per second. Groups or bundles of fibers coursing together are what are referred to as *nerves.*

Within the nervous system, neurons can link together to form a continuous chain to allow for the uninterrupted passage of a nerve impulse to its desired destination. A *synapse* is described as this connection between two nerve cells. Special chemical transmitters located at synapses (*neurotransmitters*) transfer the impulses from the end of one neuron to the receptive end of another, allowing the impulse to continue in its travels. Neurotransmitters are also found at the junctions between nerve fibers and their target muscles or organs. In dogs, organophosphate insecticide poisoning exerts its deadly effects by interfering with the normal breakdown of acetylcholine, a neurotransmitter.

The brain is the control center for the entire nervous system. Internally, it is composed of gray matter, which is simply a collection of neuron cell bodies and synapses between nerve cells; and white matter, made up of nerve fibers originating from the neuron cell bodies.

The mammalian brain is divided into three divisions; the cerebrum, the cerebellum, and the brain stem. The largest of the three, the *cerebrum,* is responsible for memory, sensory awareness, learning, and muscular movement. The *cerebellum,* located in back of and immediately beneath the cerebrum, functions to coordinate muscular activity and movement, and control body posture. The final division of the brain, the *brain stem,* serves a variety of functions. It acts as the important intermediary by relaying messages between the cerebrum, cerebellum, and the spinal cord, and influencing activities such as heartbeat, breathing, vision, and hearing. A special portion of the brain stem, called the *hypothalamus,* provides an important link between the nervous system and the endocrine system.

The spinal cord is the major highway of activity for the transmission of nerve impulses between the brain and the rest of the body. It runs along the course of the back within the spinal canal formed by the vertebral column. Like the brain, the spinal cord also contains gray matter and white matter. Large spinal nerves containing numerous smaller nerve fibers branch off from the main cord along its course and travel to respective target muscles and organs. The spinal cord can also serve as coordinating center for certain reflex activities involving the muscles of the limbs without first requiring a nerve impulse to be sent to the brain. Clinicians can often assess the extent of damage to a spinal cord by evaluating these spinal reflex arcs.

Spinal nerves branching off from the spinal cord contain two main types of nerve fibers: *somatic nerve fibers,* which carry information to and from skeletal muscle, skin, joints, and appendages (effects such as muscle contraction, produced by somatic fibers, are said to be under conscious or voluntary control from the brain); and *autonomic nerve fibers,* which innervate glands and internal organs throughout the body. Unlike somatic nerves, autonomic nerves act mainly on reflex, with little voluntary control. Blood pressure, cardiac output, breathing, gastrointestinal motility, body temperature, and hormone secretion are only some of the many vital life functions under the influence of this unique system.

Three thin layers of tissue called meninges cover both the brain and the spinal cord. Between these layers is found a special type of fluid, called *cerebrospinal fluid.* Meninges with their accompanying cerebrospinal fluid serve to protect, support, and nourish the underlying nervous tissue. Abnormal increases in the amount of cerebrospinal fluid can cause serious damage to spinal cord and brain. *Hydrocephalus* is the term used to describe such a condition affecting the brain.

Seizures

Those who own a dog that has suffered from seizures know firsthand how scary these episodes can be. A *seizure* is defined as uncontrollable behavior or muscle activity caused by an abnormal increase in the brain's nervous activities. *Epilepsy* is a term used to describe recurring seizures.

Seizural activity in dogs can be quite obvious or quite subtle. In essence, seizures should be suspected whenever a dog undergoes sporadic, unexplained behavioral changes.

Causes of Seizures

What causes seizures in dogs? The following are some potential causes:

Viral infections (e.g., distemper)

Toxoplasmosis

Fungal infections (e.g., cryptococcosis)

Epilepsy

Hydrocephalus

Brain tumor

Intestinal parasites

Low blood sugar

Low blood calcium

Insecticide poisoning

Heat stroke

Idiopathic (unknown)

Causes for seizures are so numerous that a thorough examination and blood workup by a veterinarian is warranted any time a dog exhibits seizures (Fig. 17.1). In some cases, managing or eliminating an underlying cause will eliminate the seizures. In others, such as with idiopathic epilepsy, there is no known cause, yet by ruling out the other potential causes and establishing a pattern of occurrence, most cases can be effectively managed with anticonvulsant medications. With idiopathic epilepsy, seizures can begin at any stage in life, yet, for the most part, they begin around 1 to 3 years of age. While the cause of idiopathic epilepsy is unknown, it has been shown to be inheritable in some breeds, including beagles and dachshunds.

FIGURE 17.1 Hydrocephalus, or "water on the brain," can cause seizures in affected pets.

Few seizures are actually life threatening, unless some physical harm comes to the dog as a result of the fit. The typical seizure or epileptic fit has three stages, or phases. The first of these, the *preictal* phase, is marked by anxiety and restlessness on the part of the pet. The actual period of the seizure activity, *ictus,* follows next. Its duration might be for only a few seconds or it might be minutes. Certainly the longer the seizure lasts, the more dangerous it is to the health of the pet.

The *postictal phase* following the seizure is characterized by an overall depression or confusion. Postictal dogs can appear to be blind, running into walls and objects, or they might just sleep a lot. This phase can last for a few hours or for days, with the dog returning to its normal state after conclusion of the postictal phase.

There is one seizural presentation called *status epilepticus,* which can prove fatal to a dog. This condition is characterized by a cluster of seizure events occurring in rapid succession. Unless appropriate emergency medication is administered intravenously to stop the seizures, these dogs can lapse into a coma and die. As a result, prompt recognition and action on the part of the pet owner is essential.

When attempting to diagnose the cause of seizural activity, veterinarians will first look at the age and the type of dog involved. For example, seizures occurring in dogs under one year of age commonly result from birth defects or from infectious diseases, such as canine distemper or intestinal parasites, whereas seizures occurring in a very old dog often indicate kidney failure or cancer. In smaller, toy puppies and in active hunting dogs, low blood sugar brought on by illness, stress, or overexertion can be an important inciting cause. Seizures occurring in a pregnant dog or one that has just given birth are more than likely caused by milk fever, or low blood calcium. Finally, as mentioned above, certain breeds are prone to idiopathic epilepsy.

A good history is also vital to help determine the cause of the seizures. Does the dog have access to any type of poisons? Has the dog ever suffered any type of physical trauma, such as being hit by a car, in the past? Has the intensity of the seizures gradually been getting worse or increasing in frequency? The answers to these and other questions can help a veterinarian narrow the choices a bit.

A complete blood profile and urinalysis should be performed to help rule out the metabolic and infectious causes of seizures. Radiographs and ultrasound can prove to be helpful in certain instances as well. If no underlying cause can be found, and the history supports it, a diagnosis of idiopathic epilepsy is made and treatment is started on this premise.

For cases other than idiopathic epilepsy, treatment is geared toward correcting or managing the underlying problem, such as kidney failure, poisoning, or low blood sugar. In instances in which idiopathic epilepsy is suspect, anticonvulsant medications can be used to control or even eliminate the seizural activity.

Dogs suffering from idiopathic epilepsy do not necessarily need to be on any medication unless the seizures last for more than 2 minutes at a time or occur more often than once every 2 months.

Determining the exact dosages of anticonvulsant medications might require frequent adjustments at the start in order to accommodate its individual needs. Pets taking anticonvulsant medication should have liver function tests performed at least annually, since some of these medications can damage the liver over the long term.

Paralysis

Paralysis can be defined as a disruption of the nervous system leading to an impairment of motor function and/or feeling to a particular region or regions of the body. This impairment can be in the form of a spasticity of the muscles in the involved region, or these muscles may become completely limp. In either case, the muscles involved are unable to function in the manner in which they were intended.

Paralysis involving the sensory portion of the nervous system can result in either an increased sensitivity to or a complete absence of pain. Finally, paralysis resulting in the inefficient function of certain internal organs can occur as well if the nerves supplying these structures are disrupted in any way.

Any disease or disorder that traumatizes the brain, spinal cord, and nerves has the potential to cause paralysis. In dogs, some of the more common causes seen by veterinarians include infectious diseases and parasites, being hit by a car, ruptured disks, and in the case of facial muscle paralysis, ear infections.

Treatment of paralysis is geared toward identifying and treating the underlying cause. If it has been caused by trauma, anti-inflammatory agents combined with drugs designed to draw fluid out of the central nervous system might help reverse signs of paralysis, yet their usefulness is dependent on the extent of the nervous injury and how quickly therapy is instituted.

Dogs who have sensory paralysis in a limb might require limb amputation to prevent self-mutilation to the leg. In instances where an irreversible paralysis involves more than one limb, or involves the malfunction of internal organs, pet owners must seriously consider not only their dog's quality of life as a paralytic but their own as well, before prolonged therapeutic or rehabilitative measures are undertaken.

Degenerative Disk Disease

Coursing along the length of the back, the spinal cord travels protected within the bony vertebral column. Separating each vertebra, and located beneath the spinal cord itself, are structures called *intervertebral disks.* These disks serve as cushions between each individual vertebra, absorbing shock and forming joints that allow the vertebral column to bend. Each circular disk is composed of an outer band of tough, fibrous tissue called the *annulus fibrosus* surrounding an inner gelatinous center called the *nucleus pulposus.* This latter structure is responsible for absorbing any shock placed on the disk.

Degenerative disk disease is characterized by the slow degeneration of the nucleus pulposus within one or more intervertebral disks. As these continue to degenerate, they become less resilient and can even calcify, leaving the intervertebral disk without its shock-absorbing unit. As a result, the disks so affected become very susceptible to compression damage, even from the normal day-to-day activity. In dogs so affected, continued stress or sudden trauma to the disk or vertebral column can lead to an overt tearing or rupture of the annulus fibrosus, and extrusion of the degenerating nucleus pulposus. Unfortunately, since the top portion of the annulus is much narrower than the bottom portion, this extrusion usually occurs upward directly into the spinal canal, damaging the spinal cord and associated nerves (Fig. 17.2).

Overt disk ruptures may be classified as partial or complete. In partial ruptures, the annulus can be either stretched or displaced into the spinal canal, or it can partially rupture, allowing a small amount of the nucleus within to escape and pressure the spinal cord. With complete ruptures, the entire nucleus content is allowed to escape into the spinal canal. Obviously, the consequences of such a rupture versus a partial one are much more severe.

Site of disk rupture placing pressure on spinal cord

FIGURE 17.2 Cross section of a ruptured intervertebral disk.

The region of the vertebral column most susceptible to rupture is that portion extending from the last rib to the pelvis. The neck region is another area that can be affected. In a dog suffering from degenerative disk disease, even the slightest wrong move, such as jumping off the couch or running too fast, can cause an affected disk to rupture.

Although any dog can suffer from degenerative disk disease, there do seem to be breed dispositions. The dachshund breed certainly leads the list in the number of cases reported (Fig. 17.3). Other breeds commonly afflicted with degenerative disk disease include poodles, Pekingese, and Lhasa apsos. Beagles and cocker spaniels also have a notable incidence of degenerative disk disease in their neck region.

FIGURE 17.3 Degenerative disk disease is a common cause of paralysis in dachshunds.

Problems with degenerative disk disease can show up in smaller breeds by as early as 3 years of age. In larger dogs, the onset of signs might not occur until they are 6 to 7 years old. Overweight dogs are at an especially high risk of developing complications associated with intervertebral disk disease.

The clinical signs seen with degenerative disk disease and/or disk rupture depend on the location of the lesion and the amount, if any, of the rupture that has taken place. In fact, the extent of pressure or damage to the spinal cord can be estimated on the basis of the signs seen.

Dogs with early or mild cases of disk disease causing slight pressure on the cord will be in considerable pain and reluctant to move. Many will cry or yelp when picked up. If the neck is involved, any manipulations attempted will be met with vigorous protests. These pets often prefer not to be bothered, and to isolate themselves. Appetites are usually reduced as well. Since nerve fibers responsible for coordinated muscle movement run within the outer layers of the spinal cord, owners may also notice weakness and/or incoordination when their pet attempts to walk.

With more severe disk ruptures, damage to the deeper portions of the spinal cord can become a serious factor. When this occurs, partial or complete paralysis of one or more limbs might result, depending on the location of the rupture. If the entire depth of the spinal cord is involved, these animals will also lose all pain sensation to one or all four limbs, again depending on the areas of the spinal cord involved. Such severe cases carry a very grave prognosis, since treatment at this stage is rarely successful.

In most cases, confirmation of a ruptured disk is made via a thorough examination, clinical signs, and with radiographs of the vertebral column. If the exact location of the spinal lesion cannot be pinpointed with regular radiographs, a special test, called a *myelogram,* is performed. This test involves injecting a dye directly into the spinal canal. The dye, which can be identified on a radiograph, helps to outline the cord lesion and demonstrate the extent of the disk rupture.

The type of treatment instituted for disk disease and/or rupture depends on the extent of the damage done by the disk to the spinal cord.

For those dogs showing only pain with some mild incoordination, *a strict 2-week confinement* period either at home or in a hospital setting, is a must! Afterward, short 10- to 15-minute physical therapy sessions, including swimming, can be performed twice daily to help hasten recovery and return to normal function.

For cases in which the affected dog is having great difficulty walking, strict cage confinement combined with anti-inflammatory therapy and other specific treatment is indicated. If the disease is such that the dog is unable to support weight on the limbs at all, even after medical therapy, then surgery is required to reduce the pressure placed on the spinal cord by the ruptured disk.

This surgery, called a *laminectomy* or *hemilaminectomy,* works best if performed within the first 24 hours of the injury. It involves the removal of part of the vertebra over the affected cord segment. By eliminating the enclosed space through which the spinal cord runs, the pressure on the cord caused by the inflammation is allowed to dissipate. At the same time, surgeons often elect to perform intervertebral disk fenestrations, aimed at removing the offending nucleus pulposus from the disk in question and from adjacent disks as well.

The prognosis is poor for those pets that are unable to walk and have lost deep pain sensation in their legs as a result of a ruptured disk. The loss of deep pain indicates that the entire depth of the spinal cord is invariably involved, and surgical salvage procedures are rarely successful.

In those instances where surgery is unsuccessful, or in which paralysis is permanent, euthanasia is not always the only option left to the owner. Special "wheelchairs" for dogs have been developed for dogs paralyzed by a ruptured disk or other neurological accidents. Although not for every patient, these carts can help afford mobility to select patients willing to wear the apparatus and an alternative for those owners willing to devote much time and care to their paralyzed pet. If you think such a device could be applicable to your own pet's situation, ask your veterinarian for more details regarding this and other management options available.

Pet owners can take specific measures to help protect their dogs from ruptured disks. The first and most important is to prevent obesity. Overweight dogs are prime candidates for such complications; hence, they should be placed on a strict diet to reduce this risk factor.

Jumping should be discouraged in dogs predisposed to intervertebral disk disease. Many ruptured disks result from pets jumping off and on furniture. Pets so inclined should be assisted up or down whenever possible. Even better than assisting the pet, a small chair or ramp can be placed in front of your dog's favorite piece of furniture to allow easier access.

Whenever lifting a dog with back problems, be sure to firmly support both the front and hind ends, keeping the back as straight as possible. This stabilizes the position of the spine and affords you, the handler, with better and safer control should the pet struggle (Fig. 17.4).

Surgical intervertebral disk fenestration is often used as a preventive measure in dogs with a history of intervertebral disk disease bouts. As mentioned before, this involves the penetration and removal of the nucleus pulposus from one or more intervertebral disks suspected of causing current or future problems. By doing so, the danger associated with later disk rupture is removed with the nucleus.

Vertebral Instability (Canine Wobbler Syndrome)

Seen primarily in Great Danes and Doberman pinschers, vertebral instability is characterized by instability and deformities in the

FIGURE 17.4 Whenever handling a dog with degenerative disk disease, always keep the back straight and well supported.

vertebra of the neck region, leading to pressure on the spinal cord in that region. The condition in these breeds is hereditary in nature; however, trauma can predispose any dog to canine wobbler syndrome. Signs associated with vertebral instability include incoordination, weakness, and paralysis. Pain is rarely a feature of this disease. Diagnosis of vertebral instability is made with radiographic X rays. Treatment involves the use of anti-inflammatory medication to reduce the spinal cord inflammation. Surgical decompression of the spinal cord is also warranted in severe cases.

Myelopathies

Myelopathies are degenerative diseases that strike the spinal cord and nerve fibers coursing throughout the body. These diseases involve the gradual loss of the outer, conductive coating that surrounds certain nerve fibers, called *myelin.* This loss impairs the fiber's ability to transmit nerve impulses. Seen primarily in older, larger breeds of dogs, especially German shepherds, myelopathies are characterized by muscular incoordination, weakness, and atrophy. As the nerves innervating the hindlegs are affected, a turning under or dragging of the hind feet may result. In fact, the hind-limb weakness exhibited by some dogs with degenerative myelopathy is often mistaken for arthritis of the hips or spondylosis deformans of the spine. However, unlike the others, pain is rarely a factor in this disease.

A myelopathy is tentatively diagnosed using historical findings, clinical signs, and reflex testing. Dogs afflicted with this condition will exhibit weak to absent reflex activity in their limbs. Electromyograms (EMGs) may be performed as well to evaluate electrical activity associated with the muscle tissue of the body.

Unfortunately, because an exact cause of most myelopathies, other than genetics, remains a mystery, there is no effective treatment to date. Vitamin therapy has been used in some instances to slow the progression of the disease, yet motor incapacitation is inevitable.

The Endocrine System

Within the bodies of all mammals, a complex network of glands (the endocrine system) is responsible for the production and secretion of special proteins and lipids (fats) called *hormones*. In turn, these hormones serve to regulate many vital functions within the body, from growth and development to digestion and utilization of nutrients. Like the nervous system, the endocrine system assumes a regulatory role within the body, and its proper function is essential to the overall health of the animal. Without the endocrine glands and their hormones, a state of chaos would quickly ensue within the body, as the functional harmony existing between the various organ systems would cease to exist.

Anatomy and Physiology

Hormones can be protein in nature, or they can be fashioned from special fatty components, known as *steroids*—which is one of the most misused and widely misunderstood terms in today's society.

Corticosteroids are a special group of steroids produced by the adrenal glands that are vital to many everyday functions within the body. Synthetic derivatives of this steroid group are commonly used, among other things, to reduce pain and inflammation resulting from musculoskeletal injuries.

Androgens (e.g., testosterone) and estrogens, the sex hormones that influence reproductive activity and secondary sexual characteristics, are also types of steroid hormones produced naturally within the body.

Anabolic steroids, probably the most notorious members of the steroid family, are actually synthetic (human-manufactured) derivatives of the male androgenic steroid hormones. This is the group that has been largely exploited by athletes for increased muscular strength and size.

Although all the different classes of steroids mentioned above, whether natural or synthetic, share a similar structural design, it is easy to see that their functions and effects differ greatly between classes.

Both protein and steroid-type hormones are secreted directly into the bloodstream from the glands or organs that produce them, and circulate to their specific target cells or organs, where they exert their effect. The amount of hormone required to exert its particular effect is precise. If present in too great a quantity, or if supplies are deficient, abnormal function of its target cells or organs result. As a result, hormonal activities within the body are governed by complex negative feedback mechanisms, which ensure proper blood levels at all times. Unfortunately, certain disease conditions involving the endocrine glands and organs can disrupt this delicate balance, which can pose serious health problems.

The *hypothalamus,* located at the bottom portion of the brain stem, functions as an integration center between the nervous system and the endocrine system. Nervous system functions of the hypothalamus include regulation of body temperature, emotional behavior and sleep, and control of food and water intake. As an endocrine organ, the hypothalamus secretes the hormone *antidiuretic hormone* (ADH), which controls the water balance within the body; *oxytocin,* which stimulates lactation and uterine contractions; and a variety of other hormones that exert control over the pituitary gland.

The pituitary gland produces hormones that have effects on other endocrine glands, such as the thyroid and adrenal glands. In addition, pituitary hormones also influence growth and reproductive patterns. In dogs, *Cushing's disease,* a condition characterized by an oversecretion of adrenal gland hormones, is most commonly caused by a tumor of the pituitary gland.

Hormones produced by the thyroid gland control the rate of growth and metabolism within the body, as well as reduce calcium levels within the bloodstream. Closely associated with the thyroid gland are the parathyroid glands, which produce a hormone that counteracts the action of a certain thyroid hormone by increasing blood calcium levels. This balance between the thyroid and parathyroid glands helps maintain proper blood levels of calcium at all times. Too much parathyroid hormone can result in excess resorption of bony tissue, resulting in metabolic bone disease.

The adrenal glands produce a variety of hormones, each exerting unique effects within the body. Among other things, adrenal hormones influence carbohydrate and protein metabolism and storage (cortisol, cortisone), help the kidneys regulate sodium and potassium levels (aldosterone), and control blood pressure and heart rate (epinephrine and norepinephrine). Certain organs can double as endocrine glands. The pancreas is not responsible only for producing digestive enzymes; it secretes two hormones, insulin and glucagon, both involved in carbohydrate (sugar) metabolism within the body. Insulin functions to lower blood sugar by increasing its uptake and utilization by the body organs. Counteracting the effects of insulin, glucagon increases blood sugar levels by decreasing its uptake into the liver and fatty tissue. Diabetes mellitus is a disease in which not enough insulin is produced by the pancreas, prohibiting cells and organs from extracting carbohydrates out of the bloodstream.

Other organs exhibiting endocrine functions include the stomach, which produces hormones that regulate digestion; the ovaries and testicles, which, together with the adrenal gland and placenta (in pregnant females), produce the sex hormones; the kidneys, which secrete hormones that influence blood flow and filtration within the kidneys themselves; and the thymus gland, with hormonal activity that influences the cells of the immune system.

The Use of Steroids in Veterinary Medicine

If there ever was a group of drugs that revolutionized both human and veterinary medicine, it is steroids. These chemicals are produced naturally by the body and have been produced synthetically. Although they are vital to life and can be used therapeutically in a wide variety of useful ways, steroids are also, in the public's eye, one of the most misunderstood of all drug groups. When the word *steroid* is mentioned to the layperson, images of muscle-bound athletes or of unhealthy side effects are often conjured up. Yet what most of them fail to realize is that, used correctly, steroids can be safe and unsurpassed in effectiveness in treating a wide variety of diseases and conditions.

One point to keep in mind is that *steroid* is a catchall term used to describe those compounds sharing a similar, yet not necessarily identical, biochemical makeup. For instance, glucocorticosteroids, the types used most frequently in veterinary medicine, should not be confused with anabolic steroids, which are actually synthetic derivatives of the male sex hormone testosterone (these are the steroids that have caused so much controversy within athletic circles). Although the chemical makeup of anabolic steroids may be similar to that of glucocorticosteroids, their functions and effects are not. The sex hormones, such as estrogen, progesterone, and testosterone, and the mineralocorticosteroids, probably the closest group in biochemical structure to glucocorticosteroids than any of the others, are also types of steroid hormones produced by the body.

Glucocorticosteroids

The glucocorticosteroids are by far the class of steroid used most in veterinary medicine, Some names from this group that you might be familiar with include hydrocortisone, prednisone, prednisolone, and dexamethasone. The first is a steroid produced naturally by the body; the latter ones are synthetic steroids created in the laboratory.

Glucocorticosteroids can be further classified into groups according to the duration of their effects once they are administered for treatment purposes. For instance, hydrocortisone is considered a short-acting corticosteroid, with effects lasting anywhere from 8 to 12 hours. Prednisone and prednisolone are considered intermediate-acting steroids, with durations of action up around 12 to 36 hours. Finally, corticosteroids such as dexamethasone are long-acting drugs, exerting their effects for up to 48 hours after administration.

Therapeutically, what are glucocorticosteroids used for? In veterinary medicine, their primary uses are to reduce inflammation associated with disease, to regulate immune responses, and to combat shock. They are the first lines of defense against autoimmune diseases, or those diseases caused by an overactive immune system. Pet owners probably know them best for their ability to provide prompt relief from itching and skin irritation in those dogs suffering from allergies.

Although glucocorticosteroids can prove to be useful and even life-saving in many instances, they can't be employed with indiscretion. For example, because they do have the ability to suppress the immune system, especially at high doses, glucocorticosteroids need to be used with caution or avoided altogether in those instances in which severe parasitic, fungal, or bacterial disease is present. Also, if given to a pet during pregnancy, these steroids could cause premature labor and abortion. Even their use on the eyes should be avoided in those cases where an early ulceration has occurred on one or both corneas, since doing so could actually make the ulcers worse and lead to loss of vision. Finally, as with other anti-inflammatory medications, corticosteroids can also upset the gastrointestinal tract.

Long-term, indiscriminant use of glucocorticosteroids can eventually be detrimental to the health of a pet. Granted, the natures of some diseases do require extended and sometimes even lifetime use of these compounds. In such cases, these pets must be placed on a strict treatment regimen and be monitored closely by a veterinarian while they are on the medication.

The problem with the daily use of corticosteroids rests in the fact that whenever they are administered to a pet either through injection, orally, or even topically on the skin, the body's hypothalamus and pituitary gland signal to the adrenal glands to stop their natural production of glucocorticosteroids. If the adrenal glands remain dormant for any appreciable amount of time, they might actually lose the ability to make their own corticosteroids. If this happens, and if the corticosteroid therapy is abruptly stopped, the pet's life could be endangered because of a lack of corticosteroids within the body. Similarly, as high levels of glucocorticosteroids remain in the bloodstream, over time, signs of Cushing's disease could actually develop.

Because of these potential problems, pets that must be on daily glucocorticosteroid therapy for more than 2 weeks are placed thereafter on alternate-day dosing regimens using a short- or intermediate-acting synthetic steroids, such as prednisolone, at the lowest possible dose. Giving the corticosteroid every other day instead of daily should prevent total suppression of the adrenal glands and allow the body to continue to produce its own steroids. In addition, by using the lowest dosage possible in this fashion, there is less chance of causing Cushing-type disease. If the situation ever arises where the corticosteroid therapy is to be halted, then a gradual weaning off of the medication, usually in the form of a slow reduction in dosage over four to six weeks time, is indicated.

Hypothyroidism

The thyroid gland, through production of thyroid hormones, functions to influence nutrient and oxygen utilization within the body, hence affecting overall metabolism. As a result, deficiencies in thyroid hormone or interference with its function can have profound effects on the body. In dogs, immune system malfunctions, iodine deficiencies, incomplete thyroid gland development, and pituitary gland malfunctions can all lead to a condition of hypothyroidism. Predisposed breeds include cocker spaniels, Dobermans, dachshunds, beagles, and golden retrievers.

Clinical signs associated with this disorder are varied, owing to the tremendous scope of thyroid hormone function. Dogs with hypothyroidism tend to be lethargic, sleeping a lot and tiring easily after exercise. Some exhibit a profound intolerance to cold floors or cool environmental temperatures. Puppies so affected might seem to be slow learners when it comes to training. As the skin around the face of these dogs often thickens as a result of the disease, a dog's voice might change to a lower pitch, and facial features might appear droopy or sad.

In addition, hypothyroid dogs may also have poor appetites, yet still gain weight. Over 50 percent of dogs afflicted with hypothyroidism will exhibit changes to the skin and haircoat. A loss of the undercoat occurs, resulting in a thinned, poor-looking coat. Skin thickening occurs, and secondary seborrhea is not uncommon. Finally, eye problems, neurologic disorders, repro-

FACT OR FICTION

Hypothyroidism is a common cause of obesity in dogs. **FACT.** In fact, all obese dogs should be tested for this condition. If diagnosed, the treatment is simple and rapid weight loss can be achieved.

ductive infertility, and arthritis could all have their roots in a thyroid disorder.

A veterinarian can evaluate your pet's thyroid function right at the office. A simple blood test can be used to screen thyroid hormone levels within the body (Fig. 18.1). If a problem is found, then more extensive thyroid function tests may be ordered to help determine the extent of the problem. If a dog is taking corticosteroid hormones for other problems at the time of the testing, the results could come back

FIGURE 18.1 A simple blood test can be used to assess the thyroid status of a dog.

falsely low. As a rule, however, if clinical signs correlate with blood test results, then it is safe to assume that a condition of true hypothyroidism exists.

Regardless of the underlying cause, treatment of hypothyroidism in dogs involves daily supplementation with synthetic thyroid hormone tablets. Thyroid hormone levels will need to be monitored during the initial stages of treatment to ensure that the proper dosage is being met. For the most part, this is a medication that affected dogs will need to stay on the rest of their lives. Clinical response to medicating is usually seen within 2 weeks after initiation, with resolution of signs occurring soon after.

Hyperadrenocorticism (Cushing's Disease)

Steroid hormones, specifically the class known as *glucocorticosteroids,* produced by the adrenal glands, serve over 50 vital functions within the body. Some of the more important ones have to deal with carbohydrate, protein, and fat utilization and with maintaining water and electrolyte balance within the body. Veterinarians fighting allergic reactions or inflammation in dogs rely on glucocorticosteroids for their anti-inflammatory effects when given at low dosages. Similarly, since high doses of glucocorticosteroids can suppress the immune system, they are quite useful in treatments against autoimmune diseases in dogs, including *pemphigus,* a disease that causes severe skin lesions in affected dogs.

Unfortunately, since steroid hormones help maintain a delicate balance within the body, an overproduction of these hormones within the body can upset this balance. This is precisely what happens in Cushing's disease. An overproduction of glucocorticosteroids from the adrenal glands occurs within the body, usually the result of a tumor affecting one or both glands, or, more commonly, a tumor affecting the pituitary gland. The disease is most common in dogs over 8 years of age. Furthermore, poodles, boxers, and dachshunds seem to be afflicted with a greater frequency than do other breeds.

Some of the clinical signs seen in dogs with Cushing's disease include a marked increase in water and food consumption, an increase in elimination activity, lethargy and exercise intolerance, and a generalized reduction in muscle size and tone, which, when it affects the muscles of the abdominal wall, leads to a characteristic pot-bellied appearance (Fig. 18.2).

The skin and coat changes that occur in a dog with Cushing's disease might be the first clues as to the existence of the problem. A generalized thinning of the haircoat and skin will be seen, with flakiness, pigmentation, and secondary infections. Eye problems are common in these dogs, too, with reoccurring ulcers affecting the cornea. Because high levels of steroids have a suppressing influence on the immune system, secondary infections, especially bladder infections, are often seen in these dogs as well.

FIGURE 18.2 Hair loss and a pot-bellied appearance are both frequent signs seen with Cushing's disease.

Finally, if a tumor is present in the pituitary gland at the base of the brain, neurological problems might occur as pressure is increased on the brain.

These signs can lead a clinician to suspect Cushing's disease, but it usually requires more extensive blood testing and radiographic X rays to confirm a diagnosis. Measuring actual blood levels of steroids within the bloodstream is one way to test for Cushing's disease; other methods include injecting small amounts of special synthetic hormones, designed to alter the production of steroids within the body, into the dog and measuring the body's response to them. If these hormones cannot alter the steroid production, then a diagnosis can be made.

Once a dog is diagnosed with Cushing's disease, therapy may be instituted in a number of ways. Surgical removal of the tumor in either the adrenal glands and/or the pituitary gland can be attempted, yet this is a very difficult procedure associated with many postoperative complications.

Chemotherapy can be employed to target the adrenal glands and reduce the amount of steroids being produced by them. Used correctly, this treatment can reduce or eliminate the clinical signs seen and greatly improve a dog's quality of life. Close veterinary monitoring for the appearance of side effects during the initial treatment stage is recommended. Therapy is usually required for life.

Because of the intense management required with these modes of therapy, some pet owners prefer to stick to conservative treatment when dealing with this disease in their dog. In these cases, dogs should be placed on high-protein diets to counteract protein loss caused by the disease. In addition, treating secondary problems as they arise—such as skin infections, bladder infections, and corneal ulceration—is necessary. Because the tumors responsible for Cushing's disease are usually slow-growing, most dogs can live up to 2 years with this treatment approach alone.

Hypoadrenocorticism (Addison's Disease)

While Cushing's disease is caused by too many corticosteroids circulating within the body, *Addison's disease* is caused by the exact opposite: inadequate amounts of circulating corticosteroids. This includes not only the glucocorticosteroids produced by the adrenal glands, but the mineralocorticoids as well. Because the latter are so vital at maintaining a fluid and electrolyte balance within the body, Addison's disease can be acutely life-threatening in the affected individual.

Causes of this disease in dogs can include tumors, infections, autoimmune diseases, and toxins. It can also occur secondarily to overtreatment with corticosteroids

The clinical signs seen resemble those exhibited by pets afflicted with viral or parasitic gastroenteritis: vomiting, diarrhea, and dehydration. Loss of appetite and weight loss accompanies these signs as well, yet there might be an increase in water consumption. Because the levels of sodium and potassium, two electrolytes vital to proper muscle contraction, are disrupted, profound muscle weakness, including a slowing of the rate at which the heart muscle contracts, are also observed. In severe cases, collapse of the entire circulatory system, with shock and then death, have been documented.

Diagnosis of Addison's disease can be based on the history (i.e., long-term corticosteroid therapy), clinical signs seen, and determining the ratio of sodium to potassium in the bloodstream. Marked increases in potassium and decreases in sodium are indicative of primary Addison's disease. Physical examination and electrocardiograms will reveal abnormal heart activity in these patients as well.

If Addison's disease is diagnosed or suspected, treatment should be instituted immediately. Dehydration is compensated with intravenous fluids, and injections of mineralocorticoids are administered to stabilize fluid and electrolyte levels.

For cases of primary Addison's disease, periodic injections with mineralocorticoids will be required throughout the dog's life to prevent relapses from occurring. If the condition was caused by the sudden cessation of glucocorticosteroid therapy, such therapy is reinstituted and then gradually tapered off over weeks to months.

Hyperparathyroidism

The parathyroid glands, which are closely associated with the thyroid glands in dogs, produce a hormone that is responsible for increasing calcium levels in the blood by drawing stores of this mineral from bone and other regions of the body. Hyperparathyroidism is a condition initiated by a deficiency of calcium within the bloodstream. This can result from administering diets that are high in phosphorus (nutritional hyperparathyroidism), such as all-meat diets, or, more commonly in older dogs, from increased phosphorus levels in the body caused by kidney disease. When such a calcium deficiency occurs, the parathyroid glands respond by secreting large amounts of hormone, which draws calcium out of bones in an attempt to normalize blood calcium levels. Over time, these bones become weakened and prone to stress injury.

Clinical signs of this metabolic disease in dogs include lameness, weakness, bone deformities, and spontaneous fractures. A definitive diagnosis can be made by evaluating blood calcium levels and relating them to historical or other laboratory findings (e.g., history of poor diet or kidney disease, laboratory evidence of kidney disease).

Treatment for nutritional hyperparathyroidism includes dietary modification and calcium supplementation. Unfortunately, there is no effective treatment for hyperparathyroidism caused by kidney disease except for treatment of the kidney disease itself.

Sex Hormone Imbalances

Although rare, imbalances involving testosterone, estrogen, and progesterone have been known to occur. For instance, in male dogs with excessive circulating estrogens, skin disorders, hair loss, increased skin pigmentation, enlargement of the mammary glands, seborrhea, otitis externa, and behavioral changes can result. Estrogen-secreting tumors involving the testicles, called *Sertoli cell tumors,* are the main cause of increased estrogen levels in dogs. Cryptorchid canines (those with one or both testicles retained within the abdomen) are at highest risk of developing such a tumor. Neutering those dogs so affected is the only effective way to treat this disorder. In some cases, giving testosterone supplements may be required as well for full abatement of clinical signs.

Similarly, if a female dog has too much circulating estrogens in her system, she can suffer from the same clinical signs as her male counterpart. Hair loss, seborrhea, and increased pigmentation of the skin, especially in flank areas, are common signs. Performing an ovariohysterectomy on these dogs will effectively reduce the amount of circulating estrogens and clinically effect a cure.

A condition known as *hypoestrogenism,* characterized by inadequate amounts of the estrogen hormone within the body, has been documented in older female dogs that were spayed at an early age. A gradual hair loss, especially around the hind end of these dogs, could be all that is seen in these pets. In addition, dribbling of urine has been reported in older dogs suffering from this lack of estrogen. Special medications designed to increase sphincter tone to the bladder can be employed to help diminish this latter clinical sign.

Diabetes Mellitus

Diabetes mellitus is one of the more common endocrine diseases affecting dogs. The condition is caused by a deficiency in the hormone called *insulin,* which is normally created by the pancreas. Insulin is responsible for regulating the uptake of blood sugar, or glucose, into cells and tissues of the body for use as energy. Any disease involving the pancreas, including chronic pancreatitis, can cause deficiencies in this hormone. In addition, autoimmune disease, in which the dog's body creates antibodies against its own insulin, has also been known to occur. Finally, there is evidence that, in dogs, the propensity for diabetes can be inherited. Middle-aged female dogs seem to be at greater risk.

When a deficiency in insulin does occur, this transfer of glucose from the bloodstream to the tissues does not occur; hence, blood glucose levels become elevated. At the same time, the cells, tissues, and organs of the body don't receive the proper nutrition needed to maintain their function, and begin to look for other sources of energy in the body, namely, proteins and fats. And this is where the problems start.

Dogs with this disease will exhibit an increase in water consumption and, consequently, urination. As the body calls on these alternate sources of energy, pronounced weight loss results. In addition, as body fat stores are called on and metabolized for energy, an excess of ketone bodies, by-products of fatty breakdown, accumulate within the body. In large amounts, these ketone bodies have the ability to damage the liver and to depress the nervous system, leading to depression and coma. Over time, the increased glucose levels within the blood can lead to cataracts and blindness.

Diabetic dogs have a decreased resistance to infection; as a result, they often suffer from chronic skin and bladder infections. Damage to small capillaries within the body caused by diabetes mellitus can lead to secondary kidney disease, blindness, and gangrene of the skin and extremities.

The clinical signs associated with diabetes mellitus are similar to conditions such as Cushing's disease, kidney disease, and diabetes insipidus; therefore, a thorough laboratory workup is needed to ensure a correct diagnosis. Blood tests on dogs with diabetes mellitus will consistently reveal elevated glucose levels, and evaluation of urine samples will reveal the same. Such findings, along with the ruling out of other potential causes of the clinical signs, can lead to a definitive diagnosis of diabetes mellitus.

Diabetes mellitus can be classified as either uncomplicated or complicated. Uncomplicated cases might exhibit mild to moderate signs of the disease, yet none are truly life-threatening. In contrast, dogs diagnosed with the disease and exhibiting marked depression, vomiting, diarrhea, heavy breathing, and/or severe weight loss should all be considered complicated cases and should always be considered medical emergencies. In most of these cases, the high levels of ketone acids produced as a result of increased fat metabolism lower the pH of the blood significantly enough to cause the harmful effects represented by the clinical signs. These dogs usually become severely dehydrated at the same time.

Treatment consists of immediate hospitalization with intravenous infusion of replacement fluids, medications designed to increase the pH of the blood (if, indeed, the pH is too low), and insulin. The levels of insulin given and corresponding blood glucose readings must be monitored closely, since too much insulin is even worse than not having enough. If excess insulin is given, the pet could quickly become hypoglycemic and suffer convulsions. Good monitoring and careful planning on the part of a veterinarian will help prevent this.

Often, dogs are presented with complicated cases of diabetes mellitus because of some underlying disorder adding to the problem. For instance, many of these dogs suffer from coexisting disorders such as obesity, pancreatitis, kidney disease, and heart disease. To increase the chances of recovery from a complicated case of diabetes mellitus, these disorders must be addressed at the same time.

When a pet finally comes home, it will be the owner's job to ensure that the proper insulin dosage (as prescribed by the veterinarian) is given each day and that proper adjustments are made (per veterinary instruction) as needed.

Keep in mind that it is better to give a diabetic dog too little insulin than to give too much. Adjustments to insulin dosages need to be made slowly and carefully in these uncomplicated cases. Giving too much insulin can cause insulin shock (hypoglycemia), which can be fatal. Signs of this can include trembling, weakness, incoordination, and, if it is not rapidly corrected, seizures. Owners of diabetic pets should always keep a bottle of pancake syrup or honey on hand in case of insulin shock. Two tablespoons or more given orally should be used if such a reaction is suspected.

Owners must keep accurate records each day as to their pet's urine glucose readings, insulin dosage, overall attitude and/or clinical signs that day, and appetite. These will not only come in useful in regulating insulin levels, but such records can provide a veterinarian with valuable information should a question or problem ever arise.

Strict feeding schedules for dogs with diabetes mellitus must be followed. Rations high in fiber and protein with restricted fat and special sources of carbohydrates are ideal for maintaining the diabetic dog.

Diabetic dogs must also be kept on a consistent exercise program, since fluctuations in the amount of exercise performed from one day to the other can affect blood glucose levels and make proper insulin dosing difficult. If a dog is obese to start with, it will need to be placed on a weight reduction program.

Finally, intact female dogs that are diabetic should be spayed. By eliminating female hormonal influences on glucose levels in the body, achieving and maintaining proper insulin levels will be greatly enhanced.

Diabetes Insipidus

Diabetes insipidus should not be confused with diabetes mellitus, which involves abnormal glucose metabolism. Diabetes insipidus involves abnormal water metabolism, and it occurs when there is a lack of the hormone ADH (antidiuretic hormone). ADH is normally produced by the hypothalamus of the brain, yet it exerts its effects on the kidneys, causing water to be recaptured from the kidney tubules rather than being lost in the urine. As a result, the delicate water balance within the body is maintained with this hormone's influence.

Too little ADH may be produced by the hypothalamus as the result of an inherited defect or a head trauma that damages the hypothalamus. In addition, defects present in the kidneys at birth or acquired later in life can render the kidneys unresponsive or only partially responsive to the effects of ADH. If any of these situations occur, then diabetes insipidus results.

Dogs with diabetes insipidus exhibit increased urinations, incontinence (especially at night), and an increased water consumption. Routine laboratory work usually reveals nothing too significant except for very low urine specific gravity (dilute urine). However, a laboratory workup will help rule out other potential causes of the clinical signs seen, such as diabetes mellitus, Cushing's disease, and kidney disease. If these are ruled out, then a tentative diagnosis of diabetes insipidus becomes more likely. To obtain a definitive diagnosis, special laboratory tests, such as water-deprivation tests, plasma ADH determinations, and ADH trials, are required.

Diabetes insipidus caused by poor ADH production from the hypothalamus can be treated by administering a natural or synthetic ADH supplement. These can be administered by injection or by drops applied directly into the eyes. Such treatment will be required on a daily basis to control the clinical signs. Therapy is usually for life.

Diabetes insipidus caused by kidneys that are nonresponsive to ADH is more difficult to control. Special drugs can be utilized to slow water loss and reduce thirst in dogs so affected.

Providing free access to water at all times is the most important therapeutic measure for all dogs suffering from diabetes insipidus. Doing so will help prevent dehydration and its undesirable effects from setting in as a result of the excess water loss through the kidneys.

The prognosis for most dogs with diabetes insipidus is good to excellent, assuming that medical therapy and free access to water is provided. Because these pets are prone to dehydration, any signs of illness such as loss of appetite, vomiting, or diarrhea warrant prompt veterinary attention.

Cats

If there ever was a creature that has stirred the fascination and admiration of humankind throughout the ages, it is the cat. Cat fanciers have existed for thousands of years, captivated by the personal yet seemingly independent nature of these graceful animals.

The cat is a descendant of *Miacis*, a catlike creature that lived over 40 million years ago and gave rise to not only the modern-day cat but to the dog and the bear as well. The modern cat, *Felis catus*, is a direct descendent of *Felis libyca*, the African wildcat, and *Felis sylvestris*, a European wildcat with a tabbylike appearance (i.e., with a mottled or striped haircoat).

Interestingly, over the years, the domestic cat has undergone only limited selective breeding. As a result, it has the closest ties to its "wild" ancestors when compared to other domesticated animals. Evidence of this can be seen in the similar size and anatomic features of all cats. Except for certain muzzle and coat lengths, as well as color, different breeds of cats all look alike. Compare this, if you will, to the dog, which comes in a multitude of sizes, shapes, and varieties, all brought on by selective breeding.

DID YOU KNOW?

The first evidence of feline domestication dates back over 9000 years!

Cats first associated with humans back in the Stone Age, where they probably hung around camp for food scraps and leftovers. It was not until ancient Egyptian times that humans and felines became true companions. Cats were used to hunt birds and catch fish for the Egyptians, and to rid their granaries of rats and mice. So revered did the cat become in this society that goddesses were fashioned after its image, and separate burial grounds were set aside for the mummified remains of those felines that departed from this world.

As the world trade routes opened up and the high seas became an important means of interaction between countries and peoples, the cat spread throughout the civilized world. Longhaired varieties soon developed, and became highly favored in the European community, favored that is, until the Dark Ages, when superstition began to run rampant and cats became symbols of evil and witchcraft. They quickly lost their preferred status, and the European cat population fell into decline. Unfortunately, when the Crusaders returned from the Holy Land carrying plague-laden brown rats with them on their ships, there were few cats around to meet this threat. As the bubonic plague devastated Europe, the importance of the predatory nature of the cat increased, and numbers were soon back on the rise. As they regained status in society, cats found their way back into the farmer's granaries and into the courts of royalty. To this day, in the eyes of millions of cat fanciers, they still command a royal status in our society!

Choosing the Right Cat for You

When it comes time to choose that perfect feline companion, what criteria should you follow to be certain your selection is a sound one? Some questions you should ask yourself include the following:

- Why do I want a cat in the first place?

- What type of cat do I want?

- How will my new cat affect my existing pets?

- Am I willing to devote the time and money needed to be a responsible pet owner?

Your answers to these questions will have great bearing on the type of cat you will ultimately choose.

Why Do You Want a Cat?

Regardless of breed, be they genetically pure or genetic blends, cats make great companions and can fulfill a variety of roles. Obviously, when making your selection, keep your particular wants and needs

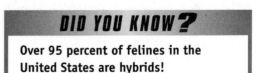

DID YOU KNOW?

Over 95 percent of felines in the United States are hybrids!

FIGURE 19.1 Cats can be just as social and loving as dogs.

in mind. Although you may want your cat to fulfill several roles, know what the primary one will be, and base your selection on that decision.

Cats for Companionship

Ask any feline aficionados you know, and they will tell you that the companionship that a cat can provide is hard to beat! Although cats have gained the reputation of being "independent" and oblivious to their owner's wants and needs, such is not always the case. Many cats that are socialized to people at an early age will form special bonds with their owners that rival those formed between dogs and people (Fig. 19.1).

Cats for Children

Cats can be an excellent tool for educating children about responsibility and about life itself! If this is your reason for wanting a cat, keep these guidelines in mind. First, for maximum benefit and enjoyment, wait until your children are at least 5 years old before acquiring a new pet. Younger children, some of whom might just be starting to crawl or walk, stand a greater chance of being accidentally hurt by a playful feline than do older children. On the contrary, older children are better equipped to learn about and/or undertake responsibilities associated with pet ownership, and can become active participants in the care of your new cat, including litterbox duties! And that is why you wanted the cat in the first place, right?

Choose a kitten with an outgoing personality, one that can stand up to the rigors of ownership by a child. Shy, introverted kittens rarely satisfy the energy requirements of children. Such cats might be difficult to socialize and could turn aggressive if mentally traumatized by an overzealous child.

Mixed breeds (domestic shorthairs, mediumhairs, or longhairs) are preferred over purebred cats as pets for children, simply because they tend to be less excitable than some of the more emotional purebreds.

If purchasing a kitten, limit your selection to one that is between 6 and 12 weeks old. Because socialization naturally occurs during this time, a greater bond will form between it and your child. Along the same lines, a cat older than 12 weeks of age should not be placed with children unless it is correctly socialized to children. One word of caution: Be certain that your child is not allowed to abuse or hurt the new pet during this sensitive socialization period. Such adverse interaction could ruin their relationship for years to come, as the kitten will have learned to associate your child with pain and abuse. It is every parent's responsibility to teach their children that their cuddly new friend is not a toy, and that it needs to be handled with loving kindness and gentleness.

Cats as Sources of Income

Unless you are planning to become (or are already) a professional cat breeder, don't purchase a cat with visions of large profits from the sale of future litters. Most novices find out real fast that breeding operations, if done correctly and humanely (and they should always be), represent a considerable investment in time and money. Be sure to find out what these investments are prior to plunging into the cat-breeding business.

If you are a novice, confine your efforts to one of the more common breeds versus some exotic, delicate breed. As a rule, you'll be rewarded with less problems with dystocia (difficult or complicated birthing). In addition, the more popular the breed, the greater the demand will be for your kittens, resulting in greater financial rewards.

But beware: When selecting your initial breeding stock, closely scrutinize the pedigree of the cat's parents. All that it takes is one genetic defect to appear in one or more of your cat's offspring, and your reputation as a breeder could be ruined!

Cats as Competitors

For cat lovers, the pleasure of ownership and/or breeding is compounded by the thrill of competition in the show ring. Competitive events involving cats have been around since the nineteenth century. Each year, events are sanctioned by a number of different cat fanciers' associations throughout the world. At such functions, serious breeders have the opportunity to earn the reputation of producing champion-quality felines, rewarding not only to the ego but also the pocketbook!

But you don't need to own a purebred cat to enter the show ring. Most events have a special show class in which an average house cat can compete. If you are interested in showing cats, there are many good books and Websites available that can show you the way. Also, contact local clubs for information regarding types of competitive events, rules and qualifications, and event schedules.

Cats as Workers

Throughout history, one of the main functions of the domesticated cat has been rodent control, and cats continue to fill this role even today. The challenge, however, of keeping cats around the homestead for this purpose alone is the increased threat of disease, including zoonotic diseases. As a result, if you own a cat for such a purpose, it is imperative that its preventive health care program be impeccable, not only for your cat's well-being, but for yours as well.

Cats as Gifts

Although your intentions might be pure and from the heart, never surprise someone with a new cat or kitten unless you are positively, absolutely sure that they want one in the first place. Think about it: Your gift to them not only includes that furry bundle of energy, but also a hearty commitment to training, time, and money. Unfortunately, too many people do fail to think about it that way, and as a result, our nation's pounds and shelters are overflowing with unwanted pets turned in by disgruntled or disinterested gift recipients. As a result, it is always best to

FACT OR *FICTION*

Cats are loners by nature. **FICTION.** Research has shown that feral cats, especially females, will actually exhibit pack behavior similar to dogs, grooming and taking care of one another! Only about 15 percent of cats will refuse to socialize at all with humans.

allow other people to come to a decision about pet ownership by themselves, and not to force it on them by your good intentions. Believe me, everyone will be happier in the long run!

What Type of Cat Do You Want?

Once you have figured out why you want a cat in the first place, you must further narrow your choices as to the type of cat you want. For starters, both purebreds and mixed breeds can make great pets, and the decision concerning genetic purity pedigree is entirely up to you. If you choose to go the purebred route, expect to pay more up front for your purchase. In addition, you run greater risk of facing genetic disorders inherent to that particular breed. Being very cautious and prudent in your selection process can minimize this risk. If you don't have your heart set on any breed in particular, reference books, magazines, or Internet sites that discuss the individual breeds and their special characteristics can help you narrow the field.

If you are like many cat fanciers, you might be less finicky about a lengthy pedigree and instead prefer a cat with a more mysterious gene pool. In fact, there are several advantages to owning mixed-breed cats (also known as *domestic shorthair, domestic mediumhair, domestic longhair*). First, because of their diluted, colorful ancestries, they exhibit a unique genetic phenomenon known as *hybrid vigor.* Because of hybrid vigor, mixed-breed cats as a group tend to be healthier and live longer than do their purebred cousins.

Another obvious advantage of choosing a hybrid is that they cost less to purchase than do purebreds.

Do You Want an Indoor or Outdoor Cat?

For some reason, many cat owners are under the false impression that a cat cannot be happy unless it is roaming free outdoors. Although this might have been the standard of thinking years back, it is time that cat owners change their attitudes toward this subject. Aside from the obvious health hazards to outdoor cats, such as car fenders and fan belts, hostile dogs, hostile humans, and infectious diseases, there is another important reason: an increased threat of zoonotic disease transmission.

As a result, while it is fine to allow your cat to spend some time outside, it should spend the majority of the day (and all of the night) inside.

How Will Your Existing Pets Be Affected?

Are there other pets in your household already? Jealousies or incompatibilities could arise that need to be anticipated before a new cat is brought home. Household dogs and small pocket pets can harbor a particular aversion to such new additions to the family!

Another important question to ask yourself if you already own a cat is whether it has ever been socialized to other cats. Unsocialized cats (and even some that are properly socialized) might refuse to accept another cat into its territory without a fight.

All newcomers should be gradually introduced to existing pets one day at a time. Keep your new cat in a separate room or enclosure, allowing initial interactions to take place only under your direct supervision. These gradual encounters should eventually help break the ice between the two.

Are You Willing to Be a Responsible Pet Owner?

Reduced time requirement is a big reason many people choose cats over dogs as pets. Cats are indeed fairly self-sufficient, seemingly needing only food, water, a clean litterbox, and very little training. While this is true in many instances, all cats still need a daily dose of attention and grooming.

The financial aspect of pet ownership is a major consideration if you are in the market for a cat. The actual cost of owning a cat, including food, supplies, and veterinary care, can cost hundreds of dollars each year, assuming that your cat remains healthy. Are you willing to accept financial responsibility for your pet's preventive health care or for treatment in an event of an injury or illness? If not, you are not ready to own a cat.

Finding the Right Cat

Once you have decided on a particular type or breed of cat, now is the time to start your search. Newspapers, pet stores, veterinary hospitals, the Internet, and word of mouth are fruitful avenues for information. If you're not interested in a purebred cat, check with the local humane society or animal shelter in your area. These are excellent places to start and are often jam-packed with mixed-breed and purebred cats alike, all eager to be adopted into happy homes. Usually, one can be yours to love for only a nominal adoption fee. As an added benefit, you will feel good knowing that you've saved an unwanted pet from an uncertain future.

If a purebred fits your fancy, check pet stores or contact cat breeders within your area. Local veterinarians and groomers can often provide specific recommendations. Magazines catering to cat owners can also be excellent reference sources for purebred cats and professional breeders. Finally, cat shows and other competitive events provide a means of giving you a firsthand glimpse of the cream of the crop and can give you the opportunity to meet prominent cat breeders in person.

Before you go shopping, do your homework. Find out what the going rate is for the particular breed you want. Choose reputable breeders who can provide you with the complete pedigrees of both parents and references of satisfied clients. This rule holds true for pet-store purchases as well. Before buying from a pet store, ask where the kitten came from and who the breeder was. Ask to see the pedigrees of both parents. Reputable pet stores will have all this information readily available for your inspection. And don't hesitate to ask for references from satisfied customers. If the store is unwilling or unable to divulge such information, look elsewhere.

Whatever you do, don't rush your decision. Remember: You are making a long-term commitment. Take your time, and pick out that special kitten or cat that is just right for you!

Prepurchase Exam

Once you think you've finally found the perfect companion, now what? For starters, you want to be sure you are getting a healthy specimen. Be sure to inquire as to the cat's vaccination and deworming history. You might be told that all of the "shots" and dewormings have been given. This might be true, but don't hesitate to ask for, in writing, dates and names of products used. Your veterinarian can then review this list for completeness during the professional prepurchase exam. Inquire as to any prior feline leukemia virus (FeLV) or feline AIDS [feline immuno-deficiency virus (FIV)] testing. Kittens can be born with these diseases, so be certain that you know their status before you buy.

Even before your veterinarian gets involved, you should perform your own prepurchase exam on the prospect. It is easy to do on site and will help illuminate many problems that might otherwise elude the untrained eye.

1. *Environment.* For starters, take note of the surrounding environment in which the kitten or cat is being kept. Does it look and smell clean, or is it filthy, with dirty litterboxes or no litterboxes at all? If the latter is true, you should question the integrity of the seller. Observe all the kittens and cats in the litter or group. Do any appear sickly, depressed, or otherwise unhealthy? An infectious disease can run rampant through such a congregation of felines, and it could be just beginning to rear its ugly head within the group.

2. *Attitude.* Now focus your attention on the actual candidate. Start with overall attitude. Does it appear active and healthy, or is it lethargic and depressed? Are breathing problems evident? Does it seem friendly and outgoing to people and to the other cats in the group, or does it seem shy and introverted? Cats destined to be good pets should take an instant fancy to people, and should outwardly show this affection. At the same time, avoid those individuals with aggressive and/or unsociable personalities.

3. *Skin and coat.* Once attitude and personality have been evaluated, check out the skin and coat. Any fleas or ticks present? How about any hair loss, scabs, or signs of infection? These could be indicators of diseases such as mange or ringworm, both of which can be zoonotic (see section on zoonotic diseases). Also, since cats are such meticulous self-groomers, an unkempt haircoat could signify parasitism or some other underlying health disorder.

4. *Lumps, bumps, or swellings.* Run your hands over the umbilical area and, on both sides, over the points where the inner thighs connect with the abdominal wall. Notice any soft, fluctuant masses? These could be hernias, especially in young kittens. Run your hands over the entire body surface, feeling for other types of lumps and bumps. Note the location of any you find. Does the belly seem distended? If so, it could be full of food, or it could be full of worms or coccidia. Check beneath the tail, looking for tapeworm segments and for evidence of diarrhea. Soiling on and around the hair in this area should alert you to a potential intestinal disorder.

5. *Other anatomical considerations.* Observe leg conformation and how the kitten or cat walks and runs. Any obvious deformity and/or lameness should be noted. In male cats, check for descent of the testicles. Both testicles should be present at birth. If they aren't, be prepared to neuter at a later date, not only for health reasons but also to prevent the passage of this inheritable trait to future generations.

6. *Head region.* Now focus on the head region. Using your eyes and your nose, check the ears for discharges or strong odors (usually a sign of infection or ear mites). Both eyes should be free of matter, with no cloudiness or redness. Compare both eyes, making sure they are of the same size, and that the kittens are of the same diameter. Glance at the nose, noting any discharges or crusts. Finally, look into the mouth. The gums should be pink. If they are white, the cat could be anemic. Look for any severe underbites or overbites, or any missing teeth. Also glance at the roof of the mouth. In a young kitten, a cleft palate is a serious birth defect, and unless it is surgically corrected, it will lead to secondary aspiration pneumonia and death.

Consulting Your Veterinarian

Let's say you've completed the exam described above and have found some potential problem areas. What do you do next? First, don't get discouraged. Many of these conditions have quick, inexpensive solutions. This is where your veterinarian comes in handy.

Don't feel awkward asking the seller to pick up the tab for a professional prepurchase exam and feline leukemia/FIV testing by a veterinarian of your choice. Those sellers confidant in the quality of their cats should have no qualms about this. If they balk, a warning light should flash in your head. And don't get suckered into a "money back" or "lifetime" guarantee on a pet as an alternative to a professional prepurchase screen. Such a guarantee doesn't protect you against the emotional distress caused by having to return a pet to which you've already grown attached.

Follow your veterinarian's recommendations as to the purchase quality of the cat in question. If the one you have your heart set on does have medical problems that can be easily corrected, ask the seller to deduct these costs from the purchase price if possible. The seller is not legally, but perhaps only morally, obligated to do so; as a result, you must decide on your next move if the seller refuses or fails to compromise. The extra expense out of your own pocketbook might be worth it if you think you have truly found the cat of your dreams! You be the judge.

Introducing Your Cat to Its New Home

You will want to do everything in your power to make your new cat feel comfortable and secure in its new home by providing some basic supplies (Table 19.1). Although most cats kept indoors have the run of the house, yours should have one special quiet area it can call its own. When you bring your new friend home for the first time, have this special area equipped with a cushioned bed or basket. For kittens, cardboard boxes work just fine, assuming that the kitten can easily enter and exit the box. Be sure that this sleeping quarter is in a part of the house away from noise and disturbances.

Your cat's litterbox should also be placed in an area in the house where interruptions are not likely to occur. For very small kittens, an aluminum pan or shallow tray may be used; for larger kittens and adult cats, your standard plastic varieties available from a pet shop work just fine.

Avoid using boxes or other cardboard devices for a litterbox. Not only do they have a tendency to leak, but their porous nature is most unsanitary to your cat. Covered litterboxes have the advantage of keeping the litter from

> **FACT OR FICTION**
>
> Cats love to play with strings and ribbons. **FACT.** And unfortunately, string foreign bodies intestinal obstructions are relatively common feline medical emergencies seen by veterinarians. As a result, keep these items well out of reach of your cat!

Table 19.1 Supply Checklist for Your New Cat

Food and water bowl	Brush
Cat (kitten) food	Comb
Collar or harness	Bed or cat house
Leash	Travel kennel
Nail trimmers	Flea control products
Identification tag	Scratching post
City license (if required)	Toothbrush/paste
Proof of rabies vaccination	Toys
Litterbox	Heartworm preventive agent
Litter	

being strewn across the floor—assuming, of course, that your cat feels comfortable enough to enter such an enclosure!

Try to match the type of litter used in your cat's previous home, but be sure that it is dust-free. Also, avoid products containing chlorophyll to mask odors, as this substance can irritate your cat's nose and prevent it from using the box. Fill the box with about 1$\frac{1}{2}$ inches of litter. For sanitation purposes as well as aesthetics within the house, make it a habit to change your cat's litterbox on a daily basis (*Note:* Pregnant women should pass this duty on to someone else, in order to reduce their risk of exposure to toxoplasmosis. The exception to this would be if special "clumping" litters are used. These can be spot-cleaned daily without having to dump out the entire box. However, regardless of litter type used, litterboxes should be emptied completely and cleaned with soap and water at least once a week to maintain sanitary conditions and to control odor.)

Unless you plan to have your cat declawed at a young age, you will also need to invest in a good scratching post to spare your furniture and fixtures from the ravages of your cat's claws. Clawing comes naturally to cats, which use such behavior to keep their nails in top condition and to mark their territory. The scratching post should be made of sturdy material and be heavy enough or braced so that it doesn't fall over when the cat attempts to scratch. A sturdy piece of soft wood is ideal for this purpose. Other commercial varieties can be obtained at a local pet store. Avoid those posts lined with thick, compliant carpet, as this might not satisfy your cat's needs, causing it to look elsewhere for a surface that will.

Your new cat's first encounters with the rest of your family are important. Be sure that initial introductions—whether with children or other adults in the family—turn out to be positive ones. Carefully supervise child-pet interactions, and stress to your children the importance of gentle play and handling. Instruct your children and other adults on the proper way to pick up and hold a new kitten. Cats should not be picked up solely by the front legs or by the neck. Instead, the entire body should be picked up as one unit, with the hind end supported, not left dangling in midair. Picking a cat up by grasping the skin over the back of the neck is acceptable as long as the hind end is supported as well.

If they had it their way, most children, and some adults, for that matter, would choose to play with a new kitten 24 hours a day. However, you need to stress the importance of a rest time for the new kitten after periods of play, and lay down strict ground rules against disturbing it during this downtime.

Catproofing Your Home

For your cat's sake, be sure to take necessary steps to petproof your home. Because cats can be very inquisitive creatures, and because they have the ability to scale heights, you will need to take even more care when you are doing this than if a dog were involved.

Keep all plants out of reach. Cats and kittens love to chew on foliage, and they also enjoy using potting soil as litter. As a result, they have the ability to quickly dispatch precious house plants in either of these manners. Also, if they decide to nibble on a harmful ornamented variety of plant, they could poison themselves. Keep electrical cords well out of reach. This might mean banishing your cat or kitten from certain areas of the house, but this is a minor inconvenience compared to a potentially fatal accident. Pins, needles, knives, rubber bands, yarn, string, ribbons, aluminum foil, cellophane, and holiday tinsel are just a few items that could cause serious health problems if ingested by cats. Inquisitive cats have been known to get their heads lodged within open cans and jars, and because cats possess a strange attraction to bags of all types, plastic bags can become death traps if entered.

Finally, because of the cat's desire to explore its environment and to see how high it can climb, washers-dryers, drawers, high ledges or balconies, hot irons on ironing boards, and stovetop burners left on can all be insidious dangers to your cat's health.

When selecting toys for your new kitten or cat, be sure that they cannot be torn apart easily and that they do not contain small parts that could be swallowed. Wrinkled paper and shoeboxes are intriguing to most cats. Rubber balls or mice too large to swallow, as well as catnip toys (again, constructed for safety), are also considered safe toys. If a string is attached to a toy in order to entice a cat to play, always remove it after the play session is over. Along the same lines, never use ribbon or laces as play items. If a cat swallows such items, these items could damage their intestines and have to be removed surgically.

Naming Your Cat

Naming your new pet should be fun and involve the entire family. You can even find entire books that are dedicated to choosing the right name for your cat. Stick to names having two syllables; this will allow your cat to differentiate between its name and those one syllable commands you might choose to teach it. You can further set its name apart from potential commands or reprimands by adding a vowel sound to the end of it. Just be creative!

Traveling with Your Cat

When transporting a cat by car, the comfort and safety of both driver and passenger must always be taken into consideration. Whether you are bringing your cat home for the first time, or simply taking it on a Sunday afternoon drive, keep these principles in mind to make the trip pleasant and safe for the both of you.

To begin, it is always recommended that, when transporting a pet by automobile, a travel carrier or kennel be used (Fig. 19.2). Not only will your pet feel more secure in a carrier, helping to reduce stress associated with the ride, but it will help minimize jostling and jolting movements that could injure your cat. This carrier should be just large enough for your cat to stand up and turn around in.

You shouldn't have to be told to keep the interior of your car well ventilated and cool. Excited or stressed cats forced to travel in hot, stuffy cars, or ones filled with cigarette or cigar smoke, are likely to suffer ill effects. Cigarette smoke in itself can be quite irritating to the eyes, nose, and mucous membranes of your cat. As a result, as a courtesy to your feline friend, refrain from smoking until you have reached your final destination. Car exhaust fumes can have the same effect as cigarette smoke. As a result, if stopped in traffic for any appreciable amount of time, crack the car windows and keep the air within the car circulating.

Never leave your cat in a parked car unattended for more than 5 minutes on days when environmental temperatures exceed 72 degrees Fahrenheit or drop below 55 degrees Fahrenheit, as heat stroke or hypothermia (respectively) could result. If you do have to leave your pet for a few minutes, be sure to leave two or more windows partially opened to allow for air circulation. In addition, the use of window shields and sun visors is strongly recommended to help temporarily keep temperatures within the car at acceptable levels.

FIGURE 19.2 Cats should always be transported in sturdy carriers.

For trips over 2 hours, be sure to take plenty of breaks to give your cat water and to stretch and exercise (this is where harness training comes in handy!). Ice can also be offered along the way to keep your cat's thirst at bay. Keep a clean towel lining the floor of the carrier, since many cats on long trips will refuse to use a litterbox if offered one.

If your cat gets car sick, try feeding a small amount of food about 30 minutes prior to your trip. Often, an empty stomach coupled with stress can predispose a pet to motion sickness. Contact your veterinarian concerning the various over-the-counter medications you can use in cats and their dosages.

For those cats absolutely terrified of the car, a tranquilizer prescribed by your veterinarian may be needed. Although this should be used only as a last resort, it can be an effective tool for taking the edge off your phobic feline and thereby make the ride much less stressful for everyone concerned.

When transporting your cat by airplane, special precautions should be taken. Always consult your veterinarian beforehand to determine whether any medical conditions your pet may have could be exacerbated by such a trip. For example, high-altitude flying and potential temperature/pressure fluctuations could prove to be harmful to a cat that may be suffering from an underlying heart disorder. Speak with your airline representatives concerning their accommodations and restrictions for traveling pets. Most will require a current health certificate prior to transport and will restrict travel if environmental temperatures are too extreme. Book nonstop flights to reduce the chances of "lost luggage." In addition, during the summer, book a flight early in the morning or late in the evening to avoid exposing your pet to midday heat. Carrying flight insurance on your cat might help increase the gentleness and care with which it is handled. The night prior to the trip, freeze some water in the travel carrier water dish to ensure your cat continued access to water during the trip. Tranquilization should be reserved only for those cats that are absolutely terrified of travel.

Training Your Cat

Once your new family member has settled into its new home, you are now ready for the next step: training. Contrary to popular belief, some cats can be just as trainable as dogs. Keep in mind, though, that the independent nature of cats can make certain training procedures a bit tricky, but if you maintain an understanding attitude toward your task, your frustrations will be minimal and your reward plentiful.

Basic Training

For starters, all cats should be trained to walk on a leash at an early age (Fig. 20.1). Why? By teaching your cat to accept a leash and harness, you will be able to institute a daily exercise program for it, keeping it fit and healthy. In addition, since allowing a cat to roam freely outdoors these days is becoming more dangerous, a leash-trained cat can enjoy the same benefits of the great outdoors, yet without the risks. Finally, many travelers find that leash training comes in quite handy at rest stops during lengthy trips.

Before you attach a leash to your kitten or cat, it must become accustomed to a halter. Because halters provide more control and security than do collars, the latter should not be used to walk a cat on a leash. Place the new halter on your cat and allow it to wear the halter around

FIGURE 20.1 All cats should be trained to a harness and leash.

the house or apartment for 10 to 15 minutes at a time. Then take it off, and repeat the process at 3-hour intervals throughout the day. Eventually lengthen the time you leave the halter on until your cat will wear it all day without a fuss.

At this point, attach a leash to the halter and allow your cat to drag the leash around for 10 to 15 minutes at a time before removing it. Repeat this procedure throughout the day for a week or so. Do not allow your cat to walk around unsupervised with the leash dangling free. If the leash becomes snagged, your cat could seriously injure itself.

Once you feel your cat has become accustomed to the leash, practice walking with it indoors using the lead for a week or two. Only after your cat gives you total compliance should you attempt the same maneuver outdoors. If everything goes as planned, be sure to reward your cat for a job well done. A scratch behind the ears or under the chin, or a favorite food treat, does wonders to help solidify and promote such desired behavior.

Other Commands

If you so desire, teach your cat commands as you would a dog. Remember: Because of the inherent nature of the feline, you can't always expect 100 percent compliance; simply take all successes and run with them! One helpful tip is to hold your training sessions when your cat is hungry. If you do, food rewards become powerful motivators for good behavior.

Litter Training Your Kitten

Kittens will be instinctively drawn to litter or dirt in which to eliminate as early as 4 to 6 weeks of age (Fig. 20.2). As a result, housebreaking a kitten usually involves minimal effort on an owner's part. Allowing access of your new kitten to its litterbox after eating, playing, waking up, or just before bedtime will help encourage repeat use. If your cat doesn't seem to catch on, there might be some reason for its reluctance to use the litterbox. If so, it is your job to find out why.

FIGURE 20.2 Most kittens will learn to use a litterbox without your help.

Socializing Your Cat

As with a puppy, a kitten's socialization period falls between 3 and 12 weeks of age. During this short time span, a kitten will learn who it is, who you are, and who and what all of those other living, moving beings in its surroundings are as well (Fig. 20.3).

If for some reason a kitten fails to be properly introduced to members of its own species, or to other species (including children) during this time, there is a good chance that the kitten will not "recognize" these individuals. Your cat will probably exhibit aggressiveness or excessive timidity toward them.

Improper or negative socialization is even worse than no socialization at all. Any traumatic experience or physical punishment that occurs between 3 and 12 weeks of age could permanently scar a

FIGURE 20.3 Socialization is just as important for cats as it is for dogs.

DID YOU KNOW ?

Cats may socialize to one breed of dog but not to another!

FIGURE 20.4 The power of socialization!

cat's personality toward a specific group or species for life (Fig. 20.4). This is one reason why all physical punishment should be avoided during this time in your kitten's life. Such punishment could permanently damage the kitten's relationship with the person doing the punishing!

Solving Behavioral Challenges

When searching for the leading cause of dissatisfaction among cat owners, problem behaviors top the list. Each year, a multitude of cats are abandoned, evicted from their homes, or even put to sleep because of annoying behavioral activities. However, by understanding why these behaviors happen and by employing special training techniques to correct such vices, cat owners can often avert such drastic actions as those mentioned above.

House Soiling

Cats exhibit two types of normal elimination behavior. The first involves urine spraying to delineate territories (the typical feline territory encompasses over 0.1 square mile) and to attract members of the opposite sex (Fig. 20.5). The second type is called "covering" behavior, in which a cat digs a hole in

FIGURE 20.5 Cats will often spray urine to mark their territory.

the soil (or litter), eliminates in it, and then covers it to mask the scent. Most inappropriate house soiling that occurs with cats involve indulgences or deviations in one or the other.

The most frequent cause of house soiling deals with the first type: territoriality and sexual behavior. Both male and female cats, neutered or not, can spray urine. A new cat in the neighborhood or a female in heat can quickly set off instinctive behavior in a male cat kept indoors and lead to inappropriate markings. Even moving into a new house or apartment in which a cat previously lived might entice your cat to go around the house and mark those areas in which a scent from the previous inhabitant is picked up.

Neutering might help control urine spraying in the repeat offender, yet, as mentioned before, it is not necessarily a cure-all. If there is a particular area in the house that your cat fancies the most for its spraying activities, do your best to prevent its access to that part of the house. Or, if you can, catch your cat in the act and punish it using a squirt from a water sprayer or a blast of air from a compressed-air canister. Then leave the sprayer or canister sitting beside the soiled object or in the room for a few days. Your cat will probably get the drift and abandon its tendencies to repeat the action. [*Note:* If plain water from your spray bottle seems to have little impact with your cat, adding a small amount of vinegar or lemon juice (2 tablespoons per cup of water) to it will impart to it an odor that is offensive to most cats.]

Feline odor neutralizers can be used on carpets and furniture to help eliminate those lingering odors that might be causing the problem behavior. They should also be used anytime an elimination accident occurs outside the litterbox. These odor neutralizers are available from your veterinarian or your favorite pet supply. Household cleaners designed to simply mask odors or those containing ammonia are of no use; in fact, the latter might actually attract your cat back to the same spot.

For those tough cases of urine spraying in which nothing seems to work, special drug therapy prescribed by your veterinarian might provide a satisfactory solution to the problem. However, such agents should be used only after other training methods have failed.

Refusal to Use the Litterbox

What about the cat that has stopped using the litterbox? There could be a number of reasons for this behavior. Some cats may not like the type or brand of litter that was put in the box. Have you changed brands lately? If so, switch back to the brand you were using before the house soiling started. Remember that the texture and scent of a litter are two factors that can influence your cat's reaction to it.

Some cats become upset if there is too much litter in the litterbox. Cats should be able to reach the bottom of their pan when digging. If you have one of these fickle cats, restocking the box with just 1-inch layer of litter might do the trick.

Still other cats will refuse to use a litterbox that, in their minds, is dirty. Check the frequency of your litter changes. If the litter is not being replaced every day, this could be the problem. If so, step up the frequency. Also, do not use strong cleansers when doing your weekly litterbox cleaning, as the residual scents from these might be just enough to send your cat off searching for another place to do its business.

Refusal to use a litterbox may also be linked to some traumatic incident, emotionally or physically, that occurred while your cat was using the box on a previous occasion. Because of this, it now associates the box or its location with the unpleasant incident. Obviously, the best way to find out if this is indeed the cause is to move the litterbox to a different location, one that is quiet and away from disturbances. For those cats that are especially emotional, buying a new litterbox might be required.

Not all causes of house soiling are psychological in nature. For instance, the presence of feline lower urinary tract disease can be the underlying cause of abnormal elimination behavior in felines. Since some of the diseases causing abnormal elimination can be life-threatening, always let your veterinarian rule out any medical causes before concentrating on behavioral causes.

Destructive Scratching

Scratching comes naturally to cats, which use this behavior to keep their retractable claws manicured and to mark their territories. As a result, scratching, although it might become destructive and annoying, should be viewed as a perfectly natural behavior.

If your cat is engaged in destructive scratching, you haven't satisfied a basic need. A scratching post is a required tool for anyone who owns a cat. In fact, it is preferable to train a cat on a scratching post right from the start instead of bringing one in to offset problem scratching activity. If your cat seems to fancy one or more particular pieces of furniture in your house, see if you can catch it in the act. If you do, use a blast of water or compressed air from a sprayer or canister to reprimand it, then leave the sprayer or canister sitting beside or on top of the piece of furniture for several days. Most cats will avoid that piece of furniture like the plague from that point on. Some persons recommend commercial cat repellents or vinegar be used on furniture to discourage scratching, but these can be messy and could stain your furniture.

For that feline that seems refractory to punishment, try placing the scratching post near its favorite piece of furniture and allow it to make a choice. Make the scratching post as plush and tempting as possible. Catnip attached to the post can help lure a reluctant cat to its new scratching post. Be sure to reward your cat for making the switch (Fig. 20.6).

Special nail covers are available through veterinarians and pet stores and can be applied to the nails of your cat to prevent scratching. Surgical removal of its front claws can also be considered to spare your house from total destruction.

Aggressiveness

Because of the inherent nature of the cat, a display of aggression toward another member of its own species, especially if a territory has been violated, is somewhat common. Aggressiveness toward humans, on the other hand, can be influenced by a number of factors, including personality defects, fear, play activity, and medical disorders. Cats that have not been properly socialized to people can be expected to

FIGURE 20.6 A scratching post can be used to spare your furniture from the ravages of your cat's claws!

show some degree of aggressiveness when feeling threatened. It is also a well-known fact that even some socialized cats just want to be left alone at times and may become aggressive if disturbed.

PERSONALITY DEFECTS

Personality defects can lead to true aggressive tendencies in cats. These are cats that have been poorly socialized to humans, or have experienced negative socialization. Nervous or hyperexcitable cats or those with extremely domineering personalities can also show aggressiveness at times. Agitated or angry cats will flag their tails and flatten their ears against their heads when approached or touched. A low-pitched growl or hiss is usually heard as well.

All aggressive cats, especially males, should be neutered. If neutering doesn't resolve the problem, then antianxiety medications can be used to help take the edge off of the pugnacious feline.

FEAR-INDUCED AGGRESSION

Fear-induced aggression rarely responds to training or reprimand. In fact, if such actions are attempted while the cat is in such a state, serious injury to an owner could result! The self-defense posture caused by fear-induced aggressive behavior is characterized by piloerection (hair standing on end), arched back, flattened ears, and hissing or spitting. Cats that feel threatened will lash out with their claws, and make short, sharp lunges at their adversaries. If they really sense danger, they often roll over on their backs, and assume a defense posture that will allow them to utilize the claws on all four feet.

Obviously, eliminating the source of fear is the first step in managing such aggression. Afterward, give your cat plenty of time alone to calm down and relax. A special food treat can be offered as well to help take its mind off of the incident.

PLAYFUL AGGRESSION

Playful aggression must be differentiated from the two previous types of aggression, since it is by far the easiest to address. This type of aggression is seen primarily in younger cats filled with youthful energy and curiosity. These cats may stalk house guests or ambush unexpecting owners when they arrive home. This behavior provides them a way to release excess energy and to practice their instinctive hunting skills. Most bites inflicted during this type of play are not meant to break the skin; however, this can certainly be a function of the game's intensity. One physical characteristic of mischievous cats or kittens is that they often carry their tails arched up over their backs or in an inverted "U" position during these play episodes.

Playful aggression can be managed by allowing your cat greater access to toys such as paper bags, ping-pong balls, or wind-up, moving figures. If you play action games with your cat using strings attached to toys, be sure to remove these strings following a play session. Finally, taking your cat out for more walks during the day can help expend some of its pent-up energy.

Negative reinforcement utilizing water sprayers or compressed-air canisters can also be used to break overzealous cats of their bad habits. As a last resort, simply isolating your rambunctious feline in another room while you have guests over will ensure that they are not met with any unexpected surprises!

MEDICAL CAUSES

Let us not forget about medical causes for aggressiveness in cats. Cats that don't feel well often just want to be left alone, and if they are disturbed, they may show aggressiveness. Diseases that affect the nervous system (including rabies), metabolic disorders, and pain can all have a negative effect on a cat's personality. If your cat has experienced a gradual or sudden change in personality, have it examined by a veterinarian in order to rule out possible medical causes for the change.

Preventive Health Care

Ensuring that your cat remains healthy and happy should be your foremost goal as an owner. To accomplish this, you must implement a well-defined preventive health care program. Both you and your veterinarian will play vital roles in its success. Immunizations, parasite control, grooming, exercise, and proper nutrition are all preventive health care measures that are important to your pet's health (Fig. 21.1).

At-Home Physical Exam

Do you worry about your cat's health even when it appears healthy? Your veterinarian can ensure that your cat is thriving by performing a thorough checkup, but what can you do between visits? Cats cannot verbalize their discomforts, and people often worry that they'll miss the early signs of illness. If you learn to examine your cat at home, you can have that all-important peace of mind between visits to the vet.

During your next visit to the pet clinic, the veterinarian will probably begin with an examination of your cat. Watch how your veterinarian performs the exam and ask to participate in the process. Discuss your desire to supplement the vet's exams with at-home checks that you will make. Your veterinarian should be pleased with your desire to provide such attention to your cat's health and should be happy to

FIGURE 21.1 Preventive health care can help your cat live a happy and healthy life.

help develop your skills. Your teamwork will provide the consistent attention to details that could prevent a tragedy.

At-home examinations are no substitute for a veterinary checkup, but doing them might one day give you a jump on treating a minor or serious condition. For convenience, these exams can be combined with regular grooming sessions (Table 21.1).

1. *Observe your cat.* Begin the exam by looking at your pet from a distance. Observe its general appearance. Watch it move back and forth. An abnormal gait with or without limping or lameness could indicate such things as nervous system problems or musculoskeletal disorders. Does your cat stand erect and relaxed? Abnormal postures such as a wide stance with the neck extended could indicate breathing difficulties. An arching of the back could mean abdominal pain. Note

Table 21.1 Physical Exam Checklist for Cats

Date _____	Temperature_____
Weight_____	

General evaluation

__Alert	__Disinterested
__Active	__Lethargic
__Healthy appetite	__Poor appetite
__Playful	__Weight loss/gain
__Lameness	__Abnormal posture
__Abnormal aggressiveness	

Skin and haircoat

__Appear normal	__Shedding
__Hair loss	__Mats
__Dull; unkempt	__Tumors or warts
__Scaly	__Parasites
__Dry	__Abnormal lumps under the skin
__Oily	__Crusts on neck and head
__Itching	

Eyes

__Appear normal	__Haziness/cloudiness
__Clear discharge	__Unequal pupil size
__Mucus discharge	__Discoloration
__Redness	__Squinting
__Eyelid abnormalities	__Protruding third eyelids

Ears

__Appear normal	__Hair loss on pinnae

Table 21.1 Physical Exam Checklist for Cats (*Continued*)

__Red; swollen	__Bad odor
__Itchy	__Masses
__Creamy, yellow discharge	__Tender
__Brown to black discharge	__Head tilt
__Head shaking	

Nose and throat

__Appear normal	__Ulceration on nose
__Nasal discharge	__Crusty nose

__Enlarged lymph nodes (feel on either side of the neck just under the jaw)

Mouth, teeth, and gums

__Appear normal	__Tooth loss
__Broken, discolored, or loose teeth	__Inflamed gums
__Foul odor	__Excess salivation
__Tartar accumulation	__Pale gums
__Growths or masses	__Ulcers
__Base of tongue inflamed	__Foreign body noted

Miscellaneous

__Abdominal tenderness	__Increased water consumption
__Coughing	__Decreased water consumption
__Breathing difficulties	__Genital discharge
__Abnormal stools	__Mammary lumps
__Straining to urinate	__Swollen limb

the position of your cat's head. A tilted head is often characteristic of a cat with an irritated or infected ear canal. A droopy head can signify depression and overall malaise.

What is your pet's attitude? Is it alert, active, and friendly, or is it lethargic, depressed, or aggressive? Sick or injured animals, especially those in pain, often show aggressive behaviors; therefore, handle them with caution. Keep in mind that normal behavior will vary among individuals and in different situations.

2. *Look for warning signs.* Cat owners should be aware of certain clinical signs that could signify serious problems in their pets. Weakness, shortness of breath, coughing, labored breathing, and, as mentioned before, a wide-based stance could be the first signs of heart or lung problems. A pale blue or purple tongue can signify poor tissue oxygenation, often the result of circulation problems. If your cat shows any of these signs, obtain a pulse by gently pressing your fingers against the upper, inner portion of a back leg, or on either side of the neck next to the trachea. The normal resting pulse for a cat ranges from 60 to 120 beats per minute. An abnormal pulse or any other signs of heart or lung problems should be reported to your veterinarian immediately.

A cat's normal temperature ranges from around 100 to 103.2 degrees Fahrenheit. Excited or nervous animals might have elevated temperatures, but a temperature due to excitement should rarely exceed 103.5 degrees Fahrenheit (Table 21.2). To take your cat's temperature, lubricate the tip of a plastic electronic thermometer with lubricating jelly. Insert the thermometer into the cat's rectum and hold it in place for at least two minutes. If the reading is higher than 103.5 degrees Fahrenheit, you should call your veterinarian for advice.

Get into the habit of weighing your cat every 3 months and record your readings. Unexplained weight loss or weight gain that is greater than 3 pounds or a pattern of continual loss or gain should prompt you to contact your veterinarian. Such fluctuations or patterns could signify some underlying medical disorder. Cats that are 8 years or older should be weighed monthly, and unexplained changes in weight should be reported to the veterinarian. Additionally, keep in mind that obesity poses the same health hazards in animals as it does in humans. An overweight cat should be put on a diet and an exercise program formulated and prescribed by its veterinarian.

Table 21.2 Potential Causes of Elevated Body Temperature in Cats

Fear or excitement
High environmental temperature
Exercise
Infection
Tissue inflammation or trauma
Autoimmune disease
Cancer
Drug reactions
Endocrine disorders (e.g., hyperthyroidism)

3. *Inspect the head region.* Using a systematic approach when performing the examination, start at the head and work toward the rear. As you go, check each body part for abnormalities. A checklist sheet might be helpful to remind you of each stop along the way, and it will be an excellent record for future reference.

Eyes. Any abnormalities you detect involving the eyes should be brought to the attention of your veterinarian. Redness, cloudiness, discharge (or drainage), squinting, or unequal pupil sizes could signify trouble. The white of the eye, called the *sclera,* should be just that—white. If inflammation is present, the scleras are usually reddened. Yellow-tinged or jaundiced scleras indicate the presence of a serious condition, such as liver failure. A thorough exam by a veterinarian is the only way to determine the cause of the jaundice. Check the cat's eyelids. Be sure that no foreign objects are irritating the surfaces of the eyes. Constant, untreated irritation can lead to corneal injuries, which are extremely painful. Eyelid abnormalities require immediate veterinary attention to

FIGURE 21.2 Protrusion of the third eyelids is a sign of illness in cats.

prevent significant eye damage (Fig. 21.2).

Ears. Inspect the ears and note any foul smell or discharge. A black or brown discharge could signify an ear mite infestation or a yeast infection (Fig. 21.3). A yellowish, creamy discharge means a bacterial infection is present. Other signs of ear disease include constant scratching at the ears, head shaking, and head tilting.

FIGURE 21.3 Treating for ear mites.

Nostrils. Discharges from the nostrils should alert you to a potential disease condition. Clear discharges usually indicate either allergies or viral infections. A green, mucus discharge usually indicates bacterial infection, which can be caused by a variety of diseases or a lodged foreign object. Bleeding from the nose could result from trauma, tumors, foreign bodies, or a blood-clotting disorder. Look for tumors and ulcerations affecting the mucous membranes of the nose. (*Note:* Nasal discharge in cats is often accompanied by a loss of appetite, because cats will not eat what they cannot smell. This might seem harmless enough; however, serious malnutrition can occur in certain cases unless the underlying disease condition is diagnosed and treated.)

Mouth. Gently open your cat's mouth by grasping the head and upper jaw with one hand, tilting the head back and using your other hand to separate the jaws. The gums and mucous membranes should be moist and pink. Pale, dry mucous membranes might indicate anemia, dehydration, or shock. If you suspect a problem, obtain a capillary refill time by pressing on the upper gum with your index finger. The gum region under your finger should turn white. Release the pressure and the gum should return to a pink color within 2 seconds. If it takes longer, consult your veterinarian. Check the mouth for swollen gums, foreign objects, tumors, ulcerations, and sores. A foul odor can be caused by all the above. Using the blunt end of a pencil or similar object, lift up the tongue to get a good look underneath. This is a common lodging site for needles, strings, and other items that cats might put in their mouths.

4. *Inspect the body.* Run your hands over your pet's entire body and feel for lumps or bumps. If you have any doubt that what you feel is normal, you should consult your veterinarian. Lumps can indicate abscesses, enlarged lymph nodes, cysts, foreign bodies, soft tissue swellings (such as hernias and bruises), or cancer. The earlier you detect and treat cancer, the better the chances are for complete recovery. Be sure to check for lumps in the mammary region of female cats (especially if they have not been spayed). The testicles of intact male cats should be examined for abnormal swellings and masses. Note any discharges from the reproductive tract. Not all discharges are abnormal, but some discharges indicate the presence of infection. Often an odor is the first noticeable sign of infection of the reproductive tract. If you have any doubt as to whether a discharge is normal, consult your veterinarian.

The stomach, intestines, liver, pancreas, spleen, and kidneys are all located in the abdomen. Gently press both sides of the abdomen just behind the ribcage. (*Note:* Some cats immediately become tense when you do this.) Slowly work your way to the hip region, gently pressing as you go. Unless you have training in palpation (the act of feeling with the hand to determine physical diagnosis), don't expect to know what you are feeling. The purpose of doing this is to detect any swelling, tenderness, pain, or obvious masses involving the abdomen. If you feel anything strange, seek the opinion of your veterinarian.

5. *Inspect the skin and coat.* Evaluate your cat's skin and coat carefully. Signs of skin problems include hair loss, itchiness, redness, oiliness, scaliness, crustiness, and infection. Look closely for parasites, such as fleas and ticks. Poor nutrition or a metabolic disorder (e.g., abnormal thyroid function) can cause a cat's hair to become dull and lifeless. The potential causes of skin and coat disorders are so numerous that a veterinarian should diagnose all such disorders. Your early-warning system will enable you to treat the problems before they become serious.

Congratulations! You have just performed a physical exam on your cat. Now that you have seen the wealth of information that can be obtained concerning a pet's health status, it is clear why all cat owners should perform these periodic physical exams on their cats. You will also find that with experience, you will be able to do the entire exam within a matter of minutes. Start practicing today!

Immunizations

The theory behind vaccinating any pet is to artificially provide that initial exposure to certain disease-causing agents, thereby priming the body's immune system before natural exposure occurs. Doing so will allow for a rapid, effective immune response if this exposure does happen, without the lag time associated with a first exposure (Fig. 21.4).

If the queen has been properly vaccinated prior to pregnancy, most kittens receive protective antibodies from her through nursing, primarily during the first 24 hours of life. These passive antibodies are important, since the immune system of a neonate under 6 weeks of age is incapable of mounting an effective response to any *antigen* (foreign invader). Around 8 weeks of age, levels of these antibodies begin to taper off, leaving the kitten to fend for itself.

If a kitten that still has adequate levels of passive antibodies present in its system is immunized, the vaccination will be rendered ineffective. For this reason, initial vaccinations for kittens are usually given around 8 weeks of age, when levels of passive antibodies are low. Vaccination as early as 6 weeks of age is warranted in those instances where the

FIGURE 21.4 Immunizations are an important line of defense against disease.

mother was not current on vaccinations, or if lack of passive antibody absorption is a possibility (such as in cases of inadequate nursing during the first hours of life).

Those feline diseases that can be vaccinated against include

Panleukopenia (parvovirus)

Herpesvirus (viral rhinotracheitis)

Calicivirus

Rabies

Feline leukemia (FeLV)

Feline infectious peritonitis (FIP)

Microsporum canis (ringworm)

Chlamydia

Bordetella

The first four vaccines are considered *core vaccines*; that is, they should be administered to every cat. The remaining vaccines are considered optional, and are given at the discretion of each individual veterinarian.

Cats may receive boosters on these vaccines; the frequency of the boosters depends on a variety of factors. Many veterinary practitioners and veterinary schools are opting to use extended vaccination schedules for cats in lieu of the traditional "yearly booster" approach. These changes in traditional protocol are based on research findings indicating that

- Certain vaccines provide extended immunity and in some cases, lifelong immunity after an initial series of immunizations.

- Vaccines administered after this immunity has been established may be neutralized and rendered ineffective by the cat's immune system.

- Repeated immunization using certain vaccine agents has been linked to allergic reactions, autoimmune disease, and feline sarcoma, a deadly form of cancer in cats.

An example of an extended vaccination schedule for cats is as follows. The first three core caccines, which include panleukopenia, herpesvirus, and calicivirus, are administered at 8 weeks of age, and then
repeated at 12 and 16 weeks of age, for a total of three kitten immunizations. (*Note:* If an intranasal or intraocular vaccine is used for these core
vaccines, vaccinations can begin as early as 4 weeks of age.) The fourth
core vaccine, rabies, is administered between 12 and 16 weeks of age.

All core vacines are boostered at 1 year of age and at 2 years of age.
After 2 years of age, boosters are administered every 3 years for the
remainder of the cat's life. The exception to this would be the rabies
vaccine, which may need to be administered each year, depending on
the laws of the state in which you live.

Optional (noncore) vaccines for cats include feline leukemia, feline
infectious peritonitis, ringworm, *Chlamydia,* and *Bordetella.* These
are used at the discretion of each individual veterinarian. For instance,
the feline leukemia vaccine should be administered to cats under 2
years of age that are living with or are in contact with FeLV-positive
cats. For kittens at risk, one immunization is given at 9 weeks of age
and another at 12 weeks of age. A booster is also administered at one
year of age. Cats under 2 years of age receive two immunizations 3 to
4 weeks apart. Cats older than 2 years generally do not need further
immunizations against the disease.

On a final note, research also suggests that individual vaccines that
provide protection against a single type of disease ("univalent" vaccines) should be administered in lieu of those that stimulate immunity
against more than one type of disease ("multivalent" vaccines). The
traditional "three-way" and "four-way" vaccines used in cats for years
are examples of multivalent vaccines. Even though it may mean more
needles for your pet. the protection conferred by univalent vaccines is
deemed superior to that of multivalent varieties.

As you can see, much has changed regarding the principles behind
immunization in cats. Continuing research is needed to determine the
best vaccine protocol for this species. Regardless of types of vaccine used
and immunization frequency, such a protocol must be one that provides
maximum protection with minimum risk to the pet. Be sure to ask your
veterinarian about the latest research findings regarding feline immunology, and about the best vaccination protocol for your particular pet.

Controlling Internal Parasites

Left undetected, intestinal parasites can rob your cat of much-needed nutrients, cause severe gastrointestinal upset, and predispose your cat to secondary disease, such as panleukopenia. To make matters worse, many internal parasites of cats are also classified as *zoonotic diseases*; that is,they can be directly communicable to humans, especially children. As a result, controlling feline intestinal parasites is a vital part of any preventive health care program.

Treatment for feline internal parasites should begin in kittens as early as 3 weeks of age. At this age, kittens might harbor immature hookworms, roundworms, or coccidia without any evidence of eggs shed in the stool. Deworming should be performed again at 6 and 9 weeks of age. More treatments might be necessary if parasite eggs are found on stool exams during later visits. Stool examinations on these kittens should be performed by a veterinarian at 6, 9, and 12 weeks of age to ensure that they are indeed free of these parasites and are not shedding eggs into the environment.

Although cats over 1 year do not necessarily need routine deworming, their stools should be examined for parasite eggs on at least an annual basis. Stool exams should also be conducted on any ill animal, regardless of clinical signs. Even when the illness is not directly caused by the worms, their mere presence and effect on the host's immune system can exacerbate any disease, regardless of cause.

Aside from routine stool checks, good environmental sanitation is another way to lessen the impact of feline intestinal parasites. Many parasite eggs that are shed into the environment via feces take days of sitting in the sun or in the right environmental conditions before becoming ineffective to other cats or to people. As a result, keeping that litterbox cleaned on a daily basis is a very effective way of protecting your pet (and yourself) from internal parasites.

Controlling External Parasites

Much confusion exists in the proper approaches to external parasite control and prevention in cats. Many different approved product types are now available for external parasite control. The key to successful control is choosing and properly using the products that provide the best possible results for the specific external parasite and environment involved.

Flea Control

Fleas are by far the most common external parasites with which your cat will have to contend. Not only can their annoying bites produce extreme discomfort and even allergic reactions, fleas are also host to the most common tapeworm that affects cats, *Dipylidium caninum.*

Flea control entails not only treatment for fleas on the pet but environmental control as well. Consult with your veterinarian concerning the best approach to take to relieve your cat of these pesky parasites.

Insecticide Sprays, Powders, Collars, and Dips

Once representing the vanguard in the war against fleas and ticks, these products are being replaced by newer, more effective agents. However, some can still be helpful in certain situations, and warrant mention here.

Flea and tick sprays, available in both liquid and aerosol forms, are useful for spot treatments. Sprays containing natural chemicals called *pyrethrins,* derived from chrysanthemums, are the preferred products over others for flea control because of their safety and efficacy if used properly. The major advantage of natural pyrethrums is that they are relatively safe for use on pets of all ages. The disadvantage is that they have poor residual flea-fighting activity, lasting only a day or so. Newer, synthetic pyrethrin products available on the market today have improved this residual activity while still maintaining a good safety margin. If pyrethrin products are used, frequent

DR. P's VET TIP

When applying any type of spray to the haircoat of a cat, avoid spraying it directly on the coat. Instead, saturate a washcloth or towel with the solution and then rub it on the haircoat. Your cat is much less likely to object to treatment that way.

spray application, on both the cat and in its environment (bedding, carpet, etc.), is imperative for effective flea control. In some instances, this means on a daily basis. Just be sure before doing so to check the label on the particular product you are using to confirm the safety of this practice. If you are in doubt, always follow label directions!

As with the sprays, pyrethrin-containing powders are preferred over others because of their low toxicity. Powders do not evaporate as do liquid products; therefore, under dry conditions, powders stay active on the hair and skin somewhat longer than do sprays. Again, frequent application is required for best results. Exposure to water inactivates most insecticide powders.

Insecticide shampoos and collars are common items in retail stores and in most veterinary clinics. However, since frequent shampoo can lead to excessively dry skin, and collars are of little use to begin with, these products are not recommended for flea control. Dips, which are simply highly concentrated preparations of insecticides are also no longer recommended for flea and tick control, because of their highly toxic nature and the advent of newer, safer products.

Second-Generation (Once-a-Month) Products

When treating for parasites on your cat, a number of products designed to be administered only once per month are now available. For instance, fipronil (Frontline) kills adult fleas on cats and helps to break the flea life cycle by killing immature fleas before they can lay eggs. This product is also effective against ticks that your cat may encounter in the woods or field. Applied as a spray or topical drops, fipronil collects within the hair follicles and sebaceous glands of the skin, providing good residual action after initial application. Imidacloprid is yet another addition to the flea-control arsenal that can be incorporated into a comprehensive flea-control program. Imidacloprid works by killing adult fleas on contact, before they can lay eggs. According to its manufacturer, this product, which is applied as topical drops on the back, retains its effectiveness even after sham-

DID YOU KNOW?

Since the advent of newer, safer flea-control products, the incidence of insecticide-related poisoning in cats has decreased dramatically!

pooing or repeated swimming. Lufenuron (Program) is a product designed to be taken internally by your cat. It exerts its flea-control action by sterilizing the fleas that bite the cat. Since they cannot reproduce, fleas are eventually eliminated (in a contained environment) via attrition. it is important to remember that lufenuron does not actually kill fleas. As a result, products that kill adult fleas must be used in conjunction with this treatment in order to achieve effective flea control. As one might expect, many veterinarians recommend this product only for those cats kepts in an indoor (contained) environment.

Natural Remedies

Throughout the years, countless natural remedies for parasite control have been touted as effective alternatives to insecticides. Some of these substances or devices are worn or applied externally; some are designed to be taken internally.

Products such as brewer's yeast, garlic, and B vitamins have all been implicated at one time or another as flea-control remedies. Unfortunately, controlled scientific studies indicate little to no benefit in flea control with these products. In addition, some natural substances can be highly toxic to cats. Check with your veterinarian before giving any natural remedy to your cat.

Certain products containing abrasive-type ingredients (e.g., silica gel and diatomaceous earth) are available for external flea control. These noninsecticidal products act by damaging the chitin exoskeleton of the flea. Desiccation (drying up) and death of the flea can result.

Moderate success has been reported with abrasive-type products. Drying and/or mild irritation of the pet's skin may occur with these products. Frequent application (four to seven times weekly) is required if these are to be used.

Electronic flea collars have limited popularity, as well as limited benefits. Although manufacturers may stand by their efficacy, scientific studies have shown that their worth in controlling external parasites is minimal. These devices are designed to emit a high-pitched sound that can't be heard by humans or cats, yet it drives fleas away. Unfortunately, aside from their relative ineffectiveness, some models might indeed deliver an audible pitch that can be heard by—and might be quite discomforting to—the cat wearing the collar.

Environmental Control

Environmental control of fleas begins in the home. You can use insecticidal foggers to get the job done, or you can employ a professional exterminator. For excellent results, use polymerized borate compounds, available under various brand names from your veterinarian or favorite pet supplier. Sprinkled on the carpets, baseboards, and/or furniture, these compounds will kill all fleas that come in contact with them. Noticeable results are usually obtained within a week after application. Best of all, these powders are odorless, easy to use, and safe for pets and children. Under normal conditions, application of this product must be performed every 6 to 12 months. Carpets must remain dry for continued efficacy; if the carpet becomes damp or is shampooed, reapplication will be necessary.

Your yard should be treated with insecticidal granules every 6 to 8 weeks during the warm months of the year. Alternating the types of insecticidal granules used with each treatment (several different types are available commercially) can improve effectivenesss of your overall control.

Tick Control

Besides fleas, the next most prevalent external parasite that your cat will likely encounter is the tick. Controlling ticks on your cat and in your environment is important for your health as well as your pet's. These unsightly parasites, which attach themselves to their host via sucking mouthparts, can transmit serious diseases such as Rocky Mountain Spotted Fever and Lyme disease to pets and to people. As far as their feline hosts are concerned, untreated infestations can also lead to skin irritation and in severe cases, blood-loss anemia.

Female ticks lay their eggs in and under sheltered areas in the environment, such as wood stumps, rocks, and wall crevices. Once hatched, the larvae, called "seed ticks," will crawl up onto grass stems or bushes and attach themselves to a host that may happen to pass by. Depending on their life cycle, immature ticks may seek out one to three different host animals to complete the maturation process into an adult.

Fortunately, because cats are such meticulous groomers, tick infestations are usually mild, if they occur at all. Since ticks are sensitive to the same type of chemicals as are fleas, treatment and control is basically the same. Certain topical once-a-month treatment for fleas in cats can be effective in controlling ticks as well. Ask your veterinarian for details. Flea and tick collars are sometimes effective at keeping ticks out of the ears. Just be sure that if one is used, it is a "breakaway" variety that is designed to snap apart in case it gets snagged on a fence or tree branch. A pyrethrin spray or powder can also be applied to your cat's haircoat prior to a trip outdoors to discourage ticks from attaching.

Certainly a thorough and consistent treatment of the yard, and if needed, house, with an approved insecticide is the cornerstone of an effective control program. Since ticks can live for months in their surrounding habitat without a blood meal, treatment should be performed every two to four weeks during the peak tick seasons in your area.

If a tick happens to attach itself to your cat, use a pyrethrin spray to kill it. Never attempt to remove ticks from your cat by applying manual pressure alone, or by applying a hot match or needle to the tick's body. Most ticks first killed by the application of a pyrethrin spray will fall off with time once they die. In some cases, you may need to manually remove the dead tick after spraying. When picking them off your cat, never use your bare hands in order to prevent accidental exposure to disease. Instead, use a pair of gloves and tweezers to grasp the dead tick as close to its attachment site as possible, then pull straight up using constant tension. Once the tick is freed, wash the bite wound with soap and water and then apply a first aid cream or ointment to prevent infection. Again, be sure that the tick is completely dead before removal; this will ensure that the tick's mouthparts come out attached to the rest of the body. If left behind, the mouthparts can cause an irritating localized skin reaction.

Preventing Feline Heartworm Disease

Heartworm disease can be a devastating disease in cats. Even though the number of worms typically found in an infected feline's heart is usually small, these worms still take up a lot of space and interfere with proper heart function. The challenge is that cats afflicted with this parasitism are difficult to treat, because killing the adult worms in the relatively small heart and lungs of cats (when compared to dogs) can cause life-threatening blockages to proper blood circulation. As a result, preventing this disease from the start is the key. And the good news is that, as in dogs, it is easy to do so. Feline heartworm preventive medication is available in tablet form, and is designed to be given just once a month. If your cat is not currently on a heartworm prevention program, call right now and schedule an appointment with your veterinarian to start one. In warmer climates where mosquitoes are present nearly year-round, heartworm preventive agents need to be given 12 months out of the year. In contrast, in those regions that experience seasonal changes and cooler temperatures, the preventive agent need not be given the entire year but only during the warmer mosquito season. Be sure to consult your veterinarian as to the proper preventive schedule to follow in your particular area (Fig. 21.5).

Before starting a cat on heartworm preventive medication, a simple blood test needs to be performed to determine whether heartworm exposure has already occurred. If the test results are negative, then your cat may be started on a preventive agent. However, if the test returns positive for heartworms, preventive medication should not be started. Giving such medication to a cat already harboring adult heartworms and heartworm larvae circulating in the bloodstream could cause dangerous adverse reactions. Furthermore, if you are currently giving your pet preventive medication and you miss a scheduled treatment, always consult your veterinarian prior to resuming the treatments. Depending on how late the treatment is, retesting may or may not be necessary. For those cats on a seasonal prevention program, blood retesting should always be performed before the first preventive medication of the season is given.

FIGURE 21.5 The mosquito is the vector for both feline and canine heartworm disease.

Dental Care for Cats

Periodontal disease, or tooth and gum disease, is one of the most common diseases affecting cats today. Symptoms can include tender, swollen gums; excessive drooling;

loss of appetite; and foul breath. More importantly, though, plaque and calculus buildup on the teeth can lead to heart and kidney disease if left untreated.

A complete dental exam should be performed on all cats at least once a year. If dental calculus is present at the gumline, your veterinarian should professionally clean your cat's teeth. Because this cleaning can be a painful procedure, especially if periodontal disease already exists, a short-acting sedative or anesthetic is essential for your cat's comfort and safety. An ultrasonic dental scaler, combined with manual scaling instruments, is used to break apart and remove the hard calculus and deposits from the tooth surfaces. Afterwards, the teeth are polished with a special paste to restore their natural smooth surfaces.

Your pet's dental care doesn't stop there, though! At-home aftercare is a vital part of your cat's dental health. Toothpaste, gels, and rinses formulated for use in felines are readily available from pet stores or veterinary offices. Choose one that contains chlorhexidine, as this antibacterial compound can remain effective for up to 12 hours after application. Human toothpaste should not be used, as it can cause stomach upset if swallowed by your pet. For best results, purchase a special "finger" brush that fits on the end of your finger. These can be purchased at any pet supply store. Apply the paste, gel, or solution to the brush, and proceed to brush your cat's teeth as you would your own, concentrating on the gumline as well as the outsides of the premolars and canine teeth. No rinsing is necessary (Fig. 21.6).

Contrary to popular belief, feeding hard food does little by itself to prevent periodontal disease. However, since dry foods generally contain less sugar than do moist foods, they won't promote periodontal disease as readily as do the latter. Special diets do exist

FIGURE 21.6 You can use your finger to apply dental paste along the gumline to help prevent periodontal disease.

that contain ingredients to help control tartar buildup in cats. Ask your veterinarian if such a diet would be right for your feline.

Remember: Good dental hygiene is important to the health of your pet. In fact, it can help it live a longer, happier life. If you have any questions concerning your cat's dental health, don't hesitate to confer with your veterinarian.

Nutrition

There can be little doubt that proper nutrition is the cornerstone of a long, healthy life for all pets. As our understanding of the link between diet and health increases each day, so does the quality of foods that are available to feed your pet. Not long ago, the diet of most cats consisted primarily of table scraps, supplemented by whatever other foods they could find while roaming freely. Today, our pets more often than not live indoors with us, and it is much more practical to feed them commercially prepared food that is complete and balanced for the particular stage of life of each pet.

While the quality of nutrition for cats has improved considerably with the increasing use of prepared pet foods, there remains a great deal you should know about choosing the proper diet for your pet from among the many thousands of brands available in this country alone. Because cats move through several "life stages" as they age, it is easiest to discuss the nutritional needs of these different life stages separately and in the order in which the cat experiences them.

Nutrition for Kittens

Kittenhood lasts for about the first year of life. During this time, the kitten requires higher levels of minerals such as calcium and phosphorus, protein, vitamins, and energy (calories) than it will as an adult. Therefore, foods fed to young, growing cats should contain these higher levels in balance with each other and with all other dietary nutrients. Such a pet food will carry a designation such as "feline growth" or "kitten food" to distinguish it from diets that contain levels of nutrients that are right for some other life stage, such as adult maintenance.

Please note that the commonly held belief that if "a little is good, more must be better" is not true when it comes to feeding pets. Diets that contain very high levels of minerals, protein, and some vitamins are not superior to those that contain only the amounts required for growth. Excesses can actually be harmful to the growing kitten, as can the practice of supplementing a good growth diet with various human foods or vitamin-mineral preparations. To be sure your kitten gets all the good nutrition it needs for good growth and development, but never too much, follow these simple guidelines:

1. Feed a high-quality, balanced commercial cat food that specifically states on the label that it is intended for growth in cats. Your veterinarian, who should examine, vaccinate, and deworm your kitten, can recommend an appropriate brand. Remember that your kitten's nutrition will influence its lifelong health and happiness. It is very important that you invest in good nutrition at this crucial life stage.

2. Do not supplement a quality, balanced food; you will almost certainly create an imbalance in your pet's diet if you do. Avoid giving table food, table scraps, or treats and snacks to your kitten for the same reason.

3. You can feed your kitten free-choice; however, follow the daily recommendations given on the food bag or can and don't exceed these amounts. Ideally, put down one-half of the recommended daily ration amount in the morning, and later on in the day, feed the second half of the daily ration. Discard any uneaten food prior to bedtime.

4. As always, keep fresh, clean water (preferably filtered) available at all times.

Nutrition for Adult Cats

At about 12 months of age, switch your pet to a maintenance diet for adults. Once your kitten is grown, its nutritional needs are reduced considerably from those during the rapid development of that first year. Continuing to feed your adult cat high levels of minerals (particularly calcium and phosphorus), protein, and energy (calories) could lead to problems later in life. Just as we are finding that excess intake of certain dietary nutrients (like phosphorus, sodium, and fat) are harmful for

DID YOU KNOW?

Cats can starve themselves to death. Whereas otherwise healthy dogs will eventually give in to hunger pressures, cats can be more stubborn. If they go without food long enough, they can develop life-threatening malnutrition and hepatic lipidosis!

humans over long periods, certain excesses might also contribute to diseases such as kidney failure, heart failure, obesity, and diabetes in adult and older cats. Also, we know that reducing the level of key nutrients in the adult's diet to meet but not greatly exceed its needs is never harmful. Good-quality, scientifically designed, adult-maintenance diets always contain these reduced and balanced nutrient levels.

Guidelines for feeding adult cats include

1. Feed a high-quality, complete, and balanced diet specifically designed for adult cat maintenance. Be aware that foods that say they are "complete and balanced for all life stages" are actually kitten foods, since they have been formulated to meet the needs of the most demanding life stage: growth. They contain excesses of most nutrients for the adult or older cat.

2. It is best not to give supplements or treats to your adult cat. If you must give an occasional food snack, low-fat cat snacks are available from your pet store or veterinarian.

3. Adult cats should be fed free-choice. Use the manufacturer's recommended feeding amounts as a starting point only. If your pet gains weight, reduce the portion offered. If your pet starts to lose weight, increase the amount you feed. Your veterinarian can help you decide what your pet's optimum weight should be. Once you know this, weigh your pet periodically to prevent weight loss or gain from becoming a problem.

4. Some cats may gain weight as they grow older, despite eating only moderate amounts of an adult-maintenance diet. For these, follow the instructions for overweight cats in this chapter.

5. The pregnant queen will need extra nutrition in the last few weeks of her pregnancy and throughout the time she nurses her kittens. Actually, she requires a good growth diet again, the

same one she needed when she was young. Provide such a food starting in the last one-third of pregnancy and continue until all kittens are weaned. Feed her free-choice and do not add vitamin-mineral supplements unless your veterinarian recommends it. As the kittens grow and begin to investigate their surroundings, they can be offered some of the mother's food, which they will gradually start to eat. This makes the transition to a kitten-food diet much easier at weaning.

6. Keep fresh, clean water (preferably filtered) available at all times.

Nutrition for the Older Cat

Once your pet reaches 7 years of age, another dietary change becomes necessary. As people and animals age, many organ systems begin to show the effects of wear and tear. The kidneys especially begin to lose the ability to handle waste materials that must be removed from the bloodstream and excreted in the urine. Even older cats that appear to be in perfect health could have kidneys that function much less effectively than they used to.

Guidelines for feeding the older cat include

1. Provide a high-quality pet food specifically designed for the older cat. Your veterinarian can advise you of any special health problems that your pet already has and any other dietary changes that might be necessary. In many cases of "old age" diseases, special foods can be prescribed along with medication to help manage these conditions.

2. If you notice your older cat gaining or losing weight, consult with your veterinarian about any changes in diet that can correct the problem. At the same time, your vet will check for any medical problem that might be contributing to the change in weight.

3. Do not supplement your older cat's diet with anything unless your veterinarian specifically recommends it. The older cat is even more sensitive than the young cat to the unbalancing effects of frequent snacks, treats, and table food added to the diet.

Dr. P's Vet Tip

Feeding your cat a high-quality, highly digestible diet will cut
down on litterbox odor as well as litterbox mess.

4. Take your "senior" for regular (at least once a year) medical checkups to catch problems early or prevent them altogether. The right diet throughout the life of your pet is an important part of a sound preventive medicine program to safeguard its health and long life.

5. Keep fresh, clean, filtered water available at all times.

Dietary Management of Disease

For years, medical research has been telling us about the benefits of eating a well-balanced diet for good health. In addition, we also know that special modification of the dietary intake in the presence of a disease state can be helpful in the treatment and/or long-term management of the condition. This same nutritional health concept can be applied to cats as well.

Many disease conditions in cats, such as obesity (yes, obesity is a disease!), heart disease, kidney disease, and gastrointestinal disease, can be effectively controlled, and sometimes even cured, just through diet modulation alone.

For example, obesity, feline megacolon, certain types of colitis, and diabetes mellitus are all conditions that warrant an increase in the amount of fiber present in the ration. Cats suffering from feline lower urinary tract disease benefit from diets that acidify the urine and contain low levels of magnesium and other trace minerals. Finally, recommended management of cats suffering from kidney disease includes diets low in protein and phosphorus.

These special diets or rations aimed at fighting or counteracting feline diseases can be purchased through your veterinarian, or can be prepared at home via veterinary-supplied recipes. In general, the commercially prepared products are preferred over the homemade rations. The cost of these diets is negligible when compared to continuing veterinary bills and the poor quality of life that would result by not providing them. Just remember to follow your veterinarian's directions closely as to amounts and frequency of administering these diets if they are indeed used.

Managing and Preventing Obesity

Obesity is certainly one of the most prevalent diseases affecting the U.S. cat population today. For years, the frequency of this health disorder was skyrocketing at an alarming pace, owing primarily to improper feeding practices. Unfortunately, owners might not realize that by encouraging their cat to get fat, they are at the same time endangering its health and unfairly reducing its quality of life.

The health-related ramifications of obesity in cats are the same as those in people. Although cats don't suffer from atherosclerosis and heart attacks like we do, obesity does place a great strain on their cardiovascular systems. Other internal organs suffer the consequences as well. Obese cats seem to suffer from more skin ailments and coat disorders than do their slim and trim counterparts. In addition, musculoskeletal disorders, including joint injuries sustained when jumping, occur with greater frequency in cats carrying around excessive baggage.

Visually, cats that are overweight aren't hard to miss. Most will sport a waist that is barely discernable and ribs that can barely be felt when their chest is touched. In addition, the skin on the abdomen of many of these cats may drag the ground! In summary, it is safe to say that the overall quality of and length of life for overweight cats are reduced, owing to the adverse effects of obesity.

Causes of Obesity

The potential causes of obesity in cats are numerous, yet the most common one is overfeeding. Because it can be difficult to force a cat to exercise regularly, many owners miscalculate their cat's caloric needs and feed too much. Also, feeding a higher calorie food to a less active or older cat that requires less energy can promote obesity as well. Furthermore, remember that cats spending much of their time outdoors might have access to food elsewhere in the neighborhood.

Proper Diet

If your cat is overweight, simply cutting back on the amount you feed will not do the trick. In fact, doing so could conceivably lead to a mild state of malnutrition and will cause your cat to be constantly hungry and hunting for food. Instead of cutting back the ration, switch to a diet that is specially formulated for weight loss. These diets are readily available from your veterinarian. They might cost a bit more than what you are accustomed to paying for cat food at the supermarket, but the switch is only temporary and the benefits to your pet immense.

These special foods have a high fiber content, which allows for calorie reduction while giving your cat that feeling of fullness after eating. Your veterinarian can assist you as far as how much and how often to feed. Keeping a daily portion of food available in a bowl throughout the day might help satisfy your pet even more. Be patient with the results. You might not realize it, but even one pound of weight loss is significant in a cat. It is vital that during the weight-reduction period you remain consistent with the feedings and avoid giving any snacks (a few kibbles of the special diet now and then can make for an excellent snack substitute).

Exercise

As with people, lack of exercise does its part to promote obesity. Cats kept indoors rarely get enough exercise—unless, of course, they are leash-trained and can be taken for daily walks. However, simply playing with your cat more when you get home or take a break from work can do its part to help burn those calories!

Skin and Coat Care

Routine grooming is essential for maintaining healthy hair and skin in cats. Be sure to allot some time each day to this task.

Brushing

Whether your cat has short or long hair, brushing the coat thoroughly on a daily basis will aid in its appearance, reduce the incidence of hairballs, and promote healthy skin. It does this by

- Removing telogen (dead) hairs from the coat, making way for new ones to grow in.

- Preventing tangles and mats.

- Stimulating sebaceous gland activity, which keeps the skin moisturized and the haircoat shiny. Brushing also helps to spread these oils across the entire skin and coat.

- Removing scale (excess keratin), which could lead to itching.

- Increasing owner awareness of the presence of external parasites or other skin-related problems.

Long- or thick-coated breeds require more diligent brushing than do shorter-coated cats, because of high shedding and matting tendencies. Minor shedding is normal year-round in all breeds. However, because the shedding cycle in cats is stimulated by changes in day length, most will occur during the spring and fall months, when the days become longer and shorter, respectively.

Long-coated cats should be brushed using a wire-pin brush or comb. For shorthaired cats, a bristle-type brush or rubber curry comb will do the trick.

Always use firm, short strokes when brushing, never forcing the brush through the coat. If you encounter a mat, don't try to forcefully remove it with the brush. Instead, try to work it free with your fingers, using one hand to free the tangle and the other to stabilize the tuft of hair to keep it from pulling the skin.

If the mat or tangle still can't be freed, insert a comb between the mat and the skin surface, then take a pair of blunt-nosed scissors and snip as much of the mat off as you can between the comb and the free end of the hair. Don't worry about cosmetic appearances. It will grow back! Mats that are left in place can cause skin infections. And always remember: If you brush your cat as often as you should, you won't have a problem with matting! Be aware that excessive matting could indicate that your cat has a problem with external parasites or with some type of skin disorder.

Bathing

Cats with normal, healthy skin and haircoats really do not require routine bathing. It's a good thing, too, since most cats abhor bathing! Actually, indiscriminate bathing can dry out the skin and predispose an otherwise healthy integument to disease. So when is bathing necessary? Our feline friends do need it when any of the following circumstances develop:

- Accumulation of excessive dirt, grease, or other foreign substances on the skin and coat

- Buildup of waxy sebum (seborrhea), which often leads to body odor
- Accumulation of skin scale (dandruff)
- Skin infections

Hypoallergenic or other mild cat shampoos are ideal for bathing cats with otherwise healthy skin and coats. For medical conditions involving skin infections and seborrhea, use only those shampoos prescribed by your veterinarian. Using the wrong type of shampoo on such skin disorders will yield poor results and might even exacerbate them. Even if your cat appears to have perfectly healthy skin, it is still prudent to consult your veterinarian in choosing a specific shampoo for it. Your vet will be able to recommend products and give you valuable tips on how to continue to keep your cat's integument (skin) in the top shape.

Prior to putting your cat into the tub or laundry sink, brush the coat thoroughly and remove any mats and tangles. In addition, always apply some type of protection to both eyes to prevent accidental soap burns. Mineral oil has been used for this purpose; however, a sterile ophthalmic ointment is preferred. Such ointment is readily available from your veterinarian or favorite pet store, and it provides greater eye protection than does plain mineral oil.

Once these preparatory measures have been taken, you can proceed with the shampoo and rinse. If a medicated shampoo is to be used, plan on allowing it to lather and remain in contact with the skin for a good 10 minutes before rinsing. After rinsing, a towel or chamois cloth can be used for drying. Blow dryers are not recommended for cats.

Nail Trimming

As part of a routine grooming program and furniture preservation effort, you should perform a nail trim on your cat every 2 to 3 weeks if indeed your cat has not been declawed (Fig. 21.7). The procedure itself is easy, assuming that you have the right equipment and that your cat agrees to cooperate. If your feline refuses to stand still for its manicure, let your veterinarian perform the deed. It will be less stressful on both you and your cat.

There are many types and styles of nail trimmers on the market today. The preferred choice is the guillotine-type nail trimmers with replaceable blades. These are available at pet stores everywhere.

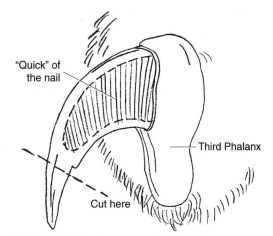

FIGURE 21.7 Keeping the nails trimmed short is one alternative to declawing.

The procedure itself is simple on the clear nails. Observe the nail to be clipped and identify the endpoint of the blood supply, or the "quick." Then, staying just in front of the quick, snip off the end portion of the nail.

Invariably, the time might come when you accidentally "quick" your pet's nail, causing it to bleed. If this occurs, there is no cause for panic. Using a clean cloth or gauze pad, apply direct pressure to the bleeding nail for 5 minutes to stop the bleeding. Alternatively, you can apply clotting powder or ordinary flour to the end of the affected nail to help stop the bleeding.

Caring for the Older Cat

It is estimated that in the United States alone, over 35 percent of all pets owned are geriatric. Depending on which veterinarian you talk to, cats are considered geriatric when they reach 7 to 9 years of age. Understand, though, that breed, genetics, nutrition, and environmental influences will all ultimately affect the aging process in a particular cat (Table 21.3).

The overall care that a cat receives throughout its life will have a great impact

DID YOU KNOW?

Like dogs, cats experience accelerated biological aging during their first few years of life versus their latter years, which is Nature's way of allowing for hastened sexual maturity and speedy propagation of the species.

Table 21.3 Chronological versus Biological Age of Cats as Compared to Humans

Cat age, years	Human age, years
1	16
2	23
3	27
4	31
5	35
6	39
7	43
8	47
9	51
10	56
11	60
12	64
13	69
14	73
15	77

on the rate of aging. Cats that are well cared for throughout kittenhood and adult life tend to suffer fewer infirmities as they grow old. Furthermore, through diligent preventive health care measures, age-related health problems can be detected early, greatly diminishing their impact. In contrast, neglecting a pet in husbandry or in preventive health care will greatly accelerate the aging process.

Physical changes seen as cats age are related to wear and tear on all body systems. Again, these are variable between individuals and breeds, and can be greatly influenced by an owner who provides good environment, proper nutrition, and routine veterinary care throughout the cat's life.

Physical Challenges in Older Cats

As with people, the overall metabolism of a pet has a tendency to slow as the years advance. This, combined with a decrease in the amount of activity, can easily predispose a geriatric pet to obesity and all its dangerous ramifications. As cats age, they don't suffer from many of the cardiovascular challenges that humans do, such as hardening of the arteries and atherosclerosis. Yet as the feline matures, the heart does become less efficient at pumping blood during exercise or stressful situations that can arise. In addition, heart disease caused by wear and tear from years of normal use is common in all older pets. It can often be related back to untreated periodontal disease during the pet's younger years.

Bone and joint challenges. Arthritis can affect older cats in the same way as it affects their canine counterparts. Since cats are relatively lightweight, joint degeneration from age-related wear and tear is seldom as profound as it would be in a dog the same age. However, it will slow an older cat down, and limit its desire to jump on and off of objects as it used to do.

Muscular challenges. The muscles of older cats tend to atrophy because of a decrease in muscle activity and age-related protein loss from the body. A loss in flexibility can also occur, causing upwardly mobile felines to slow down.

Disorders of the skin and hair. These can increase in prevalence in the geriatric cat as a result of aging effects on the hair cycle and because of metabolic and endocrine upsets.

Aging kidneys. It is a well-known fact that as a cat matures, its kidneys become less efficient at filtering the blood and ridding the body of waste products. Incredibly, however, it would take a loss of over 75 percent of the functioning capacity of both kidneys to lead to signs of kidney failure in cats. As a result, care taken early to help ease the burden placed on the aging kidneys and keep them out of this percentage range using special diets and medications will greatly enhance the longevity of a cat.

Reproductive challenges. Female cats that were not spayed at an early age are more prone to reproductive system problems, including mammary cancer and uterine infections, as they enter their geriatric years. Furthermore, as one might expect, fertility and reproductive performance tend to decrease with advancing age.

Intestinal challenges. The aging gastrointestinal tract might begin to show signs of reduced efficiency and intolerance to excesses. For this reason, flare-ups of gastritis, colitis, and constipation can become more prevalent as a pet enters its golden years. At the same time, liver function can decrease, making it more difficult to metabolize nutrients and detoxify wastes within the body.

Weakened immune systems. It is well documented that the efficiency and activity of the immune system is compromised with age. As a result, geriatric pets are more susceptible to disease, especially viruses and cancer. For this reason, preventive health care takes on an even more important meaning in these pets.

Endocrine challenges. As cats mature, the activity of the glands within the body may start to decrease, leaving the pet with hormone-related challenges. For example, *hyperthyroidism,* often caused by a tumor of the thyroid gland, is a condition that can arise in maturing cats. *Diabetes mellitus* can occur secondarily to aging of the insulin-producing cells within the pancreas.

Vision challenges. Most older cats will likely develop a slight grayish hue to the lenses of both eyes, yet this rarely causes severe vision challenges. In fact, the incidence of age-related blindness in cats is much less than that for dogs. However, as cats age, their ability to focus on objects will diminish, so they might react suddenly if approached. Don't confuse this with crankiness or irritability. A slow approach with a gentle hand accompanied by a calm voice will allow a cat with failing vision to hear and smell the familiar person approaching.

Hearing loss. Fortunately, partial or total hearing loss is not common in geriatric cats, but it can occur. It is often related to long-term, irreversible nervous changes in the inner ear. Further hearing loss occurs with senile changes or damage to the eardrum or ossicles (the bones of vibration conduction) housed within the middle ear. Wax accumulation within the ears can play a role in deafness as well.

DR. P'S VET TIP

Food palatability can be enhanced by increasing a food's odor or changing its texture. Odor can be enhanced by warming the food or by adding bouillon or gravy to it. The texture of a ration can be changed by blending it or cooking it further.

Dependence on sense of smell. The sense of smell is usually the last sense to fail in a cat. For this reason, the geriatric cat depends more and more on its sense of smell to identify people, objects, and food. Also, the senses of taste and smell are highly dependent on one another in cats. As a result, the appetite of older cats may taper off as the sense of smell becomes compromised. This can be dangerous if the cat begins to refuse food, as secondary liver disease could result. As a result, close attention needs to be paid to the appetites of older felines.

Cognitive dysfunction syndrome (senility). Senility is relatively rare in older cats, yet when it occurs, it may manifest itself as changes in sleep patterns, changes in the levels and types of social interaction desired, increased house soiling, and disorientation. Your veterinarian may be able to prescribe medications to help reduce these symptoms and improve your pet's quality of life.

The changes that occur with aging warrant special adjustments in husbandry practices and preventive health care for geriatric cats. The following four steps are recommended to be sure that your cat's geriatric years are filled with health and happiness:

1. Adjust your cat's diet to match its health needs. Your veterinarian can assist you with this switch. If your pet suffers from a specific ailment, such as heart or kidney disease, special diets can be prescribed to reduce the wear and tear on the affected organ systems. For the otherwise healthy cat, provide a diet that is higher in fiber and lower in calories. Don't forget to weigh your cat on a regular basis. Obesity is an enemy, and can significantly shorten your cat's life.

2. Keep your cat as active as possible. Consistent activity will help keep your cat's bones, joints, heart, and lungs conditioned. If your pet is suffering from a specific medical condition, always consult your veterinarian first as to the type and amount of activity that is appropriate for your particular pet.

3. Be sure to brush your pet daily. Skin and coat changes secondary to metabolic slowdown or adjustments within the body can often be managed with a stepped-up home grooming program. Along with grooming, be sure to give your geriatric pet plenty of

attention each day. As the senses start to fail, pets can become frightened by the gradual loss of sensory contact with their owners. As a result, you need to reinforce the care and companionship you are offering.

4. Semiannual veterinary checkups and periodic at-home physical examinations for aging pets are a must. Remember: Early detection of a disease condition is the key to curing or managing the disorder. Also, because of the effects of aging on the immune system, be sure to keep your cat current on its vaccinations.

Breeding Your Cat

A sound knowledge of feline reproductive principles constitutes the livelihood of the professional cat breeder. But professional breeders are not the only ones that need to know about these matters. All cat owners planning to breed their pets should do their homework first prior to proceeding with such plans. And because of the importance of preventive health care for kittens, be sure that your female cat is up-to-date with all immunizations and stool exams prior to breeding.

For an overview of the anatomic and functional features of the reproductive system, both male and female, see Chap. 31.

Puberty and the Reproductive Cycle

Puberty is defined as the age in which the queen first comes into heat, or when the male testicles first begin to produce spermatozoa. It varies with each breed, but generally occurs between 6 and 12 months of age.

As a general rule, owners should wait until a male cat (tomcat) reaches at least 12 to 14 months of age before using it for breeding purposes. For females (queens), breeding attempts should not be made until the second or third heat cycle. Even these guidelines can vary somewhat, depending on the cat's level of maturity, both mentally and physically.

The optimum breeding age for female cats is between 3 and 6 years. Kittens born to females in these age groups tend to be healthier at birth, grow more rapidly, and wean much more easily when compared to others. After 6 years, reproductive performance in the queen begins a steady decline. Tomcats, on the other hand, have greater sexual longevity than do females, yet this, too, begins to decline over the years.

The Estrous Cycle

The term *estrous cycle* is used to describe a series of events that occurs within the female reproductive tract between actual heat periods. Cats are considered seasonal breeders; that is, sexual activity becomes more active in the early spring and early fall. There are four phases to the feline estrous cycle: (1) anestrus, (2) proestrus, (3) estrus, and (4) metestrus-diestrus.

Anestrus. During this period there is no reproductive activity in the ovaries. The duration of anestrus is typically 2 to 3 months in the average cat.

Proestrus. From anestrus, the reproductive cycle enters the period of proestrus. Signs seen during proestrus are minimal, although an increased frequency in urinary activity might be seen.

Estrus. From proestrus, the queen enters into estrus, or true heat and is receptive to the tomcat. Marked behavioral changes also occur, such as increased vocalizations, loss of appetite, and elevation of the hindquarters when the queen is petted (Fig. 22.1). Queens in heat often roll around the floor and rub up against anything they can find. The duration of estrus is 10 days to 2 weeks if mating does not occur.

Metestrus-diestrus. Following estrus, the metestrus-diestrus period marks the end of sexual receptivity by the queen if not mated, or the beginning of pregnancy if a successful mating takes place. False pregnancies can occur during this period in cats in the same way they do in dogs. These are influenced by the

DID YOU KNOW?

Queens are induced ovulators, that is, mating stimulates the egg to be ovulated from the ovary, increasing the chances of a successful fertilization.

progesterone secreted from the ovary at the site where the ovulation occurred. False pregnancies can sometimes mimic the real thing, yet as the progesterone levels taper off because of unsuccessful fertilization, the signs associated with false pregnancies will slowly abate.

A tomcat sensing a queen in heat will start vocalizing to attract the female to his "territory."

FIGURE 22.1 Females in heat will elevate their hindquarters when touched.

When the female approaches, the tom will grip the skin of the queen's neck in his mouth, a move properly termed the *neck grip*. After this, mounting and copulation will take place.

Gestation

The gestation period for cats ranges from 58 to 70 days, averaging 63 days. Unfortunately, there are no simple blood tests that can confirm whether a cat is pregnant. As a result, alternate means of pregnancy diagnosis must be utilized.

Ultrasonography provides a reliable method for confirming pregnancy status as early as 28 days. If an ultrasound is not available, abdominal palpation by trained hands can often achieve similar results. Abdominal enlargement and mammary development usually become noticeable after the first month of pregnancy. If an uncertainty still exists, radiographic X rays can be used to confirm pregnancies as early as 45 days.

Care of the Pregnant Cat

Care of the pregnant cat consists of maintaining a good plane of nutrition and reducing stress as much as possible. Expectant queens should be put on a growth-type ration, similar to those used for kittens, throughout the gestation and lactation periods. Because *eclampsia,* or milk fever, is rare in cats, mineral supplements are rarely required.

During your cat's pregnancy, administer all medications only with your veterinarian's direct consent or direct supervision. Many drugs can harm both mother and unborn kittens if given during pregnancy. Always check the labels on insecticide products used for flea and tick control before applying to pregnant pets. The label should state whether that product is safe to use on pregnant pets. If this is not mentioned on the label, play it safe; don't use the product.

The Birthing Process

One of the most fascinating and rewarding experiences associated with cat ownership occurs when a queen undergoes *parturition* (the birthing process). In most instances, you need only to sit back and let nature take its course.

Although *dystocia* (difficult parturition) is not especially common in cats, it is important to be able to recognize problems that may arise in order to protect the health of both mother and offspring. Dystocia can occur in any type of cat, yet the more exotic breeds are at higher risk than others. Those cats that have suffered a prior traumatic pelvic injury are at higher risk as well.

As mentioned previously, the average length of pregnancy in the cat is 63 days. If your cat is not already acquainted with her surroundings, be sure to allow her up to 3 weeks prior to the delivery date to become familiar and comfortable with her new environment. You may choose to provide her a special bed or delivery box, yet your cat will probably seek out a birthing area of her own. Popular spots include beds (on top of or beneath), drawers, and closets.

Enlargement of the queen's mammary glands is noted 48 to 72 hours prior to delivery. A mucoid discharge from the vulva might also be seen at that time. Although in the majority of instances, your assistance in the parturition process will not be needed, some cats will seek out their owners as the time approaches. If this is the case, plan to stay with your cat until parturition is complete. However, it is important to let nature take its course and avoid interruptions during labor. Some queens have been known to delay labor for days if they feel uncomfortable with outside interference!

As the queen enters true labor and contractions become more frequent, the first placental sac will soon come into view. Following a normal birth, a green discharge will be seen. The queen will clean the membranes off the kittens and sever the umbilical cord. Do not be alarmed if the queen eats the afterbirth. This is normal behavior. The expected interval between deliveries is 5 to 40 minutes. In some cases, the entire delivery process took 1 to 2 days to complete, with no ill effects to either mother or offspring!

Stages of Parturition

Stage 1: prelabor. This stage might last anywhere from 2 to 36 hours. Signs associated with this stage include pacing, anxiety, nest building, loss of appetite, vomiting, and/or shivering.

Stage two: true labor. Signs seen when a cat enters into true labor include straining, abdominal contractions, the appearance of the placental sac, and the actual birth of the kitten.

Stage three: expulsion. The placenta might be passed with the kitten or soon after its birth. A green fluid should accompany a normal delivery.

The following guidelines (see also Fig. 22.2) are written in a quick reference, logarithmic format to help you through your cat's special time. If you ever have any questions or doubts concerning the health of your cat or one of its kittens, don't hesitate to contact your veterinarian for advice.

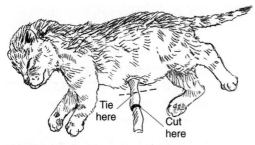

FIGURE 22.2 Correct placement of ligatures when severing the umbilical cord.

Care of Neonatal Kittens

This section is included to alert you to potential health problems that might arise in neonatal kittens (see Figs. 22.3 and 22.4). If you suspect that something is wrong, consult your veterinarian immediately. Normally, healthy newborn kittens should be doing one of two things: eating or sleeping. Crying usually indicates hunger, and should cease when the kitten is allowed to nurse. If it doesn't, something might be wrong.

Hypoglycemia

Hypoglycemia, or low blood sugar, can result from lack of adequate intake of the mother's milk. It is often seen in orphaned kittens too weak to nurse. This condition requires immediate attention, for it can lead to profound weakness, convulsions, and death.

Commercial formulas available at your veterinarian or pet store are ideal milk substitutes. The amounts needed by the kitten are printed on

FIGURE 22.3 Newborn kittens receive colostrum from their mother's milk during their first 24 hours of life. This colostrum contains antibodies that help protect the neonates against disease.

the label. However, in emergency situations, you can prepare a homemade formula from one large egg yolk and enough homogenized milk to prepare 4 to 6 ounces of formula. The mixture might be sweetened by adding one teaspoon of honey to 8 ounces of formula.

a   **b**

FIGURE 22.4 The sex of a young kitten can be determined by the distance between the anus and genitalia. This distance is shorter in the female (*a*) than it is in the male (*b*).

Feed this homemade formula according to the willingness of the kitten to accept it. A general rule of thumb is one tablespoon of formula for every 2 ounces of the animal's body weight per 24 hours. For example, a 6-ounce kitten would get three tablespoons of formula in 24 hours. Feedings should be performed every 2 hours. You can obtain a feeding syringe or pet nurser from your veterinarian or local pet store. If the neonate simply refuses to eat, tube feeding might be required. Ask your veterinarian for details. It should be emphasized that this formula is only for emergencies, and the commercial formula should be started as soon as possible.

Diarrhea

Diarrhea is another dangerous condition in newborn kittens. Sometimes, the only sign of diarrhea you'll notice is an inflamed anus, since mothers are so good at cleaning up after their young. *Toxic-milk syndrome* is one of the diseases that can cause diarrhea in neonates. "Bad" milk might result if *mastitis* (mammary gland infection) or uterine infection exists in the mother.

Affected neonates often bloat suddenly, cry frequently, run a fever, and are restless. When toxic-milk syndrome is suspected, kittens must be prevented from nursing the mother, and your veterinarian should be contacted. Oxygen, special fluids, and antibiotic injections might be necessary for treatment.

A newborn's hydration status might be easily evaluated by testing the elasticity of the skin over its back. If the skin fails to fall back to its

Flowchart for parturition in cats

Has your cat started to show ———▶ No. ———▶ Review this section and
signs of stage 1 labor?   watch for signs of stage 1
                                                       labor. Contact your
                                                       veterinarian if pregnancy
Yes.   lasts more than 63 days.

Is there any evidence of a ———▶ Yes. ———▶ Contact your veterinarian.
green, black, or red foul-
smelling discharge from the
vulva?

No.

Don't intervene prematurely.
Leave your cat alone in a
quiet environment with
minimal interruptions.
Many cats have the ability
to delay parturition if
interrupted by the
unnecessary presence of an
owner.

Has your cat started to show ———▶ No. ———▶ Contact your veterinarian if
signs of stage 2 labor?   stage 1 lasts more than 36
                                                       hours.
Yes.

Has a kitten been born ———▶ No. ———▶ Contact your veterinarian.
within 2 hours after the
onset of stage 2 labor?

Yes.

Immediately after giving ———▶ No. ———▶ Put on disposable gloves
birth, has the queen   and manually remove the
removed the placental   membranes.
membranes surrounding the
newborn?

Yes.

Has the kitten started breathing within 1 minute after birth? ⟶ No. ⟶ Hold the kitten upside-down to allow the fluid to drain from the lungs and vigorously massage the skin. A bulb syringe can be used to suction excess fluid out of the mouth and nose. If this approach is not working within 2 to 3 minutes, institute artificial respiration (CPR), and gently expand the lungs, taking care not to blow too hard into the nostril. Avoid overinflating the lungs. Continue artificial respiration and massage until the kitten is breathing on its own.

Yes.

Has the queen severed the umbilical cord? ⟶ No. ⟶ Tie off the cord with thin gauze or thread by making a knot abut $1/2$ inch from the body wall of the newborn, then sever the cord between the knot and the membranes. Discard the membranes. Treat the end of the umbilical stump with tamed iodine (see Fig. 22.2).

Has at least 2 hours elapsed between births? ⟶ Yes. ⟶ Contact your veterinarian.

No.

Following delivery and cleanup by the queen, newborn kittens will usually find their way to their mother's milk supply. You should, however, keep an eye out for kittens that might be rejected and ignored by the mother for one reason or another. For instance, this rejection might occur if the newborn's body temperature is lower than normal, if it is the runt of the litter, or if it has any physical abnormalities.

Do you suspect a rejection of a newborn?   ——→ Yes. ——→ Try warming the kitten with a blanket or well-insulated heating pad (use the low setting!), then place it back with the mother and the rest of the litter. If this does not work, you might need to hand-feed the kitten yourself. Contact your veterinarian.

No.

It is wise to have your cat examined by your veterinarian once you think that parturition is complete. A dark, red discharge might be seen from the vulva following the last birth. On the average, an entire litter is usually born within 12 hours after the onset of parturition.

natural position after being pulled up with your fingers, the kitten is most likely dehydrated. Since kittens can dehydrate seven times faster than adults, this condition can prove to be rapidly fatal if not managed immediately.

Hypothermia

Another major cause of death in neonates is *hypothermia* (*loss* of body temperature). This condition is often seen in kittens rejected by their mothers. To help prevent hypothermia, the air temperature in the kittens' environment should be maintained at or above 75 degrees Fahrenheit at all times, and care should be taken to prevent the young from being exposed to drafts and to cold floors.

Retained Urine and Feces

Finally, orphaned or neglected kittens less than three to four weeks of age can suffer from retained urine and feces, since they normally need to be stimulated by their mother to eliminate. To stimulate these necessary functions, kittens should be gently massaged in the genital and anal areas with a cotton ball soaked in warm water. This should be done after each feeding and at least once between feedings.

Kitten Mortality Complex (KMC)

This condition is more common in certain breeds of cats, including the Himalayan. Queens predisposed to KMC litters exhibit infertility, abortions, and stillbirths. For those kittens that survive parturition, most are extremely weak and poor "doers" and usually die within hours to days after delivery. Certain disease organisms, including feline leukemia, upper respiratory viruses, and feline infectious peritonitis, are all suspected as etiologies of KMC. Unfortunately, there is no effective way to treat KMC once it strikes. Supportive care is certainly warranted for those individuals affected. As far as prevention is concerned, it is recommended that all queens that have produced KMC litters in the past not be used for breeding purposes.

Elective Surgeries in Cats

Two of the more common elective surgeries (surgeries not resulting from disease or illness) performed in cats include neutering (ovario-hysterectomy, castration) and declawing. The latter procedure has come under much public scrutiny as to its necessity and humaneness. Whether you decide to have such a procedure performed on your cat is entirely up to you, but before making a final decision, you are encouraged to communicate with your veterinarian, who will be able to answer your questions regarding benefits, risks, and controversy surrounding any particular elective surgery

Anesthesia

The term *anesthesia* tends to inspire uneasiness and fear in many people. Actually, anesthesia is an indispensable tool in veterinary and human medicine, as well. It is required for the painless performance of many important procedures, including surgery, dentistry, diagnostics, and physical restraint.

There are basically two types of anesthetics that are used alone or in combination in elective and

DID YOU KNOW?

The feral cat population in the United States is estimated at over 50 million!

nonelective surgeries: *injectable anesthetics,* which are used quite often for procedures lasting for only a short period of time; and *inhalation (gas) anesthesia,* which is used for longer procedures and for maintenance.

Newer, safer anesthetic agents are now available for use in pets. However, regardless of the type of anesthetic agent used, it is important to remember that none are totally risk-free. It is difficult to predict how each pet will react while under anesthesia, yet with strict monitoring and adherence to basic anesthetic principles, many problems can be avoided.

Ideally, animals should be as healthy as possible prior to undergoing anesthesia. For this reason, laboratory work is often required to confirm the health status of your pet. Of course, certain situations will require the use of anesthesia in sick animals. It is easy to see how the risks of anesthesia tend to be greater in these patients. Older animals also tend to be at greater risk. Yet, again, with the proper laboratory workup and a good physical exam performed by your veterinarian prior to anesthesia, as well as close monitoring during the procedure, the risks associated with the anesthesia can be greatly minimized.

Owners, too, have a responsibility to help ensure the safety of a pet undergoing anesthesia. Be sure to inform your veterinarian of all medications your pet is currently taking, as well as any changes you have noted regarding your pet's behavior (more frequent urination, exercise intolerance, etc.). Don't hesitate to review your pet's past medical history with your veterinarian and to ask questions concerning the anesthesia to be used.

If the pet is to stay at home the night before the surgery, it is imperative that all food be taken away at least 12 to 18 hours prior to the scheduled procedure. Water, on the other hand, may usually be offered up to 4 hours before the scheduled anesthesia. Be sure to check with your veterinarian regarding this subject. If for some reason your pet does eat food or drink water when it's not supposed to, it is important that you relate this information to your veterinarian.

Neutering

Ovariohysterectomy (OHE) involves the surgical removal of the ovaries and uterus from an intact female cat. The common term assigned to this procedure is "spaying." OHE is a preferred method of birth control in cats, since it is easy to perform and ensures 100 percent sterility. Most veterinarians require a cat to be at least 6 months of age before undergoing such an operation.

Aside from birth control, there are many other reasons for performing an OHE on your female cat. For instance, it can prevent uterine infections in mature cats. In addition, it has been used as a behavioral modification tool to calm excited or overly aggressive cats. Finally, and very importantly, spaying a cat at an early age might reduce the risks of mammary cancer in the future.

The entire process takes anywhere from 10 to 20 minutes, depending on the skill of the surgeon and on certain patient factors. For instance, the procedure normally takes longer if the cat is in heat at the time of surgery, owing to an increased blood supply to the reproductive tract, thus requiring additional care and ligatures. The same holds true for pregnant cats. Excessively overweight cats are more difficult to spay because increased fatty tissue within the abdomen may obstruct the surgeon's view.

The technical term for neutering a tomcat is *castration* (the colloquial term is "fixing"), which involves the surgical removal of the testicles. This procedure is commonly employed for birth control, and for reducing territoriality and aggressiveness in male cats (Fig. 23.1). In general, castrations can be safely performed on a cat as early as 6 months of age.

Sterilization surgery on cats may soon be phased out and replacd with a series of special injections. Chemicals that can render the reproductive organs nonfunctional have been developed, and may offer a safer, more affordable way to neuter a pet. Ask your veterinarian for details (Fig. 23.2).

FIGURE 23.1 Castrating tomcats can sometimes help curb aggressive tendencies.

FIGURE 23.2 With animal shelters overflowing with so many unwanted pets, neutering your cat is highly recommended.

Common Concerns about Neutering

One common misconception about spaying a cat is the belief that a female needs to go through at least one heat cycle or have at least one litter of kittens before the deed is performed. Many feel that this is necessary for the proper emotional development of their cat, but in fact, it isn't. On the contrary, spaying before the first heat cycle will have no adverse effect on a cat's mental well-being, and, as mentioned earlier, can offer significant medical benefits to the cat.

Another concern that many pet owners harbor is that neutering will cause their cats to gain weight. However, poor feeding practices, lack of activity, or certain medical conditions cause obesity, not the act of neutering. By addressing these issues, you can keep your neutered cat slim, trim, and healthy!

Declawing

The decision on whether to have a cat declawed is certainly a controversial one, yet it must be based on individual circumstances. For indoor cats that refuse to use a scratching post, declawing is certainly a better solution than drug therapy, or worse yet, eviction from the home. Also, for predominately outdoor cats who spend their time indoors destroying the furniture with their claws, declawing might be the answer (Fig. 23.3). It is important to remember, however, that removal of the front claes impairs a cat's ability to climb in order to escape potential danger from hostile dogs, humans, fellow cats, or other species that might pursue them.

Declawing can be performed as early as 12 weeks of age. In fact, younger cats seem to recover much faster from the surgery than do

FIGURE 23.3 Declawing your cat may become necessary if it refuses to limit its scratching activities to its scratching post.

older cats, primarily because of the immature development of the blood supply and other supporting structures to the nails at a younger age.

Before deciding to declaw your cat, try to train it to a scratching post first. If done correctly, you might find that this may solve the problem. Also, consider keeping your cat's nails clipped short to minimize the damage caused by its scratching activity. Since cats' nails are somewhat fragile, be sure that the nail clippers you use are sharp. Guillotine-type clippers available from pet stores work best.

When clipping the nail back, be sure to stop short of the pink "quick," which contains the blood supply

🔍FACT OR FICTION

Cats that are declawed in front can't defend themselves. **FICTION.** A cat in true defense mode will utilize its back claws with utmost efficiency! What renders a feline truly defenseless is to remove these rear claws, which will also take away its ability to climb. As a result, remove only the front claws, never the back ones.

to the nail. However, if an accident does happen, the bleeding can be controlled with direct pressure to the site through the use of clotting powder, again available at a local pet store.

Finally, special nail covers are also available to minimize the damage associated with scratching activity. However, if none of the aforementioned options work, then removal of the front claws might be the only option left to preserve that happy owner-pet relationship.

Postsurgical Care for Cats

Following any type of surgery, you should receive specific instructions from your veterinarian as to the type of postsurgical care your pet requires. It is important to follow these instructions closely to ensure an uneventful recovery. Postsurgical instructions include

- Do not give your cat food or water for 30 minutes after arriving at home; doing so can cause nausea and vomiting.

- Restrict your pet's activity for 8 to 10 days or until the sutures are removed. Protect your pet from stress, such as extreme exertion, excitement, temperature fluctuations, and drafts. Traveling should be kept to a minimum.

- Check incision sites twice daily for any swelling and/or discharge. Keep them clean and dry at all times. Avoid bathing your pet until all sutures have been removed.

- Unless otherwise instructed, return to your veterinarian in 8 to 10 days for suture removal.

- If medications are dispensed, follow all label directions closely.

- Don't hesitate to call your veterinarian if any problems arise or if you have any questions regarding your pet's recovery.

CHAPTER 24

Infectious Diseases

Infectious diseases are among the most common feline illnesses seen by veterinarians. Organisms responsible for diseases in cats include a multitude of viruses, bacteria and bacterialike organisms, and fungi, and they can affect any number of different areas of the body (Fig. 24.1).

Viral Diseases

Viruses account for a high number of infectious illnesses seen in cats. Because of the lack of specific treatment measures for most viruses, prevention of these diseases through vaccinations is essential. The following are the most prevalent viral diseases seen in cats.

Parvovirus (Panleukopenia; Feline Distemper)

The feline parvovirus is found worldwide, affecting cats in much the same way as parvovirus affects their canine counterparts. The feline parvovirus causes severe gastroenteritis in affected cats, and can be fatal unless treated with haste. This highly contagious disease primarily affects unvaccinated cats less than a year old.

Spread by oral contact with infective feces, urine, or saliva, the feline parvovirus strikes the intestines with a fury, causing fever,

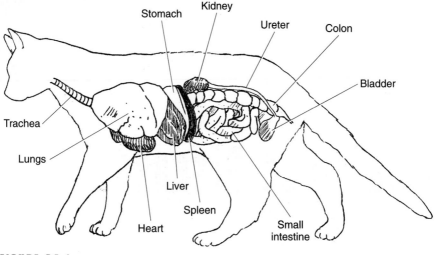

Stomach · Kidney · Ureter · Colon · Bladder · Trachea · Lungs · Liver · Spleen · Heart · Small intestine

FIGURE 24.1 The internal cat.

depression, vomiting, diarrhea, abdominal pain, and dehydration. The disease can be complicated even further as bacteria within the gut proliferate as a result of the virus and release toxins into the bloodstream. The virus itself can even spread to the bone marrow and interfere with the body's ability to mount an effective immune response to the disease. If a queen becomes infected with the parvovirus while pregnant, abortions or weak kittens could result. In many instances, these newborn kittens suffer from underdeveloped brains, causing permanent incoordination.

Diagnosis of a parvovirus infection in cats is based on history, clinical signs, and a marked reduction in the circulating number of white blood cells (Fig. 24-2).

Treatment is supportive, involving antivomiting drugs and intravenous fluids to correct and prevent further dehydration, and antibiotics to keep the secondary bacterial infections at bay. Recovery will depend on how rapidly this supportive treatment is instituted.

Feline parvovirus can be prevented through vaccination. Queens should be current on vaccinations prior to becoming pregnant, to protect unborn offspring from the virus. Finally, this virus is relatively stable in the environment, so it is a good idea to wait 3 to 4 weeks

FIGURE 24.2 Laboratory analysis of a blood sample can help confirm a diagnosis of panleukopenia.

before introducing any new kittens or cats into a house where the parvovirus has been.

Feline Infectious Peritonitis

Feline infectious peritonitis (FIP) is a unique viral disease of cats; it is unique in that the actual organ damage resulting from infection is not directly caused by the virus itself, but from the immune response to the invader.

The FIP organism is classified as a coronavirus, belonging to the same group of viruses that cause gastrointestinal disease in dogs. Cats actually can be infected with two types of coronavirus: the feline enteric coronavirus and the feline infectious peritonitis coronavirus. Although the former can cause severe gastroenteritis in affected cats, most cases are *subclinical*; that is, there are no apparent clinical signs caused by the infection. The importance of these enteric coronaviruses is not only that their presence in a feline can interfere with some standard testing procedures designed to diagnose FIP but also that the FIP coronavirus may actually be a mutation of the enteric coronavirus. If this is true, then all cats could be at risk of this disease.

Cats under 4 years and over 12 years of age seem to have a higher preponderance for this disease than do other age groups. Inhalation or ingestion of infective secretions and excretions is the primary way in which this highly contagious disease is spread from cat to cat. The virus can even be passed via the uterus from an infected queen to her kittens.

Interestingly, most cats that contract this potentially deadly viral disease rarely show signs of infection, and may actually eliminate the infection soon after exposure occurs. If they are to appear, clinical signs usually show up 2 to 3 weeks after exposure, although this can vary by months to years. Upper respiratory signs can appear for a few days, then subside without any further problems until other clinical signs appear years later.

Another interesting fact about cats infected with FIP is that many are also concurrently infected with the feline leukemia virus. Since the leukemia virus suppresses the immune system, this paves the way for clinical FIP if exposure occurs.

FIP infections are unique in that the actual virus itself does not cause specific damage to the body's organs or tissues. It is the cat's exaggerated immune response to the virus that damages the organs, tissues, and blood vessels within the body. The clinical signs that are seen depend on where this damage is done. Almost all affected cats run persistent, low-grade fevers. Insidious weight loss, and appetite loss are common as well.

Clinical FIP presents itself in three forms:

1. Wet or effusive FIP

2. Dry or noneffusive FIP

3. A combination of 1 and 2

Wet FIP. When the immune system attacks the blood vessels in response to FIP, wet FIP results. Fluid that leaks out of the damaged vessels accumulates within the chest and/or abdomen, causing nonpainful abdominal distension and/or breathing difficulties.

Dry FIP. With dry FIP, many small nodules and regions of inflammation appear in various areas of the body, including the gastrointestinal tract, the lungs and heart, the brain and spinal cord, kidneys, and/or the eyes. Obviously, with so many organ systems potentially affected, a wide variety of clinical signs, including coughing, vomiting, diarrhea, seizures, and blindness, can result.

In an effort to diagnose a suspected case of FIP, a veterinarian will rely initially on clinical signs seen, physical exam, blood samples, and perhaps microscopic examination of any abnormal fluids within the chest or abdomen. A persistent nonresponsive fever in a cat may point to FIP infection.

As mentioned, diagnosis of the FIP coronavirus using certain tests designed to detect antibodies to FIP can be obscured by the presence or absence of the enteric coronavirus.

Unfortunately, there are no effective treatments that can eliminate the FIP virus from the feline body. Modulating the immune response with steroids and certain chemotherapy drugs are only *palliative,* that is, can help provide temporary relief from clinical signs, but will do nothing to afford a cure. Survival time for cats exhibiting clinical signs can vary from days to weeks, depending on the degree of organ involvement.

Because of the lack of an effective treatment, prevention is the key with this disease (Fig. 24.3). The vaccine available for FIP still has questionable efficacy; as a result, owners should take alternate steps to protect their cats from the deleterious effects of FIP. Because FIP can gain a foothold in cats with unhealthy immune systems, it is important to keep the immune system in excellent shape. This includes keeping cats on a good plane of nutrition and being sure they are current on their feline leukemia vaccinations. Keeping cats indoors, restricting their interaction with stray felines, is another excellent way to limit potential exposure. Finally, all new cats brought into a household should test negative for the feline coronavirus.

Enteric Coronavirus

As a disease entity itself, *enteric coronavirus* (EC) can cause fever, vomiting, and diarrhea in kittens; however, if supportive care is provided, the gastrointestinal tract of these kittens usually recovers in a

FIGURE 24.3 Administering an intranasal vaccine to a cat.

few days. Yet, the primary importance of this virus is not in the disease it causes, but in the confusion it often generates when trying to diagnose a case of feline infectious peritonitis.

Feline Upper Respiratory Disease

At least six infectious agents are responsible for upper respiratory disease (URD) in cats, including *Bordetella,* the same bacterium that causes kennel cough in dogs. The primary agents in the majority of cases include the feline herpes virus (rhinotracheitis) and the feline calicivirus. Vaccinations against these two organisms are routinely administered to cats at the time of their yearly checkup. In many parts of the country, veterinarians also routinely vaccinate for *Chlamydia psittaci,* a bacterial agent that causes a condition known as *feline pneumonitis.* However, because many other less common organisms can cause feline respiratory problems besides these three, vaccination is not a guarantee against a cat contracting respiratory disease.

FELINE RHINOTRACHEITIS

Feline rhinotracheitis is caused by a herpes virus that infects the nasal passages and upper airways of the affected individual. The virus itself is very contagious, with the incubation period (the period from exposure to the appearance of clinical signs) ranging from 2 to 20 days. Kittens are usually more severely affected by acute disease than are adults. The pres-

FIGURE 24.4 Conjunctivitis is often caused by upper respiratory viruses.

ence of the feline leukemia or feline AIDS virus can also significantly increase the susceptibility to rhinotracheitis. Clinical signs associated with rhinotracheitis include sneezing, loss of appetite, conjunctivitis, oral ulcers, and nasal discharge (Fig. 24.4). The discharges might start out as clear, but then they turn thick and mucuslike as secondary bacterial infection sets in. Severe infections can result in corneal ulcers of the eye, and pregnant queens might even abort their fetuses. Rhinotracheitis in newborn kittens can be deadly, with infected kittens dying within hours to days after birth. This syndrome is better known as fading kitten syndrome.

Many cats, especially those infected when young, will suffer continued recurrences of this disease as they mature if the virus decides to set up housekeeping within the bones of the nasal passages. Purebreds such as Siamese and Himalayan are especially predisposed to these chronic, recurring infections and become effective carriers of the virus. Recurring episodes are brought on by stress due to shipping or boarding, pregnancy, or other illnesses.

FELINE CALICIVIRUS

As with rhinotracheitis, the feline *calicivirus* is a very contagious organism that can cause both acute upper respiratory disease and chronic carriers in all ages. The incubation period of the calicivirus is anywhere from 2 to 10 days. Sneezing, fever, nasal discharge, oral ulcers, and conjunctivitis are all characteristic signs of the acute disease. The chronic form of the disease can be responsible for recurring gingivitis and oral infections in infected individuals.

The feline calicivirus has also been implicated in the disease syndrome of kittens known as *limping kitten syndrome* (LKS), which is seen in kittens under 14 weeks of age and appears as a generalized arthritis (hence the name), especially affecting the back legs. This presentation of the disease will usually run its course without causing any permanent joint damage.

CHLAMYDIA

Chlamydia psittaci does not limit itself to the airways of cats; humans and birds are also susceptible to infection by this organism as well. Although this organism is not a virus, *Chlamydia* behaves very similar to the herpes virus and the calicivirus in causing disease and clinical signs. The incubation period for this organism is approximately the same as that for the calicivirus.

Chlamydia psittaci is responsive to antibiotic therapy and can be brought under control with rapid treatment. Unfortunately, as with the viruses, carrier states can occur, and recurrence of clinical signs might result secondary to stress.

DIAGNOSIS AND TREATMENT OF URD

Because viruses cannot be readily identified microscopically or cultured, diagnosis of URD in cats is based on history of occurrence and clinical signs seen. Laboratory findings from blood samples are usually nonspecific as well. If *Chlamydia* is suspected, microscopic examination of some of the cells lining the conjunctiva and/or nasal passages might reveal characteristic inclusions created by this organism. Also, because of its effect on the immune system, all cats suffering from URD should be concurrently tested for feline leukemia and the feline immunodeficiency virus.

Any sign suggestive of URD in cats warrants prompt veterinary examination and treatment to prevent serious sequela. In the case of rhinotracheitis and calicivirus, there are no specific drugs to combat these agents; however, with good supportive care, life-threatening situations can be avoided. Antibiotic therapy is usually implemented to prevent any secondary infections from setting in; antibiotics are also indicated for combating *Chlamydia* and *Bordetella* infections. If eye manifestations are present, antibiotic-containing eyedrops or ointment will help protect the eyes and speed healing.

In addition to oral and, if needed, ophthalmic antibiotics, it is vital that the nose and airways be cleared of discharge and fluid as soon as possible. Because a feline's appetite is dependent on its ability to smell its food, cats with URD will show a marked reduction in appetite, which could conceivably lead to secondary complications from malnutrition and dehydration.

Nasal discharges should be manually removed as often as possible. Human nasal decongestant sprays might be used to help break up any mucus buildup that might be present (contact a veterinarian as to types and dosages).

Humidifying the cat's room air using a vaporizer or placing the cat in a misty bathroom where hot water has been running in the shower will also assist in the breakup of mucus within the airways. If dehydration is a factor, intravenous fluid replacement performed by a veterinarian might be necessary.

Finally, good nursing care can do wonders to assure a positive outcome. Keep the ill cat warm and dry and free from stress. If required, force-feeding or tube feeding can help provide the nutrition necessary to boost the effectiveness of the cat's own immune system and shorten the convalescent period.

PREVENTION OF URD

Owners can help prevent URD in their cats by making sure that they remain current on vaccinations. Both intranasal and injectable vaccines are available to combat respiratory viruses. In multiple-cat households, prompt isolation of sick and sneezing cats might help prevent its rapid spread to other cats in the household.

Feline Leukemia Virus

Certainly one of the most devastating diseases affecting cat populations around the world is the feline leukemia virus (FeLV). The feline leukemia virus belongs to a group of infectious agents known as *retroviruses,* and it shares some characteristics with the human AIDS virus. It can occur by itself, or in combination with the *feline immunodeficiency virus* (FIV), a deadly AIDS-like virus that in itself has been spreading at an alarming rate in cats in recent years.

Like the human AIDS virus, both of these feline diseases wreak havoc on the cat's immune system, predisposing it to a wide variety of infectious diseases and to cancer.

The feline leukemia virus can be transmitted via all bodily excretions from an infected cat (Fig. 24.5). Infected queens can transmit the disease to their offspring through the placenta prior to birth or through the milk during lactation. As a result, even newborn kittens can test positive for this disease.

For other cats, close contact is required for effective transmission. As a result, feline leukemia is most prevalent in multiple-cat households and catteries.

Because of the ability of the feline leukemia virus to suppress the cat's immune system, infected felines are prone to cancer (especially lymphosarcoma and leukemia), anemia, kidney disease, and a wide variety of secondary infections such as feline infectious peritonitis, hemobartonellosis, cryptococcosis, and upper respiratory viruses. Pregnant queens might abort their kittens, or give birth to weak, unthrifty offspring that die soon after birth.

FIGURE 24.5 The feline leukemia virus is easily spread through close contact.

Even cats suffering from seemingly innocuous lesions on their skin and mucous membranes could actually be suffering from an underlying infection with feline leukemia. Finally, in some affected individuals, the only apparent signs might be lethargy, weight loss, and/or chronic gingivitis.

Diagnosis of feline leukemia is accomplished by a simple test that can be performed in a veterinarian's office. Tears and saliva can be used for initial screening purposes, but for definitive answers, a blood test should be performed.

The most common blood test used in house is the *enzyme-linked immunosorbent assay* (ELISA), which will detect the presence of virus particles in the serum. If a cat is found to be positive using ELISA, an *indirect fluorescent antibody* (IFA) test is also performed. The IFA assists in determining how long the infection has been present and whether it has reached the bone marrow.

As a rule, cats showing signs of illness that test positive for FeLV on ELISA, or seemingly healthy cats that test positive on both ELISA and the IFA test, are permanently infected with the virus. However, if a seemingly healthy cat tests positive for the leukemia virus on ELISA and negative on the IFA test, it might not be permanently FeLV-infected. In fact, many of these felines can successfully fight off and eliminate early infections by FeLV if their immune systems are functioning up to par.

Therefore the ELISA should be repeated one month later in such cats and, if the cat is still positive at this time, again at 3 months. If still positive after 3 months, the virus has undoubtedly outsmarted the cat's immune system and has set up housekeeping within the bone marrow. An IFA test at this time will usually confirm this.

When bone marrow penetration such as this has occurred, permanent infection is likely, and the majority of these individuals will become active carriers and shedders of the disease. FeLV has the ability to incorporate itself into the genetic material within host cells and remain dormant (not causing disease) for long periods of time. As a result, an infected cat might not show any adverse signs for years. However, if the immune system becomes stressed in any way, the FeLV will become active, and clinical signs will appear. In general, cats with permanent FeLV infections usually succumb to FeLV-related disease within 3 to 5 years after initial exposure.

Currently, there is no cure for the FeLV virus. Treatment is directed at relieving any clinical signs seen and eliminating secondary infections or managing cancerous conditions present. Unfortunately, however, recurrences of such diseases are common after treatment. Many experimental agents, such as interferon, antiviral drugs, and medications designed to modulate the immune system, have been employed in an attempt to eliminate FeLV itself. Unfortunately, to date, these have met with limited results. Bone marrow transplant, although helpful in some experimental instances, is not as yet a proven or practical means of treatment. The bottom line: The best treatment for feline leukemia is prevention!

Vaccines that can help protect a pet against this deadly disease are available from veterinarians. Kittens in high-risk households can be vaccinated as early as 8 weeks of age. These kittens (and those adult cats that have yet to be immunized) should receive two initial boosters 3 weeks apart.

Prior to receiving the vaccine, all cats should be tested for the leukemia virus. While such testing is not mandatory before the vaccine is given, it is always a good idea to prevent a false sense of security in an owner's mind. Remember: Because they can be born with this disease, even kittens that have no other history of exposure should be tested.

There are other control measures that you can implement to protect cats from FeLV. Testing all new cats before introducing them into a household is one. In addition, when boarding a feline or taking it to cat shows, be certain that the facility or event requires that all cats be tested free of leukemia and vaccinated prior to admission. Finally, keeping a cat indoors at night and, if it is a male, having it neutered, will help reduce potential interactions with neighborhood carriers of the disease.

A question frequently asked concerning a cat that has tested positive for FeLV is whether FeLV is transmissible to humans. To date, no antibodies to FeLV have been found in human individuals in high-exposure-risk groups such as veterinarians, cat breeders, and laboratory handlers. In addition, the incidence of cancer in humans seems to show no correlation with exposure or nonexposure to FeLV-positive cats.

However, the ultimate decision governing whether a FeLV-positive cat is to be kept in a household rests on the cat owner. Many veterinarians and researchers do recommend segregating children, pregnant women, the elderly, and immunocompromised persons from cats that have FeLV, primarily because of the other zoonotic organisms that these immune-depressed cats may be harboring. Certainly other cats within the household, even if fully vaccinated, are at risk of contracting the disease from an infected cat. However, in those situations in which none of these conditions apply, the difficult decision on whether to keep an FeLV-positive feline is a personal one, and should be influenced by an owner's individual feelings on the matter and on the cat's overall health status.

Feline Immunodeficiency Virus (Feline AIDS)

Until the late 1980s, the feline leukemia virus was the only agent linked to acquired immunodeficiency syndrome in cats—that is, until the feline immunodeficiency virus (FIV) was identified. This organism is unlike the feline leukemia virus in that it belongs to the same sub-family of retroviruses as the human AIDS virus (HIV). FIV is now known to be widespread among the cat population across the United States and around the world.

FIV behaves the same way in cats as HIV does in humans; it attacks the host's immune system and debilitates it, leaving the body wide open to secondary invaders and disease. The disease does not appear to be readily sexually transmitted in cats, and rarely is it passed on through casual contact with saliva, urine, or other body fluids, as the feline leukemia virus can be.

Instead, the main mode of transmission of FIV between cats is through penetrating bite wounds that can introduce infected saliva deep into the tissues. This method of transmission is said to be analogous to the use of a dirty hypodermic needle in humans as a means of spreading HIV between people. Needless

> ## DID YOU KNOW ?
>
> Kittens under 6 months of age can test positive for FIV if they received antibodies to the virus from their mother's milk. However, this does not mean that they are necessarily infected with the virus. They should be retested at 6 months of age to ascertain their true status. The test will usually turn up negative.

FIGURE 24.6 Cats that fight are at high risk of contracting the feline immunodeficiency virus.

to say, nonneutered male cats between the ages of 3 and 10 years that are allowed to roam about the neighborhood and fight with other cats are at greatest risk of contracting this deadly disease (Fig. 24.6).

Clinical signs associated with FIV in cats can be quite variable because of the immunosuppressive nature of the disease. Some cats might be carriers of the disease, not showing any clinical signs of illness whatsoever. In others, the only subtle signs noticed might be recurring infections (abscesses and skin infections, respiratory infections, bladder infections, etc.), weight loss, or chronic gingivitis and bad breath. Chronic, unresponsive diarrhea is another sign commonly seen in cats harboring FIV. Lymph node enlargement, loss of appetite, cancerous growths, and/or bizarre behavioral changes might also be present in an active infection. Finally, FIV renders the affected cat more susceptible to parasitic infections, such as toxoplasmosis, hemobartonellosis, and demodecosis, and their associated clinical syndromes.

Veterinarians can diagnose FIV in their own offices using a quick, easy test similar to the one used to test for feline leukemia. In fact, it is common to test for both diseases at the same time, since they can occur concurrently.

All cats presented with acute illnesses or those with chronic, recurring disorders, are prime candidates for testing. In addition, all new cats should be tested for both feline leukemia and FIV prior to their introduction into new households.

Kittens under 6 months of age can test positive for FIV if they received antibodies to the virus from their mother' milk. However, this does not mean that they are necessarily infected with the virus. As a result, they should be retested at 6 months of age to ascertain their true status.

As with feline leukemia, there is no known cure for FIV in cats. In the early stages of the disease, many infected individuals will respond well to treatments geared specifically toward any secondary problems of infections, yet as the disease progresses, even these treatments become less and less effective. Medications used to treat AIDs in humans have been used to treat FIV, yet such therapies are cost-pro-hibitive for most pet owners, and have achieved limited success at prolonging life in these cats.

Felines exhibiting pronounced clinical signs are usually in the ter-minal stages of the illness, yet even then they might slowly deteriorate over months to years. Euthanasia should be considered in these instances.

There is no vaccine currently available for FIV, yet veterinary researchers are working diligently to find one. The best ways to protect a cat from the ravages of FIV are to have it neutered and keep the cat indoors during the evening hours (the time when it is most likely to get into a fight with another cat). Cat owners should report all stray cats in the neighborhood to animal-control authorities because such animals are the most likely carriers. Finally, as mentioned above, all new cats should be tested for the disease before they are introduced into a new household.

As with feline leukemia, the question arises as to whether FIV is transmissible to humans. The general consensus of veterinary and medical researchers is that it is not. Studies analyzing individuals at high risk of exposure to FIV (veterinarians, lab technicians, multiple-cat owners) have failed to show any link between FIV and human ill-ness. Furthermore, viruses belonging to the same subfamily as HIV and FIV are quite species-specific, rarely crossing species lines.

The decision governing whether an FIV-positive cat is to be kept in a household rests on the cat owner. Many veterinarians and researchers agree that owners should consider segregating children, pregnant women, the elderly, and immunocompromised individuals from cats that are carriers of FIV, primarily because these immunosuppressed cats can be carriers of other zoonotic diseases that would not otherwise be found in a healthy cat.

Rabies

If there was ever a disease to strike fear into the hearts and minds of pet owners everywhere, this is it. Rabies is a deadly viral disease that can infect any warm-blooded mammal, including the cat. As a disease to be avoided, rabies is one of the earliest ever to be recorded, dating back to almost 2000 B.C. It is found worldwide, except in a few countries, such as Great Britain and Japan, which have strict laws designed to keep the countries rabies-free.

The incidence of rabies within the United States varies with each state, depending on the normal fauna found in that state, and on existing vaccination laws. It is estimated that 86 percent of all rabies cases occur in wildlife species of animals, with about 14 percent spilling over into the domestic pet and livestock population. It is certainly these latter groups that pose the greatest threat to public health.

Species that are commonly culprits of spreading wildlife rabies include skunks, raccoons, foxes, coyotes, and bats. Opossums are noted for their resistance to this virus, and rarely become infected. Rodents, such as rats and mice, are not significant carriers of the disease, either, since few survive encounters with rabid animals in the first place.

Skunk rabies is most prevalent in the midwestern and southwestern United States and California; raccoon rabies, in the mid-Atlantic states and southeastern United States; fox rabies, in the eastern states; and bat rabies—well, it's found in all states. Most cases seem to occur during the spring and fall months of the year.

The rabies virus is transmitted via the infected saliva of affected animals, usually through a bite wound or contamination therewith of an open wound or mucous membranes. Contrary to popular belief, however, this isn't the only way. Aerosol transmission has been known to occur as well, although the incidence of this is very low. In addition, in skunks, oral ingestion of the virus leading to an active infection has been demonstrated. Regardless of route of transmission, the disease is uniformly fatal once contracted.

The incidence of rabies in cats has increased in recent years, actually surpassing that of dogs. In fact, the majority of prophylactic rabies treatments in humans result from exposure to rabid cats. Reasons for this include poor vaccination compliance on the part of cat owners, increases in the number of stray or roaming cats, and the propensity of cats afflicted with rabies to exhibit the "furious," biting form of the disease (Fig. 24.7).

Traditionally, when rabies is mentioned, most people visualize a snarling, frothing animal snapping at anything in sight. While this is true in some instances, pet owners should understand that this represents only one of three stages that are part of the overall disease process. Depending on each individual case, viciousness might take on a prominent role, or might not occur at all. These three stages of rabies include the prodromal stage, the furious stage, and the "dumb" or paralytic stage.

The first stage, which might last from 1 to 3 days, is characterized by a noticeable change in the overall behavior of the animal. Normally friendly cats might suddenly exhibit aggressive tendencies toward their owners or toward other pets in the household. Affected individuals might also hide a lot, preferring to be left alone, and becoming upset when disturbed. Loss of appetite might become apparent, and owners might notice an increased sexual arousal and/or frequency of urination.

Once the prodromal stage is complete, the victim then enters into the furious stage. This is the

FIGURE 24.7 Because of their nocturnal and predatory behaviors, cats are at relatively high risk of exposure to the rabies virus.

stage most persons equate with a traditional rabies presentation. Cats in this stage often become quite restless, easily excited, and aggressive, losing fear of natural enemies. They might wander about aimlessly, snapping and biting at anything that moves. The character of the animal's vocalizations might change noticeably. *Pica,* or an abnormal desire to eat anything within reach (rocks, wire, dirt, feces, etc.), might become apparent as well.

As the disease enters the third stage, the swallowing reflex becomes paralyzed, making it impossible to eat, drink, or swallow saliva. This is what accounts for the excessive drooling seen in rabid animals.

The furious stage might last for up to a week before progressing into stage 3, the paralytic stage. The paralytic stage presents itself as a general loss of coordination and paralysis. A droopy lower jaw with the mouth hanging open is often characteristic. A general paralysis and death usually overtakes the unfortunate animal in a matter of hours.

Rabies should be suspected whenever a cat exhibits behavioral changes with unexplained, abnormal nervous system signs. Unfortunately, the only way to definitively diagnose a case of rabies is to have a laboratory analysis performed on the animal's brain tissue, which means, of course, euthanasia of the animal in question.

There is no known treatment for this fatal disease; as a result, stringent control and vaccination measures are a must.

All kittens should receive a rabies immunization between 3 and 4 months of age. In most states, a licensed veterinarian must administer this vaccine. Depending on the vaccine used and on the state in which you live, a booster immunization is required every 1 to 3 years. Owing to the public health implications of this disease, cat owners who fail to keep their pets current on this immunization are putting their own health at risk!

Other preventive control measures that can be taken include discouraging

---

DID YOU KNOW?

Not all pets stricken with rabies will exhibit aggressive behavior. In fact, some cats might skip the furious stage entirely, going directly from the prodromal stage into the paralytic stage. When this happens, the disease can be easily mistaken for other nervous system disorders, thereby increasing the risk of human exposure.

night roaming and keeping cats restrained on a leash and harness when walking outside. Repairing or constructing fences and enclosures to help keep wild animals out of your immediate living areas will also help reduce chances of exposure.

If a cat is bitten by a stray or wild animal, the wound must be seen immediately by a veterinarian, and, depending on when the last one was given, a booster rabies immunization should be administered. The animal should also be quarantined for at least 90 days, unless the particular animal that did the biting can be found and its rabies status deemed negative.

If the cat that was bitten by a known rabies carrier was never vaccinated, immediate euthanasia is warranted. If the owner of such a pet refuses to do so, then, for safety reasons, the pet should be quarantined for at least 6 months before it is declared uninfected.

Laws in most states spell out regulations concerning vaccinations, bites involving humans, and the ownership of wildlife in order to curb the impact of this disease. Any vaccinated cat that bites a human being should be placed in quarantine for a minimum of 10 days to observe for signs of rabies. If suspicious signs appear, the animal is then euthanized, and samples are sent to the laboratory. If the cat was not previously vaccinated against rabies, or if a wild animal is involved, euthanasia and prompt laboratory examination of the brain tissue is warranted to expedite the diagnostic process.

Euthanasia should be carried out only by veterinarians or other public health and/or wildlife officials to ensure that the sample that reaches the lab has been properly handled and stored. Certainly any person bitten by an animal should contact a physician immediately. If the situation warrants it, prophylactic rabies treatment of the bitten individual will begin and will continue until the quarantine period is over or until the specific laboratory tests are in.

It is interesting to note that because the concentration of the rabies virus in the infected cat might be low or even absent in some cases, less than 50 percent of all bites from rabies-positive animals will result in the transmission of the disease. Yet because there is no way of knowing which fall into this category, prophylactic treatment is a must, just to be on the safe side!

Finally, ownership of wild animals, especially skunks (descented or not) and raccoons, should be avoided for a number of reasons. First, there are no licensed vaccines available for these wild pets. Second, because the incubation period of rabies can last for months, owners might be exposing themselves to rabies right from the start without knowing it. Finally, in many states, it is illegal to own such pets without a permit.

Parents should always discourage children from interacting with stray animals or wildlife. Their natural curiosity could lead to a serious bite wound and much anxiety, especially if the offender is not found.

Bacterial Diseases

Infections in cats caused by bacterial organisms often occur secondarily to other disease conditions or trauma, such as bite wounds, stress, viral infections, and/or parasites. For this reason, whenever a bacterial disease is present, treatments should be directed also against any existing underlying problems.

Bacterial infections of the skin and underlying tissues represent the majority of cases seen by veterinarians. For more information on such infections and their treatment, see Chap. 32.

Fungi and Yeast

Along with viruses and bacteria, fungal organisms can produce infectious disease (mycoses) in cats. Probably the most common one that pet owners are familiar with is *dermatophytosis,* or ringworm. In addition, yeast infections can be a common problem in the ears of cats. These types of yeast and fungi that affect mainly the outer skin surfaces are termed *superficial mycoses.*

Ringworm

The most prevalent fungal organism that afflicts felines is ringworm. Three different organisms, *Microsporum canis, Trichophyton mentagrophytes,* or *Microsporum gypseum*—can actually cause ringworm. The first two are contracted from infected animals; the third, from contaminated soil.

Microsporum canis is the most common variety affecting cats. In fact, ringworm-infected cats might not show any external signs whatsoever, making them ideal transmitters of the disease to other pets in the household and to people! In some cats, the ringworm causes a circular patch of hair loss with or without an accompanying lesion on the underlying skin (Fig. 24.8).

Diagnosis of ringworm is confirmed by a fungal culture performed by a veterinarian. In many cats, ringworm infections are self-limiting and have a tendency to disappear on their own. However, because of the potential threat to humans, all cats found to be positive for ringworm should be treated. This treatment consists of chlorhexidine shampoos, and both topical and oral antifungal medications. It should be strongly emphasized that certain oral antifungal medications can cause birth defects and should not be given to pregnant cats.

DID YOU KNOW?

Ringworm is not a "worm" at all, but a skin fungus.

FIGURE 24.8 Ringworm often causes facial lesions in cats.

A vaccine does exist for ringworm, but you should consult your veterinarian concerning recommendations regarding this mode of prevention.

Subcutaneous or Deep Mycoses

In contrast to ringworm, fungal and yeast infections involving the deeper tissues of the body are termed *subcutaneous* or *deep mycoses,* depending on the depth of tissue involvement. These diseases, including sporotrichosis, aspergillosis, blastomycosis, histoplasmosis, cryptococcosis, and coccidioidomycosis, can be quite severe, and even life-threatening at times. Others exist as well, yet their importance is minor.

Inhalation of fungal spores from infected soil through the respiratory tract is the primary mode of transmission for the majority of these deeper fungi and yeast (with the exception of sporotrichosis). As a result, the first clinical signs seen usually relate to some type of respiratory problem. Many of these cats just seem to do poorly and often suffer from chronic weight loss. Others are presented to the veterinarian for a skin disorder or abscess, when in fact the skin problem is being caused by underlying drainage from the deeper fungal involvement.

Sporotrichosis

The fungus that causes sporotrichosis in cats, *Sporothrix schenckii,* can gain entrance into the body via a direct injury to the skin or by inhalation. It then spreads throughout the body by way of the lymphatic system. Cats afflicted with this soilborne organism can exhibit numerous tender lumps, nodules, and/or ulcerations anywhere on the body surface, but particularly on the extremities. Some of these lumps might actually resemble warts. In severe instances, liver, lungs, and other body organs can become involved as well. *Rhinitis,* or inflammation of the nasal passages, is also known to occur in cats suffering from sporotrichosis. Sneezing, nasal discharge, and facial swellings can result from such involvement.

Blastomycosis

Blastomyces dermatitidis is the organism responsible for this disease in cats. Eighty percent of cats affected will show some type of respiratory signs, such as a nonproductive cough. Skin involvement can occur with numerous draining lesions and abscesses, along with lymph node enlargement. Other organ systems can be affected as well. Blindness can result if the organisms spread to the eyes; and lameness, especially in the hind legs, can result secondary to bony involvement.

Histoplasmosis

Histoplasmosis is caused by the organism *Histoplasma capsulatum.* Soil contaminated with the droppings of starlings and other birds appear to be an important source of this disease in cats. Like blastomycosis, histoplasmosis can strike the respiratory systems of affected cats, leading to coughing and breathing difficulties. The gastrointestinal tract is often involved as well, resulting in chronic diarrhea. Histo-plasmosis infection can also cause bone, eye, and skin lesions.

Coccidioidomycosis

Infections with the fungus *Coccidioides immitis* are associated with the soil from the dry, desert regions of North America. As with other deep fungi, these spores are inhaled into the lungs, where the organisms set up housekeeping. If the disease remains localized in the lungs, the clinical signs usually reflect this respiratory involvement. Coughing and breathing difficulties result from invasion of the lung tissue and from enlargement of lymph nodes within the chest cavity. If the coccidioidomycosis disseminates throughout the body via the blood and lymphatics, bone infection is common. Lameness, pain, and joint swelling usually occur as a result. Oftentimes, one or more draining tracts originating from the bone infection break through the skin and create unsightly lesions.

Cryptococcosis

Unlike the three conditions mentioned above, this disease is caused by a yeast organism, *Cryptococcus neoformans,* rather than a fungus. Soil contaminated with pigeon and bat feces is a main source of these yeast organisms. Cryptococcosis in cats is mainly an upper respiratory and nasal problem. A thick, copious, continuous nasal discharge usually results, and sneezing can be a clinical sign. From the nasal passages, cryptococcosis can spread throughout the body and cause lameness, enlarged lymph nodes, nervous system impairment (seizures, coma), blindness, and skin infections.

History, physical exam findings, and laboratory tests, including radiographic X rays and biopsies of affected regions, can lead the veterinary practitioner to a tentative diagnosis of a fungal infection. Microscopic examination of body fluids or drainage for fungal spores or yeast can also be helpful. In most cases, a definitive diagnosis is made by testing a blood serum sample for antibodies against the fungal organisms in question, or, less commonly, by culturing for growth.

Several medications are available to treat fungal infections in cats. Depending on which agents are used (many are used in combination with one another), duration of treatment required is often 1 to 3 months to afford a complete cure. Radiographs and special immunologic tests can be used to monitor the response to treatment. In many cases, surgical excision of those regions infected with the fungus can afford faster recovery. The prognosis for cats is good when fungal infections are detected and treated in their early stages; guarded to poor, if dissemination throughout the body has occurred.

Parasitic Diseases

Along with infectious diseases, internal and external parasites are responsible for the vast majority of illnesses and disorders seen in cats. As a result, timely diagnosis and treatment for these pests are vital to the health of the cat.

Fleas

Fleas are by far the most common external parasite that afflicts cats. Aside from the relentless chewing and scratching they cause, fleas are also carriers of tapeworms and other diseases. As a result, the development of a good control program to combat these irritating pests is a must.

The flea life cycle includes four major stages: egg, larva, pupa, and adult stages. Both the egg and pupa stages are very resistant to insecticides, which can make complete flea control difficult. During summer months, the entire flea cycle (egg to adult) can be completed in 16 to 21 days. Heat and humidity tend to shorten this cycle period. In addition, fleas are most prolific during hot humid weather.

For more information on flea control, see page 365.

Ticks

Ticks, unlike fleas, attach themselves to the pet's skin via their mouth-parts. Ticks generally remain attached in one spot for long periods. The head, neck, and interdigital (between toes) areas of the pet are the most common sites of severe infestation. Ticks produce local irritation and even anemia in heavy infestations. They can also serve as inter-mediate hosts for disease producing microorganisms and may transmit such illnesses to the infested pet.

For more information on tick control, see page 368.

Mites

Mite infestation, commonly known as "mange," requires the expertise of a veterinarian for diagnosis and treatment.

Notoedres Mange

The most common mange mite infecting cats, *Notoedres cati,* is microscopic, and it requires special skin scrapes for its detection (Fig. 25.1). Direct exposure to an infected animal is required for its transmission.

The major symptom of notoedres mange is a sudden onset of severe itching. As the mite burrows into the host's epidermis, itching, hair loss, and scaly skin result, initially on the face, neck, and ears, and then to other areas on the body. The haircoat on these cats often takes on a "mousy" odor as well.

Treatment for notoedres mange consists of special miticidal dipping and/or systemic miticides. If dips are used, they should be performed only by a veterinarian, since toxicity can be a problem if they are not used correctly. All other cats in the household should also be treated because of the highly contagious nature of this mite.

FIGURE 25.1 Skin scrapings can be used to detect mite infestations in cats.

Demodex Mange

The *Demodex* mange mite can also affect cats as it does dogs, yet its occurrence rate in felines is quite low. If present, it causes scaly, bald regions on the skin of the head, legs, and feet. As in dogs, this type of mange infestation is caused by a poorly functioning immune system. As a result, gaining a complete cure with treatment can be difficult.

Cheyletiella Mange (Walking Dandruff)

The third type of mange that can be seen in cats is *Cheyletiella,* or "walking dandruff." This type of mange presents itself as dry, flaky skin with variable amounts of itching. On close inspection of the skin flakes, they will appear to be actually moving, hence the name. Microscopic examination of the flakes or of a skin scraping will afford a diagnosis. Once this type of mange has been diagnosed, treatment with any one of the common topical insecticidal sprays or powders will usually take care of an infestation.

Tapeworms

By far, the most prevalent species of tapeworm seen in cats is called *Dipylidium caninum,* the double-pored tapeworm. It is so common because it uses the flea as an intermediate host and because cats are so efficient at grooming themselves that they are likely to accidentally ingest fleas if they are present on the skin.

Segments from the tapeworm are passed in the feces, or actually "crawl" out onto the haircoat of the infested animal. Once outside, the segments dry out and release egg baskets into the environment. Flea larvae looking for food then ingest these eggs, and a new tapeworm begins to develop inside the flea. If the flea is ingested by the cat during chewing or self-grooming episodes, the tapeworm larvae will develop into an adult worm within the pet's small intestine (Fig. 25.2).

Although less frequent, cats can become infected with other types of tapeworms besides *Dipylidium.* For instance, the hunting habits of some felines put them at high risk of exposure to *Echinococcus granulosus,* the tapeworm responsible for hydatid cyst disease in humans.

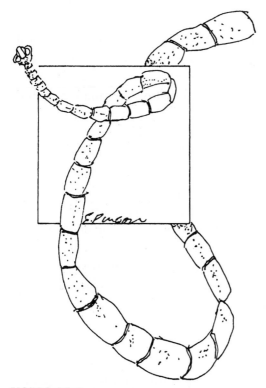

FIGURE 25.2 Tapeworms can grow to enormous lengths inside a cat!

Cats infested with adult tapeworms may or may not exhibit the typical signs associated with gastroenteritis, such as vomiting and diarrhea. Weight loss certainly can occur as the worms absorb nutrients from within the gut.

Diagnosis of a tapeworm infestation can be confirmed by actually seeing the white, moving, wormlike segments in fresh fecal material or on the haircoat around the hind region. Segments might also be seen on anal sac expression. If dried, the segments will take on a brownish, "ricelike" appearance. Microscopic examination of the stool may be helpful as well; however, because the shedding of the segments is sporadic, a negative finding cannot totally rule out an infestation.

Tapeworms can be difficult pests to treat and totally eliminate. Praziquantel and epsiprantel are two effective medications used by veterinarians to eliminate tapeworms from the intestines. Other drugs are available as well. Repeating the treatment in two to three weeks helps ensure thorough elimination.

Flea control is the best way to prevent *D. caninum.* Daily brushing is an additional means of preventing repeat infestations from occurring. Other tapeworms, including *Echinococcus,* can be prevented by not allowing cats to hunt rodents and other wild game.

Warbles

"Warbles" (*Cuterebra*) are an unusual type of parasite that can be found on, or living within, the skin of cats (Fig. 25.3). They usually appear as nodules or lumps around the head or neck region. Often, these nodules are mistaken for plain abscesses, yet on close inspection inside, an actual worm, sometimes the size of a grape, will be visible. In rare instances, depending

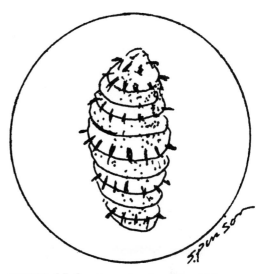

FIGURE 25.3 *Cuterebra* **larva (warble).**

on their location, these parasites can adversely affect the brain, leading to severe neurological signs.

Needless to say, such unwelcome guests need to be manually extracted by a veterinarian. In addition, the open cavity left over in the skin after extraction will usually require antibiotics to assure fast healing to take place.

Roundworms

Roundworms, known as *ascarids* or "spool worms," are thick-bodied, whitish- to cream-colored worms that can inhabit the small intestine of cats. Adult worms exist unattached within the intestinal lumen, and can grow up to 8 inches in length.

If present in sufficient numbers, roundworms can cause prominent malnutrition and gastroenteritis, with associated vomiting and diarrhea (Fig. 25.4). In addition, larval forms of the worms have the ability to migrate through the tissues when ingested and, in rare instances, cause neurological disease.

Veterinarians can diagnose roundworms by using a microscope to look for eggs in a stool sample from a cat and prescribe or recommend

FIGURE 25.4 A bloated abdomen in a kitten caused by roundworms.

treatment with any of a wide variety of deworming drugs effective at removing roundworms from the animal's intestines. Relatively inexpensive dewormers can be obtained at grocery stores and pet suppliers. Owners should be sure to consult a veterinarian before using one of these to be certain that it contains the correct ingredients for the pet's particular problem. Repeat deworming should be performed 3 weeks later to ensure that a complete kill has been achieved.

For more information on roundworms, see Chap. 7.

Hookworms

The *hookworm* is another type of parasite that can inhabit the small intestine of cats. Unlike the roundworm, which floats unattached within the intestinal lumen, absorbing nutrients through its skin, the hookworm actually uses teeth to attach itself to the wall of the intestine. Once attached, it begins to suck blood from vessels within the wall. In fact, it can become so severe that the resulting anemia and gastroenteritis could lead to an infested cat's death!

Fortunately, hookworm infestations are not very common in cats. Diagnosis of a hookworm infestation is based on looking for the presence of eggs on a microscopic stool exam. A number of safe dewormers available from veterinarians can help eliminate a hookworm infection. After the initial dose is given, a follow-up deworming should be administered 2 to 3 weeks later to ensure a complete kill.

For more information on hookworms, see Chap. 7.

Lungworms

Lungworm infections in cats are uncommon, yet they are worth mentioning. *Aleurostrongylus abstrusus* and *Capillaria aerophila* are two parasites that can live within the respiratory tract of affected felines, causing weight loss, chronic coughing, and difficulty breathing.

Because eggs or larvae from these lung parasites are passed in the stool, fecal examinations can be used by veterinarians to diagnose an infection. Radiographic X rays, microscopic examination of respiratory fluids, and direct examination of the airways using an endoscope can also lead to a diagnosis. Once this is confirmed, special dewormers can be used to tackle lungworm infestations in cats.

Paragonimus kellicotti, the lung fluke, can also infest the airways of cats, causing disease very similar to lungworms. Diagnosis and treatment are the same as for lungworms. Fortunately, this parasite is quite rare in cats.

Heartworms

As frightening as it might seem, the incidence of this disease, once thought to be limited to canines, is on the rise in cats as well. *Dirofilaria immitis,* the same mosquitoborne organism that causes canine heartworm disease, also causes the feline disease. Most cats that become infested with heartworms develop fewer than 10 worms within the heart, yet even this low number can damage the heart and lead to lung and kidney disease as they do in the dog. The main reason for this is that cats produce a more potent immune response to the parasites than do dogs, which can result in greater damage to the tissues involved.

Male cats allowed to roam outdoors are at greatest risk of contracting this disease. Many cats infested with heartworms will show no clinical signs whatsoever, with the disease being identified incidentally when these cats are brought to the veterinarian for other reasons. In more advanced cases, lethargy, breathing difficulties, coughing, vomiting, and sometimes even blindness can occur.

Special blood tests can be used to help detect heartworm disease in cats. However, because the worm burden in some cats is so low, some infections may be missed by these tests. As a result, many veterinarians base the diagnosis on chest radiographs (X rays) and ultrasound findings, which usually reveal changes in the heart and lungs characteristic of heartworm disease.

Treatment, if performed, is similar to that used for dogs. However, because of the comparatively small size of the feline heart and lungs, and the intense feline immune response to these parasites, killing the adult worms contained within the heart can actually do more harm than good. As a result, cats diagnosed with this disease, yet not showing any clinical signs, are seldom treated, but are usually placed on heartworm preventive instead to prevent additional infestation. Unfortunately, those cases exhibiting clinical signs of heartworm disease carry with them a poor to grave prognosis for recovery.

Because of the difficulty in safely treating heartworms in cats if they become infected with the disease, cat owners should consider giving their pets preventive heartworm medication on a monthly basis. Such medication is available through veterinarians.

Coccidia

Coccidia are microscopic protozoan parasites that inhabit the small intestine of affected cats. The disease caused by coccidia (coccidiosis) is characterized by diarrhea, which can rapidly dehydrate a young kitten if not brought under control.

Overcrowding and poor sanitation greatly contribute to the spread of these organisms with a group of cats or kittens. Eggs passed in fecal material can be directly ingested by another feline, leading to the development and maturation of the organisms within the gut of the new host.

Occasionally, tissue migration can occur, especially with the parasite *Toxoplasma,* leading to fever, muscle pain, and/or convulsions. Fortunately, this presentation is quite uncommon in cats.

Blood tests might be necessary for a diagnosis of toxoplasmosis; however, for most coccidian parasites, a microscopic examination of a stool specimen for eggs will suffice. Several different types of medications have been used by veterinarians to eliminate active coccidia infections in cats.

If *Toxoplasma* is involved, more extensive treatment utilizing different types of medications might be required. Certainly if dehydration or other signs are noticed, supportive hospital treatment will be needed

Good sanitation practices offer the best means of preventing exposure to coccidiosis. Routine stool checks performed by a veterinarian should also be utilized to ensure that cats remains parasite-free. As a zoonotic disease, toxoplasmosis is quite significant, especially in pregnant women. For more information, see Chap. 59.

Cytauxzoonosis

Cytauxzoonosis is found mainly across the southeastern portion of the United States in cats allowed to roam in heavily wooded areas. Ticks are thought to transmit this protozoal organism, which attacks the host's red blood cells and causes anemia. As a result, clinical signs associated with cytauxzoonosis include those related to anemia, such as loss of appetite, lethargy, breathing difficulties, and pale mucous membranes.

Veterinarians can diagnose this disorder by observing specially stained blood smears under the microscope. Unfortunately, once a diagnosis is made, there is no known effective treatment and infected cats invariably die from the disease. Good tick control and limiting access to high-risk environmental areas are the two best ways to protect a cat from this fatal disease.

Hemobartonellosis

Hemobartonellosis in cats is caused by the bacterial organism *Haemobartonella felis.* This disease, which causes a profound anemia, occurs most often in young male cats around 4 to 6 years old. Insects are thought to be the mode of transmission between these organisms and cats.

Clinical signs of hemobartonellosis include a sudden onset of depression, loss of appetite, and fever. Because of the anemia the disease causes, the gums and mucous membranes of these cats are often quite pale. The skin and whites of the eyes may appear jaundiced as well.

Diagnosis of this disease in cats can be made in a veterinary setting from the microscopic examination of fresh blood from suspected cats. Many felines suffering from hemobartonellosis also concurrently have feline leukemia. As a result, a feline leukemia test should be performed on all cats with hemobartonellosis. Hemobartonellosis is treated with blood transfusions if the anemia caused by it is severe, and with special antibiotics and medications.

The prognosis for recovery from the anemia and associated symptoms is good if treatment is instituted quickly. Unfortunately, a total cure is rarely possible with this disease, and owners should be on the lookout for stress-induced relapses, and seek prompt treatment for their felines if they should happen.

The Immune System

Without a functioning immune system, our cats would fall easy prey to every hostile organism that came around. Immunity is designed to protect against such infectious invaders and eliminate any foreign matter or cells that somehow gain entrance into the body. Preventing the growth of cancer cells and tumors is also in its job description.

The immune system itself is a complex network of cells, organs, and special chemicals. No one division overshadows another; each team member relies on the others for support. In this way, they all work in unison toward a common goal. Since the immune system of the cat is essentially identical to that of dogs, the reader is referred to Chap. 8 for more details as to the cells, organs, and functions of the immune system.

Immunosuppression

Although the immune system serves a rough and rugged function, a delicate balance does exist as far as its activity is concerned. Stress, poor nutrition, and hormone fluctuations are only some of the many factors that can deleteriously alter this activity, leading to a weakened defense system. As if this weren't enough, certain viruses, such as the feline leukemia and feline AIDS (FIV) viruses, also have the ability to suppress the very system designed to defend against them. Overcoming the body's natural defense mechanisms can lead to only one outcome, and it isn't good.

Allergies and Autoimmune Disease

Both allergies and autoimmune diseases are characterized by an overactive immune system that can irritate or damage its host's own tissues in response to an antigen invasion within the body. For example, inhalant allergies and flea allergies in cats result from an overactive immune response to pollens and to flea saliva, respectively. *Lupus erythematosus* and *pemphigus* are two autoimmune disorders that result from an overactive immune system. These two diseases often cause notable skin lesions, aside from affecting other organs of the body. *Eosinophilic granuloma complex* is another feline disease caused by an overactive immune system. Still another serious autoimmune disorder that can affect cats is *autoimmune hemolytic anemia.* This disease occurs when a cat's body produces antibodies against its own red blood cells, leading to their destruction.

Finally, the classic example in cats of an immune system gone awry is *feline infectious peritonitis* (FIP). In this disease, it is not the virus itself but rather the exaggerated immune response to it that actually proves fatal to the cat.

Allergies and autoimmune reactions can be controlled with corticosteroid medication, which, at sufficient dosages, has a suppressive effect on the immune system. However, because long-term use of these steroids can have significant side effects, such treatments should be performed only under the close, continual supervision of a veterinarian.

The Cardiovascular and Hemolymphatic Systems

The cardiovascular and hemolymphatic systems are responsible for the effective transmission of oxygen and nutrition to all organs and tissues of the body. This system is composed of the heart, the vessels that carry blood to and from the heart, the blood itself, and the lymphatic channels, which transport lymph within the body (Fig. 27.1). For a more in-depth discussion regarding the anatomy and function of the cardiovascular and hemolymphatic systems, see Chap. 9.

Feline Cardiomyopathy

Changes in the thickness and/or contractility of the muscles making up the heart are termed *cardiomyopathies.* The two main types of cardiomyopathies that cats can suffer from are hypertrophic cardiomyopathy and dilated cardiomyopathy.

In hypertrophic cardiomyopathy, the muscular heart walls become excessively thickened, shrinking the chambers of the heart and disrupting normal filling of the heart with blood. With dilated cardiomyopathy, the opposite occurs—the heart walls become thin and weak, making normal contractions difficult. Regardless of the type, a cardiomyopathy can lead to overt heart failure if progression occurs.

441

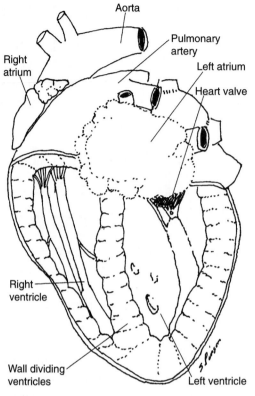

Aorta

Pulmonary artery

Right atrium

Left atrium

Heart valve

Right ventricle

Wall dividing ventricles

Left ventricle

FIGURE 27.1 The feline heart.

Cardiomyopathies seem to be more prevalent in middle-aged cats, and males seem to have a greater tendency to develop the condition than do females. In addition, Siamese, Burmese, and Abyssinian cats appear to have a higher incidence of this disorder than do other breeds. The causes of hypertrophic cardiomyopathy in cats remain unknown; however, researchers have found a link between dilated cardiomyopathy and dietary deficiencies in the amino acid taurine.

An increased lethargy and loss of appetite might be the initial signs seen in cats with cardiomyopathies. Other more advanced clinical signs can include coughing, difficulty in breathing, and overt collapse. Vomiting can also become a factor, especially if there is secondary kidney damage caused by poor blood circulation. In addition, hind-end weakness and muscular pain due to aortic thromboembolism can be seen in these cats.

These clinical signs can help lead a veterinarian to a diagnosis of cardiomyopathy in a cat. Using a stethoscope, the veterinarian can detect rapid heart rates, abnormal rhythms, and heart murmurs as well. Radiographic X rays and ultrasound show abnormal heart shapes, abnormal heart wall thickness, and, if heart failure is present, fluid buildup within the thorax in these cats.

Electrocardiograms are useful in determining the extent of any heart enlargement and to assess the electrical conduction occurring within the heart walls. If a taurine deficiency is suspected, measuring blood levels of this amino acid can prove or disprove such suspicions.

Treatment of cardiomyopathy consists of medications designed to reduce blood pressure and to increase the efficiency of heart contractions. Drugs designed to move fluids out of the lungs might also be prescribed. In cats with advanced heart failure, oxygen therapy might be necessary. Obviously, for those cats with taurine-deficiency cardiomyopathy, taurine supplementation should also be used to normalize cardiac function.

Unfortunately, little can be done to reverse the anatomic changes to the heart seen in most cardiomyopathies. With supportive treatment, however, the quality of life of affected felines can be maintained at a good level for months, even years.

Taurine and Feline Cardiomyopathy

Taurine is an amino acid that plays several important roles within the body. It is used to help inactivate toxins within the liver and—more importantly in terms of cardiomyopathy—assists in the normal contraction of heart muscle cells.

Taurine is normally synthesized within the bodies of most mammals—most, that is, except the cat. As a result, felines need to obtain their taurine through the diet. If a diet contains subnormal levels of the amino acid, then a taurine deficiency and dilated cardiomyopathy can result.

Heart disease is not the only syndrome that can result from deficient levels of taurine. Another disease, called *feline central retinal degeneration,* involves the retina of the eye and can eventually lead to blindness.

Less commonly, taurine deficiencies can produce other neurological problems, abortions in pregnant queens, neuromuscular disease in kittens, and immunosuppression.

To ward off deficiencies in this vital amino acid, cat foods should contain over 1000 parts per million (ppm) taurine in dry varieties, and greater than 2000 ppm taurine in the moist types. Cardiomyopathy related to a taurine deficiency is rarely seen in cats fed high-quality commercial cat foods.

Taurine deficiencies can also be caused by gastrointestinal disturbances interfering with the proper absorption of taurine from the intestines. This can become significant in those cats suffering from chronic inflammatory bowel disease. It is vital that these cats be on a taurine-rich diet, and that they have heart function monitored periodically by a veterinarian. Needless to say, any cat in which cardiomyopathy is suspected should have blood taurine levels checked, even if its diet is adequate in the amino acid.

For those instances in which taurine supplementation is warranted, taurine capsules can be prescribed by veterinarians. Natural food substances such as minced clams and tuna are both good sources of taurine and can be used as substitutes for the capsules if desired. Owners should ask their veterinarians for feeding amounts.

Arrhythmias

An *arrhythmia* is a deviation from the normal rate and/or rhythm of contraction of the heart. When the heart muscle fails to contract in the proper sequence, or contracts too quickly or too slowly, poor blood circulation results. Arrhythmias in cats can be caused by a number of underlying conditions, including cardiomyopathy, kidney disease, hyperthyroidism, and hypokalemia (low blood potassium).

Depending on the type of and degree of the malfunction, the effects of arrhythmias can be mild, causing few problems, or can be life-threatening. Regardless of the underlying cause, the symptoms associated with arrhythmias are similar to those seen with cardiomyopathies—namely, coughing, weakness, breathing distress, weight loss, and exercise intolerance.

Arrhythmias are diagnosed using a physical examination and an electroencephalographic (ECG) reading. Treatment involves the use of antiarrhythmic drugs while the underlying disorder is being addressed. In severe cases in which an underlying disorder cannot be effectively controlled, a cardiac pacemaker may need to be installed to provide long-term management of the arrhythmia.

Arterial Thromboembolism

Cats afflicted with cardiomyopathy suffer from impaired circulation, which, in turn, can lead to a condition known as *arterial thromboembolism*. This disorder is characterized by large blood clots that form within the left side of the heart and pass into the circulatory system, only to lodge within one or more blood vessels within the body. The most common region for this lodging to occur is where the large aorta divides into two smaller arteries that supply the hindlimbs.

When such a clot restricts blood flow to the back legs, pronounced hindlimb weakness results. The hind paws might feel cold to the touch, and the clear nails might take on a bluish hue. As the muscles of the hind end are deprived of blood and oxygen, they become firm and painful to the touch.

Diagnosis of arterial thromboembolism is based on clinical signs and physical exam findings. Ultrasound can be used to assess the condition of the heart and to identify thrombi still within the organ. A total absence or partial reduction in hindlimb pulse is diagnostic of a thromboembolism as well (Fig. 27.2).

Treatment for arterial thromboembolism is difficult at best. Surgery is usually unrewarding, and the preexisting heart disease in these cats places them at high risk for anesthesia. Medical therapy can be somewhat effective if instituted within a few hours of onset. This involves administering drugs designed to dissolve the blood clot, prevent further thrombi from developing, and restore normal blood flow.

Prognosis for a full recovery is guarded, simply because of the preexisting heart disease and because of chronic pain and tissue damage caused by the temporary loss of oxygen. However, with physical therapy and attentive nursing care, many cats experience at least partial functional restoration in 1 to 2 months. Obviously, management of the preexisting cardiomyopathy is necessary as well.

Anemia

Anemia is defined as an overall reduction in the number of red blood cells within the bloodstream relative to normal levels within that pet. This reduction can occur from a number of processes, including an

FIGURE 27.2 Cats with thromboemboli often lack a pulse in the hindlimbs.

increased destruction or decreased production of red blood cells within the body. The overall consequence of anemia is the inability of the blood to supply desired levels of oxygen to the tissues.

Signs seen in an anemic cat include intense lethargy, weakness, increased respiratory and heart rates, and a pallor of the mucous membranes. Depending on the cause of the anemia, signs related to a blood clotting disorder might be seen as well. Finally, if red blood cells are being destroyed within the body, the skin and mucous membranes might become jaundiced.

A simple blood test performed by your veterinarian can tell you if your cat is anemic. Treatment of anemia depends on the underlying cause. In severe cases, blood transfusions and oxygen therapy might be required to save the pet's life until the cause can be identified and treated. Therapy utilizing special compounds called *colloids* and other oxygen-carrying solutions can be a lifesaving as well.

Bleeding Disorders

Whenever an injury or illness compromises a blood vessel and leads to bleeding out of that vessel, a remarkable mechanism or chain reaction begins within the body in an effort to stop the leakage of blood from the damaged vessel and prevent the individual from bleeding to death. This mechanism is known as *hemostasis.*

When a blood vessel is compromised, the first reaction that occurs is constriction of the vessel to help slow blood loss. Following this, special blood cells called *platelets* begin to adhere to the injured vessel wall, forming a temporary plug. At the same time, a coagulation (clotting) pathway is activated within the body, involving a complex interaction of blood and tissue components, as well as calcium and vitamin K. The end result of this pathway is the formation of a more permanent clot at the site of injury.

Bleeding disorders can occur whenever any part of the clotting mechanism is interfered with. Diseases or substances such as toxins, drugs, cancers, autoimmune hemolytic anemia, and infectious agents, such as feline infectious peritonitis, can interfere with platelet numbers or function. In addition, kidney disease and certain inherited defects can also lead to poor platelet function and secondary bleeding.

Any disruptions of the coagulation pathway also spell trouble for hemostasis. For instance, many rodent poisons contain substances that interfere with the vitamin K component of the coagulation pathway. If a cat accidentally ingests these, its coagulation pathway will be effectively disrupted. Liver disease can lead to bleeding disorders because many of the components used in blood clotting are manufactured in that organ. Inherited defects in the coagulation pathway, such as hemophilia, are rare in cats.

Serious diseases or injuries such as feline infectious peritonitis, heat stroke, or massive trauma (such as that caused by a car) can lead to a secondary condition known as *disseminated intravascular coagulation* (DIC), in which tiny blood clots form all throughout the body. Not only are these clots detrimental to the health of the animal but DIC also leads to a depletion of the body's clotting components. This, in turn, predisposes the cat to a bleeding disorder. DIC is invariably fatal to a pet unless rapid supportive treatment is instituted.

Clinical signs of a bleeding disorder usually include noticeable bruising of the skin and mucous membranes. Blood in the urine or feces, nosebleeds, joint pain, abdominal pain, and breathing difficulties might be seen as well. Because of the variety of potential causes, a veterinarian will need to run a series of tests to determine the exact cause and to formulate a treatment regimen.

Initial treatment for any bleeding disorder entails blood transfusions until the exact cause is discerned. If rodenticide poisoning is suspected, vitamin K injections, followed by oral vitamin K tablets, will help reverse the effects of the poison. These tablets should be given daily for a minimum of 4 weeks, since the ingested poison could linger within the body and exert its effects for this length of time.

the cat is

thetized

identify an

prit. If not,

required to

prevent se

cations ass

terial infec

Feline A

Cats can su

attacks ver

seen in p

usually trig

gic reactio

other allerg

caused by

severe, cau

This, in tur

ging in affe

cat can su

asthma, reg

Along

tory of occ

ical signs

feline asth

radiograph

lungs. Lon

ring case

exhibit sca

of the lung

Treatme

asthma in

ing the so

gic reacti

corticoster

CHAPTER

28

The Respiratory System

The respiratory system works in conjunction with the circulatory system to provide oxygen to and remove carbon dioxide from the body tissues. Oxygen is the driving force behind all chemical reactions that occur internally. Obviously, life could not exist without it. As a result, the function of all body systems, including the respiratory system itself, depends first on the ability of this system to deliver its product.

In addition to this vital function, the respiratory system also serves as a means of *thermoregulation,* or body heat exchange, in the cat. Since cats can't sweat in the conventional (human) way, they rely on heat transfer out of the body through exhaled air. That is why cats pant when they get hot.

For more information on the anatomy of the respiratory system, see Chap. 10.

Rhinitis

Inflammation involving the nasal passages of cats is termed *rhinitis*. The hallmark clinical signs seen with a case of rhinitis

FACT OR FICTION

Cats purr only when they are content. **FICTION.** Cats may also purr when they are in pain.

449

include s
terial infe
the funga
and tissu
thick nas;

Nasoph

Nasophai
ated with
within th
ity. They
normal fl
breathing

Clinic
include n
lowing d
enough,
dination

Diagn
made on
ing this
However,
Because
ear canal
age. Sucl
muscles

Nasal F

Occasion
ways of
sinusitis.
grass, wh

Cats w
or bloody
the back

have inflamed lips. The inflammation associated with the disease can also spread to the back of the throat, making it difficult to swallow.

The exact cause of this disorder in cats is unknown; however, conceivably any type of chronic inflammation that attracts inflammatory cells to the area could cause such a reaction. Diagnosis of feline stomatitis is made by collecting a biopsy sample of the affected tissue and radiographing the oral cavity to determine the extent of involvement. Treatment consists of surgically removing and/or cauterizing the excess gum tissue, as well as any teeth or bony tissue affected. In especially severe cases, steroidal anti-inflammatory medications, antibiotics, and pain relievers may be used as well.

Owners can help slow the recurrence of this disorder by following a strict regimen of dental care for their cats, including the daily treatment of both teeth and gums with a paste, gel, or solution containing chlorhexidine.

Oral Ulcers

Although ulceration affecting the feline mouth and tongue can be caused by chemical or electrical burns, many such ulcers occur secondary to some underlying health disorder. For instance, infectious diseases such as feline calicivirus and feline leukemia might cause mouth ulcers and associated bad breath (Fig. 29.1). Other serious internal disease conditions such as kidney failure, diabetes mellitus, or autoimmune disease can also be manifested in this fashion as well. In all of these instances, treatment is aimed at clearing up the underlying disease syndrome if possible.

Ulcerations affecting the lips of cats can be caused by a condition known as eosinophilic granuloma complex. These red, angry-looking lesions often lead to excessive salivation and a reluctance to eat. Treatment using anti-inflammatory or immune-modulating medications can help clear up these types of ulcers; unfortunately, however, recurrence is common.

Oral Foreign Bodies

A cat's natural playful attraction to strings, threads, and ribbons could lead to health problems. As impossible as it might seem, such items can become wrapped around the base of the tongue and be partially swallowed, causing gagging, retching, salivation, and difficulty swallowing food and water. Other oral foreign bodies, such as fishhooks, needles, bones, and grass awns, can cause similar signs.

Many cats suffering from an oral foreign body will paw at their mouths or will exhibit exaggerated licking motions in fruitless attempts to dislodge the unwelcome object. Depending on the length of time that the object has been there, halitosis (bad breath) might become an obvious sign as well.

FIGURE 29.1 Oral ulcers can cause foul breath in cats.

In most instances, such a problem can be diagnosed on an oral examination, assuming, of course, that the cat wants to cooperate. If it doesn't, sedation might be required. Needles, fishhooks, and other metal objects will also show up on radiographic X rays.

Removal of the offending foreign body will afford a cure. However, if a piece of string (for instance) is extending down into the esophagus, forceful removal should be avoided. In these instances, surgical removal might be required.

Finally, for those foreign bodies that penetrated any oral tissue, antibiotic therapy should be instituted following their removal to prevent secondary bacterial infections from setting up housekeeping within the mouth.

Oral Tumors

Like other regions of the body, the oral cavity has its share of tumors and growths. A wide variety of tumors, including melanomas, sarcomas, and carcinomas, can arise within the oral cavity of cats. The most prevalent tumor occurring within the mouths of cats is the squamous cell carcinoma.

Signs associated with oral tumors in cats include halitosis (bad breath), oral bleeding, excessive salivation, and/or swallowing difficulties. In severe cases, actual facial deformities could occur secondary to the tumor growth.

Rapid recognition of the presence of an oral tumor and concurrent treatment are essential, since most oral tumors in cats, if malignant, will spread very rapidly to other areas of the body, including the lungs. For more information on oral tumors, see Chap. 60.

Esophageal Disorders

Disorders involving the esophagus will manifest themselves as difficulty in swallowing and regurgitation. Effortless regurgitation of solid food, which must be differentiated from vomiting and its associated abdominal spasms, often alerts the pet owner and veterinary practitioner to an existing problem with the esophagus. Because of their inability to properly swallow food, cats afflicted with esophageal disease are at high risk of accidentally aspirating food into their lungs, causing serious, life-threatening pneumonia.

Megaesophagus

Megaesophagus is a condition in which a generalized enlargement of the esophagus occurs, making it unable to push food into the stomach. This condition might be inherited, or seen as secondary to esophageal obstructions or to neuromuscular diseases.

Signs seen with megaesophagus include regurgitation minutes to hours after eating or drinking. Often, the undigested food will appear to be shaped like a tube or a sausage link. Certainly weight loss occurs as food is unable to enter the stomach, and, if the buildup of food and water within the esophagus is great enough, the pressure placed on the trachea can make breathing difficult as well.

Diagnosis of megaesophagus is made by physical exam, analyzing clinical signs, and by taking radiographic X rays of the esophagus or actually visualizing the enlargement with an endoscope inserted into the esophagus via the mouth.

A cat diagnosed with this disorder must be fed with its front end elevated on a chair or table to encourage gravity flow of food and water into the stomach. Feeding liquid or semisolid food will also help facilitate passage into the stomach.

Depending on the cause, some individuals do improve with time. Yet for the most part, the condition is permanent, and cat owners must be on guard at all times for potential complications.

Esophagitis

Inflammation occurring anywhere along the esophagus is termed *esophagitis.* Esophagitis can be instituted by foreign bodies that injure the organ's lining, by ingestion of caustic substances, and by reflux of stomach contents and acids up into the esophagus. In keeping with the latter cause, chronic, long-term vomiting can also lead to esophagitis.

Regurgitation, inappetence, and weight loss are the most frequent signs seen. If left untreated, damage to the lining of the esophagus could occur, causing strictures and secondary megaesophagus.

As with megaesophagus, diagnosis is made using clinical signs, physical exam findings, and endoscopic exam or radiographic X rays of the esophagus using barium as a contrast medium. Treatment of esophagitis consists of treating any primary problems that might be present, and, if stomach acid reflux is to blame, reducing the amount of stomach acid secretions and increasing the rate of gastric emptying. In addition, if the esophageal diameter has shrunk as a result of scarring of the esophageal lining, endoscopy and balloon dilatation may be needed to break down the stricture.

Esophageal Obstructions

Esophageal obstructions in the cat can occur secondary to tumors (squamous cell carcinoma), infections, strictures (as seen with chronic esophagitis), and to the ingestion of foreign objects, including bones, fishhooks, and strings.

Again, regurgitation and weight loss are the two most common signs seen in cats afflicted with such a problem. However, if a foreign body has penetrated the esophageal wall, then more generalized signs, such as fever, loss of appetite, breathing difficulties, and vomiting, might be seen as a result of secondary infection.

Obstructions can be diagnosed using radiographs and/or endoscopy. Obviously, treatment is aimed at the surgical or endoscopic removal of the offending obstruction and at treating any secondary infection.

Hairballs

The accumulation of hair within the stomach is the most common cause of vomiting in cats. Because of their self-grooming habits and the roughened nature of their tongues, cats generally are susceptible to hairballs. Incidence of this problem increases during the spring and fall months because of increased shedding (Fig. 29.2).

DID YOU KNOW?

Shorthaired cats can develop hairballs just as readily as their longhaired peers.

When the hair is swallowed, it can coalesce into a ball within the stomach and act as a gastric foreign body, irritating the stomach lining. Vomiting, often right after eating, and gagging are usually the result when this happens; coughing might also be noticed. Aside from these signs, those cats affected seem otherwise clinically normal.

Diagnosis of hairballs is based on clinical signs (and the absence of other clinical signs) and physical examination. If the vomiting is continuous or severe, radiographs of the stomach or direct endoscopic examination might be required to rule out other gastric foreign bodies common to cats, such as cloth, strings, and plastic wrap.

Another way to make a diagnosis of hairballs is to monitor response to treatment. There are numerous "cat laxatives" on the market that can be given to a cat suspected of harboring hairballs. These agents, most of which are merely flavored petroleum jelly, act to lubricate the hairball and facilitate its passage out of the stomach and into the stool. Once this occurs, the clinical signs seen should abate. In

FIGURE 29.2 Because cats groom themselves so efficiently, they are highly prone to hairball formation.

severe instances, surgical removal of a prominent hairball might even be required to effect a cure.

Pet owners can do their part to prevent hairballs in their cat. Giving laxatives in a preventive manner once or twice weekly should help keep things moving smoothly through the gastrointestinal tract. One word of caution: Mineral oil should never be used as a hairball laxative, primarily because this substance can be easily aspirated into the lungs. In addition to giving a hairball laxative periodically, brushing a cat's haircoat on a daily basis will help reduce the amount of hair available for ingestion.

Gastrointestinal Ulcers

An ulceration within the stomach or intestines occurs when the protective mucus barrier covering the inner surfaces of the gastrointestinal tract is lost or destroyed, allowing stomach acids and bile acids to erode the gastrointestinal lining.

The same type of heartburn that humans sometimes experience with this problem can affect cats as well, leading to inappetence, vomiting, and lethargy.

Gastrointestinal ulcers are actually symptoms of disease rather than a distinct disease syndrome in themselves. Sharp foreign bodies or harsh chemicals that are swallowed can scrape, injure, and (in the case of the latter) burn the stomach or intestinal lining as to cause a primary ulceration. Ulcers occur secondary to stress, infectious agents (including *Helicobacter*), intestinal parasites, and metabolic diseases such as kidney disease. Certain drugs, such as steroid anti-inflammatory medications, can also have a deleterious effect on the stomach and intestinal lining.

Diagnosis of an ulcer relies heavily on clinical signs seen and the history or evidence of an underlying disorder. Radiographs taken after the oral administration of barium can be used to pinpoint the exact location of an ulcer. In addition, direct visualization of the actual stomach and upper intestinal lining using an endoscope is another means of diagnosing ulcers in a cat.

Obviously, when formulating any treatment regimen for ulcers, any underlying source for the ulcerations must be identified and treated.

Specific ulcer treatment is aimed at reducing the amount of stomach acid secretion, and providing a protective coating over the existing ulcer until it has time to heal. Standard human antiulcer medications are very effective at reducing the amount of stomach acid secretion in cats.

Food Allergies

Allergies to foods can cause vomiting and diarrhea in cats. In many instances, it is not the natural food ingredients themselves that cause the problems, but the additives and fillers that are present in a ration.

In addition to vomiting and diarrhea, weight loss, abdominal pain, excess gas formation, and dermatitis might be seen as well. Allergies to food have also been implicated as a primary cause of lymphocytic-plasmacytic enteritis.

Food allergies are often diagnosed after other common causes of the same signs have been ruled out. Food trials might also be conducted to determine whether there is an abatement of signs. This is accomplished by administering a hypoallergenic diet exclusively for at least 8 weeks. These diets are available from veterinarians. If a cat does indeed have a food allergy, then it will need to remain on a hypoallergenic diet indefinitely.

Eosinophilic Enteritis

Eosinophilic enteritis is a disease characterized by a thickening and inflammation of the walls of the intestinal tract caused by an infiltration of white blood cells. At the same time, this infiltration can affect other organs of the abdomen, including the liver, spleen, and lymph nodes, with enlargement and inflammation. Clinical signs associated with this disorder include vomiting, diarrhea, and weight loss. The exact cause of this disorder remains unknown; however, allergies are believed to be involved.

Diagnosis of eosinophilic enteritis is made through examination of biopsy samples taken from affected organs. Treatment consists of corticosteroids to reduce the inflammatory response. Relapses following therapy are common, necessitating long-term medical and dietary management.

Inflammatory bowel disease

Inflammatory bowel disease (IBD) in cats is actually a group of chronic digestive disorders characterized by the infiltration of the walls of the bowels with inflammatory cells, leading to abnormal wall thickening and irregularities. IBD has been recognized as a significant cause of chronic vomiting and/or diarrhea in cats. As far as the etiology of IBD, research to date has failed to uncover an exact cause. Many veterinarians believe that bacterial and/or dietary proteins may stimulate an autoimmune type of reaction in these cats. This reaction, in turn, manifests as a buildup of immune cells on and within the surfaces coming in contact with these proteins. Interestingly, it has also been noted that inflammatory bowel disease occurs simultaneously in many cats suffering from hyperthyroidism.

The classic clinical sign associated with IBD in cats is chronic vomiting. Often misdiagnosed as hairballs, vomiting induced by IBD usually occurs intermittently over months to years, gradually worsening and increasing in frequency with time. In addition to vomiting, bloody diarrhea and abdominal pain are also clinical signs seen in cats suffering from IBD.

Diagnosis of IBD in cats is made through the use of a thorough history, physical exam findings, radiographs of the abdomen, and more specifically, biopsy samples from affected portions of bowel. Diagnostic techniques such as these will help differentiate this condition from other disorders that may cause similar clinical signs, including foreign bodies, hyperthyroidism, pancreatitis, lymphosarcoma, and bowel obstruction.

Treatment for inflammatory bowel disease employs the use of drugs designed to reduce the inflammatory response, as well as medications designed to locally suppress the immune system response within the gut. Administration of these medications may be required on a long-term basis to control this disorder. Most treatment regimens for IBD also require dietary adjustments using rations that are hypoallergenic. Unfortunately, the overall prognosis for cats suffering from IBD is very guarded. Lymphosarcoma is not an uncommon sequela to severe cases of IBD that cannot be controlled through medical means.

Linear Foreign Bodies

Cats are notorious for playing with and swallowing linear items such as strings, threads, and ribbons (Fig. 29.3). If, for instance, a string becomes wrapped around the tongue or remains trapped within the stomach while the remaining portion passes on into the intestine, normal intestinal peristalsis will cause the intestine to "bunch up" around the string, resulting in intestinal obstruction. Furthermore, as the intestine becomes more and more irritated, its motility will increase, creating a "sawing" action against the immobilized string. In this way, intestinal perforation and secondary peritonitis can result.

FIGURE 29.3 String foreign bodies commonly become lodged under the tongue.

Cats suffering from a lodged linear foreign body have painful abdomens and exhibit persistent vomiting, with or without diarrhea. Fever and weight loss are also accompanying signs. If intestinal perforation occurs, septic shock could result.

Diagnosis of a linear foreign body is made by physical examination and radiographic X rays. Often, a diagnosis can be confirmed by finding a free end of the object wrapped around the base of the tongue. In these instances, however, manual extraction of the foreign body through the mouth should not be attempted. Instead, the string or foreign body should be freed from under the tongue and allowed to pass down into the stomach, and then into the stool.

Often, this provides enough relief from the tension placed on the intestines to allow intestinal function to return to normal. However, if radiographs show that the intestinal bunching has not been relieved, or if the cat's clinical signs continue, then surgical exploration with removal of the foreign body and repair of any intestinal perforations might be necessary. If perforations have indeed occurred, antibiotic therapy is indicated as well to combat infection.

Intestinal Obstructions

In addition to string foreign bodies, other items can obstruct normal flow through the gut and result in clinical signs, such as lethargy, vomiting, and black, tarry stools. Swallowed foreign bodies (e.g., bones, plastic wraps, and cloth), tumors, fungal infections, and hernias are all capable of causing either partial or complete obstructions if sufficiently large or extensive. Unless the obstruction is relieved in a timely fashion, usually through surgical means, loss of blood supply to the affected portion can occur, resulting in the death of that portion of bowel, systemic infection, and shock.

Bacterial Enteritis

Two types of bacteria are responsible for most cases of feline bacterial enteritis: *Campylobacter fetus jejuni* and *Salmonella.* Although rarely a primary cause of fever, depression, and diarrhea in cats, these bacterial infections often occur secondary to other gastrointestinal diseases (e.g., feline parvovirus) and to diseases that depress the immune system (e.g., feline leukemia). Severe salmonella infections can also spread to the liver and lungs, causing abscesses and associated clinical signs. On the other hand, a primary importance of *Campylobacter* lies in the fact that it is transmissible to and can cause diarrhea in humans.

Diagnosis of salmonella enteritis can be supported by finding a marked depression in the number of white blood cells in a blood sample. In most cases, however, a positive response to treatment with antibiotics provides the best method of diagnosis for most veterinary clinicians. Because bacterial enteritis can cause profound dehydration, intravenous fluids are a must during convalescence to protect against this deadly complication.

Colitis

Problems involving the large intestine of cats are common in veterinary medicine. *Colitis* refers to the inflammation of the lining of the large intestine, resulting in diarrhea, with the feces often containing an abundance of blood and mucus. The blood seen with colitis is usually bright red, in contrast to small intestinal bleeding, which contributes to a black tarry appearance of the feces. *Tenesmus,* or straining to defecate, is another prevalent sign with colitis that is often mistaken for constipation.

Acute colitis refers to a sudden onset of signs that usually lasts only a short period of time with proper treatment. Chronic colitis is a long-term, recurring condition that might last an entire lifetime of the cat. Parasites such as coccidia are common causes of colitis in cats; dietary indiscretions and stress factors are two other prevalent sources as well.

Feline leukemia and FIV should be ruled out in any case of long-standing problems with the bowels. Less commonly, fungal infections, foreign bodies, intussusceptions, polyps, food allergies, immune system disorders, and tumors can all result in signs related to a chronic colitis.

In cats, a special type of colitis, called *idiopathic colitis,* has been known to occur. Although the exact cause of this is unknown, many researchers suspect food allergies. An unusual characteristic of idiopathic colitis is that diarrhea is rarely a clinical sign; instead, the stools appear relatively normal except for a small amount of blood and/or mucus coating the surface. Most of these cats show no other signs of apparent illness.

Diagnosis of any type of colitis is made from a predisposing history (e.g., known dietary indiscretion), existing clinical signs, and physical examination. Stool examinations and other laboratory tests, especially FeLV and FIV testing, should be performed in an attempt to identify the underlying cause of the colitis. Radiographs, including barium contrast studies, are indicated in nonresponsive, recurring cases. Biopsies obtained using an endoscope or through exploratory surgery can also prove to be helpful for establishing a definitive diagnosis. In some cases, an exact cause of the inflammation can never be discerned, even with extensive laboratory testing.

Treatment of colitis is aimed at eliminating the inciting cause. Parasites should be treated using proper dewormers and antiparasitic medications. Antibiotics can be used to help remove any disease-causing bacteria within the colon, and steroid anti-inflammatory agents might prove to be helpful in abating clinical signs.

If polyps or tumors are presented, surgical removal might be necessary to afford a cure. However, understand that in many cases of chronic colitis, especially those caused by stress or by immune system disorders, a complete cure cannot be achieved. In these cats, treatment goals are aimed at managing flare-ups as they occur, Anti-inflammatory agents, antibiotics, and local protectants such as kaolin and pectin can help provide relief from these intermittent flare-ups.

Dietary management is an important component of colitis treatment. Acute cases of colitis caused by dietary indiscretion or some infectious process respond well to administration of an easily digestible diet.

Chronic, recurring bouts with colitis may be managed by increasing the fiber content in the diet to increase the bulk of the stool that helps normalize intestinal motility. Finally, for those cases caused by food allergies, a hypoallergenic diet can help eliminate the effects of the allergy.

Feline Megacolon

Feline megacolon is a disease condition characterized by a large, distended colon that has lost its ability to contract properly. When this occurs, feces build up within the affected segment, preventing normal flow of ingesta through the intestinal tract.

Megacolon is caused by a disruption of or lack of nerve activity in the muscular walls of the colon. It might occur secondary to spinal cord trauma or other diseases affecting the nervous system, or, as in the case of some tailless Manx cats, it can be inherited.

The clinical signs associated with feline megacolon can vary. Straining to defecate is certainly the most obvious sign; diarrhea can also be seen, along with firm, hard stools. If the obstruction is severe, vomiting, dehydration, and loss of appetite can be seen as well.

Diagnosis of feline megacolon can be made on physical examination and, for confirmation, from radiographs. Treatment involves removing the fecal impaction using warm-water enemas and by infusing the colon with mineral oil.

Enemas designed for use in humans should not be used in cats, as the components of an enema can cause severe dehydration in cats. Severe cases might require surgical relief of the impaction.

There is no effective cure for this condition; as a result, preventive maintenance therapy should be used to prevent recurrences. Giving an oral hairball laxative on a daily basis will help keep fecal matter moving along nicely. Increasing the amount of fiber in the diet has also been shown to be helpful in preventing relapses.

Feline Liver Disease

Because of the important role the liver plays in the metabolism of nutrients and in the detoxification of poisonous substances, any malfunction or interference with its function can place the life of the pet in serious jeopardy. In the cat, liver damage can occur secondarily to infections elsewhere in the body (including the gastrointestinal tract), to internal diseases such as diabetes mellitus, heart disease, and cancer, and to the ingestion of toxic substances.

Hepatic lipidosis is a common type of liver dysfunction in cats that has baffled researchers for years. It is characterized by an extensive infiltration of the liver by fatty tissue that, in essence, crowds out the normal liver cells and interferes with normal liver function. Hepatic lipidosis is seen in all ages of cats, and its exact etiology is unknown;

however, obesity and/or prolonged periods of food deprivation due to loss of appetite are thought to increase the body's utilization of fats for energy, the metabolism of which is carried out in the liver.

Like so many other diseases, liver disorders can cause loss of appetite (often profound), vomiting, diarrhea, and fever in affected cats.

One unique sign often seen with liver disease, including hepatic lipidosis, is jaundice, or *icterus.* Jaundice is caused by elevated levels of bile pigments in the bloodstream and is characterized by a yellow discoloration of the skin, mucous membranes, and the blood serum.

Other clinical signs that can result from chronic, long-term liver disease include a fluid buildup within the abdominal cavity (ascites), due to increased resistance to blood flow through the liver bleeding tendencies, and anemia. Seizures, comas, and other neurological disorders can also appear with advanced cases as ammonia and other toxins are allowed to build up within the bloodstream.

Diagnosis of feline liver diseases is based upon clinical signs, physical exam findings, and upon demonstrating elevated levels of liver enzymes in a blood sample. Radiographic X rays can be used to judge the size of the liver, which gives the veterinary practitioner some idea as to the duration of the problem. In many instances, a biopsy is required to determine the actual cause of the liver malfunction.

FACT OR FICTION

Aspirin, acetaminophen, and other types of oral human pain medications are poisonous to cats. **FACT.** The feline liver, unlike that of most other species, is deficient in a certain enzyme called *glucuronyl transferase.* This enzyme is normally responsible for metabolizing and detoxifying certain therapeutic drugs that reach the liver. This is why cats are so sensitive to drugs such as aspirin and acetaminophen; even small doses can be deadly!

Treatment objectives for feline liver disease are aimed at eliminating any injurious agents that might be present, and to promote healing of the affected tissue. The liver is one of the few organs within the body that can actually regenerate itself after injury provided of course that the source of the injury is dealt with properly. Intravenous fluids are a must to prevent dehydration and its unpleasant side effects. It is vital for recovery that these

FIGURE 29.4 Sick cats that refuse to eat may require tube feeding. This particular tube passes through the nose, down the esophagus, and into the stomach.

cats be force-fed, especially in cases of hepatic lipidosis. This might require actual feedings through a stomach tube (Fig. 29.4). An easily digestible, low-protein diet with high biological value is ideal for patients suffering from a liver disorder.

Antibiotics can be used if bacterial infection is suspected; for those cases that exhibit neurological signs caused by too much ammonia in the bloodstream, they can also be helpful for eliminating ammonia-forming organisms in the gastrointestinal tract. Ascites can be treated with diuretic drugs and by reducing the amount of sodium in the cat's diet. Finally, in select instances only, steroids might be used to increase appetite and to counteract the loss of protein that can occur with liver disease.

Pancreatitis

The *pancreas* is an organ responsible for the production of essential digestive enzymes that break down foodstuffs into usable and absorbable units within the small intestine. It is also the site of production for the hormone insulin, which is vital for the conversion of sugar (glucose) to energy within the body.

Inflammation involving the pancreas is termed pancreatitis. In cats, the cause of most cases of pancreatitis remains unknown. Some cases result from abdominal trauma, tumors, intestinal obstructions, infectious diseases such as FIP and toxoplasmosis, liver and gallbladder disease, and insecticide poisoning. Infiltration of the pancreas by inflammatory cells of the body can also cause this condition.

Signs of pancreatitis include weakness, loss of appetite, excessive salivation, vomiting, diarrhea, dehydration, and abdominal pain. In addition, repeat bouts of pancreatitis can damage the insulin-producing cells of the pancreas, resulting in clinical signs associated with diabetes mellitus. Another aftereffect of chronic pancreatitis in cats can be a condition known as *exocrine pancreatic insufficiency*. Characterized by the inability of the pancreas to produce proper amounts of pancreatic digestive enzymes, exocrine pancreatic insufficiency is accompanied by a marked increase in appetite (due to poor digestion of nutrients), chronic weight loss, and diarrhea. This loose stool often contains large amounts of fat, which may cause a greasy soiling of the haircoat in the hindend.

Pancreatitis is difficult to definitively diagnose in cats. Traditional elevations in levels of amylase and lipase, two pancreatic enzymes, are not seen as consistently in cats as in dogs with the disease. Radiography, ultrasonography, and endoscopy can be employed as alternate diagnostic methods, yet even the reliability of these procedures can be inconsistent. In most instances, diagnosis is based on clinical signs seen and by a biopsy of the pancreas. If exocrine pancreatic insufficiency is suspected, specialized laboratory tests will need to be performed on a series of stool samples in order to positively identify the condition.

Cats experiencing only a mild bout of pancreatic inflammation will often recover on withholding all food and water for at least 24 hours. When treating severe cases of pancreatitis, it is imperative that all food, water, and even oral medications be discontinued for at least 48 hours. Intravenous fluids will be required as well to prevent dehydration during this time. Additionally, antibiotics, pain relievers, and medications designed to reduce pancreatic secretions are usually employed to prevent secondary complications. Certainly all underlying disease conditions contributing to the pancreatitis must be addressed as well.

On recovery, cats should be maintained on dietary rations that are low in calories and easily digestible to reduce the workload placed on the pancreas. For those cats that are overweight, increasing exercise levels and promoting weight loss will reduce their susceptibility to subsequent flare-ups. Finally, cats experiencing exocrine pancreatic insufficiency due to chronic bouts with this disease will require enzyme supplementation to their diet to ensure adequate digestion of foodstuffs takes place.

The Urinary System

In the normal, day-to-day functioning of the body, much waste material is formed as a result of metabolic activity. It is the function of the urinary system to handle and to rid the body of these waste products. In addition, through its ability to dilute or concentrate the urine, it serves to regulate fluid levels within the body.

Because of its vital function, any interference or alteration of urinary system function can quickly have serious health consequences. For this reason, prompt and proper diagnosis of urinary tract disorders in cats is essential. Periodic checkups by a veterinarian can help detect potential problems before they reach such a magnitude as to threaten the health of a pet.

For more information regarding anatomy and function of the urinary system, see Chap. 12.

Feline Lower Urinary Tract Disease

Feline lower urinary tract disease (FLUTD) [known in the past as *feline urologic syndrome* or (FUS)], is a disease syndrome of cats characterized by the formation of crystals (most commonly struvite crystals) within the urinary bladder. These crystals, in turn, cause inflammation, urinary bleeding and straining, and sometimes life-threatening obstruction to the normal flow of urine out of the bladder (Fig. 30.1).

No one knows for sure why some cats get FLUTD and others don't. Many potential causes have been hypothesized, including viruses, abnormal urinary retention, obesity, bladder defects, and—the most popular theory to date—improper diet. In reality, one or all of these factors might play a role in the occurrence of FLUTD.

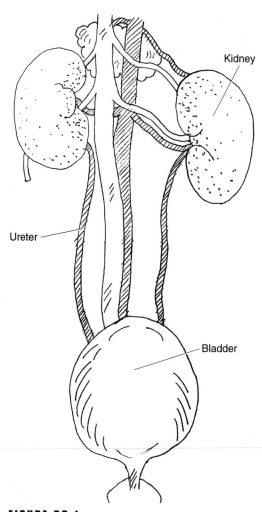

FIGURE 30.1 Lower urinary tract disease in male cats can lead to an obstruction that damages the bladder and kidneys.

If a cat is prone to this disorder, it will usually show some signs of the disease when it reaches 3 years of age. Both male and female cats are at risk of developing FLUTD; however, males have a greater likelihood of developing a life-threatening obstruction simply because the male urethra is smaller in size than that of the female and can become plugged with crystals more easily. If such an obstruction occurs, urine can back flow back into the kidneys, causing damage to these organs and also causing toxins to begin building up in the bloodstream.

Early clinical signs of FLUTD result from the irritation that these crystals cause within the bladder itself. These can include inappropriate urination in places other than the litterbox or normal elimination areas, increased licking at the genital region, straining, and frequent attempts at urination with crying or vocalization, and blood in the urine (Fig. 30.2). Cats often lose their appetites and become more irritable as well. More seriously, male cats suffering from partial or complete obstruction of the urethra can exhibit vomiting, intense lethargy, and a distended, painful abdomen.

Diagnosis of FLUTD is based on clinical signs, physical examination, and a urinalysis. An enlarged, painful bladder can also be palpated in those cats suffering from some degree of obstruction. If a bladder infection is suspected, then urine cultures might also be performed.

The obstructed cat will usually have high levels of kidney enzymes [blood urea nitrogen (BUN), creatinine] present in its bloodstream, signifying the toxin buildup and kidney destruction that is occurring. Most veterinary hospitals are equipped to monitor these enzymes.

FIGURE 30.2 Cats with urinary tract disease will lick incessantly.

If an actual obstruction is suspected, then rapid treatment is essential to save the life of the cat. Obstructed cats are immediately placed on intravenous fluids to help dilute the toxin levels within the bloodstream. A catheter is then inserted into the urethra to "unplug" it in order to reestablish urine flow. Once this flow is reestablished, the bladder is flushed repeatedly with

FIGURE 30.3 A urinary catheter may become necessary to relieve an obstruction.

sterile saline to remove any crystals that might be remaining within (Fig. 30.3).

It is up to the veterinarian's discretion as to whether to keep the urinary catheter in place for a few days. While catheterized, these cats are placed on antibiotics to prevent any secondary bladder infections from occurring as a result of catheterization. Intravenous fluids are continued in the hospital setting for 2 to 3 days after the obstruction is relieved.

For the cats that are not obstructed but are still showing signs of FLUTD, smooth muscle relaxants and anti-inflammatory medications can be used to help reduce the discomfort and urge associated with this disease. The use of antibiotics in such patients is still controversial; studies have shown that bacterial infections are present in less than 20 percent of the cases. However, if urine culture confirms the presence of such, antibiotics are, of course, indicated.

Altering the pH of the urine in order to dissolve any crystals present within the bladder is another important step in treating this disease in both obstructed and unobstructed felines (Fig. 30.4). Struvite crystal formation in cats with FLUTD is encouraged by an alkaline urine pH.

Rendering the urine more acidic will help dissolve existing crystals and help prevent the formation of new ones. On the contrary, promoting a more alkaline urinary pH will help manage oxalate crystals within the bladder. As one can see, it is vital that crystals be properly identified during the diagnostic process.

Most veterinary researchers agree that diet plays the foremost role in the creation and in the treatment and prevention of this disease syndrome. Dry diets with high contents of magnesium and ash (mineral) levels are the major culprits in promoting FLUTD in cats.

FIGURE 30.4 Urine crystals as seen under a microscope.

Unfortunately, many of the commercial supermarket brands of cat food contain these excesses. Diets specially formulated for the prevention of FLUTD can be obtained in both moist and dry forms from most veterinary offices. Because of its high calcium and mineral content, cow's milk should never be offered to those individuals prone to FLUTD.

Besides feeding a diet that acidifies the urine and is low in magnesium and ash, providing cats free access to a fresh water supply is a must. Increased water consumption will help increase the number of urinations each day, effectively keeping the bladder flushed out. In fact, most commercial diets formulated for the prevention of FLUTD have an increased salt content to promote increased water consumption. With these increased urinations comes the responsibility of cleaning the litterbox on a regular basis. Many cats refuse to urinate in a dirty litterbox, a practice that encourages urine retention and FLUTD.

Although it might not seem important, regulating the frequency of meals fed can play a direct role in the prevention of FLUTD. After a cat consumes a meal, its urine undergoes a temporary rise in pH. For those cats allowed to eat and nibble all day long (such as those fed dry foods), this might promote relatively constant alkaline urine, and thereby predispose to crystal formation. As a result, in terms of preventing FLUTD, offering one or two meals a day rather than free-choice meals is preferred.

Obese cats are more prone to FLUTD than are their slimmer counterparts, so weight control is an important preventive measure to follow as well. Overweight felines, especially those who have exhibited signs of FLUTD in the past, should be placed on reducing diets prescribed by their veterinarians, and their activity levels should be increased until the desired weight is reached. Once weight loss is accomplished, they can be switched back over to preventive-type rations.

Without proper dietary management, FLUTD can be expected to recur over 50 percent of the time. In some cats, however, FLUTD recurs over and over again, even with dietary management. In these instances, treating the symptoms when they first appear and continuing with prevention measures will usually keep such episodes from turning serious.

For those male cats with a history of recurring obstruction, a special operation known as *perineal urethrostomy* might be indicated to reduce the danger of death due to urinary blockage. This surgery involves removal of the end of the penis and widening the urethral opening, effectively allowing for free passage out of any and all crystals. Keep in mind that such a procedure is not intended to cure the FLUTD; it merely lessens the risk of severe, life-threatening complications associated with it.

Kidney Disease

The kidneys are responsible for eliminating waste products produced by the body's normal metabolism. If they fail to perform this function adequately, the body will literally poison itself. For this reason, special attention must be directed at keeping the kidneys healthy, and—if a disease state already exists—at treatment to prevent further functional deterioration.

In cats as in dogs, kidney disease is a common disorder associated with old age. In essence, through normal wear and tear, the kidneys become unable to perform their functions in the same way that they did when they were young. Worn-out kidney cells die and are replaced by scar tissue, which can't filter out toxins from the blood. When enough of these nephrons die and with sufficient buildup of toxins in the blood, the pet begins to exhibit signs of kidney failure.

DID YOU KNOW❓

It takes a loss of over 75 percent of the functioning capacity of both kidneys to lead to signs of kidney failure in cats.

But don't get the idea that older cats are the only ones that can suffer from kidney impairment. Young cats might be born with inadequate kidney function. For instance, kittens can be born with inadequately developed kidneys, or with kidneys containing open cysts embedded within the normal tissue, a condition known as *polycystic kidneys.*

Cats of all ages might suffer from other diseases or toxic agents that kill nephrons and impair renal performance. For example, bacterial infections, feline leukemia, feline infectious peritonitis, heat stroke, heart disease, and cancer are only some of the acquired conditions that can lead to kidney disease and kidney failure.

Glomerulonephritis and renal amyloidosis are two types of kidney impairment caused by overreactive immune systems in the affected cats, which actually destroy healthy kidney tissue in an attempt to eliminate infections or diseases elsewhere within the cat's body. Next, many therapeutic drugs, such as aspirin and certain antibiotics, can be damaging to the kidneys if used indiscriminately. In addition, antifreeze, or ethylene glycol, is deadly to cats when ingested because of its profound damage to the kidneys (Fig. 30.5). Finally, periodontal disease, with its associated complications, can predispose felines, both young and old, to kidney problems in the future.

The clinical signs associated with kidney disease can be quite variable, depending on the extent of damage to the kidneys. Interestingly, cats rarely show outward signs of kidney disease until at least 75 percent of the function in both kidneys is lost! As a result, when signs do finally become apparent, it is vital that therapeutic measures be taken quickly to prevent loss of the remaining 25 percent.

Sudden, acute kidney failure, the type that can result from the ingestion of a poison such as antifreeze, can lead directly into intense dehydration, shock, unconsciousness, and death without showing any other signs. Chronic, more long-term kidney disease and kidney failure rarely have such a dramatic presentation, yet such conditions can eventually turn into acute kidney failure if measures aren't instituted to prevent this progression.

Cats with chronic renal failure will exhibit an increased thirst and an increased desire to urinate. Depression and loss of

FIGURE 30.5 Antifreeze will destroy the kidneys!

appetite might also set in. In addition, since renal disease can cause stomach ulcers, vomiting might occur.

Veterinarians can diagnose kidney disease through a series of laboratory tests performed on the blood and the urine. Two blood parameters or enzymes, blood urea nitrogen (BUN) and serum creatinine, will be elevated if the kidneys are failing.

The urine specific gravity is also an important parameter that helps the veterinary practitioner determine the extent of damage to the kidneys. Under normal circumstances, the specific gravity of the urine, which measures how concentrated the urine is, should fluctuate according to the body's own needs for water. Diseased kidneys, however, are unable to conserve water for the body; hence, this specific gravity of the urine in a cat with advanced kidney disease will be diluted, even if the pet is clinically dehydrated.

Cats suffering from acute renal failure must be hospitalized and placed on intravenous fluids to correct dehydration. Other medications designed to stimulate kidney function will be given as well. If the cat survives this acute attack, support measures for chronic kidney failure must then be implemented.

Stress reduction is of vital importance in cats with chronic renal disease and/or failure. Unlimited access to clean, fresh water should be provided at all times, since deprivation could lead to an acute kidney failure crisis. Special diets that are low in protein and phosphorus should be provided to help reduce toxin buildup within the bloodstream. These are available from veterinarians. Vitamin supplementation should also be considered to replace those lost in the increased urine flow.

Since renal disease can alter, among other things, the blood levels of calcium and phosphorus, medications designed to keep levels of these electrolytes constant are used as well. If a pet is vomiting, human antiulcer medications can be employed to help settle the stomach.

The Reproductive System

iseases and conditions involving the reproductive tract are fairly rare in cats, especially males. Most of the problems that arise tend to be infectious in nature. Prompt medical attention is warranted in any disorder involving the reproductive tract. See Chap. 22 for more information concerning breeding cats.

Anatomy

The reproductive system of the female cat consists of the ovaries (which produce eggs and reproductive hormones), the oviducts (where fertilization takes place), the uterus (the site of fetal development), the birth canal, and the mammary glands. This system can become a significant source of medical challenges in mature female cats that have not been previously neutered. Influenced over the years by repeated hormonal patterns, the reproductive tissues in these cats can experience abnormal anatomical growth or secretory activity. These changes, if significant enough, predispose the pet to several serious medical conditions, including cancer. In intact females, the sites of most potential problems are the uterus and the mammary glands.

The reproductive organs of the male cat include the testicles and associated structures, the penis, prostate gland, and two bulbourethral

FIGURE 31.1 Cats can be prolific breeders; as a result, neutering is highly recommended in most instances.

glands, which contribute fluid to the semen. Fortunately, intact male cats are rarely afflicted with reproductive disorders. However, they are not immune to neoplasia and other age-related changes involving one or more of these structures.

As a general rule, neutering cats at a young age should be performed to minimize potential health challenges involving the reproductive system (Fig. 31.1).

Accidental Mating (Mismating)

The question about what to do with the female cat that is accidentally bred is not an easy one to answer. Long ago, cat owners only needed to take their pets to the veterinarian for a "mismating shot or pill." Yet because of potential undesirable side effects from using such drugs for aborting pregnancies, their use is now discouraged. Instead, the queen should be allowed to have the litter of kittens if the mating was indeed a successful one, or an ovariohysterectomy should be performed.

Metritis and Cystic Endometrial Hyperplasia Complex

Female cats over the age of 6 that have not been spayed are susceptible to the development of metritis and cystic endometrial hyperplasia complex (CEHC). *Metritis* refers to inflammation involving the lining of the uterus, whereas *pyometra* refers to a condition in which the uterus becomes grossly distended with uterine secretions and inflammatory fluid.

The causes of metritis are numerous, and can include venereal transmitted disease organisms, endocrine disorders such as diabetes mellitus, abnormal pregnancies or births, and treatment with certain types of drugs. These drugs include hormones used to prevent or terminate unwanted pregnancies, and special hormones called *progestins,* used by some veterinarians to treat certain skin and behavioral disorders in cats. In addition, intact females become increasingly susceptible to CEHC with each successive heat cycle because of the hormone progesterone secreted as a natural part of this cycle. Over time, repeated exposure of the uterus to the effects of progesterone can cause the secretory glands within the inner walls of the uterus to undergo abnormal growth (hyperplasia) and secretory activity. This, combined with the ability of progesterone to decrease uterine muscle motility, can ultimately lead to fluid accumulation within the uterus. This fluid may escape from the uterus in the form of a discharge. However, if for some reason it is not allowed to escape, a dangerous enlargement can result, with marked uterine enlargement, even to the point of rupture. Furthermore, the retained fluid can serve as an ideal medium for the growth of bacteria and other organisms, creating an infection (*pyometra*). In advanced cases, these bacteria and the toxins they produce can gain entrance into the bloodstream, causing blood poisoning. In addition, kidney failure can even occur secondary to pyometra due to the immune response mounted by the body in response to the infection.

The most prevalent clinical sign associated with metritis is a thick yellow-green to hemorrhagic vaginal discharge. In addition, constant grooming around the vaginal opening occurs frequently with cats with metritis. In advanced cases, loss of appetite, fever, and abdominal pain may arise as well. Finally, because of the close proximity of the two organ systems in female cats, secondary bladder infections can arise as a result of metritis.

Cats with pyometra exhibit similar signs seen with metritis, yet a discharge may or may not be seen. Also, true pyometra classically causes a marked increase in thirst and abdominal enlargement in affected felines. If secondary kidney disease becomes a factor, dehydration, vomiting, or increased urination frequency may be seen as well.

Diagnosis of metritis and pyometra in cats is made through the use of a history (i.e., intact vs. neutered), clinical signs observed, and laboratory workup, including blood tests, discharge cultures, abdominal radiographs, and/or ultrasound. In cases of pyometra, blood work often reveals a marked elevation of the white blood cell count and a mild anemic state. Abdominal radiographs and ultrasonography reveal a grossly distended uterus that displaces other organs within the abdomen.

The treatment of choice for metritis and pyometra is neutering. Although select cases of metritis may be treated successively with antibiotic and fluid therapy, the chances of recurrence are so high that neutering should still be considered. On the contrary, pyometra in a cat should be considered an emergency situation, and surgical removal of the offending uterus should be performed as soon as possible.

The Skin and Haircoat

The skin, or *integument,* functions to protect the body from outside foreign invaders and from loss of water. It provides a focus for the sense of touch and assists in the regulation of the temperature within the body. In addition, special modifications of the skin, such as claws and pads, provide a means of defense as well as shock absorbency.

For more information on the anatomy and function of the skin and hair, see Chap. 14.

The Itchy Cat

Many disease conditions can cause itching in the cat (Table 32.1) However, only a few disorders result in severe and/or prolonged itching. The primary symptoms of the itchy cat is scratching, biting, and/or licking at the involved skin. Early signs often noticed include wet hairs, reddened skin, miliary dermatitis, and hair loss in the affected areas. Prolonged itching results in further hair loss, excessive scaling, thickening, and discoloration of the involved skin. Secondary skin infection is not uncommon in these situations (Fig. 32.1).

Severe and/or prolonged itching is virtually always a symptom of an underlying skin disorder, such as fleas or allergies. As a result, correction of the underlying problem is imperative if the symptom of itching

Table 32.1 Common Causes of Itching and Hair Loss in Cats

Fleas
Food allergy
Inhalant allergies (atopy)
Neurodermatitis
Feline endocrine alopecia
Ringworm
Mange

is to be successfully controlled. The most common causes of itching in cats are described in the following paragraphs.

Flea Allergy

Aside from the discomfort caused by the actual bite of a flea, cats can develop an allergic response to the flea's saliva deposited in the skin during feeding. Miliary dermatitis with moderate to severe itching and hair loss usually results, especially around the head and neck and along the back near the tail. As one might guess, successful treatment of a flea allergy is heavily dependent on the ability to control fleas on the pet and in the environment.

FIGURE 32.1 Fleas and ear mites are two common reasons why cats will scratch at their heads.

Food Hypersensitivity (Food Allergies)

Food allergies are another potential cause of itching and miliary dermatitis in cats. Skin lesions related to such an allergy generally involve the head and neck, although other areas can also be affected. Food-related allergies have also been implicated in numerous gastrointestinal disorders as well. Fortunately, food allergies occur rarely.

Food allergies should be suspected any time a recent change in diet has led to the appearance of a skin condition, or if itching starts soon after eating. A definitive diagnosis of food hypersensitivity requires the exclusive feeding of a hypoallergenic diet for 8 weeks. A veterinarian can prescribe such a diet, which contains a protein source that is not commonly used in commercial cat foods. If a positive diagnosis is made, the cat will need to remain on the hypoallergenic diet indefinitely. Simply changing food brands or types is seldom of benefit in food allergy cases because most commercial foods contain similar ingredients.

Contact Allergies

The haircoat of cats normally offers an efficient protective barrier to many substances and agents that could produce an allergic reaction just by coming in contact with the skin. Unfortunately, when people step in and try to help, they can inadvertently cause problems related to contact allergies.

For instance, the most common contact allergy-producing agents are flea collars, shampoos, pet sprays, insecticides, and similar products, all of which are generally applied or used with good intentions.

Symptoms of a contact allergy include redness and swelling of the skin, with intense itching. These signs will generally develop 24 to 72 hours after exposure. Hair loss, especially with allergies to flea collars, is also a common finding.

Many times, treatment of contact allergies simply requires the removal of the offending agent. In tougher cases, administration of topical and/or systemic corticosteroids may be needed as well to reduce the associated inflammation.

Hair Loss (Alopecia)

Loss of hair either locally or generalized over the coat of a cat is another type of skin problem owners could face. As with itching, the causes of hair loss can be quite numerous, and sometimes very complex (Table 32.1). A proper diagnosis is essential for restoring the full-bodied haircoat that once was. Here are some of the potential causes of alopecia in cats.

Shedding

The normal shedding cycles for cats tend to occur in the spring and fall, yet if the cat is kept indoors, shedding could occur year-round. If normal shedding is truly the cause of the hair loss, rarely do raw spots or patches of exposed skin appear. If they do, another cause of the hair loss should be suspected. If a cat sheds excessively, brushing its coat daily will help remove the dead hairs and make way for the new ones. Failure to do this can predispose your feline to itchy skin and infections.

Any event that is associated with abnormally high amounts of stress can cause increases in shedding activity and in some cases, overt alopecia. A good example of this is the queen undergoing pregnancy or lactation. The physiologic and nutritional stress placed on the cat's body can lead to accelerated hair loss. Fortunately, in most instances, the hair will return once the stress abates.

Malnutrition

The hair cycle in cats is dynamic and active, with new hairs constantly growing in to replace old, dead hairs that are naturally shed. These new hairs require a bounty of protein and other nutrients for their proper formation and development. If these are not supplied, replacement hairs might not grow in at all, or they might be weak, brittle, and easily broken. As a result, cats suffering from poor nutrition often have scanty, lackluster haircoats, not to mention unhealthy skin. Since the source of the problem is internal in nature, the distribution of this hair loss tends to be symmetrical over the entire body.

The wrong type of diet is not the only cause of nutritionally related hair loss. Internal parasites can also lead to malnutrition because intestinal parasites can steal vital nutrients from the cat, causing the haircoat to bear the brunt of the consequences.

Obviously, providing a good plane of nutrition and correcting any internal parasite problems that might exist are the two key means of restoring normal hair growth in these cases.

Itching

As might be expected, incessant itching and scratching can cause loss of hair as well. This hair loss might be due to self-trauma from licking, chewing, and/or scratching, or it could be secondary to inflammation affecting the hair follicles themselves. The distribution of the hair loss can be localized or diffuse, symmetrical or asymmetrical, depending on the extent of the causative disorder. For instance, if hormonal disorders are to blame, the resulting hair loss is often symmetrical, affecting both sides equally. On the other hand, hair loss caused by mange or ringworm usually appears localized to certain portions of the body at first, although this hair loss can spread to other parts if the disease is left unchecked.

Identifying and correcting the underlying problem is the most important step to take for restoring the scanty coat. Realize that in many conditions involving inflammation of the hair follicle, the coat might look worse with treatment before it gets better as a result of treatment-induced shedding of already dead or damaged hair. A good plane of nutrition, one that is adequate in protein and fatty acids, will also speed replacement of the lost hair in recovered pets.

Feline Endocrine Alopecia

Traditionally, otherwise unexplained hair loss affecting neutered male and female cats has been attributed to a hormonal disorder known as *feline endocrine alopecia.* This condition is characterized by a non-itchy, symmetrical hair loss affecting the abdomen, thighs, and posterior region; however, the underlying skin in these areas appears healthy and unaffected.

Diagnosis of this disorder is based on ruling out other potential causes of hair loss and on experiencing a positive response to therapy. Treatment using special drugs can sometimes help stimulate hair regrowth in these cats.

Ringworm

Fungal infections involving the skin and hair can cause hair loss without associated itching. The most prevalent fungal infection affecting the integument of felines is ringworm. For more information regarding ringworm in cats, see Chap. 24.

Feline Miliary Dermatitis

The term *miliary dermatitis* refers to a specific way in which feline skin responds to inflammation and/or irritation. Such a skin reaction is characterized by the formation of tiny, seedlike crusts that frequent the head, neck, and tail regions of the body. In extensive cases, the entire body might be involved. Furthermore, the miliary reaction is quite itchy, and leads to scratching, rubbing, and licking of the affected skin. Hair loss often results because of these activities. Often the irritation miliary dermatitis causes is so great that the affected cat becomes easily agitated and twitches its skin when disturbed or touched.

The potential causes of miliary dermatitis are numerous. Irritation caused by external parasites is the most common cause of localized miliary reactions. Allergies, including food, inhalant, and contact allergies, are other potential causes. In addition, adverse reactions to medications and drugs, and fatty acid deficiencies in the diet have also been implicated as inciting feline miliary dermatitis.

Treatment for feline miliary dermatitis is aimed at correcting the underlying cause for the disorder, if this is known. For those cases in which an underlying cause cannot be identified, treatment with corticosteroids can provide relief from the clinical signs. Antibiotics are rarely necessary, since bacterial infection is rarely a component of this disorder.

Eosinophilic Granuloma Complex

This dermatopathy of cats is characterized by the unexplained appearance of red to yellow-brown ulcerated lesions with associated hair loss occurring at various locations around the body. On the average, it tends to strike female cats that are under 6 years of age.

When the raised, well-demarcated reddish ulcers appear on the lips of affected felines, they are termed *eosinophilic ulcers* or "rodent" ulcers (Fig. 32.2). Linear granulomas are eosinophilic granulomas that can occur anywhere on the body, but

Eosinophilic lip ulcer

FIGURE 32.2 Eosinophilic lip ulcers appear as red, angry lesions.

especially frequent the back portion of the hind legs. These ulcerations are yellowish to pink in appearance, and, as the name implies, they tend to run in a straight line down the affected portion of skin.

With both eosinophilic ulcers and linear granulomas, pain and itching do not appear to be significant factors. However, prompt treatment is still important, since some of these lesions, especially eosinophilic ulcers, can evolve to skin cancer if left alone.

Eosinophilic plaques are types of eosinophilic granuloma that are associated with intense itching. These well-demarcated, raised ulcers are often bright red in appearance and show up primarily on the abdomen and on the upper, inside portions of the back legs. Cats so affected will often lick constantly at the lesions because of the irritation and itching caused by these plaques.

Diagnosis of eosinophilic granuloma complex in cats is routinely made on physical exam and on microscopic examination of cells or tissues from the lesions. Treatment employs corticosteroids given orally or by injection for 3 to 4 weeks. In cases that don't respond to standard treatment, alternate therapy such as radiation therapy may be used in an effort to bring the lesions under control. As with miliary dermatitis, antibiotics are rarely necessary to effect a cure unless a secondary infection is present.

Stud Tail

This skin disease is seen in purebred, intact, male cats who are sexually active. It is caused by overactive sebaceous glands near the base of the tail, which cause a greasy, waxy deposit to be laid down over the skin and coat in this region. Although unsightly, this condition usually causes no pain or itching in affected tomcats.

Treatment consists of periodic cleansing of the region with a mild, hypoallergenic shampoo or soap, being sure to dry the area well after doing so. More extensive treatment regimens are seldom necessary.

Bacterial Infections

Healthy skin has several mechanisms for resisting infectious organisms. A dry, outer layer of keratin, combined with periodic shedding of dead skin cells, helps to discourage population of the skin surface with harmful bacteria. Even sebum, produced by the sebaceous glands of the skin, is antibacterial at normal concentrations. Finally, a normal population of bacteria that resides on the skin surface and in the hair follicles competitively inhibits the growth of disease-causing bacteria.

Problems can start to occur when the integument becomes traumatized, or when underlying disease alters the normal integrity of the skin. If the skin's defenses are penetrated in such a way, disease-causing bacteria found naturally on the skin (or on the teeth of other felines) can set up housekeeping.

Superficial Bacterial Skin Disease

Superficial bacterial skin disease in cats can take on a number of appearances. Feline acne is perhaps the most common type seen in veterinary circles. This disease is characterized by infection of the hair follicles and the appearance of blackheads and/or pustules on the chins of affected cats. Although the exact cause of this disorder remains unknown, many researchers feel that it is due to the cat's inability to adequately groom this area.

Treatment for feline acne consists of clipping the hair away from the chin and scrubbing the chin daily with a mild antibacterial solution containing benzoyl peroxide or chlorhexidine. Afterward, a drying agent such as alcohol or ear-cleansing solution should be applied to the chin. In severe instances, systemic antibiotics might be required to completely clear up an infection.

As far as other superficial skin infections are concerned, any at-home treatment that uses topical antibacterial creams or ointments should be first approved by a veterinarian. Avoid those preparations containing hydrocortisone or other steroid compounds. In cases where the infection is spreading or is not responding to topical medications, oral antibiotics will be required.

Cellulitis and Abscesses

Cellulitis and *abscesses* are types of deep infections that occur secondary to tissue injury, usually from bite wounds. Cellulitis involves a poorly defined region of inflammation involving the deeper layers of the skin with no apparent rim or border, whereas abscesses do have a well-demarcated line of surrounding inflammatory cells that make them stand out.

Both can be characterized by a painful buildup of pus, and usually cause fever and depression. Both can also lead to blood poisoning if not treated in a timely manner with high doses of antibiotics. Because of their isolated nature, veterinarians often lance and flush out abscesses to help speed the healing process.

Feline Neurodermatitis

Feline neurodermatitis results in hair loss and/or skin irritation due to nervous licking and chewing. The highly emotional breeds of cats, such as Siamese and Himalayans, are more prone to this disease than others.

This nervous licking and chewing can be triggered by any disruption or stress in the cat's normal daily routine, such as moving into a new home or introducing a new addition to the family. The lesions caused by this abnormal grooming activity can resemble eosinophilic ulcers, or there might be a "stripe" of hair loss on the back or sides of the body (Fig. 32.3). Often the hair loss resembles that seen with ringworm.

A diagnosis of neurodermatitis is made after carefully examining the history of occurrence, plus ruling out other causes of similar dermatological signs. If possible, eliminating or correcting the inciting cause is the best way to treat neurodermatitis. In difficult cases, therapy using antianxiety or mood-altering drugs might be necessary to calm the nervous feline and prevent the self-trauma to the skin and coat.

Feline Solar Dermatitis

Initiated by the ultraviolet rays of the sun, *feline solar dermatitis* can occur in cats with insufficient skin pigmentation to block the harmful effects of the sun-

FIGURE 32.3 Cats suffering from neurodermatitis harbor characteristic lesions.

light. Cats with white haircoats (or those with white ears and/or white faces) that live in hot, sunny climates are most prone to this dermatopathy.

Lesions usually begin at the tips and margins of the ears, yet they can also appear on the eyelids, nose, and/or lips. Hair loss, scabs, and ulcerations characterize these lesions. If left unattended, the affected skin can eventually become cancerous, and metastasize to other parts of the body.

Diagnosis of solar dermatitis is confirmed through surgically obtaining a biopsy sample of the affected areas. Treatment is geared toward reducing exposure to the sun's rays via indoor confinement and through the use of commercial sunscreen products. Corticosteroids applied topically can also help reduce any associated inflammation. For those lesions suspect of becoming cancerous, surgical removal (if possible) and/or radiation therapy is needed to prevent spreading.

Skin Lumps and Masses

Whenever a lump or mass appears on or beneath the skin of a cat, there are five possible sources:

1. An abscess

2. A hematoma or seroma

3. A cyst

4. A granuloma

5. A tumor

Obviously, because the cause can vary, a veterinary diagnosis is essential. A fine-needle aspirate of the mass, or an actual biopsy sample will assist the veterinarian in this diagnosis.

Abscesses

Abscesses are usually painful to the touch and are often associated with other signs, such as fever, depression, and loss of appetite. They also tend to be fluctuant when direct pressure is applied to them.

Hematomas and Seromas

These result from leakage of blood or serum, respectively, from damaged blood vessels. Traumatic blows to the skin can result in hematoma or seroma formation beneath the affected area of skin. The swellings caused by these are also fluctuant; because of the traumatic nature of their occurrence, they can be painful as well. In most cases, the swellings caused by hematomas and seromas will resolve on their own with time, assuming that infection does not appear in the meantime.

Cysts

A cyst is simply a well-defined pocket filled with fluid, secretion, or inflammatory debris. Unlike abscesses, cysts are seldom filled with pus or painful to the touch. Although they normally pose no specific danger to the health of a cat, especially large cysts should be surgically excised.

Granulomas

Granulomas are firm, raised masses consisting chiefly of inflammatory cells sent to the particular area by the body in response to skin penetration by a foreign substance or infectious agent. In essence, the body attempts to quickly surround and ward off the foreign invader before it can spread to other parts of the body. Thorns, insect stingers, vaccines, fungal organisms, and certain bacteria are only a few of the things that can incite granuloma formation. If a cat develops one of these growths, an attempt should be made to determine the cause of its appearance. If an infectious agent is suspected, appropriate antimicrobial therapy is indicated to prevent further development of the granuloma. Granulomas may or may not recede with time, depending on the cause. In some cases, surgical removal of the mass gets rid of the unsightly lump and its inciting cause all at the same time.

Tumors

Skin tumors or cancers can appear in a variety of types, sizes, and shapes. Common tumors that appear as a lump or mass on or beneath the skin of a cat include squamous cell carcinoma, basal cell tumors, and mast cell tumors. Fibrosarcomas have been known to occur infrequently after certain vaccines are administered. As a result, any lump that appears 2 to 6 weeks following vaccination should be brought to the attention of a veterinarian. With any lump suspected of being a tumor, it is imperative that a biopsy be performed in all instances to determine whether the tumor is malignant or benign.

Mammary tumors in cats are serious, since the vast majority of these are malignant. Most common in older, intact queens, these tumors can spread throughout the body quite rapidly unless diagnosed and treated early. Treatment involves surgical removal of the affected gland(s). For extensive tumors, chemotherapy might also be employed.

For more information on cancer and its treatment, see Chap. 60.

The Eyes and Ears

THE EYES

The sense of vision is important to nocturnal hunters such as the cat, more so than in their canine counterparts. Unique adaptations of the feline eye (Fig. 33.1) allow for this greater visual acuity. For instance, the unique slit-shaped design of the feline pupil allows it to dilate exceptionally wide in dimly lit surroundings. In addition, the ability to focus in on objects and to detect even the slightest movement is highly refined.

Certainly such visual characteristics account for the effectiveness of the feline as a hunter. As with dogs, cats also possess those ocular structures necessary to perceive their world in color. Whether they actually take advantage of their presence is doubtful. Except for the shape of the iris and pupil, the anatomy of the feline eye is essentially the same as that of the dog. For more information concerning visual anatomy and function, see Chap. 15.

As far as visual capabilities are concerned, one interesting breed to take note of is the Siamese cat. Although their eyes differ

---

DID YOU KNOW?

Color receptors in the eyes of cats enable them to see their world in greens and blues, and any combinations thereof.

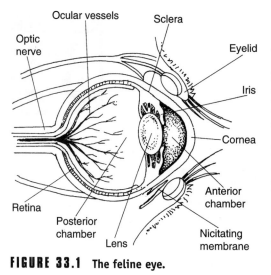

Optic nerve

Ocular vessels

Sclera

Eyelid

Iris

Cornea

Retina

Posterior chamber

Lens

Anterior chamber

Nicitating membrane

FIGURE 33.1 The feline eye.

little anatomically, if at all, from those of their brethren, research has revealed that they might perceive their world a little bit differently. While binocular vision (visualizing one scene with both eyes) is the standard for humans and most animals, Siamese cats might actually visualize two different presentations for the same scene—one for each eye. Confusing? Imagine a set of keys sitting on a countertop. That is what a person would see, a set of keys. A Siamese cat, on the other hand, might visualize two sets of keys because each eye is focusing on the set separately. Because of this apparent lack of binocular vision, depth perception is not as refined in this breed as in others. Could all this explain the unique behavior exhibited by this fanciful breed?

Corneal Ulcers

The transparent cornea enclosing the front portion of the eye is a remarkable organ in itself. Responsible for gathering light and directing it into the eye, healthy corneas are essential for proper vision. It stands to reason, then, that ulcerations (loss of surface epithelium) or scratches involving one or more corneal surfaces can seriously threaten eyesight if not managed promptly.

Corneal scratches and ulcerations in cats can occur secondary to skirmishes with other cats, dust and foreign debris entering the eyes, and other

FACT OR FICTION

Night vision in cats is far superior to that of humans. **FACT.** This assumes, however, that the moon is up. In pitch darkness, cats can see no better than we do!

types of direct trauma. Ulcerations can also occur through improper eye protection applied when bathing or dipping.

Clinical signs of a corneal ulcer include squinting and aversion to light, ocular discharge, and obvious discomfort, often signified by pawing at or rubbing the affected eye. A change in the normal color or transparency of the corneal surface also may indicate that something is wrong. Definitive diagnosis of a corneal ulcer is made by a veterinarian using a special fluorescein dye to stain the corneal surfaces. Dead, diseased corneal tissue will readily take up such stain, whereas healthy tissue will not.

Luckily, the cornea is one organ that will heal quite rapidly if treatment is administered vigorously and in a timely fashion. For ulcers involving only the superficial layers of the cornea, topical antibiotic ointments or solutions designed for use in the eyes and applied numerous times during the day will help speed healing.

Of course, if an underlying cause, such as a piece of nail, still exists in the eye, it must be removed before proper healing can take place. Superficial ulcers can heal within 36 to 48 hours with proper treatment applied.

Deep Corneal Ulcerations

Deep corneal ulcerations are treated the same way that superficial ulcerations are, yet deep ulcerations require close observation for progression or worsening of the ulcer. Bacterial cultures of such ulcers are necessary to ensure that the antibiotics being used are effective against the organisms involved.

For deep ulcers that worsen or fail to respond to conventional treatment, additional procedures might be necessary to speed healing or to prevent the cornea from actually rupturing. One procedure used consists of surgically freeing and extending a portion of the thin conjunctiva over the ulcer and actually tacking it down against the ulcer using suture material (conjunctival flap). The flap of conjunctiva provides nutrition and speeds healing to the ulcer, and also allows medications applied directly to the eye(s) to reach the ulcer unhindered. Once healing has been accomplished, the flap is released, and excess conjunctival tissue is trimmed away from the healed surface.

Special contact lenses and/or corneal tissue adhesives can also be applied over the damaged surface of the cornea. These serve to protect it from further degradation and help promote rapid healing. For difficult ulcers, actual grafts using fresh or frozen corneal tissue may be required.

Conjunctivitis

Inflammation of the thin, transparent mucous membrane lining the inner portion of the eyelids and front part of the sclera is termed *conjunctivitis.*

Conjunctivitis is the most common cause of "red eyes" in cats. Other signs seen with conjunctivitis include discharge, swelling, and, if other eye structures are involved, pain. The type of discharge present can sometimes give a clue as to the underlying cause of the conjunctivitis. For instance, a watery discharge can indicate irritation from an allergy, virus (such as feline rhinotracheitis), or contact with dirt or dust. In contrast, a cloudy discharge often links the problem to a bacterial infection, either primary or secondary to any of the causes previously mentioned.

Because conjunctivitis can be secondary to other problems, diagnostic tests performed by a veterinarian should be directed at identifying any underlying causes. Corneal staining using a fluorescent stain is usually performed to determine whether the cornea is concurrently affected.

Treatment of conjunctivitis is aimed at treating or eliminating any inciting causes, and at controlling the localized inflammation. If dust or pollens are the source of the conjunctivitis, daily flushing of the eyes with a sterile saline solution designed for use in the eyes or daily application of a sterile ophthalmic lubricant can help reduce the irritation caused by these offenders.

Ophthalmic drops or ointments containing antibiotics are warranted if a bacterial infection is present. In addition, ophthalmic preparations containing steroids can be used to reduce the inflammation present, provided the surface of the cornea is intact. Preparations containing both antibiotics and steroid compounds for use in the eyes are readily available for pets through a prescription from a veterinarian (Fig. 33.2).

In cases of conjunctivitis that don't respond to conventional therapy, a bacterial culture or sensitivity test and an eye-pressure test should be performed. The first can help determine whether the type of antibiotic ointment or solution being used is indeed the right choice; the second will help identify any underlying problems with the eyes themselves (such as glaucoma) that might be contributing to the lingering conjunctivitis.

FIGURE 33.2 Whenever applying eye ointment, keep the tip of the tube parallel to the eye to prevent accidental injury if your cat moves.

Cataracts

Fortunately, the incidence of cataract formation in cats is much less than that in dogs. When it does occur, the most common underlying cause is diabetes mellitus. As a result, any change in a cat's visual responsiveness or any obvious changes in the lens color warrants a complete veterinary medical workup.

Glaucoma

Glaucoma is a condition characterized by an increase in fluid pressure from the aqueous humor within the eye(s). In the normal eye, pressure and aqueous levels are maintained at a constant level by the continual drainage of excess aqueous humor out of the eye through tiny ports (drainage angles) located where the edge of the iris meets the cornea. If for any reason this drainage is obstructed or altered in any way, a rise in pressure within the eye can result. Unfortunately, even short-term rises in this pressure can lead to irreversible damage if not detected and treated in a timely fashion.

Conditions such as a buildup of inflammatory material within the eye secondary to FIP or feline leukemia, luxation of the lens due to trauma or cataracts, and synechia (where the iris "sticks" to the lens or cornea), can all effectively prevent the normal drainage of the aqueous humor from the eye.

Clinical signs of a glaucomatous eye include a marked redness both affecting the conjunctival tissue and the sclera; a blue, hazy cornea; a dilated, unresponsive pupil; and apparent blindness due to the increased pressure that the fluid is placing on the optic nerve. In instances where the glaucoma has been present for quite some time, enlargement of the affected eyeball might become noticeable, and actual rupture of the cornea could occur.

Diagnosis of glaucoma can be easily confirmed by a veterinarian through the use of an instrument called a *tonometer* (Fig. 33.3). This instrument, which is placed directly on the surface of the cornea, measures the exact pressure occurring within that eye. If the pressure reading is indeed elevated, then treatment should be instituted immediately to prevent lasting damage to the eye.

FIGURE 33.3   Testing for glaucoma.

Treatment for glaucoma is aimed at decreasing the pressure within the eye to an acceptable level as quickly as possible, and then stabilizing this pressure to prevent increases in the future. A veterinarian will initially use drugs designed to quickly draw fluid out of the eye and into the bloodstream to reduce the pressure within the pet's eye(s); other drugs that act by decreasing aqueous humor production and by increasing the size of the drainage angles are then prescribed and given for the long-term management and prevention of recurrence. At the same time, anti-inflammatory medications can be used topically on the eye to clear up any primary or secondary inflammation that might be aggravating the glaucoma.

In instances where a luxated lens is causing the increase in pressure, surgical removal of the offending lens should always be performed. Cryotherapy (freezing) can be used as well. This involves surgically inserting a special needle within the eye and freezing the cells within the eye responsible for the production of aqueous humor. With this technique, aqueous production can be reduced significantly.

Entropion and Ectropion

Entropion is an ophthalmic condition in which the eyelids roll inward, allowing lashes and hair to irritate the surface of the eyes. *Ectropion* is the opposite; one or more lids roll outward, exposing conjunctival tissue and predisposing it to irritation. In both instances, the surface of the affected eye(s) become irritated and damaged, and inflammation results. Kittens can be born with either of these eyelid defects, or they can acquire them later in life, usually as a result of trauma to the lid(s). Fortunately, the incidence of both conditions is quite low in cats. When it occurs, surgical correction is required to prevent permanent damage to the eyes.

Eyelid Masses

The integrity of the eyelids is vital for the protection of the eyes from environmental hazards. Any disruption or alteration in the normal lid anatomy can place vision in jeopardy And certain masses involving the lids can do just that if they become sufficiently disruptive.

Tumors are the most common types of eyelid masses seen in cats. The presence of an eyelid tumor can be very serious because it is impossible to remove one surgically without disrupting the integrity of the lid. Squamous cell carcinomas are frequently involved in this location.

As alternatives to the potential complications afforded by eyelid surgery, radiation therapy, chemotherapy, and cryotherapy (freezing) might all be employed for treatment, depending on the type of tumor that is involved.

THE EARS

The sense of hearing in the cat is much more fine-tuned than that in a human, allowing the cat to detect much higher sound pitches (up to 60

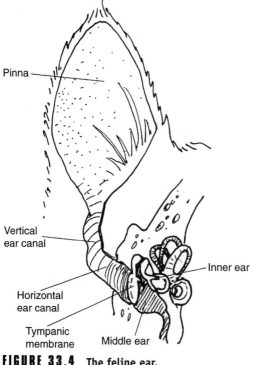

Pinna

Vertical
ear canal

Inner ear

Horizontal
ear canal

Tympanic
membrane   Middle ear

FIGURE 33.4 The feline ear.

kHz, as compared to 20 kHz for humans) that might be emitted by potential prey. Like that in the dog, the cat's hearing apparatus can be divided into three portions (Fig. 33.4): the inner ear, the middle ear, and the external ear canal and associated structures. For more information on anatomy and function of the ear, see Chap. 15.

Otitis Externa

Inflammation involving the external ear canal of an animal is called *otitis externa.* Although it occurs only infrequently in the cat, it can conceivably result from allergies, infections, foreign bodies, tumors, polyps, and ear mite infestations. Otitis externa can also lead to secondary infections within the ear canal if the inflammation persists for long enough.

DR. P's VET TIP

To help prevent treatment failures and recurrences when treating ear mites in cats, apply a pyrethrin spray to the haircoat at least once a week during the course of treatment. This will kill those industrious mites that may have evacuated the ears prior to or during treatment and are "hiding out" in the haircoat.

Signs of otitis externa involving one or both ears include head shaking, itching, painful ears, personality changes, and/or odiferous discharges from the ear canal(s). Hair loss might be noticed around the pinnae due to scratching.

Diagnosis of this condition is based on clinical signs and direct examination of the ear canals by a veterinarian. Once the exact nature of the problem is identified, specific treatment can be instituted (Fig. 33.5).

Ear Mites

Otodectes cynotis is the ear mite commonly found in the feline ear canal (see Fig. 21.3). These tiny parasites, which are transmitted by close contact with other infected animals,

FIGURE 33.5 Commercial ear cleansers can help you keep your cat's ears in tiptop shape.

live on the skin surface within the ear canal and feed on body fluids. Their presence irritates the glands lining the ear canal, leading to an increased cerumen (ear wax) production.

Secondary yeast infections within the ear often occur because of them, leading to the brown, crusty discharge so often seen with ear mite infestations. In isolated cases, intense allergic reactions to ear mites can occur, causing severe inflammation and secondary bacterial infection.

Diagnosis of an ear mite infestation is confirmed by identification of the mites directly on otoscopic exam or through a microscopic examination of an ear swab. Treatment involves the use of medications containing antiparasitic compounds, such as pyrethrins, rotenone, and/or thiabendazole. Mineral oil has also been employed as a home remedy for killing mites by suffocation. Since secondary yeast infections are commonly found with ear mite infestations, an antiyeast medication should be used concurrently with antimite preparations.

Ear mites can be difficult pests to eliminate. Daily treatment for 3 to 4 weeks might be needed to ensure a complete kill. All pets in the household, regardless of whether they are exhibiting signs of infestation, should be treated at the same time. In addition, to prevent reinfestation from the haircoat, an insecticide spray or shampoo should be used on the coat at least twice during the treatment period.

Otitis Media and Otitis Interna

Otitis media, infection involving the middle ear, usually results from a chronic, untreated, or recurring otitis externa. In such cases, the eardrum might become so diseased that it tears or ruptures completely, allowing direct access of infectious organisms into the middle ear chamber.

The clinical signs of otitis media are essentially the same as those for otitis externa, with a few notable additions. Cats so afflicted will usually exhibit a head tilt toward the side of the affected ear. In severe cases, paralysis of the facial muscles on the side of the lesion might be seen as the nerves passing through the middle ear become involved. This can result in a characteristic drooping of the eyelids, cheeks, and lips. In addition, a decreased tear production, pinpoint pupil, and protrusion of the third eyelid might be noted in the eye on the affected side.

If the infection extends from the middle ear into the inner-ear apparatus (otitis interna), the signs become even more pronounced. Since the inner ear functions in maintaining balance and equilibrium as well as hearing, cats suffering from otitis interna tend to become very uncoordinated and might fall down frequently or move in circles favoring the affected side. A characteristic twitching of the eyeball, called *nystagmus,* also becomes noticeable.

Although the clinical signs seen are often diagnostic, radiographs of the skull are quite helpful in confirming a diagnosis of otitis media or interna and determining the extent of the disorder.

Therapy for otitis media or interna must be instituted promptly to prevent permanent damage to the hearing apparatus. Oral antibiotics should be started immediately. In cases of otitis interna, continued treatment with antibiotics might be required for up to 30 days to afford a complete cure. In select cases, anti-inflammatory medications have been used to reduce signs associated with inflammation.

If it is not already ruptured, the eardrum on the affected side will usually be punctured to allow for thorough drainage of the middle-ear cavity and for the direct infusion of medications. Of course, such treatment steps must be carried out in a veterinary hospital under heavy sedation or anesthesia.

In tough, refractory cases, surgical placement of a drain in the bony tympanic bulla affords excellent exposure to the middle- and inner-ear spaces.

Ruptured Eardrums

Eardrums can tear or rupture as the result of direct trauma from a foreign body (such as a twig, cotton-tip applicator), sudden pressure changes, or most commonly, as a secondary complication due to otitis externa. Although a torn eardrum is a serious and painful condition, it will heal quite quickly provided the underlying cause of the perforation is eliminated.

Medications designed for use in the ears must be used with caution if a cat suffers from a ruptured eardrum. Not only can their application be painful, but also, as mentioned previously, certain antibiotics and solutions, if allowed direct access into the middle- and inner-ear chambers, can cause damage to the auditory nerve endings, resulting in deafness. As a result, owners must be certain to follow their veterinarian's recommendations closely.

Nerve Deafness

Infections are not the only source of deafness in cats. Nerve deafness can be inherited in some cats. This type of genetically induced deafness is seen primarily in white cats with blue eyes. In addition, age-related degeneration of the auditory (hearing-related) nerve endings can result in diminished hearing in elderly felines. Nerve deafness can also arise secondary to trauma to the ear, toxins, or treatment of the ears with certain types of medications. For instance, certain types of antibiotics, called *aminoglycosides,* may be prescribed in cats to combat certain types of bacterial infections. However, this class of drug can damage auditory nerves when used in high doses for extended periods of time. If this occurs, the damage is usually irreversible. As a result, veterinarians are especially cautious when selecting dosages and treatment durations of these and other drugs that may have similar effects on hearing.

Diagnosis of nerve deafness is based on history and special hearing tests. One such test, the brain stem auditory evoked response test (BAER), measures the brain's response to auditory stimuli and is quite helpful in the detection of hearing defects, determining the extent of any defect, and pinpointing its location. Unfortunately, no known treatment exists for nerve deafness once it is diagnosed. Most deaf cats will adapt to their condition with time. However, because of the inherent dangers associated with environmental hazards, deaf cats should not be allowed outdoors unless closely supervised or maintained on a leash and harness.

The Musculoskeletal System

The musculoskeletal system in mammals is responsible for locomotion and support, not to mention protection of vital internal organs. The components of this system include muscles, bones, and a variety of supportive structures, including ligaments, tendons, and cartilage. Disorders of the musculoskeletal system can be quite debilitating to a cat and be accompanied by a lot of pain.

For more information on the anatomy and function of the musculoskeletal system, see Chap. 16.

Arthritis and Degenerative Joint Disease

The term *arthritis* is the term used in both human and veterinary medicine to describe any type of joint inflammation. *Polyarthritis* describes inflammation involving multiple joints throughout the body. This inflammation could be accompanied by loss of cartilage or bony changes within the joint(s) in question.

Causes of arthritis in cats include infections, autoimmune diseases, and trauma. Even certain drugs, such as sulfa antibiotics, can promote joint inflammation if used indiscriminately.

Osteoarthrosis, or degenerative joint disease, describes the condition in which a cartilage defect or cartilage erosion occurs within a given joint. Although not considered a true inflammatory condition, many people use the term interchangeably with *arthritis.* Osteoarthrosis usually strikes older cats as a result of normal wear and tear associated with aging.

Stiffness or lameness involving one or more limbs is often the most obvious sign of a joint problem. In many instances, this lameness is aggravated by colder weather and prolonged periods of rest or overexertion. Affected cats might be reluctant to play or jump, and they could become more irritable when touched, because of pain. Joints might also be noticeably swollen and painful to the touch.

Diagnosis of a joint disorder is based on physical palpation of the joint(s) in question, observing the abnormal gait or movement associated with the disorder, and obtaining radiographic X rays of the joints.

Treatment approaches for arthritis and osteoarthrosis include weight control and anti-inflammatory medications. Since aspirin and acetaminophen can be highly toxic to cats, corticosteroids such as prednisone are prescribed instead for their anti-inflammatory activity.

Disease modifying osteoarthritis drugs such as the polysulfated glycosaminoglycans, glucosamine, chondroitin sulfate, and hyaluronic acid can be employed in the conservative treatment of joint diseases in cats. These agents appear to satisfactorily set the stage for healing to take place within the defective cartilage.

Infectious Arthritis

Apart from the normal wear and tear due to aging, joint inflammation can be secondary to an infectious process. Bacteria that gain entrance into the body's bloodstream can circulate to one or more joints of the body, setting up housekeeping within the joint fluid. Bite wounds resulting from fights with other cats are an important cause of infectious arthritis.

Fever, depression, and painful, swollen joints, with accompanying lameness, are prominent clinical signs seen in most cases of infectious arthritis. If allowed to progress untreated, actual degeneration of the bones making up the joint can occur, causing actual joint collapse.

Laboratory testing, including cultures of the fluid within the joint, might be needed to positively identify the offender. Once this is accomplished, specific treatment, usually involving high doses of antibiotics for 4 to 6 weeks, can then be instituted. Hot packs applied to the affected joints can also be used to help relieve some of the swelling and pain associated with the arthritis.

Limping-Kitten Syndrome

Young kittens fewer than 14 weeks of age can be afflicted with a form of infectious arthritis called "limping-kitten syndrome." Caused by the calicivirus, this syndrome presents as fever, generalized lameness, and pain, and hot, swollen joints.

Because the signs of limping-kitten syndrome are initially so severe, one would expect these kittens to suffer long-term ill effects from such a disease. Interestingly, however, prognosis for a complete recovery is excellent, since the disease is self-limiting and will disappear with time even without treatment.

Immune-Mediated Polyarthritis

Sometimes, an overactive immune system can lead to an arthritic condition. In these instances immune complexes consisting of antibodies coalesce within the joints of the body, causing inflammation. The resultant polyarthritis (arthritis affecting more than one joint) can be very painful and debilitating.

Many cats that suffer from immunity-related polyarthritis are also infected with the feline leukemia virus. As a result, other symptoms not related to the arthritis might be seen. Fever and a generalized depression are two such symptoms that are seen quite consistently.

Special blood tests and/or tests on joint fluid are used to diagnose autoimmune disorders in cats. Treatment usually consists of high dosages of steroid anti-inflammatory medications designed to curb the body's overactive immune response. Lifelong therapy might be required.

Hip Luxation

One common sequela to automobile accidents involving cats is *dislocation,* or *luxation,* of one or both hip joints. These cats are rarely able to move and experience pain in the affected regions.

Diagnosis can be made with a physical examination and radiographic X rays of the hips and pelvis. Because of the high rate of recurrence once a dislocation has taken place, surgical repair of the dislocation is preferred over the manual manipulation of the bone of the hind leg back into the hip socket. The surgical procedure most commonly used in these cats, called *femoral head and neck excision,* will eliminate recurrences of the problem and restore painless function to the affected limb.

Fractures

Most bone fractures in cats are trauma-related. In isolated instances, metabolic diseases such as nutritional osteodystrophy and bone cancers can also be underlying causes as well. In cats, the sites most often fractured include the femur (the long bone of the hindleg), the tail, the pelvis, the vertebral column, and the jaw.

Fractures can be caused by direct trauma to a bone, repeated stress placed on a bone, and disease-associated weakening of bone. They are classified as either *closed fractures,* in which no portion of bone is exposed through the skin, or *open fractures,* in which one or more of the fractured ends of bones are exposed through penetrations through the skin, creating a high risk of secondary infection. In addition, they can be further classified as to the extent of damage (complete versus incomplete), direction and location of the fracture line (transverse, oblique, physeal), and their stability following treatment (stable vs. unstable).

Bone fractures are usually accompanied by swelling, pain, crepitation, deformity, and loss of function. A fracture involving a limb will present itself as a non-weight-bearing lameness. Apparent paralysis of the hindend is seen with fractures involving the spine and/or pelvis. Facial deformity, excessive salivation, halitosis, and loss of appetite accompany fractures of the jaw.

Fractures are diagnosed on the basis of clinical signs exhibited and by radiographic analysis of the region in question. Management of the fracture will depend on the extent, stability, and location of the break. Incomplete fractures that do not affect the stability of the affected bone(s) can be treated with pain relievers and forced cage rest for 4 to 6 weeks. Complete fractures involving the entire circumference of the bone and those fractures accompanied by instability of the bone will usually require surgical intervention in order for proper healing to take place. In addition, open fractures will require antibiotic therapy in addition to surgical reduction to prevent secondary complication associated with infection from arising.

Most fractures involving the bones of the limbs, including the femur, can be stabilized with orthopedic pins and bone plates placed in or on the bone. Lower jaw fractures can usually be stabilized utilizing pins placed through the bones of the jaw as well as wires placed strategically around the lower teeth. Pelvic fractures may require pinning or bone plating if the fracture results in pelvic instability and/or the anatomy of the pelvic region and the pelvic canal (through which the colon, urethra, and reproductive structures pass) is grossly altered. Finally, fractures involving the vertebrae of the tail that result in nerve damage and loss of function to this structure can be managed by amputating the tail at or close to the fracture site.

Osteomyelitis

Infections involving bony tissue within the body are termed *osteomyelitis.* Bacterial osteomyelitis in cats usually occurs secondary to a deep bite wound or some other type of penetrating trauma. Open fractures can also predispose a cat to bone infections. Furthermore, fungal organisms such as histoplasmosis and blastomycosis can also spread from other areas of the body via the blood and infect bony tissue in cats.

Cats with osteomyelitis are lame and feverish. The affected site is usually quite painful. These signs, combined with the localized swelling that often occurs, might be mistaken for a fracture and, indeed, must be differentiated from one. To do this, radiographic X rays should be taken of the suspected skeletal region. In addition, bone biopsies might even be necessary to differentiate some cases of osteomyelitis from bone tumors, and to collect samples for bacterial or fungal cultures.

Because infections that become embedded in bone can be difficult to clear up with antibiotics alone, surgery is usually needed to actually remove those portions of bone severely affected. Drain tubes are placed as well to allow for postsurgical drainage and flushing of the site with medicated solutions.

Following surgery, antibiotic therapy might be required for 1 to 2 months; if a fungal organism is involved, medications might need to be given for 4 to 6 months.

Metabolic Bone Disease

Cats that consume diets consisting primarily of meat or those suffering from kidney disease are susceptible to a metabolic condition known as *secondary hyperparathyroidism,* which is characterized by a generalized degeneration and thinning of bone. Elevated levels of phosphorus in the bloodstream can result from the high phosphorus content of all-meat diets or by the failure of the kidneys to correctly regulate phosphorus levels within the blood. These abnormally high levels disturb the proper calcium/phosphorus ratio in the blood, and stimulate the body to draw calcium out of bony tissue in order to reestablish the desired ratio. Unfortunately, the effect of this calcium draw on bone integrity can be devastating. Cats afflicted with metabolic bone disease can experience lameness, weakness, joint deformities, and spontaneous fractures associated with weakened and brittle bones.

Diagnosis of secondary hyperparathyroidism is based on a history of dietary imbalance or the diagnosis of kidney disease, combined with the detection of elevated calcium and phosphorus levels in the blood. In addition, radiographic findings can be used to detect the bony changes caused by this disorder. Treatment of secondary hyperparathyroidism includes correcting the dietary deficit, managing any underlying kidney disease, and, in both cases, the administration of calcium supplements.

Another type of metabolic bone disease that can affect cats is called *hypervitaminosis A.* This condition is seen in those cats administered an exclusive diet of liver, which contain high levels of vitamin A. Musculoskeletal changes seen in cats experiencing chronic vitamin A toxicity include bony deformities, outgrowths, and fusion involving the vertebral column, especially in the region of the neck, and bony fusion of the joints of the limbs, resulting in pain and immobility.

A history of an all-liver diet, combined with clinical signs and radiographic analysis of the spine and limbs, can reveal conclusive evidence of hypervitaminosis A. If detected early in its development, this condition can often be reversed by switching the cat to a balanced diet. However, in advanced cases, the bony changes that occur are usually permanent, and anti-inflammatory medications are usually required for the remaining life of the cat to help ease the pain associated with the disease.

Mucopolysaccharidosis

Mucopolysaccharidosis is an inherited disorder that has been documented in Siamese cats. It results from an enzyme deficiency that allows polysaccharide carbohydrates to accumulate within the cells of the body.

The skeletal system is particularly affected, with stricken cats suffering from bony spurs on the vertebrae, arthritis and abnormal formation of the joints, and a generalized *osteoporosis,* or thinning of the bones themselves. These cats also have a characteristic "flattening" of the face, resulting from a widening of the facial structure, and, at an early age, can suffer from opacities or cloudiness involving the corneas of both eyes.

Diagnosis of mucopolysaccharidosis is made by physical examination, blood tests, and radiographic X rays of the skeletal system. A special test that detects mucopolysaccharides in the urine can also be employed in the diagnosis of this disorder.

Unfortunately, because of the inherited nature of this disease, there is no known treatment. Future generations should be protected by neutering those pets affected to prevent passage of the trait.

Myositis

Myositis is inflammation of muscle tissue that results in pain, weakness, and muscle atrophy (shrinking). Cats suffering from severe bouts of myositis are reluctant to move and can actually appear as if they are paralyzed from the inflammatory effects on the muscles. Myositis in felines can be caused by a number of different disease entities, including toxoplasmosis, bacterial infections (abscesses), hypokalemia (low blood potassium), and, rarely, autoimmune disease.

Myositis is diagnosed using clinical signs and blood tests designed to detect increased levels in muscle enzymes within the blood. In especially elusive cases, biopsy samples taken from suspected muscle tissue could help a veterinarian obtain a definitive diagnosis.

Treatment for myositis is aimed at the underlying cause. For instance, if infections are to blame, appropriate antimicrobial or antiparasitic therapy will help relieve the myositis. Anti-inflammatory medications can also be used to relieve the pain and discomfort associated with the inflammation until the underlying cause is treated.

Hypokalemic Myopathy (Potassium Depletion)

As an electrolyte, potassium serves a variety of functions within the body, including maintaining proper fluid volume and pH. Potassium is also necessary for normal muscle contraction. Many illnesses in cats can also produce deficiencies in this electrolyte, or hypokalemia, within their bodies. This is especially true for those cats suffering from kidney disease, liver disease, or diabetes mellitus.

Actual signs of hypokalemia can include weight loss, loss of appetite, constipation (due to poor motility of the muscles lining the gastrointestinal tract), muscle weakness, muscle pain, and incoordination. As the condition progresses and respiratory muscles become affected, breathing difficulties might be noted. In severe cases, death from respiratory paralysis could result.

Diagnosis of hypokalemia in a sick cat is based on a history, clinical signs, and measurements of blood potassium levels. If hypokalemia is diagnosed, treatment consists of intravenous injections of a potassium supplement to correct the immediate deficit, followed by oral supplementation as long as deemed necessary. Prognosis for recovery is good if treated early (Fig. 34.1).

Hernias

A *hernia* results from a tear or defect in a muscular wall, allowing the contents contained behind the wall to protrude through the opening in the muscle. In cats, two common types of hernias include inguinal hernias and diaphragmatic hernias.

FIGURE 34.1 Critically ill cats require supportive care to prevent secondary potassium depletion.

Inguinal Hernias

Inguinal hernias occur in the inguinal region of the abdomen, or that region where the abdominal musculature meets that of the hind legs. They are present at birth, or more commonly, can be seen secondary to trauma.

These hernias can be serious, since the herniated material often includes intestines. As a result, normal digestive processes can be disrupted. Treatment involves surgical replacement of the herniated material back inside the abdomen and suturing the defective muscle.

Diaphragmatic Hernias

By far the most serious type of hernia is the diaphragmatic hernia. The *diaphragm* is the thick wall of muscle that separates the thorax or chest cavity from the abdominal contents. Tears or ruptures occurring in this band of muscle, resulting from either inherited defects or traumatic incidents, can allow liver, intestines, and other abdominal contents to herniate through into the chest cavity. When this happens, the pressure applied to the crowded lungs and heart results in, among other things, breathing difficulties, weakness, and gastrointestinal disturbances.

Definitive diagnosis of a diaphragmatic hernia can be made by coupling history, clinical signs, and a physical examination with radiographic X-ray findings. Surgical repair of the torn diaphragm will alleviate the signs and usually result in a complete recovery.

The Nervous System

The nervous system involves a complex interaction between special elements designed to originate or to carry unique electrochemical charges to and from the various organs within the body. Like its endocrine counterpart, the nervous system initiates and regulates body functions and assures its owner of an awareness to its surrounding environment. For more information regarding the anatomy and function of the nervous system, see Chap. 17.

Paralysis

Paralysis can be defined as a disruption of the nervous system leading to an impairment of motor function and/or feeling to a particular region or regions of the body. This impairment can be in the form of a spasticity of the muscles in the involved region, or these muscles might become completely limp. In either case, the muscles involved are unable to function in the manner in which they were intended.

Paralysis involving the sensory portion of the nervous system can result in either an increased sensitivity to or a complete absence of pain. Paralysis resulting in the inefficient function of certain internal organs can occur as well if the nerves supplying these structures are disrupted in any way. If the bladder or colon is involved, this can lead to elimination disorders.

Trauma to the vertebral column and spinal cord is one of the most common sources of paralysis seen in cats. Fractured vertebrae resulting from encounters with moving automobiles, fractious dogs, or other sources can result in a partially or completely torn spinal cord in the region of the fracture(s). Neoplasia and infectious or parasitic agents can also cause inflammation and tissue damage in the spinal cord of cats, leading to functional deficits. Lymphosarcoma is probably the most prevalent tumor seen affecting this structure, and classically causes hind-end paralysis. Feline infectious peritonitis is a viral disease that can settle into the spinal cord of cats and cause clinical signs of disease, as is rabies. In addition, the toxoplasmosis and cryptococcosis organisms can attack the spinal cord as well as the brain and eyes, creating a myriad of nervous symptoms.

Diagnosis of the source of the paralysis can be made using clinical signs, physical examination findings, blood profiles (if infectious disease is suspected), laboratory analysis of the cerebrospinal fluid (CSF), and radiographs of the vertebral column. To pinpoint the exact sites of spinal cord involvement, special radiographs called *myelograms,* which entail the injection of a special dye into the spinal canal, may be employed as well.

Treatment of paralysis depends on the cause. Anti-inflammatory agents combined with drugs designed to draw fluid out of the central nervous system can help reverse signs of paralysis, yet their usefulness is dependent on the extent of the nervous injury and how quickly therapy is instituted. In some instances, surgery may be required to repair a vertebral fracture, excise an offending tumor, or remove a diseased intervertebral disk.

Cats that have sensory paralysis in a limb might require limb amputation to prevent self-mutilation to the leg. In instances where an irreversible paralysis involves more than one limb, or involves the malfunction of internal organs, pet owners must seriously consider not only their cat's quality of life as a paralytic but their own as well, before prolonged therapeutic or rehabilitative measures are undertaken.

Seizures

Owners who have a cat that suffers from seizures know firsthand how frightening these episodes can be. A *seizure* is defined as uncontrollable behavior or muscle activity caused by an abnormal increase in the brain's nervous activities. *Epilepsy* is the term used to describe recurring seizures.

What causes seizures in cats? The following are some potential sources:

- Viral infections (e.g., FeLV, FIP)
- Toxoplasmosis
- Trauma
- Fungal infections
- Cancer
- Intestinal parasites
- Low blood sugar
- Insecticide poisoning
- Heat stroke

Because the causes are so numerous, a thorough examination and blood workup by a veterinarian is warranted whenever a cat exhibits seizures. In some cases, managing or eliminating an underlying cause will eliminate the seizures. In others, such as with idiopathic epilepsy, there is no known cause, yet by ruling out the other potential causes and establishing a pattern of occurrence, one can effectively manage most cases with anticonvulsant medications.

With idiopathic epilepsy, seizures can begin at any stage in life but usually begin around 1 to 3 years of age. As mentioned before, the cause of idiopathic epilepsy is unknown; however, if it occurs in young animals, it was probably inherited. In contrast, if it occurs in older cats, some traumatic cause, such as a stroke, should be considered.

Most seizures themselves are rarely life-threatening, unless some physical harm comes to the cat as a result of the fit. The typical seizure or epileptic fit has three stages, or phases. The first of these, the *preic-*

tal phase, is marked by anxiety and restlessness on the part of the pet. The actual period of the seizure activity, *ictus,* follows next. Its duration might range from a few seconds to several minutes. Certainly the longer the seizure lasts, the more dangerous it is to the health of the pet. The *postictal* phase following the seizure is characterized by an overall depression or confusion. Postictal cats can appear to be blind, running into walls and objects, or they might only sleep a lot. This phase can last for a few hours or for days, with the cat returning to its normal state after conclusion of the phase.

There is one seizure presentation called *status epilepticus* that can prove fatal. It is characterized by a cluster of seizure events occurring in quick succession. Unless appropriate emergency medication is administered intravenously to stop the seizures, these cats can lapse into a coma and die. As a result, prompt recognition and action on the part of the pet owner is essential.

For cases other than idiopathic epilepsy, treatment is geared toward correcting or managing the underlying problem, such as kidney failure, poisoning, or low blood sugar. In instances in which idiopathic epilepsy is suspect, anticonvulsant medications can be used to control or even eliminate the seizure activity.

Cats suffering from idiopathic epilepsy do not necessarily need to be on any medication unless the seizures last for more than 2 minutes at a time or occur more often than every 2 months.

Determining the exact dosages of any of these medications for a pet might require frequent adjustments at the start in order to accommodate its individual needs. Pets taking anticonvulsant medication should undergo liver-function tests at least annually, since some of these drugs can adversely affect the liver over the long term.

Vestibular Disease

The vestibular system is a specialized portion of the nervous system found within the inner ear, brain, and spinal cord. Its duty is to maintain a state of equilibrium and balance. By communicating with the nerves supplying the eyes, limbs, and trunk, the body is able to coordinate the position and activity of these regions with movements of the head.

Peripheral vestibular dysfunction (PVD) is a disease that affects the nerves of the vestibular apparatus in the ears of cats. PVD is characterized by a sudden onset of incoordination and loss of balance, which is often accompanied by a head tilt, involuntary twitching of the eyeballs, and, in many cases, vomiting. The causes of this disorder can include trauma to the ears, skull infections,

FACT OR FICTION

When falling from heights, all cats have the natural ability to "right" themselves and land feet first.
FACT. But only if the cat has healthy ears! The vestibular portion of the nervous system, normally responsible for this remarkable reflex, can be disrupted by, among other things, ear infections and nasopharyngeal polyps. As a result, any cat harboring a severe ear mite infestation should think twice before leaping!

and tumors involving the middle or inner ear. Diagnosis of PVD is achieved using clinical signs and various laboratory tests to rule out other potential causes of the symptoms. Radiographs of the skull may be helpful in the detection of any masses or infections that may involve the inner portions of the ears. Treatment, of course, depends on the underlying cause and usually includes high doses of corticosteroid medications designed to reduce inflammation involving the vestibular apparatus.

Vestibular ataxia syndrome is seen in kittens born of queens stricken with feline parvovirus during pregnancy. Owners often are alerted to a problem when these kittens seem to have trouble in attempting to walk. The condition will not improve as these kittens mature, nor will it usually worsen.

Congenital vestibular syndrome is seen in Siamese and Burmese cats, with signs appearing anywhere from 2 to 4 weeks of age. Many of the Siamese cats affected are deaf as well.

The prognosis for Siamese cats with congenital vestibular syndrome is good, with clinical signs usually abating by the time the cat is 6 months of age. In Burmese cats, however, the prognosis is not as good, and the poor quality of life for most of these individuals will usually warrant euthanasia.

Feline Hyperesthesia Syndrome

Feline hyperesthesia syndrome ("twitchy skin syndrome") is a condition characterized by some unique clinical signs. Affected cats exhibit a rippling of the skin on their backs, especially when petted in the lower back region. They might chew or lick at their tail incessantly, and appear to be "spaced out," spontaneously darting throughout a room or house and attacking objects and owners without provocation.

The exact cause of this condition remains unknown. Some researchers feel that it is a form of epilepsy. Because "emotional" breeds such as Siamese, Persians, and Himalayans seem most often affected, other researchers believe that it is actually a behavioral disorder brought about by an upsetting experience or circumstance. Even food preservatives used in cat foods have been accused of causing feline hyperesthesia syndrome.

Medical therapy for this disorder consists of the use of antianxiety medications or sedatives in an attempt to modify the cat's behavior. Identifying and correcting any environmental upsets (including any dietary changes) that might have a possible link to the problem are needed as well.

Feline Ischemic Encephalopathy

Feline ischemic encephalopathy (FIE) is a neurological condition that has been known to strike cats. FIE is caused by a sudden disruption of blood supply to the brain, similar to a stroke in humans. Although a definitive cause has yet to be determined, cardiomyopathy, neoplasia metastasis, and even feline heartworms are suspect. Affected cats exhibit marked depression, incoordination, circling behavior, and/or seizure activity. The pupils of the eyes may become dilated, and blindness may be apparent. Acute clinical signs usually resolve within 7 to 10 days; however, residual neurologic deficits of varying degrees often remain indefinitely.

Diagnosis of feline ischemic encephalopathy is based on history and clinical signs seen, as well as ruling out other causes of similar symptoms, such as vestibular disease, feline leukemia, and poisonings. Treatment of this neurologic disorder involves the administration of high doses of anti-inflammatory medications. In addition, medications designed to dilate the brain's blood vessels and thin the blood may be employed in an effort to improve overall circulation to the affected regions of the brain.

The prognosis for survival in cats with FIE is guarded during the first 48 hours following onset of clinical signs. After 48 hours, the prognosis for survival is good, since FIE is a nonprogressive disorder.

The Endocrine System

Endocrine diseases in cats are those diseases that affect hormones or hormone-producing glands within the body. Because of the importance of hormones in metabolic regulation and function within the body, diseases affecting endocrine glands within the body can lead to a wide variety of clinical signs. In addition, proper diagnosis and treatment is essential to prevent permanent damage to the body.

Those endocrine diseases that have the greatest prevalence in cats are discussed later. Keep in mind that other less common ones do exist, which reinforces the importance of a proper diagnosis.

For more information on the anatomy and function of the endocrine system, see Chap. 18.

Hyperthyroidism

A condition of hyperthyroidism in cats is caused by an increase in circulating levels of thyroid hormones: thyroxine (T3) and triiodothyronine (T4). When it occurs, hyperthyroidism is most commonly seen in cats over 8 years of age, usually as a result of a tumor involving the thyroid gland(s). Because thyroid hormone helps regulate the body's metabolism, the clinical signs seen with hyperthyroidism can be directly related to the exaggerated increase in the cat's metabolic rate.

These symptoms may be mild to severe depending on the amount of excess hormone being secreted. Signs typically include noticeable weight loss in the presence of a voracious appetite, nervousness and hyperactive behavior, and a rough, unkempt haircoat (Fig. 36.1). Other less common signs seen include increased water consumption, regurgitation (due to rapid overeating), panting, and breathing difficulties, especially if the thyroid glands are grossly enlarged. In addition, many cats with elevated thyroid levels also suffer from inflammatory bowel disease (IBD). As a result, vomiting and/or diarrhea related to this may be seen in the hyperthyroid feline as well.

Diagnosis of hyperthyroidism is made through the evaluation of clinical signs, physical exam findings, and special laboratory tests. On physical examination, nodules can usually be palpated in the neck region because of the glandular enlargements. In addition, a rapid heart rate and pulse is often detected because of the effects of thyroid hormones upon the heart of the animal. This cardiac effect can be especially dangerous in cats suffering from concurrent cardiomyopathy. A diagnosis of hyperthyroidism can also be verified through the use of special tests designed to detect levels of thyroid hormone in the blood.

If this condition is definitively diagnosed, a number of treatment options exist. The type of treatment chosen will depend on the severity of the thyroid hormone elevation and on other underlying disease factors (such as the presence of heart disease or kidney disease). Medical treatment for hyperthyroidism involves the administration of special drugs designed to inhibit pro-

FIGURE 36.1 Hyperthyroidism causes emaciation in the presence of a ravenous appetite!

duction of thyroid hormone by the thyroid glands, thereby controlling clinical signs. Side effects from the administration of such drugs can include anemia, immune cell suppression, decreased appetite, vomiting, weakness, and itching. Since most cats must stay on this medication for the remainder of their lives, close monitoring by and periodic communication with a veterinarian is essential.

Yet another form of medical therapy that yields successive results in hyperthyroid felines is called *radioactive iodine therapy*. This type of therapy selectively destroys malfunctioning thyroid cells using radiation.

Most cats suffering from hyperthyroidism will respond favorably to medical therapy. However, if drug therapy fails to resolve the disorder and radioactive iodine therapy is unavailable, surgical removal of one or both thyroid glands (partial or complete thyroidectomy) must be performed. If extensive tumor involvement necessitates the removal of both glands, then daily thyroid hormone supplementation will be required for the remainder of the cat's life. Felines placed on such supplementation should undergo blood thyroid level monitoring every 6 to 8 months to ensure that adequate levels are being given.

An inherent risk associated with the surgical removal of both thyroid glands in cats is a complication known as *hypoparathyroidism*. This condition, characterized by low blood calcium levels, is caused by the inadvertent removal of the parathyroid glands (which are very small and tightly adhered to the thyroid glands) when the thyroid tissue is removed. Signs of low blood calcium, which normally arise within 3 days of parathyroid gland removal, include profound weakness, muscle tremors and spasms, and in some cases, seizures. Felines suffering from this postsurgical complication require prompt treatment with calcium supplements. These supplements, as well as vitamin D tablets, will be required for life to help maintain proper calcium levels within the body.

Hyperadrenocorticism (Cushing's Disease)

Cushing's disease (*hyperadrenocorticism*) is characterized by an overabundance of glucocorticosteroids circulating within the body. It is extremely rare in felines. When it does occur, increases in appetite, water consumption, and urination usually result. In addition, the typical thinning of the skin, hair loss, and pot-bellied appearance seen in dogs with Cushing's disease can be seen in cats as well.

For more information on Cushing's disease and its treatment, see Chap. 18.

Hypoadrenocorticism (Addison's Disease)

Like Cushing's disease, Addison's disease (*hypoadrenocorticism*) is rare in cats. Instead of being caused by too many corticosteroids circulating within the body, this disease is caused by the exact opposite: inadequate amounts of circulating corticosteroids. If this disease occurs in cats, it is usually the result of administration of drugs that suppress the immune system, such as synthetic corticosteroids.

Diagnosis and treatment of hypoadrenocorticism in cats is essentially the same as that for dogs. For more information, see Chap. 18.

Hyperparathyroidism

The parathyroid glands, which are closely associated with the thyroid glands in cats, produce a hormone that is responsible for increasing calcium levels in the blood by drawing stores of this mineral from bone and other regions of the body. *Hyperparathyroidism* is a condition initiated by a deficiency of calcium within the bloodstream. This can result from diet regimens that are high in phosphorus (nutritional hyperparathyroidism), such as organ-meat (liver, kidney, etc.) diets. More commonly in cats, hyperparathyroidism occurs secondary to increased phosphorus levels in the body caused by kidney disease. In response to the increased phosphorus levels, the parathyroid glands secrete large amounts of hormone, drawing calcium out of bone in an attempt to maintain the proper ratio of calcium to phosphorus within the bloodstream. Over time, the bones become weakened and prone to stress injury.

Clinical signs of this metabolic disease in cats include lameness, weakness, bone deformities, and spontaneous fractures. A conclusive diagnosis can be made by evaluating blood calcium levels and relating them to historical or laboratory findings (history of poor diet, laboratory evidence of kidney disease, etc.).

Treatment for nutritional hyperparathyroidism includes dietary modification and calcium supplementation. Unfortunately, there is no effective treatment for hyperparathyroidism caused by kidney disease except for treatment of the kidney disease itself.

Diabetes Mellitus

Diabetes mellitus is an endocrine condition in cats caused by a disruption in the normal metabolism of glucose within the body. Many cases of diabetes mellitus are caused by a blood deficiency in the hormone called *insulin,* which is created by the pancreas. Insulin is responsible for regulating the uptake of blood sugar, or glucose, into cells and tissues of the body for use as energy. Insufficient insulin levels in cats are usually seen with a condition known as *pancreatic amyloidosis,* which destroys the tissue responsible for insulin production. Diabetes mellitus can also occur if the body fails to respond properly to the insulin released (insulin resistance). Obesity is known to be a factor in such resistance. Prolonged drug therapy with corticosteroids and similar compounds has also been implicated in causing feline diabetes mellitus.

With diabetes mellitus, the proper transfer of glucose from the bloodstream to the tissues does not occur; hence, blood glucose levels become elevated. At the same time, the cells, tissues, and organs of the body don't receive the proper nutrition needed to maintain their function, and start to look for other sources of energy in the body—namely, proteins and fats. And this is where the problems begin.

Cats with this disease will exhibit increases in water consumption and urination. As the body calls on these alternate sources of energy, pronounced weight loss results. In addition, as body fat stores are called on and metabolized for energy, an excess of ketone bodies, byproducts of fatty breakdown, can accumulate within the body and blood (ketosis). In large amounts, these ketone bodies have the ability to damage the liver and to depress the nervous system, leading to unusual postures, rear-limb weakness, depression, and coma.

Diabetic cats have a decreased resistance to infection; as a result, they often suffer from chronic skin and bladder infections. Damage to small capillaries within the body can lead to secondary kidney disease, blindness, and gangrene of the skin and extremities.

Many of the clinical signs associated with diabetes mellitus are similar to those of other endocrine diseases; therefore, a thorough laboratory workup is needed to ensure a correct diagnosis. Blood tests on cats with diabetes mellitus will consistently reveal elevated glucose levels, and evaluation of urine samples will reveal the same. Such findings, along with the exclusion of other potential causes of the clinical signs, can lead to a definitive diagnosis of diabetes mellitus.

DID YOU KNOW?

Approximately 50 percent of all diabetic cats are non-insulin-dependent.

Diabetes mellitus can be classified as either uncomplicated or complicated. Uncomplicated cases exhibit mild to moderate signs of the disease, yet none are truly life-threatening. In contrast, cats diagnosed with the disease and exhibiting marked depression, vomiting, diarrhea, heavy breathing, and/or severe weight loss should all be considered complicated cases. These cases should always be considered medical emergencies. In most of these cases, the high levels of ketone acids produced as a result of increased fat metabolism lower the pH of the blood significantly enough to cause the harmful effects represented by the clinical signs. These cats usually become severely dehydrated at the same time.

Treatment for complicated diabetes mellitus consists of immediate hospitalization with intravenous infusion of replacement fluids, medications designed to increase the pH of the blood (if the pH is too low), and insulin. The insulin is given either as a large bolus or as a continuous drip in the replacement fluids. Regardless of how it is administered, the levels of insulin given and corresponding blood glucose must be monitored closely, since too much insulin is even worse than not having enough. If excess insulin is given, the pet could quickly become hypoglycemic and go into convulsions. Good monitoring and careful planning on the part of the veterinarian will help prevent this.

Often cats are presented with complicated cases of diabetes mellitus because of some underlying disorder adding to the problem. For instance, many of these cats suffer from coexisting disorders such as obesity, kidney disease, and cardiomyopathy. In order to increase the chances of recovery from a complicated case of diabetes mellitus, these disorders must be addressed and treated at the same time.

A large number of uncomplicated cases of diabetes mellitus in cats are non-insulin-dependent and do not require specific insulin therapy. In these instances, providing high fiber diets (which help regulate the absorption of glucose from the intestines) and administering oral medications designed to either stimulate insulin release from the pancreas, decrease insulin resistance, and/or slow glucose absorption from the intestines are indicated. However, if ketosis occurs at any time during treatment, insulin therapy will be needed.

At home, it will be the owner's job to ensure that the proper dosages (as prescribed by the veterinarian) of all medications are given each day and that proper adjustments are made (per veterinary instruction) as needed.

If insulin is being administered, keep in mind that it is better to give a diabetic cat too little rather than too much insulin. Adjustments to insulin dosages need to be made slowly and carefully in these uncomplicated cases. Giving too much insulin can cause insulin shock (hypoglycemia), which can be fatal. Signs of shock can include trembling, weakness, incoordination, and—if it is not rapidly corrected—seizures. Owners of diabetic pets should always keep a bottle of pancake syrup or honey around in case of insulin shock. Two tablespoons or more given orally should be used if such a reaction is suspected.

Owners must keep accurate daily records of their cat's urine glucose readings, insulin dosage (if applicable), overall daily attitude and/or clinical signs, and appetite. These will not only come in useful in regulating dosages but also can provide a veterinarian with valuable information should questions or problems later arise. Finally, strict feeding schedules for cats with diabetes mellitus must be followed to help regulate blood glucose levels and to prevent or combat obesity.

Finally, since kidney disease places an incredible burden on the affected pet's immune system, all underlying disease processes and disorders (such as periodontal disease) need to be addressed and treated.

PART

III

BIRDS

Just a few short years ago, when one thought of a household pet, a dog or cat came to mind. Not so anymore. As a substitute for these furry companion animals, birds are increasing in popularity. In fact, the pet bird population in the United States now numbers in the tens of millions and is growing every year.

Birds certainly have their place in history, where they undoubtedly served as an important food source for early humans. As human appreciation for their beauty and unique personalities grew, birds were eventually tamed as pets and, as in the case of raptors, hunters in the households of Egyptian, Grecian, and Roman elite. Ever since Christopher Columbus introduced the first parrot to the European community from one of his many voyages to the New World, their popularity as companions has been on the increase.

What accounts for the popularity of birds as pets in our day and age? For starters, they are fascinating creatures to be around. Most people fail to realize how much personality and affection a pet bird can exhibit toward its owner. And when was the last time you carried on a conversation with your dog, and it talked back to you!

Still another reason sparking the popularity of birds as pets is the increase in the number of people who live in apartments and condominiums. Space and lease restrictions against dogs and cats in many of these locations have left potential pet owners seeking options. And pet birds seem to be the perfect choice!

Many books and articles promote the virtue of birds as being fairly maintenance-free pets. Granted, maintaining a pair of finches might not require much expenditure of energy on your part, but keep in mind that husbandry for the average pet bird requires at least as much effort as that for cats and dogs. For instance, cleanliness is a key factor in bird husbandry, and daily attention to it must be given. Also, many birds, such as cockatoos and hand-raised birds, require a definite daily time commitment to satisfy their need for social interaction. Failure to do so can lead to great emotional stress, upsetting behavioral problems, and even disease.

The bottom line is this: Don't purchase a bird with the idea of a low-maintenance pet in mind. Like a dog or a cat, it will require both time and effort on your part to ensure that your relationship with your bird is a happy and healthy one.

Choosing the Right Bird for You

When purchasing or selecting a bird, there are a number of factors to consider. The first obviously is what variety of bird you want. You have many to choose from. Be sure to visit the library, local bookstore, or the Internet to thoroughly research the variety of bird you are most drawn to prior to becoming an actual owner.

Factors to Consider

The more popular pet birds come from two categories, or orders, of avians: Psittaciformes (psittacines) and Passeriformes (passerines). Psittacines include budgerigars, cockatiels, cockatoos, lovebirds, lories, lorikeets, conures, the large parrots, and macaws. The *passerine* group includes finches, canaries, and the softbilled mynahs. Another popular pet, the toucan, belongs to the order Piciformes.

> ### DID YOU KNOW?
>
> One way to differentiate psittacines from passerines is to observe their feet when they are at perch. Psittacines will perch with two toes pointing forward and two pointing backward. Passerines, on the other hand, perch with three toes pointing forward and one pointing back.

Varieties

BUDGERIGARS

Budgerigars, or "budgies," are by far the most fancied bird in America, accounting for almost 45 percent of all pet birds purchased (Fig. 37.1). They are referred to by most people as *parakeets,* yet in reality, the word *parakeet* pertains to any long-tailed parrot, including budgies, lorikeets, rosellas, and those birds belonging to the genus *Brotogeris.*

Budgerigars are hardy birds that, for the most part, have gentle dispositions. Their popularity also rests on the fact that they are inexpensive to purchase, require little space, and maintain a relatively low noise level.

Budgerigars have the capability to live 15 to 18 years in captivity. Unfortunately, because of poor husbandry practices on the part of many budgie owners, few of these birds live past 6 years of age. As far as talking is concerned, male budgerigars have the ability to learn a broad vocabulary, and can actually vocalize entire phrases and sentences at a time. Females, on the other hand, won't talk as much as will the opposite sex!

FIGURE 37.1 Budgerigars are by far the most popular of all pet birds.

COCKATIELS

The second most popular companion bird is the cockatiel. In fact, many experts feel that as a first bird for beginners, cockatiels rank among the best. Known for their affection toward their owners and their insatiable curiosity, these birds are relatively easy to maintain and can live as long as 20 years. Compared to budgies, their vocabulary is somewhat limited, yet they (especially males) can be taught to talk. In addition, the female cockatiel tends to have a more laid-back personality than do her male counterparts.

FINCHES AND CANARIES

Finches are small, lively birds. They make excellent pets, and just watching their busy activity can provide hours of enjoyment. The two most popular finch varieties for beginners include "zebra" finches and "society" finches. Because of their gregarious nature, finches should be kept in pairs.

FACT *OR* *FICTION*

Green budgerigars and gray cockatiels tend to live longer and healthier lives than do their different colored counterparts within the same species.

FACT. Green and gray are the normal colors found in wild budgies and wild cockatiels, respectively, whereas other colors are the result of mutations. Because other genetic mutations often accompany these color mutations, the longevity of these "off-colored" birds tends to be reduced.

Canaries, on the other hand, may be kept as singles and are easier to tame than finches. Another desired feature of canaries is that males have the ability to produce beautiful music and song, much to the delight of their owners. Finches can live anywhere from 6 to 10 years, and canaries even longer.

LOVEBIRDS

Lovebirds make up only a small portion of the pet bird population. These dwarf parrots originate from Africa and are tough to tame, requiring regular interaction with people to maintain any established trust between bird and owner. The peachface lovebird seems to be the most popular among the species available. Energetic and active, lovebirds have a captive life span of 5 to 10 years.

LORIES AND LORIKEETS

Having roots in Australia and the South Pacific, lories and lorikeets are known for their striking colors and playfulness. Although they are visually appealing to novice bird owners, lories and lorikeets can be considered high maintenance and are not good selections for beginners. Since they eat nectars, fruits, and vegetables, their droppings tend to be quite liquid and messy. This necessitates frequent cleanings of the cage and the contents therein. Food must be kept fresh at all times. Lories and lorikeets love to take baths, so frequent opportunities to do so should be offered. Cared for properly, these affectionate birds can live 8 to 15 years in captivity.

CONURES

Conures are a smaller variety of parrot that can make excellent starter pets for the novice. Most have outgoing pleasant personalities and can be quite affectionate. The half-moon conure from Mexico is among the most popular. Be forewarned, however, that these birds like to screech and can be quite loud at times, much to the dismay of neighbors. The average life span of a captive conure ranges from 15 to 30 years.

LARGE PARROTS

The African Grey parrot is the most popular of the larger psittacines. Fancied in ancient Rome for their outgoing personalities and impressive talking abilities, African Greys have proved to be faithful companions of humans throughout history. When raised domestically and hand-fed when young, these birds enjoy and actively seek out the attention and affection of their owners.

One unique feature of African Greys is the vocal growl they won't hesitate to exhibit when surprised or stressed. The average life span of the African Grey in the wild is 50+ years, or 18 years in captivity. Their cost is usually not quite as high as the Amazon parrot, yet many factors, including whether the bird was hand-fed and tamed when young, can influence purchase prices.

Like their African cousins, Amazon parrots are popular choices among bird fanciers, primarily because of their ready availability and to their social attraction to humans. They tend to be more expensive than the smaller psittacines and even the African Grey, with hand-reared birds bringing the highest prices. Amazon parrots can live 80+ years in the wild, yet rarely live past 20 years in captivity.

Within the Amazon parrot family, there are varieties from which to choose, including the popular double yellowhead, yellow nape, and blue-fronted Amazons. The yellowhead Amazon is a popular talker, yet is also known for its somewhat temperamental disposition. The blue-fronted Amazon parrot exhibits talking abilities that rival that of their yellowhead counterparts. Lilac-crowned Amazon parrots are a common species smuggled into the United States from Mexico. Potential purchasers of yellowhead Amazons, especially from a "shady" source, should be on the lookout, since the heads of the inexpensive lilac-crowned parrots are sometimes dyed yellow to fool potential buyers into thinking they are buying a more expensive bird.

Because of the long lifespan of Amazon parrots, purchasers of these birds are truly accepting a lifelong responsibility. However, most owners will agree that the companionship and joy that these entertaining talkers offer is well worth the commitment.

Because of the danger of the disease psittacosis (see Chap. 41) in birds that are illegally smuggled into the United States, potential buyers of Amazon parrots should buy their pets only from reputable sources.

COCKATOOS

Cockatoos are magnificent birds and are among the most intelligent and emotional members of the entire parrot family. Consequently, they demand more social attention from their owners than do other psittacines.

Cockatoos that feel neglected can become quite destructive and noisy, and can begin to pick at their feathers as a result of emotional stress. However, as current cockatoo owners would agree, the high intelligence level and outgoing personalities of cockatoos rank them among the most entertaining and devoted of all psittacine pets. The average life span of these beautiful birds in the wild is 50 to 80 years, yet only 15 to 20 years in captivity.

MACAWS

Macaws are the largest of the psittacines and among the most beautiful. Highly intelligent birds, they, too, enjoy interaction with people. Common types include blue and gold macaws, scarlet macaws, green-wing macaws, and military macaws. A fifth type, the hyacinth macaw, is the largest of all parrots (Fig. 37.2).

Because of their size, macaws do have large space requirements. This factor, along with their high cost and high maintenance requirements, make them inappropriate choices for first-time bird owners. The incredible power of this bird's beak can quickly wreak havoc on

FIGURE 37.2 Baby macaws.

DID YOU KNOW?

A large psittacine can inflict serious physical trauma on any dog or cat.

household furnishings if allowed free access to them. Cages must be sturdy! Inexperienced handlers may also learn the hard way that macaws must be approached and handled with gentleness and care. The loud shrill of these magnificent psittacines and its potential effects on one's neighbors is another factor that must be taken into account by prospective buyers of these birds. Macaws can live 50+ years in the wild, yet rarely live past 15 years in captivity.

MYNAHS AND TOUCANS

Mynahs and toucans belong to a special group of birds known as "softbills" that eat only fruits and other soft foods. Mynahs are probably the most prolific and expert talkers of all birds. Toucans, on the other hand, won't say a word. Both require fruit in their diets, which can make daily cleanup much more arduous than with parrots.

Aside from cleanup, softbills require less social attention than do most conventional psittacines, which can make them excellent choices for those owners who just enjoy having a bird in the house.

Purchase Price

Cost of ownership undoubtedly comes into play when deciding which variety of bird to buy. Purchase prices can range from less than $20 for finches and budgies to over $10,000 for some hand-raised, domestic macaws. One can expect to pay more in food, housing, and veterinary care for the larger parrots and macaws, and for a much longer period of time. Also, birds that are domestically hand-raised and hand-fed by breeders when young command higher prices than do wilder imports, simply because they generally make tamer, more desirable pets. As a result, beginners should plan on paying a little extra for such a bird.

Beware of "special deals" and abnormally low prices advertised for some psittacines. These birds could have undesirable personalities or health problems, which may account for their low price. For example, psittacines that are smuggled into the United States can often be purchased at exceptionally low prices, yet these birds are often quite wild and can be carriers of *psittacosis,* a disease that can threaten human health as well as that of the bird. As a result, always be knowledgeable of the current price trends for the variety of bird you want, and always purchase your bird from a reputable breeder or pet store.

Time

Before you purchase a bird, you should consider how much time you are willing to invest in its care. Realize that acquiring a larger parrot or macaw may constitute a lifetime commitment on your part. If you have doubts about taking on such a responsibility, stick to the smaller varieties of birds with shorter life spans, such as budgerigars or cockatiels. Even with these birds, however, realize that you are still making a 10- to 15-year commitment!

The time you need to devote daily to a pet bird will increase with the size of the bird, with the exception of the cockatoo, which seems to require the most attention of all psittacines. Failure to devote daily attention and time to these birds can lead to many serious behavioral and health problems in the future (Fig. 37.3).

Also remember that owning a pet bird may restrict or interfere with your ability to travel or vacation. Transport-

FIGURE 37.3 Many birds require lots of attention from their owners and could exhibit serious behavioral disorders if neglected.

ing your bird between temporary travel destinations is not recommended because of the high level of stress it would ultimately generate, putting your pet's health at risk. The best solution is to hire a pet sitter to care for your bird while you are gone.

Housing

Housing and space requirements should also be figured into your purchase decision. Birdcages need to be roomy enough to provide for safe, adequate movement and exercise within. In addition, realize that most pet birds will require time outside their cages, which can inevitably lead to abuses within your house or apartment. This is especially true with the larger parrots and macaws. Finally, conures, large parrots, and macaws can be quite noisy, which could pose a problem with your neighbors and/or landlord. You must also take this noise factor into account if you run an office from your home.

Age

Consider the age of the bird you are going to buy. As a rule, younger birds are more desirable than older ones simply because they are easier to tame and train, and are less likely to have difficult personality quirks. They are also more likely to develop into good talkers. If possible, purchase budgerigars and cockatiels before they are 3 months of age and larger psittacines before they are 1 year of age.

Eye color can be used as an age estimator for African Grey parrots, cockatoos, and macaws. Young birds tend to have darker eyes that turn grayish around 1 year of age, and then turn white to yellow around 3 to 4 years of age. The iris color of Amazon parrots turns from brown in young birds to a red-orange color as the bird matures.

Sex

The sex of a bird often determines its personality For example, male psittacines tend to be better talkers than do females of the same species, yet the latter are often less aggressive and more content in captivity.

Male budgies can be differentiated from females by the color of their ceres (or nostrils) and legs. The male budgie has a dark blue to lavender cere and a blue hue to his legs; the female will have a tan, pink, or light blue cere and pink legs. Male cockatiels can be identified by yellow and orange markings on the head, in contrast to the grayish coloration of the female. Most cockatoos can be sexed according to their eye color; males have black-colored eyes and females have a red-brown tint to theirs. Male zebra finches can be identified apart from the female by the red-orange patches on their cheeks and sides. On the contrary, male and female society finches and canaries are indistinguishable in terms of color. Male canaries, however, can be identified according to their ability to sing.

For conures, macaws, and the larger parrots, methods other than coloration and behavior must be used to determine sex. One of the most common methods used today is fiber-optic endoscopy to surgically sex these birds. If you wish to breed your bird at some point in the future, have this procedure performed prior to purchase, as part of the prepurchase screening, just so you can be sure of the sex and reproductive health status of your new feathered friend.

Taming and Training Your Pet Bird

Because of their highly intelligent nature, training a pet bird is not as difficult a task as it might seem. The first hurdle you must overcome, however, is the taming process. If you purchased a bird that was hand-reared, this taming no doubt has already been done for you. Your only job is to make friends with your new companion (Fig. 37.4).

Depending on the previous socialization your bird has received, it might take some time for it to become comfortable with you, so be patient. Perform this routine over and over each day. Keep each session short and positive. Remember: This relationship is based on mutual trust (Fig. 37.5).

When trying to win your way into your new friend's heart, go by way of the stomach! Use food, especially seed or pound cake, to entice your bird out of its cage and onto your hand or arm (Fig. 37.6). If you haven't already done so, get your bird's feathers clipped to prevent it from flying away while you are trying to tame it.

Once tamed, birds can be taught to do a variety of tricks using food as a reward. Be careful not to be overzealous when doling out these rewards. You don't want your pet to get fat during the training process!

FIGURE 37.4 When properly socialized, pet birds can be fun for the entire family!

Talking

Most psittacines have the uncanny ability to mimic what they hear, a skill that is instinctive. Some species are more talkative than others. Pet birds listed from most talkative to least talkative include African Grey parrots, Amazon parrots, budgerigars, cockatoos, cockatiels, conures, lovebirds, and macaws. In addition, males birds tend to exhibit a greater ability to mimic than do females.

If you want to teach your bird certain words, names, or phrases, *repetition* is the key. Although young birds are the easiest to teach, all birds can learn to speak. Practice with your bird daily, rewarding it with food for a desired response. When you are not there, a tape recording of the word or phrase repeated over and over again is an effective training tool you can leave with your bird. Just be sure you don't leave it on during the night, disturbing your bird's rest. With enough repetition and practice, you will soon find your bird talking like a pro!

Proper Nutrition

There is no doubt that, aside from good sanitation, nutrition leads the list as the most important factor in keeping pet birds healthy. Birds should be allowed access to a high-quality diet twice a day, early morning and late evening, to better satisfy the instinctive food gathering rituals that they exhibit in the wild.

FIGURE 37.5 As part of its training program, don't allow your bird to bite you, even in play.

The most common misconception held among novice owners regarding avian nutrition is that perching birds can be sustained on a diet of seeds alone. Granted, seeds add to the nutritional requirements of birds, yet an all-seed diet or even one where seeds are simply offered as treats is inadequate for captive birds and will eventually lead to serious health problems.

FIGURE 37.6 Food is one of the most effective training aids for birds.

Seeds are high in fat and carbohydrates, yet relatively low in protein and certain essential amino acids. Many obese birds became that way because of too much seed, and consequently, too much fat, in their diets. Seeds alone are also deficient in certain vitamins, including vitamins A, D_3, and B_{12}. The hulls of seeds, which are rich in B vitamins, are often removed prior to consumption, thereby further reducing the seed's nutritional value.

As far as essential minerals are concerned, seeds are deficient in iodine, calcium, and other trace minerals, yet high in phosphorus. For birds fed seed-only diets, this high level of phosphorus can lead to musculoskeletal disease. Old, moldy seed can also cause aspergillosis.

The Best Dietary Choices

A number of high-quality formulated feed mixtures suitable for your particular variety of bird are now available commercially, and are the diets of choice for pet birds. Ask your veterinarian to recommend the mixture best suited for your bird. Because of the wide variety of high-quality bird rations available on the market today, formulating your own mixtures at home is no longer recommended. Limited amounts of green vegetables (such as bell peppers, collards and mustard greens, broccoli, and alfalfa sprouts), yellow vegetables (such as squash and carrots), and fruit (including apples, grapes, and bananas) can still be offered as treats to birds being fed a high-quality formulation. As a rule, these should not exceed 15 percent of your bird's total daily food intake. All foods offered to your bird should be as fresh as possible (Fig. 37.7).

(*Note:* Softbills, lories, and lorikeets require special fruit and nectar diets. Be sure to discuss these dietary needs with your veterinarian.)

FIGURE 37.7 Fruits and vegetables are important parts of your psittacine's diet.

Supplements

All birds should also be fed a vitamin supplement containing vitamin D_3, and a mineral supplement that provides extra calcium to the diet. Cuttlebone, mineral blocks, or crushed oyster shells can be used as sources for calcium. As for vitamin supplements, these are readily available from pet stores and can be added directly to food or water. If added to the water, remember to change the water daily to prevent bacterial growth.

The Finicky Eater

What happens if your bird appears to be hooked on seeds and refuses to eat its high-quality ration? The first thing to remember is that birds can become malnourished because of food refusal following abrupt changes in diet. For example, finches, which consume about one-third of their body weight per day in food, can die within 48 hours if they choose to go on a hunger strike! Since taste and smell are poorly developed in birds, sight recognition plays an important role in food desirability. Your bird might not like what it sees.

> ## DR. P's VET TIP
>
> A useful tool for coaxing a finicky bird to eat food other than seeds is pound cake. Most birds will readily accept this tasty treat, which, when used to camouflage or cover up new types of foods, can be used to entice the bird into eating them. Over the next few days, gradually reduce the amount of pound cake offered. Pound cake is also useful as a vehicle for giving oral medications to birds!

Any radical changes to your bird's diet should take place gradually over a 7- to 10-day period. If your bird is addicted to seeds, try to wean it off of them by offering a formulated diet with no seeds in the mornings, and then offering a small amount of seed in the evenings. Leave this seed in the cage for only a few hours, then remove it. Keep repeating this exercise, gradually reducing the amount of seeds and increasing the formulated diet that you are offering.

Other Nutritional Requirements

Grit is often offered to pet birds as an aid to digestion. Commercial grit usually consists of crushed shells and/or limestone. This substance does its work in the bird's gizzard, helping to crush and grind food, making it acceptable for digestion. Not much is actually needed for this purpose—only a few pieces over a week's time. In fact, allowing access to too much grit at one time can actually cause serious health problems, especially in birds that are already ill.

The need for grit in captive birds is still controversial among veterinarians, with many feeling that it is not necessary for those birds fed a well-formulated diet. Ask your veterinarian to decide whether grit is necessary for your particular bird.

Twigs from apple, maple, oak, elm, or cherry trees should also be offered to pet birds. Chewing on these will not only help keep their beaks in fine shape but also contribute essential trace minerals to the diet.

Finally, fresh water should be offered at all times. Smaller birds consume anywhere from a teaspoon to tablespoon of water per day; larger birds, up to 1 ounce (30 milliliters) per day. Filtered or purified water is ideal, and considering the small amount of water the average bird drinks in one day, offering such water is worth the extra cost.

Housing Your Pet Bird

Cages

The cage you select for your bird should be large enough to enable your bird to fully extend its wings and flap them without the tips touching the sides (Fig. 37.8). In addition, your bird must be able to perch without its tail feathers touching the floor or sides of the cage. The larger the cage the better, for a large cage will allow your bird more opportunity for exercise. Many experts recommend birdcages with flat tops versus those with domed tops, since the latter have been implicated in toe and beak injuries from those regions on top where the metal bars converge. If you plan on using an antique or custom-made cage, be certain there is no chance of exposure to lead-based paint and/or solder that might have been used in its construction.

Regardless of the type of cage you choose, the metal bars of the cage should not be spaced sufficiently wide apart to allow your pet to escape or, worse yet, cause injury if it attempts to squeeze through them. For smaller birds, this usually means spacing no greater than 7/16 inch and for larger parrots, no greater than 1 inch.

For safety, the door leading into the cage should open in an outward direction away from the cage, instead of opening inward or sliding up and down. Also, if the door has a spring action, remove the spring and allow the door to swing freely.

Finally, make sure that the cage you choose is constructed in such a way that it is easy to access and clean. Having to clean an entire cage through the small entry door can be difficult and tedious, and could lead to dereliction of duty!

FIGURE 37.8 Your bird's cage should be large enough to allow it to fully extend its wings without touching the sides.

CAGE LINING

Paper towels or commercial cage pads can be used to cover the bottom of the cage. Newspaper should not be used, since news ink, if ingested, can be harmful to birds. This lining should be cleaned daily to maintain good sanitation. However, always take note of the number and characteristics of the droppings on the liner before throwing it away. As will be pointed out later, these droppings can be useful indicators of your bird's health status (see Chap. 39).

PERCHES

Every pet bird needs a perch to sit on, and choosing the right type will help prevent foot problems from developing later on. Ideally, more than one perch should be provided, each of a different diameter and hardness to provide variety for the bird's feet (Fig. 37.9).

The best perches you can offer are simple tree branches of varying widths from northern hardwood, citrus, or eucalyptus trees. Be sure to

FIGURE 37.9 Be sure to provide your bird with multiple perches of differing diameters.

wash, disinfect, and dry these before placing them in the cage for the first time. Perches shaped like tree branches and made of nontoxic plastic are also available commercially. If you plan to use a painted perch, make certain that a lead-free paint was used. Avoid perches designed with a sandpaper covering (supposedly designed to keep the nails in shape) or those covered with ridges. These are hard on the feet, and can lead to foot problems, including bumblefoot (see Chap. 41).

For sanitary purposes, be sure to position the perches within the cage away from food and water dishes. Like anything else, perches will need to be periodically cleaned and sanitized when they get dirty. Be sure to keep a few spares on hand to minimize the time you must spend on cage cleaning.

CAGE COVERS

Pet birds need at least 12 hours of darkness per day during which to rest and sleep. As a result, a cage cover will be needed to help ensure that your bird gets the beauty sleep it needs. For greatest effectiveness, the cover itself should be made out of a dark fabric. One word of caution: Be sure your bird is at perch before putting on the cage cover. If it is not, it could have difficulty finding the perch in the dark—many a bird has suffered injuries trying to do so.

Toys and Accessories

Toys and accessories for your bird can include small branches, pinecones, rawhide chews, corncobs, and other nontoxic items. Glass mirrors are not recommended for any bird, especially large ones, since the reflection can frighten or anger the bird and lead to a self-sustained injury. In addition, watch out for lead weights contained in some toys. These can be an innocent source of lead poisoning in birds. Finally, food and water dishes should be durably constructed to withstand abuse!

Sanitation

Impeccable sanitation is another key to effective bird husbandry. Cages should be thoroughly cleaned from top to bottom and perches cleaned and rotated at least once a week. Food dishes and water dishes should be cleaned and disinfected on a daily basis. Toys should also be either cleaned or rotated on a daily basis.

Use nontoxic soap and water for cleaning, and afterward, apply a disinfectant. Quaternary ammonium disinfectants, available from most cleaning-supply stores, work well for this purpose. You can use household bleach, diluted $1/4$ cup per gallon of water, as an alternative. Just be sure to rinse all items and surfaces thoroughly with tap water to remove all disinfectant residues.

Avian Anatomy and Physiology

In order to understand the behavior that our pet birds exhibit, and the diseases and disorders that they may encounter, we need to touch on a brief overview of avian anatomy and physiology.

Birds possess some unique features, both externally and internally, that set them apart from the rest of the animal kingdom. For the most part, these variations are geared toward making the bird's primary mode of transportation, flight, easier and more efficient (Fig. 38.1).

The Digestive System

Birds have a short, efficient digestive system. The beak is actually a lightweight substitute for the mammalian cheek, teeth, and lips. It can be used as an effective weapon; the strength contained in the jaws of the larger parrots and macaws is enormous and can lead to serious injuries if the inexperienced handler is not careful.

The tongue of birds, as in mammals, helps manipulate food to the back of the throat, where it can enter the esophagus. As food passes down the esophagus, it enters the *crop*. The crop represents an out-pouching of esophagus at the point just before it enters the chest cavity. It serves as a temporary storage place for food. Canaries have no crop.

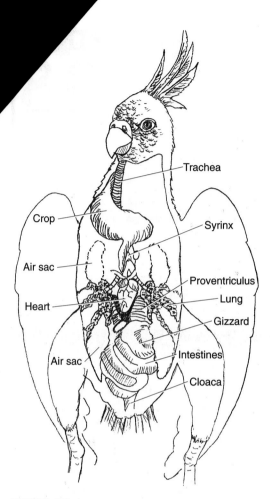

FIGURE 38.1 **The internal organs.**

Labels on figure: Trachea, Crop, Syrinx, Air sac, Proventriculus, Heart, Lung, Gizzard, Air sac, Intestines, Cloaca

From the crop, food then passes into the *proventriculus,* or *glandular stomach,* and then into the *ventriculus,* or "gizzard." Within the gizzard of the bird, strong muscular contractions, combined with ingested grit, serve to grind up food. Digesta leaves the ventriculus and enters the small intestine, where most of the nutrient absorption takes place. Afterward, it passes into the large intestine. The terminal portion of the large intestine is termed the *cloaca.* It is here that fecal matter is mixed with urates and urine from the urinary system, all of which then pass out through the external opening of the cloaca, called the *vent.*

As far as accessory digestive organs are concerned, the liver, pancreas, and gallbladder (when present) serve similar functions in birds as they do in mammals.

The Respiratory System

The unique respiratory system of the bird begins with the nares, which are two small slits located in the upper portion of the beak. These mark the external entrances into the nasal cavity The trachea extends from the back portion of the mouth down toward the chest cavity and splits off into two branches as it nears its destination. At this bifurcation is located the *syrinx*. This organ corresponds to our vocal cords and is responsible for a bird's singing and talking abilities.

From the syrinx, tube-like bronchi enter into the lungs. Birds have no func-

tional diaphragm that separates the chest and abdominal cavities; as a result, they rely on the active movement of the ribcage for expansion and contraction of the lungs. This is one reason why gentle restraint is a must when handling pet birds.

Finally, attached to and surrounding the lungs are unique structures called air sacs. Serving as large storage areas for air during respiratory activity, air sacs contribute to the aerodynamics of flight. Interestingly, some of these sacs actually communicate with the cavities inside certain bones, filling them with air. This is why a fractured bone can lead to inflammation of the air sacs, called *airsacculitis.*

The Urogenital System

The kidneys and ureters of birds function in essentially the same way as those of mammals. Birds have no urinary bladder, which would only serve to weigh them down in flight. Instead, the ureters empty their contents directly into the cloaca, which, as mentioned previously, communicates to the outside through the vent.

The reproductive system of the male bird, or cock, consists of testicles and associated structures, *ductus deferens,* and a copulatory apparatus. Female birds, or hens, have two ovaries, yet the left ovary is usually the only one active. When the egg, or yolk, is ovulated from the ovary, it enters the oviduct. In most birds, the left oviduct is the only one that is functional. Within the oviduct, the *albumen,* or "whites" of the final egg are added to the yolk. From the oviduct, the unfinished egg enters into the uterus. It is within the uterus that the hard shell is added. From here, the egg is transferred through the vagina to the cloaca, and from there is laid through the vent. Females lay eggs in groups known as *clutches,* the size of which depends on the species involved.

The Endocrine, Circulatory, and Nervous Systems

These three organ systems are very similar to those in dogs and cats. Heart rates in birds can range anywhere from 175 beats per minute for large macaws to over 1000 beats per minute for small finches and canaries. Birds do have lymphatic channels within their bodies that serve an immune capacity, yet they lack actual lymph nodes.

The Musculoskeletal System

As you might suspect, the muscles and bones of birds are geared toward efficient flight. The skeleton of the typical bird is very lightweight, making flying easier. As mentioned earlier, some of the bones are actually air-filled, communicating directly with air sacs.

DID YOU KNOW?

When at perch, a bird crouches and bends its legs. This action causes the flexor tendons in the legs to draw in and lock the toes around the perch so tightly that the bird can actually go to sleep without falling from the perch!

The muscles making up the breast of the bird, which are responsible for wing motion, are not surprisingly the largest and strongest in the body. Wasting of these muscles secondary to disease will cause the large *keel bone* or breast bone to protrude and become easily palpable.

The Integumentary System

In contrast to most mammals, the skin of birds is very thin and has minimal blood and nerve supply. In addition, this skin contains no glands per se, except for a special one located near the base of the tail called the *uropygial gland.* The oils produced by this gland are used by the bird during self-grooming, or *preening,* to lubricate and smooth the feathers (Fig. 38.2). Contrary to popular belief, these oils do not waterproof the bird.

The legs and feet of birds are covered in scales. The beak, which corresponds to teeth, cheeks, and lips seen in dogs and cats, is made up of a tough, horny material. The *cere is* a soft tissue structure located at the top portion of the beak. Often used to sex smaller psittacines, overgrowth of this structure could signify nutritional imbalances or parasitic infestations.

The feathers of birds are not only necessary for flight but also play an important role in the regulation of body temperature and in courtship displays. In addition, the overall structure and overlap of feathers helps waterproof the bird and protect it from the elements.

Two Types of Feathers

Contour feathers make up the majority of feathers seen on the head, wings, body, and tail of a bird. The flight feathers are contour feathers, and can be further

FIGURE 38.2 Preening is a natural way for birds to keep their feathers in top shape.

broken down into the *remiges,* which include the primary and secondary flight feathers of the wings, and the *rectrices,* or those flight feathers making up the tail. *Semiplumes* are smaller contour feathers that blend in with the second main type of feathers, the *down feathers,* the small, soft feathers found beneath the contour feathers. These serve as effective insulators against environmental temperature fluctuations. In addition, some species, such as cockatiels and cockatoos, have special down feathers called *powder down feathers.* These give off a fine powder that the bird uses in preening.

DID YOU KNOW?

During winter months, finches sport well over 3000 contour feathers!

Molting

Birds go through a molting period one or more times a year in which feathers are lost and then replaced (similar to shedding in dogs and cats). Molting usually occurs seasonally, depending on species. Signs of an impending molt include an increase in preening activity, not to mention the increased number of feathers that will be seen lying at the bottom of the cage. Molting birds may become noticeably lethargic, as the process uses up lots of calories! Some birds will lose most of their feathers all at once; others will lose them more gradually. The entire process usually takes 4 to 6 weeks to complete.

The new feathers that grow in after a molt are encased within feather sheaths, which are eventually shed once eruption is complete. These new feathers also have a rich blood supply that will disappear when the feather reaches its mature length. If a growing feather is accidentally injured and begins to bleed, the entire feather should be plucked from its shaft. This will stop the bleeding, and allow for a new feather to replace the damaged one. On the other hand, mature feathers that are plucked will not be replaced until the next molt.

As indicated above, the molting period for birds is very stressful. Otherwise talkative birds might choose to remain silent during this time, and songbirds might stop singing. It is important that you take appropriate husbandry actions to ensure that other sources of potential stress are avoided. Be sure to provide extra privacy and warmth during this time. Also, increasing the protein, fat and calcium in diets offered to birds in molt will help ensure that the molt is a successful one and that the new feathers are bright, shiny, and healthy.

Abnormal molting can result in new feathers that are ragged or incomplete, or ones that contain abnormal markings or streaks caused by improper feather development (stress bars). If you suspect that your bird has had an abnormal molt, contact your veterinarian right away.

Vision and Hearing

Eyes

The bird's sense of vision is generally sharper and more acute than that of their furry household counterparts. This is to be expected, considering the maneuverability required for flight and the keen visual perception necessary for safe takeoffs and landings. For example, the eyesight of birds of prey is so acute that they can pick up even the slightest movements on the ground from hundreds of feet up in the air! Researchers also believe that certain species of birds even have the ability to perceive and differentiate colors in their environment.

Anatomically, the eyes and ocular components of birds and those of cats and dogs are essentially the same. There are, however, some unique features of the avian eye worth mentioning.

For starters, the muscles that control eye movement in birds are somewhat small and underdeveloped. As a result, birds must cock, tilt, and turn their heads when trying to focus in on a subject. The iris of the bird eye is also unique in that the bird can, at any time, voluntarily control the size of its pupil. This could account for the exceptional visual acuity displayed by birds, especially birds of prey while in flight. Finally, unlike the eyes of other companion animals, birds have small bones situated within the sclera of the eyes, giving the bird's eye its characteristic shape.

Ears

The structure of the avian ear is also similar to that of dogs and cats, except that it lacks a pinna and has a much shorter ear canal. Located just behind and below the eyes, the ears are rarely a source of health problems in birds. However, because of the ear's importance in maintaining balance and equilibrium, infections or injuries can seriously impair a bird's ability to fly and should be suspected if flight difficulties arise.

Preventive Health Care

As with dogs and cats, the best treatment for any avian disease or injury is prevention (Fig. 39-1). With birds, this takes on a special importance when you consider that they have the ability to hide signs of disease quite effectively, and when evidence of illness does appear, subsequent treatment efforts are often futile. As a result, bird owners can and should play an active role in preventing disease in their pets. Listed below are 11 effective ways to do so:

1. Avoid overcrowding. Housing too many birds in a cage that is too small will not only lead to sanitation problems but also increase the chances of physical trauma and injury.

2. Clean food and water bowls on a daily basis.

3. Keep fresh food and water in the bowls at all times. This might mean replacing the food and water more than once a day. Use filtered or purified water if possible.

4. Provide adequate ventilation in and around your bird's living quarters. Environmental temperatures should be kept between 60 and 85 degrees Fahrenheit, and cages should be placed clear of any drafts in the room. If there are smokers in the household, be sure that such smoke is kept away from your bird.

FIGURE 39.1 All birds should receive regular veterinary checkups as part of a complete preventive health care program.

5. Be sure your bird is getting adequate amounts of sleep. Keep bedtimes constant and predictable.

6. Feed a well-balanced diet. What more can be said!

7. Don't let your bird mingle with its wild peers. Wild birds can transmit infectious diseases such as avian pox and internal parasites.

8. Quarantine new birds brought into the household for 6 to 8 weeks before introducing them to an existing bird in the house. A new-bird checkup by your veterinarian is also warranted to help detect any diseases or parasitism already present.

9. Minimize other sources of stress as much as possible. Avoid moving your bird's cage to a different location unless absolutely necessary. Keep the cage free from drafts, as these can quickly lead to stress and respiratory problems in exposed birds. Remember that dogs and cats in the household can place a great deal of stress on some birds, so it makes sense to keep them separated. Also, other sources of stress such as loud noises and blaring music should be kept to a minimum.

10. Vaccines do exist against some of the more common diseases seen in pet birds. For instance, vaccines against avian pox, polyomavirus, and Pacheco's disease are available, and might be effective in preventing the spread of disease within

FACT *OR* *FICTION*

You shouldn't kiss your bird. **F**ACT. Pet birds can develop serious bacterial infections from contact with human saliva.

aviaries, or in those instances in which access to wild birds cannot be controlled. Ask your veterinarian for details.

11. Unnecessary and close physical contact between humans and birds could expose the bird to various infections; avoid such contact if possible.

Preventing Injury or Accidental Poisoning

Aside from the aforementioned tips for preventing disease in pet birds, there are also steps bird owners can take to minimize the chances of injury or accidental poisoning involving their feathered pet within the home.

> **DID YOU KNOW?**
>
> One common source of poisoning in birds during the holiday season is ornamental dough, used to make Christmas tree decorations. This dough contains high levels of salt, which, if consumed by an unsuspecting bird, can cause rapid dehydration, diarrhea, and neurologic signs.

Flying Hazards

To prevent your bird from embarking on an unexpected trip outdoors, get into the habit of keeping all doors and windows closed. In addition, place conspicuous stickers on clear glass doors, windows with the curtains or shades drawn, and mirrors to help prevent midair collisions.

Feather-clipping should also be performed periodically, especially after molting, to help limit your bird's ability to fly freely within the house.

Other Household Hazards

Other hazards that the average house can pose for pet birds include exposed lightbulbs, ceiling fans, and hot stove burners or ovens. Poisonous substances that your pet bird could encounter inside your home include toxic plants, alcohol, pesticides, crayons, pencils, mothballs, chocolate, cedar, redwood, and tobacco. Toilet bowl cleaners that are hung within the tank can pose a special hazard to the innocent bird that sees the open toilet lid and decides it is time to take a bath.

Noxious fumes emitted from paint, cleaners, cigarettes, and even from the nonstick coating of certain types of cookware (when heated) can quickly overcome a bird if adequate ventilation is not available. Jewelry and other small metal items may be eaten by a curious bird, with unfortunate consequences. You must also guard against and eliminate potential sources of lead poisoning, such as lead-based paint, caulking, ceramic glazing, linoleum, and curtain weights. Even excess lead in the water supply (caused by lead-lined pipes) can lead to lead toxicity in a pet bird if levels are high enough.

DID YOU KNOW?

Many perfumes and colognes can be toxic to birds.

The clinical signs of lead poisoning can vary, depending on the amount consumed. General signs include lethargy, vomiting, diarrhea, and increased urination. Also, neurologic signs, such as seizures, apparent blindness, tremors, excitability, and lack of coordination, are usually a tipoff to lead poisoning in birds.

Diagnosis of lead toxicity can be made using radiographic X rays, and actually seeing the lead particles within the gastrointestinal tract. Prompt therapy using the antidote EDTA (ethylenediaminetetraacetic acid) can help relieve the clinical signs in these birds. Surgical removal of the remaining lead particles may also be necessary.

Restraint

When it comes to physical restraint of a bird, the ultimate goal is to cause the least amount of stress to your bird as possible. As a result, knowing how to safely restrain your bird is a must!

There are three important principles regarding bird restraint that owners must be aware of:

1. Birds have no muscular diaphragm to help them breathe, so they rely on active movements of the ribcage to draw and expel air to and from the lungs. Grasping a bird too tightly can severely restrict its breathing ability, and could lead to death through suffocation.

2. Birds, especially overweight budgerigars, can experience a phenomenon known as *cardiac racing* if they are extremely stressed

or frightened. The heart rate in these birds can increase to such a high level that the heart itself can't pump blood properly, and death can result. As a result, certain measures should be taken to ease excitement as much as possible.

3. Birds that are exhibiting signs of illness are poor candidates for any kind of restraint, except when needed for treatment. These birds are already so stressed out that even the slightest anxiety attack could lead to death.

Proper Procedure for Restraint

Before reaching into a cage or carrier to capture a bird, be sure that all toys, perches, and bowls have been removed. Also, make certain all doors and windows in the room are closed. For smaller birds, dimming the room lights can help immensely in their capture, since most are reluctant to fly in the dark.

Camouflage your hand when capturing a bird to prevent it from becoming hand-shy in the future. A towel, or for larger birds, a pair of welders gloves works just fine. Reach into the cage slowly and intently, waiting until the bird grasps the cage bars with its beak as it tries to avoid your approach. Then grasp the bird's head between your thumb and forefinger (Fig. 39.2). Let the bird chew on the towel if it chooses. Remember: The key to capturing and handling pet birds is to gain control of the head right from the start.

For small birds, gently cradle the body with your remaining fingers and the palm of your hand. For large birds, wrap them up completely in a towel, leaving their head exposed, yet under the control of your hand. Keeping the bird in an upright position will facilitate their breathing (Fig. 39.3).

FIGURE 39.2 Restraining a budgerigar.

FIGURE 39.3 Using a towel to restrain a large parrot.

At-Home Physical Exam

The physical exam is a useful tool that you can use to assess the overall health of your bird. It can be performed prior to purchase, and thereafter at periodic intervals, preferably at least four times per year. In addition, your bird should receive a complete professional checkup by your veterinarian at least twice a year.

At-home or prepurchase physical exams are easy to do and take little time. Owners should be cautioned, however, that if their pet is showing obvious signs of illness, veterinary attention is warranted at once. Here is the reason why. As mentioned previously, birds have an incredible ability to mask signs of illness to protect them against predators looking for sick and wounded prey on which to feast. However, such a tendency presents a problem in that birds kept as pets will also exhibit the same type of instinctive behavior, and illnesses might brew for months before a bird owner has any indication that something is wrong. Unfortunately, by the time the sickness overwhelms the bird's ability to mask its signs, subsequent treatment efforts often are unrewarding. Therefore, as an owner of one of these extremely stoic creatures, you must be constantly on the lookout for early, subtle clinical signs that can alert you to an illness. Performing periodic at-home physical examinations on your bird will assist you in these efforts. This same examination technique can also be used for your prepurchase screening, and can alert you to any health problems before any cash changes hands.

If possible, these exams should be performed without physical restraint, in the comfort of your bird's own surroundings. For a closer look, see if your bird won't stay perched on your hand or arm while you perform the exam, or, in the case of a prepurchase exam, on the seller's arm. However, if the subject simply refuses to cooperate, physical restraint might need to be employed.

Examine Droppings

Every examination should start with a good look at your bird's droppings in the cage. Have they changed in color or consistency? Normal bird droppings consist of three fractions:

1. A formed fecal fraction, which will appear green if the bird is eating seed; brown if eating pellets
2. A white, creamy urate fraction
3. A liquid urine portion

Again, the consistency and color of the droppings can vary with the type of diet the bird is on, so learn what is normal for your particular bird. Abnormal droppings are characterized by changes in frequency, volume, color, and consistency. Birds can have anywhere from 20 to 40 droppings per day. A decrease in the frequency of elimination or in the volume of the fecal portion is a good indicator of a decrease in food consumption, which could be secondary to disease and stress. Keep in mind that birds can't go without food for more than 2 to 3 days at a time without suffering serious health consequences.

Gastroenteritis usually causes the fecal portion to be liquid, whereas pancreatic disease can cause the feces to be bulky and gray in color, due to inadequate digestion of food. On the other hand, undigested seed and/or grit in the feces points to a potential problem in the gizzard region of the digestive tract. Pea-green stools are often seen with psittacosis or other serious infections. Finally, overt blood in the feces could signify a tumor or an ulcer somewhere within the digestive tract.

Changes in the urate and urine fractions of the droppings can also result from underlying disease. Urates having a yellow-green tinge often reveal the presence of an underlying liver disorder. Also, increases in the amount of urate or urine produced can be caused by, among other things, kidney disease and diabetes mellitus. Finally, lead poisoning should be suspected if blood is noted in the urine.

Observe Your Bird

Observe the way your bird carries itself. Does it seem uncomfortable on the perch? Is it shifting its weight back and forth? If so, it could have sore feet or it could be acting restless because of an underlying illness. Are there any signs of lameness? Certainly musculoskeletal injuries and gout are two leading causes of lameness in birds. In addition, internal tumors can cause paralysis in one or both legs, resulting in apparent lameness.

How about your bird's posture? Is it upright and attentive? Is it active? Birds that are ill often appear sleepy and exhibit unsteadiness at perch. A decrease in singing or vocalization could also indicate problems.

WEIGHT

How is your bird's weight? For small birds, weight can be monitored using a small postal scale or food scale. Excessive weight gain is as undesirable and unhealthy in pet birds as it is in dogs and cats. Obesity tends to be a problem in budgerigars more than in other species of birds. What is thought to be weight gain must be differentiated from internal masses or swellings. Have your veterinarian check it out. On the other hand, apparent weight loss could mean that your bird's appetite is off or it could mean dehydration, both signifying disease.

One key indicator of disease is the status of the large breast muscles. Disease often produces a wasting of these muscles, which results in a protruding keel (breast) bone that is easily palpable.

EYES

The eyes should be bright, shiny, and sharp. Look for signs of irritation and/or swelling. Green discharges coming from the eyes or crusty material surrounding the eye are indicators of infections. Clear discharges could indicate an allergy problem or a foreign body in the eye. Cataracts, which are common in older psittacines, will appear as a cloudy space within the pupil of one or both eyes. Are the eyelids droopy? This could be the result of a former eye infection, especially in cockatiels.

FACIAL AREA

The beak, nares, and cere should be smooth and free of growths and discharges. Discharges from the nares could indicate an active *airsacculitis*. Sneezing could be a sign of an early respiratory infection. Does the beak seem to be wearing evenly? Does it close properly? How about its length? Overgrown beaks can be a sign of liver disease in birds. A scaly, flaky beak could be infected. The mite *Knemidokoptes* should also be suspected if the beak appears crusty and scaly.

BREATHING

The respirations of a bird should be barely noticeable. Also, healthy birds breathe with their mouths closed. Labored respirations with or without open-mouth breathing signify serious respiratory distress. A wheezing or clicking sound is also indicative of respiratory disease in birds, as is tail bobbing when at perch.

WINGS AND PLUMAGE

Observe the wings and plumage. A droopy wing might be injured or held that way because of sheer weakness. The feathers of a healthy bird should appear crisp, sleek, and bright and should lie smoothly against the body. Ruffled feathers could indicate cool environmental temperatures or worse, illness. Are any feathers missing or broken? Broken tail feathers might mean that your bird's cage is too small. Missing or misshapen feathers can result from an abnormal molt or from feather picking.

Look at the feathers around the vent. Pasting of the feathers with fecal material should alert you to a potential gastrointestinal disorder. At the same time, observe the head feathers and those around the mouth for signs of matting and pasting. This could indicate regurgitation and/or vomiting.

FEET AND LEGS

Check the feet and legs for signs of irritation, inflammation, or tissue proliferation. The feet should be smooth. Keep in mind that poor perch selection and maintenance are the most common causes of foot problems in pet birds.

Overgrown nails can also adversely affect perching, and can pose a danger to the bird's health if they get caught in the cage. Also, leg bands on confined birds can do more harm than good and should be removed.

If your physical examination reveals any abnormalities, seek the advice of your veterinarian. Avoid further handling of your bird until you get it to your veterinarian, since unwarranted handling could kill a seriously ill bird. Transport your bird to the veterinary hospital in its cage (very important!). Don't clean the cage before you go, as your veterinarian will want to observe the character of your bird's droppings and all toys, food, and medicine that have been offered. However, you should empty water dishes and remove grit and perches from the cage prior to transport. Cover the cage for warmth and to minimize stress. If it is cold outside, warm your car up first before loading your bird.

Nail Trimming

The nails of your bird should be kept at a proper length, since overgrowth can cause nail breakage and predispose the legs and feet to injuries. Most of the time, the nails stay worn down by themselves as a result of normal perching activities. However, disease can sometimes cause overgrowth to occur. If your bird is otherwise healthy, yet suffering from nail overgrowth, take a close look at the perches in the cage. Soft, narrow perches can contribute to this problem.

You can trim the nails of your bird using a pair of dog or cat toenail clippers. For smaller birds, use a set of human nail trimmers. Before performing this procedure, always have clotting powder on hand in

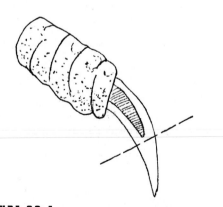

FIGURE 39.4 The dashed line indicates where to cut a bird's nail.

case you cut a nail too short. This is readily available from your veterinarian or a local pet supplier.

Simply capture and restrain your bird (assuming it is not ill), then snip off the sharp ends to the nails (Fig. 39.4). If one or more of the nails starts to bleed, apply clotting powder to the bleeding tips. Keep the bird restrained for a minute or two before putting it back in its cage to be certain the bleeding has stopped.

Beak Care

Healthy birds will keep their beaks in shape through normal eating habits and by chewing on soft wood and toys within their cages. The absence of such items within the cage, as well as injuries, various diseases, and poor nutrition, can all lead to uneven beak wear and/or overgrowth. Budgerigars seem to be the pet birds that are most in need of periodic beak trims (Fig. 39-5).

FIGURE 39.5 A budgie suffering from an overgrown beak.

Beak trimming should be performed only by a qualified avian veterinarian. At the same time, your veterinarian can show you how to perform minor touchups at home to keep your bird's beak looking nice.

Feather Clipping

Feather clipping is a procedure performed on pet birds to limit their flight capabilities. This not only prevents inadvertent escape out of an open window or door but also protects the birds from hazards associated with flight within the house (such as ceiling fans).

To minimize stress and possible harm to your bird, have your veterinarian perform this procedure. If you are determined to do it on your own, you should at least receive hands-on training from your veterinarian, who can show you several methods of doing so. The first method involves starting from the tip of the wing, skipping the first two or three primary feathers, and then using scissors to cut the remaining primaries down to the level of the covert feathers. Secondary flight feathers may be left intact. Scissors are then used to clip the very outer edges of the remaining flight feathers to prevent their adherence to one another (Fig. 39.6). An alternate method of deflighting pet birds is to strip every other flight feather bare, leaving only a shaft. This effectively eliminates adherence between the feathers, making it difficult to fly.

Evaluate your bird's flight capabilities after the clipping. If it is still able to fly well, secondary feathers may need clipping. In some instances, the opposite wing will need to be clipped as well. In general, the smaller the bird, the harder it is to keep them from flying.

Feather clipping must usually be repeated every 6 to 8 months, or 6 to 8 weeks after the start of a new molt. If clipping is to be performed soon after molting, use caution to avoid the new blood feathers that have come in. If one of these is accidentally clipped and begins to bleed, the feather should be plucked from its shaft and temporary pressure applied to the follicle to stop the blood flow. A new feather should replace it in 6 to 8 weeks.

Permanent flight-restraint procedures that can be surgically performed by your veterinarian include pinioning, which involves amputation of a portion of the wing, and tenotomy, a procedure in which the tendon of the main extension muscle of the wing is severed, rendering the wing nonfunctional.

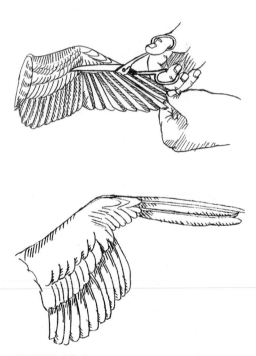

FIGURE 39.6 One method of feather clipping to prevent flight.

Bathing

Most birds enjoy periodic water baths, so provide them with the opportunity. A shallow bowl filled with water can be placed in the cage for this purpose. Some birds would rather use the kitchen sink containing a small amount of water for their bath once allowed out of their cage. Other birds find toilet water attractive, which is fine as long as no detergents or automatic cleaners are present within the water (these can be highly toxic to the unsuspecting bird).

Many owners choose to use a spray bottle filled with water to give their bird a daily mist bath. If you do so, be sure the spray bottle you use did not previously contain any chemicals or residues that could harm your bird.

Finally, some birds enjoy showering with their owners. If this is the case, the temperature within the shower should not exceed 98 degrees Fahrenheit. To be safe, leave the bathroom door opened slightly to allow your bird an easy exit if the need arises.

Avian Reproduction

For many bird owners, breeding pet birds represents the ultimate in fun and fulfillment. For others, it means a source of income, since offspring from a good breeding pair can demand attractive prices, depending on the species involved. Regardless of motives, breeding birds is not difficult if proper nutrition and husbandry are followed. Occasionally, though, birds may have trouble reproducing, and the potential causes are numerous. These and other breeding considerations are the focus of this chapter.

"Sexing" Your Bird

Certainly the first item on a successful breeding agenda is to be sure you know the sex of your bird(s). This might sound funny, but for many birds, especially the larger psittacines, the sex can't be reliably determined by physical appearance.

Most small psittacines, finches, and canaries can be sexed using physical appearances and/or characteristic behavior. For instance, male budgies can be differentiated from females by the color of their ceres. The male budgie has a dark blue to lavender cere, whereas the female will have a pink or tan cere.

Similarly, male cockatiels can usually be identified by yellow and orange markings on the head, in contrast to the grayish coloration of the female. Cockatoos can often be sexed according to the color of their eyes; males have black eyes and females have red-brown eyes. Male zebra finches can be identified by characteristic red-orange patches on their cheeks and sides.

Not all finches can be differentiated sexually by their coloration. For instance, both male and female society finches look similar. However, behavior can be used to identify male society finches, which will often sing and dance in the presence of a female. The same holds true for male canaries, which can be distinguished by their unprecedented singing ability when spring is in the air.

For larger psittacines such as conures, macaws, African Grey parrots, and Amazon parrots, special lab tests and/or surgical procedures are required to accurately determine the sex of these birds. One such test veterinarians can use is called a *fecal steroid analysis,* which tests for sex specific hormones within the bird's feces. This test is noninvasive, easy to perform, and fairly accurate.

Another sexing method that is popular and can be used to actually view and identify the reproductive organs within the bird's abdomen is called *endoscopy.* With this method, a bird is placed under light anesthesia and a tiny incision is made in the bird's side, into which a fiberoptic device can be inserted. Once inside, the endoscope can be used to visualize the ovaries or testes. One big advantage endoscopy has over other methods of sexing psittacines is that while the endoscope is inside the abdomen, the veterinarian can also assess the overall internal health and breeding condition of the bird in question. For example, endoscopy can be used to detect excessive fat within the abdomen, abnormally developed reproductive organs, and infections, all of which can affect breeding performance. The disadvantage of this procedure, of course, is the risk associated with using anesthetics, although this risk is generally quite low in the hands of an experienced veterinarian. It is up to each individual bird owner to weigh the benefits and risks of having an endoscopic procedure performed. Also, it is a good idea for potential bird owners who are purchasing birds specifically for breeding purposes to arrange with the seller to have the procedure performed as part of the prepurchase exam, if it has not already been done.

Proper Breeding Conditions

Because breeding can place much stress on pet birds, be sure to have your bird examined by a veterinarian before you begin breeding it. Breeding birds that are ill can endanger both their individual health and the collective health of their offspring. Also, because of the stress factors involved, birds should never be bred during a molting period.

The breeding cage and nesting box that you select should be spacious enough for two birds to move around in comfortably. The nesting box should be equipped with a perch or a ledge preceding the entryway into the box. Depending on the species involved, you will also want to obtain soft nesting material such as straw or cotton to place within the nest contained within the box to prevent the eggs from rolling around and help absorb moisture and fecal matter. Food and water bowls should be kept spotless as usual, and a water bath should be provided, since many birds enjoy this activity during the incubation and preweaning periods.

Breeding Finches and Canaries

Finches and canaries will reach sexual maturity anywhere from 4 to 8 months of age. The mating season for these passerines takes place in the spring. For purposes of introducing a new male to your existing female (or vice versa), a special breeding cage or nest box with a wire or wooden divider separating it into two compartments should be offered. Your local pet store should have such cages on hand. The male should be placed in one side of the cage and the female in the other. Keep the divider in place for seven to ten days, allowing the two to get to know each other. Once this time is up, remove the divider and allow the two to interact (Fig. 40.1*a, b.*).

A nest made of wicker or plastic needs to be placed in the nesting box. Most pet stores carry a suitable selection of these. Dried grass, straw, cotton, or a thin blanket is all suitable nesting materials to place within the nest itself. String, thread, or hair should be kept out of the nest, since these could wrap around and cause injury to a bird's legs and toes.

Incubation

Females will usually lay one egg per day over a period of 2 to 7 days.

Because it is less stressful and easier on the female to have the eggs in a clutch that all hatch at the same time, carefully remove the first one or two eggs that are laid in the nest and replace them with fake or "dummy" eggs, available at most pet stores. The eggs that are removed should be kept in a cool environment and placed on soft cotton padding to prevent inadvertent damage. Once subsequent eggs are laid, the eggs that were originally

a

b

FIGURE 40.1(a, b) Typical housing used when breeding finches and canaries. Note the slide-out partition. A breeding nest should also be placed within the cage.

removed can then be placed back into the nest to be incubated by the female and hatched. At the same time, you might want to again separate the male from the female to provide her with a relaxed atmosphere.

The incubation period for the eggs after laying is approximately 14 days, give or take a few. During that time, the female will sit on them to provide the desired temperature for their development. To determine whether the eggs are fertile, you can hold them up to a bright light and observe their color. Fertile eggs will appear red from within, which corresponds to developing blood vessels in the embryo. Nonfertile eggs will have no such appearance. If you know that an egg is nonfertile, you can remove it from the nest and replace it with a dummy egg.

Hatching

Once the incubation period is completed, the eggs will begin to hatch. When this starts to occur, resist the temptation of assisting in the delivery. Mother Nature can do just fine on her own.

Baby finches and canaries are born featherless and unable to see. The eyes should open up after a week; feathering should be completed by week 2. By 4 weeks of age, the hatchlings are ready to be weaned and leave the nest.

Nutrition

Throughout the incubation period and the preweaning period, your female bird should be kept on a high plane of nutrition in order to reduce stress. Egg biscuit or yolks from hard-boiled eggs provide an excellent source of added nutrition for the mother with young, and should be fed twice daily in addition to her regular ration.

Once the eggs hatch, a soft nestling food should be added to the diet to provide the chicks with a source of nutrition. These nestling foods are available commercially, but if you can't find a commercial brand right away, use white bread dipped in boiled whole milk as a temporary substitute. Keep your bird's food bowl filled with this food, and replace it daily with a fresh supply.

Foster Parents

Sometimes, mother finches and canaries abandon their eggs or refuse to feed their young. If this happens, remove the female from the nest and give the male a chance to rear and feed the young. If this doesn't seem to be working, a foster parent might be necessary. Society finches can make great foster parents for abandoned offspring, and can save you the time and effort associated with hand-raising the young.

Breeding Budgerigars

Budgies reach sexual maturity at 6 months of age, yet they should be at least one year old or showing mature coloration prior to breeding. The mating season for budgerigars is year-round, with spring being the most favorable time. The female should be introduced into the breeding cage a few days prior to the male to allow her to become comfortable with her surroundings. Males in courtship will try to impress the female by dancing around and bobbing their heads. As the couple becomes more and more comfortable with each other, they will start sharing food and feeding each other.

After the two have had several weeks to become acquainted, a nesting box should be placed on the floor of the breeding cage (Fig. 40.2). Within the nesting box, a wooden tray or plastic bowl can be used as a nest, with a small amount of pine chips or straw provided for nesting material.

Incubation

Female budgerigars will lay one egg every other day for a total of three to six. The incubation period for the eggs is approximately $2^{1}/_{2}$ weeks, with the hen staying within the box the entire time. Once this period is completed, the eggs will begin to hatch.

Hatching

Baby budgerigars, like most birds, are born featherless and blind. The eyes of these chicks open up after a week, and feathering should be completed by 4 weeks. By 6 weeks of age, they should be starting to fly and ready to leave the nest. Once they start to fly, young budgies should be separated from the parents and placed in their own enclosures.

Nutrition

Throughout the incubation and preweaning periods, the female budgerigar should be kept on a high plane of nutrition in order to reduce stress. Egg biscuit or the yolks from hard-boiled eggs provide an excellent source of added nutrition for the mother with young, and should be fed twice daily as a supplement to her regular ration.

Female budgies feed their young a special type of milk produced in the proventriculus of the digestive tract. This substance is rich in protein and other nutrients beneficial to the chicks. In addition, the male budgies will usually help in the feeding process as well, transferring partially digested food to the female, who in turn, feeds it to the hungry mouths of her offspring.

Foster Parents

For especially large clutches, another budgie can be used to serve as a foster parent to ensure that the chicks are getting the proper attention and nutrition they need. Such foster parents can save you much time and effort, considering the hand-rearing alternative.

FIGURE 40.2 A typical nesting box used for budgies.

Breeding Cockatiels

Cockatiels are quite similar to budgerigars as far as reproductive management is concerned. Once sexual maturity is reached at 6 to 12 months, the mating season for cockatiels occurs year-round; springtime is optimal. For best results, birds should be at least 18 months of age before attempting to breed. The female cockatiel should be introduced into a breeding cage a few days prior to the male to allow her to become comfortable with the surroundings. As the two become more acquainted with each other over a week's time, a nesting box can be introduced into the cage. Within the nesting box, a wooden tray or plastic bowl can be used as a nest, with a small amount of pine chips or straw provided as nesting material.

Incubation

Female cockatiels will lay one egg every other day for a total of 4 to 10 eggs. The incubation period for the eggs after they have been laid is approximately 2¹/₂ weeks, with the male often taking turns with the female sitting on the eggs. For especially large clutches, eggs can be removed from the nest and placed with foster parents.

Hatching

Once the incubation period is completed, the eggs will begin to hatch. Baby cockatiels are born featherless and blind. The eyes of these chicks open up after a week, and feathering should be completed by 4 to 5 weeks of age. At 6 weeks of age, they should be starting to fly and ready to leave the nest. Once they start to fly, young cockatiels should be separated from the parents and placed in separate cages.

Nutrition

Throughout the incubation period and the preweaning period, the female cockatiel should be kept on a high plane of nutrition in order to reduce stress. Egg biscuit or the yolks from hard-boiled eggs provide an excellent source of added nutrition for the mother with young, and should be fed twice daily along with her regular ration.

Breeding Parrots

The mating season for parrots such as Amazons and African Greys is year-round; springtime, as usual, is the most optimal time. Birds should be mature when bred, which means at least 2 years of age for smaller parrots and at least 6 years of age for larger varieties. The female parrot should be introduced into a breeding cage a few days prior to the male to allow her to become comfortable with her surroundings. The two should be allowed to become acquainted with each other over a week's time, but don't expect to see much courtship display by the male. A wooden nesting box with a portion of the floor concave in shape can be introduced into the cage after the introductory period. Hardwood shavings can be offered as nesting material to absorb wastes and to keep eggs from rolling (Fig. 40.3).

FIGURE 40.3 One example of breeding accommodations for larger psittacines. The nestbox needs to be of sturdy, stable construction to resist wear and tear!

Incubation

Parrots will lay one egg every 1 to 2 days for a total of two to six eggs. The incubation period for the eggs is on the average four weeks, with the male often taking turns with the female sitting on the eggs. For especially large clutches, eggs can be removed from the nest and placed with foster parents.

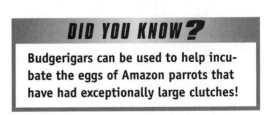

DID YOU KNOW?

Budgerigars can be used to help incubate the eggs of Amazon parrots that have had exceptionally large clutches!

Hatching

Once the incubation period is completed, the eggs will begin to hatch. Baby parrots are born featherless and blind. The eyes of these chicks open up in 10 to 14 days, and feathering and weaning should be completed by 12 to 14 weeks.

Nutrition

Throughout the incubation and preweaning periods, the female parrot should be kept on a high plane of nutrition in order to reduce stress. Egg biscuit or the yolks from hard-boiled eggs provide an excellent source of added nutrition for the mother with young, and should be fed twice daily along with her regular ration.

The male parrot will also sometimes assist in the feeding of the young, transferring softened food to the mouth of the female, who, in turn, transfers it to the awaiting mouths of her hungry offspring.

Reproductive Challenges

As with other pets, birds can have their share of breeding problems. Infertile eggs, eggs with thin shells that crack easily, and fertile eggs that fail to hatch are often the products of poor nutrition and/or unsanitary environmental conditions. Egg binding (see Chap. 41) can occur secondary to obesity and other illnesses, or from sheer exhaustion due to overlaying.

Improper mating or lack of mating between two birds can be an indicator of a stressful environment, perhaps due to a lack of privacy. Occasionally, the personality of each mate might not be compatible with the other, causing either the male or the female to ignore, or in especially tense cases, fight with the other. Also, in larger psittacines, be sure that each has been properly sexed, since this is a common cause of breeding failures.

Avian Diseases and Disorders

This chapter covers some of the more common afflictions seen in pet birds. General signs of illness in birds include the following:

Decreased appetite or water consumption

Weakness

Fluffed-up feathers

Broken, bent, or lost feathers

Labored breathing

Reluctance or inability to perch

Loss of muscle mass on breast

Shifting leg lameness

Abnormal lumps, bumps, or swellings

Change in color or character of droppings

Vomiting or regurgitation of food

Overgrown beak and/or nails

Discharges from eyes or nares

Prolonged molting period

As mentioned previously, the appearance of one or more of these symptoms warrants a consultation with your veterinarian.

Most of the diseases discussed in this chapter are grouped according to major organ systems affected. However, it is important to note that many of them, especially the infectious diseases, can affect multiple tissues and organs at a time, resulting in a potpourri of clinical signs. For this reason, the infectious diseases are presented in their own section within this chapter and are not listed under the respective organ systems that they affect.

Respiratory Tract Diseases

Refer to Chap. 38 for details regarding the anatomy and physiology of the avian respiratory system. Respiratory tract disease is undoubtedly the number 1 health disorder seen in birds. The causes are numerous, and can include viral, bacterial, and/or fungal etiologies.

Regardless of cause, clinical signs that indicate a respiratory problem in a bird include an increased breathing rate, tail bobbing, labored or open-mouthed breathing and abnormal respiratory sounds, nasal or eye discharge, and loss of voice. Other nonspecific signs, such as ruffled feathers, reluctance to fly, and a depressed, sleepy attitude, could also accompany these signs.

If respiratory disease is suspected, rapid diagnosis and treatment of the underlying cause are imperative for a happy ending. Supportive care designed to reduce stress, combined with appropriate antibiotic therapy and, if needed, oxygen therapy, are the benchmarks for treating respiratory disease in birds. For increased effectiveness, antibiotic therapy can be delivered using a *nebulizer,* a device that converts medications into a fine mist that can then be inhaled directly into the respiratory tract.

Aspergillosis

Aspergillosis is caused by a fungal organism that is normally found in the bird's environment. Because of this ubiquitous nature, disease caused by this organism is usually seen only in those birds that become highly stressed because of poor sanitation and/or poor nutrition. Old, moldy seeds and foods are major sources of this organism.

The disease caused by aspergillosis is primarily respiratory in origin, with infected birds exhibiting clinical signs such as sneezing, nasal discharge, and breathing difficulties. Occasionally, the organism will spread to other organs within the body, leading to a wide variety of clinical signs.

Diagnosis of aspergillosis is based on history (e.g., poor husbandry), clinical signs seen, and physical examination. Radiographic X rays can be used to confirm lung and/or air sac involvement, and cultures of respiratory secretions can help isolate and identify the causative organism.

Treatment of aspergillosis is often successful if the disease is caught in its early stages. Antifungal medications can be employed to combat such an infection. Certainly a change in nutrition, sanitation, and other husbandry practices are warranted at the same time.

Airsacculitis

The term *airsacculitis* refers to inflammation and functional impairment of the air sacs. The most frequent culprits causing airsacculitis include infectious diseases (bacteria, fungi, and viruses), parasites such as air sac mites, and traumatic rupture of the sacs themselves. Diagnosis can be made using radiographic X-ray findings. Nebulization of antibiotics can be an effective mode of treatment for airsacculitis.

> **DID YOU KNOW?**
>
> The air sacs are not only important for aerodynamics but also function to help deliver oxygen to the tissues and to dissipate the tremendous amount of body heat generated by the act of flying.

Gapeworms

The "gapeworm," *Syngamus trachea,* is a parasite that can inhabit the wall of the trachea in finches and canaries. Its colloquial name is derived from the clinical sign it causes in affected birds, namely, an open-mouthed "gape" due to interference with normal airflow down the trachea.

The parasite gains entrance into the body through infected soil or, in some cases, via ingested earthworms and insects harboring the worm larvae. From the gastrointestinal tract, the larvae migrate to the trachea. These migrating larvae can also cause pneumonia along the way. A variety of medicines can be used to treat gapeworms. In fact, in larger birds, manual removal of the worms by a veterinarian can often be accomplished. Because of the damage and distress gapeworms cause in birds, early treatment is a must.

Digestive System Diseases

See Chap. 38 for details on the anatomy and physiology of the digestive system in birds.

Specific signs of gastrointestinal disease usually include regurgitation, vomiting, diarrhea, and/or weight loss. Some of the more prevalent diseases affecting this system in birds include those discussed below.

Candidiasis

Candidiasis is not a primary disease syndrome, but rather a disease seen secondarily to long-term antibiotic therapy, malnutrition, and/or poor husbandry. This yeast organism causes lesions and ulcers in the mouth, esophagus, crop, or even the proventriculus. A characteristic white film, or plaque, usually covers the ulcerated areas.

Birds afflicted with candidiasis often regurgitate food due to the irritation caused by the lesions. Others may exhibit only nonspecific signs of illness, such as depression, ruffled feathers, and decreased appetite. Candidiasis is a serious disease in baby cockatiels, as it can quickly lead to death.

Diagnosis of this disease can be made by your veterinarian by identifying the characteristic plaques within the mouth or throat, and by examining swabs taken from the mouth and other affected areas, and demonstrating the yeast organisms under the microscope. Once this condition is diagnosed, specific antifungal treatments can then be instituted. Correcting husbandry shortcomings is also a must to prevent recurrences.

Sour Crop

Diseases affecting the crop invariably lead to one clinical sign common to all birds affected: regurgitation. One of the more prevalent conditions affecting this region is known as "sour crop," which occurs when the crop becomes inflamed and ulcerated, usually secondary to bacterial or fungal overgrowth within. Birds affected with sour crop will regurgitate foul-smelling food that has been sitting and fermenting within the irritated crop. Spoiled or moldy feed is thought to play a role in the development of this condition. Continual tube feeding can also predispose the crop to infection.

Treatment involves removing the crop contents using a feeding tube, and then repeatedly flushing out the crop using a special mixture of baking soda (1 teaspoon) plus kaolin and pectin ($1/2$ teaspoon mixed into 8 ounces of water).

Appropriate therapy for bacterial and/or fungal infections that may be present is also necessary. Feeding should be resumed in small increments several times a day until the crop heals. Sour crop can be prevented by observing good hygiene when tube feeding pet birds, by not overfeeding, and by feeding only fresh rations.

Crop and Gizzard Impaction

Impaction of the crop is another problem that can occur in pet birds. It can result when birds are allowed to engorge themselves on seed or grit, causing a grossly overdistended crop. Impaction can also occur secondary to infections, tumors, foreign bodies, and enlarged thyroid glands, all of which can affect the crop's contractility and ability to empty.

Palpation of the crop region will confirm a diagnosis of impaction. If this condition is diagnosed, treatment is aimed at emptying the crop of its contents and treating any underlying disease condition present. In severe cases, surgical removal of the crop contents and/or partial removal of the crop itself might become necessary.

Like crop impactions, impactions of the gizzard can be seen in birds that overfeed on grit or seeds. For instance, sick birds have a tendency to engorge themselves on grit. As a result, all grit should be removed from the cage of an ill bird.

Signs of a gizzard impaction include scant, bloody droppings that may have undigested seeds in them. Radiographic X rays can be used to reveal grit buildup within the gizzard. As mentioned above, surgery might be required to alleviate the impaction.

Macaw Wasting Disease

Probably the most infamous psittacine diseases affecting the gastrointestinal tract of birds is termed *macaw wasting disease* (MWD). As the name implies, this condition, which is characterized by an abnormal distension of the proventriculus, is seen mostly in macaws, although other psittacines can be affected. The exact cause of this disease syndrome is still unknown, but a virus is suspect. Researchers do know that it is a disorder characterized by poor nerve supply to the proventriculus and other organs, leading to muscular degeneration and weak contractions.

Once signs appear, the course of the disease is usually short. Sick birds will exhibit weight loss and muscle wasting, especially along the breast. Regurgitation can occur as the crop becomes affected, and as other normal digestive processes are disrupted, diarrhea containing undigested seed is seen. Birds severely afflicted exhibit incoordination and other nervous system signs. A radiographic X ray that reveals a distended proventriculus is diagnostic for MWD.

Unfortunately, there is no treatment available. As a supportive measure, these birds should be put on a liquid diet to promote normal passage of nutrients through the gastrointestinal tract.

Gastrointestinal Parasites

The most prevalent worm seen in the intestinal tract of psittacines is the roundworm, or *ascarid.* Affected birds often exhibit signs of unthriftiness, poor growth, weight loss, and sometimes diarrhea. Birds pick up infestations through contact with infected fecal material. In some cases, earthworms can act as intermediate carriers for the parasite.

Diagnosis can be difficult, and repeated examinations of stool specimens under a microscope might be necessary to identify the characteristic eggs. Once infestation is diagnosed, treatment using a dewormer is usually effective. Thoroughly steam-cleaning the cage a few days after treatment will help prevent reinfestation originating from the bird's own droppings.

THREADWORMS

If ascarids are the most common internal parasite seen in birds, *Capillaria* (the threadworm) runs a close second! These hairlike worms live in the small intestines. In canaries and finches they can inhabit the esophagus and crop as well. Transmitted between birds through contact with infected soil or with earthworms, threadworms cause loss of appetite, weight loss, and profuse diarrhea—often bloody—in affected birds.

Microscopic examination of fluid from the crop or of a stool specimen can lead a veterinarian to a diagnosis of threadworms in a pet bird. Again, treatment for this parasite is similar to that for ascarids.

OTHER INTESTINAL PARASITES

Other worms that can affect pet birds include tapeworms and stomach worms. Both have the ability to cause diarrhea and generalized unthriftiness in birds.

Tapeworms can be easily treated with special dewormers once identified in the stools. Stomach worms burrow into the lining of the proventriculus and gizzard, and can actually cause perforations if allowed to persist. As a result, expedient diagnosis and deworming can be lifesaving.

Other intestinal parasites that can adversely affect the health of pet birds include flagellates (*Trichomonas*), coccidia, and *Giardia*. The

> **DID YOU KNOW?**
>
> *Giardia* is the most common human intestinal parasite worldwide.

Giardia organism can cause high mortality rates in baby budgerigars and cockatiels affected with the organism, and has been implicated as the cause of cockatiel feather syndrome.

All three of these latter parasites can cause pronounced unthriftiness, lethargy, and gastroenteritis. Trichomonas can also infect the throat, causing oral exudates and breathing difficulties (*frounce*). Microscopic examination of a fecal sample can help your veterinarian establish a definite diagnosis and institute a proper treatment regimen.

Other Intestinal Diseases

While infectious and parasitic diseases can play major roles in gastrointestinal disease, poisonings, such as lead poisoning or plant toxicity, can also cause their share of intestinal upset, and usually lead to profound diarrhea. A good history combined with microscopic examination of droppings can often reveal the cause of the problem, or at least rule some out. Once a diagnosis has been established, appropriate treatment measures can be instituted.

Constipation can be a problem in dehydrated birds, overweight birds, or in those birds that eat too much grit. It can also affect females getting ready to lay eggs, due to pressure placed on the rectum from the maturing egg. Treatment consists of administering mineral oil or adding more fruit to the diet, and correcting any underlying problems.

Prolapse of the cloaca out of the vent can occur secondarily to egg laying and to straining, as seen with persistent diarrhea or constipation. Mild prolapses can often be replaced with minimal effort; more extensive ones might require surgery.

Liver Disease

Liver impairment in birds can present itself as a variety of clinical signs, including weight loss, seizures, abdominal enlargement, diarrhea, regurgitation, and blindness. Various infectious diseases, such as psittacosis, Pacheco's disease, and salmonellosis, can all adversely affect the liver. In addition, ingestion of toxic substances can also impair liver function.

DID YOU KNOW?

Overgrown toenails can be indicative of liver disease in birds.

Demonstrating elevated levels of liver enzymes in a blood sample is indicative of a liver disorder. Treatment is generally aimed at the underlying cause.

Neurologic Disorders

Disorders of the nervous system in birds can manifest themselves in the following clinical signs: Seizures, weakness, paralysis, incoordination and inability to perch, weight loss, vomiting, and abnormal posturing. Conditions that can induce such signs in pet birds include trauma, malnutrition (especially vitamin deficiencies), infectious diseases (such as Pacheco's disease, psittacosis, exotic Newcastle disease), liver disease, proventricular wasting syndrome, parasites, and toxic substances such as lead or insecticides. Budgerigars suffering from tumors of the kidneys or pituitary gland can also exhibit neurological signs.

Seizures caused by epilepsy have been diagnosed in budgerigars and certain Amazon parrots. During an epileptic fit, these birds may fall off the perch, shiver, rock back and forth, and appear to be in a trancelike state. Some birds may even exhibit abnormal aggressive tendencies. Anticonvulsant medications, similar to those used in cats and dogs, can be administered to control the seizures.

Because of the wide variety of potential causes, a proper diagnosis by a veterinarian is essential for establishing an exact source of a seizure. Once this has been done, an appropriate treatment, if available, can be instituted.

Cardiovascular Diseases

Fortunately, noninfectious diseases affecting the heart are not seen much in pet birds. Certainly older birds can suffer from the wear-and-tear effects of aging;

> **DID YOU KNOW?**
>
> Older birds on fatty diets can develop atherosclerosis of the blood vessels just as humans do!

chronic heart disease is one such effect. The two clinical signs seen most in these birds suffering from heart disease include exercise intolerance and breathing difficulties.

Parasites

Interestingly, parasites that inhabit the bloodstream are common in birds. Types include microfilaria, trypanosomes, *Hemoproteus, Plasmodium,* and *Leukocy-*

> **DID YOU KNOW?**
>
> Up to 50 percent of otherwise healthy caged birds harbor some type of bloodborne organism!

tozoon. Fortunately, most of the blood parasites seen in birds are harmless to their hosts, except when those birds are ill or highly stressed. In these individuals, bloodborne parasites can cause clinical disease, usually in the form of anemia or impaired blood circulation, and will require specific treatment.

Endocrine Malfunctions

Endocrine malfunctions resulting in diabetes mellitus, adrenal gland insufficiency, and hypothyroidism have been known to occur in pet birds. Because of their systemic nature, clinical signs associated with these disorders can be quite variable and originate from multiple organ systems. Diagnosis can be achieved through the use of laboratory blood testing.

Eye Disorders

Eye disorders can afflict birds of all ages. Traumatic eye injuries resulting from flight injuries, fighting, foreign objects, and burns can disrupt the outer corneal surface of the eye, leading to corneal ulcerations and abrasions. Corneas so affected usually appear cloudy and opaque, with the bird reluctant to keep its eye open. Certainly such a condition can seriously threaten eyesight if not managed promptly with ophthalmic antibiotics and other medications.

Conjunctivitis is another type of eye problem seen in pet birds. Swelling and inflammation of one or both conjunctival membranes are most often associated with respiratory infections in birds. In addition, cockatiels have been known to suffer from bacterial conjunctivitis, which can cause ocular discharge and swollen, protruding conjunctival membranes. Such infections usually respond to antibiotic eyedrops.

Inflammation of the internal structures of the eye, called *uveitis,* can be seen secondary to any generalized disease. If allowed to continue untreated, a cataract in the affected eye could result. A *cataract* is an opacity of the lens within the eye that does not allow light to penetrate to the retina, ultimately resulting in vision loss. Not all cataracts are caused by inflammation or infections. They can be inherited as well, especially in canaries.

The avian poxvirus causes serious eye disease in birds. The eyelids of these birds become scabbed shut, and corneal ulcers, conjunctivitis, and uveitis can result. Manual removal of these scabs can lead to intense scarring around the eyes and lids if the bird survives. Treatment is aimed at combating secondary infection with antibiotic ointments for the eyes, and at preventing the lids from becoming scabbed shut using daily warm-water lid washes. Vitamin A supplementation is thought to also be of some help in these birds.

Finally, parasites known as *conjunctival worms* can set up house-keeping within the eyelids and conjunctival sacs of unfortunate cockatoos and macaws. Affected birds are seen constantly rubbing and scratching at their eyes. Antiparasitic drugs can be used to get rid of these pesky parasites. However, if treatment is not prompt, these worms could actually penetrate the eye itself, making removal all the more difficult and threatening vision in the affected eye(s).

Ear Problems

The ears are rarely a source of health problems in birds. However, because of the ear's importance in maintaining balance and equilibrium, infections or injuries can seriously impair a bird's ability to fly and should be suspect in such cases.

Disorders of the Skin and Feathers

Diseases of the skin and feathers are major concerns for most bird owners, not only for the health of their pets but for cosmetic reasons as well. Disorders involving the integument and feathers are among the most frequent seen by veterinarians and can be among the most challenging to treat. Feather loss and skin involvement might signify a primary disorder, or they might occur incidentally to an unrelated disease process. The goal is to find out which it is!

External Parasites

Dogs and cats are not the only species that can suffer from external parasites. Pet birds can have their share as well.

Knemidokoptic mange is a skin and feather disease caused by a mite that burrows into the skin and feather follicles. In parrots and other psittacines, these parasites manifest disease as deformities and overgrowth of the beak, and deformities of the legs, feet, and nails (Fig. 41.1). In fact, severe infestations can actually lead to sloughing of the toes and nails!

FIGURE 41.1 Abnormal growth on the cere caused by mite infestation.

Canaries and finches can also be infested with this parasite, yet their legs and feet are affected more often than are their beaks. Lesions caused by this mite have been known to take on a characteristic "honeycomb" appearance. Itching is usually not seen with this disease.

Your veterinarian can diagnose this condition by taking skin scrapings of affected skin and examining them under the microscope for the presence of mange mites. Treatment using topical insecticides should be applied to the affected regions every 3 days for five treatments total, then repeated weekly until the lesions have cleared. Systemic antiparasitic drugs, given orally or injected, have also been shown to be even more effective in eliminating these mites. During the treatment process, loosened scabs should be removed and the beak, if affected, should be kept trimmed.

Other mites that pester pet birds less frequently include red mites, feather mites, *Myialges,* and *Ornithonsyssus,* the northern mite. The tracheal mite, *Sternostoma tracheacolum,* can inhabit the upper airways of birds and can cause loss of voice and some breathing difficulties. Air sac mites can also cause breathing difficulties and coughing in affected birds. A characteristic "smacking" sound emitted from these birds should alert owners to a potential problem involving these mites. Systemic drugs administered by your veterinarian is the best treatment for these mites as well.

Feather Picking

Feather picking is one of the most frustrating syndromes affecting pet birds (Fig. 41.2). Characterized by a loss of or damage to the feathers below the neck, this condition can exert devastating cosmetic effects on a prized pet. It is important to realize that feather picking is a sign of some other underlying problem, which must be addressed before the disfiguring habit can be stopped.

Medical illnesses can certainly play a role in the development of feather picking. Diseases that need to be ruled out as causes are numerous, and include the following:

Endocrine diseases (such as hypothyroidism)

Infectious diseases (poxvirus, psittacosis)

Poor nutrition

Food allergies (especially to seeds)

Contrary to popular belief, external parasites such as feather mites are rarely a cause of feather picking in pet birds. However, internal parasites such as roundworms and tapeworms must be ruled out as potential causes. *Giardia* infections have also been implicated as a cause of feather picking in cockatiels and budgerigars.

Another reason why a bird might pick at its feathers is stress due to emotional upset. Birds that have moved into a new home or those that are being handled excessively and unwillingly have been

FIGURE 41.2 Feather picking can have devastating effects.

known to start feather picking. Often, a new addition to the family will trigger an emotional episode, resulting in feather loss. Finally, if a bird does not receive enough attention on a daily basis, it might turn to feather picking to relieve its frustration.

Treatment for feather picking is directed at the underlying cause. If a medical reason exists, appropriate medications can be used to clear up both problems at the same time. Improved nutrition and husbandry are a must in all instances. In some birds, feather picking might lead to secondary bacterial infections of the feather follicles. As a result,

Dr. P's Vet Tip

For the emotional bird prone to feather picking, try leaving a radio or television on while you're not at home. Just hearing a familiar, consistent noise is often enough to thwart the nervous anxiety that can lead to this bad habit.

antibiotic therapy might be needed to treat this secondary problem.

For those cases that are psychologically induced, an owner can take a number of measures to curb their bird's anxiety. Sometimes simply moving the cage to a different location with more privacy is all that is necessary to calm an upset bird. Providing a larger cage with lots of safe toys and more room to move around also helps in some instances.

If lack of attention is the suspected cause, the obvious solution is to increase the amount of time you devote to your bird each day. If you haven't done so already, get your bird on a regular schedule of feeding, exercise, and sleep. This will help reduce its stress level.

Finally, if you are having difficulties fulfilling your time commitments to your bird, you might want to even go so far as to purchase your bird a feathered companion with which it can play and interact in your absence.

In especially tough feather-picking cases that are psychologically induced, your veterinarian may prescribe tranquilizers for your bird. Special collars designed to prevent the bird's access to its feathers can also be used to temporarily spare the remaining feathers from a similar fate while the underlying problem is being worked on. Please note that these collars should be used only for temporary relief and should not be relied on on a long-term basis. Because birds wearing these collars cannot preen themselves, owners must be sure to remove the sheaths from any new feathers that grow in. Any feathers that have been traumatized and broken should be pulled out to allow the new ones to grow in.

Psittacine Beak and Feather Disease

This disease, first identified in cockatoos years ago and subsequently in other parrot species, is caused by the psittacine circovirus (Fig. 41.3).

Affected birds suffer from feather loss and deformities in new feathers attempting to replace those lost. The beaks and nails of these birds are also affected and often chip, split, or fall off as a result of the disease.

Diagnosis of psittacine beak and feather disease is made by obtaining biopsy samples and performing microscopic examinations of deformed feathers and affected follicles. Unfortunately, an effective treatment for this disease is not available. Affected birds eventually die as a result of secondary complications and infections associated with this disease.

FIGURE 41.3 Psittacine beak-and-feather disease.

French Molt

Seen in budgerigars and other smaller psittacines, this condition is characterized by the abnormal development or overt absence of tail and flight feathers. The exact cause is unknown, although a genetic viral etiology is suspected. Unfortunately, as with the previous disease, there is no effective treatment.

Feather Cysts

Bulging nodules under the skin that contain abnormal feather shafts are characteristic of feather cysts. Their exact cause is unknown, but they have been shown to be genetic in nature in canaries. Feather cysts must be differentiated from other lumps and bumps that can arise on the skin of a bird, such as abscesses, tumors, and cysts affecting the feather follicles themselves. Once a feather cyst is diagnosed, treatment consists of surgical lancing or removal of the cysts as they occur.

Hormone-Induced Feather Loss

Feather loss can occur secondary to hormonal influences. In male canaries and budgies, a testosterone deficiency can cause such a loss.

Accordingly, administration of testosterone hormone for 4 to 6 weeks will usually prevent further feather loss.

Deficiencies in thyroid hormone (*hypothyroidism*) due to iodine deficiencies or inflammation of the thyroid gland can, among other things, lead to feather loss. Treatment consisting of daily administration of a thyroid hormone supplement in the bird's water is usually quite rewarding.

Overgrown Beak and Cere Changes

In a year's time, the beak of a healthy budgerigar should grow 2 to 3 inches; that of a larger psittacine should grow 1 to 1^1/$_2$ inches. The normal length of the beak is usually well maintained by the normal wear and tear from eating and from chewing on wood and other hard objects in the bird's cage. As a result, when beak overgrowth occurs, it is usually a sign of underlying disease. Genetic deformities can predispose a bird to beak overgrowth, as can other diseases such as malnutrition, bacterial and fungal infections, trauma, tumors, and liver disease.

MITES

The *Knemidokoptes* mite is a common instigator of beak overgrowth in budgerigars. Characteristically, this mite causes proliferation and crusting not only of the beak but also of the cere, face, neck, and legs. Fortunately, these mites can be treated effectively with miticides.

BROWN HYPERTROPHY

Unexpected changes in the color of the cere can be caused by a condition known as *brown hypertrophy* of the cere. This condition is seen primarily in budgerigars and is characterized by a brown, crusty thickening of the cere region, often becoming unicornlike in appearance. The exact cause of brown hypertrophy is unknown. Removal of the crusts and application of a skin-softening cream or lanolin to the region might help cosmetically, but you should count on the condition to recur.

INTERNAL TUMORS

Internal tumors can also cause a brownish discoloration of the cere in budgerigars. However, in most of these instances, there are other clinical signs, such as weight loss, neurologic defects, and an apparent abdominal mass will be seen as well.

Tumors of the Integument

Lipomas and papillomas are the two most common types of tumors affecting the integument of pet birds.

Lipomas are fatty tumors that can appear on the breast, abdomen, wings, and neck of pet birds, especially budgerigars. These tumors can get so large that they interfere with flying, walking, and perching. *Hypothyroidism* is thought to be one of the predisposing causes of lipomas. Diet might also play a role in their development. Feeding white millet on a regular basis has been shown to reduce the size of lipomas in select instances. Large and encumbering lipomas will need to be removed surgically.

Papillomas are warty proliferations that can affect many species of pet birds. The neck, toes, lower beak, and uropygial region are commonly affected. These pink-to-white growths are often covered with dry, brown crusts that can be easily removed. As far as the papilloma is concerned, surgical removal will ensure a cure.

Oiled Feathers

We have all seen and heard of the devastating effects spilled oil can have on a bird. The harmful effects of oil are numerous. The bird's insulating mechanisms are lost, and the oral cavity and vent become clogged with the substance, creating breathing and eating difficulties. Oil is also toxic to birds and can quickly lead to dehydration, gout, and organ failure in affected birds. See Chap. 42 for management of birds exposed to oil and other petroleum products.

Musculoskeletal Disorders

Lameness, the primary clinical sign seen with musculoskeletal disease, can be caused by a wide variety of illnesses and syndromes. Certainly one prevalent cause of lameness is sore feet due to poor perches. Perches that are too large or are covered with ridges or sandpaper are the major culprits.

Nutritional deficiencies, such as vitamin A deficiencies, can also lead to unhealthy skin on the bottom of the feet and, eventually, to lameness. Filthy living conditions and perches can cause bacterial infections of the feet. Other causes of lameness can include arthritis, gout, *Knemidokoptes,* tight-fitting leg bands, abdominal tumors, bone tumors, and bone fractures.

Gout

Gout, a condition causing lameness in pet birds, is characterized by a disposition to uric acid in the tissues and joints. Diets high in protein, dehydration, kidney disease, and vitamin A deficiencies have all been implicated in causing gout. Besides obvious lameness, joint swellings, and flight difficulties, gout can also lead to weight loss, diarrhea, and breathing difficulties as other organs within the body become affected.

Diagnosis of gout is based on clinical signs seen and on laboratory detection of abnormal levels of uric acid within the tissues. Treatment consists of lowering protein levels and increasing vitamin A levels in the diet; providing low, soft perches; and adding allopurinol to the drinking water daily. Analgesics such as aspirin can be added to the drinking water to reduce the discomfort. Unfortunately, not much can be done with the uric acid deposits that already exist within the tissues; therefore, the overall prognosis for recovery is poor.

Broken Bones

Broken wings and legs often result when birds fly into sliding glass doors, windows, and mirrors that are not properly marked. Ceiling fans can also cause broken bones in pet birds. Obviously, one of the best ways to protect your bird from such injuries is to keep its wings clipped to impair its flying abilities.

Poorly designed cages can also be implicated in many cases of broken bones. Cages that are too small or those that have narrow bar spacings or convergences in which a nail or wing could be trapped pose the biggest hazards.

Birds with broken wings will droop the affected wing or allow it to drag the ground when walking. If a break is suspected, immobilize the wing by pinning it against the bird's body using gauze wrap or a small towel. Be sure not to wrap it so tightly that you impair your bird's breathing. Transport your bird immediately to the veterinarian. For leg fractures, a toothpick or pencil can be used as a temporary splint while you transport your bird to the veterinarian.

Reproductive Disorders

Refer to Chap. 40 for information about the reproductive system in pet birds.

Egg Binding

Egg binding is the most prevalent challenge seen involving the reproductive organ system. Failure or inability of a maturing egg to be expelled from the reproductive tract characterizes this condition. It occurs more frequently in small birds, such as budgerigars, canaries, and finches. Predisposing factors to egg binding include obesity (especially in budgerigars), exhaustion from repeat layings, and the presence of any underlying disease process. Also, calcium deficiency in the diet can lead to the formation of soft, thin-shelled eggs that can easily become bound.

Clinical signs of egg binding include tail wagging, swaying and unsteadiness while at perch, abdominal swelling, and a penguinlike stance, with the bird resting its weight on its tail with its legs spread apart. Some of these birds might show signs of leg paralysis due to the pressure the egg is placing on the nerve supply to one or both legs.

Egg binding can be diagnosed using clinical signs, physical examination, and radiographic X rays. Treatment involves calcium injections and/or removing the contents of the egg with needle and syringe prior to manual extraction. In some cases, actual surgical removal might be required.

Specific medical therapy can be instituted to help prevent future egg-binding episodes in pet birds. Ask your veterinarian for details.

Tumors

Occasionally birds, especially budgerigars, can suffer from tumors affecting the structures of the reproductive tract. Signs associated with such growths include inability to fly, abdominal enlargement, breathing difficulties, and, characteristically, leg paralysis. Unfortunately, once clinical signs are manifested, surgical treatment is generally unrewarding.

Infectious Diseases

Infectious agents account for many of the disease conditions seen in pet birds. These agents can occur as primary disease entities, or they can occur secondary to stress, poor nutrition, and/or poor sanitation. Regardless of the organism involved, infectious diseases can be quite deadly to pet birds.

Psittacosis

Psittacosis, or *chlamydiosis,* is a serious disease in birds that must be considered whenever a bird becomes ill. Not only can it become life-threatening if it remains undetected, but it also can pose a health threat to an owner. It is caused by the organism *Chlamydia psittaci,* which is transmitted from bird to bird (and from bird to man) via dried feces and nasal discharges. Ingestion or inhalation of infected particles directly exposes birds.

Many birds, especially cockatoos, can become carriers of the disease, not showing any outward signs until stressed. Psittacines that are smuggled into the United States from Mexico and other countries without passing through a quarantine station are important sources of this zoonotic disease. Because of this, when purchasing a bird, always do so from a reputable source. If you do, the birds you choose will usually have already been tested for psittacosis, and should pose no health threat to your family.

Psittacosis has been known to cause severe and sometimes fatal flu-like illness in people. The disease can be transmitted by both exotic birds and pigeons, and can be caught by humans breathing infective aerosols from dried bird droppings.

The history of a bird affected with psittacosis usually involves recent exposure to other birds and to some stressful situation. Many will suffer from chronic, intermittent, low-grade illnesses and fail to fully regain their health.

The clinical signs of psittacosis include depression, muscle wasting, poor feathering, regurgitation, sneezing, nasal and eye discharges, and breathing difficulties. Psittacine birds will usually exhibit a classic sign: lime-green diarrhea. In addition, the urate portion of the droppings often takes on a yellow hue, signifying liver inflammation. Heart disease can also occur secondary to infection with the psittacosis organism.

Your veterinarian can diagnose psittacosis using laboratory tests. Increases in the number of white cells in the blood, evidence of anemia, and elevated liver enzymes in the blood can all point toward psittacosis. Specific diagnostic tests, including fecal cultures, selected antibody screens, and tissue stains, are also useful in the diagnosis of this disease.

Treatment of this disease involves the use of special antibiotics that are added to the bird's feed or water. Treatment might be necessary for 30 to 45 days or, in some birds, for an entire lifetime. During their convalescence, sick birds must be isolated from others to prevent transmission of the disease and to reduce stress.

Because of its zoonotic potential, owners should always practice good hygiene when caring for a bird with psittacosis. Cages and utensils should be thoroughly disinfected on a daily basis, using a quaternary ammonium compound or a dilution of bleach (1/4 cup of bleach per gallon of water).

Owners can prevent unwelcome surprises by having all new psittacines examined and tested for psittacosis prior to bringing them into the household. This is especially true for birds with questionable origins. If you have other birds in your household, it is a good idea to keep new birds away from these existing pets for 2 to 3 weeks before introducing it to the others. This will protect your existing birds not only from the threat of psittacosis but also from the threat of other diseases.

Exotic Newcastle's Disease (Avian Distemper)

Exotic Newcastle's disease (END) has been effectively eradicated from the United States, but it bears mentioning, since not all new birds entering the country pass through quarantine stations as they should. This viral disease is spread by ingestion or inhalation of the infective virus in food, in water, or on the hands of a handler. Among the psittacines, cockatoos and cockatiels are especially susceptible to END.

Clinical signs of the disease in affected birds include depression, loss of appetite and weight, breathing difficulties, nasal and eye discharges, diarrhea, and nervous system signs, such as incoordination, weakness, and paralysis.

If END is suspected in a pet bird from history and clinical signs, the United States Department of Agriculture is notified immediately, and the bird is placed in quarantine at a USDA facility. Unfortunately, there is no effective treatment for this disease.

Pox (Avian Diphtheria)

Avian pox is a viral disease characterized by severe respiratory and skin disease. Almost all birds can be infected with a poxvirus; the most likely candidates are canaries, finches, parrots, and pigeons. Cockatoos and cockatiels are relatively resistant to the disease. Exposure to the pox organism occurs via inhalation or by skin penetration, usually secondary to trauma. Insects, especially mosquitoes, can even spread the disease between susceptible birds. Pox seems to be a nagging problem in exotic bird quarantine stations.

The clinical signs associated with a pox infection include sneezing, breathing difficulties, discharges from the eyes and nose, and ulcers or scabs in the mouth, on the face, or on the extremities. The eyes of affected birds are often inflamed and painful. With severe involvement, death can ensue 1 to 7 days after clinical signs appear.

Diagnosis of a pox infection is based on clinical signs seen and microscopic examination of infected tissues and fluids. Unfortunately, not much can be done for treatment. Preventing secondary infections with antibiotics and treating any eye involvement is certainly warranted.

A vaccine can be used to help protect canaries against the ravages of canary pox. In addition, owners can help reduce chances of transmission by preventing their pets' access to wild birds (or vice versa), by controlling mosquitoes, and by quarantining all new birds before introducing them into the household.

Polyoma Papovavirus Infection (Budgie Fledgling Disease)

The *polyoma papovavirus* has been implicated as the cause of budgie fledgling disease, a highly fatal syndrome that affects young birds less than 4 weeks of age. The disease is transmitted through contact with infected droppings and other body fluids. Mother-to-egg transfer has also been documented. Fledglings stricken with this disease suffer from a severe gastroenteritis with accompanying diarrhea. The heart, liver, and kidney become additional targets for the virus as well.

Because of the disease's intensity and the lack of an effective treatment, these young birds usually die within 1 to 2 days after the onset of signs. Those rare birds that do survive often experience stunted growth and feather development.

Pacheco's Disease (Inclusion Body Hepatitis)

Pacheco's disease is caused by the psittacine herpes virus, which causes severe illness in affected birds. It is seen most often in newly imported and illegally smuggled birds. Transmission between birds occurs through contact with infected feces, usually from contaminated food and water bowls. Some birds can become carriers of this disease, with stress playing an important role in the appearance of clinical signs.

The clinical signs seen with Pacheco's disease are the result of liver, spleen, gastrointestinal, and respiratory involvement. Bright yellow diarrhea, yellow-green urates, vomiting, breathing difficulties, nasal discharges, depression, and a generalized wasting are all signs that can be seen with this disease. Incoordination and head tilting can also occur if the nervous system becomes involved. In severe instances, sudden death might occur.

Diagnosis of Pacheco's disease is made using history and clinical signs. Fecal cultures for the herpes virus can be performed as well. Unfortunately, definitive diagnosis is often made only after the bird has died.

There is currently no effective treatment for Pacheco's disease, although the effectiveness of certain human antiviral drugs against this disease agent is being tested in the laboratory.

A vaccine for Pacheco's disease does now exist and is available through veterinarians. As with psittacosis, new birds should be quarantined and screened for Pacheco's before introduction into the household.

Bacterial Infections

The bacterial organism *Salmonella* and others can cause significant disease in pet birds, particularly those stressed because of poor husbandry and nutrition. Pigeons are effective carriers of salmonellosis, yet rarely show any signs of infection. In contrast, pet birds that become infected can suffer from severe clinical signs and syndromes, some of which include depression, diarrhea, breathing difficulties, arthritis, and bone infections. Salmonellosis and other bacterial infections are spread from bird to bird via contact with infected fecal material. Rodents and certain insects such as cockroaches can also play an active role in the spread of these diseases.

General Treatment of Sick Birds

Keep in mind that a sick bird is fragile, and requires lots of attention and care to ensure that a proper recovery takes place. Because of the importance of minimizing stress, many veterinarians encourage convalescence at home in the environment in which the bird is most comfortable. As a result, owners should know how to best care for a sick or injured bird during that all-important convalescent period.

Care for Sick Birds

The cornerstone of any treatment regimen for birds is to reduce stress as much as possible. For starters, this means that handling should be kept to a minimum at all times during the recovery period (Fig. 42.1).

If applicable, remove other birds from the cage. It is essential to keep the cage environment between 85 and 90 degrees Fahrenheit and adequately humidified (Fig. 42.2). A heating pad set on low may be placed beneath (not *in*) the cage. Be sure that a towel or blanket separates the pad from the metal of the cage and clear the

Dr. P's Vet Tip

Ill birds have a tendency to overindulge in grit. As a result, if your bird is sick, remove all grit from its cage.

FIGURE 42.1 Unless administering a treatment, keep handling of sick birds to an absolute minimum.

cage of grit. Always use a thermometer to monitor cage temperature.

An incandescent light-bulb can also be installed overhead to provide extra warmth. Avoid using white bulbs because the bright light they emit will interfere with sleep. Instead, use a 40- to 60-watt green bulb. It can provide a source of heat, while at the same time respecting your bird's seclusion.

A cage cover can be used for the convalescing bird to help provide additional seclusion and warmth. It should cover three-fourths of the cage during the day and the entire cage at night. It is vital that convalescing birds receive at least 12 hours of undisturbed rest per day.

Also, lower perches to make access easier and to reduce the chances of injury from falling. Place food and water within the bird's easy reach.

Tube Feeding

If a bird refuses to eat or drink on its own, tube feeding might be necessary. Before doing this, however, try to hand-feed your bird.

Warmed baby food or oatmeal may be sufficiently enticing to stimulate an appetite. To encourage drinking, add sugar or honey to your bird's water, and offer it with a dropper or small syringe. This is especially helpful if medications are to be administered in the water. (If you decide to add sugar or honey to the water, be sure to change the water

FIGURE 42.2 One method of humidifying a bird with respiratory disease.

twice a day to prevent bacterial growth.) Commercial electrolyte replacement fluids can also be administered to help prevent dehydration.

If tube feeding becomes the only solution, you will need some special supplies. A soft rubber feeding tube and plastic syringe are ideal for the job and can be obtained from your veterinarian. As an alternative, a metal feeding tube can be acquired and used for tube feeding purposes. The main advantage that the metal tube has over the rubber tube is its rigidity. However, a big disadvantage is that too much pressure applied with a metal feeding tube during passage could actually damage or perforate the crop. They are also more expensive and not as readily available as rubber ones.

A speculum will be needed if a rubber tube is used to keep the mouth open during the feeding and to prevent the bird from biting off

DR. P's VET TIP

To allow for easier tube feeding if only one pair of hands is available, keep rubber tubes in your freezer between feedings. This will make them rigid, making them easier to pass into the crop.

the tubing. For small birds, a paper clip inserted into the mouth horizontally, and then turned up on its side, works great. For larger birds, an empty syringe case with a hole punched in the sealed end large enough for tube passage functions as an effective mouth speculum. Again, your veterinarian can provide you with one of these.

Numerous nutritional formulas are available for tube-feeding birds. A limited number of premixed commercial formulas are available on the market, yet they might be difficult to find. One formula for tube feeding that can be blended right at home includes the following:

Dog food (adult formula)	1 cup
High-protein baby cereal	1 cup
Banana	1
Honey	1 teaspoon
Vitamin-mineral supplement	1 teaspoon

These ingredients should be blended with water to form a slurry that passes easily through the feeding tube. Feedings should be performed every 6 to 8 hours. Consult your veterinarian as to amounts to feed your bird. As a general rule, finches and canaries should receive 1/4 to 1/2 milliliter of formula per feeding; budgies should receive 1/2 to 3/4 milliliter of the formula per feeding; cockatiels, 3 milliliter of formula per feeding; small parrots, 5 milliliter of formula per feeding; medium to large parrots, 10 milliliter of formula per feeding; and macaws, 15 milliliter of formula per feeding.

Refrigerate homemade formulas between feedings, and replace them every day. Always warm the formula to room temperature and double-check the temperature before feeding. Formula that is too hot could burn the esophagus and crop, whereas formula that is too cold could actually cause a detrimental drop in the bird's body temperature.

The steps involved in tube feeding are as follows:

1. Gently restrain the bird with one hand using a towel and extend the neck. Use your other hand to control the speculum and the feeding tube. Measure the approximate length of tubing it will take to pass from the bird's mouth to its crop (Fig. 42.3) and mark the stopping point directly on the tube using tape or a permanent-ink marker.

2. Attach the feeding syringe filled with the desired amount of formula to the tube, and expel any air present within the tube. With the bird held upright, insert the speculum into its mouth. Pass the feeding tube through the speculum starting from the left side of the bird's mouth and progressing toward the right side of the throat. As you pass the tube, feel for the tube in the esophagus as it passes down. This will help ensure that the tube is in the correct place and not in the airways. Insert the tube the premeasured distance (Fig. 42.3).

3. Slowly administer the desired amount of food. Palpate the crop for fullness. It should not feel tight, but rather still slightly fluctuant to the touch. Once finished, withdraw the tube. If the bird regurgitates food at any time during the feeding, withdraw the tube immediately. Be sure to clean and disinfect the equipment after each feeding and put leftover formula back into the refrigerator. Discard any unused commercial formula after 48 hours.

FIGURE 42.3 Prior to passing a feeding tube, measure the approximate length of tubing it will take to pass from the bird's mouth to its crop. The crop will be situated near the forwardmost tip of the breastbone (keel bone). (Refer to Fig. 38.1.) Mark the proper length directly on the tube using tape or a permanent-ink marker.

Hand-Raising Baby Birds

At some time you might be faced with hand-raising a baby bird, perhaps because the mother bird has abandoned the baby or was abusive toward it. Many bird breeders choose to hand-raise new offspring in order to stimulate the parents to produce more eggs. Birds that are hand-raised as babies are also tamer and generally make better pets.

Hand-reared baby birds must be kept warm, and a good way to do this is to either place a heating pad (low setting) under the portion of the box in which the baby is being kept, or by using a 75-watt lightbulb clamped overhead. Always use a thermometer to monitor environmental temperatures. For the first 10 days of the baby bird's life, the environmental temperature should be kept between 90 and 95 degrees Fahrenheit. Afterward, it can be dropped to about 85 degrees Fahrenheit for the next 30 days. Once the bird is feathered, maintaining an environmental temperature of around 75 degrees Fahrenheit is ideal.

The floor of the box should be kept spotless at all times. Paper towels or soft facial tissue can be used as floor covering. Wood shavings are not recommended, since birds may eat them.

Feedings need to be performed at regular intervals, depending on the age of the bird. Just-hatched birds will receive nourishment from the yolk sac for up to 12 hours and seldom require feeding during this time. Once feeding is to commence, an eyedropper or syringe can be used to deliver the food mixture. Commercial formulas should be used. However, if one is not readily available, then the following formula can be substituted:

Baby food, including	
High-protein cereal	1 cup
Vegetable (any type)	1 teaspoon
Fruit (any type)	1 teaspoon
Lowfat milk (powder)	1/4 cup

This formula should be blended with warm water to form a mixture that can easily be fed using a syringe or dropper. The water used to prepare the feeding formula should not be soft water because of its high salt content. Purified or filtered water is the best. Additionally, a vitamin-mineral supplement can be added to the mixture, dosing according to the supplement's label instructions. Keep the formula refrigerated when not in use. Discard unused homemade formula on a daily basis.

Warm your bird's food up to 100 degrees Fahrenheit before feeding. When administering food into your bird's mouth, have the bird facing you and slowly squirt the food into the mouth aiming from your right to your left. This will help guide the food down the esophagus instead of the trachea. Give just enough food to lightly distend the crop; don't overfill! The idea is to have the crop three-quarters empty by the time the next feeding rolls around. If a meal sits in the crop too long, it can predispose to crop infection. If you find that the crop is not emptying properly, try cutting back on the amount you are feeding, or add more water to the formula. Also, recheck the temperature of the food. If the formula is too cold, crop emptying can be delayed. Do not force-feed a bird that is reluctant to eat. If its appetite remains depressed, call your veterinarian for instructions.

Feed birds 1 to 7 days of age every 2 hours (feed only once or twice during the night to avoid totally interrupting your bird's sleep). When the bird is 7 to 21 days old, feed it every 4 hours; at 3 to 6 weeks of age, feed three times daily. When the bird is 6 to 8 weeks of age, feed it twice daily. Birds over 8 weeks of age should not require more than one hand-fed meal, given at bedtime. At this age, they will usually start eating and drinking on their own.

Emergency and First Aid Procedures in Birds

Because any injury or illness in a bird can lead to serious complications and even death, you must be prepared in the event of an emergency involving your pet (Fig. 42.4). Some of the more common emergency situations that might arise include bleeding, broken bones, respiratory distress, and poisonings. As far as first aid is concerned, minor injuries such as bleeding toenails or minor lacerations

FIGURE 42.4 Any injury or apparent illness in a bird should be treated as a medical emergency.

can be effectively doctored at home. On the other hand, those first aid procedures related to more serious injuries or illnesses are only palliative, and must be followed up immediately with a visit to your veterinarian. Remember: The life of an injured or ill bird is fragile and could easily be lost unless prompt action is taken.

Ideally, transport your bird to the veterinary hospital in its original cage. Remove all perches and empty all water containers prior to moving. Also, place a cover over the cage for seclusion and warmth. If your bird is so debilitated that it cannot stand or balance itself, gently wrap it in a towel large enough to prevent movement. Keep the temperature within the car above 85 degrees Fahrenheit to minimize stress.

First Aid for Birds

BLEEDING (HEMORRHAGE), CUTS, AND WOUNDS

Apply direct, firm pressure over the area for a minimum of 5 minutes using a cloth, towel, or article of clothing. Be aware of how you are restraining your pet; don't grasp it so tightly that breathing is impaired.

After applying pressure for 5 minutes, remove the covering and observe for further bleeding. Reapply pressure if necessary or apply a clotting cream or powder (if a toenail is involved). Do not use clotting powders or creams on other open wounds. Instead, gently wash the wound with soap and water, and rinse thoroughly. Apply an antibiotic ointment to the wound. In addition, if the wound is large, cover it with a sterile dressing. If the wound and/or bleeding is severe, wrap your bird in a towel and transport it to your veterinarian.

BREATHING DIFFICULTIES AND NASAL DISCHARGE

These two clinical symptoms indicate respiratory disease or heart disease, both of which can be rapidly fatal if not treated promptly. Do not try to treat these symptoms at home. Take your bird to your veterinarian immediately.

DIARRHEA AND CONSTIPATION

Bird owners should not attempt to treat diarrhea in birds at home, because of the high probability of an underlying infectious disease.

The longer you postpone professional treatment, the greater the chances are for your bird's condition to worsen.

For the constipated bird, try adding mineral oil or more fruit to the diet. If the problem persists for more than 2 days or if the bird shows other signs of illness, immediate veterinary attention is indicated.

CLOACAL PROLAPSE

If such a prolapse occurs, gently clean the prolapse with warm water and soap, and rinse well. Coat and lubricate the prolapsed region with lubricating jelly and attempt to gently push it back in. Then take your bird to your veterinarian. If it won't go back in easily, discontinue your attempts and enlist the help of your veterinarian. Prolapsed birds should be placed on antibiotics to prevent secondary infections from developing.

EGG BINDING

There is no specific treatment that you can do at home for an egg-bound bird. This condition requires immediate veterinary attention.

OILED BIRDS

Loosely tape your bird's mouth shut to prevent ingestion of the oil. Flush the eyes, nose, and mouth to remove any oil that may be present. Using mild dishwashing liquid, wash the feathers thoroughly and

Dr. P's Vet Tip

Nontoxic mechanic's waterless hand cleanser can be an effective tool for removing oil and dirt from the feathers of birds. Just be sure to dry the feathers thoroughly after use.

rinse well. Repeat as necessary. Blot the feathers dry using a towel, and take your bird to your veterinarian for further treatment.

POISONINGS

If the poison was ingested, rush both bird and poison container to your veterinarian as soon as possible. If the poison contacts the skin and feathers, rinse the bird well with copious amounts of warm water and blot dry with a towel. Transport to your veterinarian at once, being sure to take the poison container with you.

SEIZURES

Wrap a seizuring bird gently in a towel to prevent self-injury. Transport immediately to a veterinarian.

EYE INJURIES AND DISORDERS

If a noxious substance gets in the eye, gently flush the eye liberally with an ophthalmic solution or tap water. Use a tissue or soft cloth to wipe away any discharge or foreign matter from the skin surrounding the eye. Transport to your veterinarian.

HEAT STROKE AND SMOKE INHALATION

Quickly remove the bird from the offending environment and provide free access to fresh air. Fan the bird to increase air circulation. For heat stroke, wrap the bird in a cool (not cold) moistened towel and transport it immediately to your veterinarian.

FRACTURES AND BROKEN BONES

For broken wings, immobilize the wing by pinning it against the bird's body using gauze wrap or a small towel. Be sure not to wrap so tightly as to impair your bird's breathing. Transport it immediately to your veterinarian. For leg fractures, toothpicks, pens, or pencils can be used as temporary splints while you transport your bird to the veterinarian.

PART IV

EXOTIC PETS

For the purpose of this book, any creature that doesn't bark, meow, or fly falls into the category of "exotic pet." In reality, most of these pets are not truly "exotic" or unconventional, owing to their ever-increasing popularity and numbers in households across the country. As American lifestyles change, it appears that pet preferences may be changing as well!

Popular exotic pets include rabbits, guinea pigs, small rodents (gerbils, hamsters, mice, and rats), chinchillas, prairie dogs, hedgehogs, ferrets, pot-bellied pigs, reptiles, amphibians, invertebrates, and fish. Each one of these pets has special husbandry, nutritional, and preventive health care requirements that are essential for its health and happiness. It is vital that prospective owners do their research *before, not after,* obtaining such a pet. Veterinarians are becoming more specialized in exotic medicine, and can serve as excellent information resources for first-time owners.

Keeping an exotic pet healthy and happy is not difficult and can be loads of fun. The following chapters are designed to touch on the main points of husbandry and health care of the more popular exotic species seen today. If more in-depth information is needed, consult your veterinarian or pet health care professional.

Rabbits

The domestic rabbit that we are all familiar with, *Oryctolagus cuniculus*, is actually a descendant of the European wild rabbit. Rabbits have been used for centuries for food and pelts, yet their importance and popularity as delightful house pets is rapidly increasing. Well over 50 breeds exist from which to choose, depending on aesthetic preference. Common breeds kept as pets include several varieties of Angoras, lop-eared, and dwarf rabbits. Many of the popular lop-eared rabbits have ears that hang all the way down to the floor! In addition, rabbits come in three basic sizes: large, medium, and small, with the larger rabbits weighing in as much as 15 pounds! Docile and easy to handle, rabbits are relatively easy to care for. Many can be trained to perform tricks and even walk on a leash! As with other pets, the key to disease prevention and control in these creatures is good husbandry. Well maintained, the average rabbit can live to be 5 to 10 years old.

Restraint

When handling a rabbit, grasp the loose skin over the shoulder and neck region with one hand, and support

DID YOU KNOW?

Lagomorphs (rabbits) and rodents can be differentiated by their teeth. Lagomorphs have four upper incisor teeth, whereas rodents have only two.

FIGURE 43.1 When holding a rabbit, always maintain support of its powerful hind legs to prevent injury.

the hind legs against your chest with the other (Fig. 43.1). Not only will this keep you from being bitten or scratched, but it is also necessary to prevent accidental injury to the back and spine of the rabbit. A rabbit that is restrained with its rear legs unsupported can kick and thrust with such force as to actually fracture its spine in the struggle!

Housing

Rabbits can be allowed free access to the house and can be readily litter-trained. If a litterbox is to be supplied, use only pelleted paper or non-toxic organic litter in the box. Standard clay or gravel can be harmful if ingested by your rabbit. With rabbits that are allowed to roam freely, realize that they can be quite destructive with their teeth and nails. Rabbitproof your home as you would for any new puppy or kitten.

If your rabbit is to be kept in a cage, be sure it provides plenty of room in which to move around. Metal cages can be purchased commercially or can be constructed out of wire mesh (Fig. 43.2). This wire mesh should be 1 × 2 inches on the sides and no more than 1/2 × 1 inch on the floor.

Because wire mesh is hard on the feet of rabbits, supply a plastic or metal resting board to place over a portion of the cage floor. This will provide your rabbit with both a space for resting and a space for activity. Cover this portion of flooring with straw or aspen shavings. Just remember to remove all feces and urine that may accumulate on a daily basis. To ensure utmost sanitation, a tray filled with cat litter or other absorbent material can be placed beneath the open flooring to capture urine and fecal material that passes through the wire mesh. Many cage setups have sunken flooring beneath the wire mesh that slides out and makes cleanup much easier (Fig. 43.3).

FIGURE 43.2 One example of a housing setup that can be used for a dwarf rabbit.

Cages should be placed in well-ventilated areas to prevent buildups of ammonia fumes emitted from urine. If kept outdoors, it should also provide protection against the wind and other elements.

Rabbits enjoy environmental temperature that range between 65 and 80 degrees Fahrenheit. Temperatures exceeding 85 degrees are not well tolerated.

Sipper bottles suspended from the sides of the cage should be used in place of water bowls, since sippers prevent fecal contamination of the water supply and also reduce the chances of sore hock and other moisture-related diseases. Cages, food bowls, and water dispensers should be cleaned

FIGURE 43.3 A classic outdoor rabbit hutch with plastic sheeting on the side to protect against the wind.

and disinfected at least twice weekly. Chlorhexidine or a quaternary ammonium compound diluted in a 1:10 solution (1 part ammonium to 10 parts water) can be used as the disinfectant. Be sure to rinse well after application. For cages located outdoors, waste material should be removed at least every other day to keep it from attracting flies and other insects.

Nutrition

Commercial rabbit pellets can be purchased for your rabbit, along with unlimited amounts of hay. All food offered should be as fresh as possible and be free of mold. The daily allotment should be offered free-choice for consumption throughout the day. In addition to pellets, small portions of dark green or yellow vegetables (e.g., broccoli, brussels sprouts, alfalfa sprouts, carrots, squash) and fruit (e.g., apples, melon, strawberries) should be offered daily. (*Note:* To prevent digestive upset, green, leafy vegetables should not be offered to young rabbits under 6 months of age.)

As always, provide plenty of clean, fresh water delivered through a water sipper that hangs from the side of the cage. Both food (uneaten) and water should be changed daily.

Because a rabbit's teeth are in a constant growth mode, provide a hardwood chew block and/or tree branches (e.g., elm, maple, birch, apple, pear, peach) to help keep the teeth worn down properly and to satisfy its desire to chew (Fig. 43.4). Avoid branches from trees such as cedar, redwood, cherry, and oleander, as these can be poisonous.

One behavior of rabbits that might surprise new owners is *coprophagy*, or the consumption of their own fecal material. This usually occurs during the morning hours. This practice shouldn't be frowned

FIGURE 43.4 A rabbit's incisor teeth are constantly on the grow and need to be worn down through normal chewing activity. As a result, rabbits should be provided with plenty of hardwood chew blocks and/or tree branches to help keep the teeth in top shape.

on, as it actually increases nutrient utilization and absorption within the rabbit's body.

Reproduction

Justifiably, the rabbit has been accused of being one of the most prolific breeders of all time. One reason for this fecundity is that the female rabbit, or doe, is *polyestrous,* that is, continually in heat. Rabbits are also induced ovulators, which means that an egg is released from the ovary only on copulation.

Three weeks after breeding, a hay-filled nesting box should be introduced into the cage for the doe to make final preparations for birth. It must be large enough for the doe to easily stand in and be equipped with a doorway to allow for the doe and her babies to come and go as they please. Pregnancy in does lasts 28 to 34 days.

The number of offspring to be expected is around three to nine. Baby rabbits, or pups, are born in the nest naked, blind, and helpless, yet are usually well cared for by the doe. Eyes will open up at around 10 days of age.

After the birth, the doe's food allowance should be increased gradually over a week's time to compensate for lactation. Do not increase it suddenly, as this can lead to serious gastrointestinal problems. In 3 weeks, the nest can be removed from the cage. Weaning will occur 3 to 4 weeks after its removal. Young rabbits reach puberty at 4 to 10 months of age.

Orphaned pups or those that have not been fed properly during the first 2 days of life can be raised on commercial milk replacements intended for puppies and kittens. Feedings should be offered every 8 to 12 hours, up to a daily amount of 10 to 20 milliliters of formula. Pups should be stimulated to urinate and defecate after feeding by massaging their anal regions with a cotton ball soaked in warm water. Most young rabbits can be weaned onto commercial pellets as early as 3 weeks of age. As always, warmth, sanitation, and tender loving care are vital whenever raising orphans.

Preventive Health Care

Routine vaccinations are not required for rabbits, but annual veterinary checkups and stool checks are highly recommended. The nails

FIGURE 43.5 Treat ear mites in a rabbit as you would in a cat.

should be trimmed monthly (or more frequently if needed), and the haircoat should be brushed at least twice weekly (longhair varieties more frequently). Rabbits will shed their haircoats every 3 to 4 months. Feline hairball laxative should be administered weekly to prevent hairball formation. While administering this medication, take note of the teeth for any apparent overgrowth. If detected, contact your veterinarian. Fleas and ear mites can be controlled using safe topical products designed for puppies and kittens (Fig. 43.5).

Adult does can be spayed to prevent further pregnancies and to reduce the incidence of uterine cancer as they grow older. Similarly, bucks can be neutered when they are 8 to 12 months of age. Ask your veterinarian for more details.

Strict sanitation, environmental control, and high-quality rations must be given top priority in order to prevent disease. Keep a close eye on your pet's behavior, eating habits, elimination habits, and physical characteristics. Notify your veterinarian of any changes. Care should be taken to prevent obesity, which can have the same deleterious effects in rabbits as it does in humans. And don't forget to offer a liberal dose of attention to your pet each day to help fulfill its mental and emotional needs.

Diseases and Disorders of Rabbits

The following are some selected diseases and disorders seen in rabbits. Remember that others do exist, which is why a definitive diagnosis should be made by a qualified veterinarian. Identifying and treating diseases in their early stages is the key to successful treatment and cure (Table 43.1).

Table 43.1 Diseases and Disorders of Rabbits

Disease or disorder	Clinical signs	Treatment and comments
Respiratory disease		
Bacterial rhinitis/ pneumonia (snuffles; pasteurellosis)	Sneezing; nasal and eye discharge; breathing difficulties; head shaking	Common in stressed rabbits; treat with antibiotics
Gastrointestinal diseases		
Malocclusion of teeth ("slobbers")	Excessive salivation; inability to eat; weight loss; lip lacerations	Trim incisor teeth every 2 weeks
Hairballs	Loss of appetite; abdominal pain	Treat using laxatives; surgical removal sometimes needed; prevent with brushing, hairball laxative weekly
Mucoid-enteropathy	Abdominal pain and distension; diarrhea; arched back; dehydration	Highly fatal in young rabbits; exact cause unknown; treat with antibiotics to prevent secondary infection; replace fluids; high-fiber diet might help

Table 43.1 Diseases and Disorders of Rabbits (*Continued*)

Disease or disorder	Clinical signs	Treatment and comments
Coccidiosis	Abdominal pain and distension; loss of appetite; diarrhea; jaundice; weight loss	Associated with poor sanitary conditions; treat with sulfa drugs
Bacterial enteritis	Diarrhea; weight loss; jaundice	Associated with poor sanitary conditions; also can be associated with improper antibiotic therapy; treat using a select group of antimicrobial agents
Skin and coat diseases		
"Sore hocks" (bacterial dermatitis)	Moist, ulcerated skin lesions on hind feet	Caused by trauma from wire floors, environmental filth; treat with antibiotics; change environmental conditions
Ringworm	Hair loss; crusts on head, ears	Treat with antifungal medications
Ear mites	Head shaking; scratching at ears; crusts and scabs in ears; hair loss on head and neck	Very common problem in pet rabbits; treat with ear mite medication; ivermectin for tough cases
Mange (*Sarcoptes*)	Intense itching; hair loss on face, ears, genitalia	Very contagious to other rabbits; treat with safe insecticidal shampoo; ivermectin for tough cases
Fleas, ticks	Itching; hair loss; anemia	Treatment same as that for cats

Table 43.1 Diseases and Disorders of Rabbits (*Continued*)

Disease or disorder	Clinical signs	Treatment and comments
Pox viruses	Warlike growths on face, legs, and feet; swollen eyelids; eye discharge; subcutaneous lumps	Transmitted by biting insects; no treatment; wartlike growths usually regress on their own
Reproductive system diseases		
Pregnancy toxemia	Loss of appetite; depression; seizures in pregnant or lactating does	Cause unknown; high mortality; support with antibiotics
Uterine adenocarcinoma	Infertility; weight loss; loss of appetite; vaginal discharge	Common in older females; spay if not metastasized
Urinary system diseases		
Normal urine	Urine cloudy, thick; often orange or brown in color	
Nephroma	Loss of appetite, depression; variable signs (associated with kidney disease)	Usually benign, yet affects kidney function
Neurological diseases		
Parasitic encephalitis	Tremors; convulsions; incoordination	Can be caused by exposure to raccoon, roundworms, or other infected rabbits; cuterebra larvae can also cause similar signs

Table 43.1 Diseases and Disorders of Rabbits (*Continued*)

Disease or disorder	Clinical signs	Treatment and comments
Musculoskeletal diseases		
Splayleg	Inability to walk; support weight; one or all legs can be affected	Can be genetic or traumatic in origin; treatment generally unrewarding
Spinal fractures	Paralysis of hind end and hind legs	Caused by improper handling or trauma; treatment generally unrewarding

Guinea Pigs

Cavia porcellus, the guinea pig, is a native of the south American continent, where it was raised by the Incas for food and for religious sacrifice. Introduced into Europe centuries ago, the guinea pig became popular as a laboratory animal, then as a pet. In the United States, the same functions hold true today. As pets, there are a number of popular breeds from which to choose, including the *English,* characterized by smooth, short hair; *Peruvians,* which have long, silky hair; *Abyssinians,* which sport short, coarse hair arranged in multiple whorls; *crested,* which are similar to English guinea pigs but with a white crest on the head; and *Teddys,* characterized by coarse, kinky hair. Guinea pigs also come in a variety of colors, such as solids, agouti, Himalayan, and tortoise shell.

Like hamsters, guinea pigs have no tails. Good-natured, they rarely bite, yet will emit a loud squeal when frightened or handled. They are easy to maintain, and require minimal preventive health care. They do require periodic brushing and nail trims. In addition, their front teeth may require trimming if overgrowth occurs. Guinea pigs average about 1 to 2 pounds in weight when fully grown, and can live up to 8 years when well cared for.

FIGURE 44.1 Use two hands when lifting your guinea pig.

Restraint

Restraint of the guinea pig is similar to that of rats. The shoulder and chest regions can be encircled with one hand and the hind end supported with the other hand as you lift. Be sure to control the guinea pig's hind feet and rump to prevent it from scratching you (Fig. 44.1).

Housing

Male guinea pigs can be housed with females, yet two males living together will fight. Housing for guinea pigs should consist of a wire cage at least 12 inches high and providing at least 2 square feet of space for each pig. The smooth flooring of the cage can be lined with aspen shavings (avoid cedar shavings), commercial rodent bedding, or hay. Bedding should be spot-cleaned daily and changed completely every week. Most guinea pigs appreciate a hiding box or enclosure made of plastic, ceramic, or wood in which to crawl and hide when the feeling arises (Fig. 44.2). Also, guinea pigs like to climb. Providing multilevel shelving within the cage would make your pet extremely happy!

Water delivery systems should be kept up off of the cage floor for sanitary purposes. Since some pigs might actually regurgitate food backup into the water sipper, be sure to check and maintain the patency of such devices on a daily basis. A sturdy, chew-resistant food bowl is a must. The entire cage and its contents should be thoroughly cleaned and sanitized weekly using soap and water.

Guinea pigs do not tolerate heat and humidity very well. Ideal environmental temperature for them is around 70 degrees Fahrenheit. Temperatures exceeding 80 degrees Fahrenheit can quickly lead to heat stroke.

FIGURE 44.2 Provide your guinea pigs with lots of places in which to hide!

Nutrition

Guinea pigs must have adequate amounts of vitamin C in their diets, since their bodies are not capable of synthesizing the vitamin internally. Commercial guinea pig rations, in pellet form, can more than satisfy this requirement if the pellets purchased are fresh. However, to be safe, offer fresh fruits (e.g., one quarter of an orange or apple) and vegetables (e.g., collard greens, parsley, kale) along with the regular pelleted rations to ensure adequate amounts of vitamin C in the diet. Like rabbits, guinea pigs also enjoy gnawing on carrot sticks.

Because a guinea pig's teeth are in a constant growth mode, provide a hardwood chew block and/or tree branches (e.g., elm, maple, birch, apple, pear, peach) to help keep the teeth worn down properly and to satisfy its desire to chew. Avoid branches from trees such as cedar, redwood, cherry, and oleander, as these can be poisonous.

Clean food bowls daily, as some guinea pigs enjoy defecating therein. Also, provide plenty of clean, fresh water delivered through a water sipper that hangs from the side of the cage (Fig. 44.3).

Reproduction

Female guinea pigs cycle every 16 days and, if mated, will carry the developing offspring for an average of 68 days. Females that are not bred until after 6 months of age have a higher incidence of birthing complications than do those bred earlier in life. If a pig is not bred before this time, its pelvis might fuse together, making passage through the birth canal difficult. As a result, a C-section operation might be necessary to deliver the litter. Also, pregnant guinea pigs are especially susceptible to heat stroke if environmental temperatures are not kept well regulated.

FIGURE 44.3 A water bottle that hangs from the side of the cage is the most sanitary method for delivering water to your guinea pig.

Litter sizes usually range from one to eight cavies. Baby guinea pigs are born with eyes open and with hair. This enables them to be weaned almost immediately if the situation warrants it. However, survival rates are better if babies are weaned around 3 weeks of age (Fig. 44.4). Sexual maturity in guinea pigs is reached at 3 months of age.

FIGURE 44.4 Young guinea pigs are weaned at 3 to 4 weeks of age.

Preventive Health Care

Routine vaccinations are not required for guinea pigs, but an annual veterinary checkup is highly recommended. The nails of guinea pigs should be trimmed monthly (or more frequently if needed), and the haircoat should be brushed at least twice weekly (longhair varieties more frequently). Monitor your pet's teeth monthly for any apparent overgrowth. If detected, contact your veterinarian. Fleas can be controlled by spot-treating with safe, topical products designed for puppies and kittens.

Guinea pigs can be prolific breeders, so many owners opt to have their pets neutered to prevent their households from becoming over-populated with these cute creatures!

Strict sanitation, environmental control, and high-quality rations, including vitamin C supplements, must be given top priority in order to prevent disease in guinea pigs. Always keep a close eye on your pet's behavior, eating habits, elimination habits, and physical characteristics. Notify your veterinarian of any changes. Care should be taken to prevent obesity, which can have the same deleterious effects in guinea pigs as it does in humans. And be sure to offer your pet a liberal dose of attention each day to cater to its mental and emotional health.

FACT *OR* **FICTION**

A guinea pig that rubs its rump on the ground has worms. **FICTION.** In reality, it is just marking its territory!

Diseases and Disorders of Guinea Pigs

Table 44.1 shows selected diseases and disorders seen in guinea pigs. Stress, overcrowding, improper nutrition, and poor sanitation all play important roles in the development of many diseases, especially the infectious ones.

DID YOU KNOW?

The same *Bordetella* organism that causes kennel cough in dogs can cause life-threatening disease in guinea pigs. As a result, it is always a good idea to have a *Bordetella* vaccine administered to any dog or cat living in the same house as a guinea pig.

Table 44.1 Diseases and Disorders of Guinea Pigs

Disease or disorder	Clinical signs	Treatment and comments
Infectious diseases		
Salmonellosis	Weight loss; conjunctivitis, diarrhea	Often transmitted via contaminated food (greens); treat with antibiotics; good sanitation; wash greens prior to feeding
Streptococcosis	Enlarged lymph nodes ("lumps"); variable signs and organ involvement; breathing difficulties	Treat with antibiotics
Bordetella bronchiseptica	Nasal discharge; breathing difficulties	Same organism that causes canine cough; treat with antibiotics
Lymphocytic choriomeningitis virus	Poor growth; eye discharge; locomotion difficulties; seizures; breathing difficulties	Transmitted by wild rodents; no treatment available; zoonotic disease
Adenovirus	Breathing difficulties; nasal discharge; weight loss	No treatment available
Inclusion conjunctivitis	Eye crusting, discharge in young guinea pigs; swollen eyelids	Treat with topical eye ointments; will usually clear up without intervention
Digestive system diseases		
Malocclusion of teeth ("slobbers")	Excessive salivation; inability to eat; weight loss	Usually involves premolars and molars; causes include nutritional deficiencies, genetics; file down overgrown teeth—repeat every 3 weeks

Table 44.1 Diseases and Disorders of Guinea Pigs (*Continued*)

Disease or disorder	Clinical signs	Treatment and comments
Hairballs	Loss of appetite; abdominal pain; palpable mass within abdomen	Surgical removal necessary
Coccidiosis	Abdominal pain and distension; loss of appetite; diarrhea; weight loss	Associated with poor sanitary conditions; treat with sulfa drugs
Bacterial enteritis	Diarrhea; weight loss; abdominal pain	Associated with poor sanitary conditions; also can be associated with improper antibiotic therapy; treat using a select group of antimicrobial agents
Hemorrhagic syndrome	Jaundice; diarrhea; blood clotting problems	Seen in pregnant pigs; caused by uterus disrupting liver function; treat by C-section;* vitamin K therapy
Skin diseases		
Pododermatitis	Moist, ulcerated skin lesions on feet	Caused by trauma from wire floors, environmental filth; treat with antibiotics; change environmental conditions
Hair loss	Can occur anywhere on the body	Causes can include skin parasites, chewing ("barbering"), fighting, pregnancy, ringworm
Ringworm	Hair loss; crusts on head, ears, back	Treat with antifungal medications

Table 44.1 Diseases and Disorders of Guinea Pigs (*Continued*)

Disease or disorder	Clinical signs	Treatment and comments
Mange (mites)	Intense itching; hair loss on face, ears; seizures	Very contagious to other pigs; treat with safe insecticidal shampoo or dip
Fleas, ticks, lice	Itching; hair loss; anemia	Treatment with pyrethrin spray
Reproductive disease		
Pregnancy toxemia	Loss of appetite; depression; seizures; breathing difficulties in pregnant or lactating pigs	Obesity, genetics, stress, fasting can play a role; treat with dextrose
Urinary diseases		
Urethral obstruction	Inability to urinate; painful abdomen; irritable behavior; blood-tinged urine	Seen in older males; obstruction must be manually removed
Kidney disease	Weight loss; loss of appetite; variable clinical signs	Common in older pigs; treatment generally unrewarding
Nervous system diseases		
Hind-end paralysis	Inability to walk and support weight on hind legs	Often due to spinal fracture or spinal cord damage secondary to pregnancy, vitamin C deficiency, arthritis; treatment depends on severity

Table 44.1 Diseases and Disorders of Guinea Pigs (*Continued*)

Disease or disorder	Clinical signs	Treatment and comments
Musculoskeletal diseases		
Hind-leg fractures	Inability to bear weight on hind leg; dragging leg	Caused by foot getting caught in flooring of wire cage, other trauma; treatment depends on severity
Myopathy	Reluctance to move; depression	Due to vitamin E deficiency; treat with vitamin E supplements
"Stiff wrist" syndrome	Bone deformities; muscular stiffness; abnormal posture	Due to magnesium deficiency; treat by correcting ration

*Cesarean section.

If your guinea pig shows signs of illness, do not give it any medications unless prescribed by your veterinarian. For instance, antibiotic preparations containing penicillin or erythromycin can be deadly if given to guinea pigs.

Remember that with the appearance of any clinical signs, a definitive diagnosis should be made by a qualified veterinarian. Identifying and treating diseases in their early stages is the key to successful treatment and cure. Sick guinea pigs are fragile creatures, and require prompt veterinary attention.

CHAPTER 45

Hamsters and Gerbils

The most popular species of pet hamster is by far the golden (Syrian) hamster (*Mesocricetus auratus*). Its smaller cousin, the Chinese (striped-back) hamster (*Cricetus griseus*), is probably next in popularity. Hamsters are native to both the European and Asian continents. They are larger than gerbils and lack tails. Depending on the variety, hamsters can sport either a long or a short haircoat, and come in variety of colors, including brown, cinnamon, white, and blends thereof.

Hamsters can be fun and loving pets, providing hours of enjoyment and fascination just watching their busy activity. Notorious escape artists, hamsters are most active at night (sometimes to the dismay of their owners!) and like to sleep during the day. The average lifespan of a hamster in captivity is approximately 2 years.

Gerbils can be differentiated from hamsters by their smaller size and by the presence of a hairy tail. The presence of hair on the tail can also be used to differentiate gerbils from mice, which have hairless tails. The Mongolian gerbil, *Meriones unguiculatus,* is by far the most popular type. It is native to the deserts of Mongolia and China. Because of their origin, gerbils possess many unique features, including a very low daily water requirement. Like camels, gerbils can regulate water reserves within their bodies quite efficiently, and can go for days without water (Fig. 45.1)! Gerbils tend to be friendlier than hamsters, rarely biting the hand that feeds them. They are curious creatures, yet rarely try to escape. Unlike hamsters, they enjoy daytime as well as nighttime activity. Gerbils that are well cared for can live 4 years or more in captivity.

FIGURE 45.1 One unique feature of the gerbil is that it has a very low daily water requirement.

Restraint

When handling or restraining hamsters, use caution because some may have a tendency to bite. Grasp the skin over the shoulder and neck region with the thumb and first two fingers of one hand and support the body with the other hand. For restraining hamsters that are known biters (this includes sick hamsters), be sure to grasp as much skin as you can.

Gerbils are much easier to handle than hamsters because of their friendly and gentle dispositions. Most will climb right into an open hand; others might need to be restrained similar to mice (see Fig. 45.2). Never pick up a gerbil by its tail. If you do, the skin covering the tail could come off in your hand, leaving your rodent friend in an unhealthy predicament!

DID YOU KNOW?

During winter months, hamsters might become lethargic and appear ill (or even dead) if environmental temperatures drop to below 50 degrees Fahrenheit. But don't fret! These hamsters are only thinking about hibernating, and a little warmth and rousing will soon bring them back to life!

Housing

Hamsters, especially females, should be housed individually, owing to their somewhat belligerent behavior toward cagemates. Adult gerbils placed in a cage together for the first time may fight as well. However, gerbils that were raised together for the first 2 months of life will coexist quite comfortably within the same enclosure (Fig. 45.3).

FIGURE 45.2 When picking up a gerbil by the tail, be sure to grasp it at the base—instead of the end—of the tail.

Housing accommodations for hamsters and gerbils can be readily purchased from a local pet store or pet supplier. Well-ventilated wire or plastic cages with solid flooring are preferred. For hamsters, setups containing divided compartments connected with tunnels work well also. Cages with wire mesh flooring should be avoided because they can be hard on the feet and, in the case of gerbils, be a source of

FIGURE 45.3 Gerbils are happiest when kept in pairs.

tail injuries. Finally, hamsters are notorious escape artists, so be certain that all cage outlets are secured at all times!

Aspen shavings or commercial rodent bedding can be used to line the bottom of the cage and help absorb waste material. This bedding should be changed at least twice weekly. Cedar shavings should not be used, as the oils contained in cedar can be irritating to the skin and

FIGURE 45.4 All small rodents should be provided with an exercise wheel to help keep them fit and trim!

mucous membranes of rodents. Be sure to also provide nesting material consisting of shredded tissue or cotton.

Exercise wheels, toys, and makeshift huts or sleeping quarters should be installed for your pet's enjoyment (Fig. 45.4). When choosing a wheel for gerbils, select one constructed of plastic. Avoid metal wheels with spokes, since these can cause serious injuries to tails if they become intertwined in them.

Both hamsters and gerbils should be provided with 12 hours of light and 12 hours of darkness each day. Environmental temperatures should be kept around 70 degrees Fahrenheit for maximum comfort. Humidity should not exceed 50 percent.

Nutrition

Rations for a hamster or gerbil should consist of commercial rodent pellets with a few treats such as sprouts, fruits (avoid oranges) such as raisins, or nuts thrown in for good measure. Seeds can be offered as treats as well, but only in limited quantities. Some pets will prefer to eat the seeds over their regular ration, leading to nutritional imbalances and obesity. At the same time, be careful not to overfeed regular rations. Obesity causes the same ill effects in these small animals as it does in larger ones. Hamsters are notorious for gathering and storing food, which may trick you into thinking that you aren't feeding enough.

Food dispensers can be attached directly to the side of the cage. This method of food delivery is much more sanitary than simply placing a food bowl on the floor of the cage. Water sippers can also be attached to the side of the cage. Just be sure that both food and water are within easy reach and that the delivery end of the water sipper remains patent. Many hamsters and gerbils die each year because food and water sources are innocently placed out of reach or are inefficient at delivering their products!

Natural wood blocks or sticks for chewing should be placed in the enclosure as well to help keep the incisors worn down and healthy.

Reproduction

Male hamsters can be differentiated from females by the presence of two dark, pigmented spots on the hip regions. These identify the location of hip glands used for marking territory and attracting females.

Female hamsters experience a heat cycle every 4 days. Toward the end of her heat period, a white discharge might be seen coming from the vagina. This is normal and should not be mistaken for an infection. Male hamsters should be introduced into the cage at this time.

Because it could take a few days for the female to become adjusted to the male, watch for aggressiveness on her part, and remove the male immediately if it occurs. Reintroduce him the next day, following the same precautions.

Once breeding takes place, the gestation period is approximately 18 days. Litter size normally ranges from 6 to 10 pups. They are born hairless and blind. Although not common, cannibalism of offspring by young females has been known to occur if the new mother becomes disturbed during the first week after giving birth. This can be aggravated by owners handling the young during the first week of life, improper nesting material, cage cleanings, and difficult access to food and water. As a result, be sure to leave mom alone and undisturbed with her pups for the first week, except, of course, to provide her with food and water. Hamster pups reach weaning age in 3 to 4 weeks and should be removed to their own housing at that time. Puberty is achieved at 8 weeks of age.

The breeding habits of gerbils are similar to those of hamsters. Interestingly, male and female breeding pairs form strong bonds that can last a lifetime. Male gerbils can be differentiated from females by the distance between the anal opening and the genital opening; the distance for the male is much longer.

Females undergo a heat period every 4 to 5 days, and once bred, they experience a gestation period of approximately 24 days. Litter sizes usually range from four to five pups, which, like hamsters, are born hairless, blind, and helpless. A full coat of hair is usually in place by day 10, and the eyes open around day 18.

Cannibalism is not as serious a problem in gerbils as in hamsters. However, it can occur if she becomes stressed or ill. Pups are weaned at 21 to 24 days, and will reach sexual maturity themselves at about 12 weeks of age.

Preventive Health Care

FIGURE 45.5 Stress, improper nutrition, and poor sanitation play important roles in the development of disease in hamsters and gerbils.

Strict sanitation, environmental control, and high-quality rations must be given top priority in order to prevent disease (Fig. 45.5). Keep a close eye on your pet's behavior, and its eating habits, elimination habits, and physical characteristics. The teeth should be examined monthly for overgrowth. Also, the appearance of an unkempt haircoat should alert you to a potential health problem. Notify your veterinarian of this or any other noticeable changes. (*Note:* Remember that hamsters kept in cold temperatures might undergo behavioral changes and appear lethargic or lifeless. Increasing the environmental temperature will restore these hamsters to normal behavior and activity.)

Diseases and Disorders of Hamsters and Gerbils

The following are some selected diseases and disorders seen in hamsters and gerbils. Sick hamsters are generally very irritable and can bite! Stress, improper nutrition, and poor sanitation play important roles in the development of many diseases, especially infectious diseases. Remember that with the appearance of any clinical signs, a definitive diagnosis should be made by a qualified veterinarian. Identifying and treating diseases in their early stages is the key to successful treatment and cure (Tables 45.1 and 45.2).

DID YOU KNOW?

Gerbils that are frightened or stressed might exhibit spontaneous epileptic seizures. This tendency for seizure is an inherited trait seen in some strains of gerbils, but don't be alarmed if this happens to your pet. The convulsions will subside on their own, and they require no specific management.

Table 45.1 Diseases and Disorders of Hamsters

Disease or disorder	Clinical signs	Treatment and comments
	Digestive system diseases	
Malocclusion of incisor teeth	Excessive salivation; inability to eat; weight loss; nasal discharge	Trim incisors every 8–12 weeks as needed
Salmonellosis	Weight loss; diarrhea; variable signs and organ involvement	Often transmitted via contaminated food (greens); treatment rarely helpful
"Wet tail"	Weight loss; diarrhea; ruffled fur; dehydration; rectal prolapse	Can be rapidly fatal; treat with antibiotics and fluids to correct dehydration
Antibiotic-induced colitis	Severe diarrhea, dehydration, death	Bacterial overgrowth in intestines caused by improper selection of antibiotic
Tapeworms	Weight loss; poor appetite; diarrhea	Rarely causes severe disease; treat with anti-tapeworm medication

Table 45.1 Diseases and Disorders of Hamsters (*Continued*)

Disease or disorder	Clinical signs	Treatment and comments
Skin diseases		
Streptococcosis, staphylococcosis	Enlarged lymph nodes, abscesses	Often secondary to fight wounds; treat with antibiotics; lance
Mange (mites)	Hair loss, scaling, especially along back and face	Often appears secondary to other diseases; treat with insecticidal products as in cats
Musculoskeletal diseases		
Cage paralysis	Weakness; inability to move or lift head	Caused by nutritional deficiency; treat with vitamin supplementation
Other diseases		
Neoplasia	Variable signs, depending on organ systems involved; weight loss; loss of appetite	Tumors are not uncommon in hamsters; often affect glands within the body; treatment depends on organ system involved
Amyloidosis	Weight loss, dehydration, loss of appetite	Causes kidney failure in affected hamsters; common disease

Table 45.2 Diseases and Disorders of Gerbils

Disease or disorder	Clinical signs	Treatment and comments
Digestive system diseases		
Malocclusion of incisor teeth	Depression; inability to eat; weight loss	Trim incisors every 8–12 weeks as needed
Tyzzer's disease ("wet tail")	Weight loss; diarrhea; ruffled fur; dehydration	Can be rapidly fatal; treatment generally unrewarding once signs appear
Salmonellosis	Weight loss; diarrhea; ruffled fur; dehydration	Treatment is generally unrewarding
Skin diseases		
Mange (*Demodex*)	Hair loss, scaling, especially at base of tail and rear legs	Often appears secondary to other diseases; treat with acaricides as in cats
Dermatitis	Moist skin lesions, abscesses; hair loss, abrasions on nose	Usually secondary to poor husbandry and sanitation; self-induced trauma; parasites; antibiotics might be needed for secondary bacterial infections
Respiratory system diseases		
Upper respiratory infection and pneumonia	Sneezing; breathing difficulties; chattering; conjunctivitis	Often caused by stress and poor husbandry; treat with appropriate antibiotics

Table 45.2 Diseases and Disorders of Gerbils (*Continued*)

Disease or disorder	Clinical signs	Treatment and comments
Urinary system diseases		
Kidney disease	Weight loss; increased water consumption; increased urination	Common in older gerbils; no effective treatment
Nervous system diseases		
Epilepsy	Spontaneous seizures	Certain strains of gerbils highly susceptible; no treatment necessary
Other diseases		
Neoplasia	Variable signs, depending on organ systems involved; weight loss; loss of appetite	Tumors are not uncommon in older gerbils; treatment depends on organ system involved

Mice and Rats

Although more popular as laboratory research animals, mice and rats are occasionally kept as pets. They are relatively easy to care for, and most have gentle dispositions, making them easy to handle. The mouse, *Mus musculus,* and the rat, *Rattus norvegicus,* originated from the Asian continent, but soon spread with man throughout the world. They are both nocturnal creatures, becoming most active during the twilight hours. However, some mice may choose to be quite active during the day as well. Both have hairless tails, a fact that helps differentiate the mouse from its rodent cousin, the gerbil. While most pet rats are pure white or white with black or brown "hoods," pet mice can be found in a variety of colors, including white, black, brown, and tan. The captive life span for mice and rats is around 2 to 4 years.

Restraint

Mice and rats are usually quite gentle and can be handled without much trouble. Feistier pets can be picked up and restrained by grasping the base of the tail with one hand and, as you lift, encircling the back and ribcage with the other hand. For mice, you can also use your thumb and index finger to grasp the scruff of the neck. Be ready: Most rodents will urinate and/or defecate when handled (Fig. 46.1).

FIGURE 46.1 Restrain a mouse by grasping the scruff of the neck and the base of the tail.

Dr. P's Vet Tip

When handling a belligerent rodent, use a paper towel or cloth to protect your hands as you grasp the neck region. In this way, if the rodent turns its head to bite, it won't be able to reach your fingers.

Housing

Mice and rats can be housed in any type of cage or container, provided there is enough room to maintain good sanitary conditions and to allow for an exercise wheel, nesting area, and feeding area. Mice tend to be escape artists, so the enclosure must be secure. Rats are social creatures and can be kept together, regardless of sex, with minimal hostilities (Fig. 46.2). Male and female mice usually can be housed together, but male mice should not be housed together because of their tendency to fight.

You can buy wire-mesh rodent cages for your pet mouse or rat at your favorite pet store. A 5- to 10-gallon aquarium-type enclosure with a wire-screened top can be used as well. Smooth plastic or metal floors are preferred over wire mesh, as the latter can pose hazards to both feet and tails. The floor of the cage should be lined with 2 to 3 inches of aspen shavings or commercial bedding. This bedding should be changed at least twice weekly to maintain good sanitation. Nesting material offered can consist of facial tissue, pieces of cloth, or cardboard.

DID YOU KNOW?

Cedar shavings should not be used as bedding for exotic pets, as the oils contained within the wood can be quite irritating to the skin and mucous membranes of these pets.

Exercise wheels, toys, and makeshift huts or sleeping quarters should be installed for your pet's enjoyment. When choosing a wheel for mice and rats, try to select one constructed of plastic. Avoid metal wheels with spokes, since they can cause serious injuries to tails that become intertwined.

Ideally, the temperature of the room in which you house your rodent should be kept between 70 and 75 degrees Fahrenheit, with a

FIGURE 46.2 Rats are social creatures and often enjoy human interaction.

humidity of around 55 to 60 percent. Twelve hours of both light and darkness should be provided daily.

Nutrition

Rations for mice and rats should consist of commercial rodent pellets with a few vegetables or fruit pieces added. However, these treats should not exceed 5 percent of the total daily ration. Some mice and rats may prefer the treats over the regular ration, leading to nutritional imbalances. At the same time, be careful not to overfeed regular rations, since obesity causes the same ill effects in these small animals as it does in larger ones.

The average mouse will consume about 3 to 4 grams of food per day; rats will consume 10 to 20 grams. Dispensers that hang suspended from the side of the cage can be used to deliver water and food. This method of delivery is much more sanitary than simply placing a food or water bowl on the floor of the cage.

Be sure the sources of food and water are easily reachable and that the delivery end of the water sipper remains accessible. Failure to heed this advice could lead to death from starvation or dehydration, especially in small or weak animals.

Natural wood blocks or sticks for chewing should be placed in the enclosure as well to help keep the incisors worn down and healthy.

Reproduction

Male mice and rats can be differentiated from females on the basis of their external genitalia and by the distance between the anal and genital openings (longer in males). Female mice and rats experience a heat cycle every 4 to 6 days. Once they have been bred, the gestation period is approximately 21 days. Litter size normally ranges from six to twelve. Baby mice and rats, like other rodents, are born hairless and blind. New litters should not be disturbed for at least 3 days after birth. Weaning occurs at 3 to 4 weeks, with the young reaching sexual maturity close to 2 months of age.

Preventive Health Care

Strict sanitation, environmental control, and high-quality rations must be given top priority in order to prevent disease in mice and rats. Monitor behavior, eating habits, elimination habits, and physical characteristics closely and notify your veterinarian of any noticeable changes.

Diseases and Disorders of Mice and Rats

The following are some selected diseases and disorders seen in mice and rats. Stress, overcrowding, improper nutrition, and poor sanitation play important roles in the development of many diseases, especially infectious diseases. Exposure to insects, wild rodents, and other animals can lead to disease transmission to your rodent as well. Remember that with the appearance of any clinical signs, including changes in activity levels, food or water consumption, or character of droppings, a definitive diagnosis should be made by a qualified veterinarian. Identifying and treating diseases in their early stages is the key to successful treatment and cure (Table 46.1).

Table 46.1 Diseases and Disorders of Mice and Rats

Disease or disorder	Clinical signs	Treatment and comments
	Infectious diseases	
Bacterial infections	Enlarged lymph nodes; abscesses; breathing difficulties; conjunctivitis; weight loss; loss of appetite	Treat with antibiotics; lance abscesses

Table 46.1 Diseases and Disorders of Mice and Rats (*Continued*)

Disease or disorder	Clinical signs	Treatment and comments
Infectious diseases		
Sialodacryoadenitis	Swelling in neck region due to inflamed salivary glands	Seen in rats; caused by virus; antibiotics for secondary infections
Pox virus	Sloughing of tail and/or digits of feet	No treatment available
Skin diseases		
Ringtail syndrome	Ulcerated lesion at base of tail	Seen in mice; caused by low humidity; treat by maintaining humidity at 50%
Traumatic wounds	Sores and wounds on ear pinnae and tail	Usually caused by fighting between males; treat by separating males
Mange	Hair loss, scratching especially around head and ears	Seen primarily in mice; treat with pyrethrin insecticide
Ringworm	Hair loss; scaliness	Treat with antifungal medications
Mammary tumor	Lumps; ulcerated tissue in mammary region of females	Must be surgically removed
Respiratory diseases		
Upper respiratory disease and pneumonia	Sneezing; chattering; nasal discharge; breathing difficulty; depression; eye discharge	Can be viral or bacterial in origin; treat with antibiotics; occasional sneezing may occur in healthy rats

Table 46.1 Diseases and Disorders of Mice and Rats (*Continued*)

Disease or disorder	Clinical signs	Treatment and comments
Gastrointestinal diseases		
Enteritis	Diarrhea; rectal prolapse	Pinworms, protozoal organisms, bacteria can all cause; treat according to source
Nervous system diseases		
Vestibular syndrome	Head tilt; circling	Often seen secondary to respiratory infections; treat with antibiotics

Chinchillas

Chinchillas (*Chinchilla lanigera; Chinchilla brevicaudata*) are members of the rodent family and close relatives of the guinea pig. These fascinating creatures boast compact bodies; squirrellike tails; large, batlike eyes; pronounced, thin, erect ears; and, of course, the famous thick, soft, velvety haircoats. Chinchillas were once native to the high, rocky slopes of the Andes Mountains, stretching from Peru to the tip of Chile. The Chincha Indians inhabiting these slopes valued the chinchilla's fur as clothing for protection against the bitter Andean cold. As Spanish influence spread across the South American continent, chinchilla fur soon became a valuable export item to Europe. As a result, chinchillas were harvested to near extinction up to the early part of the twentieth century. Today, Chile is the only country still harboring a native population of chinchillas, which is under government protection. Chinchillas first began to appear in the United States in the early 1900s, where they were and are bred and raised commercially for their valuable fur.

As the demand for natural fur declines in the United States, more and more chinchillas are finding

DID YOU KNOW?

Because their auditory apparatus is very similar to that of humans, chinchillas are popular laboratory models for hearing studies in people.

their way into homes as pets. As a rule, they are clean creatures and harbor little odor. Fun, active, and full of personality, they love to interact with people they know and trust. Chinchillas enjoy being petted and scratched and often emit a soft cooing sound when such attention is afforded them. Their long, heavily muscled hind legs enable them to sit up on their haunches while nibbling on a morsel, and hop around like a kangaroo when the feeling arises! Their acute sense of hearing can cause them to become easily frightened or startled when they are confronted with loud noises or high-pitched sounds. When frightened, a chinchilla may let out a cry and scurry for cover. In fact, if the fright turns into anger, this cry could actually turn into a surprisingly belligerent bark or growl.

The standard chinchilla is blue-gray to dark gray in color, although mutant color variations do exist. These include charcoal, black, brown, beige, and white. Chinchillas weigh in at approximately 400 to 800 grams (with females often weighing more than males) and average about 14 inches in length from head to tail. Their lifespan in captivity averages 10 years, although there have been reports of some living to be 20!

Restraint

Chinchillas are fairly easy to handle and require no special restraint techniques. They rarely bite when handled gently; however, they have been known to nip at a finger when frightened or startled. When picking up a chinchilla, grasp it gently at the base of the tail with one hand and scoop up the body under the belly using the other hand (Fig. 47.1). Chinchillas that are handled roughly can "slip" their fur, leaving large tufts of hair in the hands of the handler. This is a natural defense mechanism designed to leave potential predators with mouthfuls of hair!

Housing

When selecting living quarters for your chinchilla, keep in mind the dry, cool climate from where your friend originated. Ideal environmental temperature for chinchillas is between 55 and 65 degrees Fahrenheit. Temperatures can drop to as low as 32 degrees Fahrenheit for short periods of time without ill effects as long as the humidity

FIGURE 47.1 Method of restraint for chinchillas.

is kept low and the room is draft-free. Environmental humidity should be kept at 40 percent or lower. A humidity gauge attached to your pet's enclosure can help ensure that this requirement is being met.

Select a relatively remote, peaceful location within the home in which to place the cage. Since chinchillas are nocturnal creatures, distance the cage far enough from your family's sleeping quarters so as not to be disturbed by your chinchilla's nighttime activities.

Chinchillas need lots of room to move and roam in, so select a spacious enclosure. To prevent destruction due to chewing, your pet's cage should be constructed of metal instead of wood. Chinchillas love to climb. Providing multilevel cages or shelving within a single cage would make your chinchilla extremely happy (Fig. 47.2)! The smooth flooring of the cage can be lined

DR. P'S VET TIP

Chinchillas require lower environmental temperatures than do most other rodents, a factor that must be taken into account during hot summer months. Keep your chinchilla's cage in a portion of your home that can be closed off easily and kept well air-conditioned.

FIGURE 47.2 Because Chinchillas love to climb, multilevel caging makes them extremely happy!

with aspen shavings or commercial rodent bedding. Cedar chips should not be used, as these can irritate the respiratory tract of rodents. Change this bedding at least twice per week to maintain proper sanitation. If you plan on owning more than one chinchilla, they need to be housed separately, as chinchillas housed together within a confined space (especially two males) can become quite bellicose to one another.

Provide your chinchilla with plenty of places in which to hide and burrow. Wooden hide boxes, ceramic enclosures, or a 4- to 6-inch portion of PVC (polyvinyl chloride) pipe work great. Even better, an actual arrangement of smooth-edged rocks can be configured within the cage to create crevices and hiding places that simulate your chinchilla's natural habitat. Obviously, make sure that the rocks are firmly seated and secured to prevent accidental injury to your pet from falling rocks.

Another important accessory you'll want to provide your unique friend on occasion is a dust bath. In the wild, chinchillas clean their coats by rolling or dusting in volcanic ash found along the mountain slopes. The purpose of such behavior is to rid their special coat of excess oils. Captive chinchillas also need to roll in dust for the same reason. An 8×10-inch pan or dust bin with edges high enough to prevent dust from flying out yet low enough to allow the chinchilla to easily enter is ideal. Fill the pan with 2 to 3 inches of sanitized chinchilla dust purchased from a pet store. This finely granulated dust is the closest you will come to mimicking volcanic ash. Some experts use a home mixture consisting of 9 parts silver sand and 1 part fuller's earth. Just know that regular sand or dirt won't do the trick .

Offer your chinchilla its dust bath three times per week. Leave the bath in the cage for 1 to 2 hours, then remove it. Dust baths should never be left as permanent fixtures within cages not only for sanitary purposes but also because overbathing can lead to eye irritation. Dust can be reused if it is free from fecal or urine contamination when removed from the cage. Because chinchillas are creatures of habit, offer their dust baths on set schedules each week.

Both hay racks and water delivery systems should be mounted on the sides of the cage and kept off the floor. Be sure to verify the patency of such devices on a daily basis. The entire cage should be thoroughly cleaned and sanitized weekly.

Nutrition

In the wild, the chinchilla's natural diet consisted of grasses, shrubs, roots, and the occasional berry. Fortunately, special food pellets designed for chinchillas are commercially available and make feeding a balanced diet quite easy. It should be noted that chinchillas like to grasp food pellets with their forepaws and eat from their hands. As a result, the size of the pellet offered is important. Short-pelleted foods are difficult for the average chinchilla to handle, and will lead to malnourishment.

Pellets should be offered in a sturdy, hard plastic, metal, or ceramic food dish. Feed your chinchilla approximately $1/2$ ounce of pellets in the morning and again in the evening. In addition to pellets, you can supplement your pet's diet with nuts, raisins, or dried cherries. However, such supplementation should not exceed 15 percent of your chinchilla's daily dietary intake.

Because their digestive tracts are designed to ferment foodstuff in the lower portion of the bowel, chinchillas require a good source of dietary fiber. For those kept as pets, hay provides the best source of this nutrient. The average chinchilla will consume up to one cup of hay per day. Chinchillas that are not provided adequate dietary fiber will develop potentially life-threatening enteritis. Hay racks should be hung from the sides of the cage and kept full at all times to help prevent such a problem.

Finally, because a chinchilla's teeth are in a constant growth mode, provide a hardwood chew block and/or tree branches (e.g., elm, maple, birch, apple, pear, peach) to help keep the teeth worn down properly and to satisfy the chinchilla's desire to chew. Avoid branches from trees such as cedar, redwood, cherry, and oleander, as these can be poisonous.

Reproduction

The age at which chinchillas reach puberty depends on the time of year they were born. For example, chinchillas born in spring will often reach puberty 4 to 6 months later, whereas those born in the fall months can take up to a year to reach sexual maturity. Breeding season runs between November and May each year. Females cycle every 6 to 7 weeks during this time.

When introducing male and female chinchillas to each other, always supervise the initial interaction. Females that feel uncomfortable with a potential mate can become aggressive and do much harm to him. This is especially true when a younger male is paired with an older female.

Gestation for chinchillas lasts an average of 111 days. A small nesting box containing straw may be offered to the pregnant female nearing parturition. However, when the time comes, she may simply choose to give birth directly on the floor bedding. The average litter size is two, although litters of up to five have been known to occur. Birth usually occurs in the morning hours. Newborn kits are born fully furred, with eyes and ears functional, and a full complement of teeth. Chinchilla kits are usually eating pellets as early as 7 days of age, although full weaning won't occur until 3 to 5 weeks of age. Note that once parturition has taken place, the female chinchilla will enter into heat again several days later.

Preventive Health Care

As with guinea pigs, routine vaccinations are not required for chinchillas, yet a routine annual visit to your veterinarian is highly recommended. Always pay attention to your pet's behavior, eating habits, elimination habits, and physical characteristics. Notify your veterinarian immediately of any changes. Obesity can be a problem in pet chinchillas, so monitor your pet's weight frequently.

As a rule, chinchillas are hardy creatures and rarely suffer health problems. Most unthriftiness and ill health seen are direct results of poor diet and poor housing conditions. Taking special care to ensure that these two husbandry factors are optimized is the best defense against illness or injury in chinchillas.

The chinchilla's soft, velvety haircoat requires little maintenance aside from its dust baths during the week. Weekly brushing using a soft cloth is also recommended to help remove any obvious dirt and shed hair from the coat. Your chinchilla will enjoy it as well!

Chinchillas enjoy exploring their environments with their mouths and will chew to maintain their long incisor teeth at proper length. As a result, don't allow your pet to roam the house unsupervised, as one encounter with an electrical cord or similar hazard could spell disaster.

As mentioned previously, chinchillas that don't receive adequate amounts of fiber in their diets are highly predisposed to serious digestive disturbances. Any abrupt changes in diet can also cause enteritis. If introducing a new food to your chinchilla, always do so gradually over several days. If diarrhea develops, contact your veterinarian immediately.

Hot, humid conditions can pose a definite health threat to chinchillas. The ideal environmental temperature for them is around 60 degrees Fahrenheit. Temperatures exceeding 85 degrees Fahrenheit can quickly lead to heat stroke.

Diseases and Disorders of Chinchillas

Table 47.1 shows selected diseases and disorders seen in chinchillas. If your chinchilla shows signs of illness, do not give it any medications unless prescribed by your veterinarian. Remember that with the appearance of any clinical signs, a qualified veterinarian should be allowed to make a definitive diagnosis. Identifying and treating diseases in their early stages is the key to successful treatment and cure.

Table 47.1 Diseases and Disorders of Chinchillas

Disease or disorder	Clinical signs	Treatment and comments
Bacterial enteritis	Diarrhea; listlessness; dehydration; rectal prolapse	Nonspecific, including antibiotics, fluid replacement, and increases in dietary fiber; often fatal condition; usually due to unsanitary living conditions, poor diets, or abrupt dietary changes
Pneumonia	Breathing difficulties; swollen neck; nasal discharge; depression	Treat with antibiotics and fluids; improve housing conditions, including ventilation and temperature
Fur chewing	Fur on lower portion of body short, "lion's mane" appearance (due to self-mutilation); moth-eaten appearance (barbering by cage mate)	Possible causes include boredom, poor nutrition, stress due to poor husbandry, heredity, hormonal disorders, and/or fungi; separate cage mates to prevent barbering; offer fatty acid and/or zinc supplements
Malocclusion (tooth overgrowth)	Drooling; weight loss; loss of appetite; crooked, curling teeth; runny eyes; bleeding from mouth	Trim teeth under sedation; allow access to chew blocks or other chewing material to help "file down" teeth

Table 47.1 Diseases and Disorders of Chinchillas (*Continued*)

Disease or disorder	Clinical signs	Treatment and comments
Paraphimosis (hair rings)	Male infertility; irritation and swelling of penis and prepuce due to hair wrapped around these structures	Manually remove ring using sterile lubricant; check for recurrence monthly
Heat prostration	Rapid, open-mouth breathing; extreme weakness	Immerse in cool water; seek veterinary care immediately; can occur when environmental temperatures exceed 80°F, especially with high humidity
Metal toxicity	Weakness; weight loss; seizures	Caused by excess consumption of lead and/or zinc; usually secondary to chewing on galvanized metal or objects containing lead
Abscesses	Swellings on or beneath skin	Surgical removal or drainage; treat with antibiotics; usually secondary to injuries or bite wounds
Bacterial encephalitis	Seizures; incoordination	Caused by poor sanitation or food contamination; poor prognosis, even with treatment with antibiotics

Table 47.1 Diseases and Disorders of Chinchillas (*Continued*)

Disease or disorder	Clinical signs	Treatment and comments
Ringworm	Hair loss, dermatitis	Oral antifungal drugs; antifungal agent added to dust bath
Bloat	Reluctance to move; recumbency; lethargy; loss of appetite	Decompress bloat using stomach tube; caused by overeating fruit or green feed; can also occur secondary to enteritis
Constipation	Straining; unable to defecate	Increase fiber in diet; administer laxative (i.e., mineral oil) to facilitate passage
Conjunctivitis	Red, irritated runny eyes	Caused by upper respiratory infection or irritation from dust; treat with antibiotics (oral and/or topical); reduce the number of dust baths offered each week

Prairie Dogs

Prairie dogs are members of the rodent family that once flourished across the western and southwestern portions of the United States. Each year, more and more of these unique, fun-loving creatures are finding their way into hearts and homes across the country as pets as their numbers in the wild decrease dramatically. In the wild, prairie dogs are viewed as pests by farmers and ranchers because they compete with livestock for food and dig holes and burrows that can make walking or running hazardous to livestock and horses. As a result, prairie dogs have been hunted and poisoned to the point where their numbers in the wild have decreased dramatically. In fact, the black-tailed prairie dog could become an endangered species, which could put their legality as pets in question (Fig. 48.1).

Four species of prairie dogs reside in the United States, including the Utah prairie dog, the white-tailed prairie dog, Gunnison's prairie dog, and the black-tailed prairie dog. Of the four, the black-tailed prairie dog (*Cynomys ludovicianus*) is the most popular choice as a pet. Whereas the other three varieties are native to the high plains, pastures, and mountainous slopes in and around the Rocky Mountains, the black-tailed prairie dog resides more in the lower plains and short grass prairies of the southwestern United States. As a result, it seems to adjust better to captivity than do the other three.

FIGURE 48.1 Labeled as pests and frequently exterminated by farmers and ranchers, an increasing number of prairie dogs are finding refuge as pets in homes across the country.

Depending on species, coat colors can range from red to brown to yellow buff, with all having black hairs interspersed throughout the coat. White patches on the tail and other coat patterns help distinguish one species from another. A close cousin of the squirrel, the prairie dog sports a stout body, relatively short legs, large black eyes, and small ears. The front paws possess remarkable dexterity and are used to grasp and hold food as it eats. Its short tail will flicker and flag if the prairie dog becomes agitated or threatened.

These unique creatures are diurnal in nature, being especially active in the early morning and late afternoon hours. Prairie dogs communicate with one another and with their owners through a series of chirps, chatters, yips, snarls, and squeals. Prairie dogs are social pets, and will often nudge noses with each other (or with their owners) as an outward sign of affection (Fig. 48.2). As far as their size is concerned, prairie dogs can grow to 15 inches in length and weigh up to 2 pounds when fully grown. When properly cared for, life span in captivity averages 8 years.

DID YOU KNOW?

Prairie dogs get their name from the shrill barking sound that they make when excited or alarmed.

Prior to purchasing one of these pets, be sure to contact your state's wildlife agency to be sure that it is legal to own a prairie dog in your particular state. Also,

FIGURE 48.2 Prairie dogs like to nudge noses as an outward sign of recognition and affection.

realize that wild prairie dogs have been known to harbor hantavirus and fleas that carry bubonic plague. As a result, always purchase your prairie dog from a rep-

Dr. P's Vet Tip

If you want to win your way into your prairie dog's heart, rub or scratch its belly!

utable source and be sure that it has been quarantined for at least 6 to 8 weeks before bringing it home.

Restraint

Prairie dogs that have been socialized to people possess sanguine personalities that make them relatively easy to handle. If a prairie dog has not been socialized or is acting nervous, roll it up in a towel with its head exposed before picking it up. This maneuver will not only protect you from being bitten but will also calm and relax your pet. An agitated prairie dog will emit a variety of sounds, including its characteristic "bark," and will flip its tail in annoyance. Wearing thick welder's gloves can also protect your hands against an overly aggressive prairie dog.

Housing

Because of their highly social nature, prairie dogs should ideally be kept in pairs rather than as solitary pets. When selecting housing for your prairie dog, keep in mind the natural habitat from where it came. Wild prairie dogs live in sophisticated underground tunnel systems.

As a result, the more you can simulate burrowing and tunneling conditions, the happier your prairie dog will be. Two or three large rodent or rabbit cages connected together via tunnels provide the ideal captive environment for prairie dogs. Also, your pet should have its own separate "apartment" somewhere within a cage into which it can retire if it so desires. Hay or aspen shavings deep enough for your pet to burrow should be supplied as well. Cedar chips should not be used, as these can irritate the respiratory tract of prairie dogs. Change this bedding at least twice per week to maintain proper sanitation.

The ideal environmental temperature at which to house your prairie dog is 70 degrees Fahrenheit. Although certain species of prairie dog that naturally live in the higher elevations hibernate during the cold, winter months, the black-tailed prairie dog does not. However, a decrease in activity may become apparent if your prairie dog is subjected to low environmental temperatures.

Nutrition

In the wild, prairie dogs eat grasses, cactus, shrubs, seeds, and the occasional insect. In captivity, prairie dogs should be offered a wide variety of food choices, including hay, alfalfa cubes, and commercial pellets formulated for squirrels and other rodents. Fruits can be offered as an occasional treat.

Both hay racks and water delivery systems should be mounted on the sides of the cage and kept off the floor. Be sure to verify the patency of water sippers on a daily basis. The entire cage should be thoroughly cleaned and sanitized weekly.

A hardwood chew block and/or tree branches (e.g., elm, maple, birch, apple, pear, peach) should be offered for your pet to chew on. These will help keep its incisors, which are in constant growth mode, worn down to proper length and prevent problems with overgrowth and malocclusion.

Reproduction

Prairie dogs will average one litter per year with a gestation lasting 27 to 33 days. Average litter size is five, with pups born blind, hairless, and helpless. However, they will begin to develop quite rapidly under their mother's nurturing care. Weaning takes place 3 to 6 weeks after birth. The average litter size is four. Young prairie dogs reach sexual maturity at 2 to 3 years of age.

Preventive Health Care

Routine vaccinations are not required for prairie dogs, but an annual veterinary checkup is highly recommended. Always pay attention to your pet's behavior, eating habits, elimination habits, and physical characteristics. Notify your veterinarian immediately of any changes. Obesity can be a problem in prairie dogs kept as pets, especially during the winter months, so monitor your pet's weight closely.

Most unthriftiness and ill health seen in prairie dogs is due to poor diet and/or living environment. Taking special care to ensure that these two husbandry factors are optimized is the best defense against illness or injury in prairie dogs.

Offer your prairie dog plenty of attention each day. And keep your pet's nails trimmed to keep them from getting snagged and to keep you from getting scratched!

Neutering your prairie dog can help reduce anxiety as well as prevent reproduction-related health disorders as your pet matures. If surgery is to be done, however, your pet must not be obese. Slimming down obese prairie dogs prior to surgery reduces anesthetic and surgical risks, and makes the procedures much easier to perform.

Diseases and Disorders of Prairie Dogs

Table 48.1 shows selected diseases and disorders seen in prairie dogs. If your prairie dog shows signs of illness, do not give it any medications unless prescribed by your veterinarian. Remember that with the appearance of any clinical signs, a qualified veterinarian should be allowed to make a definitive diagnosis. Identifying and treating diseases in their early stages is the key to successful treatment and cure.

Table 48.1 Diseases and Disorders of Prairie Dogs

Disease or disorder	Clinical signs	Treatment and comments
Dietary-induced enteritis	Diarrhea; listlessness; dehydration	Often caused by change in diet, poor-quality diet, lack of fiber, or overeating; bismuth subsalicylate, yogurt, and/or antibiotics used to treat; fluid replacement to correct dehydration
Coccidiosis	Diarrhea; listlessness; dehydration	Treat parasite with sulfa drug; improve sanitation
Pododermatitis	Lameness; ulcerated feet	Due to rough flooring and/or poor sanitation; improve both conditions; treat with antibiotics
Malocclusion	Drooling; weight loss; loss of appetite; sores surrounding mouth	Caused by overgrown or poorly aligned teeth; clip or file teeth as needed
Rhinitis	Sneezing; nasal discharge; breathing difficulties	Usually caused by allergies; foreign matter in nasal passages, tumors or dental disease; treat with antihistamines and/or antibiotics; nasal flush
Prepucial occlusion	Swollen, painful prepuce; prepucial discharge, urine leakage	Seen in intact males; caused by an accumulation of debris within the prepuce; treat by douching prepuce with chlorhexidine or tamed iodine; antibiotics if necessary; prevent with castration

Table 48.1 Diseases and Disorders of Prairie Dogs (*Continued*)

Disease or disorder	Clinical signs	Treatment and comments
Osteochondroma	Swelling involving bone	If extremity is involved, amputation of affected limb; otherwise poor prognosis
Cardiomyopathy (heart disease)	Breathing difficulties; lethargy; weight loss; loss of appetite	Often seen in obese prairie dogs; other causes thought to include poor nutrition, tooth infections, genetics; treat with special medications designed to ease workload on heart
Ringworm	Nonitchy, patchy hair loss; flaky skin	This fungus can be transmitted to people; treat in prairie dogs with medicated shampoos and rinses; oral antifungal agents if needed
Fleas	Itching; reddened skin; hair loss	Fleas carried by wild prairie dogs can be vectors for bubonic plague
Odontoma (dental tumor)	Excessive salivation; strong mouth odor; nasal discharge; breathing difficulties	These tumors carry with them a grave prognosis for recovery

Hedgehogs

While pocket pets come in all colors, shapes, and sizes, there are none as unique-looking as the hedgehog. Sporting elongated snouts and coats covered with short spines up to $3/4$ inch in length, these small creatures can make delightful pets! Harboring a sweet, gentle, and even somewhat shy personality, hedgies love to interact with people they know and trust.

Hedgehogs are found naturally across the European, Asian, and African continents. Two types are generally kept as pets, the European hedgehog (*Erinaceus*) and the African hedgehog (*Atelerix*). The European hedgehog is a highly favored resident of British gardens, where it serves to protect precious flowers and plants from insects. The African hedgehog, on the other hand, is the preferred pet within the United States. It should be noted that in certain areas throughout Europe and the United States, hedgehogs are protected by law. As a result, if you are contemplating the purchase of one of these cute pocket pets, be sure to check local laws and ordinances prior to bringing one home.

The short, sharp spines of the hedgehog extend all along its head and back (except to a small band on the head). In contrast, the muzzle, chest, stomach, and leg regions are covered with a fine, soft white hair.

In the wild, hedgehogs are found in a wide variety of colors, ranging from cream to black, with multiple variations in between. Those kept as pets will usually have a mixture of white and gray-brown spines, giving them a characteristic salt-and-pepper color. Some individuals may sport white spines exclusively, giving them a snowflake appearance. Adult African hedgehogs are 5 to 8 inches in length, weighing in at around 300 to 600 grams. European hedgehogs are 12 to 14 inches long and can weigh up to 1200 grams. The average lifespan of the captive hedgie is 3 to 8 years.

Hedgies are inherently curious animals, loving to lumber and waddle around and stick their noses into any new place they can find. As they are nocturnal creatures, pet hedgehogs will tend to sleep during the daylight hours and emerge at night to eat and play.

Restraint

Gentle restraint is needed with these sensitive pets. When feeling frightened or threatened, hedgies may struggle when handled or simply tuck their nose and legs in tightly against their bodies and roll up into a compact "ball of spines." As you can imagine, this provides formidable protection against any interaction. Although they rarely bite, a few hedgehogs may hiss or squeal. Hedgies that are properly socialized to people as infants will rarely display this behavior if approached slowly and handled gently.

> **Dr. P's Vet Tip**
>
> If your hedgehog rolls up into a ball, a gentle stroking against the grain of the spines along the rump will usually entice your pet to uncurl itself.

Gloves may be worn to protect your hands from the sharp spines (Fig. 49.1). When lifting your pet, encircle the shoulder and chest regions with one hand and support the hind end with the other hand. Be sure to control the hedgehog's hind feet and rump to prevent it from scratching you. Because the spines are indeed sharp, care must be taken to resist the temptation to drop one of these pets if a finger accidentally gets pricked.

FIGURE 49.1 A glove may be worn when handling your hedgehog to protect your hand against its sharp spines.

Housing

Housing for your hedgehog can consist of a wire cage or hutch with solid flooring, or a glass aquarium. If the latter is used, it must be at least 20-gallon capacity and have a wire covering to prevent escape and to provide open-air ventilation. Bedding can consist of commercial pelleted bedding, aspen shavings (avoid cedar), or hay. It should remain clean and dry; as a result, plan on changing it at least twice weekly. For multiple hedgie households, plan on housing individuals separately to prevent fighting.

Situate the cage in a warm room free from drafts. Ideal room temperature should be around 80 degrees Fahrenheit. European hedgehogs kept in captivity may go into hibernation if temperatures drop below 60 degrees Fahrenheit for any appreciable length of time. Keep your hedgehog's home out of direct

> **DR. P's VET TIP**
>
> Large travel carriers make good homes for pet hedgehogs, offering portability, good ventilation, and easy maintenance.

sunlight, as temperatures over 90 degrees Fahrenheit can predispose it to heat stroke. Also, hedgehogs don't care for bright lights or loud noises, so situate your pet's abode away from brightly lit areas and noisy activity centers within the home. Offer plenty of hiding places for your hedgehog to frequent. A piece of PVC (polyvinyl chloride) pipe, wooden box, or ceramic enclosure can be placed in the cage to provide such a hiding area. Your hedgehog will enjoy an exercise wheel as well. Commercial exercise wheels designed exclusively for hedgehogs should be used, as wire-spoked wheels designed for rodents can cause leg injuries.

Nutrition

The elongated nose of these spiny creatures harbors a keen sense of smell that assists the wild hedgehog in rooting out insects, spiders, worms, snails, and other tasty morsels. For pet hedgies, commercial diets are now available and should be used. Enlist the help of your veterinarian if you have trouble locating a source for such diets. Contrary to popular belief, cat food by itself does not provide a nutritionally balanced diet for hedgehogs. Feed once daily, preferably in the evening. Discard any uneaten food the next morning. You can also supplement your pet's diet with a teaspoon of banana, apple, boiled egg, and/or the occasional cricket or mealworm. However, to prevent obesity, supplement the diet no more than twice weekly. Avoid feeding snails or slugs, for these can harbor parasites that can be harmful to your hedgehog. Fresh water should be available at all times, preferably contained within a sipper bottle mounted to the side of the enclosure. If your hedgie won't use a sipper, a small, sturdy water dish can be used as a substitute.

Reproduction

The mating season for African hedgehogs occurs year-round. Juvenile hedgehogs will reach puberty usually before 9 months of age. Following mating, the length of gestation is 35 to 37 days. The average litter size is four. Baby hedgehogs are born deaf and blind, with eyes and ears becoming functional between 14 and 20 days of age. Care must be taken not to disturb females with litters, as stress can lead to cannibalism of newborn hedgies by the mother. Weaning takes place between 4 and 6 weeks of age.

Preventive Health Care

Routine vaccinations are not required for hedgehogs, but an annual veterinary checkup is highly recommended. Always pay attention to your pet's behavior, eating habits, elimination habits, and physical characteristics. Notify your veterinarian immediately of any changes. Obesity can be a problem in pet hedgehogs, so monitor your pet's weight frequently.

Most unthriftiness and ill health encountered in pet hedgehogs is a direct result of a poor diet and poor housing. Taking special care to ensure that these two husbandry factors are optimized is the best defense against illness or injury in hedgies.

Offer your hedgehog plenty of attention each day. A great way to do this is to gently groom your pet's spiny coat using a soft cloth or a soft bristle tooth brush. Doing so will not only keep the skin and coat healthy but will also help tighten the bond of friendship between you and your spiny friend. Also, keeping your hedgie's teeth cleaned and nails trimmed are two other husbandry methods that will increase your pet's quality of life.

Hedgehogs exhibit a unique behavior known as "anting" or "anointing." Anting is often seen when new objects are placed within a hedgehog's cage. The hedgehog will approach the object and begin to produce copious amounts of saliva, which it then spreads onto its skin and spiny coat. The exact reason for this unusual behavior is not known. Some experts feel that it might play a role in territorial marking or predator avoidance; others feel it may simply be the way an excited hedgehog says "hello" to a new object! Regardless, it is normal behavior and is no cause for alarm (Fig. 49.2).

Diseases and Disorders of Hedgehogs

Table 49.1 shows selected diseases and disorders seen in hedgehogs. If your hedgehog shows signs of illness, do not give it any medications

FIGURE 49.2 Normal "anting" behavior in a hedgehog.

unless prescribed by your veterinarian. Remember that with the appearance of any clinical signs, a qualified veterinarian should be allowed to make a definitive diagnosis. Identifying and treating diseases in their early stages is the key to successful treatment and cure. Sick hedgehogs are fragile creatures, and require prompt veterinary attention.

Table 49.1 Diseases and Disorders of Hedgehogs

Disease or disorder	Clinical signs	Treatment and comments
Bacterial or parasitic enteritis	Diarrhea; listlessness; dehydration	Antibiotics; antiparasitics, fluid replacement; improve sanitation
Obesity	Weight gain; listlessness; lameness	Evaluate diet; dietary portion control; eliminate "snacks"; pregnancy and neoplasia can cause weight gain as well

Table 49.1 Diseases and Disorders of Hedgehogs (*Continued*)

Disease or disorder	Clinical signs	Treatment and comments
Musculoskeletal disease	Lameness; reluctance to move	Arthritis, fractures, overgrown nails, foot infections, obesity are among common causes; treat according to cause; keep nails trimmed
Dental disease; gingivitis	Drooling; weight loss; loss of appetite	Have teeth professionally cleaned, followed by daily brushing at home; antibiotics as necessary; normal "anting" behavior will also cause drooling
Fatty liver syndrome	Diarrhea; weight loss; loss of appetite; sudden death	Decrease amount of fat in diet; supplement diet with B complex vitamins
Rhinitis; pneumonia	Sneezing; congestion; breathing difficulties	Can be bacterial, fungal, or viral in etiology; treat with appropriate antibiotics or antifungal agents; fluid therapy; oxygen therapy in severe cases
Neoplasia	Nodules or masses on or beneath skin; ulcerations; abdominal enlargement; foul breath; drooling; weight loss	Increased incidence of tumors in hedgehogs over 3 years of age; treat according to type of tumor

Table 49.1 Diseases and Disorders of Hedgehogs (*Continued*)

Disease or disorder	Clinical signs	Treatment and comments
Skin parasites	Broken quills; flaky skin; irritability	Identify parasite and treat with appropriate medication; improve environmental sanitation and parasite control
Hypothermia	Listlessness; loss of appetite; lameness	Seen when environmental temperatures drop below 50° F; treat by warming pet with towel wrap or place on covered heating pad (low setting); increase environmental temperature appropriately

Ferrets

Ferrets are popular as pets in the United States, with thousands of households obtaining one or more of these curious, rambunctious creatures each year. Ferrets belong to the same family as do minks, skunks, and weasels. Several different species exist, yet *Mustela putorius furo* represents the most common pet species. This particular ferret is a direct descendant of the European polecat.

For centuries, ferrets have been used by humans for a variety of tasks, including pest control and, more popularly, hunting. Only in the past century has their role as house pet been established. Insatiably curious, ferrets love to roam and explore their environment, especially tight-fitting nooks and crannies. They also can be quite playful and mischievous. Ferrets love to gather up items and store them in predetermined hiding places. They are smart animals, and can be leash-trained quite easily (Fig. 50.1).

Ferrets exist in a variety of color patterns, including (but not limited to) sable, albino, siamese, cinnamon, cream, and silver mitt. Many sport black faces, tails, and legs as well. Male

DID YOU KNOW❓

Ferrets are illegal to own or require ownership permits in many cities and states. Be sure to inquire about this prior to bringing one home.

ferrets reach weights of up to 6 pounds; females average 2 to 4 pounds. Weight increases are common during the fall and winter months as ferrets store up fat for the winter. This weight is usually lost when spring arrives. The life span of a ferret in captivity is 5 to 9 years.

FIGURE 50.1 Ferrets require plenty of daily exercise to allow them to expend their abundance of stored energy!

Restraint

Most ferrets are mild-mannered and can be handled with minimal restraint. One hand can be used to grasp the scruff of the neck or encircle the forequarters, pushing the forelegs together as the ferret is lifted from the cage or carrier. The other hand should support the hindquarters. Never lift a ferret solely by the scruff of its neck without supporting its hind end (Fig. 50.2). And never lift by its tail. Those are two good ways to injure your pet and/or get bitten!

Housing

Ferrets can be housed in any type of enclosure that allows them ample room to move about freely. You can house more than one ferret together, but be aware that males might fight with each other.

Wire cages of various sizes are readily available from most pet stores. Choose one with smooth flooring, as wire-mesh floor surfaces can be tough on ferret feet. The bottom of the cage can be lined with aspen shavings (no cedar) or commercial bedding material. A small box or hideaway constructed of plastic or wood can be placed in one corner of the cage to provide a place for recluse and sleep. Ferrets also love blankets or old cotton undershirts in which to cuddle up and hide.

Ferrets can be trained to use a litterbox. As a result, a litter pan or tray can be placed at one end of the cage to help maintain cleanliness. Be sure to change this litter at least twice weekly.

FIGURE 50.2 When lifting a ferret by its scruff, always support its hind end with your other hand.

For those ferrets kept exclusively in cages or pens, provide a daily exercise period to allow them to expend their abundance of stored energy. Offer plenty of safe toys to play with and play tunnels in which to explore.

Nutrition

Ferrets should be fed a commercial mink or ferret ration. Be sure the food you choose is not high in fiber because ferrets have difficulty digesting it. Fruits and vegetables should be offered as treats only sparingly, owing to their relatively high fiber content. Ferrets prefer six to eight meals throughout the day rather than one or two large meals. Water bowls should also be kept full at all times. Choose a water bowl weighted at the bottom to resist spilling. Also, because ferrets can develop hairballs, a feline hairball laxative should be administered to your ferret weekly.

Reproduction

Male ferrets are called *hobs*; females are referred to as *jills*. Sexual maturity for both occurs at approximately 8 to 10 months of age. The breeding season for ferrets runs from March to August, the time period in which the reproductive cycle of the jill is active.

Prior to breeding, place a wooden or plastic nesting box, complete with bedding material, within the cage or den. It should be large enough to allow the jill to move about freely and lie down comfortably. As jills come into heat, vulvular discharge and swelling will be noted. Female ferrets are induced ovulators; that is, the egg is ovulated only upon copulation. Hobs should be introduced to the jill only long enough for copulation to take place, and then they should be separated. Hobs and jills can inflict serious injury on one another if left together, and the former can even go so far as kill the offspring when they arrive.

The gestation period for ferrets is approximately 42 days. Litter size ranges from five to eight "kits." They are born blind and hairless. To prevent infant rejection or, worse yet, infanticide, try not to disturb or handle a jill and her box unnecessarily during the first 3 weeks after parturition except for cleaning and feeding purposes. Feline milk replacements should be added to the jill's diet to give an added nutritional boost during the lactation period. Starting at 6 weeks, kits can be gradually weaned off of the jill using canned cat food mixed one to one (1:1) with a commercial feline milk substitute.

Orphaned or abandoned kits can be raised by hand using the same feline milk substitute. Feedings should be performed at least every 2 hours for the first week and every 4 hours for the next 3 to 4 weeks. Orphans need to be stimulated to eliminate after each feeding. This can be accomplished using a warm, moist cotton ball and gently massaging the anal and genital region. Starting at 3 weeks of age, the orphan can be slowly weaned onto solid food using the formula mentioned above. As with any orphaned animal, warmth, sanitation, and lots of tender loving care are needed.

The reproductive cycle

DID YOU KNOW?

Nonspayed female ferrets that are not bred when they come into heat can die from anemia!

of jills is unique in that jills must be bred in order for estrogen levels within their bodies to decline, allowing them to go out of heat. This becomes significant because jills that are not bred can develop life-threatening anemia and blood-clotting problems caused by persistently high estrogen levels. As a result, owners must be sure to have their jills bred each breeding season, or have their veterinarian administer a special injection each time to bring them out of heat. Another more preferable alternative is surgical spaying, which can be performed as early as 6 months of age.

Preventive Health Care

Ferrets should receive routine medical checkups just like dogs and cats (Fig. 50.3). For ferrets less than 4 years old, these visits to the veterinarian should be made annually. For ferrets older than 4 years, increase the visits to twice per year.

Ferrets are very susceptible to the canine distemper virus and should be vaccinated against this disease using a ferret-approved vaccine starting at 6 to 8 weeks of age. Booster immunizations should be administered at 12 weeks and 16 weeks, and then annually. A rabies vaccine should be administered on an annual basis as well.

The same types of intestinal parasites that can affect dogs and cats can infest ferrets. As a result, routine stool examinations should be performed annually by your veterinarian, and deworming medication should be administered if deemed appropriate.

Ear mites are very common in ferrets. As a result, owners need to be on constant lookout for these pests. Ferrets infested with these mites will shake their heads and have a brown-black discharge in the affected ear(s). Ear mite medication applied directly to the ears is the most effective method of eliminating an ear mite infestation.

Ferrets are also susceptible to heartworm disease. As a result, in those areas with large concentrations of this disease, a heartworm preventive medicine should be administered. Contact your veterinarian for his/her recommendations for your particular area.

Routine surgical procedures performed on ferrets include neutering and descenting. Neutering hobs will help reduce their aggressiveness and reduce body odor. If not to be bred, jills should be spayed as

FIGURE 50.3 Ferrets should see their veterinarians for routine medical checkups as do dogs and cats.

well to eliminate the dangers of persistent estrus. Both procedures can be performed at 6 months of age.

Descenting can be performed at the same time as neutering to help reduce obnoxious odors emitted from ferrets. This involves the removal of the anal sacs. This procedure, combined with frequent baths using a hypoallergenic shampoo, can help control your ferret's odor.

FACT *OR* FICTION

Descenting a ferret will remove its characteristic odor. FICTION. Descenting is really a misnomer, since the surgical removal of the anal sacs rarely eliminates odor completely. Secretions from glands in the skin beneath the tail also account for the characteristic odor of a ferret.

Finally, because ferrets like to dig, their nails should be trimmed short on a weekly basis.

Diseases and Disorders of Ferrets

Some selected diseases and disorders seen in ferrets are listed in Table 50.1. Remember that others do exist, which is why definitive diagnosis should be made by a qualified veterinarian. Identifying and treating diseases in their early stages is the key to successful treatment and cure.

Table 50.1 Diseases and Disorders of Ferrets

Disease or disorder	Clinical signs	Treatment and comments
Infectious diseases		
Canine distemper	Fever; loss of appetite; nasal and eye discharge; convulsions	No treatment available; prevent by vaccinating
Human influenza	Fever; nasal discharge; sneezing; breathing difficulties	Can be transmitted by humans; treat with antibiotics and antihistamines
Retroviral infection	Signs vary with organ involved; can cause cancer; anemia	Some ill ferrets have tested positive for the feline leukemia virus
Skin diseases		
Skin parasites (fleas, mites, ear mites)	Itching; hair loss; inflamed ears	Treat with pyrethrin-type insecticide
Mast cell tumors	Itching; hair loss; reddened raised skin lesions	Can occur along with other tumors; surgical excision
Digestive system diseases		
Intestinal parasites (hookworms, roundworms, tapeworms, Giardia, coccidia)	Weight loss; loss of appetite; vomiting; diarrhea	Treat with dewormer similar to those used in cats

Table 50.1 Diseases and Disorders of Ferrets (*Continued*)

Disease or disorder	Clinical signs	Treatment and comments
Proliferative bowel disease	Green, mucoid diarrhea; weight loss; prolapsed rectum; incoordination	Age of onset is around 4–6 months; treat with antibiotics; might be zoonotic disease
Hairballs; gastric foreign bodies	Vomiting, loss of appetite	Treat hairballs as in cats; foreign bodies might need to be removed surgically
Insulinoma	Profound weakness; increased salivation; seizures	This tumor of the pancreas causes low blood sugar; surgical removal of tumor necessary
Reproductive system diseases		
Aplastic anemia	Weakness; loss of appetite; bruising; hemorrhaging; dark, tarry stool	Caused by persistent heat cycle; treat with hormones, blood transfusions, bone marrow stimulants; prevent by spaying at 6 months of age
Pregnancy toxemia	Lethargy; dehydration; black tarry stools; hair loss	Seen in jills on poor plan of nutrition; treat with Cesarean section; fluids; antibiotics; improve nutrition
Urinary system diseases		
Urolithiasis	Blood-tinged urine; straining to urinate; depression	Treatment is the same as for cats

Table 50.1 Diseases and Disorders of Ferrets (*Continued*)

Disease or disorder	Clinical signs	Treatment and comments
Cardiopulmonary diseases		
Heartworm disease	Weakness; coughing; breathing difficulties	Treat and prevent the same as in dogs
Congestive heart failure	Weakness; coughing; breathing difficulties	Treat as in dogs
Eye diseases		
Juvenile cataracts	Cloudy eyes; vision difficulties	Seen in young ferrets; surgical removal of cataract might be needed to restore vision

Miniature Pot-Bellied Pigs

Miniature pot-bellied pigs (MPBPs) can trace their origins to the jungles of Vietnam and China. First introduced into the United States in 1985, they have gained a loyal following over the years. The popularity of miniature pot-bellied pigs can be attributed to the fact that they can make adorable, fun-loving pets. Not only are they relatively clean and odor-free (unlike domestic pigs) but miniature pot-bellied pigs are intelligent, affectionate, and easy to train and house-break (Fig. 51.1).

But miniature pot-bellied pigs are certainly not for everyone. For starters, they represent an initial purchase investment of hundreds, or even thousands, of dollars. Also, armed with a keen sense of smell, miniature pot-bellied pigs love to root, which can absolutely wreak havoc on carpets. Certainly those who pride themselves on expensively landscaped lawns should think twice about allowing a miniature pot-bellied pig access to their grounds!

Before making the decision to purchase a pot-bellied pig, check the laws of your particular city or municipality concerning these pets. In some areas, miniature pot-bellied pigs are still considered livestock rather than companion animals, and zoning restrictions may apply.

DID YOU KNOW?

A pot-bellied pig is one of the cleanest pets you could own!

FIGURE 51.1 Miniature pot-bellied pigs are not only relatively clean and odor-free but are also intelligent and affectionate pets.

Miniature pot-bellied pigs come in basic black or black with white markings. The ideal standard for the pot-bellied pig calls for a weight of less than 50 pounds and a shoulder height of less than 14 inches. However, many pot-bellied pigs kept as pets in the United States exceed these standards. Maximum weight allowed for official registration of the adult pig is 95 pounds and maximum shoulder height is 18 inches. The snout of the pot-bellied pigs tends to be longer than those of domestic pigs, and their ears stand erect. Their eyesight is not as keen as that of dogs and cats, yet they have an exceptional sense of smell. The life span of a miniature pot-bellied pig is comparable to that of a cat or dog.

As with any pet, you will want to be sure the candidate that you are considering is healthy before purchasing it. Health problems to look for in miniature pot-bellied pigs include skin disorders, malformed snouts, breathing difficulties, retained testicles, lameness, hernias, and in newborns, *atresia ani,* or lack of an anal opening. To be safe, have your veterinarian perform a physical exam on your selection prior to purchase to evaluate your pig's health status.

Restraint

Because of a predisposition for hip and other musculoskeletal injuries, miniature pot-bellied pigs should be handled with care. When picking one up, be sure to cradle the pig's neck and hind end between your own body and forearm, just as you would a dog or cat. The legs of the pig should be allowed to hang free. Never grab or pick up a pig by its fore or hind legs, as this can cause joint dislocations. Get ready: Some pigs let out an ear-piercing squeal when restrained or picked up!

Housing

Miniature pot-bellied pigs can be housed just like a dog. However, whether kept indoors or outdoors, the ideal environmental temperature for a miniature pot-bellied pig is

around 70 degrees Fahrenheit. If they get too cold, pigs tend to get irritable and stressed, tearing at their bedding and burrowing in order to get warm. On the other hand, if environmental temperatures get too hot, an MPBP can succumb to heat stroke quite rapidly. As a result, if a pig is to be kept outdoors, plenty of shade and fresh water should be provided. Finally, pigs love to root, so be sure to provide your porcine access to an area with soil or dirt to satisfy this craving.

Training

Miniature pot-bellied pigs are intelligent creatures that can be trained just like dogs. Training is most effective when a pig is acquired at a young age (less than 8 weeks of age) and allowed to form an emotional bond (socialize) with you. Using simple commands, rewards, and praises, you can teach your pig many things, including litter training, leash training, and even tricks.

Nutrition

Miniature pot-bellied pigs should be fed commercially available rations designed for pigs. Fruits, vegetables, and vitamins should be added as well to provide supplementation and variety. To avoid the dangers of salt toxicity, water must be easily accessible at all times. Obesity is a common health problem in pot-bellied pigs, yet can be avoided by adhering to strict dietary moderation.

Reproduction

Miniature pot-bellied pigs reach puberty at 6 to 7 months of age. Heat in the female occurs every 21 days and lasts 2 to 3 days. Your veterinarian can assist you in timing the breeding between the sow and boar to achieve best results. If the mating is successful, the gestation period for pot-bellied pigs is approximately 114 days.

Two weeks prior to parturition (farrowing), a noticeable "drop" in the abdomen of the sow will be noted. At this time, a farrowing crate for the sow should be provided. Contact your veterinarian for assistance in crate design and dimensions for your particular pig. Crates should be roomy enough to allow free movement of both sow and offspring. The sow can be kept in this crate until farrowing occurs. Be sure to remove her from the crate three to four times a day for exercise and eliminations.

Litter sizes can range from 4 to 12, depending on the maturity of the sow. At birth, piglets weigh about 16 ounces. Because of a predisposition to anemia, neonatal piglets should receive injections of an iron supplement daily for the first 3 days of life. The sharp needle teeth that these piglets possess should be clipped back as well to prevent inadvertent injury to the sow and other offspring.

Neonatal piglets are extremely susceptible to hypothermia. As a result, keep environmental temperatures maintained between 85 and 95 degrees Fahrenheit until weaning takes place at 4 to 6 weeks of age. In addition, piglets under 2 weeks of age should be observed for signs of hypoglycemia (low blood sugar). This condition, characterized by depression and coma, is a medical emergency and requires immediate veterinary intervention.

Preventive Health Care

Like dogs and cats, miniature pot-bellied pigs require routine preventive health care to keep them healthy and happy. MPBPs should be vaccinated against the common diseases seen in domestic pigs, including erysipelas (caused by *Streptococcus pyogenes*), transmissible gastroenteritis (TGE), atrophic rhinitis, and leptospirosis. Piglets should be vaccinated for these diseases starting at 6 weeks of age, and again at 9 weeks of age. Booster vaccinations should be given at six months of age, and then annually thereafter. If you intend to breed your pigs, contact your veterinarian for special vaccination schedules for sows and boars.

In addition to vaccinations, pigs need to have regular stool checks performed for internal parasites. Roundworms, whipworms, and nodular worms are the most frequently found parasites inhabiting the gastrointestinal tract of these pigs. If any worms are detected, appropriate medications can be administered and repeated in 3 weeks to ensure a complete kill.

Miniature pigs that are to be introduced to households containing dogs should be blood-tested for the pseudorabies virus. This virus is extremely deadly to dogs, which can contract the disease from otherwise healthy pigs.

Piglets less than 6 weeks of age are very prone to developing anemia and low blood sugar. Iron supplements and additional sources of glucose may be administered to prevent these problems. Since most piglets acquired as pets are older, this should not be a concern for most new pig owners.

Miniature pigs should be brushed daily with a soft-bristle brush to help control seborrhea and flaking. Hypoallergenic shampoos can be used if bathing is required. Periodic trimming of the tusks (if present) and hooves should be performed as needed.

Much to the jealousy of dog and cat owners, fleas have nowhere to hide on miniature pigs, so flea control is rarely necessary. However, the skin of miniature pot-bellied pigs is very sensitive to sunlight and cold temperatures, and owners should take care to shield their pig's skin from these environmental factors.

Routine surgical procedures performed on minature pot-bellied pigs include spaying, castration, and removal of sharp canine teeth (Fig. 51.2). These procedures are generally performed before 4 months of age.

> ## Dr. P's Vet Tip
>
> Because pot-bellied pigs are prone to sunburn, use SPF-30 (sun protection factor level 30) sunscreen on yours if it is to be exposed to direct sunlight for a prolonged period of time.

FIGURE 51.2 Clipping the sharp needle teeth on a miniature pot-bellied pig.

Diseases and Disorders of Miniature Pot-Bellied Pigs

The following are some selected diseases and disorders seen in miniature pot-bellied pigs. Remember that others do exist, which is why a definitive diagnosis by a qualified veterinarian is always needed on a sick pig. Identifying and treating diseases in their early stages is the key to successful treatment and cure (Table 51.1).

Table 51.1 Diseases and Disorders of Miniature Pot-Bellied Pigs (MPBPs)

Disease or disorder	Clinical signs	Treatment and comments
	Infectious diseases	
Erysipelas	Characteristic red, diamond-shaped skin lesions; depression; fever; lameness; conjunctivitis	Can lead to heart disease and arthritis if not treated early; treat with penicillin antibiotics
Transmissible gastroenteritis	Diarrhea; vomiting; fever; dehydration	Caused by a coronavirus (similar to that in dogs and cats); treat secondary problems with antibiotic and fluid support

Table 51.1 Diseases and Disorders of Miniature Pot-Bellied Pigs (MPBPs) (*Continued*)

Disease or disorder	Clinical signs	Treatment and comments
Leptospirosis	Depression; fever; weakness	Causes anemia and kidney failure in affected pigs; treatment consists of antibiotics and blood transfusions if needed; zoonotic disease
Hemophilus	Breathing difficulties; blood-stained foam from mouth and nose; fever; coughing	Rapidly fatal if not treated promptly with appropriate antibiotics
Skin diseases		
Sunburn or frostbite	Reddening of the skin; ulcerations	MPBPs quite susceptible to environmental insults
Seborrhea	Dry, flaky skin	Caused by nutritional deficiencies, intestinal parasites, mange. environmental conditions; treat according to cause
Mange (mites)	Itching; small red raised bumps on skin	Oral ivermectin and topical dips used to treat
Greasy pig disease	Greasy skin surface; reddened wrinkled skin; scabs; dehydration	Caused by bacteria; highly fatal in young pigs; treat with antibiotics
Musculoskeletal diseases		
Posterior weakness or stiffness	Stiff gait; lameness; can't support weight on hind legs	Conformation of MPBP and improper restraint techniques make them prone to muscle pulls, ligament tears, hip dis-

Table 51.1 Diseases and Disorders of Miniature Pot-Bellied Pigs (MPBPs) (*Continued*)

Disease or disorder	Clinical signs	Treatment and comments
Musculoskeletal diseases (*Continued*)		
		location, other musculoskeletal injuries; treat depending on problem
Infectious arthritis	Stiffness; lameness; fever	Can be caused by a variety of organisms; treat with appropriate antibiotics
Osteomalacia	Weakness; inability to stand	Caused by calcium deficiency; seen in nursing or postnursing sows
Nervous system disease		
Bacterial encephalitis	Depression; circling; seizures; abnormal gait and posture; blindness; aggressiveness	Can be caused by a variety of organisms; treat with appropriate antibiotics
Shaker pig disease	Tremors, convulsions; shaking	No treatment needed; most recover spontaneously
Salt poisoning	Depression; circling; seizures; abnormal gait and posture; blindness; aggressiveness	Caused by water deprivation, then allowing free access to water; treatment generally unrewarding
Respiratory system diseases		
Atrophic rhinitis	Snout deformity; sneezing; bloody nasal discharge	Associated with bacterial infections of the nasal passages in neonatal or newly

Table 51.1 Diseases and Disorders of Miniature Pot-Bellied Pigs (MPBPs) *(Continued)*

Disease or disorder	Clinical signs	Treatment and comments
Respiratory system diseases *(Continued)*		
		weaned pigs; infection can be treated with antibiotics yet clinical signs often persist
Pneumonia	Mouth breathing; bluish hue to skin	MPBP very susceptible to pneumonia; stress often leads to secondary bacterial infections; other causes include pseudorabies virus, roundworms, lungworms, cleft palate; treat depending on cause
Digestive system diseases		
Motion sickness, excitement overeating	Vomiting	No treatment needed
Neonatal diarrheal disease complex	Severe diarrhea; dehydration; abdominal distension and pain	Can be caused by bacteria (colibavillosis), parasites (coccidia), viruses (transmissible gastroenteritis virus); treat with antibiotics, fluids
Intestinal parasites	Bloody diarrhea; dehydration	Can include roundworms, whipworms, nodular worms, tapeworms; treat using appropriate dewormer

Table 51.1 Diseases and Disorders of Miniature Pot-Bellied Pigs (MPBPs) (*Continued*)

Disease or disorder	Clinical signs	Treatment and comments
Rectal prolapse	Prolapsed rectum; diarrhea; abdominal distention	Caused by parasitism, chronic diarrhea and straining, coughing; treatment involves replacing prolapse and antibiotic therapy; treat underlying cause
Atresia ani	Inability to defecate due to lack of external anal opening	Congenital disease; no effective surgical treatment
Urinary system diseases		
Cystitis or nephritis	Increased urination; straining to urinate; bloody urine	Can be caused by bacterial infections, kidney-worms, toxins; treat depending on cause
Prepucial diverticulum	Urine dribbling in male MPBPs	Small pocket in prepuce traps urine and leads to clinical signs; manually empty pocket, surgical correction of diverticulum
Urinary calculi	Straining to urinate; bloody urine	Surgical removal of calculi usually required
Reproductive system diseases		
Cryptorchidism	One or both testicles retained within the abdomen	Quite common; castration recommended
Vaginitis and uterine infections	Vaginal discharge; increased urination; fever; depression	Bacteria usual source of the problem; treat with medicated douches; antibiotics

Table 51.1 Diseases and Disorders of Miniature Pot-Bellied Pigs (MPBPs) (*Continued*)

Disease or disorder	Clinical signs	Treatment and comments
	Other diseases	
Hernias (umbilical, inguinal, scrotal)	Soft tissue swelling or lump on belly; swollen scrotum; diarrhea; painful abdomen	Surgical repair of hernia required

Reptiles

While the thought of keeping a snake or lizard as a pet might send shivers up the spine of some, most fanciers agree that reptiles can be enjoyable and fascinating alternatives to the more conventional pet species. The husbandry involved in keeping these scaly companions healthy is not difficult. In fact, just by knowing the proper nutritional and environmental requirements for the particular reptile species in question, most health problems can be avoided. By the way, captive-bred snakes make better pets and thrive in captivity much more so than do their wild counterparts.

Before obtaining a reptile as a pet, visit a local library or pet shop, or browse the Web to read up on your particular selection. Also, you can contact a local zoo and talk to an expert on reptiles. Finally, a veterinarian should be able to supply you with valuable information concerning the husbandry and health of the reptile species you are considering purchasing.

CARE OF SNAKES

Although thousands of snake varieties exist, the ones most commonly kept as pets include pythons, boa constrictors, garter snakes, milk snakes, king snakes, and corn snakes (rat snakes). Obviously, ownership of venomous snakes should be restricted to those persons having special training in the husbandry and handling of these species. As a result, the information contained in this section focuses on the more popular nonpoisonous varieties mentioned above. As with most other exotic pets discussed in this chapter, pet snakes will thrive in those environments that are climate-controlled, are sanitary, and offer high quality sources of nutrition for their inhabitants. Many snakes kept in such conditions can live a healthy 10 to 20 years!

Restraint

Most snakes become accustomed to being handled by their owners without requiring any special restraint techniques. However, if a snake seems to be aggressive or hyperactive, restrain it by first gripping the snake just behind its head to gain control of this region. The body should then be supported with the other hand (Fig. 52.1). Gloves can be worn if necessary to protect the hands. Also, to be safe, never handle a very large constrictor snake, especially one with a belligerent attitude, if no one else is around.

Housing

Pet snakes can be categorized several different ways, depending on the type of living environment in which they are normally found in the wild.

FIGURE 52.1   When holding your snake, gently support its body and control its head.

These can include arboreal snakes such as boa constrictors and Burmese pythons, which prefer living in trees; semiaquatic snakes such as garter snakes, which enjoy living both in water and on land; and terrestrial snakes like ball pythons and king snakes, which prefer solid ground.

DID YOU KNOW?

A snake flicks its tongue out of its mouth to pick up chemicals in the air, then returns it to a special structure within its mouth, called *Jacobson's organ*. This organ is the snake's "nose," helping it to scent nearby prey.

Most snakes kept as pets can be housed in converted glass aquariums or custom acrylic enclosures. As a rule, provide at least $3/4$ square foot of living area per foot of snake housed within. Secure, well-ventilated tops are needed as well to prevent premeditated escape. These tops should be constructed out of peg board, acrylic, or plastic instead of wire mesh, as the latter can cause snout abrasions. The configuration and setup provided within the enclosure itself should cater to your snake's individual preferences, whether they are arboreal, terrestrial, or semiaquatic. Regardless of the type, plan on thoroughly cleaning and disinfecting the floor, walls, and contents of your pet's home at least twice monthly.

Keep in mind that the two most crucial factors in providing a proper artificial environment for any reptile are temperature and humidity. In the wild, reptiles regulate their body temperatures (as necessary for various physiological functions) by changing their position in accordance with changes in environmental temperatures. As a result, snakes might choose to bask in the sun on a branch or rock to raise their body temperature, or to seek out shade to lower their body temperature. In captivity, such options should be available as well.

An incandescent lightbulb with a reflector can be positioned over one end of the cage containing a basking branch or rock. Temperatures in this "hot" region should remain a consistent 93 to 97 degrees Fahrenheit. (*Note:* Commercially available "hot rocks" should not be used within the enclosure, since these can burn the underside of snakes.) Temperature gradients elsewhere within the enclosure should range from 85 to 70 degrees Fahrenheit. Heating pads can be placed beneath selected sections of the aquarium to achieve these temperature gradients. Ceramic heating elements can be utilized as well.

Aquarium thermometers should be placed at multiple locations within the cage to monitor these temperatures throughout.

A humidity gauge should be centrally located in your snake's enclosure, away from heat and light sources. Relative humidity should be maintained between 40 and 70 percent. Environmental humidity kept too low can cause dehydration and shedding challenges. On the contrary, humidity kept consistently too high can predispose a snake to potentially harmful fungal and bacterial growth.

Artificial turf, indoor/outdoor carpet, aspen chips, or butcher-block paper can be used to line the floor of your snake's terrarium. If either of the first two are used, keep two or three clean pieces available as backups to quickly replace soiled ones. Excretions and any uneaten food should be removed daily, and the flooring should be changed at least every other day. A quaternary ammonium compound or chlorhexidine diluted 1:10 with water is an ideal disinfectant for cleaning and soaking soiled pieces of flooring. If you have only one piece of turf to work with, be sure to rinse and dry it completely before placing it back into the cage. Failure to do so could predispose your snake to skin irritation and disease.

For arboreal species, provide plenty of branches of different types and sizes on which your snake may climb. Smooth rock formations, hollow logs, or other hiding areas should be placed at different temperature locations within the enclosure. Burrowing snakes, such as sand boas, will also need a substrate into which they can burrow. Aspen shavings or other commercially available substrates designed for snakes serve this function quite nicely.

Another item needed for your snake's home is a sturdy ceramic or plastic water bowl large enough for the snake to crawl into. The bowl should contain a water level shallow enough as to not completely submerge the snake's body. Use filtered water as a water source to prevent chlorine irritation to your pet's skin. Change the water and clean the bowl on a daily basis.

Nutrition

Young, growing snakes should be fed at least twice weekly. As snakes mature, their feedings can be dropped to once every week or two. Standard food items for larger snakes include mice, rats, chicks, and rabbits. Smaller snakes can be fed insects (pesticide-free!), small mice, frogs, salamanders, small lizards, and earthworms. With the exception of smaller insects, do not serve live prey to your snake. Even the smallest of prey, if hostile enough, can cause serious, even life-threatening, injuries to a snake (Fig. 52.2). Instead, offer fresh prey that has been dispatched just prior to feeding. Frozen prey can be used as well; just be sure to thaw it out completely prior to feeding.

Don't handle your snake for several days following a meal to prevent a stress-related disruption of the digestive process. In addition, many snakes might become irritable and bite if disturbed following a good meal!

Keep careful records of the feeding activity of your snake. In this way, loss of appetite or any disruption in the normal feeding habits caused by illness can be noticed and addressed promptly.

Shedding

Shedding (*ecdysis*) is the process in which new skin is formed beneath the old and the latter is subsequently discarded. All reptiles (and amphibians) shed. In snakes, it usually occurs every 1 to 3 months depending on the age and size of snake involved. Snakes that are about to shed their skin will seem to lose their appetite and become somewhat lethargic a week or two prior to the event. As new skin develops beneath the old, the old skin will turn "opaque" for a few days, then return to its normal appearance. After several days, the old skin comes off. Keep accurate records of your snake's shedding activity (Fig. 52.3). Any changes in your snake's individual shedding pattern could be a sign of illness and warrants a trip to your veterinarian.

FIGURE 52.2 Live prey should not be fed, as it could seriously injure your snake.

FIGURE 52.3 Shedding usually occurs every 1 to 3 months, depending on the age and size of snake involved.

To prevent inadvertent damage to the new skin, do not handle your snake while it is shedding until the process is complete. If an incomplete shed occurs, place your snake in a shallow water bowl and soak the nonshed regions for 1 to 2 hours. This should help the snake complete the shed.

Occasionally, the skin covering the eyes of a snake will fail to shed with the rest of the skin. These retained eyecaps might need to be manually removed. However, this should be performed only with the help of a qualified veterinarian, since, if done incorrectly, permanent damage to your snake's eyes could result.

CARE OF LIZARDS

Like snakes, a wide variety of lizard species adorn households across the country. Popular ones include geckos, chameleons, and, of course, iguanas. Iguanas belong to the Iguanidae family of reptiles. Out of this family, the most notable member to be kept as a pet is the green iguana.

FIGURE 52.4 An effective method for restraining smaller lizards.

Fascinating creatures to observe, lizards are hardy and fairly easy to care for. This is assuming, of course, that an owner is well versed in the environmental and nutritional needs of these special reptiles.

Restraint

As a rule, handling of pet lizards should be kept to a

minimum. Lizards are incredibly strong for their size and can be difficult to manage if they put up a fight (Fig. 52.4)! When restraining large lizards, grasp the neck area and control the forelegs all with

one hand, and with the other hand, encircle the belly of the lizard to lift. Never pick up a lizard by its tail. If you do, you might find yourself holding the tail as your reptile scurries off in the other direction!

Housing

Lizards may be kept in aquariums or similar enclosures with secure, mesh screening over the top to prevent escape (Fig. 52.5). As a rule, most lizards prefer to be housed alone, and may become aggressive toward any new additions. They can be arboreal (living on trees or plants) or terrestrial (living on land) in nature. The decor of the enclosure should reflect your lizard's personal preference.

Temperature and humidity are two crucial factors when providing a proper artificial environment for any reptile. In the wild, reptiles regulate their body temperatures by changing their body position and/or location in accordance with changes in environmental temperatures. As

FIGURE 52.5 A typical terrarium setup for lizards.

a result, a lizard might choose to bask in the sun on a branch or rock to raise its body temperature, or to crawl into the shade to lower the same. In captivity, these options should be available. For this reason, the cage you keep your lizard in should provide both warm and cool regions.

An incandescent lightbulb with a reflector can be positioned over one end of the cage containing a basking branch or rock. Temperatures in this "hot" region should remain between 93 and 97 degrees Fahrenheit. Commercially available "hot rocks" should not be used within the enclosure, since these can burn reptiles.

Temperatures gradients elsewhere within the enclosure should range from 85 to 70 degrees Fahrenheit. Heating pads can be placed beneath selected sections of the aquarium to achieve these temperature gradients. Ceramic heating elements are most effective as well. Aquarium thermometers should be placed at multiple locations within the cage to monitor environmental temperatures throughout.

A humidity gauge should also be centrally located within your lizard's enclosure, away from light and heat sources. Relative humidity should be maintained between 65 and 90 percent for most arboreal lizards (including iguanas), and 20 to 40 percent for terrestrial species, such as the leopard gecko.

Although incandescent lighting may provide a source heat and light, it does not supply the full spectrum of light that lizards require to maintain both their mental and physical health. The ultraviolet rays of the sun are required for the synthesis of vitamin D_3 in the skin of lizards. If not enough of vitamin D_3 is synthesized, nutritional bone disease can result. Most lizards kept in captivity are deprived of direct exposure to natural sunlight, and require an artificial source of "sunlight." Contrary to popular belief, placing your pet's enclosure next to a sunny window is not sufficient, since glass can interfere with the effective transmission and absorption of the sun's ultraviolet rays. Instead, an unfiltered black light fluorescent tube should be mounted approximately 2 feet above your reptile's basking site to provide these much needed rays. These tubes are readily available at most pet stores. [*Note:* These are different from black light blue tubes, which are of little value and should not be used. Approximately 10 hours of this light should be provided for your lizard on a daily basis. Be sure no glass or plastic comes between the light source and the reptile (mesh screen is okay).] To

ensure maximum effec-
tiveness, black lights
should be replaced every 6
months (Fig. 52.6).

Butcher-block paper,
which is inexpensive and
easy to change, can be used
to line the floor of your
lizard's home. If used, it
should be changed daily. As
an alternative, artificial turf

FIGURE 52.6 Iguanas and other lizards require special lighting in order to keep them healthy.

or indoor/outdoor carpeting can be used as well. Keep two or three
clean pieces available as backups to quickly replace soiled ones. Excretions should be picked up daily, and the flooring should be changed
and cleaned at least three times a week. A quaternary ammonium compound or chlorhexidine diluted 1:10 with water is an ideal disinfectant
for cleaning and soaking soiled pieces of flooring. If you have only one
piece to work with, be sure to rinse and dry it completely before placing it back into the cage. Failure to do so could predispose your reptile
to skin irritation and disease.

For arboreal species, provide plenty of branches of different types
and sizes on which your lizard can climb. Smooth rock formations,
hollow logs, or other areas in which your lizard can hide should be
placed at different temperature locations within the enclosure.

Some lizards enjoy substrate into which they can burrow. Pelleted,
recycled newspaper (available at most pet stores) or commercially available substrate designed for reptiles serves this function quite nicely.

Another item needed for your lizard's home is a water bowl with easy
access. The bowl should be large enough to hold your lizard and contain
a level of water that would cover approximately two-thirds of its body.
Use filtered water as a water source to prevent chlorine irritation to your
pet's skin. Change the water and clean the bowl on a daily basis. Note
that chameleons will rarely drink water from a bowl. They will, however,
lick up water droplets from the sides of the enclosure. As a result, keep
the sides of the cage well misted throughout the day. Even better (and
less labor-intensive), consider installing a drip system (available commercially) to provide a constant source of water to your finicky pet. To
maintain proper sanitation, give your lizard's cage flooring, walls, and
contents a thorough cleaning and disinfecting at least twice monthly.

Nutrition

Nutritionally related bone disease due to poor feeding practices is common in captive lizards, especially green iguanas (Fig. 52.7). For herbivores like the green iguana, feed a varied diet consisting of

85 percent dark, leafy green vegetables, such as mustard greens, cilantro, collards, grape leaves, spinach, broccoli, etc.

5 percent fruit, such as bananas and pears

10 percent protein source, such as dry dog food, monkey chow, or hard-boiled eggs

In addition, a balanced vitamin-mineral supplement designed for herbivorous lizards should be sprinkled on the vegetables for added protection against nutritional bone disease.

The daily diet of a carnivorous species of lizard should consist of prey such as baby mice (pinkies), chicks, rabbits, insects, and/or mealworms, depending on the size of the reptile (Fig. 52.8). With the excep-

FIGURE 52.7 Nutritionally related bone disease due to poor feeding practices is common in captive iguanas.

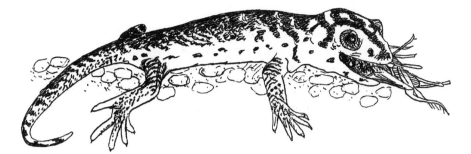

FIGURE 52.8 Crickets provide an excellent meal for most small reptiles.

tion of insects (ants, crickets, grasshoppers) and mealworms, all prey should be prekilled prior to feeding. If insects are offered, make certain they are pesticide-free. Like their herbivorous cousins, these lizards should receive daily balanced vitamin-mineral supplement as well.

Plan on feeding both herbivorous and carnivorous lizards at least once daily. Remove and discard all uneaten food at the end of the day. Water should be offered free-choice at all times. Many lizards will eliminate in their water dishes. As a result, be sure to change it daily.

CARE OF THE PET CHELONIAN

Turtles and tortoises are also popular reptiles kept as pets. They belong to the reptilian order *Chelonia,* with hundreds of different species existing. The most common chelonians kept as pets include box turtles, snapping turtles, and various aquatic turtles. If well cared for, some turtles can live over 20 years in captivity (Fig. 52.9)!

Restraint

Most turtles can be easily and safely handled by grasping the edges of the shell with one hand and supporting the underside of the turtle, or plastron, with the other. Note, however, that snapping turtles and certain

FIGURE 52.9 Certain turtles can live over 20 years in captivity with proper care!

other species of turtles do require special precautions when lifting or handling to avoid being bitten and/or scratched. For instance, a snapping turtle should be picked up only by the base of its tail. Since turtles are unable to reach around and bite effectively because of their shell, this approach is the safest. Less aggressive turtles can be handled safely by grasping the sides of the shell near the hind end, as far away from the head as possible.

Housing

Turtles can be kept in 10- to 20-gallon aquariums or other similar enclosures. Semiaquatic turtles require both water to swim in and land to crawl on within their artificial environment. Both regions need to be easily accessible. Large, round gravel can be used to create the "land" portion of the environment. Sand, aquarium gravel, or wood chips should not be used, as these may be ingested by a bored pet. A hiding spot should also be provided at one end of the land mass. Aquatic turtles obviously need less land and more water in which to swim and feed. It needn't be deep, just enough for the turtle to be able to submerge itself. The only water that terrestrial turtles need is that provided within a shallow water dish (Fig. 52.10).

All water should be filtered prior to adding to the vivarium to avoid the hazards of contamination. In addition, plan on complete water changes twice per week. A filtration system can be installed to help keep the water clean; however, this does not replace essential twice-weekly water changes. Environmental temperature, including water temperature, should be kept between 75 and 85 degrees Fahrenheit at all times (this includes any new water added). Abrupt changes in water temperature can be harmful to turtles. Also, if environmental temperatures fall too low, most turtles will go off feed

FIGURE 52.10 Turtles should have free access to water at all times.

and could become malnourished. As a result, be sure to use an aquarium thermometer to help monitor this important parameter.

Smooth rocks or branches suitable for climbing and basking should be provided for both aquatic and semiaquatic turtles. Floating platforms are appealing to these pets as well. Plenty of hiding places should be offered, and situated at various locations within the vivarium or terrarium. Enclosures, including fixtures, should be thoroughly cleaned and disinfected weekly using soap and water or a 1:10 dilution of chlorhexidine. After cleaning, rinse thoroughly to be sure no chemical residues are left that could be harmful to your turtle.

Turtles, like other reptiles, regulate body temperature according to physiological needs. As a result, a simple setup including an incandescent light bulb and reflector situated over a basking site within the terrarium should be used to create a "hot spot" of around 85 to 90 degrees Fahrenheit. Also, a heating pad can be placed beneath one section of the enclosure to create a thermal gradient within the enclosure. Thermometers can be placed in strategic locations within the enclosure to monitor temperatures.

Chelonians, like their lizard cousins, also require a source of ultraviolet light in order to synthesize vitamin D within their bodies, thereby preventing nutritionally related bone disease (see section on care of lizards).

Nutrition

The diet of aquatic turtles should consist of a variety of foodstuffs, including small fish, worms, insects, water plants, and dark green, leafy vegetables. Aquatic turtles like to eat their meals while in the water. Box turtles, on the other hand, prefer to eat on land. They, too, enjoy and need the same type of well-balanced diet as do their aquatic cousins, with the addition of some dark green or yellow vegetables and fruit. A balanced vitamin-mineral supplement should be added to the diet of all turtles for added protection against nutritional bone disease.

Preventive Health Care for Reptiles

Pet reptiles can benefit from annual veterinary checkups just like other pets. In addition to a physical examination, stool checks and/or

> ## Dr. P's Vet Tip
>
> The humidity within your reptile's environment can be raised by increasing the size of the water container within the enclosure, partially covering the screen top (if present) to reduce ventilation, misting the sides of the enclosure, and/or moistening the substrate. On the contrary, to reduce the humidity, use spot lamps or fans to promote evaporation, replace moist substrate with dry substrate, and/or increase ventilation within the enclosure.

cultures should be performed to ensure that your pet is and remains free of infection or parasitism.

Reptile owners should realize that the pet reptiles can be carriers of salmonella, a bacterium that can cause food poisoning and severe diarrhea in humans. A commonsense approach to handling and hygiene is essential to prevent zoonotic transmission (see Chap. 59).

Strict sanitation, environmental control (including temperature and humidity), and high quality rations must be given top priority in order to prevent disease in reptiles. Keep a close eye on your pet's behavior and movements, eating habits, elimination habits, and physical characteristics. Notify your veterinarian of any changes you see.

Diseases and Disorders of Reptiles

The vast majority of diseases and disorders seen in reptiles kept as pets are caused by improper sanitation, inadequate lighting, and/or poor nutrition. If your pet is exhibiting clinical signs or any type of strange behavior, take it to your veterinarian immediately for a checkup. If your veterinarian does not work on reptiles, ask for a referral to one in your area who does. Identifying and treating diseases in their early stages is the key to successful treatment and cure. Some of the more common diseases and disorders seen in reptiles are listed below. Others do exist, which is why a definitive diagnosis should be made by a qualified veterinarian (Table 52.1).

Table 52.1 Diseases and Disorders of Reptiles

Disease or disorder	Reptiles primarily affected*	Clinical signs	Treatment and comments
Vitamin D deficiency	L, T	"Rubber jaw"; limb and spine deformities; fractures; paralysis	Review and correct diet—vitamin-mineral supplement; provide source of ultraviolet light
Vitamin D excess	L	General malaise; bone abnormalities	Overuse of vitamin D supplement; treat by discontinuing supplement
Nutritional secondary hyper-parathyroidism	L, T	Same as above	Caused by calcium-phosphorous imbalances; treatment same as above
Gout	L	Lameness; general malaise	Caused by improper diet, water deprivation, kidney disease; no treatment
Vitamin A deficiency	T	Swollen eyelids; eye and nose discharge; breathing difficulties	Seen in turtles on all-meat or all-vegetable diets; treat by changing diet, vitamin A supplement, antibiotics
Pneumonia	L, T, S	Gaping and breathing difficulties; nasal discharge; swollen eyelids	Can be caused by bacteria, fungi, or parasites; treatment depends on cause
Skin parasites (mites, ticks, etc.)	L, T, S	Variable, including weakness, loss of appetite	Can cause anemia; treat locally with safe insecticide

Table 52.1 Diseases and Disorders of Reptiles (*Continued*)

Disease or disorder	Reptiles primarily affected*	Clinical signs	Treatment and comments
Retained eye cap	S	Eye opacity, irritation	May be retained after shedding; moisten, then peel off gently
Mouth rot (infectious stomatitis)	S	Loss of appetite; open-mouth gaping; white discharge within the mouth	Occurs secondary to mouth trauma and other diseases; treatment involves local flushing and antibiotics
Amebiasis	L, T, S	Loss of appetite; regurgitation; loose, abnormal stool; weight loss	Seen in reptiles kept in groups; can be spread by cockroaches; treat with amebicide and antibiotics
Septicemia	L, T, S	Loss of appetite; weakness; lack of muscle tone	Often secondary to stress and other diseases; treat using antibiotics and correcting underlying cause
Lumps and bumps	L, T, S	Abnormal body shape; lumps and bumps	Suspect food ingestion, eggs, abscesses, tumors

*L = lizard; T = turtle; S = snake.

Amphibians

Amphibians have always been highly favored as pets. The word *amphibios* means "double life," as these creatures are adopted for life both on land and in water. Adult amphibians will spend most of their time on land, only to return to water to reproduce. The offspring that result will, in turn, remain in their aqueous surroundings until maturity. Amphibians, like reptiles, are cold-blooded, meaning that their internal body temperatures fluctuate with environmental temperatures.

Over 2500 varieties of frogs and toads exist throughout the world (Fig. 53.1). The class Amphibia includes frogs, toads, salamanders, and newts. Frogs and toads are tailless amphibians that possess long, strong hindlimbs. Those that dwell in trees also sport prominent suction disks on the digits of their toes to be used for climbing and clinging. Salamanders and newts, on the other hand, possess short, relatively weak legs that protrude almost perpendicular to their bodies (Fig. 53.2). They also possess a long tail that assists them in their movements. Instead of walking or jumping like frogs, salamanders wiggle and slither toward their intended destinations.

Although the toad is considered a type of frog, they differ in a number of ways. Frogs possess bodies that are more streamlined and elongated than those of toads. The legs of frogs are elongated and ideal for

FIGURE 53.1 Over 2500 varieties of frogs and toads exist worldwide.

FIGURE 53.2 Salamanders have short legs that protrude almost perpendicular to their bodies.

leaping and swimming, whereas those of toads are shorter and used for walking and stalking prey. The skin of the frog is smooth and shiny, in contrast to the thick, dry, and knobby skin of the toad. When laying eggs, frogs will do so in clusters, while toads will lay their eggs in long chains. Finally, frogs come in a wide variety of shapes and colors, including black, various shades of green, and the bright oranges, reds, and yellows of the tropical varieties. Most toads, on the other hand, sport a basic brown color or shades thereof, providing them with the optimum camouflage within their terrestrial surroundings.

Like frogs and toads, salamanders and newts come in all sorts of shapes, sizes, and colors. Over 300 species exist worldwide. The major difference between the salamander and the newt (which is actually a type of salamander) is that the salamander prefers to dwell on land, returning to water only to breed. On the contrary, newts like to spend the majority of their time in aquatic settings. Realize, of course, that when speaking of any type of amphibian, there are always multiple exceptions to the rule!

The top two goals in the life of any amphibian are to (1) find food and (2) keep from drying out. Adult amphibians not only breathe through a set of lungs but also respire through their skin and mucous membranes. For this reason, the outer surfaces of most amphibians

DID YOU KNOW?

The body slime of the slimy salamander is almost as sticky as glue!

are coated with slimy mucus that allows them to retain the skin moisture necessary for proper oxygen exchange. Loss of surface moisture due to dehydration, low humidity, and/or high environmental temperatures can be deadly. This is why amphibians are primarily nocturnal creatures, seeking out food during the nighttime hours and retreating to cool, sheltered areas during the day.

Amphibians can be purchased from pet stores or gathered from their natural habitats. However, before doing the latter, familiarize yourself with local laws and ordinances regarding ownership of native amphibian species. If you accidentally grab hold of an endangered species, you could be faced with a stiff penalty. Remember also that if you purchase or obtain an amphibian that is not native to your region, under no circumstances should you release it back into the wild. Placing such an individual into a foreign habitat could lead to the spread of new diseases and parasites that could potentially wipe out your local ecosystem!

Restraint

If you want a pet that you can cuddle and carry around with you all day long, an amphibian is probably not the right choice for you. There are three good reasons for this: (1) the skin of frogs and salamanders is a sensitive, delicate organ and can be easily traumatized by repeated handling; (2) certain frogs, toads, and salamanders can release toxins from their skin that can be quite irritating to eyes and mucous membranes; and (3) amphibians can be carriers of bacteria and parasites that can be transmitted to humans through close contact.

If you must pick up your amphibian, don a pair of disposable gloves. Be sure the gloves are free of surface powder, as this can be quite irritating to the sensitive skin of amphibians. For best results, moisten your gloved hands prior to handling. Use cupped hands to gently scoop up your pet. Avoid squeezing it to prevent its escape. That act alone probably causes more injuries to captive amphibians and reptiles than all other sources combined! Because of their slimy skin, amphibians can easily slip out of your hands and fall to the ground, causing serious injury or death. As a result, always keep your hands near a supporting surface just in case you lose your grip (Fig. 53.3).

FIGURE 53.3 Method of restraint for larger amphibians.

DID YOU KNOW?

Frogs will sometimes urinate when handled. Their purpose for doing so is to reduce their body weight as much as possible, allowing them to jump farther and swifter should the opportunity to escape arise!

If transporting your amphibian more than a few yards, use a small container filled with moss as your means of transport. Be sure your container has a lid containing holes to allow for ventilation. If transporting for a prolonged period of time, mist your traveler every 20 minutes to prevent dehydration.

Housing

Although amphibians are quite adaptive to any environment in which they are placed, do your best to duplicate the environment from which your pet originated. Keep in mind that maintaining a constant environmental temperature and proper humidity within the living quarters are essential to your amphibian's health and well-being. If in doubt, ask for housing advice from your local pet store that sells amphibians. They will be able to assist you in a design of a functional and fun habitat for your amphibious friend.

The type of setup needed will obviously depend on the type of amphibian owned. For instance, tree frogs will need homes that are taller than those of their ground-loving peers, complete with plenty of tree branches and foliage on which to climb. "Gilled" aquatic amphibians will require an aquarium environment very similar to that of tropical fish, complete with water filtration systems. Terrestrial species may require a terrarium that consists of only a small container of water. For those in between, commercial kits are available that can transform any enclosure into a vivarium containing both aquatic and land areas (Fig. 53.4). All water added to an amphibian's abode should be filtered, salt-free, and chlorine-free, with a pH somewhere between 6.5 and 8. Salt (as found in "soft" water), chlorine, and an improper pH can be extremely irritating to the sensitive skin of these animals. Aquarium water test kits available at pet stores can be used periodically to ensure the water quality within your pet's habitat.

Most amphibians are typically housed in glass aquarium-type enclosures fitted with secure tops that prevent escape and allow for adequate ventilation. Acrylic tops containing multiple ventilation holes and secure fasteners are ideal, as these allow for visual pleasure while helping to maintain temperature and humidity within the enclosure. Plastic snap-on lids available at most pet shops can also be used as inexpensive alternatives to acrylic, yet are not quite as effective at regulating internal environment.

The size of the aquarium used will depend on the size of the amphibian in question, as well as the number of them to be kept therein. If you are planning on housing more than one amphibian within a particular enclosure, make certain that they are of the same species and of the same size. Never house frogs and salamanders together and never house a larger amphibian with a smaller one, even if they are of the same species. If you do, you may wake up one morning and find the smaller of the two missing and the larger one with a satisfied smirk on its face!

FIGURE 53.4 An example of a vivarium setup for amphibians. Note both the land and water portions.

Sphagnum moss is ideal for lining the floor of your pet's living quarters. Moss helps contain moisture and humidity within the enclosure, while providing your amphibian with a soft surface and an ideal medium in which to burrow. Even better, placing a 1-inch layer of gravel beneath the moss will allow water and waste to filter through the moss, helping to keep it clean. Adorn the mossy floor of the living space with smooth rocks, simulated wooden branches, and silk plants (these latter two items are easier to clean and maintain than the real things), thereby providing plenty of places to hide or climb.

To prevent accidental dehydration in an unsuspecting frog or salamander, situate the enclosure within your home so as to keep it out of direct sunlight and well away from incandescent heat sources. Fluorescent lighting provides the ideal light source, as it gives off very little heat. Since amphibians are nocturnal, they should be provided with at least 12 hours of darkness each day.

A thermometer and humidity gauge are always standard equipment when housing amphibians. Temperate amphibian species require temperatures ranging between 60 and 70 degrees Fahrenheit, with humidity around 75 to 80 percent. Tropical varieties need temperatures between 75 and 80 degrees Fahrenheit, with humidity at 85 to 90 percent. If environmental temperature is too high and/or humidity is too low, dehydration becomes a definite threat. On the contrary, if temperatures drop too low, overall activity, including eating, will diminish.

For land portions of a vivarium, a heating pad placed under the tank can help regulate temperatures. Standard aquarium heaters can be used to heat the water within the tank. Do not use heat lamps, as these will quickly dehydrate your pet. Humidity can be maintained by lightly misting the sphagnum moss with water at least two times per week. Don't overmist, as this can lead to harmful fungal growth.

Clean your pet's home on a daily basis. [*Note:* Always wear disposable gloves when performing these duties to protect yourself against diseases that can be spread by these types of pets (see Chap. 59).] Remove any uneaten food or debris left over from the day before and change the water in the water bowl (if used) daily. Remove soiled moss as needed, and plan on replacing the entire moss bedding every 3 weeks. For those enclosures with water reservoirs, perform a complete water change twice weekly. All wastewater should be siphoned from the bottom in order to remove organic debris that has settled to the bottom of the tank. Thoroughly clean the walls and fixtures inside the enclosure on a monthly basis. Use a mild soap when doing so and be sure to rinse all areas thoroughly, as soap residues can irritate and damage the skin of amphibians.

Nutrition

Feeding live food to your frog or salamander is recommended in order to stimulate and promote normal natural feeding behavior. Crickets are the ideal food, as they are inexpensive and easy to obtain. Crickets can be purchased from most pet stores or can be gathered from around your home. Just be sure, however, that all crickets you feed are pesticide-free. One day prior to offering them to your pet, feed the crickets tropical fish food or a commercial cricket diet loaded with nutrients to booster their nutritional value.

Terrestrial amphibians can also be fed fruitflies, mealworms, and aphids. Some of the larger toads may even make a meal of baby mice if offered to them! Aquatic amphibians enjoy earthworms, insect larvae, and small fish. Obviously, their food should be fed to them in the water. Feeding your amphibian once a day should be sufficient. Remove any uneaten food from the previous day prior to feeding a fresh meal.

You will soon discover that each frog or salamander will develop its own individualized eating habits. Some will prefer slow-moving prey while others enjoy the thrill of the chase. For instance, toads usually prefer to wait passively for prey to cross their paths, whereas frogs often take a more aggressive approach.

Preventive Health Care

Pet amphibians can benefit from annual veterinary checkups just like other pets. In addition to a physical examination, stool checks and cultures should be performed to ensure that your pet is and remains free of infection or parasitism. Because amphibians can be carriers of zoonotic organisms, special precautions should be taken when handling these pets (see Chap. 59).

Strict sanitation, environmental control (including temperature and humidity), and high-quality rations must be given top priority in order to prevent disease in amphibians kept as pets. Keep a close eye on your pet's behavior and movements, eating habits, elimination habits, and physical characteristics. Notify your veterinarian of any changes that you see.

Diseases and Disorders of Amphibians

Improper sanitation, inadequate environmental parameters (such as temperature and humidity), and/or poor nutrition cause the vast majority of diseases and disorders seen in amphibians. If your pet is exhibiting clinical signs or any type of strange behavior, take it to your veterinarian immediately for a checkup. If your veterinarian does not work on amphibians, ask for a referral to one in your area who does so. By identifying and treating diseases in their early stages, successful treatment and cure is much more obtainable. Below are some of the more common diseases and disorders seen in amphibians. Others do exist, which is why a veterinary diagnosis is essential (Table 53.1).

Table **53.1** Diseases and Disorders of Amphibians

Disease or disorder	Clinical signs	Treatment comments
Red leg disease	Reddened skin on underside of pet; ulcers on toes; bloating; cloudy eyes	Treat with antibiotics; salt baths; sanitize amphibian's environment
Edema syndrome	Generalized swelling or bloating of the body; breathing difficulties; weakness	Can occur because of liver disease, skin disease, toxins; also seen in amphibians living in and around distilled water; treat by veterinary removal of fluid with needle and syringe; salt baths; treat underlying cause

Table **53.1** Diseases and Disorders of Amphibians (*Continued*)

Disease or disorder	Clinical signs	Treatment comments
Water mold disease	White to brown cotton-like lesions on skin; weight loss; lethargy; breathing difficulties	Seen in amphibians housed in water kept below 70°F; diagnose with skin scraping; elevate water temperatures to above 70°F; salt baths
Dehydration	Weight loss; emaciation; lethargy; dull, dark skin; sunken eyes; incoordination	Seen in terrestrial amphibians kept in high temperatures; also in amphibians with skin disease; treat with water and electrolyte baths
Parasitic disease	Skin ulceration and lesions; diarrhea; weight loss; breathing difficulties	Due to poor husbandry and stress; treat with antiparasite drugs and antibiotics; clean and sanitize enclosure; improve nutrition
Hypothermia	Listlessness; loss of appetite	Maintain proper environmental temperatures
Poisoning	Skin lesions; seizures; skin color change; bloating; breathing difficulties	Sources can include disinfectant residues, vegetation or food contaminated with insecticides; contaminated water; remove inciting cause; support through good nutrition and husbandry

Table **53.1** Diseases and Disorders of Amphibians (*Continued*)

Disease or disorder	Clinical signs	Treatment comments
Bacterial skin infection	Nodules on skin; weight loss; skin ulcers	Treat with appropriate antibiotics; improve sanitation
Metabolic bone disease	Deformities of jaws and/or limbs; limb fractures	Due to imbalance of calcium, phosphorus, and other vitamins and minerals in diet; treat or prevent by feeding or dusting food source with supplement prior to feeding to amphibian

Invertebrates

"Invertebrate" is the term used to describe any animal that is devoid of a backbone. Among the countless numbers that exist, the most popular ones kept as pets are tarantulas, scorpions, and hermit crabs. Spiders and scorpions both belong to the class Arachnida, whose members sport two body segments and four pairs of legs. Hermit crabs are members of the class Crustacida, and are cousins of lobsters and shrimp.

Prior to getting an invertebrate as a pet, do your homework first. Check out books and Websites to become an expert on your favorite type. Also, talk to pet-store owners who specialize in the sale of these type of animals. Their knowledge and experience in husbandry practices are invaluable. Look at the different living arrangements they have set up for the invertebrates that they sell. This will give your some great ideas that you can apply to your own pet's housing setup.

TARANTULAS AND SCORPIONS

Certainly the most popular of all arachnids kept as pets are tarantulas. With their hairy legs and bodies, multiple eyes and quick, sudden movements, tarantulas are formidable in appearance. Yet despite their scary features, tarantulas make great pets. They are relatively easy to maintain and can display unique and entertaining personalities. In the wild, tarantulas can be found resting within foxholes deep within the ground or clinging to trees trunks and branches. Those persons living in "tarantula country" know that you can also find them climbing the sides of homes and buildings after a drenching rain! As a rule, tarantulas are hearty pets, with some living to be as old as 15 years with diligent care.

When selecting your tarantula, there are many species from which to choose. If you are a beginner, consider purchasing a Mexican redleg or Chilean rose tarantula, both known for their docility. Four other popular pet tarantulas include the pinktoe, redrump, whitecollared, and the curlyhaired tarantulas. Purchase a captive-bred tarantula versus capturing your own so that you will have some idea of the spider's temperament ahead of time.

As far as scorpions are concerned, thousands of species live in the deserts, semiarid regions, and tropical climates across the world. They can be found burrowed underground or hiding under rocks or fallen logs. Scorpions possess powerful pinchers that can deliver a mighty pinch if they latch onto a finger. They also have that infamous stinger attached to the end of their tails that can inflict painful wounds in a blink of an eye. Some scorpions deliver highly toxic poisons that can be quite dangerous to humans. As a result, always obtain your scorpion from a reputable source to ensure that the variety you are choosing is safe to handle.

The large emperor scorpion is a popular choice among beginners. Black in color, these scorpions can reach over 5 inches in length! When selecting yours, choose one that appears active, alert, fat, and healthy, not one that is thin and lethargic. If well cared for, scorpions can live 10 to 12 years in captivity.

Restraint

As a rule, arachnids should be handled as little as possible. When you do it, gentle restraint is needed.

Tarantulas that are handled roughly or startled could bite! Although their venom usually produces no more of a reaction than would a bee sting (depending on species), some persons can be allergic to the venom and suffer more severe reactions. It is always a good idea to wear gloves when handling your spider, not only to protect against bites but also to prevent irritation to the hands. The body and legs of tarantulas are covered with tiny hairs that act not only as sensors but also as defense weapons. This is particularly true of the barbed hairs covering the spider's abdomen. By scraping their abdomen with their hind legs, tarantulas can actually flick these tiny hairs at a perceived threat, including your hands. If these hairs embed themselves in the skin, they can be quite irritating and cause a rash. Tarantulas that are stressed or threatened are the ones most likely to exhibit this type of behavior when handled.

To hold your spider, place your hand down flat palm-up in front of it, then gently coax it onto your hand using your other hand to tap the rear end and push it forward. You can also gently lift your tarantula by its abdomen with its head facing away from you, keeping your free hand beneath your spider to create a platform on which it can stand (Fig. 54.1).

As a rule, gloves should be worn whenever handling a scorpion to protect your hands against being stung should your scorpion become agitated or frightened (Fig. 54.2). They will also protect your scorpion, as you are less likely to drop your pet if it lashes out at you. Coax your scorpion into your outstretched gloved hand as you would a tarantula, or you can pick it up by the base of the tail.

If you do get bitten or stung by your arachnid, by all means do not panic and drop it to the floor. Instead, gently place your pet down onto a stable surface, then

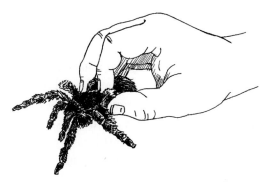

FIGURE 54.1 The proper way to lift your tarantula. Always keep it close to a supporting surface to prevent injury if it is accidentally dropped.

FIGURE 54.2 Scorpions can inflict nasty stings with their tails if they feel threatened.

treat your wound as you would any other sting or wound (don't hesitate to contact your physician for further directions). Note that abdominal rupture due to fall-induced trauma is one of the most prevalent injuries seen by veterinarians in these types of pets.

Housing

Arachnids can be housed in glass terrariums or simply clear plastic storage containers with snap-on lids. If you plan on owning more than one, they will need to be housed separately to prevent fighting or worse yet, cannibalism!

When choosing an enclosure, keep in mind that length is more important than height. The shorter the walls are, the less chance of injury from falling. Covers must provide adequate ventilation and prevent escape. Screen tops should not be used, as these can injure delicate legs and appendages.

As with all invertebrates, maintaining proper temperature and humidity within any enclosure is of the utmost importance. Standard equipment for all enclosures will include a thermometer and a humidity gauge. For most arachnids kept as pets, temperatures should not be allowed to fall below 72 degrees nor exceed 85 degrees Fahrenheit. Also, the humidity should be kept above 55 percent. Hot rocks should not be used as heating devices within your pet's enclosure, as these can cause serious burns. Instead, a heating pad placed one-third of the way under the enclosure (kept on low setting and covered with a towel for extra insulation) can be used to provide a temperature gradient within the enclosure that your arachnid will enjoy. In order to maintain proper humidity, lightly mist the substrate (until it barely clings to your finger when touched) and the sides of the enclosure with filtered water every few days. Housing facilities should be kept out of direct sunlight and away from drafts to prevent uncontrollable temperature and humidity fluctuations. No special lighting is required for your eight-legged friend!.

(*Note:* Depending on species, wild tarantulas and scorpions can live in habitats ranging from tropical rainforests to dry, arid deserts. As a result, to be sure the abovementioned guidelines fit for your particular species, consult your pet store professional.)

The best substrate to use on the floor of a terrestrial arachnid's home is vermiculite. It can be found at most lawn and garden centers. In most instances, a 3- to 4-inch layer of vermiculite will suffice to allow your pet to burrow into if it so desires. Vermiculite is also excellent at retaining moisture, thereby helping to maintain proper humidity within the enclosure. For tropical or forest dwelling varieties, a layer of sphagnum moss should line the bottom of the terrarium to provide an excellent cushion in case of an accidental fall.

Regardless of the substrate used, be sure to keep your arachnid's home pristine by removing any soiled substrate and uneaten food every day. A complete substrate replacement should be done every 6 weeks, or any time mold growth or substrate discoloration is detected. Before adding new substrate, give the inside of the enclosure a thorough cleaning with soap and water. Be sure to rinse and dry well to eliminate any residues.

For your arachnid's pleasure, you can further adorn its abode with smooth-edged rocks, silk plants, and plenty of places to hide. Cork bark, PVC piping, and/or an inverted clay flower pot with an entry hole in the bottom can provide excellent shelter into which your pet can retreat if it feels like doing so. Small caves made out of rock are also appreciated by most arachnids. Just be sure that there are no sharp edges on any items you place inside the enclosure. If you own a tree-dwelling species, you'll need to provide it with plenty of branches and foliage onto which it can climb.

Provide a shallow water dish for your spider or scorpion. Be sure that it is easily accessible and contains a water level shallow enough to prevent accidental drowning.

Nutrition

The basic meal plan for the captive tarantula or scorpion consists of crickets or grasshoppers (pesticide-free, of course), with the occasional moth, beetle, or mealworm thrown in for variety (Fig. 54.3). Larger species may even enjoy the occasional lizard or baby mouse. Regardless of what is fed, remove any uneaten prey if it has not been dispatched within 3 hours of feeding. For prey that has been killed by the spider or scorpion, remove any eaten or undigested portions from the enclosure within 24 hours after feeding.

Adult tarantulas and scorpions should be fed about every 3 days, whereas immature ones should eat at least every other day to provide proper nutrition for growth. Also, the warmer the environment in which your invertebrate is kept, the faster it will grow and consequently, the more food it will require.

Four to five crickets per week will be sufficient for most arachnids. For best results, feeding should be done at night to satisfy your pet's nocturnal hunting habits. Offer one or two crickets per meal. Never put more than two crickets at a time in with your tarantula, because they may collectively "gang up" on your pet and harm it. The same holds true for scorpions, although their pinchers allow them to defend themselves much more effectively. Again, keep in mind that no food is to be offered during the molting process, as this is the time when your arachnid is most vulnerable to attack.

Molting

From time to time arachnids will molt and shed their outer skeletons (exoskeletons). This is how they grow in size and keep their protective coverings fresh. In

FIGURE 54.3 Tarantulas will crush their prey and cover them with digestive juices.

younger individuals, molting may take place every month or so. In adults, molting occurs less frequently, usually every 12 to 18 months.

Prior to beginning a molt, your tarantula's color will darken, becoming almost black in appearance. Activity and appetite also diminish 1 to 2 weeks prior to the event. Avoid handling your spider once these signs appear, and during the actual molting process. The same rule holds true for offering live food. Regardless of size, live prey can seriously injure a spider that is in active molt. As your spider starts its molt, it may turn on its side or back and appear almost dead. Don't panic, as this is normal. Proper humidity within your spider's enclosure is essential for a successful molt. As a result, check the humidity gauge within the tank daily and, if needed, apply a light mist to the vermiculite and to the side of the enclosure. Avoid misting your spider directly.

Molting is considered complete once your arachnid's new exoskeleton has tanned and hardened. At this time, you can resume feeding your pet live food.

Preventive Health Care

Healthy tarantulas and scorpions should appear alert and active and have all appendages intact. (*Note:* If your pet does happen to lose a leg to an accident, don't fret. Otherwise healthy arachnids will regenerate the lost appendage after several molts.)

The abdomen should be plump and the legs fully functional, not curled in on themselves. In tarantulas, hair should not be missing except perhaps on the abdominal surface. The skin of an arachnid should not be blotchy in appearance or have any white spots on it. Those arachnids that move slowly, appear emaciated, and remain antisocial are probably harboring an illness. Always remember that dehydration due to poor environmental management and abdominal rupture caused by falling are the two most common causes of death in tarantulas and scorpions. Take care to protect your pet against both of them.

HERMIT CRABS

Hermit crabs are fascinating pets that can provide hours of enjoyment just observing their behavior and antics. It quickly becomes apparent that

DID YOU KNOW?

Some hermit crabs live on the ocean floor some 2000 meters below the surface!

each crab possesses a distinct and unique personality. They are fairly easy to maintain as pets, assuming, of course, that proper care and nutrition is afforded them.

Restraint

When picking up your crab (which should be done infrequently), grasp it by the shell with its front end pointing away from you. If your pet happens to latch onto you with its claw, by all means do not let go! Instead, make a gentle attempt to pry open the claw in order to release your finger. If this doesn't work, run lukewarm water over the claw until your crab releases its grip. (*Note:* Never attempt to extract your crab from its shell. If you try to do so, it will resist with all its might and, more than likely injure itself in the process.)

Housing

Hermit crabs are usually housed in 10- to 20-gallon glass aquarium enclosures, with securely fastened acrylic tops containing multiple air vents. Large plastic boxes with tops containing plenty of ventilation holes or slits can also be used. Three to four inches of sand can be used to line the bottom of the enclosure. This should allow your crab enough room to burrow. Be sure to spot-clean this sand on a daily basis. As mentioned previously, keep an eye out for food buried beneath the surface. A complete change in substrate should be performed every 2 weeks. Because hermit crabs are mostly active at night, there are no special lighting requirements. Environmental temperature should be kept between 72 and 85 degrees Fahrenheit. Humidity within the enclosure should be kept above 80 percent. A moist sponge can help maintain humid conditions within your pet's home, as well as provide an alternate source of drinking water. Natural sponges are preferred over the artificial ones. Also, keeping your crab's living quarters out of direct sunlight and drafts will help prevent unpredictable changes in temperature and humidity.

Keep in mind that hermit crabs also love to cruise, climb, and jump, so the inside of your crab's home should provide amenities that cater to these needs. Smooth rocks and/or pieces of driftwood can be used to provide for places for your crab to climb and hide. Silk plants can also be added to spruce up the surroundings. Keep climbing surfaces low enough in elevation to prevent accidental injury if your pet slips and falls. If you want to go the extra mile for your crab, mist its sand with saltwater (available from your local pet store or aquarium shop) daily to more closely simulate its natural environment. This will also help to maintain proper humidity within the enclosure.

Hermit crabs enjoy company, so keeping two or more together will help prevent boredom. Just remember to provide at least three shells (of varying sizes) per crab to allow for plenty of new home choices. Avoid painted or decorated shells as these can be harmful to hermit crabs.

Nutrition

Hermit crabs will eat just about anything you put in front of them. However, to ensure a high plane of nutrition, they should be fed only commercial rations designed for hermit crabs. These are available at most pet stores specializing in exotic and aquatic animals. These commercial diets can be supplemented with cornmeal, oats, apples, bananas, grapes, beans, and lettuce and even moist dog food. In addition, most hermit crabs love peanut butter!

Whatever you use for food and water dispensers, they should be easily acces-

> **Dr. P's Vet Tip**
> Do not give bread to hermit crabs, as it can clog their gills and cause them to suffocate.

sible. Metal jar lids should not be used, as these can rust and can contaminate your crab's food and water. Clam shells can make ideal food and water bowls, and can also act as a source of calcium for your crab. Just be sure to keep water levels shallow enough to prevent drowning.

All uneaten food should be removed prior to the next fresh meal. Be aware that a crab will bury food just as a dog will bury a bone. As a result, you may have to do some digging in order to accomplish this task!

Molting

Your hermit crab will undergo a molt every 12 to 18 months (or more frequently if immature) in order to shed its exoskeleton. Molting is necessary for continued growth and for regeneration for any limbs they may have been lost since the previous molt. As an impending molt approaches, you may notice your pet becoming less active or less social. It may bury itself in the substrate a week or two prior to the actual molt. Molting hermit crabs are quite susceptible to attacks by pugnacious cagemates; therefore, all cagemates not undergoing molt should be removed until the process is complete. It is also vital that the humidity in the enclosure be kept at a proper level to assist your crab in its molt. Realize that every time your crab undergoes a molt, it will require a bigger shell. As a rule, the rounder the shell is, the better. Be sure it has plenty from which to choose.

Preventive Health Care

FIGURE 54.4 A good diet, a clean habitat, and plenty of shells from which to choose a home will allow your hermit crab to lead a happy and healthy life.

Hermit crabs are relatively easy to care for and keep healthy. If provided with a good diet, a clean habitat, and plenty of shells from which to choose a home, your hermit crab will lead a happy, contented, and healthy life. In fact, when well cared for, it is not unusual for these pets to exceed 10 years of age in captivity (Fig. 54.4)!

DISEASES AND DISORDERS OF INVERTEBRATES

The vast majority of diseases and disorders seen in invertebrates kept as pets are caused by improper sanitation, poor nutrition, and excessive or improper handling. Table 54.1 lists some of the more common diseases and disorders seen.

Table 54.1 Diseases and Disorders of Invertebrates

Disease or disorder	Clinical signs	Treatment and comments
Dehydration	Gaunt, thin appearance; legs curled inward	Lower temperature and increase humidity accordingly; mist pet every 4 hours; move cage if exposed to direct sunlight; treatment often unrewarding if dehydration severe
Lethargy; loss of appetite	Same	Could be due to impending molt or illness; look for signs of illness, such as emaciation, dehydration, skin lesions; treat as appropriate
Malnutrition	Gaunt, thin appearance	Review and correct nutrition; be sure food is easily accessible
Skin infections	Blotchy skin; white patches	Usually due to unsanitary living conditions or improper temperature and/or humidity; treat by correcting underlying problem; apply antibiotics and antifungals
Injured or lost appendages	Same	No treatment needed; will be replaced after several molts

Table 54.1 Diseases and Disorders of Invertebrates (*Continued*)

Disease or disorder	Clinical signs	Treatment and comments
Dark color change	Same	Impending molt; normal
Circular hair loss on abdomen	Same	Normal in tarantulas; due to "throwing" hairs
Abdominal rupture	Obvious trauma to abdomen; protruding contents	Often occurs when dropped from a height; no treatment
Insecticide poisoning	Seizures; lethargy; death	Usually occurs when pet comes in contact with an insecticide sprayed in close proximity to its enclosure or fed insects contaminated with insecticide

Tropical Fish

Looking for a pet that doesn't eat much, requires no training whatsoever, will not bring fleas into your house, and can actually lower your blood pressure? Welcome to the world of tropical fish. More and more, these fascinating aquatic creatures are finding their way into the hearts of pet lovers all across the country. In fact, it is estimated that aquariums adorn approximately one out of three households in the United States alone.

Another key indicator of the popularity of tropical fish in this country is the amount of money spent on them each year. Retail sales of tropical fish and supplies are in the hundreds of millions of dollars per year, with no signs of stopping. So what makes these scaly creatures so fashionable as pets? What's the attraction to owning an aquarium filled with tropical fish?

To begin, aquariums, especially the freshwater variety, are really fairly easy to care for, regardless of what some people might say. With a basic knowledge of aquarium management and tropical fish husbandry, anyone can successfully create and propagate a self-contained aquatic environment. Tropical fish themselves are virtually maintenance-free, requiring only food and a clean, suitable environment in which to live. Unlike dogs, they don't require lots of attention on your part, yet you'll find that once you have your aquarium started, they'll

FIGURE 55.1 Aquariums and tropical fish can provide hours of enjoyment and relaxation.

receive loads of it nonetheless (Fig. 55.1).

Maintaining an aquarium filled with tropical fish is a relatively inexpensive endeavor when compared to other types of pet ownership. Aside from initial start-up costs needed for equipment and supplies, the yearly cost of food, maintenance, and new fish rarely places a strain on the average household budget. Fish do not require yearly trips to the veterinarian to keep them healthy, which, as any responsible dog or cat owner knows, can add considerably to the owner's yearly pet expense account.

Finally, people who own tropical fish as pets can plan on reaping the same benefits and sharing in the same joy and satisfaction that come with owning a pet. Aquariums can provide their caretakers with entertainment for hours on end and can contribute to our knowledge of an environmental ecosystem so very different from our own. As educational tools for children, aquariums can't be beat. They are a fun way to teach kids about aquatic life and also provide a means of teaching responsible pet ownership at an early age.

There is one more benefit to owning an aquarium that you might find fascinating. Medical research has actually shown that aquariums can be effective stress-management tools. That is, reduced anxiety levels and lowered blood pressure can result from spending just a few minutes each day observing the steady, flowing movement

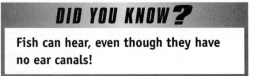

DID YOU KNOW?

Fish can hear, even though they have no ear canals!

of aquarium life. Considering today's hectic world, this benefit alone is a good enough reason to rush out and get an aquarium started right away!

Getting Started

There are two types of aquarium environments that tropical fish hobbyists have to choose from: freshwater and saltwater. Since the latter variety requires a greater level of care and expertise (and expense) to ensure success, our discussion, for all practical purposes, is limited to the freshwater aquarium. This is by far the most popular and practical type for children and beginning hobbyists.

In order to create a first-rate freshwater aquarium for yourself or for your kids, you'll need to spend some money on proper equipment and supplies. Of course, you'll need a tank, along with ancillary supplies such as substrate for the bottom of the tank, plants (real or artificial), aquarium cover with fluorescent lighting, thermometers, tank cleaning equipment, and fixtures for your fish to use for shelter. In addition, a good water-quality control system, including water filtration and aeration devices, is a must.

Aquarium Tanks

Aquarium tanks are available in all shapes and sizes, from small goldfish bowls to 200-gallon reservoirs. Obviously, the size of the aquarium will dictate how many fish will be allowed to dwell within, as well as the amount of time necessary for care and cleaning. Regardless of the gallon capacity that you choose (the 10- and 20-gallon varieties are the most popular), it is best to select a tank that is rectangular in shape instead of one that is round or one that is tall and narrow, since the amount of oxygen exchange that occurs between the outside air and the water in the tank is directly proportional to the size of the air-water interface dictated by the shape of the tank (Fig. 55.2). Tropical fish thrive much better in tanks with large surface areas on top, simply because the oxygen levels in these tanks are greater. If a bowl-type aquarium is to be used, be sure to fill it only to the halfway mark with water, in order to achieve the greatest possible surface area for this exchange of oxygen between the air and the water to take place.

FIGURE 55.2 A rectangular tank allows for better surface-to-air interface than does a round tank.

Avoid aquarium tanks that use metal in their frame construction. Metal, if exposed to water over a period of time, could corrode and become a major source of contamination of your tank water. The more glass in the tank, the better. In fact, aquarium tanks composed entirely of glass with silicone-sealed edges and corners are preferred over others. Some enthusiasts prefer acrylic over glass, simply because of its durability, but the major disadvantage to acrylic is that it tends to scratch easily when cleaned and can become quite unsightly over time.

You will need to equip your aquarium tank with a cover, preferably one with a hinged access door. The purpose of aquarium covers is to keep dust, silt, and other airborne contaminants out of the water, and to keep the fish in! Some of the fancier models come equipped with fluorescent light sources and reflectors, which not only play a useful role in the temperature regulation within the tank but are also desirable if you so choose to propagate live plants and vegetation within your aquarium.

Finally, you will need to establish a location within the house to place your new aquarium. Any location will do as long as the tank is not exposed to direct sunlight or environmental pollution. Be sure that the table or stand on which you place your aquarium is sturdy; a 10-gallon aquarium filled with water and ancillary supplies can weigh in excess of 80 pounds!

Ancillary Supplies

Two inches of gravel, stone, pebble, or sand can be used as a bottom lining for your tank to provide an anchoring substrate for plants and shelters and to serve as anchoring points for the tank's biological filter (explained later) (Fig. 55.3). If the gravel or substrate you are planning on using was used in a previous aquarium, be sure to boil it thoroughly to disinfect it before placing it into your tank. The choice between real and artificial plants is entirely up to you. The main advantage of artificial over natural is ease of maintenance and durabil-

FIGURE 55.3 Sloping the gravel within the tank will cause waste to drift and accumulate at one side of the tank, where it can be more easily removed.

ity. However, for a more aesthetic and natural look to your aquarium environment, live flora can't be beat.

If you'll recall Biology 101, live plants can act as a source of oxygen for your fish through the process called *photosynthesis.* They also provide a source of food for some fish, as well as a place to lay their eggs. If you desire real vegetation over the artificial kind, you'll need to be sure to match it with the type of fish you want to keep in the aquarium. For more information about proper matching, ask a local tropical fish dealer or aquarium shop, or consult your local library, bookstore, or the Internet.

Using live plants also means that you'll need to provide a light source for them. Many aquarium covers contain built-in lighting. Ideally, artificial light sources such as fluorescent lighting (approximately 3 watts per gallon of water) should be used instead of natural lighting, since the latter can be difficult to regulate properly. Eight to ten hours of light each day should be enough to allow your plants to thrive in their watery environment. Be aware, however, that too much lighting is not good and can cause harmful temperature fluctuations within the tank, leading to algae growth.

Finally, every aquarium needs a variety of fixtures and structures designed to provide shelter and security for its finned inhabitants. You can certainly be creative in this department; however, you must also use some caution. If the object you're placing in the aquarium is made of plastic instead of glass or ceramic, be sure that it is nontoxic (including

Table 55.1 Equipment and Supplies Needed for a Freshwater Aquarium

Tank (size based on preference)
Lighted tank hood
Water heater
Thermometer
Gravel
Undergravel filter
Air pump and tubing
Plants, rocks, and decorations
Fish net
Pitcher or bucket

artificial plants!). The same goes for painted fixtures. To be safe, these items should be purchased from an aquarium supply house or pet store instead of trying to supply them yourself from everyday household items (Table 55.1).

Water Quality Control

Before introducing any fish into your new aquarium, you must make certain that the water you are putting them in is of the highest quality possible. Now this doesn't mean that you'll need to invest in an expensive purification system or purchase stock in a bottled water company. On the contrary, ordinary tap water from the kitchen faucet works just fine as a water source for your aquarium. However, you need to take certain measures to ensure that this water is (and, once in the aquarium, remains) of satisfactory quality to ensure success.

Ordinary tap water is classified as being either "hard" or "soft," depending on the amounts of minerals dissolved within. Test kits are available from aquarium shops that can tell you whether your water supply is hard or soft. Most tropical fish prefer water that is on the soft end [about 40 to 60 ppm (parts per million)]. If you live in an area with hard water, make sure that it is softened before being introduced into the tank. There are several ways to do this. First, the most efficient way (and the most expensive way) is to purchase a water softener that can be hooked into your house's water supply, and will provide a continuous supply of soft water. Other alternatives to purchasing one of these machines or filters include boiling the water first to remove the mineral deposits, or mixing distilled water in with your untreated water to effectively dilute out the hardness.

In addition to correcting water hardness, you must also neutralize or remove the chlorine or chloramine normally added to most water supplies. This is achieved by adding commercially available tablets or powders to the water that are designed specifically for this purpose.

Water temperature is a vital parameter that warrants a fish owner's special attention. In fact, improper maintenance of water temperature is one of the more common causes of aquarium failure that many amateurs encounter. Just because fish are called "tropical" fish doesn't necessarily mean that they automatically thrive in warmer temperatures. In fact, warmer water carries less oxygen, and some of the more sensitive species of tropical fish will do quite poorly in excessively warm water. As a general rule, most tropical fish do well with water temperatures maintained around 75 to 80 degrees Fahrenheit. However, before purchasing many different types of fish for your tank, it would be wise to find out what the ideal temperature is for each species. If the temperature ranges differ significantly, then one species will thrive at the expense of another.

Rapid temperature fluctuations should be avoided at all costs, since these can be quite harmful to fish. Keep this in mind when replacing water within the aquarium. Be sure the water you add is at the same temperature as the existing tank water. And don't worry about the natural thermal layers associated with water. Your aerator pump will keep the water circulating enough to prevent significant temperature gradients from being established.

The best way to maintain narrow temperature margins within your tank is to invest in an aquarium water heater and a quality thermometer. If possible, avoid mercury thermometers. Although they are quite accurate, should the thermometer break and the mercury enter the water, your entire fish population could be fatally poisoned within a matter of minutes.

Fish, like people, rely on oxygen to sustain life. And since fish rely on their water supply for this source of oxygen, it stands to reason that the aquarium enthusiast be sure that the oxygen supply remains adequate. The most common method of ensuring well-oxygenated aquarium water is to install an aerator pump within the tank. These water aerators draw in air from the outside and "bubble" it into the water, helping to stimulate oxygen exchange. The circulating action of these pumps also helps increase total water contact with the outside air at the surface of the tank, thereby allowing greater amounts of oxygen to be absorbed into the system. An efficient aerator pump should exchange about 2 liters of air per 1 liter of water every hour. One interesting point to remember is that the fish are literally breathing the air you breathe; nicotine, fumes, and other pollutants in the air being pumped into the aquarium can have adverse effects on the health of some fish. As a result, take care to shelter your aquarium away from those obvious sources of air pollution.

Live plants, which release oxygen into their surrounding environment through photosynthesis, can also make a significant contribution to the oxygen levels within the aquarium. Also, keeping water temperatures from becoming warmer than the desired ranges and preventing fish overcrowding can both have a positive impact on this aspect of water quality.

Again, the very shape you choose for your aquarium tank (remember the air-water interface) can directly affect the oxygen content of the water, and hence, its overall quality

Filter Systems

In addition to water aeration pumps, a filter system is needed within the aquarium to remove solid and chemical contaminates from the water before they build up to harmful levels. These filters can be classified as either mechanical filters or biological filters. *Mechanical filters* hook onto the outside (or sometimes inside) of the aquarium and actively pump water through a filtering substance, such as filter wool or activated charcoal. Ideally, the capacity of the filter should be such that the entire water content of the tank can pass through it and be filtered every 2 hours. If mechanical filters are used, it is important to replace the filter material on a regular basis, preferably every 3 weeks.

The other type of filter is the *biological filter.* Compared to the cost of a good mechanical filter, the cost of a biological filter is negligible. Yet it can be an even more effective weapon at waste control than its mechanical, more expensive counterpart. A biological filter consists of nothing more than a porous plastic tray that is placed beneath 2 to 3 inches of gravel or substrate lining the bottom of the aquarium. This tray serves as a gathering site for bacteria found within the tank. These bacteria are "biological garbage gobblers" and break down organic wastes that are passively carried through the filter by the normal water circulation within the tank created by the air pump. In this way, Nature does the cleaning for you, the natural way!

Aquarium filters function to keep levels of ammonia and nitrites, two highly toxic substances derived from organic waste, within acceptable ranges. Ideally, the pH of the water should be kept between 6.8 and 7.5, and nitrite levels should be kept to an absolute minimum. Special test kits are available from aquarium shops and should be used to monitor these parameters. Unhealthy rises in pH and nitrite levels in newly established aquariums can often be traced back to an underdeveloped biological filter. Overcrowding and overfeeding can play a significant role as well, and these conditions should be corrected promptly.

When setting up a biological filter in a new tank, start with no more than four small fish as your pioneer population. Because new biological filters can take 3 to 6 weeks to become fully established and functional, daily water rotations (in which 20 percent of the tank water is removed and replaced) should be performed during this time to dilute out offending substances. After 6 weeks, you can begin to add more fish.

For established tanks, regardless of whether you use a mechanical filter, a biological filter, or both, plan on removing and replacing 25 to 30 percent of the water within the tank with seasoned tap water (hardness and chlorine removed) every 4 weeks. This rotation will help eliminate impurities that can't be filtered properly, as well as help ease the burden on the filters themselves (Fig. 55.4). A simple bucket or pitcher can be used to accomplish this task. Remember: Change no more than 30 percent at a time instead of the entire tank to prevent from upsetting the environmental equilibrium that has already been established in the aquarium.

Cleaning your Aquarium

How often does an aquarium need to be cleaned? The answer to this is "almost never," assuming, of course that the water-quality control measures above are kept in force. Aeration, filtration, periodic partial water changes, and scavenger fish (explained below) should do the cleaning for you on a continual basis. Keeping the cover closed on your aquarium will help prevent dust and dirt from the outside from soiling the water.

Water that appears gray and cloudy has too much bacteria in it. Such a presentation is caused by a poor filter, overcrowding, or overfeeding, or by failure to properly rotate the water each month. On the other hand, water that appears green and cloudy indicates too much algae. This is caused by excessive exposure to light and by an increase in nitrogen in the water. In both instances, the frequency of water rotations performed must be temporarily increased to regain water quality. Soap-free cleaning pads are useful for scraping off any algae that may have accumulated on the aquarium glass, artificial plants, or stationary fixtures within your tank. Avoid using soaps or detergents to clean your aquarium. Of course, to prevent a recurrence of either problem, the underlying causes must be addressed as well.

FIGURE 55.4 Water rotations help eliminate impurities and support the tank's biological filter.

Selecting Fish for Your Aquarium

As you know, there are countless varieties of tropical fish to choose from when populating your aquarium. The choice is really a matter of your preference and taste. Some people prefer ones with exotic coloring or patterns; others prefer larger varieties over the smaller ones. In addition, some species are more sensitive and delicate than others, and might require more attention and maintenance than you are willing to devote.

One thing you'll want to be very careful of is not to overstock your aquarium with fish. Tank overcrowding is right up there with poor water quality and temperature fluctuations as a major cause of aquarium failures. As a general rule, you should have no more than one inch of fish per one gallon of water. Exceed this ratio, and oxygen content and water quality will suffer.

The various tropical fish species can be classified into groups according to their aggressiveness toward other fish. For instance, goldfish, guppies, and mollies are all known for their mild-mannered temperaments, whereas angelfish can be considered semiaggressive, sometimes making a meal of fish small enough to swallow. Bettas and paradise fish are highly aggressive fish and won't hesitate to pick a fight with any fish in the tank. Regardless of which species you prefer, obviously you don't want to mix aggressive or semiaggressive fish with nonaggressive fish. In fact, if you decide to stock your tank with more aggressive varieties, you'll need to be observant of individual personalities to prevent your serene, peaceful aquarium setting from becoming a battleground!

Besides the more ornamental varieties, you'll want to stock your aquarium with one or more scavenger fish. These fish will inhabit the bottom of the tank or cling to its sides and feed on the algae and leftover food particles. As a result, these scavenger fish play an important role in maintaining water quality. Some of the more popular names include the *cory catfish,* the *suckermouth cats,* and the *coolie loach.* Large, freshwater snails are effective scavengers as well and can be introduced into an aquarium setting for this purpose.

Each type of fish you choose will often have its own little idiosyncrasies as to ideal food, water temperature, pH, and other water conditions. For best results when selecting tropical fish (keeping your desires in mind as well), ask your tropical fish retailer or specialist for recommendations on which tropical fish varieties will work best for you.

What to Look for

When selecting your fish at the aquarium shop or pet store, there are a few items to look for to ensure that you receive healthy pets. First, observe the way a particular fish behaves in its current aquarium setting. It should be active and alert and glide smoothly through the water when swimming. Fish that act lethargic or swim in a crooked or sideways pattern should be avoided.

Anatomically, all fins should be erect and intact, and the fish's belly should be slightly rounded versus sunken. Look for blotchy, discolored skin, ulcerations, or any other obvious signs of disease or parasitism. Eyes should be bright, not cloudy. If one fish in a particular tank is showing signs of illness, assume that all within that tank have been exposed to the disease, and avoid selecting fish from that tank altogether.

> ### Dr. P's Vet Tip
>
> When purchasing fish from a pet store, check out the water color in the tank containing your potential selections. Water that appears yellow, blue, or green could be medicated, indicating a disease outbreak in the tank. If so, move along to the next tank!

Your Pets' New Home

Once you've purchased your new friends, you'll want to slowly introduce them to their new home. Again, be sure all pumps and filters are in place and in working order. The transport container containing the fish should be lowered into the tank water, which should already be at the desired temperature (check your thermometer). Leave the container suspended like this for a good 15 to 20 minutes to allow for a gradual temperature equalization between the two water compartments. Once this is accomplished, open the transport container and allow the fish, at their leisure, to enter into their new domain.

Aquarium owners should make it a point to keep handling and disturbances to a minimum once the fish are set in their environment. The common urge among many beginners to tap on the aquarium glass to get a particular fish's attention should be suppressed! Avoiding this type of behavior will help keep stress levels low and make for a much healthier, happier environment.

If for some reason a fish needs to be removed from the tank, a small net should be used. As an alternative, a plastic storage bag with small holes punched in its bottom makes an excellent fish-catcher. Regardless of which you use, be as slow, deliberate, and patient as possible when trying to capture a fish, thereby keeping stress to an absolute minimum.

Feeding Your Fish

Prepackaged fish food is readily available, and comes in all forms and fashions, such as processed, frozen, or freeze-dried. As a general rule, you should feed only that amount of food that will be consumed within a 3-to 4-minute period. Leftovers are not good, and will eventually build up to such levels at the bottom of the tank as to start adversely affecting the water quality within the tank. Two feedings, one in the morning and one in the afternoon, should suffice to satisfy even the heartiest of appetites!

Diseases and Disorders of Tropical Fish

Selected diseases and disorders seen in tropical fish are listed in Table 55.2. Healthy fish should have smooth, glistening skin surfaces and should exhibit steady, controlled movement within the aquarium. Diseased fish, aside from exhibiting obvious external signs, will exhibit unusual swimming and behavioral patterns. For instance, excessive drifting, circling, hiding, curling, or bottom-sitting are all signs of disease and should alert you to a potential problem.

Stress, poor water quality and failure to quarantine new additions to the aquarium are the two leading factors leading to disease outbreaks within aquariums. If disease does rear its

> ### Dr. P's Vet Tip
> When treating tropical fish suffering from white spot or velvet parasites, gradually raise the water temperature to 82 degrees Fahrenheit to speed up the life cycle of these parasites and expedite the cure.

Table 55.2 Diseases and Disorders of Tropical Fish

Disease or disorder	Clinical signs	Treatment and comments
Diseases related to water quality		
Ammonia and nitrite toxicity	Death of existing fish; inability to keep new additions alive	Caused by improper biological filters; treat by establishing filter; daily water change for 2–3 weeks to keep ammonia and nitrite concentrations low
Diseases		
Velvet	Yellow pollenlike spots on skin; scratching against rocks	Purchase commercial velvet treatment; raise water temperature to 82°F (slowly)
Ich (ichthyophthirius)	White spots or pustules on skin; fish scratch against rocks	Known as "white spot disease"; purchase commercial treatment; slowly raise water temperature to 82°F
Chilodenella; other protozoans; flukes	Excessive body mucus production; damaged gills; irritable behavior; gill rubbing	Treat by adding formalin to water (1 milliliter per 10 gallons of water), then changing water 8 hours later; fish in terminal stages of illness could die from treatment
Hexamita	General unthriftiness; white, stringy feces; thinning	Common in angelfish; treat with metronidazole (250 milligrams per 10 gallons of water)

Table 55.2 Diseases and Disorders of Tropical Fish (*Continued*)

Disease or disorder	Clinical signs	Treatment and comments
Diseases		
"Hole in the head"	Ulcerations on head and sides of body	May be associated with *Hexamita*; treat with frequent water changes, metronidazole; rarely causes death
Tapeworms	General unthriftiness; thinning	Treat by adding the drug praziquantel to water (90 milligrams per 10 gallons of water)
Bacterial diseases		
Aeromonas pseudomonas	Ulcerations on skin; unthriftiness	Often occur secondary to parasites or other diseases; treat with antibiotics added to water
Columnaris disease	Gray-white patches on skin; fraying or loss of fins and tail	Treat with frequent water changes and antibiotics added to the water
Septicemia	Reddish hue to skin; lethargy; unthriftiness; bulging eyes; bloat (dropsy)	Treat with antibiotics; generally unrewarding; improve water quality
Viral diseases		
Lymphocystis disease	White, raised plaques on surface of skin and tail	No treatment available; isolate infected fish; sanitize aquarium

FIGURE 55.5 A number of over-the-counter remedies are available to treat tropical fish diseases.

ugly head within your aquarium, it is important that the disease be identified and treated quickly. Treatment for disease outbreaks generally consists of isolation of infected fish, partial or complete water changes performed on a prescribed schedule, and/or the addition of specific medications to the water within the tank (Fig. 55.5). If you seem to be having chronic problems keeping your fish healthy, contact your local veterinarian for advice or, if your vet is not versed in aquarium management and fish diseases, for referral to the proper resources that you need to answer your questions and find a solution.

Other Interesting
Pet Topics

An Introduction to Holistic Pet Care

Just imagine having the best of both worlds when it comes to your pet's health care! That's exactly what you get when you merge conventional Western medicine with holistic or "alternative" medicine. When over 40 percent of Americans utilize alternative medicine for themselves and spend billions of dollars each year on holistic treatments and remedies, it's no wonder that the popularity of veterinary holistic treatments for pets and their ailments is increasing as well. And as this popularity rises, so does the need for continued education and research in order to identify and refine specific indications, techniques, benefits, and limitations of holistic treatments in our furred, scaled, and feathered friends.

The philosophy of holistic veterinary medicine is one of wellness and disease prevention. Holistic approaches are geared toward stimulating the body's own natural resources and internal mechanisms to afford self-healing and self-protection against disease. Holism not only targets the physical needs of a particular pet but also takes into account the emotional and mental needs of that pet. These needs can be influenced by such factors as breed characteristics, individual personalities, socialization, environmental influences, and disease states that may alter the biochemistry within the body and adversely affect emotional and mental well-being.

To many followers of holism, this school of thought is in direct contrast to the traditional Western approach to veterinary medicine, namely, to target and treat diseases or symptoms only as they arise. Such treatments are felt to be too standardized, failing to take into account patient differences other than those of species, breed, and/or body weight. In conventional veterinary medicine, patients are grouped together by species according to their reaction to disease and to the pharmacological, medical, and/or surgical management of such reactions. In contrast, holistic philosophy theorizes that no two individuals have identical responses to disease manifestations. Therefore, treatment approaches must be customized to each individual patient.

However, to close one's mind on traditional veterinary medicine is to naively discard the facts that they stand true. Let's face it—because of conventional veterinary preventive and therapeutic approaches, a multitude of infectious diseases that at one time killed countless pets have been eradicated or controlled through conventional vaccination programs. Injuries and illnesses that just a few short years ago meant certain death or disability to an unfortunate pet so affected can today be cured or managed with remarkable conventional therapies and techniques. Life span and quality of life are on the increase for today's pet, primarily because of the advances made in traditional veterinary medical knowledge and its application.

Holistic opinions have certainly had their influence on traditional veterinary medicine. For instance, veterinarians have been prescribing aloe vera for years for the treatment of burns and skin irritations. Curricula within veterinary schools and teaching hospitals across the country are placing greater emphasis on the understanding of animal mental health and its role in disease creation, prevention, and cure. And the use of nutraceuticals and dietary management for disease prevention and treatment has become highly favored among traditional veterinary practitioners in recent years.

It goes without saying that both traditional medicine and holistic medicine have their inherent strengths as well as their weaknesses. And this brings up a great point: When traditional and holistic medicine are used in synergy, their combined strength serves to diffuse any weaknesses that one or the other may possess! The use of both traditional and holistic approaches to patient care has been coined "complementary" veterinary medicine. Make no mistake about it: Acute life-threatening injuries or illnesses are still best handled by traditional methods. However, chronic, long-term health challenges that have responded poorly to traditional methods can and should be approached holistically.

To find a holistic veterinarian in your area, contact your local or state veterinary associations. You can also contact the American Association of Holistic Practitioners, the official licensing board of veterinary holistic practitioners. Whenever choosing a veterinary holistic practitioner for your pet, ask the following questions:

- Is your veterinarian a licensed veterinarian who has specific training in the holistic specialty you are seeking?

- How extensive is your vet's holistic training?

- How long has your vet been practicing holistic medicine?

- Can references or success stories be provided with whom you can make contact or follow-up?

- What are your vet's feelings toward conventional veterinary medicine? Does he/she practice complementary medicine?

- Is your vet able to explain the reasoning behind any procedure that may be prescribed or performed?

The more popular types of holistic medical approaches or tools used in veterinary medicine include botanical (herbal) medicine, nutritional medicine, homeopathy, chiropractic care, and acupuncture.

Botanical (Herbal) Medicine

The use of herbs to fight disease dates back far beyond the advent of modern medicine as we know it. Ancient people throughout the world, especially the Chinese and other Eastern cultures, utilized herbs to treat illnesses and injuries arising from hunting and gathering, armed conflict, and recreational activities. Written documentation on the use of herbs for medicinal purposes apparently first appeared in ancient Egyptian culture. By 1000 B.C., this knowledge had made its way across the ocean to Greece, whereupon Greek scholars such as

Socrates, Pliny, Dioscorides, and Krateus expanded on it, refined it, and recorded their findings in a *Materia Medica.* During the Middle Ages, European and Middle Eastern practitioners continued to expound on the works of the Greeks and helped solidify the foundation of the modern herbal *Materia Medica.*

Certainly the usefulness of an herbal remedy in the past depended on that herb's availability in a particular geographic location. Unfortunately, herbal practitioners within the United States found many of the herbs contained in the Old World *Materia Medicas* could not be found in the New World. However, thousands of years before Columbus set foot on the shores of the Americas, local herbs had been used by Native American tribes to prevent and combat disease. This knowledge of New World herbal remedies was quickly assimilated into the new EuroAmerican culture and ultimately grew with subsequent westward expansion, leading to the formation of a *Materia Medica* dealing specifically with native New World herbs.

Thanks to the knowledge imparted by these pioneers in botanical medicine, today's veterinarians have valuable weapons at their disposal. Indeed, herbs can provide a powerful formulary against disease in pets (see Table 56.1). In fact, many of the active ingredients found in herbs are the same ones used in today's modern drugs. These active components include tannins, polysaccharides, glycosides, alkaloids, turpoids, and essential oils. Drug companies extract and isolate these constituents from the whole plant, then potentiate their strength in a laboratory, rendering them highly effective (and highly toxic). However, there has been a paradigm shift in recent years regarding herbs and their active ingredients. Scientists are now recognizing the therapeutic importance of certain "phytochemical" constituents found in whole plants that are absent in isolated extracts. Research is finding that these constituents may not only improve the effectiveness of the active ingredients within a patient's body but also lessen the risk of harmful side effects that the ingredients may cause.

Herbal remedies may be eaten, ingested as/or with liquids, or applied externally as poultices. Both fresh and dried herbs can form the foundation for a particular remedy. However, with the exception of topical poultices (such as aloe vera poultices for burns), most herbal products used in veterinary medicine are made from dried herbs.

Table 56.1 Herbs Commonly Used in Veterinary Medicine*

Common name	Scientific name	Used to treat or prevent
Aloe	*Aloe barbadensis*	Burns; dermatitis
Astragalus	*Astragalus membranaceous*	Immune system depression and stress
Bilberry	*Vaccinium myrtilis*	Diseases of blood vessels and eyes
Bitter melon	*Momordica charantia*	Diabetes mellitus
Black cohosh	*Cimicifuga racemosa*	Inappropriate urination behavior in cats
Black walnut	*Juglans nigra*	Heartworms and other internal parasites
Boswellia	*Boswellia serrata*	Arthritis
Calendula	*Calendula officinalis*	Skin and ear irritations; stomach ulcers
Cranberry	*Vaccinium macrocarpon*	Urinary tract infection
Echinacea	*Echinacea purpurea*	Immune system depression and stress
Eleutherococcus	*Eleutherococcus senticosus*	Weakness; age-related "slowing down"
Eyebright	*Euphrasia officinalis*	Eye inflammation
Garlic	*Allium sativum*	Infections, parasites, cancer
Ginger	*Zingiber officinale*	Carsickness; nausea
Ginkgo	*Ginkgo biloba*	Senile changes, diseases of heart and vessels
Goldenseal	*Hydrastis canadensis*	Infections; liver disease; cancer
Green tea	*Camellia sinensis*	Cancer
Gymnema	*Gymnema sylvestre*	Diabetes mellitus
Hawthorn	*Crataegus oxycantha*	Heart disease

Table 56.1 Herbs Commonly Used in Veterinary Medicine* (*Continued*)

Common name	Scientific name	Used to treat or prevent
Maitake	*Grifola frondosa*	Cancer; immune system depression
Milk thistle	*Silybum marianum*	Liver disease
Red raspberry	*Rubus idaeus*	Pregnancy support
Reishi	*Ganoderma lucidum*	Immune system depression and stress
Saw palmetto	*Serenoa repens*	Prostate disease/enlargement
St. John's wort	*Hypericum perforatum*	Mental/behavioral disorders
Tea tree	*Melaleuca alternifolia*	Ringworm; skin disorders
Turmeric	*Curcuma longa*	Inflammation; liver disease; cancer
Valerian	*Valeriana officinalis*	Mental or behavioral disorders

Note: When used improperly, many herbal remedies can be harmful to pets. As a result, all herbal preparations should be administered by (or under the guidance of) a licensed veterinarian trained in herbology.

These dried herbs are crushed and formed into pills or enclosed within gelatin capsules, made into tealike preparations, or pulverized and mixed with alcohol to form elixirs (Fig. 56.1). Herbal elixirs can be administered to pets in the same way as any other liquid medication, or they can be added directly to a pet's food. Pills and gelatin capsules can be administered directly or cleverly disguised in a treat.

Factors that can affect herbal potency include the method of drying used, the age of the herbal preparation, and the stage at which the plant was originally harvested. For example, dandelion leaves are most effective if harvested before flowering, whereas blue violet is best collected after flowering. Herbs that have not been dried properly may be contaminated with mold, which can certainly adversely alter their effectiveness. Also, the older the herbal preparation, the greater is the chance of a loss in potency due to natural degradation or mishandling. As a rule, potency of herbal remedies will tend to diminish rapidly after one year on the shelf. In order to improve shelf life, herbal products should be stored in dark, airtight containers and in cool, dry locations away from direct light.

When addressing an illness, veterinary herbalists rarely use only a single herb, but rather use a combination of herbs. Doing so offers two powerful advantages: (1) combining certain herbs will create a synergistic attack against the targeted disorder, and (2) herbal combinations can be

FIGURE 56.1 Dried herbs are first crushed and then formed into pills, enclosed within gelatin capsules, or further pulverized and mixed with alcohol to form elixirs.

used to help dilute out undesirable side effects that may be caused by one or more herbs in the formula.

Herbal treatments in animals are usually prescribed for no more than 2 to 4 weeks at a time. Standard dosages are usually continued for 2 to 3 days following the disappearance of clinical signs, and then slowly tapered off over a week's time.

Herbal remedies cannot be used indiscriminately, nor, as mentioned above, should they be used on a long-term basis. Realize that adverse interactions can occur with existing medications that your pet may be taking. Also, certain herbal remedies, given at improper dosages, can cause significant bodily harm. For instance, white willow and white oak bark contains salicylates and can be highly toxic to cats. With more people turning to the Internet as their source for information, it is vital to remember that although this resource and others can indeed provide valuable information concerning herbs and their application in pets, they can also be the source of dangerous misinformation concerning dosages, duration of treatment, and applications of herbal treatments. For your pet's sake, always validate any information you may gather with a veterinary professionally trained in botanical medicine and, of course, never administer a herbal preparation without first consulting a veterinarian.

FIGURE 56.2 The holistic mindset strives for finding and feeding the most natural diet available.

Nutritional Medicine

A holistic approach to nutrition includes the feeding of a "natural"-type food ration and/or the use of nutraceuticals (Fig. 56.2). Many advocates of alternative veterinary medicine believe that many of the health challenges seen in pets today are the result of processed diets loaded with preservatives and by-products.

As emphasized in previous chapters, good nutrition is the foundation for any preventive health care program designed for pets. The holistic mindset strives for finding and feeding the most natural diet available. This ideal ration should

- Be cooked utilizing low temperatures. This will help preserve the food's nutritional value and prevent vital nutrients from being destroyed by high heat.

- Undergo minimal processing, again helping to retain as many of the original nutrients as possible.

- Consist of high-quality, fresh ingredients, including meats, grains, and vegetables. These ingredients should be highly bioavailable (easily digested and assimilated) and contain no by-products.

- Contain no artificial colors or flavorings, as these are viewed as potentially harmful agents when used on a long-term basis.

- Use only natural preservatives such as vitamins E and C. Artificial preservatives such as BHT and ethoxyquin should be absent from the ingredient statement.

■ Contain no refined sugar or excess amounts of salt, both of which are used primarily as flavor enhancers.

From a holistic point of view, a high-quality ration will contain multiple protein sources, and have all protein sources utilized within the food specifically identified on the ingredient statement. In other words, if beef is used as the primary protein source, it will be stated as such on the label. On the contrary, the words "meat" or "beef by-products" indicate that parts other than high-quality muscle tissue were used in the food's formulation. The holistic veterinary nutritionist also wants a protein source that is free from hormone or antibiotic residues. Unfortunately, the only way to be certain whether this is the case is to do your research on the particular supplier in question. Many pet owners even go so far as to have samples of the food independently tested for such residues (although significant costs are usually attached to such a procedure). Also, ethoxyquin is a chemical preservative used to prevent rancidity in pet foods. Holistic rations should have the statement "ethoxyquin-free" printed on the bag.

Many holistic pet owners prefer homemade diets for their pets, often using raw sources of protein. However, with the tremendous number of natural pet food products reaching the market everyday, such homemade preparations are not necessary. In fact, there are several disadvantages to preparing homemade diets, including the time it takes to prepare them, the potential for spoilage or nutritional imbalances, and parasite transmission from tainted ingredients.

Nutraceuticals are defined as food compounds that have scientifically proven health benefits when used at predetermined therapeutic dosages. When used properly, these nutritional supplements can help support healing processes within the body and even help prevent disease (Fig. 56.3). Just some of the nutraceutical agents commonly used in veterinary medicine include glandulars (actual extracts of glandular tissue), antioxidants, bioflavonoids, sulfated glycosaminoglycans, ω-3 fatty acids, probiotics, DHEA (dehydroepiandrosterone), coenzyme Q, *dl*-phenylalanine, creatinine, lactoferrin, vanadium, and DMG (dimethylglycine). Refer to Table 56.2 for a more complete listing of popular nutraceuticals used in veterinary medicine and their indications for use. Because dosages are empirical, consult your veterinarian prior to giving any nutraceutical agent to your pet.

Homeopathy

Homeopathy is considered by many to be the most controversial of all alternative medical practices. The homeopathic movement found its origins in eighteenth-century Europe. Its founder, a German physician by the name of Samuel Hahnemann

FIGURE 56.3 The use of nutraceuticals in veterinary medicine is on the rise.

(1755–1843), promoted homeopathic medicine as an alternative to the conventional medical approaches of that day. Indeed, back then, these conventional orthodox methods of treating disease were in themselves quite crude and sometimes brutal. Blistering, purging, blood letting, heavy-metal treatments, and crude surgical procedures were all accepted practices of the day, and often did more harm than good. Hahnemann viewed homeopathy as a less risky alternative. He also felt that orthodox medicine was being driven by symptomatic treatment of disease rather than by the treatment of the patient as a whole being. As one can imagine, Hahnemann received harsh criticism from his more orthodox peers.

The homeopathic movement made its way to the United States in the early part of the nineteenth century, and slowly gained a loyal following. Well-known proponents of the day included Mark Twain, Daniel Webster, William Cullen Bryant, and John D. Rockefeller. In 1844 the American Institute of Homeopathy was founded. In fact, this was the first national medical society formed in the United States. Interestingly, the American Medical Association was founded 2 years later. One reason for this was to counter the threat that the homeopathic movement posed to conventional medicine!

Table **56.2** Popular Nutraceuticals Used in Veterinary Medicine*

Nutraceutical	Used to treat or prevent
Blue-green algae	Viral infections; cancer; immune depression
α-Lipoic acid	Eye disorders; diabetes; circulatory disturbances
Arginine	Heart disease; liver disease; cancer; diabetes
Bioflavonoids (pycnogenol, rutin, etc.)	Eye disorders, age-related degeneration; allergies
Carnitine	Heart disease; liver disease, submaximum athletic endurance
Creatinine monohydrate	Submaximum athletic performance and endurance; muscle wasting
Coenzyme Q10	Heart disease; tooth and gum disease
Dehydroepiandrosterone (DHEA)	Immune disorders; obesity
DL-Phenylalanine (DLPA)	Arthritis; generalized or specific pain
Dimethylglycine (DMG)	Epilepsy
Enzymes (bromelain, papain, etc.)	Pancreatic enzyme deficiency; inflammatory disorders
Fiber supplements	Constipation, diabetes, bowel inflammation; hairballs; anal sac impaction
Glutamine	Bowel inflammation
Chondroitin sulfate	Arthritis; bladder disease
Glucosamine	Arthritis; bladder disease
Lactoferrin	Feline stomatitis
Lysine	Herpes infections of the eye
Magnesium	Heart disease; neurologic disease

Table **56.2** Popular Nutraceuticals Used in Veterinary Medicine*
(*Continued*)

Nutraceutical	Used to treat or prevent
ω-3 fatty acids	Allergic skin disease; heart disease; arthritis; cancer
Phosphatidylserine	Senility
Probiotics	Food allergies; immune system disorders and suppression; diarrhea
Taurine	Heart disease; liver disease; epilepsy
Vanadium	Diabetes mellitus
Vitamin C (ascorbic acid)	Allergies; immune system disorders; cancer; cataracts

Note: When used improperly, some nutraceuticals can be harmful to pets. As a result, all nutraceuticals should be administered by (or under the guidance of) a licensed veterinarian trained in nutritional therapy.

Information regarding the various homeopathic remedies has been amassed through trial-and-error applications and case studies. These findings or "provings" can all be found in the *Homeopathic Pharmacopoeia*. Within this book, first published in 1897 and updated regularly, homeopathic remedies are listed in "rubrics," which are flowcharts or listings of particular disease symptoms cross-referenced with those homeopathic preparations that produce similar symptoms in the patient.

Classical homeopathy of the type promoted by Hahnemann emphasizes single remedies to be given for specific symptoms. In recent years however, classical homeopathy has been giving way to newer schools of thought that promote combination remedies versus single remedies. The theory behind combining homeopathic remedies is that in doing so, synergy is increased, resulting in a greater chance of treatment success.

Homeopathy was and remains so controversial because its principles have yet to be proved scientifically. One challenge that traditional veterinarians have with homeopathic approaches is that standards have yet to be established that take into account the species, breed, and size of the patient being treated. For example, a small kitten and a large horse may both be prescribed the same remedy at the same potency! Many medical doctors write off apparent homeopathic successes in humans as "placebo effects." Unfortunately, this does not explain the anecdotal successes achieved in certain clinical cases involving animals. Certainly any scientist or research practitioner would agree that when working with living organisms, countless variables exist that we do not understand or recognize. Perhaps it is one or more of these variables that accounts for homeopathic treatment successes when they occur.

Homeopathy is based on the *law of Similars,* or "like cures like." This law contends that agents that cause disease symptoms at standard doses can cause the body to mimic those symptoms when introduced in extremely diluted doses and stimulate the body to cure the underlying disease.

The goal of the veterinary homeopath is to support and strengthen the pet's "vital force." This vital force is responsible for maintaining health and internal harmony within the body. According to homeopathic principles, clinical signs, which are recognized as simply outward expressions of disease and not diseases in themselves, are caused by imbalances affecting this vital force. As the vital force attempts to restore its own balance, clinical signs start to appear. Subtle clinical signs result from a weak vital force response. Severe, pronounced symptoms are indicative of a strong vital force response. Homeopathic treatment is designed to stimulate and strengthen the vital force into restoring its internal balance. When in balance, the vital force is able to effectively call on the natural body defense mechanisms to rise to the occasion and eliminate the disease from the body.

Homeopathic theory contends that focusing treatment efforts toward the elimination of symptoms will not adequately treat the underlying disease. In fact, treating symptoms without addressing the underlying disease is believed to drive the disease even deeper into the body, thereby strengthening the disease itself and weakening the vital force. Instead, if one will assist the body's vital force in regaining its balance, both the disease and the symptoms will disappear.

Veterinary homeopathic remedies are administered to animals either as tiny pellets (crushed and placed on the tongue) or elixirs. For best results, they should not be given with meals. Remedies are formulated

FIGURE 56.4 Homeopathic remedies are formulated using herbs, extracts, heavy metals, minerals, toxins, or any other substance that has the potential to stimulate the "vital force."

using herbs, extracts, heavy metals, minerals, toxins, or any other substance that has the potential to stimulate the vital force at homeopathic concentrations (Fig. 56.4). If administered at full strength, many of these substances could harm or even kill a patient! However, when diluted the homeopathic way, they purportedly stimulate the body to heal itself.

Dilutions are performed in a stepwise fashion, with the preparations succussed (shaken) after each dilution in order to increase potency and vibrational energy. This process of dilution followed by succession is termed *potentiation.* According to homeopathic theory, the more dilute the remedy, the more powerfully it acts to stimulate natural healing. Because of their diluted and energized natures, homeopathic remedies are said to be very sensitive to temperature fluctuations, chemicals, strong odors, and light, and need to be stored carefully.

Homeopathy and Prevention of Infectious Disease

Homeopathic preparations designed as substitutes for vaccines to prevent infectious diseases in pets are called nosodes. These preparations consist of diseased tissue or substances produced by the disease condition. Like other homeopathic preparations, nosodes are diluted and succussed for potency. Homeopathic nosodes are available for most of the diseases that are routinely vaccinated for in dogs and cats. In addition to protecting against disease, nosodes are used by homeopathic practitioners to treat disease.

Nosodal therapy is viewed with much suspicion and concern by traditional veterinary medical researchers, who question its effectiveness against these devastating diseases in dogs and cats. Many homeopathic practitioners believe that vaccinations weaken the vital force of the patient, thereby actually increasing patient susceptibility to the disease agent. However, in defense of traditional thinking, such a view does not fit very well with clinical and research evidence. Vaccinations indeed do what they are intended to do: Protect against infectious diseases. Because of diligent vaccination programs, diseases such as canine distemper have been virtually eliminated in the pet dog population. Are vaccinations always effective and safe? Of course not. Idiosyncrasies in the biochemical makeup of individuals, as well as variations in the types and qualities of vaccines utilized, can lead to unexpected and detrimental responses when a vaccine is administered. For various reasons, a vaccine could be rendered ineffective once introduced into the body. Or, a patient could experience an adverse response ranging from severe life-threatening anaphylactic shock or immune complex formation to the development of vaccine related tumors, such as feline sarcoma. However, with extended vaccination schedules available for dogs and cats, and continuing improvements in vaccine quality, the incidence of such adverse reactions will continue to decrease. Certainly if a pet has displayed sensitivity to one or more conventional vaccines, it may be considered a candidate for an alternative approach to preventive health care. Yet the effectiveness of nosodal therapy as this alternate approach is still highly questionable.

Chiropractic Care

A rapidly growing segment of veterinary alternative health care is chiropractic care. Since chiropractic care is so popular among the human population, it is no wonder that many pet owners are seeking it for their pets as well. As far back a Hippocrates, spinal manipulations were used on people and pets to treat a wide variety of disorders. Modern human chiropractic medicine traces its roots back to Canada in the late nineteenth century to an individual by the name of Daniel D. Palmer (1845–1913). Palmer went on to establish a college of chiropractic in the United States in 1898 and subsequently published a textbook in 1910 entitled *The Science, Art and Philosophy of Chiropractic*. Information gleaned from Palmer and his predecessors has formed the foundation for modern veterinary chiropractic. Initially, chiropractic procedures on pets were performed by chiropractors working in collaboration with veterinarians. Today, however, you will find an increasing number of veterinarians themselves receiving actual training in chiropractic theories and techniques as they apply to animals.

Chiropractic philosophy maintains (and rightly so) that all organ systems within the body are controlled by the nervous system. It does so through elaborate control systems (including those responsible for hormone production and release) and complex feedback mechanisms that coordinate all body functions and responses, including those related to health and to disease. Any disruption of the free flow of nerve impulses throughout the body can disrupt homeostasis within the body and lead to poor immune function and subsequent disease.

The focus of chiropractic medicine is centered on the spinal column, that portion of the central nervous system through which nerves course to and from the brain. More specifically, chiropractors target motor units along the spinal column. Each motor unit consists of two adjacent vertebrae and all the nerves, muscles, ligaments, blood vessels, and ancillary structures associated with the joint formed by the two vertebrae. Either a *malarticulation* or a *fixation* of one or more of these motor units can disrupt the free flow of nerve impulses. Such deviations from the normal anatomy and/or structural mechanics of the spinal column put pressure on and irritate the spinal cord, causing pain and/or preventing the body from mounting an effective response against other diseases. In addition, loss of motor unit mobility can slow the flow of spinal fluid, leading to malnourishment and degeneration of vital muscles, nerves, and other structures associated with the motor unit.

Chiropractic adjustments are used to treat lameness, hip dysplasia, intervertebral disk disease, nonspecific joint pain, muscle spasms, and poor flexibility in pets. In addition, chiropractic therapy has been shown to be effective against gastrointestinal illness, musculoskeletal trauma, stress-induced exhaustion, and certain types of paralysis in pets (Fig. 56.5).

The type and extent of clinical signs seen are dependent on the site(s) and severity of malarticulation or fixation. If a primary pressure site is not relieved in a timely fashion, other sites may subsequently appear as the animal tries to compensate for the pain and lack of motion through altered posture and locomotion.

FIGURE 56.5 Chiropractic care has been used to treat certain types of paralysis in pets.

Chiropractic treatment consists of adjustments made to affected motor units. No drugs or surgery are used. An adjustment is defined as a sudden controlled thrust delivered at a precise direction and depth to a specific contact point along the vertebral column. The goal of such a maneuver is to realign the vertebra and to relieve pressure on the surrounding tissue.

The veterinarian will examine the gait and posture of the patient for obvious asymmetries and lameness. Hands-on palpation will be performed next in an attempt to localize regions of pain, muscle spasms, swellings, and or temperature variations along the spinal column and extremities. Afterward, the clinician will assess the overall alignment of the vertebral column and the range of motion and mobility of the various joints. Once the degree of malalignment(s) or joint fixation(s) has been assessed, the direction and point of contact for the adjustment can be determined. Adjustments are performed on animals by using thumb pressure, joint stretching, or a special instrument called an activator, designed to make the adjustment process easier. If a pet is in a great deal of pain, manipulations may need to be performed under sedation or anesthesia.

Following chiropractic adjustments, many animals become more active and playful, exhibit increased appetites, and desire more interaction with their owners. The number of chiropractic adjustments required will depend on the severity and duration of the problem and the age of the patient. As a rule, the younger the patient, the fewer the adjustments needed to correct a malarticulation or fixation.

Acupuncture

The word *acupuncture* is derived from the Latin word *acus,* which means "needle," and *punctura,* which means "to prick." Acupuncture involves the stimulation of specific points on the body in order to produce chemical and physical responses within the body. This ancient form of medical therapy is thought to have originated in the Far East over 7000 years ago. Because of the close interdependence of humans and animals throughout the ages, it has no doubt been used as a form of veterinary medicine for thousands of years as well. Ancient civilizations certainly practiced acupuncture on their animals, as evidenced by the antiquated acupuncture charts that exist for a wide variety of species, including horses, camels, water buffaloes, and even elephants!

The ancient Chinese explained acupuncture in terms of Ch'I, yin, yang, acupuncture points, and meridians. *Ch'I,* the life force or life energy, moves throughout the body via channels called *meridians.* These meridians run in pairs throughout the body and are associated with the major organ systems within the body. They also interconnect with hundreds of acupuncture points on the body surface. These points correspond to those areas where the meridians containing Ch'I course closest to the body's surface.

Ch'I is believed to be bipolar in nature, with the positive ("male") forces called *yang* and the negative ("female") forces called *yin.* In order for the health of an individual to be maintained, a balance between yin and yang is needed. Any imbalance, disruption, or disturbance in these forces will create disease. The purpose of acupuncture is to reestablish the normal flow of Ch'I throughout the body, thereby restoring the balance between yin and yang. This, in turn, will restore health to the individual.

In the Western orthodox world, acupuncture points are known to be electrically discreet entities located in predictable regions of the body. These include areas where nerves enter into deep-muscle tissue and where peripheral nerves emerge from openings in bone. Also, it has been observed that certain disorders of the internal organs muscles and bones can cause spontaneous "tender spots" to appear on the surface of the body. These tender spots are believed to correspond directly to acupuncture points. And although meridians have yet to be actually identified scientifically, tests utilizing special radioactive markers injected directly into select acupuncture points demonstrate a predictable flow within the body that could very well correspond to the meridians themselves.

Several theories have been proposed in an attempt to explain the effects that acupuncture can have on animals (and people). The first theorizes that stimulation of an acupuncture point directly blocks the transmission of pain sensation along select nerve fibers within the body. A second theory postulates that chemicals called *endorphins* are released on stimulation of an acupuncture point. Endorphins, which are up to 100 times more potent than morphine, effectively block pain sensation and can circulate in the bloodstream for several hours at a time, providing a lasting effect. Endorphins can also influence the body's hormonal system, stimulating the release of various hormones (including steroids and epinephrine) that can have positive effects on all organ systems within the body. Still another theory proposes that acupuncture stimulation causes select sensory nerve endings to transmit nerve impulses to the spinal cord and brain, and then back out again to glands located throughout the body. On stimulation, these glands release hormones into the bloodstream that can exert various influences on the organ systems within the body.

More than likely, the actual mode of action for acupuncture is created by a blend of two or more of these theories. Interestingly, for acupuncture to work, an animal's nervous system must be intact. Studies involving patients suffering from nerve damage have revealed that the beneficial effects normally gained by stimulation of a particular acupuncture are actually negated by the damage.

Scientific research such as this, coupled with innumerable clinical success stories, has rendered acupuncture an accepted therapeutic tool for today's veterinary practitioner. In fact, the American Veterinary Medical Association now recognizes veterinary acupuncture and veterinary acutherapy as legitimate forms of veterinary medicine. While acupuncture is certainly not a "magic pill," it can present a viable alternative in those medical cases where conventional therapy has failed.

Acupuncture has been used with success in pets to control pain associated with intervertebral disk disease, trauma, hip dysplasia, and other forms of arthritis. In addition, it may also help speed healing in animal patients stricken with conditions such as allergies, epilepsy, nerve injuries, chronic respiratory disease, and disorders of the stomach and intestines. Acupuncture has also been used as a source of local anesthesia for pets undergoing minor surgical procedures, and as a tool to help minimize blood loss during such procedures. One of the most exciting applications of acupuncture in small-animal medicine is the use of shock point GV-26, a governing vessel meridian point, for the treatment of shock and cardiovascular collapse. This point is located at the *philtrum,* that indented portion of the upper lip just below the nose. In those animals that have stopped breathing or have suffered cardiac arrest, stimulation of this point can be a lifesaver (Fig. 56.6)!

The International Veterinary Acupuncture Society (IVAS) establishes a *code of ethics* and provides acupuncture certification within the profession. To help ensure competency when choosing a veterinary acupuncturist, always select one who has been certified by a veterinary acupuncture specialty organization such as the IVAS.

The competent veterinary acupuncturist believes in integrating veterinary acupuncture with the practice of orthodox Western veterinary medicine and always makes a complete clinical assessment of the patient prior to using acupuncture. This is vital because acupuncture can mask or alter clinical signs, sometimes making an otherwise obvious diagnosis difficult to recognize.

Stimulation of an acupuncture point in a pet can be achieved using several different methods. These include the use of needles, heat sources, finger pressure, vacuums ("cupping"), electrical currents, or lasers (Fig. 56.7). Certainly needles are the most common tools used to stimulate acupuncture points; 25- to 34-gauge stainless needles, some

FIGURE 56.6 Acupuncture "shock" points often used in emergency situations.

up to 5 centimeters long, are used to perform acupuncture on dogs and cats. The acupuncture points needing stimulation and the condition being treated will determine the actual needle gauge and length selected. Needles are usually inserted $1/8$ to $1/2$ inch into the particular point on the skin. For added benefit, the needles, once inserted, can

FIGURE 56.7 Laser acupuncture being performed on a patient.

be stimulated using a heat source (moxibustion) or electrical charge. Applying heat to an acupuncture point can be especially effective in treating arthritic conditions in dogs. Special electronic heating devices are available for such therapy in small animals.

The duration of a veterinary acupuncture treatment usually ranges from 1 to 30 minutes. During treatments, many pets become sedate and quite relaxed. Treatments are administered two to three times per week until desired results are seen. In chronic conditions, weeks or months of serial treatments may be necessary to effect positive results.

Implants may be inserted into specific acupuncture sites to provide continuous stimulation of those locations. For example, metallic beads implanted near the hip joints are said to be effective in select cases for treating pain associated with hip dysplasia. Also, gold beads implanted near the head region have been used to treat seizures in dogs (Fig. 56.8). *Aqua acupuncture,* performed by injecting liquid solutions containing sterile saline, vitamins, herbal preparations, or select therapeutic compounds directly into acupuncture points, is another popular method of achieving continuous stimulation.

Correctly locating a particular acupuncture point is much more important than the type of stimulation used on that point. When an acupuncture point is correctly identified and stimulated, initial reactions that may be seen in a pet include a bending at the waist, a raising of the tail, and sounds of relaxation, such as a heavy sigh. Some animals may even inadvertently eliminate on the spot!

There are few side effects associated with proper acupuncture therapy. Adverse effects could potentially occur if too many acupuncture points are stimulated at one time, if the wrong point is stimulated, or if a particular point is overstimulated. The most common side effect that could be seen with acupuncture is a temporary exacerbation of the disorder being treated, especially if the treatment is for pain. If this occurs, the adverse response will usually subside within a day or two. Other side effects of acupuncture therapy can include burns (if heat is used) or infections at the sites of acupuncture stimulation. Of course, accidental injury caused by an anxious or improperly restrained

FIGURE 56.8 Implanting a gold bead into an acupuncture site using a hypodermic needle.

pet probably poses the greatest risk associated with acupuncture treatment.

Under the direction of a qualified veterinarian, you can safely perform a technique called *acupressure* at home on your pet. This form of acupuncture involves stimulating acupuncture points using finger pressure instead of needles. This can be quite helpful in helping to relieve muscle spasms and to eliminate localized pain. When stimulating such a point using acupressure, use a steady, massaging circular motion. Pressure should be maintained for 30 to 60 seconds prior to moving to the next point in the treatment sequence. An entire session should take no more than 5 to 6 minutes. Sessions can be repeated two to three times per day, or as often as directed by your veterinarian.

CHAPTER

57

Ten Super Strategies for Reducing the Cost of Pet Ownership

If you currently have a pet living at home, or have ever owned one in the past, you've no doubt discovered that pet ownership can be an expensive proposition. Between the cost of food, supplies, and medical care, expenses can run into the hundreds, if not thousands, of dollars each year, depending on the type of pet you own and how many pets adorn your household. However, there is good news! There are strategies that you can employ that can help soften the fiscal challenges you may encounter. Here are 10 of them that you can put to use immediately.

Strategy 1: Purchase Pet Health Insurance or Self-Insure Your Pet
Unexpected injuries or illnesses can rapidly generate hundreds of dollars in unanticipated expenses. Such costs can no doubt cause financial and emotional strain, leading to painful decisions that an owner

may regret later on. As a result, pet fanciers need to protect themselves against such circumstances

Years ago when pet health insurance first appeared on the market, it was too downright expensive for the extent of coverage it offered the consumer. Well, times have changed, and so has pet health insurance. Today, every owner should consider it as a viable option to help cover the costs of veterinary care. Obviously, when comparing the various pet health insurance programs available, look closely at the deductibles offered and services covered. A good policy should provide the option of covering not only major medical or surgical procedures, but preventive health care as well.

If you consider yourself financially disciplined, self-insuring your pet can save you even more money. By socking money away each month into a special interest-bearing account designated for your pet's health care, you can build up a resource that you can turn to in the event of an emergency. In the best-case scenario, your pet will glide through life unscathed, and you'll never have to touch the fund, leaving you with a nice savings account that you can use as you please. This is certainly in stark contrast to insurance premiums, which must be paid regardless of your pet's health status. On the flip side, if you indeed have to draw from the account, you will have the peace of mind knowing that the money is there and that any decisions that you must make in that moment of crisis will not be solely determined by the balance in your checkbook.

But you say, "Doc, I have enough trouble saving money as it is! How am I going to find money to set aside for such a fund?" Well, believe it or not, it's there if you look for it! Are you a slave to an expensive habit? Would you be willing to give it up temporarily until your pet's account is funded? Give up one soda a day or skip one meal per week and save over $200 per year, money that you can deposit into your pet's account! Check out your weekly movie entertainment from the local library instead of renting it from the video store, and add another $250 per year. Have a garage sale and use the proceeds you earn as a source of capital for your pet's personal health plan! As you can see, the possibilities are endless! Just take a close look at your own personal lifestyle and brainstorm possible sources of savings.

Strategy 2: Be Realistic by Planning Ahead   Whenever talking money and pets, it is vitally important to your family and to your financial well-being to determine ahead of time how much you are willing to pay for veterinary medical care in the event of an unexpected injury or illness involving your pet. Even if you have insurance, it may not pay the entire bill. No one should ever be emotionally "guilted" into a personal financial crisis. Yet spontaneous emotional decisions can prove to be very expensive. Obviously this does not mean that we are released from our obligations as responsible pet owners, but rather that we should prepare ourselves in advance of that unexpected moment, should it occur.

Strategy 3: Select Your Pet Wisely   Obviously, the type of pet you choose to share your life with will determine the level of financial commitment you'll need to make. This crosses not only species lines but also breed lines. For instance, owning a dog will no doubt cost more than owning a guinea pig. In addition, owning an African gray parrot will entail greater husbandry-related expenditures than would owning a budgie. Large dogs will consume more food than their smaller peers, and will be more expensive to medicate in the event of an illness.

When selecting a dog or cat, keep in mind that the more diverse the gene pool, the heartier the individual tends to be (a phenomenon known as *hybrid vigor*). This translates into a reduced chance of a genetically related illness rearing its ugly, expensive head later on. If this is of concern to you, stick to mixed breeds or to one of the top five purebred breeds of dogs and cats.

Be sure to set limits on the number of pets you own. While every stray dog or cat that crosses your path may pull your heartstrings, be realistic. Do you have the time and the financial resources to properly devote to so many pets? If so, then go for it. If not, then find good homes for your "lost and founds" before you become emotionally attached to them.

Strategy 4: Obtain Your Pet from a Reputable Source Only   That $10 puppy you purchased at the flea market or grocery store parking lot could be a carrier of a massive veterinary bill if it is harboring a virus, mange, or internal parasites. Also, the parrot you purchased from that roadside stand could be a carrier of psittacosis, a serious disease in both parrots and humans! Purchasing your pet from a breeder or pet store isn't an automatic guarantee of quality, either.

Always check references on potential pet vendors. And always insist on a prepurchase evaluation of the pet by a qualified veterinarian of your choice prior to exchange of any money. If the vendor is reputable, this won't be a problem at all. Have your veterinarian verify the shot and deworming records of your prospective purchase. Often pets that are sold as having "all of their shots" may in fact have missed an important booster or deworming, leaving you holding an unexpected bill.

Unless you are planning to enter your pet into AKC (American Kennel Club)-sanctioned competitive events, there is no need to pay the extra expense associated with purchasing a pet with "papers" unless you can verify the reputation and record of the breeder. Because the AKC has no real regulatory enforcement of quality standards outside of its sanctioned events, purchasing a pet with papers is not a guarantee of quality. If purchasing your pet from a breeder who is renowned for quality or from a reputable pet store, it may be worth paying more for an "AKC" puppy. However, if purchasing your pup from a backyard breeder, forget the papers. The mere fact that a dog is AKC-certifiable is no justification for jacking up the purchase price by hundreds of dollars!

Strategy 5: Be a Wise Pet Food Buyer   For many pet owners, food purchases make up the majority of pet-related expenditures each year. As a result, using a little savvy when purchasing pet food can save you tremendous amounts of money. For starters, buy quality. Feeding your pet a high-quality diet versus a cheap low-quality brand can be compared to you eating plenty of fruits, vegetables, and whole grains versus eating a diet full of fast food. Feeding high-quality rations does not have to be more expensive, either. The feeding portions will be much smaller than those of a poorer-quality ration, making your food purchases last longer. Also, by comparing labels, you'll be able to discern which diets have similar ingredients and nutritional values, despite differences in price. Like human food producers, pet food manufacturers often market identical rations under several different labels and several different price points. And don't be influenced by advertising. For instance, avoid lamb-and-rice diets unless your veterinarian specifically prescribes one. Despite what pet food manufacturers may claim, most of these "hypoallergenic" foods found on the market today have limited use in the treatment of food-related skin allergies and itching. Yet they generally cost more than other formulations. Don't pay for something you don't need!

Here's another rule of thumb: Buy your pet food in bulk. You can realize significant savings by purchasing food this way. The larger the bag you buy, the lower the cost is per ounce. Once a bulk bag is opened, simply transfer the contents into resealable plastic containers to keep the food fresh and nutritious for later use.

By the way, while on the subjects of food and money, don't feed your pets table scraps or bones! These serve no nutritional purpose whatsoever and can lead to expensive bouts of pancreatitis, periodontal disease, and digestive disturbances.

Strategy 6: Become an Informed Pet Owner   With the wealth of information available at your fingertips via books, periodicals, and the Internet, there is no reason to plead ignorance when it comes to your pet's husbandry and health care. Two special questions to research and find answers for are (1) what constitutes a real veterinary medical emergency and (2) what, if any, over-the-counter remedies are available to treat the various conditions you may encounter with your pet. Verify any answers you find with your veterinarian. By gathering such information long before you need it, you can save yourself hundreds of dollars over the life of your pet in unnecessary trips to the veterinary hospital.

Strategy 7: Remember that Bigger Is Not Always Better   Veterinary hospitals come in all shapes and sizes. Just remember that in any business, fees charged are usually directly related to the amount of overhead involved. Indeed, if you opt to pay higher fees for pet care, just be sure you're paying for superior quality of care, not just superior real estate. Let's face it: There are not many differences in vaccine administration or spay/neuter skills between veterinarians. As a result, don't be afraid to price-shop for these routine procedures. Many clinics offer regular vaccination and spay/neuter clinics as a public service to their communities. If you are afraid that your veterinarian will get mad at you for shopping around, get over it. It's your money, not your vet's!

Strategy 8: Always Ask for an Estimate   Whether your pet is receiving routine preventive maintenance or being treated for an actual injury or illness, you have the right to know the costs associated with the procedures to be performed. The purpose is not to question your veterinarian's judgment or fees, but to avoid misunderstandings or unexpected financial surprises. The advantage of a written estimate is that it will reveal to you those areas that may lend themselves to cost savings. For example, is a hospitalization charge included on the estimate? If so, will there be somebody at the hospital throughout the night to monitor your pet's condition? If not, don't hesitate to question this charge. If your pet's condition is not life-threatening, there is no need for you to incur overnight hospitalization charges, since no one will be present to care for your pet, anyway. Take your pet home for the night with detailed instructions from your veterinarian on how to play nursemaid. This could save you anywhere from $10 to $30 per day, depending on the hospital. Will your pet require medications? Perhaps a written prescription could be a source of cost savings.

Estimates on preventive health care procedures are extremely important since the fees associated with these services can vary widely between veterinary practices. For instance, some clinics include an office charge with vaccination fees whereas others charge only for the vaccinations themselves. If your pet has already had a physical examination within the past 6 months, another one may not be necessary. Many clinics include a laboratory charge with their fee for teeth cleaning. Again, if routine bloodwork was performed within the last 6 months, repeating it on an otherwise healthy animal may be an unnecessary expenditure. If you have a question regarding a fee, don't be afraid to raise it. If your veterinarian becomes defensive, it may be time to look for another veterinarian. True veterinary professionals will not be offended by such questions; in fact, they encourage such open lines of communication with their clients.

Strategy 9: Form a Neighborhood "Pet Club"   Associating yourself with other pet owners in your neighborhood can provide you with incredible informational and financial leverage. Have periodic meetings with your "club," either in person, by phone, or by email! Use the time to share information, ideas, and recommendations on pet husbandry, preventive care, veterinarians, groomers, trainers, and pet-supply retailers. Pool resources with club members to purchase food and supplies in bulk, taking advantage of volume discounts. You can also organize a pet-sitting cooperative with other club members and save megabucks in boarding fees. Get creative and brainstorm with your compadres. The possibilities of saving money by working together are extraordinary!

Strategy 10: Barter for Bucks   Do you have a particular skill or training that would prove useful to your veterinarian or local pet supply owner? If so, talk to them about the possibility of setting up an equitable barter program. Bartering will help preserve your cash flow, and in most cases, save you money. For example, do you have sales and marketing expertise? For clients who can offer their veterinarians practical tips on how to market and promote their practices, a barter arrangement is probably only a handshake away. Are you skilled at carpentry, plumbing, or other types of handy work? If so, you are a valuable asset to any business. Considering this was the way our ancestors conducted business, the possibilities are endless. But there is only one way you'll ever become an effective barterer—learn how to ask!

Increasing Your Pet's Longevity

t goes without saying that eating right, getting plenty of exercise, and eliminating bad habits can add years to our lives. Well, believe it or not, the same principles apply to our pets. As a result of recent advancements in veterinary medicine and a growing public awareness concerning responsible pet ownership, pets are living longer today than at any time in the past (Fig. 58.1). Want to find the fountain of youth for your pet? Here are some proven tips that can lead you and your pet right to it!

Avoid Junk Food

No matter what the pet food companies tell you, you can't beat the new premium-type diets on the market today. Lots of research and little filler go into these products, making them popular recommendations of veterinarians across the country. Regardless of the type of pet you own, you have many types and brands to choose from. The choice is yours. However, when in doubt as to which one would be best for your pet, don't hesitate to ask your veterinarian. And though the expense of such rations may seem inflated at first, most pet owners find that the amounts consumed per feeding are much less than those for nonpremium foods, making the actual per-feeding cost for the two types of rations about the same.

FIGURE 58.1 The key to boosting your pet's longevity is to practice responsible pet ownership from the time your pet is young.

Think Thin

Obesity causes the same ill effects in pets as it does in people. Pets pushing the scales to their maximums are more prone to, among other things, heart disease, kidney disease, liver disease, and diabetes. They also become sluggish, tire easily, and seem to just crave more and more food (sounds familiar, doesn't it?).

The two biggest culprits underlying obesity in pets are indiscriminate feeding practices and lack of exercise. Feeding table scraps, too many snacks, or in the case of birds, too many seeds, is probably the worst thing you could do for your pet. Not

a

FIGURE 58.2 (*a, b*) Daily exercise will help your pet live longer.

only do these upset the nutritional balance of your pet's daily requirement, they often cause gastrointestinal upset as well. Not only that; you're going to create a pet that constantly begs or scavenges for food, which always goes over big when you're entertaining guests for dinner.

If your pet is indeed fat, simply cutting back on snacks and the amount of food you feed might not be enough. There are, however, some great weight-loss diets available that can help your pet lose the added poundage while at the same time satisfying its appetite. Ask your veterinarian for a recommendation on such a diet, since requirements could vary depending upon the age of your pet.

Exercise, Exercise, and More Exercise

Exercise offers the same benefits to pets as it does to humans: cardiovascular fitness and weight control. Twenty to thirty minutes of moderate exercise daily (walking, chasing the Frisbee or toy mouse, running on an exercise wheel) will help keep your pet slim, trim, and healthy (Fig. 58.2).

For dog owners, walking or jogging is an excellent way to keep canines fit and trim. Just remember that unless you own a Russian wolfhound, stride-for-stride, your dog is going to have to work harder than you do, so be sure you don't overdo it. Heat stroke and/or musculoskeletal injuries can be unfortunate side effects to such marathon exercise sessions.

b

FIGURE 58.2 (*a, b*) Daily exercise will help your pet live longer.

Cats that are leash-trained from the start can also benefit from controlled exercise. For those that are not, a designated daily play session will help elevate the heart rate and burn calories. The same holds true for pot-bellied pigs. Just don't allow your porcine to get overheated!

Getting a bird or exotic pet to willfully exercise can be a challenge, and requires a great deal of creativity on your part. However, it can be done. Certainly birds whose feathers have not been clipped can be offered free flight time each day. Just be sure that all windows and doors are closed and secured, all stove burners are off, access to mirrored surfaces has been denied, and other household hazards have been isolated. In addition, for all birds, including those with clipped feathers, installing several perches, each at a different height within the cage, can provide exercise value by encouraging them to move from perch to perch. However, for sanitary reasons, avoid situating one perch directly beneath another.

For rodents, an exercise wheel should always be provided. Most will catch the exercise fever right away without any coaxing from you! Other pocket pets can be taken from the confines of their cages and, for a defined period of time, allowed free access to a room or a portion thereof. This allows them to scurry and explore with their movement unimpeded by the bars of a cage. Of course, make sure that such a room or space is escape-proof and free of potential hazards.

As a corollary to this longevity tip: Give your pet plenty of attention each day. The easiest way to stress out your pet is to ignore it. So keep this in mind the next time you come home from work. Take some time to interact with your faithful companion.

Work on That Smile

Excessive dental tartar and gingivitis play important roles in heart and kidney disease in pets. To make matters worse, most dogs and cats show signs of periodontal (tooth and gum) disease by the time they're only 3 years of age! This is why it's so important to keep your pet's dental tartar under control (Fig. 58.3).

Simply feeding your pets hard food or biscuits won't do the trick alone. In fact, many of these foodstuffs may actually promote plaque and tartar formation, and subsequent periodontal disease. Surprised? You shouldn't be. Just think about what your teeth would look like if you never brushed your teeth or had a dental cleaning performed, and you'll get the picture.

You should have a dental checkup performed on your pet every time you visit your veterinarian (at least annually). If it's necessary, have your pet's teeth professionally cleaned and polished while you're there. When you get your pet home, make it a point to incorporate some type of dental care into your pet's daily routine, whether

FIGURE 58.3 Cleaning your pet's teeth daily is not difficult and yields tremendous health benefits!

brushing with toothpaste specifically formulated for pets or using special pet mouthwashes containing chlorhexidine. Also, there are a plethora of toys and chew items available on the market today that are designed to assist in pet tartar control. The more of these your pet has access to, the better!

Let Them Know Who's Boss

Proper obedience training will keep your dog off the streets—literally. Dogs that dart off despite their owner's commands to the contrary, or dig escape tunnels out of their backyards, are prime candidates for being hit by a car.

Pet owners need to teach their dogs to respond to the basic commands to stop, sit, stay, and heel. No dog is too old to be taught these commands, yet for those old, crusty canines set firmly in their ways, a good obedience school might be just what the doctor ordered.

Carpet versus Concrete

Make no mistake about it: Pets kept indoors are healthier than those kept outdoors. For instance, indoor dogs are psychologically healthier because of the increased contact with their pack members (their owners). In addition, they are less prone to physical illnesses such as infectious diseases, skin disorders, gastroenteritis induced by dietary indiscretions, and environmental afflictions such as heat stroke and car fenders.

Along the same lines, making your cat an indoor pet will keep it safe from car tires, and significantly reduce its risk of contracting deadly diseases such as feline leukemia, feline infectious peritonitis, and feline AIDS.

Finally, birds kept indoors escape the risk of exposure to infectious diseases such as avian pox and internal parasites, as well as stealthy feline predators.

An Ounce of Prevention is Worth a Pound of Cure

Preventive health care is a proven boost to longevity in pets. Such care includes keeping your pet current on its vaccinations and parasite preventive medications (if applicable), having routine checkups performed, adhering to sound grooming and husbandry principles, and heeding those longevity tips previously mentioned.

Also, if you haven't already done so, consider having your pet neutered. Besides the advantage of population control, there can be health benefits as well. For example, female dogs neutered prior to their second heat have a reduced risk of mammary cancer as they get older. In addition, male dogs that are neutered may have a reduced incidence of certain cancers as they mature when compared with their intact peers. In fact, neutering totally eliminates the possibility that these dogs will develop testicular cancer as they age. Finally, because neutering can reduce aggressiveness and anxiety in select instances, it may help reduce the chances of injury from fighting or self-inflicted trauma.

Zoonotic Diseases

"Doctor, I think my dog has a cold. Can I catch it?" In veterinary practices across the country, questions such as this one are common. And although the answer to this particular question is "no," there are numerous other diseases that can indeed be transmitted from family pets to their owners. Such diseases are properly termed zoonotic diseases.

Children are at greatest risk of contracting a disease from the family pet, primarily because of their inherent curiosity and often less-than-desirable hygiene habits (Fig. 59.1). However, adults are susceptible as well. Failing to provide adequate preventive health care for pets greatly increases the chance of exposure to one or more of these diseases. Refer to Table 59.1 for a listing of some of the zoonoses carried by dogs, cats, birds, and exotic pets.

Animal Bites and Scratches

Besides the potential for rabies transmission, a bite (Fig. 59.2) from a pet can also lead to severe bacterial infections and tissue damage in the affected individual. Likewise, scratches, especially those inflicted by cats, can be just as bad as, if not worse than, those injuries caused by teeth. For instance, cat-scratch fever, a disease that can cause fever

FIGURE 59.1 Children are especially susceptible to zoonotic diseases.

and swollen, painful lymph nodes (lymphadenopathy), can be transmitted to an unsuspecting owner by the mere scratch of a cat harboring the organism on its nails.

If your pet bites you or a member of your family, don't delay! Seek medical attention immediately.

Rabies

Certainly the most infamous of all zoonoses is rabies. This is an incurable, fatal viral disease that attacks the nervous system of its unfortunate host. The rabies virus is excreted in the saliva of infected animals and transmitted to other animals and to people via bite wounds and through contamination of open wounds or sores. Although rabies is restricted primarily to wild or feral carnivores, cases occasionally spill over into the domestic and stray dog and cat population, thus providing the important link between wildlife rabies and human rabies.

Because rabies cannot be cured, the key here is prevention. Obviously it's very important to keep all dogs, cats, and ferrets current on their rabies vaccinations. In addition, don't allow your pets to roam free outdoors at night, since this is the time when they are most likely to interact with wild animals. Use common sense: Discourage your children from playing with or petting stray animals. Avoid touching dead or dying bats that may be lying on the ground (Fig. 59.3). And don't keep wild animals such as descented skunks or raccoons as pets.

Table 59.1 Zoonotic Potential of Various Pet Species*

Dogs	Rabies
	Dermatophytes
	Roundworms
	Hookworms
	Tapeworms
	Leptospirosis
	Bacterial enteritis (*Giardia, Salmonella*)
	Tickborne illnesses
	Mites
	Heartworms
	Fleas
Cats	Rabies
	Dermatophytes
	Roundworms
	Hookworms
	Tapeworms
	Bacterial enteritis (*Giardia, Salmonella*)
	Tickborne illnesses
	Mites
	Cat-scratch fever
	Toxoplasmosis
	Heartworms
	Fleas
Birds	Psittacosis
	Bacterial enteritis
	Yersinia pseudotuberculosis
	Erysipelothrix dermatitis

Table 59.1 Zoonotic Potential of Various Pet Species* (*Continued*)

Reptiles	*Salmonella*
	Bacterial enteritis
	Bacterial dermatitis
	Various fungal diseases
	Tickborne illnesses
Amphibians	Bacterial enteritis
	Salmonella
	Leptospirosis
	Trypanosmiasis
Ferrets	Bacterial enteritis (*Giardia, Salmonella*)
	Dermatophytosis
	Tuberculosis
	Influenza A
	Mites
	Rabies
	Heartworms
	Fleas
Rabbits	Bacterial enteritis
	Dermatophytosis
	Tularemia
	Rabies
	Tapeworms
	Mites
	Fleas
Rats, mice, hamsters, gerbils	Tapeworms
	Dermatophytosis

	Meningitis	
	Allergies	
	Fleas	
	Bubonic plague (rats)	
Guinea pigs	Dermatophytosis	
	Mites	
	Allergies	
	Fleas	
Chinchillas	Dermatophytosis	
	Meningitis	
	Fleas	
	Bacterial enteritis	
Prairie dogs	Bubonic plague	
	Dermatophytosis	
	Rabies	
	Meningitis	
	Fleas	
	Mites	
	Bacterial enteritis	
	Hanta virus	
Pot-bellied pigs	Bacterial enteritis	
	Roundworms	
	Hookworms	
	Tapeworms	
	Leptospirosis	
	Rabies (rare)	

Note: The majority of these diseases are rare in pets born and raised in captivity.

FIGURE 59.2 Animal bites are the most common "zoonotic" encounters experienced.

Because of their high susceptibility to rabies, to do so is to ask for trouble!

Intestinal Worms

Hookworms, roundworms, and tapeworms can pose serious health threats to humans if exposure to infective eggs or larvae occurs. For example, certain types of hookworms can be transmitted from pets to people by contact with soil or sand contaminated with infective hookworm larvae. These larvae have the ability to penetrate and burrow into the outer layer of exposed skin, usually the feet, legs, and/or hands, causing intense itching. The term for this condition is *cutaneous larval migrans.* Adult hookworms have also been known to infect the human intestinal tract, leading to a chronic enterocolitis.

Roundworms can be transmitted by contact with soil contaminated with egg-laden feces. If these eggs are consumed, the larvae hatch within the gut and begin to migrate throughout the organs and tissues of the body. The disease caused by these larvae, called *visceral larval migrans,* is much more serious than that caused by the hookworm. In fact, blindness, seizures, and other serious maladies can result. This is especially true in children, or in those individuals with compromised immune systems. If there is one good reason for having your family pet routinely dewormed and checked for parasites, this is it!

Dipylidium caninum, the most common tapeworm seen in dogs and cats, can infest the intestinal tract of people who accidentally consume a flea that contains the tapeworm larva. Pet owners can avoid such exposure by controlling fleas on their animals. More seriously, though, hydatid cyst disease, caused by the tapeworm *Echinococcus* (Fig. 59.4), can be contracted by humans through contact with tapeworm eggs shed by dogs and cats harboring the adult form of these worms. On ingestion, the tapeworm larvae emerge from the eggs and migrate throughout all tissues and organs of the body, including the brain. The resulting damage can be deadly if not detected and managed soon enough. Dogs can become infested with adult *Echinococcus* tapeworms by eating meat

FIGURE 59.3 The bat is an important vector for the rabies virus.

from cattle, sheep, or pigs infected with the larval form of the disease. As a result, prohibiting the consumption of raw meat and offal by pets is the surest way to keep the risk of this disease low.

Heartworms

Rarely, humans can be infected with *Dirofilaria immitis,* the canine and feline heartworm. The heartworm larvae, which gain entrance into the body via a mosquito bite, do not migrate to the heart as they do in pets, but rather to the lungs. Here, they can form coinlike lesions that have been mistaken on human chest radiographs for tuberculosis or cancer. Fortunately, the actual inflammation and disease caused by these lesions is rarely severe.

Besides using mosquito repellents and practicing environmental control, you can reduce the chances of exposure to heartworm-laden

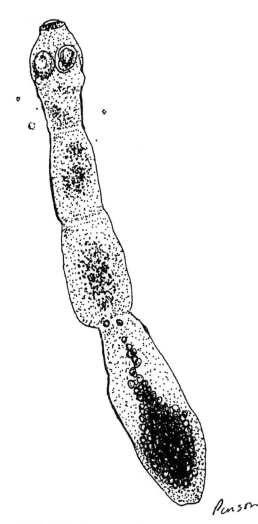

mosquitoes by keeping your dog and cat current on their heartworm preventive medication and encouraging other pet owners to do the same as well.

Ringworm

Ringworm (dermatophytosis) is not a worm at all; it is a fungus that attacks the skin, hair, and nails of both humans and animals. In humans, it typically causes red, itchy skin lesions. Pets can transmit this disease to owners by direct contact with their infected skin and coat. An outbreak of ringworm within a household can often be traced back to the family cat, since felines are common carriers of this disease.

Because of its zoonotic potential, ringworm must always be ruled out as the cause of distinct hair loss in the family pet. An exam

FIGURE 59.4 The *Echinococcus* **tapeworm is the cause of hydatid cyst disease.**

and/or fungal culture performed by your veterinarian can verify or dispel such suspicions.

Infectious Diarrhea

Campylobacteriosis, salmonellosis, and giardiasis are three infectious diseases among many that can cause diarrhea in pets. They also happen to be three major infectious causes of diarrhea recognized in people. Transmitted via infected feces, these organisms have the ability to cause severe cramping, nausea, and diarrhea in exposed people. As a result, protect yourself and your family from such diseases by observing good hygiene practices when handling pets, especially exotics. In addition, always seek prompt veterinary care for any diarrheic animal.

Toxoplasmosis

Shed in the feces of infected cats, toxoplasmosis is one of the most common zoonotic diseases around. In the United States alone, up to 40 percent of the adult population have already been exposed to this disease. The majority of cases occurring in people are subclinical in nature (don't show any signs) and often pass undetected.

However, if a pregnant woman who has never been exposed to toxoplasmosis contracts this parasite, it could pose a serious threat to the health of the fetus. If infection occurs early enough in pregnancy, mental retardation in the unborn child can occur. For this reason, if you are pregnant, avoid activities that involve working with soil or sand (your garden might serve as a litterbox for a neighborhood cat), and avoid changing or cleaning cat litterboxes. Contact your obstetrician for more detailed information regarding this disease.

Leptospirosis

The leptospirosis organism that infects dogs can infect humans as well, causing severe chills, fever, anemia, kidney damage, eye damage, and occasionally brain damage. Exposure to infected urine and other secretions or tissues is the primary method of transmission to people. Since the efficacy of the canine vaccine is questionable, keeping dogs away from potential sources of the disease, including livestock and farm tanks or water pools, is the best way to guard against this disease.

Flea- and Tickborne Illnesses

Fleas and ticks have proven to be effective vectors for a variety of diseases that infect humans (Fig. 59.5). Because pets can be reservoirs for

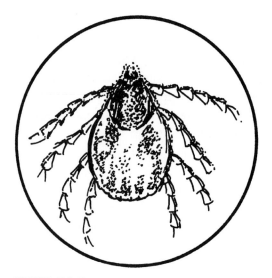

FIGURE 59.5 Ticks are notorious vectors for zoonotic diseases.

fleas and ticks within households, owners who fail to undertake adequate external parasite control measures could be placing their own health and their family's in jeopardy.

As mentioned previously, fleas are important vectors for tapeworms in dogs and cats. The chances of a person developing tapeworms following ingestion of tapeworm-infested feces are low; nonetheless, it can occur, especially in children. As a result, minimizing exposure to fleas is a must.

Fleas are also the primary mode of transmission for the plague organism *Yersinia pestis,* the same disease that achieved historical infamy during the Middle Ages. In the southwestern portions of the United States, plague still occasionally rears its ugly head. Cats and prairie dogs carrying the organism or plague-laden fleas pose the greatest threat to human health in these areas. In humans, signs of plague include sore, swollen lymph nodes, fever, seizures, and/or coughing due to pneumonia. Fortunately, if detected early enough, plague can be treated quite effectively with modern medicine. Again, an ounce of prevention is worth a pound of cure, and flea control is the key to protecting your family against this serious disease.

Three of the more infamous tickborne illnesses that can affect people include Rocky Mountain Spotted Fever, ehrlichiosis, and Lyme disease. Again, pets can act as reservoirs for ticks carrying the causative organisms. Clinical signs of these diseases in humans can include malaise, headaches, chills, painful muscles and joints, and organ failure. Owners wishing to reduce their chances of exposure to these diseases should practice strict tick control, and never remove a tick from a pet with bare hands.

Mites

The *Sarcoptes, Notoedres,* and *Cheyletiella* mange mites that normally infest housepets can also cause disease in people. As in pets, these mites can cause itchy, irritated skin lesions in exposed individuals. Fortunately, such infestations rarely last long and will usually clear up on their own. Pet owners can help shield themselves from such infestations by having all skin lesions involving itching and/or hair loss that might appear on a pet properly diagnosed and treated by their veterinarian.

Psittacosis

Psittacosis is a serious zoonotic disease of pet birds that can cause severe respiratory and flulike illness in humans. Complicated cases can even result in life-threatening inflammation of heart and brain tissue. Caused by the organism *Chlamydia psittaci,* psittacosis is transmitted from birds to humans through the ingestion or inhalation of dried particles from infected feces or discharges. Birds that are smuggled into the United States pose the greatest threat to those unsuspecting pet owners who purchase their birds from roadside stands and other questionable sources. To protect yourself from this disease, be sure that you purchase only birds that have been legally imported and have passed the mandatory quarantine procedures. For additional peace of mind, a laboratory test available from your veterinarian can help confirm the negative status of your new pet.

Control Summary

Although the diseases listed above represent some of the more important zoonoses that parents and pet owners should be aware of, it is certainly not all-inclusive. The following guidelines reiterate and expand on those preventive measures previously mentioned and will help protect you and your family from zoonotic diseases. Be sure that your children understand why these measures are important. By doing so, you can ensure that your family's relationship with your pet will remain a healthy one (Fig. 59.6).

FIGURE 59.6 Be sure that your pet's relationship between you and your family remains a healthy one!

- Purchase your pets (especially birds and exotics) from reputable sources only.

- Insist on a veterinary checkup before finalizing a purchase on any pet.

- Parents and children alike should always wash their hands thoroughly after handling family pets, especially prior to meals.

- Avoid "kissing" pets or being licked on the face by them. After all, you don't know where their mouths have been!

- Avoid interactions with stray or wild animals, alive or dead!

- Clean up and dispose of all animal waste promptly. Waste left unattended in a yard can be a source of infection to pets and people for years to come!

- Keep children's sandboxes covered when not in use, and keep other play areas free of animal excrement.

- Wear disposable gloves when handling reptiles and amphibians.

- Control fleas and ticks on your pet.

- If the area in which you live is at high risk for Lyme disease, consider having your dog vaccinated against this disease.

- If a pet becomes ill, minimize handling and seek veterinary help immediately. Always separate ill animals from young children.

- Have pets routinely examined, vaccinated, and checked for worms by your veterinarian. Birds and exotics should be checked for both external and internal parasites, and their stools should be checked for infectious organisms. New puppies and kittens should be routinely dewormed starting at 3 weeks of age. If applicable, be sure that your pet is on heartworm preventive medication.

Cancer in Companion Animals

Since the early 1980s, veterinary medicine has made tremendous advances in the diagnosis, treatment, and prevention of disease in pets. For instance, because of public education and sophisticated vaccines, the incidence of viral disease in companion animals has decreased dramatically. Another frequent cause of death—bacterial disease—can now be combatted more effectively than previously with new generations of antibiotics. In addition, both veterinarians and breeders have learned much about the control and elimination of genetic defects through selective breeding, and leash laws and responsible owners have greatly decreased the incidence of pets killed by trauma. Indeed, pets, like their owners, are living longer lives.

Yet there is one disease that, despite our efforts, remains one of the leading causes of death in older pets. That disease is cancer. Fortunately, veterinarians know a great deal more about the diagnosis and therapy of neoplastic disease in small animals than they did 20 years ago. In fact, the field of veterinary oncology (the study of cancer) is one of the fastest-growing segments of the profession today. However, there is still much to be learned about the origins and susceptibilities of this notorious killer.

FIGURE 60.1 A cancer cell undergoing uncontrolled division.

Tumor Definition and Types

A *tumor* or *neoplasm* is an abnormal growth of tissue containing cells that proliferate more rapidly than those of the normal tissue from which they originated. These cells are not subject to the same control mechanisms that keep normal cell growth in check (Fig. 60.1). Normal cells grown in laboratory tissue culture medium will cease growing when they have made contact with surrounding cells and/or filled their container. This is called *contact inhibition,* and it explains, for instance, why our liver grows to a certain size and doesn't keep growing until we burst. Tumor cells, on the other hand, don't display the same respect for boundaries. For example, in laboratory tissue cultures, they grow relentlessly, tumbling over each other and spilling over the edges of their containers.

Benign Tumors

Benign tumors are "well differentiated" tumors, differing only slightly in appearance and behavior from their tissue of origin. These tumors are slow-growing and noninvasive, do not spread throughout the body, and will often have a fibrous tissue capsule surrounding them.

All of these characteristics make benign tumors easy to surgically remove in most cases. Unless allowed to grow to a huge size, they seldom pose a threat to life. However, they might cause significant problems if they are located within a vital organ. In fact, the most significant alteration that a benign tumor makes in its host organism is that of encroachment on surrounding normal tissue, leading to obstruction or replacement of the innocent (nontumorous) tissue by the tumor.

To identify a benign tumor, the suffix -*oma* is used. For example, a benign tumor of osseous (bone) tissue would be called an *osteoma,* and a benign tumor of fibrous tissue would be called a *fibroma.* The term *adenoma* is used to describe a benign tumor of a glandular structure, such as a mammary gland (mammary adenoma) or the thyroid gland (thyroid adenoma). The term *papilloma* or *polyp* is applied to wartlike projections originating from epithelial surfaces such as skin or intestinal lining.

Malignant Tumors

Malignant tumors, in contrast to benign tumors, grow rapidly. Malignant tumors send spreading fingers into the surrounding normal tissue, making it difficult to surgically remove the entire tumor. As a result, they frequently regrow after surgery. Malignant cells demonstrate marked *dedifferentiation* or *anaplasia.* In other words, they do not look like the cells from which they originated.

Malignant tumors are commonly referred to as *cancer.* Cancers of epithelial or glandular structures are referred to as *carcinomas,* while cancers of other tissues are referred to as *sarcomas.* The major danger of a malignant tumor rests in its ability to metastasize, or spread throughout the body. Vital organs in distant locations can be invaded, often resulting in rapid death.

Carcinomas, as a rule, spread via the lymph vessels, although some can skip the lymph nodes and go directly into blood vessels. An example of a carcinoma in dogs that can metastasize either by lymphatics or blood is the mammary carcinoma.

Sarcomas usually metastasize via the bloodstream. Organs that are frequent sites of bloodborne metastasis include the liver and lungs, both of which can be rapidly overwhelmed by the tumors.

We have all seen or heard of people who have been seriously debilitated by cancer, and pets are affected similarly. A malignant tumor can cause what is called the *cachexia* of cancer. With cachexia, the animal literally starves as the tumor grows and steals the body's nutrition. Hemorrhage, pain, fever, and infection are also frequent secondary effects of cancer.

Some tumors produce side effects on the host through the production and release of hormones. These tumors cause the secretion of dangerously high levels of hormones. For example, an *insuloma* of the pancreas produces excessive amounts of insulin. Animals with this tumor will experience very low blood sugar levels, resulting in weakness and/or seizures. Also, thyroid adenomas in cats can produce excessive amounts of thyroid hormone, leading to nervousness, weight loss, and diarrhea in affected animals.

Causes, Occurrence, and Diagnosis of Cancer in Pets

What do we know about the occurrence of cancer in pets? Most people are very surprised to learn that dogs and cats have a higher incidence of many tumors than do humans. For example, dogs experience 35 times as much skin cancer as do humans, 4 times as many breast tumors, 8 times as much bone cancer, and twice the incidence of leukemia.

Only a few types of cancer are seen more frequently in humans than in small animals. For instance, the rate of occurrence of lung cancer is 7 times higher in humans, and gastrointestinal malignancies occur 13 times more frequently in humans than in dogs and cats.

Breed Predilections (Dogs)

Through careful statistical evaluation by veterinary researchers, certain breed predilections for cancer have been noted. If asked which breed of dog has the highest incidence of cancer, a veterinarian would undoubtedly reply "the boxer." When a sick, aged boxer turns up at the hospital, the attending veterinarian suspects a tumor almost immediately. Other dog breeds that can have a high incidence of cancer include Boston terriers, cocker spaniels, and wire-haired fox terriers. Breeds with a relatively low incidence of cancer include beagles, poodles, collies, and dachshunds.

Why do some breeds have a high incidence of cancer while some are rarely affected? The answer to that question is still elusive. One hypothesis deals with the immune system of these pets. The boxer's immune system is thought to be less able to mobilize resistance against cancer cells than the immune systems of many other breeds. It is also hypothesized that the high incidence of cancer in breeds such as the cocker spaniel and boxer is related to heavy inbreeding decades earlier that effectively weakened the breed's immune capabilities.

Some types of tumors are more prone to develop in one type of dog than in others. For example, the giant breeds such as the St. Bernard and the Great Dane, have a much higher incidence of osteosarcoma (a very malignant bone tumor) than does the general canine population. Dogs with lightly pigmented noses are prone to develop carcinomas in that area, probably due to long-term exposure to the ultraviolet rays of the sun. Finally, black dogs have a comparatively higher incidence of melanomas (pigmented malignant tumors) than do their light-colored peers.

Finally, the sexual status of a dog can predispose to certain types of cancer. The female dog that is not spayed has a sevenfold greater chance of developing mammary tumors than does the dog that is ovariohysterectomized early in life. Intact male canines are more likely to develop certain types of cancers, such as perianal and testicular tumors, as well.

Age Predilection

It is well noted that the incidence of cancer increases with advancing age. Cells that continually divide throughout life have a greater chance of undergoing a spontaneous genetic mutation due to cell-division "accidents" and the effects of carcinogens, or cancer-causing agents. Also, age-related depression of the normal immune response interferes with its ability to kill cancer cells that may spontaneously arise within the body. As a result, older pets will, by nature, have a higher incidence of cancer than will their younger neighbors.

Other Causes of Cancer in Pets

Some tumors affecting pets are contagious. For instance, the transmissible venereal tumor in the dog is spread by implantation during breeding, and a virus is known to cause the canine oral papilloma tumor of young dogs. In cats, cattle, mice, and poultry, a virus causes lymphosarcoma, but no virus has as yet been recovered from the lymphosarcoma of canines or humans. Finally, a virus that is quite widespread among the cat population causes feline leukemia and its associated neoplastic conditions.

Unfortunately, the causes of most types of tumors still remain a mystery. This is one area in which more research is desperately needed. Until veterinary professionals know the cause of a disease, attempts at "shotgun" treatment will be symptomatic at best and will seldom lead to a cure.

Diagnosing Cancer in Pets

The diagnosis of cancer is not always as straightforward as it would seem. Some animals may exhibit clinical signs for months before the actual cancer can be found. However, several methods are available that can be used to pinpoint and diagnose neoplastic disease in pets:

1. *Physical examination.* Many tumors can be diagnosed on physical examination alone using visual observation and/or manual palpation.

2. *Radiography (X rays).* Both plain films and contrast techniques can be used to demonstrate tumors of the lung, gastrointestinal tract, bladder, and other internal organs. Sometimes a radiograph can be pathogonomic (completely typical) for a particular type of tumor, as in the case of bone tumors. Multiple nodular masses in the lung would suggest bloodborne metastasis of a malignant tumor somewhere else in the body. However, in most cases, a tumor visualized on a radiograph must be biopsied to rule in or rule out malignancy.

3. *Ultrasonography.* The use of ultrasonic waves to visualize structures within the body is commonplace in modern veterinary medicine, and is a valuable tool for diagnosing internal cancers. Ultrasound is a very reliable method to help differentiate tumors from benign cysts. It is also useful in evaluating the sizes of internal organs. One area in which ultrasonography is not of much value is in the evaluation of the lungs, since ultrasound waves cannot effectively pass through air-filled structures.

4. *Cytology.* Examination of cells pulled from body cavities, mammary gland secretions, nasal exudates, respiratory secretions, bone marrow, lymph nodes, or various "lumps and bumps" is a popular method of diagnosing neoplastic disease. Cytological examinations are especially effective in ruling out other causes of lumps and bumps, including abscesses, cysts, and granulomas.

5. *Biopsy.* Biopsy is the most common and the most definitive way to make the diagnosis of cancer in animals. Gross and microscopic examination of a neoplasm by a competent veterinary pathologist can be expected to yield an accurate diagnosis 90 percent of the time. Misdiagnosis can occur if the sample of tissue submitted is too small or if an area of the tumor that was selected for biopsy does not contain viable cells. For example, osteosarcoma is frequently misdiagnosed because these tumors contain a great deal of dead tissue and reactive fibrous tissue. If these "benign" areas of the tumor are inadvertently biopsied, the pathologist will not find malignant cells.

6. *Endoscopy or laparoscopy.* Fiber-optic endoscopes are valuable diagnostic tools in the fight against cancer. With these instruments, tumors in the esophagus, stomach, bronchi, liver, spleen, and other organs can be visualized without dangerous exploratory surgery. Biopsies of tumors can also be obtained with these instruments.

7. *Nuclear medicine.* Nuclear scans of the liver, thyroid, lung, spleen, kidney, and bone are used in veterinary colleges and highly specialized veterinary hospitals to diagnose cancer. Radioisotopes with short half-lives are used, and anesthesia of the pet is rarely required. These scans have few adverse effects on the pet.

8. *Blood tests.* The diagnosis of certain types of neoplastic disease can be assisted by results obtained through the microscopic and biochemical analysis of a pet's blood (Fig. 60.2). For example, an increase in serum cholesterol and the enzyme alkaline phosphatase is typically found in canine Cushing's disease, which is caused by a tumor of the adrenal gland or pituitary gland. Similarly, cancer of the bone marrow (leukemia) can be diagnosed by finding tumor cells in the bloodstream. Finally, specific blood tests can be used to confirm or discount suspected cases of feline leukemia or feline immunodeficiency virus infections in sick cats.

Prognosis

Once cancer has been diagnosed in a pet, the prognosis for survival with treatment versus without treatment must be considered. One factor to consider is that these pets will frequently be older, and other diseases, such as heart and kidney disease, might be present. Therefore,

FIGURE 60.2 Certain types of neoplastic disease can be diagnosed through the microscopic and biochemical analysis of a pet's blood.

the first objectives in deciding whether to treat a pet with cancer should be to identify all the underlying conditions that may be present, and assess the severity of those conditions. If a pet has progressive kidney or heart disease, it is unlikely that it will live through major surgery. Even the animal's small secondary problems can become major primary problems once cancer treatment has started. For example, a pet might be coping well with hookworm infestation until chemotherapy depresses its immune system. At this point, a raging bloody diarrhea might develop. As a result, before initiating treatment, other problems must be taken care of first if at all possible.

Another factor that figures into the prognosis is the behavior of the particular tumor afflicting the pet. Ideally, biopsies should be performed on all tumors to determine information about growth patterns and likelihood of metastasis.

Finally, if a tumor is malignant, the extent of the disease's spread must be determined. With most sarcomas, chest radiographs are necessary because the lungs are frequent sites of bloodborne metastasis. With carcinomas, both lymph nodes and lungs should be evaluated closely, since either or both sites can be involved at the time of presentation to the veterinarian. With tumors that affect the oral and nasal cavities, skull radiographs are necessary, since prognosis is not as good if there is much bone destruction and invasion. Finally, if a lymph node is enlarged, cytology should be performed on it to determine whether it is enlarged due to tumor metastasis. Tumors that have metastasized throughout the lymphatic system carry with them a grave prognosis.

Treating Cancer in Pets

Treatment techniques for cancer have multiplied rapidly in recent years. Previously, a pet with a malignant tumor received surgery, and if that tumor grew back or spread to other organs, the pet was probably put to sleep. However, other options are now available. A combination of therapies, including chemotherapy, radiation therapy, immunotherapy, and/or surgery, is now the optimum protocol to achieve control of a malignancy (Fig. 60.3).

Surgery

If a tumor is localized and easily accessible, surgery is still the best method to effect a cure. If a highly malignant tumor involves an extremity, amputation of the affected limb may be needed to save the life of the pet. The goal of all cancer surgeries is to remove all malignant cells (or as many as possible) before any spread occurs to regional lymph nodes or other organs. With some malignancies, however, total removal may not be possible. In these instances, surgery must be combined with other forms of therapy in order for treatment to be effective.

Radiation

Many tumors are controllable, if not curable, through the use of radiation. Radiation can be administered using radioactive implants (brachytherapy), or externally, using radiation beams (teletherapy). Regardless of method used, radiation will destroy the DNA (deoxyribonucleic acid) of cells so that they can no longer reproduce. To be affected by radiotherapy, a tumor should

1. Be of a radiosensitive cell type
2. Involve no vital radiosensitive organs, such as the gastrointestinal tract
3. Have readily definable borders
4. Be slow to metastasize

Frequently, radiotherapy is combined with surgery to ensure that residual microscopic foci of disease that might have been left by the surgeon are killed.

Chemotherapy

In the past, the expense of chemotherapy had prohibited its widespread use in veterinary medicine. However, today a multitude of

FIGURE 60.3 Be sure to discuss all cancer treatment options thoroughly with your veterinarian.

affordable anticancer drugs are readily available for use in pets. These drugs work to kill tumors by several mechanisms, including fragmenting the chromosome strands within the tumor cells and inhibiting cell division.

Of course, the actions against tumor cells also cause changes in normal cells, with significant side effects in the animal being treated. These side effects can include severe bone marrow depression, nausea, vomiting, hair loss, and hemorrhage. The objective of the veterinarian is to achieve a drug dosage that is strong enough to control or cure the tumor while minimizing these side effects.

Some tumors are very responsive to chemotherapy. For example, the average lifespan after diagnosis of a lymphosarcoma in a dog is 56 days; however, with chemotherapy, the life expectancy can be increased to about a year.

On the other hand, tumors such as fibrosarcomas and osteosarcomas are notoriously resistant to chemotherapy. Human oncologists are controlling many of these highly malignant tumors with expensive drugs that cost hundreds of dollars per treatment, but these agents have had (understandably) very limited use in pets.

One disadvantage of chemotherapy is that it is relatively ineffective against large tumors. With these tumors, the number of neoplastic cells must first be reduced by either surgery or radiation therapy before chemotherapy can be effective.

Immunotherapy

Immunotherapy is a newer form of cancer therapy that shows great promise in the fight against this disease. This type of therapy is based on the premise that in many cancers, growth of the tumor is a result of a defect in the pet's immune system. Had immunity been normal, the tumor growth should have been suppressed early in its development. As a result, immunotherapy utilizes various drugs and vaccines (biological response modifiers) to stimulate the pet's immune system to fight the cancer. One form of immunotherapy, monoclonal antibody therapy, has shown promise as an effective adjunct therapy in the treatment of canine lymphoma and other cancers. *Monoclonal antibodies* work by binding to cancer cells and triggering the body's immune system to destroy the cells to which they are attached. Since these antibodies are very specific in the types of cells they bind to, normal cells within the body remain unharmed. Research is currently focusing on even newer applications for monoclonal antibody therapy, as well as newer forms of immunotherapy in general, such as gene therapy.

Treatment Summary

Both surgery and radiation therapy are excellent treatments for localized cancers. However, even if only a few tumor cells have escaped beyond this local area, the treatment will fail. If this is suspected, then chemotherapy will be used in combination with surgery and/or radiation therapy. Chemotherapy is also recommended if the tumor is of the type that readily metastasize. The combination of all the abovementioned therapies can pack a powerful "one-two punch" against neoplastic disease in animals. Adding immunotherapy to the foray will further enhance remission in select cases.

Nutritional support of the cancer patient can play a key role in the success of any treatment protocol. Scientific diets are available from veterinarians that can help reverse cancer cachexia, enhance immune function, and may actually inhibit tumor growth in certain instances. For example, studies have shown that high levels of ω-3 fatty acids in the diet of animals can help inhibit the growth and spread of tumors. As a result, if you have a pet with cancer, be sure to provide it with the proper nutritional support, including ω-3 fatty acids, to help combat the disease.

Even with the advances made in the fields of cancer therapy and support, there is still much to learn about cancer, its origins, and its behavior. As we become more knowledgeable in these areas, more effective treatments can be developed. Perhaps 30 years from now, veterinarians and pet owners alike will be able to look with amazement (and a little disdain) at the "primitive" methods now used to control cancer in pets.

Specific Types of Neoplasia in Dogs and Cats

As mentioned previously in this chapter, countless types of neoplasms can arise in dogs and cats; however, certain types appear more frequently than others.

Adenomas are tumors affecting glandular structures within the body. Adenomas arising from the sebaceous glands of the skin account for the largest percentage of tumors affecting dogs. There is no sex predilection for these tumors, and most occur in animals over 9 years of age. Sebaceous gland adenomas are cauliflower, wartlike growths and are pink to orange in appearance, although some may be pigmented. Sites most commonly affected include the limbs, trunk, eyelids, and head. In most cases, they are benign in character and pose little threat to the health of the pet.

Diagnosis of sebaceous gland adenomas is based on physical appearance and biopsy test results. Treatment consists of surgical excision, cryotherapy, and/or heat therapy. Once removed, they rarely recur in the same location. However, they may appear elsewhere on the body. In those instances in which multiple adenomas exist on a particular pet, treatment is sometimes bypassed altogether, unless the tumors appear to be growing extraordinarily fast or become ulcerated or traumatized.

Adenomas can also arise from modified skin glands in the region of the anus (perianal glands) and anal sacs of dogs. Seen most often in dogs over 11 years of age, perianal gland adenomas are nine times more likely to occur in male dogs than in females. The reason for this is that the activities of these glands are normally modulated by sex hormones, mainly the male hormone testosterone. Interestingly, female dogs afflicted with Cushing's disease may be predisposed to these tumors because disease-induced elevated levels of testosterone are produced by the adrenal glands.

Most tumors involving the perianal glands are benign in nature; however, malignancy (adenocarcinoma) can occur, especially if the tumor involves the anal sac. As a result, diagnosis of these tumors should always include biopsy evaluation to determine their status. The treatment of choice for benign adenomas is castration to remove the source of hormonal influence. In addition, in extensive cases, surgical excision, chemotherapy, and even radiation therapy can be used to attempt a cure. Therapy with estrogen compounds is often used to treat malignant adenomas and also female dogs that may be afflicted with benign or malignant tumors. Prognosis for recovery is good to excellent with benign tumors; guarded to poor with malignancies.

Cats can be affected with several different types of adenomas as well. Two of the more common forms of adenomas and adenocarcinomas seen in cats include ceruminous gland tumors, which affect the ears and ear canals; and thyroid adenomas, which are responsible for the development of hyperthyroidism.

Tumors involving the mammary glands, including mammary adenocarcinomas, are quite common among both canines and felines. Owing to the hormonal influences on mammary tissue, female dogs and cats are more likely to develop such tumors than are males. These neoplasms can arise from a number of cell types within the mammary tissue itself, and can be benign or malignant in nature. Malignant mammary neoplasms grow quite rapidly, and tend to invade and cause inflammation in and around surrounding tissue. Metastasis to other organs such as the lungs, liver, bone, and kidney can occur as well. Mammary tumors appear as hardened, sometimes painful swellings usually involving the last two glands of the mammary chain, although the others may also be affected. Local lymph node enlargement, especially in the groin region, may become noticeable as well. A fluid discharge from the affected nipples may occur, and, if metastasis takes place, breathing difficulties, coughing, swollen limbs, vomiting, and/or diarrhea may arise.

The treatment of choice for any type of mammary tumor is surgical excision. This may involve simply removing the mass if only one location along the mammary chain is affected, or in the case of multiple locations, the entire gland or a large portion thereof may need to be removed. Since mammary tumors are usually highly malignant in cats, radical mastectomies are indicated in all cases. Regional lymph nodes are removed as well if metastasis is suspected. On biopsy of the affected tissue, subsequent chemotherapy is recommended if the tumor is deemed malignant.

It should be noted that female dogs that are spayed prior to their first heat-cycle experience a dramatically reduced incidence of mammary cancer when compared to those females that were allowed to go through one or more heat cycles. As a result, this is a great way to prevent this devastating form of cancer.

Lipomas are relatively common tumors in dogs that can arise from fatty tissue anywhere in the body. Dachshunds, cocker spaniels, poodles, and terriers seem to be especially predisposed to this type of tumor. The most prevalent sites of occurrence include the subdermal (beneath the skin) fatty tissue on the belly and chest regions. Lipomas present as soft, fluctuant round masses that are adhered tightly to surrounding tissue. As a rule, lipomas rarely pose a health risk to a dog, unless they become secondarily infected or achieve such a size as to mechanically interfere with normal body functions. This can occur within the body cavities, where lipomas arising from fat adhere to body organs or from membranes lining the cavities form large space-occupying masses that can impinge on surrounding organs.

Surgical removal is the treatment of choice for lipomas, yet they can sometimes be difficult to completely excise because they tend to infiltrate into surrounding muscles and tissues. As a result, recurrences following surgery are not uncommon. In many instances, if tumor growth is minimal and there is little to no interference with normal body function, lipomas are left untreated.

The malignant form of fatty tumors, *liposarcomas,* are rare in dogs, yet must be ruled out whenever a fatty mass is discovered. Veterinarians can distinguish lipomas from liposarcomas through cytology and biopsy procedures. If a malignancy is diagnosed, liberal surgical excision of the mass and a portion of the surrounding tissue is indicated in an effort to completely remove the cancer. Chemotherapy is indicated as well.

Another prevalent form of neoplasia in cats and dogs is malignant *lymphoma-lymphosarcoma* (LSA). In fact, this is by far the most common form of neoplasia found in cats. This type of cancer involves the neoplastic proliferation of lymphocytes in sites throughout the body, including the lymph nodes, digestive tract, skin, spleen, liver, and kidneys.

In dogs, the primary clinical sign associated with malignant lymphoma typically includes a generalized swelling of the lymph nodes throughout the body, especially noticeable on the neck, shoulder, hindlimb, and inguinal regions. Other nonspecific signs may appear as organ systems within the body that are adversely affected.

In cats, LSA is usually seen concurrently with FeLV infections. There are a number of different presentations or forms of this particular neoplastic condition in felines. *Alimentary LSA* affects primarily the intestines and associated lymphatic tissue. Other organs within the abdomen can be affected as well. Symptoms commonly seen with alimentary LSA include loss of appetite, weight loss, vomiting, diarrhea, bloody stool, jaundice, and/or constipation. The *mediastinal* form of LSA presents itself as the proliferation of a large tumor within the chest cavity. As one might expect, prominent signs seen with this form include breathing difficulties, coughing, pleural effusions, chest wall incompressibility, and swallowing difficulties. *Multicentric LSA* affects lymph nodes and tissue in multiple sites throughout the body, all at one time. The signs seen with this type are variable, depending on the organs most heavily involved. Prominent swelling of the lymph nodes, including those situated beneath the skin, is usually seen with this form of LSA. *Atypical LSA* is a form of LSA that is limited to solitary organs or organ systems within the body. Such solitary sites may include the skin, eyes, spinal cord, muscles, brain, and kidneys. Obviously, symptoms exhibited will reflect the organ(s) involved. Finally, *lymphocytic leukemia* is a type of LSA characterized by the growth and proliferation of neoplastic lymphocytes within the blood and bone marrow, often affecting secondary structures such as the spleen and liver. Symptoms associated with lymphocytic leukemia tend to be nonspecific in nature, and can include anemia, jaundice, loss of appetite, weakness, fever, and organomegally (enlargement of internal organs).

Diagnosis of malignant lymphoma in dogs and cats can be achieved through lymph node cytology and biopsy, radiographs of the abdomen and chest, and ultrasonography of the same. FeLV testing of affected cats will often yield positive results, although not always.

Treatment for malignant lymphoma for both dogs and cats involves chemotherapy, radiation therapy, and in select cases, immunotherapy. Unfortunately, the prognosis for a long-term remission (extending beyond 6 months) is poor for most patients.

Myeloproliferative disorders and *leukemia* are a family of disorders seen primarily in cats and characterized by a neoplastic proliferation of the cellular components of the bone marrow, including the white blood cells, red blood cells, and platelets. Again, the feline leukemia virus is the culprit responsible for most myeloproliferative disorders seen in cats. Symptoms associated with these disorders are often related to anemia and blood clotting disorders (weakness, labored breathing, pale mucous membranes, loss of appetite), as the proliferating cells, especially white blood cells, within the bone marrow interfere with the normal production of red blood cells and platelets. In addition, certain myeloproliferative disorders are characterized by the abnormal production of the red blood cells and platelets themselves, leading again to those signs mentioned previously, and also to an enlargement of the spleen and liver. Definitive diagnosis of a myeloproliferative disorder or leukemia is made on evaluation of the blood and a biopsy sample of the bone marrow. Chemotherapy is the treatment approach of choice. Bone marrow transplants, although not readily performed on cats, can be useful as well.

Melanomas are neoplasms seen most often affecting the integument of dogs, with a special predilection for the lips, tongue, gums, oral cavity, eyelids, and the digits of the feet. Arising from pigment-producing epithelial cells, melanomas may be either benign or malignant in nature. In fact, the degree of malignancy exhibited by these tumors seems to be directly correlated with where they are located. For example, melanomas involving the mouth and oral cavity tend to be more malignant than those affecting the digits or eyelids. Male dogs seem to have a higher occurrence of this type of skin tumor than do females.

Benign melanomas appear as darkly pigmented nodules or skin blotches with well-defined borders. Rarely do they exceed one inch in diameter. Malignant melanomas, on the other hand, appear as rapidly growing, often ulcerated masses or nodules that may or may not be pigmented and can reach greater sizes. These cancers often metastasize via the blood and lymph to various organs throughout the body, including the liver, lungs, spleen, brain, spinal cord, heart, and bone. As with other tumors, definitive diagnosis of a melanoma and whether a malignancy exists is accomplished through biopsy and microscopic examination of the tumor. Radiography, ultrasonography, and lymph node biopsies may all be used to help determine the extent of metastasis if a malignancy is diagnosed. Treatment involves the surgical removal of the tumor and radiation therapy. Chemotherapy has proved to be of limited use in the treatment of malignant melanoma. Unfortunately, malignant melanomas have usually undergone metastasis by the time they are first recognized, and tend to recur after surgical removal. As a result, an overall prognosis for cure is poor.

Although melanomas are not common in cats, *basal cell tumors* are. In fact, these are the most prevalent skin tumors seen in cats. These tumors, which are usually benign in nature, present as a firm, raised nodule with or without an ulcerated surface. They may also be heavily pigmented, appearing brown to black in color. Basal cell tumors originate from the deeper layers of the skin, hair follicles, and/or sebaceous glands. Sites most often affected include the skin of the head, neck, ears, and shoulder regions. These tumors can usually be treated quite successfully with surgical removal of the tumor, chemotherapy, and/or radiation therapy.

Still another type of neoplasia that can arise from the skin epithelial cells of dogs and cats are *squamous cell carcinomas* (SCCs). Areas of skin lacking pigment or subject to repeated trauma or irritation are especially susceptible to SCC development. The oral cavity, tonsils, lips, nose, eyelids, external ear, and limbs are common sites of occurrence. SCC can involve the nails and toes as well.

A squamous cell carcinoma may appear as a slightly raised mass, often with an ulcerated surface, or it may actually resemble a papule or wart. As a rule, these tumors are slow to spread to other organs, yet usually readily invade surrounding tissue. Diagnosis is achieved through biopsy evaluation of the actual tumor. Surgery, cryotherapy, hyperthermia, chemotherapy, and radiation therapy are the most effective ways to treat SCC in dogs and cats.

Mast cell tumors (*mastocytoma*) may present as solitary or multiple skin nodules, some of which may be ulcerated and pigmented. Seen primarily in dogs, such tumors may be located anywhere on the body, yet those located around the reproductive structures and on the digits of the feet seem to exhibit a higher degree of malignancy than do those in other locations.

Mast cell tumors are especially significant because the cells making up the tumor are filled with granules containing histamine and several other powerful chemicals that can have profound effects on the body if released from the cells. Some of these effects include gastrointestinal ulcers, interference with normal blood clotting, and kidney inflammation. Diagnosis of a mast cell tumor can often be made on cytological examination and biopsy of a tumor sample. In addition, evaluation of the blood often reveals abnormalities related to the release of histamine and other granules, such as low platelet counts, anemia, and elevations in white blood cells.

Treatment for mast cell tumors employs a wide variety of techniques because of the stubborn nature of this neoplasia. Surgical excision of the visible mass along with a generous portion of healthy tissue surrounding the mass (to ensure complete removal) is usually the first step taken. Veterinary surgeons must exercise extreme care when handling these tumors, since excessive handling could cause a massive release of granules from the tumor that can induce shock and collapse. Following surgical recovery, radiation therapy and chemotherapy may be employed to help reduce the chances of recurrence and metastatic growth. Cryotherapy is also employed in those instances in which surgical excision of the tumor is incomplete or impossible.

Osteosarcoma (OSA) is a highly malignant tumor involving the bones and joints. This tumor is quite destructive in nature and metastasizes readily to other organs of the body, especially the lungs. Locally, bone destruction with infiltration of surrounding tissues occurs in most cases. The most common site of involvement in dogs is the forearm, yet the tumor can also appear on the hindlimbs and even facial bones. In cats, the hindlimbs and skull are the areas most often affected.

Clinical signs associated with OSA include limb swelling and lameness. Coughing, breathing difficulties, and other signs related to internal organ involvement may also be seen if metastasis has occurred. Diagnosis can usually be made with clinical signs and with radiographs of the affected bones. Of course, biopsy evaluation is needed to confirm such a diagnosis.

Treatment for an osteosarcoma invading the bone of a limb involves aggressive surgical intervention, including amputation of the affected limb or special surgical techniques designed to preserve limb integrity while allowing for tumor removal. Chemotherapy should follow surgery to slow or eliminate metastatic disease. If chemotherapy is not instituted, most pets diagnosed with OSA and treated with surgery alone will die within one year following diagnosis.

Fibrosarcomas are malignant tumors arising from the fibrous tissue located just beneath the skin. They usually present as solitary, irregular masses on or protruding from the skin. Their surfaces may or may not be ulcerated. In addition, fibrosarcomas have been known to develop at sites of vaccine administration along the back and flank regions of cats. When they occur, fibrosarcomas aggressively invade local tissue, and secondary metastasis to the lungs and lymph nodes is not uncommon.

Diagnosis of fibrosarcomas is made through biopsy evaluation. Treatment usually involves a combination of surgery, radiation therapy, and chemotherapy; surgery is the most important of the three.

Hemangiomas and *hemangiosarcomas* are neoplasms seen primarily in dogs that arise from the cells within the blood vessels. Common sites of occurrence include the spleen, heart, liver, and skin, although any organ within the body can be affected if metastasis via the blood takes place. Hemangiosarcomas tend to be very malignant and often ulcerate as a result of rapid growth. German shepherds, boxers, Scottish terriers, and Airedale terriers seem to have the highest incidence of this tumor type.

Clinical signs associated with hemangiomas and hemangiosarcomas involving the skin include the appearance of soft, friable masses, usually on the chest or extremities. If the spleen or other internal organs are involved, symptoms seen include weakness and depression, abdominal swelling, breathing difficulties, progressive emaciation, enlarged lymph nodes, and/or nosebleeds. Overt collapse and shock can occur secondary to excessive bleeding typically from the spleen.

Diagnosis of these blood vessel tumors is based on clinical signs and tumor biopsy results. Surgical excision or cryotherapy can be utilized on hemangiomas with favorable results. Hemangiosarcomas, on the other hand, provide a greater treatment challenge because of their invasive and metastatic nature. Often, amputation of an entire limb may be required because of the tumor's invasiveness. Removal of the spleen is indicated in cases of splenic hemangiosarcoma. Chemotherapy can be employed postsurgically, yet the prognosis for a lasting recovery still remains poor.

Bladder tumors are relatively common in dogs. They can arise from a variety of different tissues that constitute this organ. The two most prevalent bladder neoplasms include transitional cell carcinomas and squamous cell carcinomas. Female dogs seem to be affected more than males.

Tumors present within the urinary bladder can predispose to secondary infection and urolith formation. In instances where the tumor is especially large, it can obstruct the outflow of urine and cause associated complications. Clinical signs of a bladder tumor include bloody urine, straining to urinate, and painful urinations. Diagnosis is achieved through an evaluation of the urine as well as contrast radiographs or ultrasonography of the bladder. Biochemical evaluation of the blood may reveal elevated kidney enzymes if the kidneys have been damaged by an obstruction to urine flow.

Benign and malignant bladder tumors are best treated by surgical excision if their location and involvement permit. Unfortunately, most malignant bladder tumors are highly metastatic; as a result, the chances of recurrence after surgery are high. For this reason, both chemotherapy and radiation therapy may be employed after surgery to help reduce the chances of this recurrence and to attack any spread that may have taken place.

First Aid for Dogs and Cats

This appendix is designed to instruct the pet owner on first aid for dogs and cats, and on the recognition of clinical signs and true emergency situations that involve your pet. By no means is this appendix intended to replace professional veterinary care. On the contrary, it simply provides a reference source for temporary management of minor and major emergencies until a veterinarian can see the pet.

All drugs, medications, and dosages mentioned herein are based on the author's recommendation, and are not necessarily the recommendation of the product's manufacturer or distributor.

Would you know the correct way to perform CPR on your cat, how to administer first aid to your dog if it is hit by a car, or what to do if your pet swallows a poisonous substance? If not, here is your opportunity to learn. The ultimate goal of any first aid is simple: to treat and/or stabilize the patient's condition until professional medical care can be obtained.

What to Do in an Emergency Situation

If you do encounter a sudden injury or illness in your pet, don't panic! This will only hinder your first aid efforts. The first thing you need to do is to determine whether a life-threatening situation exists.

a

b

c

FIGURE A.1 (*a–c*) **Applying a muzzle.**

Cessation of breathing or heartbeat, severe bleeding, poisoning, and shock all demand immediate attention. Once the pet's condition has been stabilized, you can then direct your attention toward other, less serious problems.

Always approach injured or ill animals slowly and with caution. Use a calm, reassuring voice and move slowly. Remember that animals that are frightened or in pain might bite. For dogs, apply a muzzle made out of sturdy gauze roll or another suitable item (a necktie, leash, belt, etc.) in order to protect yourself (see Fig. A.1). Note: Never use a muzzle on an animal that is vomiting, choking, convulsing, or having breathing difficulties. For cats and dogs that have facial conformations that render muzzles useless, use heavy-duty gloves to handle the animal. If a muzzle or pair of gloves is not readily available, drape a blanket or thick towel over the animal's head prior to handling. Keep in mind that sharp teeth and claws can penetrate even the most durable of materials!

Don't forget to telephone your veterinarian concerning your pet's injury or illness, no matter how trivial it seems. Not only will you receive helpful advice; this will also give the veterinarian time to prepare for the arrival of your pet. If your veterinarian refers after-hours emergencies to an emergency clinic, keep that telephone number handy at all times.

Never delay in seeking professional help after you have initiated first aid. Sadly, many people choose to postpone further treatment of their pet, whether it is due to inconvenience or money. Often, these delays only serve to increase treatment costs and decrease treatment success rates. Remember: With pet ownership comes the responsibility of taking care of that pet's medical needs. Therefore, for your pet's sake, don't delay in seeking veterinary assistance.

Finally, it is important to minimize stress and handling as much as possible once first aid has been rendered. To help keep cats

FIGURE A.2 A towel wrap and a firm neck grip can be useful when restraining an anxious cat.

FIGURE A.3 Use extreme care when transporting a pet with a suspected spinal injury.

calm, transport them to the veterinary clinic in a box, a pillowcase or a towel (Fig. A.2). If you suspect head or spinal injury, use a piece of board or plywood, window screen, or a similar firm surface on which to move the injured pet (Fig. A.3).

Keeping these general first aid principles in mind, let's now focus our attention on specific emergencies commonly seen in dogs and cats, and on the first aid steps that can be applied to each situation.

Table A.1 Items for a First Aid Kit

Stretch bandage	Bulb syringe
Tamed iodine	Lubricating jelly
Saline solution	Plastic digital thermometer
Sterile eye ointment	Clotting powder
Bandage tape	Reusable cold pack
Clean hand towel	12-cc* syringe
Muzzle	Disposable gloves
Sterile wound dressings	Hydrogen peroxide
Forceps and tweezers	Feeding tubes
Scissors	Commercial pet piller
Cotton balls and swabs	

*Cubic centimeter.

Table A.2 Useful Conversions

1 milliliter (mL)	=1 cubic centimeter (cc) (cm^3)
1 teaspoon (tsp)	= 5 milliliter (mL)
1 tablespoon (tbs)	= 15 milliliters (mL)
1 ounce (oz)	= 30 milliliters (mL)
1 pound (lb)	= 454 grams (g)
1 kilogram (kg)	= 2.2 pounds (lb)

First Aid Kit and Home Remedies

Table A.1 lists some supplies that will come in handy in the event of either a minor or a major emergency involving your pet. Most of these items can be obtained at a local pharmacy or grocery; other items can be purchased through your veterinarian. Table A.2 provides a quick-conversion chart for metric and English measurement standards. Table A.3 lists over-the-counter medications that can be used in the event of an emergency. Please note that the usage and dosages here are those the author recommends and not necessarily those of the product's manu-

Table A.3 Useful Over-the-Counter Medications for Dogs and Cats*

Medication	Indication	Dosage
3% hydrogen peroxide	To induce vomiting; general wound cleanser	1 teaspoon per 10 pounds
Syrup of ipecac	To induce vomiting	1 teaspoon per 20 pounds
Bismuth subsalicylate (dogs only)	Vomiting; mild diarrhea	1 teaspoon per 15 pounds or 1 tablet per 40 pounds
Kaolin and pectin	Mild diarrhea	1 teaspoon per 10 pounds
Buffered aspirin (dogs only)	Fever and inflammation; mild to moderate pain; arthritis	1 adult tablet (5 grains) per 40 pounds
Acetaminophen (dogs only)	Same as aspirin	1 adult tablet per 25 pounds
Antihistamines	Mild cough; allergies; allergic reactions	Contact your veterinarian for dosages
Vegetable oil	Constipation; hairballs	1 teaspoon per 5 pounds mixed in food
Epsom salts	Constipation (dogs only); as a soak to reduce swelling and inflammation	For constipation, 1 teaspoon per 10 pounds, dissolved in water and given orally; same dilution for soaks
Milk of magnesia	Vomiting; constipation; deactivate poisons	2 teaspoons per 10 pounds mixed with water
Activated charcoal	Deactivate poisons	1 gram per pound mixed with water
Petroleum jelly	Hairballs; constipation	$1/2$ teaspoon per 10 pounds

*Note: Always consult your veterinarian before administering any of these over-the-counter medications to your pet.

Table A.4 Normal Values

Species	Temperature (degrees Fahrenheit)	Pulse (beats per minute)	Respirations (per minute)
Dog	99.5–102.5	60–120	12–22
Cat	100–103.2	80–140	20–30
Small bird	108–112	600–800	75–100
Large bird	108–112	200–300	30–50
Rabbit	102–103.5	175–210	50–75
Guinea pig	100–102.5	250–300	80–90
Small rodents	95–101	350–600	80–150
Chinchilla	102–103	200–350	45–80
Prairie dog	97–102.5	85–300	50–100
Hedgehog	97–100	200–300	45–100
Ferret	100–103	200–250	80–100
Pot-bellied pig	100.5–103	80–100	15–30

facturer or distributor. Table A.4 lists some important physiological data that you need to know in order to assess the status of an injured or ill pet.

In addition to keeping your first aid kit well equipped, be sure to write down the number of your veterinarian and nearest animal emergency clinic and keep them posted in a conspicuous location for quick reference.

FIGURE A.4 Administering a pill to a cat.

First Aid Techniques for Dogs and Cats

The pages that follow present information on common emergencies and first aid needs that you may encounter at some point in time. Priorities for each situation are identified in order to increase the effectiveness of your efforts.

Administering Oral Medications

To administer tablets, start by lubricating the tablet with lubricating jelly or butter. Open your pet's mouth by placing your hand over its top jaw, with your thumb and fingers situated behind the upper canine teeth. Now tilt the head back, and press inward and upward with your thumb and fingers. This will cause your pet to open its mouth. Next, with fingers of your free hand (which is holding the pill), pull down gently on the lower jaw and place the pill far back on the center of the tongue, using your fingers or, better yet, a commercial pet piller. Now close your

a

b

FIGURE A.5 (*a,b*) Administering a pill to a dog.

FIGURE A.6 Administering liquid medication to a cat.

FIGURE A.7 When administering liquid medication to a dog, "tent" the skin of the cheek to form a pocket, then insert the medication into the pocket.

pet's mouth and stroke its throat to encourage it to swallow the pill (Figs. A.4 and A.5).

To administer oral liquids, first hook your finger between the skin at the corner of the mouth and the teeth and "tent" the skin of the cheek out away from the gumline. Insert the syringe, dropper, or spoon into the pocket formed, pointing your pet's muzzle upward, and deliver the medication slowly. Keep the head pointed up until the medication has been swallowed. Do not deliver liquid medications directly onto the tongue or into the back of the throat. To do so could cause your pet to accidentally choke (Figs. A.6 and A.7).

Allergic Reactions

Allergic reactions can occur following administration of medications, vaccinations, or exposure to chemicals and environmental irritants or to snake or insect bites. The degree of reaction can vary considerably with each incident. Mild to moderate allergic reactions are often accompanied by intense itching, hives, soreness, minor swelling, one or two episodes of vomiting, fever, and lethargy. Signs can show up minutes to hours (usually no more than 6 hours) following exposure to the offending substance (Fig. A.8).

A severe allergic reaction (called *anaphylactic shock*) constitutes a true medical emergency. This type of reaction usually appears seconds to minutes after the animal's exposure to the offending agent. Signs of this type of reaction include breathing difficulties, protracted vomiting, shock, collapse, and unconsciousness.

FIGURE A.8 Acute allergic reactions are often accompanied by intense facial swelling.

Signs of Allergic Reaction

Intense itching

Facial swelling

Hives

Vomiting

Lethargy

Breathing difficulties

Fever

Collapse

Priorities

Ensure a patent airway.

Check respiration rate and pulse.

Perform CPR if needed.

Manage shock if present.

Administer an antihistamine if possible.

Obtain veterinary assistance as soon as possible.

First Aid Flowchart

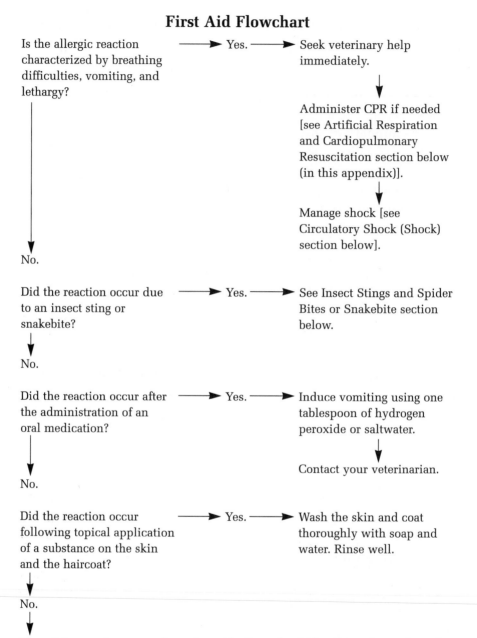

Is the allergic reaction characterized by breathing difficulties, vomiting, and lethargy? ———► Yes. ———► Seek veterinary help immediately.

Administer CPR if needed [see Artificial Respiration and Cardiopulmonary Resuscitation section below (in this appendix)].

Manage shock [see Circulatory Shock (Shock) section below].

No.

Did the reaction occur due to an insect sting or snakebite? ———► Yes. ———► See Insect Stings and Spider Bites or Snakebite section below.

No.

Did the reaction occur after the administration of an oral medication? ———► Yes. ———► Induce vomiting using one tablespoon of hydrogen peroxide or saltwater.

Contact your veterinarian.

No.

Did the reaction occur following topical application of a substance on the skin and the haircoat? ———► Yes. ———► Wash the skin and coat thoroughly with soap and water. Rinse well.

No.

For mild to moderate reactions, first aid efforts should be directed at making the pet comfortable. Giving the pet a *cold-water bath* or *oatmeal bath* often helps relieve itching. An antihistamine should be administered. Contact your veterinarian for specific medications and dosages (see Table A.3).

Application of Dressings and Bandages

A *dressing* is a protective covering that is placed directly over a wound. It can be made of any material. Ideally it should be sterile or at least very clean. It can be used to control bleeding, to absorb blood

FIGURE A.9 Applying a dressing to a wound.

and other fluids, and to minimize wound contamination (Fig. A.9).

Dressings are held in place by bandages. The most useful bandages are made of gauze or elastic. Both types can be secured with tape, safety pins, or clips. A bandage should be tight enough to keep the dressing in place, yet not so tight that it interferes with circulation. Swelling and discoloration at the affected site should prompt you to loosen the bandage (Fig. A.10).

Artificial Respiration and Cardiopulmonary Resuscitation

The combination of artificial respiration and external heart massage is termed *cardiopulmonary resuscitation* (CPR). You should perform

FIGURE A.10 Bandaging a lacerated paw.

a

b

FIGURE A.11 (*a, b*) **Checking for a pulse.**

artificial respiration if your pet has stopped breathing. In addition, if the heart has stopped beating, you must institute external heart massage in conjunction with the artificial respiration. (*Note:* Never apply heart massage if the heart is still beating. To do so could actually lead to heart failure.) The purpose of CPR is to supply oxygen to the lungs and to keep the oxygen-laden blood circulating throughout the body until the pet resumes these functions on its own.

You can take your pet's pulse in one of several different ways (Fig. A.11). The first is to place your fingertips on your pet's chest just behind the point of the elbow, press inward, a feel for the heartbeat. Another area to feel for a pulse is in the groin region, or more specifically, in the middle of either leg just below its junction with the abdomen. A third location would be on either side of the trachea, in the groove formed by the trachea and the muscles of the neck.

Priorities

Ensure a patent airway.

Perform artificial respiration, if needed.

Perform external heart massage, if needed.

Obtain veterinary assistance.

First Aid Flowchart

Is your pet breathing? ——▶ Yes. ——▶ Direct your attention to specific problems.

↓

No.

↓

Use your finger to clear the mouth of any blood, mucus, vomitus, or other debris (Fig. A.12).

↓

Tilt the head back to straighten the airway, then clasp the mouth shut with your hand and place your mouth over the animal's nose and mouth, forming a tight seal. Blow into the nose with four quick, strong breaths, expanding the chest each time (if a neonate is involved, deliver gentle puffs of breath to prevent overinflation of the lungs). If you don't see the chest expand, repeat the first two steps, then try again (Fig. A.13).

FIGURE A.12 Ensure a patent airway by extending the neck, gently pulling out the tongue, observing the oral cavity, and, if necessary, sweeping the mouth with your fingers.

↓

Did the chest expand? ——▶ No. ——▶ See Breathing Difficulties and Choking section below.

↓

Yes.

↓

Release the seal, allowing your pet to fully exhale.

↓

Administer one breath every 4 seconds until normal breathing resumes or until veterinary assistance is obtained.

First Aid Flowchart (*Continued*)

Is a heartbeat or pulse detectable? ──────────► Yes. ──────────┐

↓

No.

↓

Perform another artificial respiration.

↓

Does your pet weigh less than 20 pounds? ──────► No. ──────┐

↓

Yes.

↓

If a cat or small dog (<20 pounds) is involved: *Grasp your pet's chest just behind the elbows* with your hand (thumb on one side, fingers on the other). Your pet should be lying on its right side.

↓

In a smooth, rhythmic fashion, firmly compress the chest at a rate of one compression per second. Each compression should last approximately $1/2$ second. Remember to release your grip after each compression. Do not use excessive force when performing this procedure, for to do so could damage ribs or internal organs. As a general rule of thumb, the chest should be compressed about 2 inches on each side. For toy dogs, puppies, and kittens, compress the chest no more than 1 inch per side.

After every four compres-
sions, perform another
artificial respiration.
Remember to use gentle puffs
of breath for neonatal puppies and kittens.

No.   Yes.

If a larger dog (>20 pounds)
is involved:

Lay the dog on its right side.
Place the heel of your hand
on the ribcage just behind
the elbow, then place your
other hand on top of the
first hand.

Firmly and smoothly com-
press the chest 3 to 4 inches
using both hands. Perform
one compression every second. Each compression
should last approximately
$1/2$ second. After every four
compressions, perform an
artificial respiration.

Check your pet's pulse every
2 minutes.

Continue this sequence until the heartbeat resumes or until veterinary care is
obtained (Fig. A.14).

FIGURE A.13 Artificial respiration is performed by blowing air directly into the nostrils.

FIGURE A.14 When giving CPR, perform a chest compression once every second (60 compressions per minute). After every four compressions, perform an artificial respiration.

Bleeding and Deep Wounds and Punctures

Priorities

Control bleeding.

Check respiration rate and pulse.

Perform CPR if needed.

Manage shock if present.

Bandage wounds.

Obtain veterinary assistance as soon as possible.

First Aid Flowchart

Is there a foreign body within or protruding from the wound? ⟶ Yes. ⟶ Do not attempt to remove it. If possible, wrap the wound to help stabilize the foreign body and limit its movement.

No.

Is there active bleeding from the wound? ⟶ No. ⟶ Perform CPR if needed (see Artificial Respiration and CPR section above).

If a chest wound is involved, see Chest Wounds section below.

If the wound involved the abdomen, see Intestinal and Abdominal Injuries and Pain section below.

Do not attempt to clean wound. Apply a dressing and bandage (see Application of Dressings and Bandages section above).

Manage shock [see Circulatory Shock (Shock) section above].

Transport to your veterinarian at once.

Yes.

Is the wound on an extremity? ⟶ No. ⟶ Apply direct pressure to the wound using a clean piece of cloth, towel, or piece of clothing.

Yes.

Do you suspect a limb fracture, characterized by crepitation, abnormal limb position or mobility, swelling, pain, and/or loss of function? ⟶ Yes. ⟶ Apply direct pressure to the wound to stop any bleeding, then cover the wound with a dressing and bandage.

See Lameness and Fractures section below.

No.

Elevate the wounded limb above the level of the heart.

Apply direct pressure to the site of bleeding for eight minutes using a piece of cloth, a towel or washcloth, an article of clothing, or any other form of compress.

If CPR is needed, affix or tie the compress to the site of the wound using a piece of cloth, belt, or tie, and begin CPR immediately

Is the wound still bleeding ⟶ No.⟶ Apply a dressing and ban-
after 8 minutes of pressure? dage (see Application of
Dressings and Bandages sec-
tion above).

Manage shock [see
Circulatory Shock (Shock)
section below].

Transport to your veterinarian immediately.

Yes.

Affix a tight pressure
compress directly over
the wound using a bandage.
Apply pressure to the
appropriate pressure points
located in the armpit and/or
groin to reduce the blood
flow to the wound.

Manage shock [see
Circulatory Shock (Shock)
section below].

Transport pet to your
veterinarian immediately.

Breathing Difficulties and Choking

Signs of Breathing Difficulties or Choking

Coughing

Gagging

Wide-base stance with head and neck extended

Open-mouth breathing

Pale or purple gums and mucous membranes

Forceful expansion and contraction of the ribcage

Priorities

Ensure a patent airway; relieve choke if present.

Check respiration rate and pulse.

Perform CPR if needed.

Manage shock if present.

Obtain veterinary assistance as soon as possible.

First Aid Flowchart

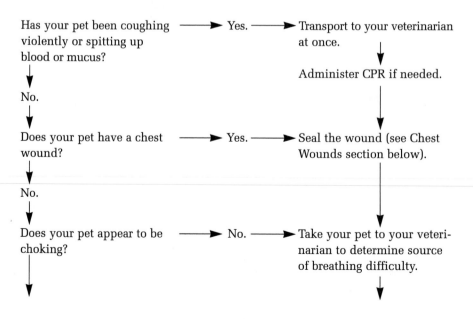

Has your pet been coughing ⟶ Yes. ⟶ Transport to your veterinarian
violently or spitting up   at once.
blood or mucus?
                                                  Administer CPR if needed.
No.

Does your pet have a chest ⟶ Yes. ⟶ Seal the wound (see Chest
wound?   Wounds section below).

No.

Does your pet appear to be ⟶ No. ⟶ Take your pet to your veteri-
choking?   narian to determine source
                                                  of breathing difficulty.

Yes.

Institute CPR if necessary.

Carefully open the mouth.
Use a tongue depressor or
pen to flatten the tongue. Do
not use your finger.

Is an obstruction visible? ⟶ Yes. ⟶ If you see a foreign object,
attempt to dislodge and
remove it with a pair of
tweezers or small needle-
nose pliers.

No.

Does your pet weigh over ⟶ No. ⟶ Place a hand on each side of
20 pounds? the chest near the last three
ribs with your fingers facing
toward your pet's head.

Yes.

Straddle the pet with your
legs, and interlock your hands
beneath the chest.

Apply a quick, forceful
squeeze inward and for-
ward. [*Caution:* Too much
force can fracture ribs and
cause internal injuries (Fig.
A.15).]

FIGURE A.15 Applying quick, forceful pressure
on either side of the chest near the last three
ribs can be used to dislodge a foreign object
caught in the airways.

↓

Apply a forceful, upward-and-inward motion, actually lifting the pet off of the ground. The objective is to create a forceful expulsion of air from the lungs. ⟶ Repeat until the foreign object is dislodged.

↓

Institute CPR if necessary.

↓

Rush your pet to a veterinarian immediately.

Burns

THERMAL BURNS

Signs of Thermal Burns

Skin redness

Blisters

Charred skin

Singed haircoat

Priorities

Manage shock if present.

Reduce contamination and prevent infection.

Obtain veterinary assistance as soon as possible.

First Aid Flowchart

Was the burn caused by
exposure to flame or heat? ⟶ No. ⟶ See Chemical Burns
subsection below.

↓

Yes.

↓

Is the skin blistered or
broken? ⟶ No. ⟶ Apply cold water or an
icepack to the affected area
for 15 minutes.

↓ ↓

Yes. A small amount of topical
anesthetic cream can be
applied to help soothe the
burn.

↓

Do not immerse the burned
region in water or apply any
medication to the burned
surface.

↓

Apply a sterile, nonadherent
dressing and bandage (see
Application of Dressings and
Bandages section above).

↓

Manage shock if present [see
Circulatory Shock (Shock)
section below].

↓

Seek veterinary attention
immediately.

CHEMICAL BURNS

Signs of Chemical Burns

Skin redness

Blisters

Ulcers

Moist skin and haircoat (where chemical contact was made)

Priorities

Neutralize or remove offending chemical.

Reduce contamination and prevent infection.

Manage shock if present.

Obtain veterinary assistance as soon as possible.

First Aid Flowchart

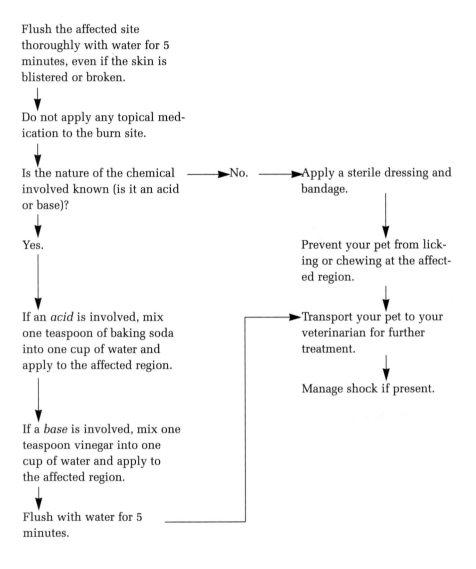

Flush the affected site thoroughly with water for 5 minutes, even if the skin is blistered or broken.

↓

Do not apply any topical medication to the burn site.

↓

Is the nature of the chemical ——▶No. ——▶Apply a sterile dressing and
involved known (is it an acid   bandage.
or base)?

↓

Yes.   Prevent your pet from licking or chewing at the affected region.

If an *acid* is involved, mix one teaspoon of baking soda into one cup of water and apply to the affected region. ——▶Transport your pet to your veterinarian for further treatment.

Manage shock if present.

If a *base* is involved, mix one teaspoon vinegar into one cup of water and apply to the affected region.

↓

Flush with water for 5 minutes.

Chemical Burns to the Eye

Priorities

Dilute the offending chemical.

Prevent further trauma to the eye.

Manage shock if necessary.

Obtain veterinary assistance as soon as possible.

First Aid Flowchart

Flush the affected eye(s) thoroughly with copious amounts of water for 5–10 minutes.

↓

Keep your pet from rubbing the affected eye(s).

↓

Do not apply any ointments to the eye(s). To do so could seal in the caustic agent and cause further damage.

↓

Seek immediate veterinary assistance.

Chest Wounds

Priorities

Control bleeding and seal the wound.

Check respiration rate and pulse.

Perform CPR if needed.

Manage shock if present.

Obtain veterinary assistance as soon as possible.

First Aid Flowchart

Is the wound a sucking chest wound, characterized by a rush of air from the wound opening and breathing difficulties?

No.

If a minor cut or laceration is involved, see Cuts and Lacerations; Bleeding Toenails section below.

If a deep wound or puncture is involved, see Bleeding and Deep Wounds and Punctures section above.

Yes.

With a piece of gauze, a clean cloth, or article of clothing, seal the wound by applying firm pressure. This will also help control bleeding.

Apply a bandage around the chest to secure the seal material (Fig. A.16). Be sure the bandage does not inter- fere with normal chest expansion needed for breathing.

Give CPR if needed (see sec- tion on CPR above).

Transport your pet to your veterinarian as soon as possible.

FIGURE A.16 Bandaging a chest wound in a cat.

Circulatory Shock (Shock)

Circulatory shock is a life-threatening situation often associated with trauma and other serious medical disorders in animals. Prompt attention to this condition is vital. With shock, the blood fails to circulate properly throughout the body. As a result, the tissues and organs do not get enough oxygen to maintain their normal functions. Causes of shock can include excessive bleeding, heart disease, infection, and severe stress and pain due to trauma or any major illness. Shock needs to be treated with intravenous fluids, colloids, and medications administered by a veterinarian; therefore, the sooner you get your pet to your veterinarian, the better are its chances of survival.

Signs of Circulatory Shock

Rapid heart rate

Weak, thready pulse

Cold, pale mucous membranes

Dry, shriveled tongue

Weakness

Stupor or unconsciousness

Panting

Subnormal body temperature

Priorities

Check respiration rate and pulse.

Keep patient warm and calm.

Seek medical assistance immediately.

First Aid Flowchart

Are any signs of shock ———▶ No. ———▶ For other problems, see
present?   appropriate sections.

↓

Yes.

↓

Be sure the mouth and airways
are clear of obstructions.

↓

Control any bleeding using
direct pressure, pressure points,
or a tourniquet (see Bleeding
and Deep Wounds and
Punctures section above).

↓

Obtain a temperature using a
rectal thermometer. Leave the
thermometer in place for 3 minutes before taking a reading.

↓

Is the body temperature ———▶ Yes. ———▶ Use blankets, towels, or hot-
below 99.5°F?   water bottles (empty 2-liter
                                            soda bottles filled with
                                            warm water work great) to
                                            attempt to raise body tem-
                                            perature to 100–102°F.

↓   ↓

No.

↓

Maintain your pet's body   Monitor temperature every 5
temperature by covering it   minutes.
with a blanket or towel.

↓   ↓

Once the temperature reaches 100°F, remove all external sources of heat and cover with a dry blanket or towel.

Minimize stress. Talk to your pet using a calm, reassuring voice.

Institute adjunct first aid procedures for severe injuries or infection (see appropriate sections).

Seek immediate veterinary help.

Constipation

If your pet appears to be having difficulty with a bowel movement, constipation might be to blame. Isolated incidents can be treated at home initially, yet if the problem persists, recurs frequently, or is accompanied by lethargy, abdominal pain, or vomiting, a medical exam is warranted. Remember: Many people mistake urinary problems for constipation [see Straining to Urinate (Urinary Obstruction) section below]. If you are in doubt, contact your veterinarian.

Signs of Constipation

Straining to defecate

Passage of dry, hard feces

Painful abdomen

Priorities

Differentiate constipation from urination difficulties.

Relieve constipation.

First Aid Flowchart

Has your pet been urinating normally? ———▶ No. ———▶ Seek veterinary assistance immediately.

Yes.

Has constipation been a problem for more than 48 hours? ———▶ Yes. ————————

No.

Is your pet exhibiting abdominal pain, lethargy, and/or vomiting? ———▶ Yes. ————————

No.

Administer hairball laxative or petroleum jelly orally at one teaspoon per 10 pounds every 4 hours.

Vegetable oil may also be used to relieve constipation. The dosage is one teaspoon per 10 pounds (mixed with food).

Do not attempt to give an enema at home.

Cuts and Lacerations; Bleeding Toenails

Priorities

Control bleeding.

Clean and medicate wound.

Bandage to prevent further contamination.

First Aid Flowchart

Is the wound a puncture, is ⟶ Yes. ⟶ See Bleeding and Deep
it greater than $^1/4$ inch   Wounds and Punctures
deep, and/or is it bleeding   section above.
profusely?

↓

No.

↓

Is a toenail involved?   ⟶ Yes. ⟶ Apply direct pressure to the
                                            nail for 5–10 minutes.

↓   ↓

No.   Apply silver nitrate, clotting
                                           powder, or flour to the
                                           exposed end of the nail (Fig.
                                           A.17). (*Caution:* Silver
                                           nitrate stings!)

↓

If minor bleeding is occurring, apply direct pressure
to the wound for 5 minutes,
using a sterile gauze or
clean cloth.

↓

↓

Use a mild hand soap and water or hydrogen peroxide to clean the wound. (If clippers are available, apply a water-soluble lubricating gel to the wound, then clip the hair from around the wound before cleaning.)

↓

Rinse the wound thoroughly with tap water. Gently blot the wound dry, preferably with a sterile gauze.

↓

Apply an antibiotic ointment or cream to the wound three times a day for 5–7 days to help prevent infection. Bandaging is optional, yet it might help prevent your pet from licking or chewing (see section on dressing and bandaging above).

↓

Are signs of infection, including swelling, heat, pain, redness, and/or pus, present? ——→ Yes. ——→ Seek immediate veterinary care.

↓

No. ————————————————————→ If healing is not occurring within 5–7 days, consult your veterinarian.

FIGURE A.17 Bleeding from a toenail can be easily controlled and is no cause for alarm.

FIGURE A.18 Tent the skin along the back to determine dehydration status. If it does not snap back into place within 2 seconds after you release your grip, your pet is dehydrated.

Dehydration

A state of dehydration can occur in dogs and cats whenever there is excessive fluid loss from the body. Conditions that can predispose the animal to dehydration include the following: water and food deprivation, burns, large wounds, increased frequency of urination, vomiting, diarrhea, bleeding, increased salivation, and excessive panting. When a pet becomes dehydrated, its blood becomes very thick. As a result, the heart is required to work extra hard in order to pump blood through the blood vessels to the organs throughout the body. In severe cases of dehydration, circulatory shock and subsequent organ failure can result [see Circulatory Shock (Shock) section above].

Skin elasticity can be tested by gently lifting the skin along your pet's back, then releasing it. If it fails to return to its normal position within 2 seconds, then your pet is dehydrated (Fig. A.18).

All suspected cases of dehydration should receive prompt veterinary care. Simply allowing the animal unlimited access to water will not correct the condition. On the contrary, intravenous fluids and colloids administered by your veterinarian will be needed to stabilize your pet while the underlying cause of the dehydration is determined.

Signs of dehydration

Weight loss

Loss of skin elasticity

Dry mucous membranes

Sunken eyeballs

Depression

Priorities

Manage shock if present.

Obtain veterinary assistance as soon as possible.

Diarrhea

Like vomiting, the danger of diarrhea rests in its ability to rapidly dehydrate the animal. Because the potential causes of diarrhea are so numerous, any case that lasts more than 48 hours should be seen by a veterinarian. If, however, the animal appears markedly depressed or dehydrated (see Dehydration section above), or exhibits vomiting or blood in the stool at any time, don't delay. Take the pet to your veterinarian at once. Intravenous fluids, colloids, and medications may be required until a diagnosis can be made.

Priorities

Prevent further diarrhea and dehydration.

First Aid Flowchart

Has the diarrhea been present for more than 48 hours? ——► Yes. ——► Veterinary evaluation is needed.

↓

No.

↓

Is there blood in the stool? ——► Yes. ————

↓

No.

↓

Is your pet depressed or vomiting? ——► Yes. ————

↓

No.

↓

Take away all food for 24 hours.

↓

Administer a kaolin-pectin mixture orally (see Table A.3 for dosage).

↓

After 24 hours, resume feeding using a bland diet (see Vomiting section below) for the next 2–3 days.

Drowning

Priorities

Ensure a patent airway.

Check respiration rate and pulse.

Perform CPR if needed.

Manage shock if present.

Obtain veterinary assistance as soon as possible.

First Aid Flowchart

Is your pet unconscious? ⟶ Yes. ⟶ See Unconsciousness section below.

↓

No.

↓

If possible, hold your pet upside-down by the hind legs for 20 seconds to allow the water to drain from the lungs.

↓

Wrap your pet in a blanket or towel to keep warm.

↓

Administer CPR as needed (see section on CPR above).

↓

Transport to your veterinarian immediately.

Electrical Shock

Before proceeding with first aid, remember that your safety comes first. Disconnect the power supply to the appliance or turn off the main electrical switch. Use a long pole or similar item to safely move the pet away from the electrical source.

Signs of Electrical Shock

Breathing difficulties

Unconsciousness

Burns noted on the lips, tongue, and corners of the mouth

Priorities

Ensure a patent airway.

Check respiration rate and pulse.

Perform CPR if needed.

Manage shock if present.

Obtain veterinary assistance as soon as possible.

First Aid Flowchart

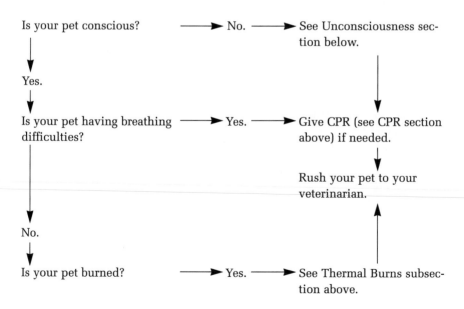

Eye Disorders and Injuries

Any injury to the eye(s) must be regarded as a medical emergency. The same is true for any redness or irritation you note in the eye(s). Prompt first aid administered at home, followed by immediate veterinary care, will help reduce the chances of partial or permanent blindness. With any eye injury, consider taping your pet's front paws or front legs together to help prevent the pet from rubbing at and further traumatizing the eye.

Signs of Eye Injury or Irritation

Redness

Drainage or discharge

Cloudiness

Protrusion of third eyelid

Squinting

Pawing or rubbing eye(s)

Eye Foreign Bodies, Scratches, and/or Bleeding

Priorities

Remove any foreign matter if indicated (see flowchart below).

Control bleeding.

Prevent self-trauma.

Manage shock if present.

Obtain veterinary assistance as soon as possible.

First Aid Flowchart

Is there a foreign body → Yes. → Do not attempt to dislodge
penetrating the eye?   the object.

No.

                                        Prevent your pet from fur-
                                        ther traumatizing the eye.

Is there active bleeding from → Yes. → Apply direct yet gentle pres-
the eye or eyelid?   sure to the site of the bleed-
                                        ing using a sterile dressing,
                                        a soft clean cloth, or an arti-
                                        cle of clothing.

No.

Is there foreign matter or → No. → Seek veterinary assistance
discharge in the eye?   immediately.

Yes.

Gently flush the eye liberally
with an ophthalmic solution
or tap water to clear the eye
of foreign matter.

Use a tissue or soft cloth to
wipe any discharge or
remaining foreign matter
from the eye.

Eye Prolapse (Eye out of Socket)

Priorities

Keep the eyeball moist.

Prevent further trauma to the eye.

Manage shock if necessary.

Obtain veterinary assistance as soon as possible.

First Aid Flowchart

Apply sterile ophthalmic solution (such as contact lens solution), ophthalmic ointment (if available), or plain tap water in order to keep the eyeball moist (Fig. A.19).

$\downarrow$

Do not attempt to push the eye back into its socket.

$\downarrow$

Prevent your pet from rubbing or further traumatizing the eye.

$\downarrow$

Watch for signs of shock and treat accordingly (see section on circulatory shock (shock) above).

$\downarrow$

Seek immediate veterinary assistance.

FIGURE A.19 A sterile ointment can be applied to an injured eye to provide additional protection until veterinary help can be obtained.

Fishhooks

Priorities

Remove fishhook if possible.

Control bleeding.

Prevent infection.

First Aid Flowchart

Is the fishhook embedded in ⟶ Yes. ⟶ Do not attempt to remove
the mouth or eye?   the hook.

↓

No.

↓

Try to minimize movement
and prevent self-inflicted
trauma.

↓

Advance the hook until the
barbed end is exposed.

↓

Snip off the end of the barb   Seek veterinary help.
with wire cutters (Fig. A.20).

↓

Remove the remaining por-
tion of the hook by gently
backing it out of the entry
site.

↓

All puncture wounds
should be seen by your veterinarian to help prevent
infection.

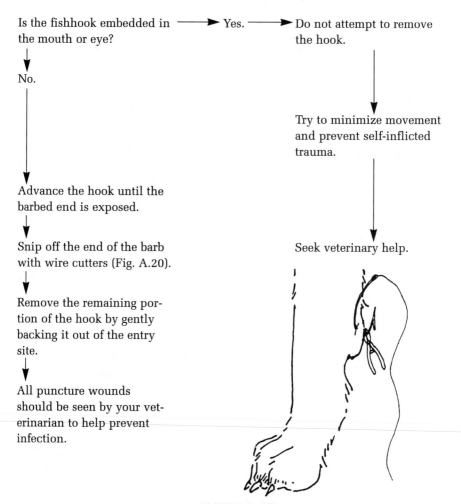

FIGURE A.20 Remove a fishhook by first snipping off the barbed end, then backing the shaft
back out of the wound.

Heat Stroke

Unfortunately, most cases of heat stroke seen in dogs and cats are due to owner neglect. As most people know, leaving a pet in a car on a hot day can lead to heat stroke and death in a relatively short period of time. This condition is also seen in pets left outdoors, restrained on chains or ropes, without adequate shelter, shade, or water.

Under hot, humid conditions, dogs and cats are very susceptible to overheating because of their limited ability to "sweat." Panting is the only way they can effectively get rid of excess body heat, and it is easy to see how this mechanism can be overwhelmed by high temperatures. Overexercise and obesity are two other predisposing factors to heat stroke.

In a true case of heat stroke, a pet's temperature will often exceed 106 degrees Fahrenheit, and if the animal is left untreated, this can result in permanent brain damage or death. Your prompt action is essential.

Signs of Heat Stroke

Elevated body temperature

Rapid respirations

Bright red mucous membranes

Thickened saliva

Vomiting

Diarrhea

Recumbancy

Unconsciousness

Priorities

Reduce body temperature.

Perform CPR if needed.

Manage shock if present.

Obtain veterinary assistance as soon as possible.

First Aid Flowchart

Is your pet conscious? ⟶ No. ⟶ See Unconsciousness section below.

↓

Yes.

↓

Take your pet's temperature using a lubricated rectal thermometer. Leave it in place at least 3 minutes before taking a reading.

↓

Does the temperature exceed 103°F? ⟶ No. ⟶ Move your pet indoors or to a cool, shady area outdoors.

↓   ↓

Yes.   Offer plenty of water, in small portions only.

↓

Move your pet indoors or to a cool, shady area outdoors.

↓

Immerse your pet in a bathtub filled with cold water or spray down with water from a hose. Use of cold packs or ice packs is also recommended.

↓

Monitor rectal temperature every 5 minutes. When the temperature reaches 103°F or if more than 20 minutes elapses from the time first aid is instituted (whichever comes first), discontinue the cooling procedure.

↓

↓

Offer small amounts of
water.

↓

Seek immediate veterinary
care. Manage shock (see section on shock above) and
administer CPR (see section
on CPR above) if needed.

Hypothermia and Frostbite

Hypothermia and frostbite can occur in any animal exposed to cold
temperatures for extended periods of time. Hypothermia is often seen
in neonatal puppies and kittens that are not kept sufficiently warm by
their mother. Frostbite, when it occurs, usually affects the tips of the
ears, tail, and/or scrotum. Blisters may or may not be present.

Signs of Hypothermia

Lethargy

Drowsiness

Unconsciousness

Weak pulse

Shallow breathing

Shivering

Subnormal body temperature

Signs of Frostbite

Same as above, plus pale skin, blisters, and hair loss

Priorities

Raise and stabilize body temperature.

Prevent or treat frostbite.

Perform CPR if needed.

Manage shock if present.

Obtain veterinary assistance as soon as possible.

First Aid Flowchart

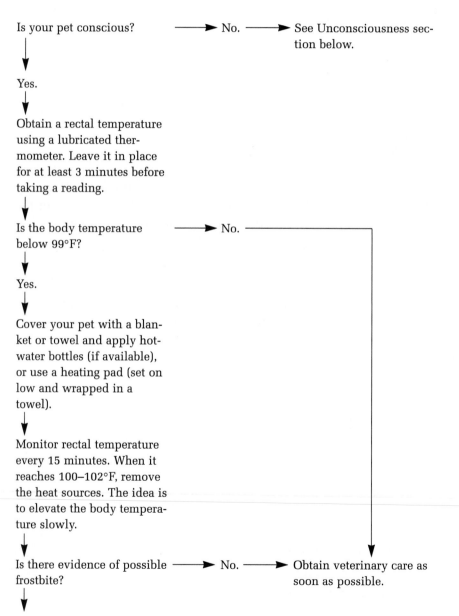

Is your pet conscious? ——▶ No. ——▶ See Unconsciousness section below.

Yes.

Obtain a rectal temperature using a lubricated thermometer. Leave it in place for at least 3 minutes before taking a reading.

Is the body temperature below 99°F? ——▶ No.

Yes.

Cover your pet with a blanket or towel and apply hot-water bottles (if available), or use a heating pad (set on low and wrapped in a towel).

Monitor rectal temperature every 15 minutes. When it reaches 100–102°F, remove the heat sources. The idea is to elevate the body temperature slowly.

Is there evidence of possible ——▶ No. ——▶ Obtain veterinary care as
frostbite? soon as possible.

Yes.

↓

If a portion of the body is
suffering from frostbite, try
to quickly rewarm the affected area by immersing it in
warm water. *Do not* rub the
affected area.

↓

Keep the injured part elevated if possible.

↓

Apply a dressing and ban-
dage to the region (see section on dressing and
bandaging above).

Ingestion of a Foreign Substance or Object

Ingestion of a foreign object must be considered any time a pet shows
sudden abdominal pain, vomiting, and/or diarrhea. Also, this possibility must be ruled out in those animals with a history of chronic
vomiting. Because of their inherent curiosity, puppies and kittens are
the ones most likely to swallow foreign objects.

Signs of Ingestion of a Foreign Object or Substance

Abdominal pain

Vomiting

Diarrhea

Gagging

Excessive salivation

Dehydration

Priorities

Induce vomiting if indicated.

Manage shock if present.

Obtain veterinary assistance as soon as possible.

First Aid Flowchart

Is the ingested object or substance a potential poison? ⟶ Yes. ⟶ See Poisoning section below.

↓

No.

↓

Did the ingested object have pointed or potentially sharp edges? ⟶ Yes. ⟶ Do not induce vomiting.

↓   ↓

No.   Seek veterinary assistance.

↓   ↑

Is your pet vomiting, or showing other signs of illness? ⟶ Yes. ⟶

↓

No.

↓

Feed your pet a piece of bread to help coat and bind the object.

↓

Induce vomiting (see Poisoning section below).

↓

If the object is not vomited back up or has not passed in the stool within 24 hours after ingestion, or if your pet shows any signs of illness or pain during that time, veterinary intervention is required.

Insect Stings and Spider Bites

Signs Associated with a Bite or Sting from an Insect or Arachnid

Localized redness, swelling, and pain

Lameness

Excess salivation

Breathing difficulties

Priorities

Administer antihistamine (see Table A.3).

Prevent infection.

Obtain veterinary assistance as soon as possible.

First Aid Flowchart

Is your pet having breathing difficulties, vomiting, abdominal pain, or other signs of illness? ⟶ Yes. ⟶ See Allergic Reactions section above.

Institute CPR (see CPR section above).

Manage shock (see Shock section above).

Obtain veterinary care.

No.

Is a stinger evident in the wound? ⟶ Yes. ⟶ Remove the stinger with a pair of tweezers.

No.

Apply a cold pack or icepack to the affected area for 15 minutes to control swelling and pain.

(Continued)

↓

Apply baking soda or
calamine lotion to the site.

↓

An antihistamine should be
administered.

↓

Contact your veterinarian
for specific medication and
dosage (see Table A.3).

↓

Monitor the site for infection (see section on cuts and
lacerations above).

Intestinal and Abdominal Injuries and Pain

Signs of Internal Abdominal Injury and/or Abdominal Pain

Lethargy

Weakness

Abdominal tenderness

Blood in urine or feces

Panting

Bloated abdomen

Arched back

Vomiting and diarrhea

Priorities

Check respiration rate and pulse.

Perform CPR if needed.

Manage shock if present.

Minimize further wound contamination.

Obtain veterinary assistance as soon as possible.

First Aid Flowchart

Are abdominal contents exposed?

↓

No.

↓

In all cases of abdominal injury or pain, consult your veterinarian at once, even if no signs of internal injuries are present. These signs might not show up for 12–24 hours after an injury.

↓

Administer CPR if needed (see section on CPR above) and manage shock (see section on shock above).

↓

Seek immediate veterinary help.

Yes.

Gently rinse the exposed organs with tap water.

↓

Carefully place any exposed organs back into the abdominal cavity.

↓

Pack the wound with a moist towel or cloth.

↓

Apply an encircling bandage to the abdomen to keep the pack in place (Fig. A.21).

FIGURE A.21 Support sling for an abdominal wound.

Lameness and Fractures

Causes of lameness in dogs and cats can include muscle strains, tendon and ligament sprains, abscesses, foreign bodies, tumors, arthritis, bruises, dislocations, and fractures. In all instances, the exact cause of the lameness should be determined by your veterinarian.

Priorities

Control bleeding if present.

Prevent further injury or wound contamination.

Stabilize any fractures present (if possible).

Manage shock if present.

Obtain veterinary assistance as soon as possible.

First Aid Flowchart

Are signs of potential fracture present, including abnormal limb position or mobility, localized pain, bruising and/or swelling, or crepitation (the crackling feel made when two ends of bone rub together)?

No. → Have your pet's lameness evaluated by your veterinarian.

↓
Yes.
↓

Is the fracture open, with ends of bone protruding through the skin?

Yes. → Do not attempt to replace the exposed ends of bone or to clean the wound.

↓

Control bleeding if present (see Bleeding and Deep Wounds and Punctures section above).

↓

Apply a dressing or bandage
(see appropriate section
above).

No.

Is the fracture located below
your pet's elbow or knee?

Yes.

Immobilize the fracture by
applying a splint to the
affected region (fractures
above the elbow and knee
are difficult to stabilize with
a conventional splint). A
rolled-up magazine affixed
to the limb with adhesive
tape or cloth (see Fig. A.22)
makes an excellent splint.
Other materials that can be
used as splints include
sticks, rulers, yardsticks,
tongue depressors, etc.
Avoid taping or tying directly over the fracture site.

FIGURE A.22 One method of temporary fracture stabilization using a rolled-up magazine.

No.

Seek veterinary assistance
at once.

Nosebleed

Although most nosebleeds seen in dogs and cats are due to trauma, some can occur secondary to tumors or infections within the nasal cavity.

Priorities

Control bleeding.

If bleeding persists, take to veterinarian to determine cause.

First Aid Flowchart

Elevate your pet's nose by pointing it straight up into the air.

↓

Apply pressure to the openings of both nostrils with your thumb and forefinger and maintain for 5 minutes. Depending on the size or the nostrils, gauze may be packed within the nostrils to control the bleeding.

↓

Is the nosebleed due to ⟶ Yes. ⟶ See Trauma section below.
trauma?

↓

No (or unknown).

↓

Have your veterinarian thoroughly examine your pet to determine a cause.

Poisoning

Poisoning, whether accidental or malicious in nature, is a common emergency situation in small animals. Prompt management is essential to ensure the health of the pet.

Any chemical, drug, or plant found within and around the home should be regarded as a potential poison to the household pet. For instance, antifreeze can quickly cause kidney failure in a pet that consumes only a small portion of the liquid (which, by the way, has a pleasing taste to animals). Aspirin and acetaminophen are very poisonous to cats because of this animal's limited ability to metabolize or break down those drugs (Table A.5).

Table A.5 Drugs and Medications that Can Be Highly Toxic to Cats

Aspirin
Acetaminophen
Ibuprofen
Iodine
Coal tar shampoo
Organophosphate insecticides
Phosphate enemas
Primidone

Other causes of poisoning in pets can include rat, snail, roach, and predator poisons; food items such as chocolate and salt; and living creatures such as salamanders and toads. Ingestion or application of flea sprays and other insecticides also account for a significant percentage of reported cases of poisonings.

Finally, many household plants can cause nausea, vomiting, diarrhea, heart problems, convulsions, coma, and/or death if eaten by dogs or cats. See Table A.6 for a list of some of the house and ornamental plants that can be hazardous to your pet.

Table A.6 Ornamental Plants that Can Be Hazardous to Pets

Aconite	Hydrangea
Amaryllis	Iris
Azalea	Jerusalem cherry
Bittersweet	Jonquil
Caladium	Larkspur
Castor bean	Laurel
Common box	Lily-of-the-valley
Crown-of-thorns	Narcissus
Daffodils	Nightshades
Daphne	Oleander

Table A.6 Ornamental Plants that Can Be Hazardous to Pets (*Continued*)

Dumbcane	Philodendron
Elephant ear	Pine needles
English holly	Precatory bean
English ivy	Rhododendron
Euonymous	Rose bay
Foxglove	Skunk cabbage
Honeysuckle	Wisteria
Hyacinth	Yew

Signs of Poisoning

Vomiting

Diarrhea

Depression

Unconsciousness

Convulsions

Muscle tremors

Abdominal pain

Drooling

Panting

Priorities

Ensure a patent airway.

Check respiration rate and pulse.

Perform CPR if needed.

Determine the type of poison involved.

Dilute or neutralize the poison.

Manage shock if present.

Obtain veterinary assistance as soon as possible for specific antidote (if available).

First Aid Flowchart

Was the poison swallowed? ———▶ No. ———▶ If the poison was absorbed through the skin, flush the affected area with copious amounts of water. If the entire body was exposed, wash the entire body with soap and water, and rinse thoroughly.

Yes.

Try to identify the poison. If available, read the label on the container and follow its directions pertaining to accidental poisoning. Contact a veterinarian immediately and explain what the poison was and how much was consumed.

Is the poison a caustic substance, or petroleum-based (see Table A.7)? Does the label specify "Do not induce vomiting"? Is your pet severely depressed, unconscious, or convulsing? ———▶ Yes. ———▶ Do not induce vomiting!

No.

(Continued)

Table A.7 Poisonings in Which Vomiting Should Not Be Induced

Bathroom cleaners	Glues and adhesives
Drain cleaners	Laundry bleach
Dry-cleaning fluids	Metal cleaners
Fire extinguisher fluids	Oven cleaners
Fuels (gas, oil, kerosene)	Paint and varnish removers
Furniture polish	Rust removers

Induce vomiting using hydrogen peroxide (1 tablespoon), salty water (1–2 tablespoons of salt per cup of water), or syrup of ipecac (0.5 milliliter per pound). Dilute the remaining poison by giving 2–3 cups of water orally

Dilute or deactivate the poison by giving activated charcoal (mix 1 gram per pound with water to form a souplike slurry), milk (1–2 cups), egg whites (two per pint of water), vinegar (use if poison was a base; 2 tablespoons), and/or milk of magnesia (use if poison was an acid; 1–2 teaspoons mixed with water) (Fig. A.23).

FIGURE A.23 A veterinarian administering activated charcoal via a stomach tube to neutralize a poison.

↓

If necessary, administer CPR
(see CPR section above), and
manage shock (see section
on Shock above).

↓

Transport your pet to your
veterinarian as soon as possible for further treatment.
Be sure to save the label or
container that the poison
was in, and take it with you
to the veterinary clinic.

Salivation (Drooling)

Excessive drooling can indicate nervousness, nausea, or some disorder
involving the mouth or facial muscles. These disorders can include
dental disease, jaw fractures, mouth infections, rabies and other diseases that affect the nervous system, mouth tumors, throat obstructions, and foreign bodies. If an obstruction or foreign body is involved,
carefully attempt to dislodge and/or remove it with tweezers or small
needle nose pliers, keeping your safety in mind at all times. Another
cause of excess salivation in dogs and cats is mouth irritation due to
the consumption of medications, poisons, plants, insects, or reptiles
(especially toads). In these instances, thoroughly rinse the pet's mouth
out with copious amounts of water, taking care not to force any water
down the animal's airways. Follow appropriate first aid measures if
poisoning is suspected (see Poisoning section above). In all cases of
excessive salivation, consult your veterinarian.

Priorities

Determine the cause of the salivation if possible.

Consult your veterinarian as to an appropriate course of action.

Seizures (Convulsions)

A seizure should be suspected whenever an animal's behavior is altered or involuntary muscle activity is noted. Some possible causes of seizures include idiopathic epilepsy, poisoning, liver and kidney disease, infections, tumors, hypocalcemia (low blood calcium seen in pregnant and nursing mothers), and low blood sugar (sometimes seen in hunting dogs and young puppies and kittens). A thorough physical exam and tests performed by your veterinarian might be necessary to identify the actual cause. There is not much that you, as an owner, can do for a convulsing pet except prevent the animal from hurting itself and others. If your pet has been previously diagnosed as having epilepsy, your veterinarian may prescribe medication to be given at home per rectum to your pet in the event of a seizure.

Signs of Seizures

Uncontrollable, involuntary muscle activity

Altered or abnormal behavior

Priorities

Keep your pet from injuring itself.

Prevent injury to yourself.

Perform CPR if needed.

First Aid Flowchart

Restrain your pet by wrapping it in a
blanket or towel.

↓

Do not apply a muzzle.

↓

Do not attempt to give anything orally
to the animal.

↓

Has epilepsy been previously diagnosed
in your pet?

↓   ↓

Yes.   No.

↓   ↓

If applicable, administer anticonvulsant   Transport your pet to your
medication per rectum according   veterinarian immediately for
to your veterinarian's instructions.   proper diagnosis and
                                                     treatment.

↓

Transport the pet to your veterinarian if
more than two seizures occur within a
24-hour period, if an individual seizure
lasts over 5 minutes, or if depression,
breathing difficulties, or unconsciousness occur following the seizure.

Snakebite

Clinical signs associated with snakebite are related to the type of snake involved, the amount of venom injected into the animal, and the location of the bite wound. The venom of pit vipers, such as rattlesnakes and water moccasins, causes tissue damage and destroys red blood cells. On the contrary, coral snake venom often causes little pain or swelling; however, it does affect the animal's nervous system, and difficulty swallowing, depression, paralysis, and death are common sequels to the bite of this snake.

Snakebites that occur on the head and neck can be more serious since they can cause direct damage to many vital structures in these regions and interfere with breathing. Furthermore, bites in these areas are difficult to manage with conventional first aid. Regardless of the location of the bite, institute first aid immediately and do the best you can.

Signs of Snakebite

Fang puncture wounds

Pain

Swelling

Breathing difficulties

Paralysis

Priorities

Slow the spread of venom.

Clean and bandage wound.

Check respiration rate and pulse.

Perform CPR if needed.

Manage shock if present.

Obtain veterinary assistance as soon as possible.

First Aid Flowchart

See Bleeding and Deep
Wounds and Punctures sec-
tion above.

Keep your pet as calm as possible to
prevent the rapid spread of venom
throughout the bloodstream.

↓

Apply a muzzle if the pet is in a great
deal of pain.

↓

Clean the bite wound with soap and
water. Apply an antibiotic ointment to
the area.

↓

Is the bite on an extremity? ⟶ No.

↓

Yes.

↓

Affix a tight pressure compress directly
over the site of the bite with a bandage.
A piece of cloth or clothing can be used
as bandaging material.

↓

Apply a cold pack or icepack over the
affected area for 10 minutes. Remove for
10 minutes, the apply a second time for
10 more minutes.

↓

Manage shock (see Shock section above)
and give CPR (see CPR section above) if
needed.

↓

Seek veterinary care immediately.

Straining to Urinate (Urinary Obstruction)

Both cats and dogs can suffer from a condition in which crystals composed of certain minerals form within the urinary tract and irritate the lining of the tract. In dogs, these crystals can coalesce into actual stones within the bladder, ranging from the size of small BBs (as from a BB gun) to the size of a baseball! In male dogs, stones can prevent the animal from urinating properly, a condition that can prove to be fatal if not treated promptly. Bladder stones are not as common in the cat, yet the crystals themselves are large enough to create a life-threatening obstruction to urine outflow in male cats.

Obstructions are more likely to occur in males because the male's urethra (that portion of the urinary tract that transports urine from the bladder to the outside) is much narrower than that of the female. Consequently, stones and crystals are more likely to become lodged within the male urethra.

If a urinary obstruction is not relieved promptly, death can result as a result of toxin buildup within the bloodstream, kidney failure, and/or ruptured bladder. Thus, seek veterinary care at once. Don't delay!

Signs of Urinary Problems

Frequent attempts at urination with minimal to no results

Bloody urine

Enlarged, painful abdomen

Panting

Priorities

Manage shock if present.

Seek veterinary attention at once.

Trauma

Frequent sources of trauma encountered in small animals include automobiles (tires, fenders, fan belts), gunshot wounds, fights with other animals, falls or jumps from elevations, and blows from blunt objects (Table A.8). Whatever the source of trauma, you should follow the first aid steps outlined below.

Priorities

Ensure a patent airway.

Control bleeding.

Check respiration rate and pulse.

Perform CPR if needed.

Manage shock if present.

Bandage wounds.

Obtain veterinary assistance as soon as possible.

Table A.8 Injuries and Disorders Commonly Resulting from Automobile Impact

Fractures
Lung contusions and fluid buildup
Ruptured organs and internal bleeding
Concussion
Diaphragmatic hernia
Shock

First Aid Flowchart

Is your pet conscious?

↓

Yes.

↓

No.   See Unconsciousness sec-
                                 tion below.

↓

Handle all injured animals
with caution. If possible,
apply a muzzle.

↓

Are wounds or active ———→ Yes. ———→ Apply direct pressure to
bleeding present?   stop bleeding. See Bleeding
                                     and Deep Wounds and
                                     Punctures section above.

↓

No.

↓

Is your pet showing signs of ———→ Yes. ———→ Manage shock (See
shock, including pale, dry   shock section above).
mucous membranes; a dry,
shriveled tongue; panting; a
weak, thready pulse; and/or
a subnormal temperature?

↓

No.

↓

Do you suspect any broken ———→ Yes. ———→ See Lameness and Fractures
bones as evidenced by lameness,   section above.
localized swelling or pain,
abnormal limb position or
mobility, and/or crepitation
(a crackling feel made when
two edges of bone rub together)?

↓

↓
No.
↓

Are signs of spinal or head ——► No. ——► Transport your pet to your
injury present, including   veterinarian for a general
paralysis and inability to   evaluation.
move, loss of pain sensation,
incoordination, unequal
pupil size, convulsions,
and/or bloody or clear
discharges from the mouth,
nose, or ears?

↓
Yes.
↓

Is your pet convulsing? ——► Yes. ——► Wrap it in a thick blanket or
                                                     towel to prevent self-inflict-
                                                     ed injury [See Seizures
                                                     (Convulsions) section].

↓
No.
↓

Slide your pet onto a board,
piece of plywood, stiff piece
of cardboard, window
screen, or taut blanket.

↓

Transport to your veterinarian at once. ◄——————

Unconsciousness

Priorities

Ensure a patent airway.

Check respiration rate and pulse.

Perform CPR if needed.

Manage shock if present.

Obtain veterinary assistance as soon as possible.

First Aid Flowchart

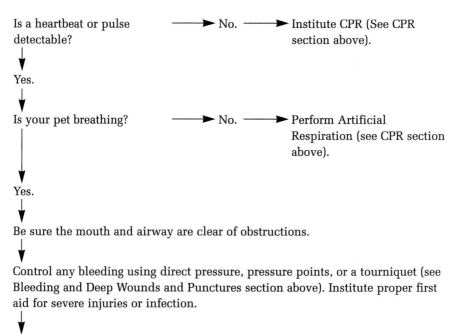

Is a heartbeat or pulse detectable? ———▶ No. ———▶ Institute CPR (See CPR section above).

Yes.

Is your pet breathing? ———▶ No. ———▶ Perform Artificial Respiration (see CPR section above).

Yes.

Be sure the mouth and airway are clear of obstructions.

Control any bleeding using direct pressure, pressure points, or a tourniquet (see Bleeding and Deep Wounds and Punctures section above). Institute proper first aid for severe injuries or infection.

Cover the pet with a blanket or towel. *Do not* use heaters or electric blankets.

Vomiting

Vomiting, the forceful expulsion of food or stomach secretions through the mouth, is actually a symptom of some underlying disorder. Dietary indiscretions, infections, worms, foreign bodies, bloat, metabolic diseases (such as kidney disease), and poisonings are just a few of the many disorders that can be characterized by vomiting.

Remember that puppies and kittens can dehydrate seven times faster than adult animals. As a result, any case of persistent vomiting in a young animal should be especially regarded as a medical emergency.

Vomiting should be differentiated from regurgitation, which can be defined as the effortless expulsion of food or saliva from the mouth due to a disorder of the esophagus. This distinction is important since the causes of the two are different.

Signs of Impending Vomiting

Increased salivation

Vocalization

Violent contractions of the abdominal muscles

Priorities

Manage poisoning if applicable.

Obtain veterinary assistance as soon as possible for persistent vomiting.

First Aid Flowchart

Has your pet vomited more ——→ Yes. ——→ Take away all food and
than two times in the past   water.
24 hours?

No.   Seek veterinary help.

                                                     If you suspect ingestion of a
foreign substance or object,
see Ingestion of Foreign
Substance or Object section
above.

Does your pet also have ——→ Yes.
diarrhea?

No.

Administer milk of magnesia or bismuth subsalicylate. See Table A.3 for
dosages.

Contact your veterinarian before giving any other type of oral medication to your
pet.

Offer only small amounts of water to prevent overdrinking and subsequent
stomach upset.

Feed your pet a bland diet for the next 24–48 hours. Such a diet is available
from your veterinarian or can be prepared at home using 4 parts boiled rice and
1 part boiled lean meat, chicken, or egg.

INDEX

So that you will find it easier to use, the index for this book is divided into four sections: *General*, *Birds*, *Cats*, and *Dogs*. Please note that those entries in **bold** are emergency/first aid terms. The special emphasis on these words should make it easier for you to find the crucial information you would need in the event of an emergency.

General Index

Birds

Cats

Dogs

ABOUT THE AUTHOR

Chris C. Pinney, D.V.M., has authored eight books and served as veterinary host and advisor for television news-magazines and syndicated radio talk shows. Dr. Pinney is also the author of the first edition of this book, titled *The Illustrated Verterinary Guide for Dogs, Cats, Birds, and Exotic Pets*. He practices veterinary medicine in Houston, Texas.